Instructor's Solutions Manual

to accompany

Forecasting Principles and Applications

Stephen A. DeLurgio, Sr.
Bloch School
University of Missouri–Kansas City
http://forecast.umkc.edu
delurgio@cctr.umkc.edu

Irwin McGraw-Hill

**Boston   Burr Ridge, IL   Dubuque, IA   Madison, WI   New York   San Francisco   St. Louis
Bangkok   Bogotá   Caracas   Lisbon   London   Madrid
Mexico City   Milan   New Delhi   Seoul   Singapore   Sydney   Taipei   Toronto**

Irwin/McGraw-Hill

A Division of The McGraw·Hill Companies

Instructor's Solutions Manual to accompany
FORECASTING PRINCIPLES AND APPLICATIONS

1 2 3 4 5 6 7 8 9 0 QSR/QSR 9 0 9 8 7

ISBN 0-256-21680-0

http://www.mhhe.com

21ST CENTURY FORECASTING

In the mid 1960s when they were professors in the mathematics department at Dartmouth, John G. Kemeny and Thomas Kurtz developed the BASIC computer language, "and saw to it that all departments of the college had terminals with which the students could have ready access to the computers. As a result, the productivity of the students increased so markedly that it became necessary to assign as homework those problems that a few years ago would have been sufficient for a senior thesis." *
Professor Kemeny was subsequently appointed to president of Dartmouth. However, his pioneering experience taught the world the effectiveness of learning and applying complex concepts via computers.

It is hoped that this book assists in continuing the experiences of Kemeny and Kurtz into the 21st century. To a great extent, my motivation in writing this book is the goal that our undergraduate and graduate students will routinely do homework assignments "that a few years ago would have been sufficient for a seniors thesis."

* Robert G. Brown, *Source Book in Production Management,* The Dryden Press, Inc. Hinsdale, Ill., 1970, p.176.

TABLE OF CONTENTS

INTRODUCTION

This Manual provides solutions to all end-of-chapter problems in the first edition of <u>Forecasting Principles and Applications</u>. In a few chapters, the solutions to Minicases have not been provided but instead are available directly from me, either through phone, the email addresses below, or the U.S. Postal Service.

ELECTRONIC VERSION OF THIS MANUAL

All chapters of this Manual can be obtained from me on a diskette in a Microsoft Word 7.0 format which can easily be converted to other formats. In addition, all of the other resources identified below are available on diskette to actual adopters if they will contact me directly. Having the Instructor's Manual in electronic format is an effective way in which to develop class lecture notes.

SOFTWARE DIFFERENCES

The calculations of this manual depended primarily on the statistical procedures of $RATS_{tm}$, SAS_{tm}, $ForecastPro_{tm}$, and Microsoft $Excel_{tm}$. Several of these programs provide many more digits than are necessary or significant in the original data. Students and other users may obtain slightly different answers depending on their software. Most examples in the body of the textbook, particularly those of Chapters 7 to 13 on ARIMA and MARIMA were run in RATS, SAS and SPSS, where it was confirmed that in all cases RATS and SAS gave identical numerical results. Those chapter examples run in SPSS gave slightly different results, but were nonetheless not statistically significantly different than those shown in this textbook. However, as with SPSS, those using ForecastPro, Soritec, Minitab, TSP, Gauss, etc, should expect some differences and should prepare students to not worry when these differences are minor. We have tried to make this book as generic as possible so that it is accessible to you and your students no matter what software product you use. With that in mind, consider some of the compatibility issues and additional resources available from the Irwin/McGraw-Hill (http://www.mhhe.com) website and my website, http://forecast.umkc.edu.

ASCII COMPATIBILITY

I have found that the ASCII data sets on the book's data disk are compatible with the ASCII import facility of SPSS and Microsoft Excel. I would hope that this compatibility will exist with other statistical packages that allow ASCII or MS-DOS text formats as inputs. To facilitate this, all alphabetic comments on the data disk files are in the last rows of each data file on the books data disk.

WEBSITE RESOURCES

In addition to the material in this Manual and the book's diskette, I maintain several directories of resources on my website (http://forecast.umkc.edu). These are all available to you and in the case of materials which are not related to homework, these materials are available to your students. These resources consist of the following subdirectories:

IM: This subdirectory contains all WORD for Windows95 files of this instructor's manual. This subdirectory will only be available to instructors who contact me via email, phone, etc. It will not be available to your students unless you mistakenly give them the password to that directory. If this becomes a problem, then we will eliminate this subdirectory.

RATS: This is a subdirectory of several hundred RATS programs that were used to run many of the examples in this book. I do not guarantee that you will find a program for every example or problem in the book, however, many will be there. In most cases, these will be very "clean" programs that will be useful to you and your students. I encourage you to download these for your own use and to make these available to your students when you deem this appropriate. There will be one subdirectory available to the public including your students and another only for Instructors, please contact me about how you can either get to the Instructor's subdirectories or have me mail you 3.5" MS-DOS compatible diskettes with this information.

FCP: Every data set on the textbook disk has been converted to a *.wk1 format for ForecastPro$_{tm}$ and is available to you and your students. These files are copyrighted for use with this book. Only the data exists in these files, not the FCP audit trails etc.

SAS: This is a subdirectory that has command line programs for many examples, but no end-of-chapter problems of the book. The majority of these files pertain to Chapters 7 to 13. Additional programs will be added over time.

LAN: This is a Lectures And Notes subdirectory of ASCII or WORD documents that are useful in generating lectures or for handouts. This is an evolving directory and as is true for all directories, you are welcome to submit materials to the website for inclusion in any of these directories. Full attribution will be given to all who submit materials for use of others on the website.

M7: A Minicase *-7 subdirectory will be maintained to assist students in completing their Minicase assignments whether chosen from this book or from their own data. In this directory I have placed most of the solutions to Minicase *-7, International Airline Passengers data. This is the original data set from Brown, Box, Jenkins, and Reinsel. I have chosen this as a typical example because this series is analyzed in so many other textbooks. Also, this minicase is often used in my lectures. The examples of Minicase *-7 become effective ways for students to learn about how and why each minicase is completed.

THE DIFFICULTY OF PROBLEM SETS AND MINICASES

ESTIMATED DIFFICULTY

Elementary   Medium   Hard   Very Hard   Bad

At the beginning of each chapter I have rated each problem on the scale given above. This scale is defined roughly as follows:

Elementary: Questions answered almost verbatim from the book. Usually taking only about 5 minutes or so to complete.

Medium: Questions that might take a few minutes to understand. Usually taking about 5 to 20 minutes to complete.

Hard: Questions that might take 15 to 45 minutes to complete, typically requiring the use of software or reference to multiple chapters.

Very Hard: Questions that might take 30 minutes to 2 hours to complete, almost always requiring software analysis.

Bad: So far there have only been about 2 questions which are Bad because of mistaken labels on the columns of the data on the data disk file. In addition, one question was found to be too advanced for the chapter in which it resided. These questions are clearly marked in bold and underlined at the beginning of each chapter in this Manual.

Even though I have rated these questions, there may be dramatic differences (i.e., great variance) in the difficulty of some problems depending on the software available to students. Thus, it is important for you to review all problems with a difficulty rating of Medium to Very Hard before assigning such problems to insure that the rating is correct for your students. For example, because SAS and ForecastPro both generate prediction intervals as standard output, some problems which might take an hour or more using other software might only take 5 minutes using SAS or ForecastPro. I rated these questions using a typical statistical forecasting package that has an easily learned command programming language like RATS, SAS, or Minitab. **Consequently, if your software is not as flexible as RATS and SAS, then some medium-to-hard problems might literally be Very Hard and even impossible using your software.**

USING REVIEW PROBLEMS

Each set of chapter-end problems begins with a section called "Review Problems Using Your Software." These problems have been included in the book to facilitate use of review problems as introductory material for students. By using these problems we can ease our students into the material more easily. You should consider using more of these review questions as the difficulty of the chapters increase. It is highly recommended that you use these review problems for the more complex chapters on econometrics, intervention analysis, and MARIMA modeling. Students receive immediate feedback when completing their assignments.

COMMENTS ABOUT ERRORS

We have all used books with typographical and even conceptual errors in them. I have tried to insure that neither typos nor conceptual errors exist here. Please accept my apologies for any that might be there. In the context of continuous improvement, I will make all errors known to others through an errata sheet and errata file available to all adopters of this book either mailed directly from me or Irwin/McGraw-Hill or downloaded from the website. Please make me aware of any errors you find by either faxing them to me at 1-816-235-6506, or emailing them to: delurgio@ cctr.umkc.edu or sad@forecast.umkc.edu. Thank You

ACKNOWLEDGEMENTS

I want to acknowledge the efforts of others who have indirectly or directly supported this endeavor. Many individuals have already been acknowledged in the text book   In addition, I would like to acknowledge Tom Doan and Sue Bessonny of Estima for assisting my students with student versions of RATS; a product which is available at a very reasonable price to all students. I have been using software such as RATS and SAS in teaching forecasting for the last 25 years. Because of software providers such as Estima, Automatic Forecasting Systems (AutoBJ), Business Forecasting Systems (ForecastPro), SCA, Smart Forecasts, Sorities, Minitab, SAS, SPSS and many other excellent products, we are able to present more effective and efficient forecasting courses. I have appreciated the technical assistance of David Riley of Automatic Forecasting Systems in answering a number of questions concerning his excellent software. Again, I have appreciated the assistance of Carl Bhame of American Software Inc. and R.G. (Bob) Brown of Material Management Inc. (now affiliated with Greystone Software) for having provided guidance over the years. I appreciated the valuable reviews of the textbook completed by Trisha Van Slyke. Again, special thanks to my brother Louis J. DeLurgio Jr. of IBM and my sons Patrick and Steve for maintenance of the website http:// forecast.umkc.edu. As always, I owe a debt of gratitude to the graduate students of UMKC who have had to endure early manuscript pages as their textbook. In addition, my wife has been very understanding and patient in enduring the quadratic loss function that results from significant positive bias in my forecasts of manuscript completion dates. Finally, let me thank you for using or considering this textbook and manual and your patient understanding about errors of any type.

Steve DeLurgio
Henry W. Bloch School of Business
University of Missouri - Kansas City
Kansas City, MO 64110
V:1-816-235-2311
F:1-816-235-6506
email:delurgio@cctr.umkc.edu
       sad@forecast.umkc.edu
url:http://forecast.umkc.edu

RATS COMMANDS

Most of the enclosed problem solutions use RATS input commands and outputs. Much of RATS is self-documenting or self-evident in input and output, thus, **I am confident that you will have absolutely no problems in understanding 99.99% of the enclosed RATS output**. If you are skeptical, then skim a few chapters to alleviate your concerns. However, there are several aspects of RATS that may not be obvious. These RATS-specific commands are:

SET commands are analogous to the BASIC programming language LET commands, however in RATS one can specify the range of observations over which the SET command is operable. For example:

SET FORE 12 48 = ACTUAL(T-12)

This command sets a forecast of periods 12 to 48 equal to the actual of twelve (T-12) periods ago. Consider the following obvious command which creates a new variable which is the natural logarithms of SALES.

SET LSALES 1 100 = LOG(SALES)

The standard RATS regression command is

LINREG depvar / residuals
#constant indepvars

where depvar and indepvars are any variables used as dependent and independent variables respectively and / represents fitting a model over all possible observations. If specific observations are to be used, then the format is:

LINREG depvar 13 48 residuals
#constant indepvars{1}

As shown above, RATS has a flexible way to specify lags of independent variables, where {1} denotes that the dependent variable is to be lagged one period. Similarly, many lags can be included in the braces as shown below:

LINREG depvar / residuals
#constant indepvars{0 to 6}

Cochrane-Orcutt Iterative Least Squares, COILS is run in RATS using:

AR1 depvar / residuals
#constant indepvars

After regression output you may see a command

PRJ fit 1 48
PRJ fore 49 60

This is a command that must follow a LINREG command and this creates either fitted or forecasted values depending on the observation numbers included after the variable name (e.g., 1 48 as shown above). In the above two command lines, two new variables are created, "fit" and "fore," obviously any variable name can be used here.

Cross correlations are run in RATS using the following command:

CROSS outvar invar

Where this calculates the CCF(k) for the variables OUTVAR(t+k) versus INVAR(t).

ARIMA
RATS uses the BOX command to fit ARIMA and MARIMA models. This command is nearly identical to the regression command and is very simple, however consider some RATS specifics:

BOX(diff=1,sdiff=1,ma=1,sar=1,constant) SALES 1 100 RES

This command fits the following model: $ARIMA(0,1,1)(1,1,0)^S$, where "sdiff" means take seasonal first differences and "diff" means take first-order, nonseasonal differences. Now the coefficients for ma1 and sar1 will be shown in the output as $MA\{1\}$ and $SAR\{1\}$. This model is fitted to observations 1 to 100 and the residuals are saved in a variable called RES.

A MARIMA model is specified very similarly to an ARIMA model - The following command models a first-order Transfer Function of an output variable SALES as a function of an input variable ADVERT, in addition an AR(1) Noise Model of first differences is fitted.

BOX(diff=1,input=1,ar=1,constant,apply) SALES 1 100 RES
#ADVERT 0 1 0
(in general 0 1 0 are s r b as developed in Chapters 12 and 13, the word input=1 means that there is one input variable as defined in the # line and the word "apply" means apply all differences to the output and input variables).

With a MARIMA model, the coefficients associated with an input variable (i.e., ADVERT) are shown in the output as either:

N_ADVERT{0}
D_ADVERT{1}
where N_ADVERT is the coefficient commonly designated as omega,
where D_ADVERT is the coefficient commonly designated as delta for a first-order transfer function.

Finally, RATS can create forecast and fit variables after ARIMA (i.e., BOX) and COILS commands using the FORE command; its use will be obvious in the problem sets. For example, the following two forecast commands create a fitted variable called FIT1 and a forecasted value called, FOR1, each of which are applied from periods 1 96 and periods 97 to 120 respectively.

```
FORE 1
#EQ1 FIT1
FORE 1 24 96
#EQ1 FOR1
```

As stated, I do not believe you will have any problems with 99.99% of the RATS input or output in this Instructor's Manual. However, if you have any problems interpreting any output in this IM, please do not hesitate to contact me via phone or email. I will respond immediately.

                                        Steve DeLurgio

TYPICAL SYLLABUS

QA 545
Forecasting Theories and Applications

Stephen A. DeLurgio, Ph.D.
Room 404 Bloch Bldg
University Phone: 816-235-2311
FAX: 816- 235-6506
EMail: delurgio@cctr.umkc.edu
         sad@cctr.umkc.edu
Website: http://forecast.umkc.edu

Time and Room:

Monday Night from 7:00 to 9:45 Instructional Technology Room, Rm 114 and Computer Classroom ·¹, approximately half time in classroom and half time in computer classroom.

Focus:

Computer based forecasting methods - theory and applications.

Description of Course:

A study of the principles and applications of alternative forecasting methods. Typical methods included are smoothing and decomposition time series methods, regression methods, econometric models, intervention analysis, and univariate and multivariate autoregressive integrated moving average methods (ARIMA building methods popularized by Box and Jenkins), artificial neural networks, and forecasting expert systems.

Prerequisites:

A basic statistics course such as QA 308 or QA 508. Those taking this class should have successfully completed a statistics course. Those who are more quantitatively challenged than others will find that the applications track requires less quantitative knowledge.

Texts:

DeLurgio, S. A., <u>Forecasting Principles and Applications</u>, Irwin/McGraw-Hill, Burr Ridge, Il. 1998, inclusive of a diskette of 245 time series and about 50 *.WK1 templates.

RATS Software is optional, however, you are urged to purchase this software for the convenience of completing assignments at work or home. This computer software is taught in the class.

Tracks:

Applications and Theory Tracks - To accommodate those with various quantitative backgrounds, I have created two tracks in the course. The applications/managerial track is for those who do not view quantitative methods as their forte', thus, it is less quantitatively rigorous. The managerial track is designed to accommodate those who feel uncomfortable with quantitative materials but who want to learn principles of forecasting. The theory track may be the most efficient for those with quantitative/mathematical backgrounds. These tracks are distinguished by the level of statistical rigor which is needed to earn a grade. One track is not easier or harder than another, but they differ in terms of the type and number of tests versus forecasting projects required of the student.

Software:

All software is available in our computer laboratory and computer classroom. This course teaches you how to use RATS^{tm}, Regression Analysis and Time Series (RATS), and ForecastPro^{tm} for Windows. RATS programs and EXCEL or Quatro Pro, or Lotus 123 (i.e., *.wk1) software will be made available to students. In lieu of these other software packages, SAS (Statistical Analysis System) software and programs will be available to students. SAS programs prewritten by me and others will be available to students so that they can learn SAS in the context of forecasting. Finally, SPSS is available in our computer lab and its TREND program is an excellent way to learn forecasting.

Some Highlights: Some of the interesting aspects of this class include:

> * Being able to understand the basic, underlying theories of many different forecasting methods.
> * Learning a powerful statistical package which is much easier to use than a spreadsheet. Learning basic-to-advanced forecasting methods that are presented in an intuitive manner.
> * Understanding forecasting/time series principles which relate to personal and professional financial planning, investments, marketing, general management, international business and human resource management.
> * Learning contemporary forecasting methods such as Artificial Neural Networks using software developed by the author. I believe that these methods are presented as intuitively as possible, thus, making them understandable and usable by manager and analyst like.
> * Using the forecasting WEBSITE (http://forecast.umkc.edu) developed for this course. It will assist you in learning more about forecasting applications throughout the world.
> * Using 250 specifically selected time series from marketing, finance, operations, and general management to study actual applications of forecasting. For example, the October 1987 crash, 1993 Midwest flood, and other notable events are studied in the context of time series analysis and forecasting. These time series are included with the book and are on the Website.
> * Using one of the most sophisticated forecasting expert systems, Forecast Pro(tm) which will be made available to you in our lab or a free demo version for use with Windows 3.1.
> * Owning and using extremely sophisticated software that until 20 years ago would have cost $20,000 for you to purchase.

Background:

This course studies the essentials of effective statistical forecasting methods. In a very general sense, all decisions are based upon forecasts. Many decision makers use unscientific methods of forecasting to arrive at decisions, and often such methods are effective. However, if the decision maker possessed a knowledge of more scientific approaches, the effectiveness of his or her decisions should be enhanced. It is for these reasons that managers, engineers, economists, and analysts should study statistical forecasting methods. In addition, few topics are as inherently interesting to as large a number of disciplines as forecasting. This course tries to further refine and stimulate your interest and success in forecasting.

Important forecasting applications are studied in the areas of financial planning and analysis, marketing research, sales forecasting, operations planning and analysis, and accounting/financial forecasting, international management including market forecasting, sales forecasting, and the analysis of stock prices.

Statistical forecasting methods and applications have taken on significantly greater importance in the last decade. This is due in part to greater competitiveness in business and the wider availability of low-cost, high-technology computer software and hardware. Microcomputer based statistical and forecasting packages rival and often exceed those currently available on mainframe computers. Computer-based management information systems, integrated production information control systems, marketing and financial information systems all require forecasts as inputs for long-term to immediate-term planning, execution, and control.

While this course covers a full range of forecasting methods, it concentrates on the most widely used methods of forecasting including simple smoothing, econometric, and Box-Jenkins (ARIMA Building) methods. These methods are important tools in production, marketing, finance, engineering, and economics. The emphasis of the course will be on the principles and applications of successful forecasting.

Grading:

The course grade will be determined from the following formulas depending on your track:

	Applications	Theory
Forecasting Project or Case Analysis	50%	25%
Homework	20%	20%
Midterm	30%	30%
Final	0%	25%
	100%	100%

Forecasting projects or case analysis are to be undertaken by groups of one or two students, preferably two students, one theory oriented the other applications oriented. The scope of these projects will be discussed early in the semester. You should select a time series of interest to you for study in this class. If you do not have a project of interest, the book includes 9 different projects.

BRIEF COURSE OUTLINE

I. Introduction
   A. Forecasting Models and Methodology
   B. Elementary Statistics: A Review
   C. Introduction to the Regression Model

II. Univariate Time-Series Methods
   A. Smoothing and Extrapolation of Time Series
   B. Exponential Smoothing -Holt-Winters Method
   C. Linear ARIMA (i.e., Box-Jenkins) Time-Series Models
   D. Identification of ARIMA Models
   E. Estimation of ARIMA Models
   F. Diagnosing ARIMA Models
   G. Forecasting with ARIMA Models

III. Multiple Regression and Econometric Methods
   A. Two-Variable (Bivariate) Regression Model
   B. The Multiple Regression Model
   C. Using Multiple Regression Models
   D. Serial Correlation and Heteroscedasticity
   E. Instrumental Variables and Two-Stage Least Squares
   F. Forecasting with a Single Equation Regression Model

IV. Multivariate ARIMA Time Series Models
   A. Intervention (Impact) Assessment
   B. The Cross-Correlation Function
   C. Prewhitening
   D. Model Identification
   E. Model Estimation
   F. Model Diagnostics
   G. Model Forecasting

IV. Other Methods and Contemporary Topics
   A. Artificial Neural Networks
   B. Cyclical Forecasting
   C. Qualitative and Technological Forecasting Methods

V. Forecasting Software and Applications are Integrated Throughout
   A. Financial Applications
   B. Marketing Applications
   C. Operations Applications
   D. Accounting Applications
   E. General Planning Applications

Forecasting projects are to be undertaken by groups of one or two students, preferably two students. The scope of these projects will be discussed early in the semester.

You are to select a time series of interest for your study in this class from the minicases identified in this book. To lessen the load of doing a minor research project, you should select your data and partner for your research project during the first two weeks of class.

PERIOD	DATE	TOPIC	READING ASSIGNMENT
1	AUG 25	Introduction to Course Grading, Forecasting Projects and Software - RATS and Sources of time series.	Chap. 1
		Sources of Data	Appendix A
	SEP 1	Holiday, Labor Day - Statistics Review	Chap. 2
2	SEP 8	Statistical Fundamentals	Chap. 2
		ACFs and Q-statistic	
		Outlier Adjustment	Appendix B
3	SEP 15	Simple Linear Regression	Chap. 3
4	SEP 22	Simple Smoothing Methods	Chap. 4
5	SEP 29	Decomposition	Chap. 5
		Schwartz Bayesian Criteriod	Part of Chap. 17
		Introduction to ForecastPro	
6	OCT 6	Trend-Seasonal and Winters'	Chap. 6
7	OCT 13	ARIMA Model Building Methods I	Chap. 7
8	OCT 20	ARIMA Model Building Methods II	Chap. 7
9	OCT 27	ARIMA Building Methods III	Chap. 8
10	NOV 3	Econometric and Regression Applications I	Chap. 10
11	NOV 10	Econometric and Regression Applications II	Chap. 11
12	NOV 17	ARIMA - Intervention	Chap. 12
13	NOV 24	MARIMA - Transfer Functions	Chap. 13
14	DEC 1	Cyclical Forecasting/Qualitative/Technological	Chap. 14/15
15	DEC 8	Neural Networks	Chap. 16

16 FINAL EXAM FOR THEORY TRACK, TIME TO BE ANNOUNCED

1 AUG 25   **Introduction to Course** Grading, Forecasting Projects and
Computer Software RATS and Sources of time series data available   Chap. 1

2 SEP 8   **Statistical Fundamentals**   Chap. 2
ACFs and Q-statistic for Random Series, Random Walks (e.g., stock prices), Trending Series, and
Seasonal Series.

3 SEP 15   **Simple Linear Regression**   Chap. 3
Assumptions of Regression Analysis, Durbin-Watson Statistic, Modeling Lead-Lag Relationships
with Cross Correlation Coefficient. US and German Stock Indexes.

4 SEP 22   **Simple Smoothing Methods**   Chap. 4
Simple and Seasonal Exponential Smoothing Methods. Forecasting and Smoothing Time Series such
as Births and Marriages.

5 SEP 29   **Decomposition**   Chap. 5
Classical Additive and Multiplicative Decomposition Methods, Interpreting Seasonal Indexes,
identifying cyclical influences. Applying these methods to many different time series.

6 OCT 6   **Trend-Seasonal and Winters'**   Chap. 6
Using Differences to Achieve Stationarity andEffective Forecasts
Holt-Winters Smoothing. Applying these methods to many different time series.

7 OCT 13   **ARIMA Model Building Methods I**   Chap. 7
ACF and PACF identification of models, identifying random walks, trends, seasonality, and trend-
seasonal series.

8 OCT 20   **ARIMA Model Building Methods II**   Chap. 7
Estimating ARIMA Models, US Stock Index, Demand for FAD product, Stock Prices, Demand for
Dairy Product, Achieving Variance Stationarity,

9 OCT 27   **ARIMA Building Methods III**   Chap. 8
Estimating More Complex ARIMA Models, the extraordinary versatility of ARIMA methods,
modeling Demand for Animal Pharmaceuticals, Common Stock Prices, Utility Electricity Demand,
Japanese Stock Index, among others.

10 NOV 3   **Econometric and Regression Applications I**   Chap. 10
Multicollinearity and Serial Correlation Adjustment Procedures Such as Cochrane-Orcutt, many
other time series concepts in regression analysis such as heteroscedasticity, elasticities, dichotomous
variables, Goldfeld-Quandt test, and Partial F-test. US versus UK Stock Index relationship,

11 NOV 10   **Econometric and Regression Applications II**   Chap. 11
Path Analysis, Granger Causality, Causality Requirements, Structural Equations, and Two Stage
Least Square Methods. Building Materials Requirements.

12 NOV 17   <u>**ARIMA - Intervention**</u>   Chap. 12
   Modeling Different Types of Interventions - Midwest Flood, October 1987 Stock Market Crash,
   Many other Interventions.

13 NOV 24   <u>**MARIMA - Transfer Functions**</u>   Chap. 13
   Modeling Complex and Dynamic Relationships Using Transfer Functions.   Daily IBM stock prices
   NY versus London, Lumber Sales, Automobile Market Share

14 DEC 1   <u>**Cyclical Forecasting/Qualitative/Technological**</u>   Chap. 14/15
   Topics to be determined by Student interests and projects.

14 DEC 8   <u>**Neural Networks**</u>   Chap. 16
   Understanding how Artificial Neural Networks model extremely complex mathematical and logical
   relationships, forecasting Automobile Prices based on automobile characteristics.

As an introduction to the types of problems and cases used throughout the book, consider the following
minicase time series graphs.

<u>SOME OF THE MINICASES USED THROUGHOUT THIS BOOK</u>

While not shown here, I distribute graphs of the 9 minicases to stimulate interests in these or other minicase
projects.

PROBLEM SOLUTIONS

PROBLEMS

ESTIMATED DIFFICULTY

Elementary	Medium			Hard			Very Hard		Bad

1 M	2 M	3 M	4 M	5 E	6 E	7 M	8 M	9 M	10 M
11 M	12 M	13 M	14 M	15 M	16 M	17 H	18 M	19 M	20 M
21 M	22 M	23 M	24 H	25 H					

Minicases are all Medium difficulty.

1-1. Choose an organization and identify the common forecasting system characteristics of Figure-1.

Type of Application:	AIRLINE
Data Collection:	Passengers making reservations and flying on each flight
Information Processing:	Accumulation of flight utilization rates (actual percentage of seats that are occupied) and absolute number of passengers.
Forecasting Model:	Forecast of passengers by flight (i.e., time and route of each flight).
Operational Goals and Plans:	Maximum customer service subject to low operating cost, low investment in facilities and equipment, and highest ROI and EPS.
Allocation Decision:	Optimal allocation of aircraft, pilots, attendants, and ramp service personnel in order to achieve the operational goals and plans.

1-2. Do you accept the near universality or commonality of forecasting data suggested in Figure 1-1? Can you think of an actual organization which would not benefit from more accurate forecasts?

Yes, we do accept the near universality and commonality of Figure 1-1. We are hard pressed to name an organization which would not benefit from improved planning as a result of better forecasts.

1-3. Do organizations you are familiar with have formal forecasting systems? Speculate why or why not?

Many organizations have formal systems, while others have informal uncoordinated forecasting systems. I am aware that at several universities there is no coordinated forecasting process. The bookstore uses one set of enrollment figures to estimate the number of books based on historical ratios, individual departments and deans use other sets of numbers, which are not coordinated with the central administration's set of numbers. The central administration may have an individual from institutional research who compiles past enrollments by class and projects future enrollments using some very basic models. In some cases, these forecasts of enrollments are used in faculty hiring decisions such as where new faculty positions will be allocated or the replacement of a retiring professor with another professor in that discipline.

Many organizations have coordinated and comprehensive forecasting systems because they recognize the potential benefits from such systems. In contrast, many organizations do not have formal forecasting systems because of several reasons including; they do not recognize the benefits from these systems, they view such systems with great distrust because they fear the loss of control or power when a coordinated forecasting system is in place, they are only comfortable with ill-defined political processes, or they are relatively uneducated in forecasting and planning. Some managers resist forecasting because they will not be able to "control or manipulate" the numbers to their advantage.

1-4. Explain the management decision hierarchy of Figure 1-2 and how it relates to forecasting.

The framework of Figure 1-2 was first introduced by Robert Anthony of Harvard's business school. It presents the generic management functions of most organizations. These generic functions are strategic planning, managerial planning, operational planning and control, and finally, transaction processing. The hierarchy of Figure 1-2 illustrates the importance of forecasts in providing the needed information for "informed" decision making in the organization. Column two of Figure 1-2 shows four forecasting horizon lengths that are inputs to the four hierarchical decisions and functions of almost all organizations.

1-5. What is a forecast? What characteristics should a good forecast have?

A forecast is an estimate of the future value of an activity that provides an expected value (i.e., mean) a range, and a probability statement associated with that range. In addition there are many other desirable attributes of a forecast that are developed throughout this book, the most important characteristic is that the forecast is representative and accurately estimates the future.

1-6. Explain the differences between dependent and independent demands and how these relate to forecasting.

Independent demand must be forecast, because it cannot be calculated. For example, the number of students that will take a course may have to be forecast. In contrast, dependent demand can and should almost always be calculated. In our example, the demand for books at a university bookstore and the demand for classrooms are dependent demands and therefore can be calculated from the independent demand forecast of the number of students who are expected to enroll in a class.

1-7. List and define the common time series patterns described in the book. Also, define typical causes of these time series patterns.

Trend - long-run general movement caused by long-run technological, demographic, social, political, and economic influences.

Cyclical - variations from the trend that typically last approximately 3 to 10 years; caused by cyclical business, economic, and technological life cycles. Cyclical variations are recurrent, but not periodic. That is, there is no known or fixed period, thus, they are the second hardest pattern to predict. The most difficult component to predict is irregular or random variations.

Seasonal - are variations which are recurrent and periodic. These are caused by manmade conventions and holidays as well as the climatic influences of weather. Some seasonal variations have a period greater than 1 year. For example the seasonal influences of the Olympics (i.e., 4 years) as well as some cash crops that have seasons greater than one year. There are many time series which have seasonal periods of less than a year, including lunar seasons, 24 hour seasonality and so on.

Irregular - these are influences which are unpredictable such wars, strikes, hurricanes, tornadoes, competitor stock outs, equipment breakdowns, terrorist acts, and so on.

Autocorrelated - these are influences that result from relatively small changes in the time series that randomly walk up and down because of a number of influences including the momentum of large markets. The characteristics of a random walk include extremely high autocorrelations and a nonconstant good predictor of the next actual. As we shall learn, highly autocorrelated series can be nonseasonally autocorrelated and/or seasonally autocorrelated.

Planned and unplanned events or interventions can be subsets of seasonal and irregular influences. For example, if a promotion takes place at the same time each year, then it will induce seasonality into the time series (i.e., reduced air fares or lower long distance charges during evenings). If the planned or unplanned event takes place with no known period, then it is an irregular event that may or may not be predictable. Obviously, when the event is planned, its date is well known, and assuming that those responsible for planning and forecasting are aware of the date, then the forecast can be adjusted appropriately.

1-8. What is an outlier and why are they so important? How do outliers relate to planned and unplanned events and interventions?

Outliers are very large values in a series that are not representative of the pattern of interest - the pattern which embodies the past and future behavior of the time series. Outliers in the statistical quality control sense are values that are statistically out of control (e.g., more than three standard deviations away from their expected values). Planned and unplanned events can both yield outliers. If either of these events can be forecasted, then that expected change in the pattern (i.e., event forecast) should be used to adjust the final forecast, for example by adding or subtracting the appropriate value of the event. We should estimate and retain the magnitude of the effects of these outliers and interventions so that they can be used to adjust forecasts. This is discussed in greater detail in book Appendix B.

1-9. Give an example of a forecasting hierarchy using an example different than that of Table 1-2?

Again, using an airline as an example:

Long-horizon forecast, strategic planning: Forecasts of the number of passengers using current and potential hub cities for flights and where those passengers want to fly. For example, some southern cities continue to undergo very rapid increases in populations, these represent expanding markets for the airline.

Medium horizon, managerial planning: Having identified general markets that the airline wants to expand into or exit from, forecasts must be made of the number of passengers, fares, and required facilities needed to serve that market. Then, finance, marketing, and operations must determine which hubs will be most profitable, easily marketed, efficiently operated, and yield the highest return on investment.

Medium-to-short horizon, Operational planning and control: Using historical time series of recent passenger use of existing routes, forecasts of passenger demand for existing and new routes are generated. Based on these forecasts for the next several months "equipment" and personnel are allocated to the most effective hubs.

Immediate horizon, transaction planning: Using the number of passengers that have booked a flight and forecasts of those who will actually show up, personnel schedules and equipment allocations are made hourly and daily to ensure that there are adequate resources to provide high levels of customer service while not exceeding the budgets resources available.

1-10. Briefly explain the three general types of forecasting methods. Make up or relate to examples which are different from those of this chapter.

The three general types of forecasting methods are univariate (time series), multivariate (causal), and qualitative (subjective or technological). Univariate forecasts use a simple model of the past patterns of a time series as a predictor of the future behavior of the time series. For example, the demand for a cold remedy might be estimated solely based on past, highly seasonal patterns in demand.

Multivariate forecasting models use the past relationship between one or more other variables to predict the value of the dependent variable. At times we attempt to model causal relationships, but more commonly, only predictive relationships result. For example, the demand for a cold remedy might be estimated using weekly weather forecasts that predict temperature and precipitation. These forecasted independent variables are then used to generate the forecast of the dependent variable.

Qualitative forecasting methods include a number of subjective methods where the opinions of experts or surveys of customers are used to forecast new products and new technologies. For example the demand for cellular mobile phones was dramatically underestimated even though consumer surveys and expert opinions were used to estimate this demand.

1-11. Describe the scientific method and how it relates to forecasting?

The scientific method consists of the systematic pursuit of knowledge through formal problem recognition and formulation, data collection through objective observation or experimentation, and the formulation and testing of specific hypotheses. The definition of the scientific method is very similar to the flow chart of Figure 1-18 on page 27.

1-12. Describe the seven steps of the forecasting process development in this Chapter.

Referring to Figure 1-18 we see the following seven steps:

I. Problem Definition: Define the problem needing solution, the decisions to be made and boundaries of the system being modeled or controlled.

II. Information Search: Define the system in greater detail including possible cause and effect relationship through initial fact finding and data acquisition.

III. Hypothesis/Theory/Model Formulation: Further refine the model and use graphical exploration of the relationship being modeled.

IV. Design the Experiment to Fit and Validate the Model: Select in and out-of-sample observations and the method for judging validity.

V. Execute the Experiment: Fit in-sample models and forecast out-of-sample models.

VI. Analyze the Results: Are the assumptions of the model correct, do results support theory? Compare in and out-of-sample statistical results.

VII. Ongoing Use of the Model: Implement the model as part of a larger system, monitor the model to detect out of control situations, when appropriate, provide ways of incorporating judgment into the forecasts.

1-13. Someone states that management intuition in forecasting is not legitimate; how do you respond to this?

The term intuition may have a negative connotation to some, however, if we accept the definition of intuition as encompassing instinctive or subjective knowledge, then intuition is a legitimate way to adjust a forecast. Sometimes managers "just knows" something is likely to occur without being able to explain why. Managers frequently use subjective judgment in adjusting forecasts.

1-14. Briefly describe any practical forecasting activities that you have personally been involved with or know about.

The answers to this question will vary depending on whether students are undergraduate or graduate and on their professional experiences. Any type of planning that the student has been involved with will likely involve forecasting. So even if they are unable to identify a specific forecasting activity, it is likely they will know of practical forecasting activities in many routine decisions. These activities include: buying a car, buying a computer system, choosing a university and a degree program, asking someone out on a date, even very mundane things such as applying the brakes on a car involve a forecast or prediction of what will happen.

This question is a good lead in for the instructor who has first hand knowledge about forecasting.

1-15. If you are to analyze an actual series in your use of this book or as a research project, identify that series and the source of the data. What types of patterns do you believe will dominate that series?

The answer to this will vary by student depending on his or her choice of time series.

1-16. Choose a time series of interest to you on the enclosed data disk, plot this series and identify which common time series patterns are included in it. What is the dominant pattern? Explain the cause of this dominant pattern.

Assume that a random walk time series has been chosen, assume that it is IBMMN.DAT, monthly stock prices of IBM. This is a good time to introduce random walks and the problems of forecasting this time series. There is quite a contrast between one period and 12 period forecasting accuracy with such time series.

Another interesting time series is SERIESD.DAT, a series of soft drink sales. This series is seasonal and cyclical. That is, during year 3, there appears to have been a short cyclical downturn.

The famous International Airline Passengers series of minicase 1-7 is an interesting series illustrating seasonality, trend, and variance nonstationarity.

1-17. Go to your University or local library and choose a time series from a government publication such as the Survey of Current Business, Federal Reserve Bulletin, or the Historical Statistics of the United States from Colonial Times to 1970. Be sure to include at least 48 observations if it is a monthly time series. Plot this series and identify common patterns in it. What is the dominant pattern? Explain the cause of this dominant pattern.

Again, the answer to this question will vary by student and his or her chosen time series.

1-18. Identify what has to be forecasted at a university for short-term planning and scheduling purposes and for long-term planning purposes.

Short-term planning: Student enrollment, books for each class next semester, classroom schedules, part time and full instructors.

Long-term planning: The mission of the school, degrees that will be offered, the physical facilities that are necessary for each degree program, the number of students at the university in each discipline, the number of faculty by discipline, the allocation of teaching, research, service dollars and emphasis, the required administrative structure and many other longer range activities.

1-19. Identify the short-term independent and dependent demands in your organization. (If you are a full time student then your organization is your school.)

The example of a university fits well here. The short-term independent demands consist of the number of students enrolling in classes. The short-term dependent demands include books, classrooms, seats in the classrooms, computers in labs, as well as number of part time and full time instructors.

Another example is an animal pharmaceutical. The independent demands are orders received from feedlots, veterinarians, and ranchers. Also, for some drugs, the demands for drugs is dependent upon the weather, particularly temperature and humidity. The dependent demands are for drug ingredients, packaging, transportation, federal inspections and testing of drugs etc.

1-20. Using two selected series from the following list and their graphs from the text, identify what is the dominant pattern? Explain the cause of this dominant pattern.

a) Figure 1-3, Printer paper demand, SERIESA.DAT. Series A displays a relatively random pattern, where there may be no better model than the mean. There appears to be a slight increase in years 3 and 4.

b) Figure 1-4, World wide air fatalities, WWFATAL.DAT. This series is rather random, and while we might like to believe that there is a downward trend in fatalities, only time will tell. Also, these fatalities represent the total number of passengers who die in commercial aircraft accidents. This is a good opportunity to discuss fatalities per passenger mile or flying time as well as the number of miles flown worldwide. Also, the great variability caused by the effect of a large airline disaster may make this series particularly difficult to forecast accurately.

c) Figure 1-5, Advanced Microcomputer sales, SERIESC.DAT. The dominant pattern in series C is trend, as we might expect. We might have expected some strong seasonality for this product, but none is there. This might be indicative of the types of customers (i.e., large corporations) that are buying this product.

d) Figure 1-7, Monthly soft drink sales, SERIESD.DAT. Soft drink sales are classical seasonal series with peaks in the summer and troughs in the winter.

e) Figure 1-9, Demand for daily trout tags, TROUT.DAT. The demand for trout fishing is very seasonal in Missouri. For the series of Figure 1-9, the season runs from March 1 to October 31, with strong repeating seasonality from weather, summer starting, Memorial Day, Father's Day, 4th of July, and Labor day. Early and late in the season, weather influences demand greatly because a combination of rainfall (sometime snowfall) and low temperatures discourages the angler from fishing.

f) Figure 1-10, Composite index of leading indicators, LEADIN.DAT. Cyclical influences and trend dominate this series.

g) Figure 1-11, Daily stock prices (stock unknown) SERIESB.DAT. Series B is not seasonal but highly autocorrelated, so much so that it is a random walk.

h) Figure 1-12, Daily IBM stock prices, IBMMN.DAT. IBMMN.DAT is a random walk.

i) Figure 1-16, Monthly AM-FM radio sales, SERIESF.DAT This series is dominated by trend and seasonality.

j) Figure 1-17, Monthly Demand for Electricity, MEGAWATT.DAT. This series is dominated by trend and seasonality. In addition, the series has variance nonstationarity where the peaks and troughs of the series increase as the level of the series increases. The percentages and logarithms of these types of series are most often analyzed because the series is undergoing a multiplicative seasonality which is eliminated or modeled using percentages or logarithms.

1-21. Plot selected time series from problem 1-20 using software chosen by you or your instructor. Confirm that the patterns identified in the text are evident in your plots.

Answers will vary by student/software and all of these plots are in Chapter 1.

1-22. Using selected time series from the following, plot the same figures using your own software. Confirm that the patterns or relationships of the text are evident in your plots.

a) Figure 1-6, German and U.S. Stock indexes, USGERM.DAT. These series can be found in Figure 3A-1 of page 137 in the text.

b) Figure 1-8, Quarterly Births and Marriages in the U.S., BIRTHMAR.DAT.

c) Figure 1-13, Big City Bookstore, BIGCITY.DAT

1-23. Using selected time series from the following, plot these series and identify the common patterns in each. What is the dominant pattern? Explain the causes of the pattern.

a) JAPAN.DAT, the Japanese Stock Index, can be found in Chapter 8, Figure 8-12 where logarithms of the series are plotted. This time series is dominated by its trend which reverses during the last part of the series. While not obvious, the series has variance nonstationarity which is very clear if one takes first differences. The rapid and sustained growth in the Japanese economy accounts for the early strong trend. Some domestic problems in the Japanese economy during the 1990's accounts for the subsequent decline. Over a longer period of analysis, this series might appear as random walk, only time will tell.

b) BLOOD.DAT, the daily demand at a blood bank, can be found in Figure 12-7 of page 505. This time series is completely random until period 135 when the blood bank expanded its market. This series can be modeled a number of different ways including regression analysis using dummy variables or intervention methods as in Chapter 12.

c) ELECT.DAT, the monthly demand for consumer electronics is shown in minicase 10, Figure M1-10 in this instructor's manual.. It is dominated by trend and seasonality. Also, there appears to be some slight variance nonstationarity as the peak to trough values seem to increase as the level of the series increases. Later, in Chapter 6 and 7 we will study logarithms as a way to eliminate the variance nonstationarity.

d) ERRORS.DAT, the hourly defects in the output of an in control chemical process is not plotted in the text. When plotted, the 185 observations of this time series clearly has an outlier in an early period. Except for this outlier, this series appears to quite random and nearly perfectly centered on zero.

e) SALES.DAT, the quarterly manufacturer's sales in the U.S. consists of 93 quarterly observations. This series displays at least three time series patterns, trend, cyclical, and seasonal variations. Also, there appears to be some variance nonstationarity as variations get larger when the series level increases. However this series may be more complex than that. (Note: Possibly a GARCH model might be necessary to model this nonstationarity, however, this is much too early to discuss this in a technical way.)

1-24. Define the purpose of each of the Roman Numeral steps of the forecasting process shown in Table 1-5.

Please refer to Table 1-5 for this answer.

1-25. Review the General Outline of the Forecasting Implementation of Table 1-5. List those sections which you do not understand and speculate on their meaning. Be prepared to discuss the meanings of those you do and do not understand.

The answer to this question will vary by students. Typically, students have problems with sections IV and V. Many however want to gloss over the importance of I. Problem Definition.

MINICASES USED THROUGHOUT THIS BOOK

MINICASE 1-1. Kansas Turnpike, Daily and Weekly Data.

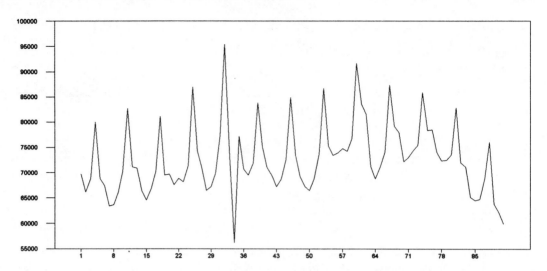

Fig. M1-1A. Daily Vehicle Usage With Peaks on Fridays and the Fourth of July Peak

1) What dominant sales patterns? Seasonality by day of the week is quite strong. Weekly seasonality and trend is quite strong in the weekly series.

2) What are the peak and trough periods? Daily, peaks on Fridays and troughs on Wednesday, much as would be expected. Interestingly, the peak day is Friday July 2 and the trough is Sunday, July 4th. Weekly seasonal peaks and troughs depend on holidays and climatic seasons. There are peaks before and after holidays and the summer. Troughs occur on the days of holidays and because of cold weather and poor highway conditions.

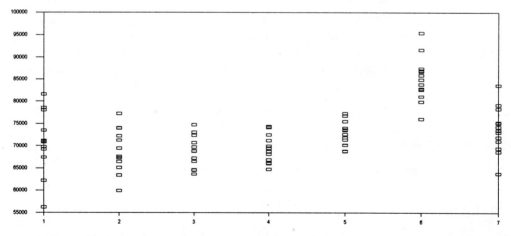

Fig. M1-1B. Daily Vehicle Usage Starting On Sunday =1, Peak on Friday = 6.

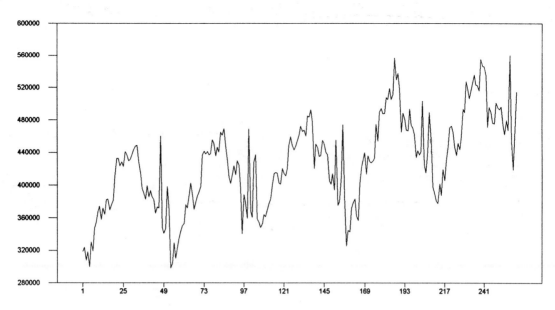

Fig. M1-1C. Weekly Usage for 5 Years- Note Holiday And Summer Peaks, Winter Troughs

3) What are the causes of these dominant patterns? Seasonality is caused by climatic conditions, work weeks, holidays, and other human habits. The peaks during Summer, Thanksgiving, and Christmas are extra-ordinary. Other holidays will have peaks and troughs, but not as strong.

4) Does the series follow the patterns that you expected? Answer yes or no and explain why or why not. Seems to be exactly what I would have expected, and possibly stronger. We draw inferences from our own travel habits, in some cases correctly and in others incorrectly.

5) What are the social and economic causes of activity? Are these changes evident in the time series. This was adequately answered in 4).

6) Speculate on what other information would be useful for forecasting this time series. How would you forecast this series using time series analysis, how about causal analysis?

Other information could include sporting events at the University of Kansas (Lawrence) and Kansas State University (further west in Manhattan), major conventions in Kansas City, for example the FFA (Future Farmers of America Convention, who said Kansas City is a Cow Town?), major sporting events in Kansas City for example the Royals Baseball and Chiefs Football games might influence traffic.

A daily time series model: $Y_t = f(Y_{t-1}, Y_{t-7}, Y_{t-364}, Y_{t-365}, \text{Holiday Effect})$

A weekly time series model: $Y_t = f(Y_{t-1}, Y_{t-364}, \text{Holiday Effect})$

A causal model would include the factors we discussed above. See also the minicase solution of Chapter 3.

MINICASE 1-2. Air Passengers by Quarter.

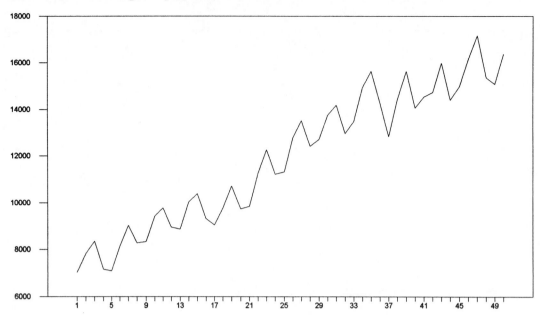

Fig. M1-2. Passenger Revenues by Quarters for 50 Quarters, Air Transport Association

1) The dominant sales patterns are trend and seasonality. Note: this is a time series of passenger revenues, not passengers.

2) Quarters I and IV are low and II and III are high.

3) Except for holiday affects like Thanksgiving, Christmas, and New Years, the trough quarters are the first and last of the year because of weather and the peaks caused by vacation plans during the summer quarter.

4) The series does follow the pattern expected because airfares and demand follow these patterns.

5) Vacation, business, and personal travel plans dominant the demand for air travel. Also, weather influences the desirability (demand) and availability (supply problems because of winter storms) of air travel. Who wants to fly to O'hare during a blizzard?

6) Other useful information includes: Air Fares, weather conditions, major world events like Olympics, terrorist bombings, etc.

A time series model: $Y_t = f(Y_{t-1}, Y_{t-4}, \text{Holiday Effects})$

A causal model might take into consideration air fares, corporate and personal incomes, major world events, the number of aircraft in service (e.g., whether an airline has gone bankrupt or not, etc.). See also the minicase solution of Chapter 3.

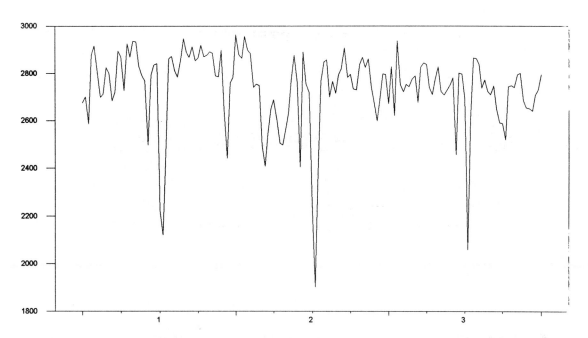

Figure M1-3. Hospital Census of Medical and Surgical Patients by Week of the Year

MINICASE 1-3. Hospital Census by Week.

1) Seasonality dominates this series.

2) Thanksgiving, Christmas, and New Years are trough months. Other seasonal patterns are not as strong

3) The causes of these patterns include holidays, physician work schedules, the seasonality of some types of accidents, diseases, physician conventions, weather conditions.

4) The seasonality is not as strong as I would have thought. In fact this series is one of the more difficult ones to achieve high accuracy (i.e., low errors).

5) For some it is surprising the extent to which physician work schedules and medical conventions influence surgeries. The holiday effect is as would be expected. In looking at holiday effects it is important to recognize that some holidays are 51, 52, and 53 weeks apart depending on the particular calendar effects, this is particularly true for Thanksgiving. Also, Easter, Passover, and Moslem holidays vary considerably from a 52 week periodicity.

6) Other information that is valuable includes the number and types of physicians who are affiliated with the hospital and unusual weather conditions that might influence demand.

A time series model: $Y_t = f(Y_{t-1}, Y_{t-52}, \text{Holiday Effects})$

A causal model might take into consideration the factors listed in 5) and 6). Note that this is a series which cannot be forecasted as accurately as most other minicases. See also the minicase solution of Chapter 3.

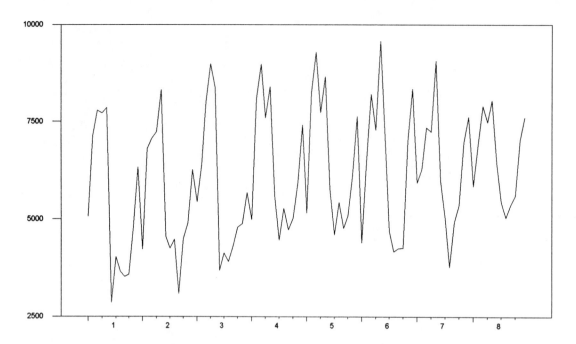

**Fig. M1-4. Eight Years of Monthly Demand at Henry Machler's Hideaway Orchids. MINICASE 14.
Henry Machler's Hideaway Orchids.**

1) Seasonality dominates this series, but no trend, Henry refused to significantly expand his business.

2) Jan. to May are increasing with May being a peak month. Also, December is a peak month. In the Summer demand is considerably lower. Some increases in November.

Thanksgiving, Christmas/New Years, and particularly Mother's Day are peak holidays.

3) The causes of these patterns include the large influx of northerners (i.e., snowbirds) arriving after the first of the year and holidays. Summer troughs are caused by northerners leaving and high temperatures and high humidity. Also, proms during May might increase demand somewhat, however, these are orchid plants, not corsages. Finally, Mother's Day causes the peak weekend of the year.

4) The pattern is a little stronger than I would have thought during May. However the pattern follows the anticipated seasonality of great demand on Mother's day.

5) The holiday effect is as would be expected. In looking at holiday effects it is important to recognize that some holidays are 51, 52, and 53 weeks apart depending on the particular calendar effects, this is particularly true for Thanksgiving. Easter, Passover, and Moslem holidays vary considerable. Thus, some minor peaks might occur during these holidays.

6) Other information that would be valuable include unusual weather conditions and the week of the religious holidays that might influence demand.

A time series model: $Y_t = f(Y_{t-1}, Y_{t-52}, \text{Holiday Effects})$

A causal model might take into consideration the factors listed in 3) and 5). See also the minicase solution of Chapter 3.

MINICASE 1-5. Your Own Forecasting Project.

Obviously responses to this vary depending on the project chosen. I always urge students to select a real world project of their own, particularly the sales of their own company, if they are working. Because students often can not find good data at their own companies or are not working, I have developed these minicases. The TROUT.DAT time series represent a time series which can be used by students, obviously, there are many other possibilities.

MINICASE 1-6. Midwestern Building Materials

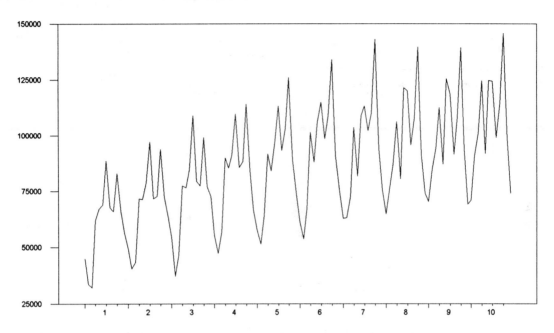

Fig. M1-6 Monthly Demand for Building Materials

1) Seasonality and trend dominate this series.

2) July and October are peak months. Troughs are in the Winter months with coldest weather in the Midwest.

3) The causes of these patterns include the large number of do-it-yourself (DIY) and professional home building projects that need building materials.

4) The pattern is not as I would have expected. I would have expected to find a peak in the Spring and one in late Summer/early fall. While a little surprised, it should be noted that the largest one month peaks in July and October are driven by promotional activity.

5) The summer or climatic influences explain much of this pattern along with vacation times and longer days for after-work home or do-it yourself projects.

6) Other information that would be valuable include unusual weather conditions and promotional and advertising campaigns of the company.

A time series model: $Y_t = f(Y_{t-1}, Y_{t-52},$ Holiday Effects, Promotional Effects, Weather Effects.)

A causal model might take into consideration the factors listed in 3), 5), and 6). See also the minicase solution of Chapter 3.

MINICASE 1-7. International Airline Passengers

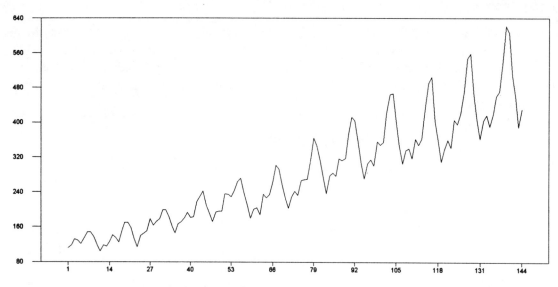

Fig. M1-7. Monthly International Airline Passengers - 12 Years, 144 Months

This is the much analyzed time series of R. G. Brown and G. E. P. Box and G. M. Jenkins. Thus, students may find this time series analyzed in many textbooks. This may or may not be desirable depending on your purpose in assigning minicases. This is a logical candidate for full class analysis or discussion as an example case used throughout the semester. You can use the minicase solutions presented in this instructor's manual as an example for student projects.

1) The dominant sales patterns are trend, seasonality, and variance nonstationarity.

2) January and February are trough months and July and August are the peak months.

3) Except for holiday affects like Thanksgiving, Christmas, and New Years, the trough months are the first and last months of the year because of weather and greater vacation plans during the summer.

4) The series does follow the pattern expected because airfares and demand follow these patterns.

5) Vacation, business, and personal travel plans dominate the demand for air travel. Also, weather influences the desirability (demand) and availability (supply problems because of winter storms) of air travel. Again, who wants to fly to O'hare during a blizzard?

6) Other useful information includes: Air Fares, weather conditions, major world events like Olympics, terrorist bombings, etc.

A time series model: $Y_t = f(Y_{t-1}, Y_{t-12}, \text{Holiday and Promotional Effects})$

A causal model might take into consideration air fares, corporate and personal incomes, major world events, the number of aircraft in service (e.g., whether an airline has gone bankrupt or not, etc.).

It can be useful to introduce variance nonstationarity at this time because of the very strong nonstationarity of this series. See also the minicase solution of Chapter 3.

MINICASE 1-8. Automobile Sales

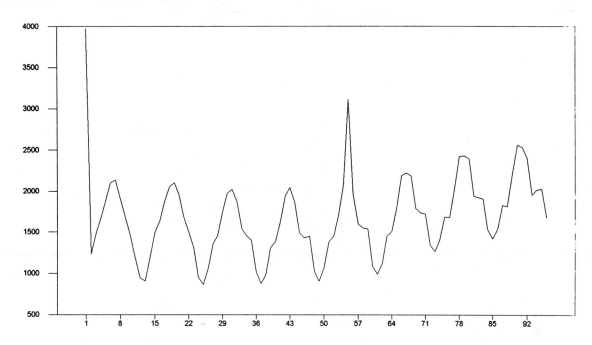

Fig. M1-8. Monthly Auto Sales Series with Two Outliers, Both Need to be Adjusted.

1) The dominant sales patterns is seasonality and level nonstationarity, it seems to be randomly walking, outliers should be adjusted for further analysis. Book Appendix B can be referred to as needed to adjust outliers.

2) December and January are trough months and June and July are the peak months.

3) We assume that the causes of the peaks are Summer promotions to unload new cars before the new model year is announced in late September or October. The trough months appear to be weather related.

4) The series does not follow the pattern I had expected because a higher demand was expected in October as a result of the announcement and availability of new cars for the new model year. Comparison of this time series with car production information published in the Wall Street Journal and by the Department of Commerce might help clarify this situation. However, summer promotions of overstocked cars does account for the peaks in June and July.

5) Weather, vacation, business, and personal travel plans influence the demand for cars. Also, these underlying causes of demand are greatly influenced by promotional campaigns by the car manufacturer, this is likely the case at this company.

6) Other useful information includes promotional campaigns and expenditures of the company, the advertising budget of this company compared to that of the industry, quality and consumer survey results, etc

A time series model: $Y_t = f(Y_{t-1}, Y_{t-12},$ Holiday and Promotional Effects)

A causal model might take into consideration personal incomes, unemployment rates, gas prices, major world events, , promotions and holidays. See also the minicase solution of Chapter 3.

MINICASE 1-9. Consumption of Distilled Spirits

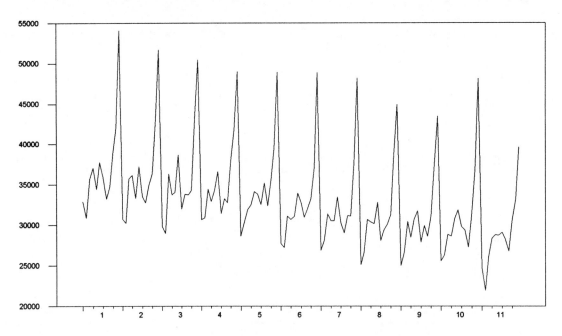

Fig. 1-9. Monthly Distilled Spirits for Eleven Years

Distilled spirits are alcoholic beverages other than beer and wine. This is a time series of shipments.

1) Negative trend with pronounced seasonality.

2) Peak months are October, November, and December with troughs in January, February, and September.

3) Clearly, holiday demand for "spirits" are the greatest determinants of seasonality. The long run decline in trend is a result of greater health concerns and the possibility of other forms of drink or spirits entering the market. Possibly, beer, soft drinks, or even drugs are displacing "spirits" as the vice of choice.

4) Yes, it follows the expected pattern.

5) The social causes are the traditions and habits of having alcoholic drinks during the holidays. Also, the decline might represent improved health consciousness, religious convictions against the use of alcohol, the results of anti-drinking campaigns for automobile drivers and college students.

6) Other information that might be helpful includes advertising budgets for alcohol, and the competition from beer and soft drinks.

A time series model: $Y_t = f(Y_{t-1}, Y_{t-12}, \text{Holiday and Promotional Effects})$

A causal model might take into consideration the other factors listed in 5) and 6). See also the minicase solution of Chapter 3.

MINICASE 1-10. Discount Consumer Electronics

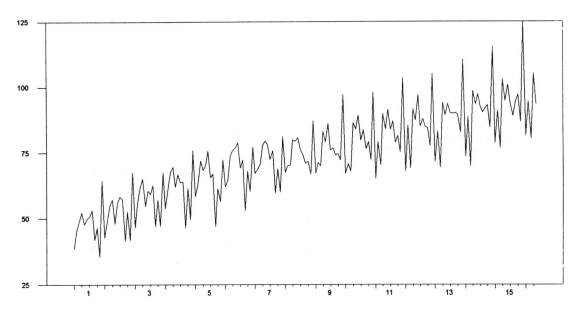

Fig. 1-10 Discount Consumer Electronic Sales for Fifteen Plus Years

1) Trend, high seasonality, and possibly variance nonstationarity.

2) Peaks occur in December, April, June to August, and October. Other months are troughs.

3) and 5) The peak in December is very predictable, the other peaks are likely caused by promotions related to the start of school (June to August) and promotions in April and October.

4) The series behaves as expected.

6) Other information includes promotional budgets, consumer surveys and quality surveys of the company's products, and cyclical influences.

A time series model: $Y_t = f(Y_{t-1}, Y_{t-12})$

A causal model might consider the other factors listed in 5) and 6). See also the minicase solution of Chapter 3.

CHAPTER 2
STATISTICAL FUNDAMENTALS FOR FORECASTING

I. PROBLEMS

ESTIMATED DIFFICULTY

Elementary		Medium		Hard			Very Hard		Bad
1 E	2 E	3 E	4 E	5 E	6 E	7 E	8 E	9 M	10 E
11 E	12 E	13 E	14 E	15 E	16 E	17 M	18 M	19 M	20 E
21 E	22 M	23 E	24 E	25 M	26 M	27 M	28 M	29 M	30 M
31 M	32 M	33 M	34 M	35 M	36 M	37 M	38 M	39 M	40 M
41 M	42 M	43 E	44 M	45 M	46 M	47 H	48 H	49 M	50 H
51 H	52 H	53 H	54 H	55 H	56 H	57 H	58 H		

Minicases are all Hard

2-1. The past patterns of a time series are assumed to be samples of all past patterns and likely (or is it hopefully) samples of future patterns. Thus, past patterns become a forecast of the future pattern.

2-2. One reason graphs are so important is the excellent pattern recognition abilities of educated analysts, abilities that are difficult to duplicate in software. That is, the analytical abilities of computer software and expert systems are only as good and as comprehensive as those who have programmed them, thus there are limitations to all forms of automated analysis.

2-3. See pages 38-41 for discussions on past relative frequencies (and probabilities), theoretical frequencies (and probabilities), and subjective probabilities in the text.

2-4. A good forecast yields point and interval estimates along with the probability of the interval. When errors are normally distributed then the forecast and RSE provide an estimate of the probability distribution of possible future values and errors. When errors are not normally distributed, then the past residuals provide a rough estimate of the out-of-sample error distribution. However, we should emphasize that normally, the RSE is only an estimate of the one-period forecast error, not the m-period ahead error which is expected to have a greater error.

2-5. A good forecasting model will reduce the risk (i.e., chance) in having a large error, but the process of forecasting is still very much like the classical definition of a game of chance. An x% chance for a small error and a (100-x)% chance of making a large error. We desire that x be as large as possible.

2-6. Elementary question easily answered by referring to the chapter. Emphasize the efficiency of the median when extreme values bias the mean.

2-7. The standard deviation describes the scatter of values about the mean and takes on its greatest significance when probability statements (i.e., confidence intervals) are made. Fortunately, the mean and standard deviation of the ND define the whole distribution and allow the generation of probability statements in forecasting. The RSE is a standard-deviation-like calculation where the deviations are forced to be about a center value of zero. The RSE is the square root of the mean of square deviations from zero whether the mean is zero or not.

2-8. Elementary question easily answered in the chapter. Also, see question 2-4.

2-9. Prediction intervals are confidence intervals with the additional assumption that past relationship will remain valid into the future. In the classical sense, a confidence interval is based on the assumption that a sample has been taken from a population and inferences are being made about that same population. In contrast, with a prediction interval in forecasting, the future may be a different population than the past, thus, the prediction interval carries with it the additional assumption that the past relationship (i.e., population) will remain valid into the future, this is a tenuous assumption.

2-10. Assumption 1, the forecasting model validly represents the past. Assumption 2, the past repeats into the future, or alternatively, the relationship of the past remains valid into the future. Clearly, assumption 2 is the more tenuous of the two. On average, we believe the past will repeat, however in a specific application it may not.

2-11. See page 51- fitting yields estimated coefficients, forecasts use these estimated (i.e., fitted) coefficients.

2-12. See pages 52-53.   2-13. See page 54.   2-14. See pages 54-56.

2-15. See page 60.   2-16. See pages 60 to 61.   2-17. See page 62.

2-18. See page 64.   2-19. See page 66.

2-20. The correlation coefficient only measures linear association, thus it is possible to have perfect nonlinear associations and zero linear correlation (i.e., a zero correlation coefficient). Graphs and nonlinear transformations can be useful in detecting nonlinear association.

2-21. See page 59 for the definition/formula of a covariance, an autocovariance is simply the substitution of lagged values of the Y_{t-k} for X_t in equation 2-16.

2-22. An autocorrelation is the measured linear association between a variable and lags of itself. Autocorrelations can be measured using several different formulas including equations 2-19 and 2-20. An ACF is an approximation of the Pearson correlation coefficient, typically, but not always calculated using equation 2-20.

2-23. Using the 2 standard error approximation formula of equation 2-23, the statistical significance test for an ACF at lag 10 equals $2/\sqrt{100} = .2$. In fact, this is the approximate 2 standard errors for ACF(k) for k = 1 to 25 (i.e., n/4). However, as pointed out on page 69 there are other formulas used in some statistical software.

2-24. The 2 standard errors of the ACF is approximately .2, thus an ACF(12) of .4 with a sample size of 100 is statistically significant. The borderline of significance is .2 when using a t-value of 2 to define significance. However, if n were less than 48, then this test becomes more unreliable because the lag of 12 becomes larger than 25% of the observations.

2-25. a. see Figure 2-11, b. see Figure 2-12, c, see Figure 2-13, d. see Figure 2-14, e. is not shown in the chapter but would appear as Figure 2-11 with the possibility of statistically significant spikes at unexplainable lags.

2-26. First 10 Presidents Mean = 77.4, Median = 78.5, and Mode = about 79. Last 10 Presidents, Mean = 71.9, Median = 69.5, and Mode about 63.5. The last 10 presidents died earlier than the first 10 presidents. I believe the responsibilities and worries of the last 10 presidents exceeds those of the first 10 presidents. However, others might argue that the change in life style to a more sedentary less physical and less aerobic life style since the turn of the century has probably taken its toll on the last 10 presidents. Finally, we should be careful to recognize that this is such a small sample that statistical inferences must be made cautiously. A simple t-test can be applied as a test of the difference between two means.

2-27. As shown below the standard deviation of the last 10 US presidents is greater than those of the first 10

MEAN	MEDIAN	MODE	STDEV	RANGE	MIN	MAX	MODIFIED MEAN	
77.4	78.5	79	7.560129	23	67	90	77.125	FIRST 10
71.9	69.5	63.5	11.63758	33	57	90	71.5	LAST 10
-5.5	-9	-15.5	4.077453	10	-10	0	-5.625	Difference

2-28. Statistics for Series A (note, MAD is not shown in the textbook, that section was eliminated) also, I cannot explain why the data disk series A has a standard deviation of 64.557 while that in the text is reported as 64.53, probably .56 was misread as .58:

Mean = 850.083   Standard Deviation = 64.557   MAD = 51.5833

2-29. ACFs for lags 1 to 4.

```
Series A ACFs    1:     0.17836372   0.22958561   0.07381349   0.1236553
Series B ACFs    1:     0.92738782   0.82500408   0.69318668   0.56357321
Series C ACFs    1:     0.85576952   0.81985284   0.76108393   0.69478066
Series D ACFs    1:     0.7916396    0.4837161    0.0857388    0.2919505
Marriages ACFs   1:    -0.1249580   -0.7113432   -0.1088449    0.8753146
```

2-30. ACFs for lags 1 to 12.

```
Series SA
1:    0.1783637    0.2295856    0.0738135    0.1236553    0.0192867    0.17184
7:    0.0809283   -0.0054841    0.0240859    0.1466917    0.1710868    0.18924
Series SB
1:    0.9273878    0.82500408   0.6931866    0.56357321   0.4485275    0.34153
7:    0.2503443    0.1740164    0.1153646    0.0869779    0.0855050    0.08734
Series SC
1:    0.8557695    0.81985284   0.76108393   0.69478066   0.64169966   0.57053
7:    0.5480687    0.46904717   0.4197087    0.3613606    0.3156404    0.27039
Series SD
1:    0.7916396    0.4837161    0.0857388   -0.2919505   -0.5732188   -0.66895
7:   -0.5894663   -0.3541970   -0.0733358    0.2110712    0.4449199    0.51070
Marriages
1:   -0.1249580   -0.7113432   -0.1088449    0.8753146   -0.1027594   -0.61304
7:   -0.1067595    0.7433771   -0.0721973   -0.5131195   -0.0975169    0.62172
```

2-31.

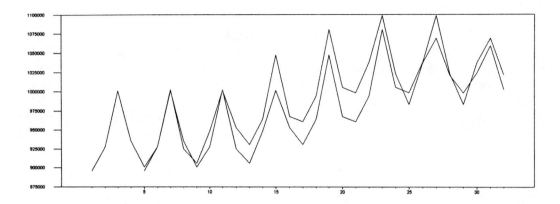

Fig. P2-31a. Births$_t$ and Births$_{t-4}$

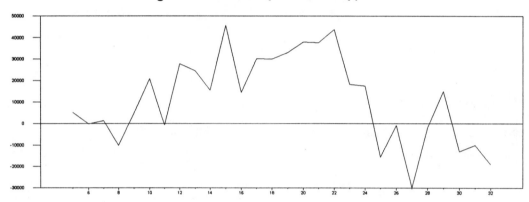

Fig. P2-31b. Errors in using Births$_{t-4}$ to forecast Births$_t$

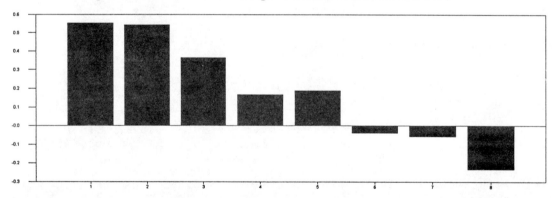

Fig. P2-31c. Autocorrelations of the Errors of Fig. P2-31b.

The simple seasonal random walk model for births is inferior to that for marriages, because Births have a pronounced trend. Thus, as shown in Fig. P2-31b, most of the errors are positive. However, one might argue that Births is also a random walk because of the decline in 1991 and 1992, however, this may reflect some cyclical influence. Note, based on the statistics below, this model does explain a significant amount of the original variance (53994^2) as a function of last years value ($RS\hat{E} = 23021^2$).

```
Series          Obs    Mean          Std Error    Minimum     Maximum
BIRTHS          32     988380.69     53994.4228   896013.     1098868.
FORECAST        28     983756.50     55526.0239   896013.     1098868.
ERRORS          28     11515.68      20299.3287   -29868.     45647.
RSE = 23020.80
```

2-32. Statistics on Series SB: Mean = 750.25   Sample Standard Deviation = 184.139   MAD = 148.896

2-33. Series B Naive Model: a. RSE=53.174   MPE = 1.06   MAPE = 6.71

b. One period ahead forecast errors are fairly low with this model with the statistics given above. The R-square is .914 which is very respectable. However, as measured by the DW and Q-statistics, this model does have considerable autocorrelation left in the residuals as shown in the plot below. Thus, R-square can be improved as we shall study later. The mean percent and mean absolute percent errors are equally good.

Durbin-Watson Statistic = 0.922785   Q(11-0) = 36.342462   Significance of Q =0.00015

c. At a 95% confidence level about 2.01 times RSE equals the prediction interval for 47 degrees of freedom, this equals 106.88. (Note: t (for 47 degrees of freedom) = 2.01 with Significance Level 0.0502)

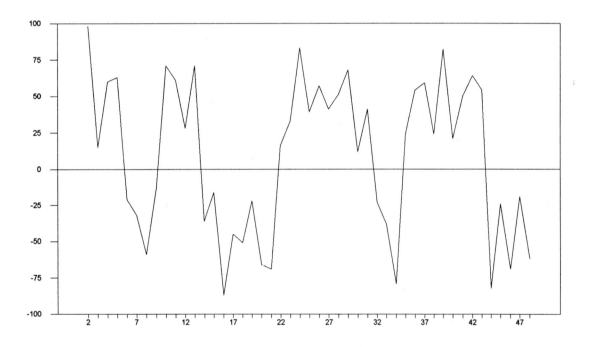

Fig. M2-33. Residuals of a Naïve Model for Series B.

2-34. Series B, using three period lag as a forecast, $Y = Y_{t-3} + e_t$

a. RSE = 126.625   MPE = 2.043   MAPE = 16.000

b. This model is not nearly as accurate as the naïve model of the previous problem. This emphasizes the need to match the correct patterns and the problems in achieving accurate forecasts for multiperiod-ahead forecasts with random walks. Because the RSE is so much higher for this model than that of 2-33, its prediction intervals are much greater.

2-5

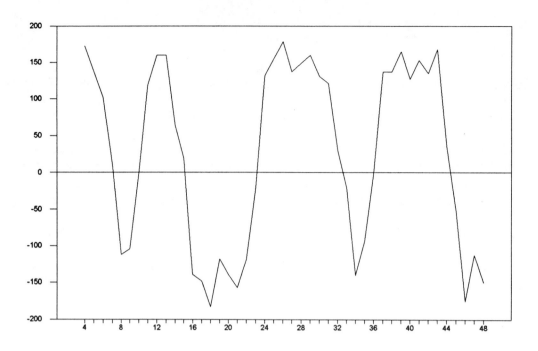

Fig. M2-34. Residuals of a Three-Period Lag Model for Series B.

2-35. a) Model 1, ME=66.00   RSE1 = 80.424   MPE1 = 7.2242   MAPE1 = 7.286 7

   Model 2, ME=3.875   RES2 = 77.353   MPE2 = .0647   MAPE2 = 7.6463

b) The errors are shown in Fig. P2-35 below.

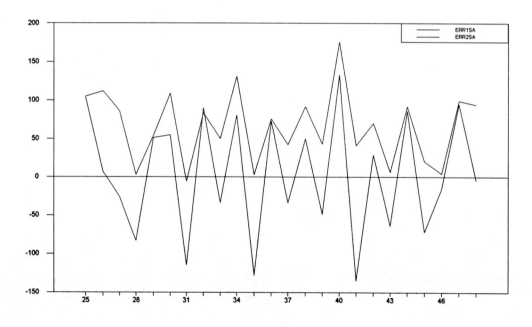

Fig. P2-35

c) Model 2 is the better of the two as measured by the ME and RSE. Model 1 suffers from bias caused by the slightly lower values in periods 25 to 48. MAPE1 is better than MAPE2. If the bias in Model 1 were removed, it would be the better model.

2-36. a) ME=14.32, MPE=1.52%, MAPE=7.05,MSE=4015.4,RSE=63.367, b) The naïve model forecasts relatively accurately except for bias. The S=175 while RSE is only 63.367., c) 95% intervals are approximately +/- 1.96*63.367. As shown in the figure below, errors are rather random, but have a nonzero mean of 14.32, this bias results from the trend in the time series.

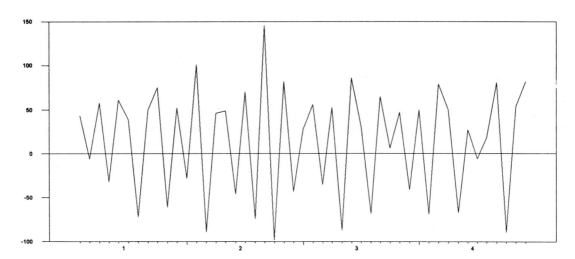

2-37. a) ME1=9.08   MPE1=1.06%, MAPE1=6.711, MSE1=2827.42,   RSE1=53.17,
         ME2=120.53, MPE2=10.51%, MAPE2=27.275, MSE2=51560.9,   RSE2=227.07

b) Clearly the random walk model is better, the twelve-period-ahead model performs much worse as shown by the ME and RSE. c) Because it walks randomly, it is very difficult to get accurate multiperiod forecasts.

2-38. a), b), c): ME1=-2.42, MPE1=-1.16%, MAPE1=10.54, MSE1=5715.03, RSE1=75.6
                  ME2=2.89,   MPE2=-1.59%, MAPE2=18.62, MSE2=15378.4, RSE2=124.0

d) Using all error statistics Model 1 is the superior of the two models because of the regularity in the 12-period seasonality.

e) If the patterns in a series repeat and are modeled, then relatively accurate s-period ahead forecasts can be obtained.

2-39. The following is a Covariance\Correlation Matrix generated by RATS, correlations above the diagonal, covariances below the diagonal.

	SALES	ADVERT	COMP
SALES	301.0555555556	0.9642120216	0.2123391439
ADVERT	122.7500000000	53.8333333333	0.4262095104
COMP	28.4722222222	24.1666666667	59.7222222222

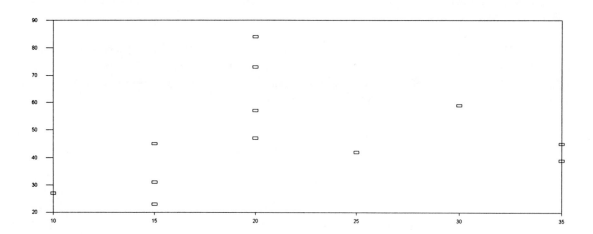

Fig. P2-39. Sales vs Competition

The low correlation between Sales and Competition is supported by the graph. Note: the output of RATS like the output of several other statistical packages, does not use n-1 in the denominator of the covariance calculations, however, a better, unbiased estimate of the covariance is obtained by using n-1 instead of n in the denominator, see for further discussion, pages 23 to 27 of Pindyck and Rubinfeld. Because n versus n-1 are canceled out in the calculation of correlation coefficients, the correlation coefficients will be the same whether n or n-1 is used.

2-40.   See the correlation matrix of problem 2-39. Advertising and Competition are positively related.

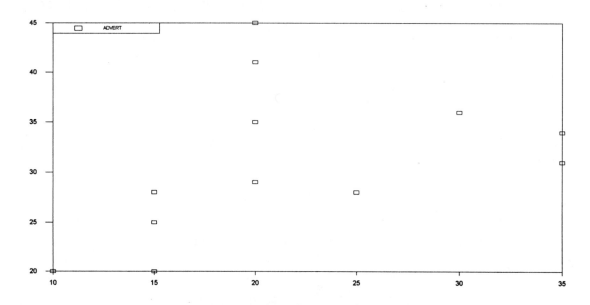

Fig. P2-40. Advertising Vs. Competition

2-41. Y and X2 are perfectly related with correlation coefficient of 1.0.

2-42.   The following is a Covariance\Correlation Matrix using RATS which uses n, not n-1 in the denominator of covariance calculations. As shown, there is a perfect negative correlation between the two variables. To adjust covariance for n-1 versus n simply take (-1.333333333*3)/2=-2 and product of the standard deviation of Y times the standard deviation of X is 2, thus the -1 correlation coefficient.

```
        Y                              X
Y    0.66666666667            -1.0000000000
X   -1.33333333333             2.66666666667
```

2-43 Autocorrelations of Series BIRTHS, note the extremely high ACFs at 4 and 8 in the figure below.

1: 0.47873   0.12478   0.450530   0.79780   0.30760   -0.03372   0.25574   0.5089503

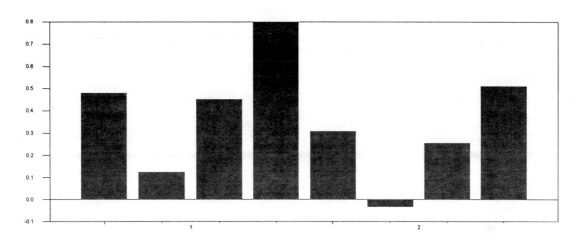

2-44. The correlation between births and marriages is .530, which is not particularly high for 32 observations. A statistical significance test is: t= .530/((1-.53^2)/(32-2))^5 = 3.42328, t-table with 30 df and α=.01 = 2.750, so we infer that this correlation is statistically significant. While births and marriages are correlated, this correlation is not extremely strong. This may be true because it may be lagged values of marriages which is highly correlated with births. Nonetheless, there is some association between the two variables, however, marriages do not literally cause births but are highly associated with births.

2-45. The error statistics for this model are: ME=-1843.75, MPE=0.00, MAPE=2.00, RSE=13257.16

The standard deviation of marriages is quite high at 116,739.84 compared to only 13,257.16 for the RSE of this model. Thus, this is very useful model. To generate 95% confidence intervals for 1 to 4 period ahead forecasts, the prediction interval would be +/- 2.048*RSE = 2.048*13257.16 = 27150.66368 (Note that the t-value, df=28, alpha=.05 = 2.048)

2-46. See pages 75 and 76.

2-47. Same as question 2-31.

2-48. The model works better for marriages than births because marriages is essentially a random series while births has a trend or is a very slow random walk. If the bias were removed from the births model by including a trend constant then this model would perform nearly as well at that model for marriages.

2-49. ACFs: -0.2234043   -0.6170213   0.3936170
Pearson Correlation: -0.2500000   -0.9113224   0.80295507

The significant difference results from the differences in the number of observations in numerator and denominator of the ACF formula.

2-9

2-50. Using IBM Closing Prices for only the 96 observations from 1985 to 1992.

	Obs.	Mean	Std Dev	Min.	Max
Closing Prices	96	117.569	22.600	50.375	168.375
Forecast	96	117.569	22.600	50.375	168.37
Error	95	−0.905	7.920	−28.250	15.750
Percent Error	95	−1.3	7.5	−35.0	11.7
Absolute PE	95	5.7	5.1	0.000	35.5
Error^2	95	62.891	103.384	0.000	798.062

MSE = 62.891, RSE= 7.930 This yields a 95% prediction intervals about a 1.96*7.930=15.543

IBM Series, Monthly Data From 1985:01 To 1992:12 Autocorrelations

```
 1: 0.88826324 0.78368415 0.67534806 0.59384517 0.52150672 0.47498365
 7: 0.44660907 0.42664097 0.42699445 0.42251265 0.40748716 0.39367774
13: 0.38528914 0.38615817 0.39253119 0.39799345 0.36064754 0.31082932
19: 0.25325461 0.20538728 0.14793133 0.12014522 0.12701674 0.15327337
```

ERRORs, Monthly Data From 1985:02 To 1992:12 Autocorrelations

```
 1:  0.1421292  0.0280623 -0.0685377 -0.0222448 -0.1094374 -0.1440195
 7: -0.1416931 -0.1646427 -0.0703313  0.0842165 -0.0362106 -0.0545060
13: -0.0450689  0.0081177  0.0434300  0.2769450  0.1619082  0.0535362
19: -0.0049039  0.0492293 -0.0899510 -0.1296504 -0.1617373
```

The is a strong random walk pattern to the original series and none left in the error series.

2-51. Using IBM Closing Prices for only the 96 observations from 1985 to 1992.

	Obs.	Mean	Std Dev	Min.	Max
FORE2	96	117.569	22.600	50.375	168.375
Error2	93	−2.278	15.034	−57.625	31.625
PE2	93	−3.4	14.3	−60.3	20.3
APE2	93	10.5	10.3	.10	60.3
ERROR2^2	93	228.771	432.272	0.016	3320.641

MSE = 228.771, RSE= 15.125, This yields a 95% prediction intervals about a 1.96*15.125=29.645

ERROR2, Monthly Data From 1985:04 To 1992:12, Autocorrelations

```
 1:  0.6886384  0.3058023 -0.0792196 -0.1834420 -0.2617115 -0.3158205
 7: -0.3305584 -0.2545313 -0.1353697 -0.0392429 -0.0444919 -0.0724514
13: -0.0734052  0.0597820  0.2291724  0.3672704  0.3324278  0.2169739
19:  0.0607358 -0.0650777 -0.2085074 -0.2496008 -0.1785828
```

There is a strong autoregressive pattern left in the errors of this model.

2-52. Clearly the random walk model is better. However, note that there may be some variance non-stationarity in the errors, so as expected, probably logarithms of the original series should be analyzed. This may or may not be too early to introduce this concept here.

2-53. Series	Obs	Mean	Std Error	Minimum	Maximum
DATE	144	68087.88889	34665.80345	12982.00000	123192.0000
CLOSE	144	250.73146	97.69219	107.09000	435.7100
FORE	143	249.43790	96.79010	107.09000	431.3500
ERROR	143	2.14098	12.24367	-70.04000	41.8700
PE	143	0.00738	0.04696	-0.27817	0.1164
APE	143	0.03407	0.03303	0.00006	0.2782
ERROR^2	143	153.44297	462.11425	0.00010	4905.6016

MSE = 153.44, RSE = 12.39, This yields a 95% prediction intervals about a 1.96*12.39=24.28. However, note that this series has a pronounced variance nonstationarity, thus the logarithms of this series should be analyzed. This topic can be introduced here or later.

SP500, Monthly Data From 1981:01 To 1992:12 Autocorrelations

```
 1: 0.97404509 0.94847330 0.92492960 0.90266899 0.88242728 0.85887861
 7: 0.83814191 0.81413993 0.79126780 0.77117074 0.74816635 0.72458650
13: 0.70002737 0.68029896 0.65745827 0.63575575 0.61318558 0.59074367
19: 0.57113471 0.54936727 0.52973352 0.51217687 0.49537493 0.48253461
25: 0.46977140 0.45754783 0.44675927 0.43610515 0.42249256 0.40323628
31: 0.38349483 0.36368952 0.34877845 0.33154943 0.31404334 0.29367162
```

There is a strong random walk in the original series and none remains in the errors below.

ERRORs, Monthly Data From 1981:02 To 1992:12 Autocorrelations

```
 1: -0.0072799 -0.0218619 -0.1220852 -0.1270963  0.0853855 -0.0716907
 7:  0.0694777 -0.1383627 -0.0778456  0.1025380  0.0180809 -0.0540047
13: -0.0165311  0.0119511 -0.0380225 -0.0680780  0.0134290 -0.0817239
19:  0.0155725 -0.0357349 -0.0851942  0.0222087 -0.0663520  0.1169549
25:  0.0277327  0.0734298  0.0187481  0.0125113  0.0773472 -0.0428583
31: -0.0397974 -0.0633037  0.0299924  0.0799746  0.1757273
```

2-54.

Series	Obs	Mean	Std Error	Minimum	Maximum
DATE	144	68087.88889	34665.80345	12982.00000	123192.00000
CLOSE	144	250.73146	97.69219	107.09000	435.71000
FORE2	141	246.94745	95.15748	107.09000	424.21000
ERROR2	141	6.30440	21.06718	-99.50000	49.53000
PE2	141	0.02137	0.08438	-0.43205	0.19909
APE2	141	0.06312	0.05973	0.00086	0.43205
ERROR2^2	141	480.42400	1114.32663	0.01960	9900.25000

MSE = 480.42, RSE = 21.92, This yields a 95% prediction intervals about a 1.96*12.39=42.96. However, note that this series has a pronounced variance nonstationarity, thus the logarithms of this series should be analyzed. This topic can be introduced here or later.

ERROR2, Monthly Data From 1981:04 To 1992:12, Autocorrelations

```
 1:  0.6156586  0.1853903 -0.1983755 -0.1878489 -0.0644481 -0.0581060
 7: -0.0691286 -0.1364092 -0.0742645  0.0030583  0.0146244 -0.0177361
13: -0.0572809 -0.0618674 -0.0768024 -0.1120400 -0.0966416 -0.1008255
19: -0.0876042 -0.1079585 -0.1202646 -0.0620965 -0.0019593  0.1179018
25:  0.1371698  0.1520004  0.1260222  0.1035834  0.0630084 -0.0376648
31: -0.0797526 -0.0640485  0.0892345  0.1903537  0.1937668
```

There is some pattern left in the errors of this model.

2-55. Clearly the random walk model is better. However, note that there is variance nonstationarity in the errors, as expected, probably logarithms of the original series should be analyzed. This may or may not be too early to introduce this concept here.

2-56. Japan Stock Index from U.S. Department of Commerce

Series	Obs	Mean	Std Error	Minimum	Maximum
DATE	271	1980.861402	6.533174	1970.010000	1992.070000
CLOSE	91	1651.145055	473.922546	839.400000	2589.40000C
FORE	90	1656.927778	473.338127	839.400000	2589.400000
ERROR	90	3.236667	87.605284	-286.100000	183.20000C
PE	90	0.002022	0.051410	-0.156083	0.097663
APE	90	0.039829	0.032294	0.000468	0.156083
ERROR^2	90	7599.887444	13428.836742	0.810000	81853.210000

MSE = 13428.84, RSE = 115.88, This yields a 95% prediction interval of about +/-1.96*115.88=227.12. However, note that this series has a pronounced variance nonstationarity, thus the logarithms of this series should be analyzed. This topic can be introduced here or later.

Closing Prices for Monthly Data From 1985:01 To 1992:07, Autocorrelations

```
 1:   0.9600830   0.9089909   0.8591373   0.8095098   0.7626996   0.7153645
 7:   0.6698457   0.6244944   0.5812690   0.5350126   0.4814246   0.4282537
13:   0.3766316   0.3308323   0.2914082   0.2541389   0.2160396   0.1750586
19:   0.1299487   0.0883367   0.0449704  -0.0021522
```

ERRORs, Monthly Data From 1985:02 To 1992:07 Autocorrelations

```
 1:   0.3786583   0.0704692  -0.0825649   0.0458593   0.1128943   0.0128281
 7:   0.0057192   0.0074723   0.1525929   0.1280983  -0.0039829  -0.0104068
13:  -0.0867028  -0.0394787   0.0294993   0.0408477   0.0850864   0.0736632
19:   0.0327746   0.0526146   0.0280302   0.1031846
```

There is still some slight pattern left in the ACFs of the errors. In addition, do not overlook the problems with variance nonstationarity.

2-57.

Series	Obs	Mean	Std Error	Minimum	Maximum
DATE	271	1980.86140	6.53317	1970.01000	1992.07000
CLOSE	91	1651.14505	473.92255	839.40000	2589.40000
FORE2	88	1667.09886	473.77746	839.40000	2589.40000
ERROR2	88	10.87955	190.59330	-538.80000	363.70000
PE2	88	0.00448	0.11376	-0.33101	0.19581
APE2	88	0.08738	0.07238	0.00000	0.33101
SERROR2	88	36031.376	57146.81	0.00000	290305.44000

MSE = 57146.80, RSE = 239.05, This yields a 95% prediction interval of about +/-1.96*239.05=468.55. However, note that this series has a pronounced variance nonstationarity, thus the logarithms of this series should be analyzed. This topic can be introduced here or later.

ERROR2, Monthly Data From 1985:04 To 1992:07, Autocorrelations

```
 1:   0.7675898   0.3919264   0.0928535   0.0451409   0.0685798   0.0595056
 7:   0.0578328   0.0966308   0.1569847   0.1482982   0.0578185  -0.0383146
13:  -0.0855874  -0.0535113   0.0172903   0.0907815   0.1252745   0.1229815
19:   0.0991457   0.0958966   0.1003638   0.1166467
```

There is an extremely strong pattern left in the errors of this model. Eliminating the variance nonstationarity will not eliminate this strong pattern.

2-58. Clearly the random walk model is better. However, note that there is variance nonstationarity in the errors, as expected, probably logarithms of the original series should be analyzed. This may or may not be too early to introduce this concept here.

II. MINICASES

MINICASE 2-1. Kansas Turnpike, Daily Data using m2-1.wk1 spreadsheet.

Including the Fourth of July

MEAN	72706.37	68616.77	69320.85	72683.77	85046.08	73689.38	70794.77	68793
STDDEV	6972.597	3456.538	3077.408	2805.976	4975.683	5046.961	6687.509	4826.49
		TUE	WED	THU	FRI	SAT	SUN	MON
	RATIOS	0.943752	0.953436	0.999689	1.16972	1.01352	0.973708	0.946176

Without the Fourth of July Week, deleting June 30th to July 7th.

MEAN	72580.79	68441.33	69307.75	72299.92	84182.33	73736.17	72007.5	68090.5
STDDEV	6523.075	3549.271	3213.869	2549.448	4053.111	5268.434	5284.985	4291.144
		TUE	WED	THU	FRI	SAT	SUN	MON
	RATIOS	0.942968	0.954905	0.99613	1.159843	1.015919	0.992101	0.938134

The fact that Friday and Saturday are peak days was not surprising. The only extremely significant holiday was the Fourth of July. This holiday had a large effect on demand. In general we would expect every major holiday to affect traffic on the turnpike. In addition, big football weekends in Lawrence and Manhattan Kansas as well as professional football and baseball in Kansas City will affect traffic. Other major conventions in K.C. might affect traffic. A logical model for forecasting this series would include measures such as the same day last year, holiday measures for those holidays that move from one day to another from year to year, as well as indicator variables denoting major sporting events.

If the assumptions of ANOVA are true, then a F-test can be used to test the statistical significance of the means or seasonal factors. Alternatively, a nonparametric ANOVA as discussed in Chapter 5 can be used. Finally, consider the following regression results using dummy variables.

```
linreg veh / res
#constant wed to mon
Dependent Variable VEH - Estimation by Least Squares
Usable Observations      91        Degrees of Freedom     84
Centered R**2       0.595373       R Bar **2    0.566471
Uncentered R**2     0.996353       T x R**2        90.668
Mean of Dependent Variable       72706.373626
Std Error of Dependent Variable  6972.596951
Standard Error of Estimate       4590.963498
Sum of Squared Residuals         1770463450.6
Regression F(6,84)                     20.5997
Significance Level of F            0.00000000
Durbin-Watson Statistic            0.728602
Q(22-0)                          130.143353
Significance Level of Q            0.00000000
     Variable             Coeff        Std Error      T-Stat      Signif
*********************************************************************
1.   Constant         68616.769231   1273.304177     53.88875   0.0000000
2.   WED                704.076923   1800.724036      0.39100   0.69678973
3.   THU               4067.000000   1800.724036      2.25854   0.02650364
4.   FRI              16429.307692   1800.724036      9.12372   0.00000000
5.   SAT               5072.615385   1800.724036      2.81699   0.00604118
6.   SUN               2178.000000   1800.724036      1.20951   0.22985874
7.   MON                176.230769   1800.724036      0.09787   0.92227136
```

MINICASE 2-2. Air Passengers by Quarter.

	TOTAL				
MEAN	11916.59	11171.13	12281.89	12725.03	11520
STDDEV	2921.163	2957.452	3019.655	3029.689	2764.873
RATIO	1	0.937443	1.030654	1.067842	0.966719
		QTR1	QTR2	QTR3	QTR4

The greatest air passenger revenue is in the third, summer vacation quarter. Because quarters are being used, these results occur because of holidays and the impact of travel habits during different seasons of the year. Nothing really was surprising here. These seasonal factors can be used as described in Chapter 5 on classical decomposition.

MINICASE 2-3. Hospital Census by Week.

Series	Obs	Mean	Std Error	Minimum	Maximum
CENSUS	157	2736.153	166.826	1902.000	2964.000

The following set commands define each of the variables in the following table.

```
set l52census 53 157 = census(t-52),
set l1census 2 157 = census(t-1)
set error52 53 157 = census - l52census,
set  error1 53 157 = census - l1census
set se52 = error52**2,
set se1 = error1**2,
set pe1 = error1/census,
set ape1 = (abs(error1))/census
set pe52 = error52/census,
set ape52 = (abs(error52))/census
```

Table of Mean Values of the variables defined in above set commands.

Series	Obs	Mean	Std Error	Minimum	Maximum
CENSUS	157	2736.153	166.826	1902	2964

Statistics for Observations 53 to 104

Series	Obs	Mean	Std Error	Minimum	Maximum
CENSUS	52	2710.03846	193.11685	1902.00000	2964.0000
L52CENSUS	52	2777.09615	168.99719	2122.00000	2948.00
L1CENSUS	52	2709.78846	193.01045	1902.00000	2964.0000
ERROR52	52	-67.05769	155.20845	-422.00000	290.0000
ERROR1	52	0.25000	170.36983	-464.00000	485.0000
SE52	52	28123.13462	41090.94611	25.00000	178084.0000
SE1	52	28467.75000	58610.93004	1.00000	235225.0000
PE1	52	-0.00224	0.06879	-0.20586	0.2015
APE1	52	0.04508	0.05163	0.00036	0.2059
PE52	52	-0.02721	0.05947	-0.16846	0.0978
APE52	52	0.04919	0.04270	0.00172	0.1685

The mean squared error of model 2, (mean of SE52) is slightly better than that of model 1. The percent error for model 2 is not as good as the PE for model 1, the same is true for APE. As mentioned previously, this is one of the more difficult time series to forecast.

Correlation Matrix
52/Year Data From 2:01 To 2:52

	CENSUS	L52CENSUS	L1CENSUS
CENSUS	1.000000000000	0.639849268401	0.610637416061
L52CENSUS	0.639849268401	1.000000000000	0.347322428464
L1CENSUS	0.610637416061	0.347322428464	1.000000000000

Both correlations are statistically very significant at a .01 level as shown below:

$$t_{Y_tY_{t-1}}= .61/[(1-.6106^2)/(52-2)]^{.5} = 5.46 \qquad t_{Y_tY_{t-52}}= .6399/[(1-.6399^2)/(52-2)]^{.5} = 5.89$$

I would have expected the 52 week lag model to have been better. However, this data is not as well behaved as the other minicase data. The correlation between the variables confirm the results above, it is ambiguous which model is better for one-period ahead forecasts. However, note that the 52 week model yields forecasts that are actually 52 week ahead forecast. Thus, for longer-term forecasting, it is the better of the two models. Consequently, the 52-week lag model has the greatest utility of the two models. This brings up the interesting situation that for short period forecasts, the one-period lag model might be used, however for longer-period forecasts, the 52 week lag model should be used.

MINICASE 2-4. Henry Machler's Hideaway Orchids.

Because of the very high values about Mother's Day, we solve this problem after adjusting values for Mother's Day. We will take each day of the week centered on Mother's day and replace them with the mean of the same day of the week before and after Mother's Day as shown in the following data. Also, note that the problem asks for performance over only 12 weeks of usable data, instead it should have said over the 19 weeks of usable data; thus, 19 week results are shown below.

Adjusting Mother's Day Extreme Values of Series SALES 7/Year Data From 1:01 To 20:07
Minimum Value is   37.07 at 20:07   Entry 140
Maximum Value is 1057.96 at 6:04   Entry 39
print 39 39

ENTRY	DAY	DATE	SALES
6:04	39.00	50981.00	1057.96

Let's create a new variable called nsales for adjusted new sales.

```
set nsales = sales
set nsales 36 42 = (sales(t-7) + sales(t+7))/2
```

Calculating the appropriate error statistics using the following set commands.

```
set l7nsales 8 140 = nsales(t-7),   set l1nsales 2 140 = nsales(t-1)
set error7 8 140 = nsales-l7nsales, set error1 8 140 = nsales - l1nsales
set se7 = error7**2,                set se1 = error1**2
set pe1 = error1/nsales,            set ape1 = (abs(error1))/nsales
set pe7 = error7/nsales,            set ape7 = (abs(error7))/nsales
```

Statistics for these variables are:

Series	Obs	Mean	Std Error	Minimum	Maximum
DAY	140	70.50000	40.55860	1.00000	140.000
DATE	140	59861.71429	13312.99412	40181.00000	81881.000
SALES	140	227.51014	145.73797	37.07000	1057.960
NSALES	140	216.88561	118.73406	37.07000	559.310
L7NSALES	133	214.78229	116.55441	37.61000	559.310
L1NSALES	139	218.17924	118.16914	37.61000	559.310
ERROR7	133	2.75474	68.93769	-238.35000	161.890
ERROR1	133	-0.98451	165.06455	-375.47000	422.480
SE7	133	4724.26105	7393.09007	0.04410	56810.725
SE1	133	27042.41593	42591.53559	13.72702	178489.350
PE1	133	-0.35398	1.18185	-7.49561	0.875
APE1	133	0.73654	0.98813	0.02349	7.496
PE7	133	-0.08106	0.47297	-2.36639	0.683
APE7	133	0.31810	0.35829	0.00159	2.366

The seven-period-lag model performs much better than the one-period-lag model in all statistics. (Note that PE and APE are not expressed in percentages, but in ratios.)

Correlation Matrix 7/Year Data From 2:01 To 20:07

	NSALES	L7NSALES	L1NSALES
NSALES	1.000000000000	0.831388833055	0.054528918782
L7NSALES	0.831388833055	1.000000000000	0.049375508812
L1NSALES	0.054528918782	0.049375508812	1.000000000000

Only the seven-period forecasted/fitted values are statistically significantly related to actual sales.

$$t_{Y_tY_{t-1}} = .0545/[(1-.0545^2)/(132-2)]^{.5} = .6223$$

$$t_{Y_tY_{t-7}} = .8314/[(1-.8314^2)/(132-2)]^{.5} = 17.059$$

The higher correlation between the seven-period lags and adjusted sales (nsales) confirms the greater accuracy of this approach. We recommend the seven-period-lag model for short and long term forecasting There really were not any surprises in this data.

MINICASE 2-6. Midwestern Building Materials

This is a series with strong trend and seasonality. The series does not seem to have strong variance non-stationarity and thus is a good series for those wanting to avoid such complexities at this time. The following set command define the variables of interest here.

```
set L1sales 2 120 = sales(t-1),     set L12sales 13 120 = sales(t-12)
set error12 13 120 = sales-l12sales,set error1 13 120 = sales - l1sales
set se12 = .001*error12**2.0,        set se1 = .001*error1**2.0
set pe1 = error1/sales,              set ape1 = (abs(error1))/sales
set pe12 = error12/sales,            set ape12 = (abs(error12))/sales
```

Statistics for observations 13 to 108

Series	Obs	Mean	Std Error	Minimum	Maximum
DATE	96	556.5000	230.3577	201.0000	912.0000
SALES	96	86793.9583	23374.0157	37094.0000	143024.0000
L1SALES	96	86662.4375	23509.3392	37094.0000	143024.0000
L12SALES	96	82004.4271	23769.4362	31984.0000	143024.0000
ERROR12	96	4789.5312	4858.0102	-6384.0000	15200.0000
ERROR1	96	131.5208	21083.2848	-49005.0000	40956.0000
SE12	96	46294.0367	51929.7822	38.0250	231040.0000
SE1	96	439891.9370	518525.5984	32.0410	2401490.0250
PE1	96	-0.0250	0.2365	-0.5275	0.3991
APE1	96	0.2033	0.1217	0.0025	0.5275
PE12	96	0.0592	0.0636	-0.0907	0.2619
APE12	96	0.0717	0.0490	0.0014	0.2619

Because of the strong seasonality in the series, the 12-period lag model does better than the one-period lag model in fitting as measured by the MSE and MAPEs. (Note that PE and APE are not expressed in percentages, but in ratios.)

Now in forecasting, Y(t-1) is unknown after 1 period, thus for model 1.

```
set ferror1 109 120  = sales-l1sales(108)
set fse1 = .001*ferror1**2
set fpe1 = ferror1/sales
set fape1 = (abs(ferror1))/sales
```

Statistics for observations 109 to 120.

Series	Obs	Mean	Std Error	Minimum	Maximum
ERROR12	12	5419.0000	3211.0668	-843.0000	11754.000
SE12	12	38817.2652	35603.0741	270.4000	138156.516
PE12	12	0.0516	0.0281	-0.0068	0.094
APE12	12	0.0528	0.0257	0.0068	0.094
FERROR1	12	11055.5000	22289.3610	-23116.0000	51739.000
FSE1	12	577638.3918	761195.6455	3876.9610	2676924.121
FPE1	12	0.0657	0.2081	-0.3261	0.355
FAPE1	12	0.1740	0.1224	0.0214	0.355

The 12-period-lag model performs better than the one-period-lag model in all forecasting statistics. (Note that PE and APE are not expressed in percentages, but in ratios.) Note however, that both models do not adequately model trend and the nonstationarity variance. Depending on your purpose in assigning this series, these concepts can be introduced here.

MINICASE 2-7. International Airline Passengers

This problem can be used to introduce level and variance nonstationarity. The following set commands define the variables of interest here.

```
set lpass = log(pass)
set L1pass 2 144 = lpass(t-1),      set L12pass 13 144 = lpass(t-12)
set l12pas = exp(l12pass),          set l1pas = exp(l1pass)
set error12 13 144 = pass - l12pas, set error1 13 144 = pass - l1pas
set se12 = error12**2.0,            set se1 = error1**2.0
set pe1 = error1/pass,              set ape1 = (abs(error1))/pass
set pe12 = error12/pass,            set ape12 = (abs(error12))/pass
```

Statistics for observations 13 to 132

Series	Obs	Mean	Std Error	Minimum	Maximum
PASS	120	276.075000	102.233639	114.000000	559.000000
LPASS	120	5.551572	0.377767	4.736198	6.326149
L1PASS	120	5.541295	0.382108	4.736198	6.326149
L12PASS	120	5.430353	0.391702	4.644391	6.224558
L12PAS	120	245.908333	94.942087	104.000000	505.000000
L1PAS	120	273.683333	102.548778	114.000000	559.000000
ERROR12	120	30.166667	16.909712	-8.000000	68.000000
ERROR1	120	2.391667	32.590223	-101.000000	76.000000
SE12	120	1193.583333	1053.345982	0.000000	4624.000000
SE1	120	1058.991667	1631.255868	0.000000	10201.000000
PE1	120	0.004530	0.107263	-0.250000	0.200000
APE1	120	0.090261	0.057537	0.000000	0.250000
PE12	120	0.112381	0.056671	-0.042553	0.273256
APE12	120	0.113748	0.053850	0.000000	0.273256

The fit of the one period model is better than the 12-period model.

Now in actual forecasting, Y(t-1) is unknown after 1 period, thus for model 1 the multiperiod ahead forecasts should be inferior. This is illustrated in the following table where again the set commands define each variable.

```
set ferror1 133 144 = pass - l1pas(132), set fse1 = ferror1**2
set fpe1 = ferror1/lpass,                set fape1 = (abs(ferror1))/lpass
```

Statistics for observations 133 to 144

Series	Obs	Mean	Std Error	Minimum	Maximum
ERROR12	12	47.833333	17.580120	13.000000	74.0000
SE12	12	2571.333333	1553.282116	169.000000	5476.0000
PE12	12	0.099875	0.033485	0.031026	0.1410
APE12	12	0.099875	0.033485	0.031026	0.1410
FERROR1	12	114.166667	77.737125	28.000000	260.0000
FSE1	12	18573.500000	22780.137143	784.000000	67600.0000
FPE1	12	18.271997	11.970295	4.693146	40.4170
FAPE1	12	18.271997	11.970295	4.693146	40.4170

The 12-period-lag model performs better than the one-period-lag model in all forecasting statistics. (Note that PE and APE are not expressed in percentages, but in ratios.) Note however, that both models do not adequately model trend and the nonstationarity variance. Depending on your purpose in assigning this series, these concepts can be introduced here.

MINICASE 2-8. Automobile Sales

This series is tainted by two large outliers, thus, these must be corrected before it can be analyzed correctly. The following set commands in RATS are used to change the extreme values in a time series. This illustrates the outlier adjustment procedure applied to observations 1 and 55, which are adjusted to equal the value in period 12 and the mean of the values of period 43 and 67 respectively.

```
set sales 1 1 = sales(13),
set sales 55 55 = (sales(43)+sales(67))/2
set L1sales 2 185 = sales(t-1),
set L12sales 13 185 = sales(t-12)
set error12 13 185 = sales - l12sales,
set error1 13 185 = sales - l1sales
set se12 = error12**2.0,
set se1 = error1**2.0
set pe1 = error1/sales,
set ape1 = (abs(error1))/sales
set pe12 = error12/sales,
set ape12 = (abs(error12))/sales
```

Statistics for Observations 13 to 173.

Series	Obs	Mean	Std Error	Minimum	Maximum
DATE	161	93.00000	46.62081	13.00000	173.000
SALES	161	1599.59938	445.36997	446.00000	2558.000
L1SALES	161	1599.06522	446.10956	446.00000	2558.000
L12SALES	161	1642.05901	411.70717	704.00000	2558.000
ERROR12	161	-42.45963	152.70236	-340.00000	286.000
ERROR1	161	0.53416	242.21626	-482.00000	467.000
SE12	161	24975.99689	26577.78325	0.00000	115600.000
SE1	161	58304.59938	65219.74652	36.00000	232324.000
PE1	161	-0.01506	0.18085	-0.70486	0.497
APE1	161	0.13584	0.11985	0.00288	0.705
PE12	161	-0.04550	0.13311	-0.57848	0.217
APE12	161	0.09989	0.09880	0.00000	0.578

Because of the high first-order autocorrelation, the one period lag model performs better than the 12-period lag model for one period ahead forecasting. (Note that PE and APE are not expressed in percentages, but in ratios.) (Note that PE and APE are not expressed in percentages, but in ratios.)

Now in forecasting, Y(t-1) is unknown after 1 period, thus for model 1.

```
set ferror1 174 185  = sales - l1sales(173),    set fres1 = ferror1**2
set fpe1 = ferror1/sales,                       set fape1 =(abs(ferror1))/sales
```

Statistics for observations 174 to 185

Series	Obs	Mean	Std Error	Minimum	Maximum
ERROR12	12	-143.66667	119.16019	-312.00000	8.00000
SE12	12	33656.00000	38172.16774	0.00000	97344.00000
PE12	12	-0.16309	0.11931	-0.38043	0.00895
APE12	12	0.16459	0.11705	0.00000	0.38043
FERROR1	12	11.00000	304.94441	-380.00000	533.00000
FRES1	12	85362.83333	96583.65408	196.00000	284089.00000
FPE1	12	-0.12416	0.43506	-0.85202	0.39220
FAPE1	12	0.32831	0.29749	0.01724	0.85202

The 12-period-lag model performs better than the one-period-lag model in all forecasting statistics. (Note that PE and APE are not expressed in percentages, but in ratios.)

MINICASE 2-9. Consumption of Distilled Spirits

The following set commands define the variables which follow:

```
set L1ship 2 132 = ship(t-1),
set L12ship 13 132 = ship(t-12)
set error12 13 132 = ship - l12ship,
set error1 13 132 = ship - l1ship
set se12 = .001*error12**2.0,          set se1 = .001*error1**2.0
set pe1 = error1/ship,                 set ape1 = (abs(error1))/ship
set pe12 = error12/ship,               set ape12 = (abs(error12))/ship
```

Statistics for observations 12 to 120.

Series	Obs	Mean	Std Error	Minimum	Maximum
SHIP	108	33466.52778	5738.66886	25010.00000	51680.000
L1SHIP	108	33521.62037	5906.94767	25010.00000	54090.000
L12SHIP	108	34141.34259	5787.92740	25010.00000	54090.000
ERROR12	108	-674.81481	1375.23744	-4270.00000	4650.000
ERROR1	108	-55.09259	7242.43343	-23390.00000	11820.000
SE12	108	2329.14120	3559.09192	0.10000	21622.500
SE1	108	51970.20278	123841.48905	0.00000	547092.100
PE1	108	-0.02255	0.24131	-0.91806	0.242
APE1	108	0.13806	0.19876	0.00000	0.918
PE12	108	-0.02121	0.04033	-0.13805	0.097
APE12	108	0.03536	0.02861	0.00028	0.138

The 12-period lag model is a better fit than the one-period lag model. (Note that PE and APE are not expressed in percentages, but in ratios.)

Now in forecasting, $Y(t-1)$ is unknown after 1 period, thus for model 1.

```
set ferror1 121 132 = ship - l1ship(120)
set fse1 = .001*ferror1**2
set fpe1 = ferror1/ship
set fape1 = (abs(ferror1))/ship
```

Statistics for observations 121 to 132.

Series	Obs	Mean	Std Error	Minimum	Maximum
L12SHIP	12	31201.66667	6076.41765	25600.00000	48140.000
ERROR12	12	-2342.50000	2375.79508	-8510.00000	-290.00
SE12	12	10661.34167	20358.71751	84.10000	72420.100
PE12	12	-0.07852	0.07015	-0.21474	-0.010
APE12	12	0.07852	0.07015	0.01023	0.215
FERROR1	12	-7850.83333	4424.22763	-14750.00000	2920.000
FSE1	12	79578.22500	58178.03979	8526.40000	217562.50
FPE1	12	-0.29752	0.18567	-0.67168	0.074
FAPE1	12	0.30980	0.16229	0.07368	0.672

The 12 period lag model is a much better model than the one period lag model based on all statistics but the percent error which is not a criteria which normally dominates other error statistics such as the APE, mean squared error, and RSE. (Note that PE and APE are not expressed in percentages, but in ratios.)

MINICASE 2-10. Discount Consumer Electronics

The following set commands define the variables which follow:
```
set L1sales 2 185 = sales(t-1),
set L12sales 13 185 = sales(t-12)
set error12 13 185 = sales - l12sales,
set error1 13 185 = sales - l1sales
set se12 = .001*error12**2.0,            set se1 = .001*error1**2.0
set pe1 = error1/sales,                  set ape1 = (abs(error1))/sales,
set pe12 = error12/sales                 set ape12 = abs(error12))/sales
```

Statistics for observations 13 173

Series	Obs	Mean	Std Error	Minimum	Maximum
SALES	161	73.93853416	14.49423302	41.57400000	115.46300000
L1SALES	161	73.74992547	14.41885427	41.57400000	115.46300000
L12SALES	161	70.61217391	14.85112347	35.49600000	110.45100000
ERROR12	161	3.32636025	2.75992375	-3.52300000	11.24900000
ERROR1	161	0.18860870	13.35447476	-36.77400000	30.97700000
SE12	161	0.01863454	0.02073094	0.00000130	0.12654000
SE1	161	0.17726986	0.28090934	0.00001664	1.35232708
PE1	161	-0.01438759	0.18840807	-0.51951334	0.37821217
APE1	161	0.14083987	0.12548329	0.00201913	0.51951334
PE12	161	0.04735513	0.04226835	-0.04865081	0.15852816
APE12	161	0.05145538	0.03713399	0.00058654	0.15852816

The 12-period lag model is a much better model than the 1-period lag model. (Note that PE and APE are not expressed in percentages, but in ratios.)

Now in forecasting, $Y(t-1)$ is unknown after 1 period, thus for model 1.
```
set ferror1  174 185  = sales - l1sales(173),  set fse1 = .001*ferror1**2
set fpe1 = ferror1/sales,  set fape1 = (abs(ferror1))/sales
```

Statistics for observation 174 to 185

Series	Obs	Mean	Std Error	Minimum	Maximum
L12SALES	12	92.51158333	10.29238254	76.99100000	115.46300000
ERROR12	12	2.72200000	2.74176768	-1.34300000	9.40600000
ERROR1	12	-0.10825000	20.66003397	-43.25800000	38.06100000
SE12	12	0.01430013	0.02383550	0.00168740	0.08847284
PE12	12	0.02730780	0.02448726	-0.01508701	0.07532694
APE12	12	0.03213855	0.01692185	0.01389751	0.07532694
FERROR1	12	-7.89241667	11.80353270	-22.66700000	21.74300000
FSE1	12	0.19000334	0.19218009	0.00447323	0.51379289
FPE1	12	-0.09673914	0.12363227	-0.28172113	0.17412648
FAPE1	12	0.12910968	0.08549543	0.02009673	0.28172113

The 12 period lag model is a much better model than the one period lag model based on all statistics but the percent error. (Note that PE and APE are not expressed in percentages, but in ratios.)

I. PROBLEMS

ESTIMATED DIFFICULTY

Elementary	Medium	Hard	Very Hard	Bad

1 M   2 M   3 M   4 M   5 M

2B-1. No Patterns in Series A, Strong Patterns in B to D, Births, and Marriages as shown by their graphs, ACFs, and Q-statistic, note that k=n/4

Series A, Monthly Data From 1:01 To 4:12, Autocorrelations

```
    1:   0.1783637   0.2295856   0.0738135   0.1236553   0.0192867   0.1718366
    7:   0.0809283  -0.0054841   0.0240859   0.1466917   0.1710868   0.1892378
Ljung-Box Q-Statistics  Q(12)  =   13.2733.  Significance Level 0.34949650
```

Series B, Monthly Data From 1:01 To 4:12, Autocorrelations

```
    1:  0.92738782  0.82500408  0.69318668  0.56357321  0.44852754  0.34153029
    7:  0.25034438  0.17401648  0.11536468  0.08697796  0.08550503  0.08734277
Ljung-Box Q-Statistics  Q(12)  =   148.0391.  Significance Level 0.0000000
```

Series C, Monthly Data From 1:01 To 4:12, Autocorrelations

```
    1:  0.85576952  0.81985284  0.76108393  0.69478066  0.64169966  0.57053351
    7:  0.54806874  0.46904717  0.41970875  0.36136060  0.31564044  0.27039188
Ljung-Box Q-Statistics  Q(12)  =   232.4798.  Significance Level 0.0000000
```

Series D, Monthly Data From 1:01 To 4:12, Autocorrelations

```
    1:   0.7916396   0.4837161   0.0857388  -0.2919505  -0.5732188  -0.6689535
    7:  -0.5894663  -0.3541970  -0.0733358   0.2110712   0.4449199   0.5107036
Ljung-Box Q-Statistics  Q(12)  =   154.4009.  Significance Level 0.0000000
```

Series BIRTHS, Quarterly Data From 1:01 To 8:04, Autocorrelations

```
    1:   0.4787316   0.1247812   0.4505308   0.7978032   0.3076034  -0.0337215
    7:   0.2557449   0.5089503
Ljung-Box Q-Statistics  Q(8)   =    59.4052.  Significance Level 0.0000000
```

Series MARRIAGE, Quarterly Data From 1:01 To 8:04, Autocorrelations

```
    1:  -0.1249580  -0.7113432  -0.1088449   0.8753146  -0.1027594  -0.6130366
    7:  -0.1067595   0.7433771
Ljung-Box Q-Statistics  Q(8)   =    90.8147.  Significance Level 0.0000000
```

2B-2. As shown below, the residuals of the marriage model appear to be white noise.

Series ERRORM, Autocorrelations

```
      1:   0.0026670   0.2458110   0.1350704  -0.2033804  -0.0759279  -0.1054829
      7:  -0.2506138
Ljung-Box Q-Statistics   Q(7) = 7.1607.   Significance Level 0.41233695
```

2B-3. A graph of the errors of the birth model, the ACFs, and Q-statistic all denote that there is considerable pattern left in the errors. This pattern results from the trend or strong autoregressive behavior of the residuals. We will model this behavior later in the book.

Series ERRORB, Autocorrelations

```
      1:   0.5534012   0.5436880   0.3644939   0.1665461   0.1887389  -0.0396486
      7:  -0.0588985
Ljung-Box Q-Statistics   Q(7)  = 26.0125.   Significance Level 0.00050109
```

2B-4. The Q-statistic is much lower for the residuals, however, we have not achieved white noise residuals. This pattern results from the strong autoregressive behavior of the residuals. We will model this behavior later in the book.

```
set error 13 48 = seriesd - seriesd(t-12)
```

Error, Autocorrelations

```
      1:   0.7840854   0.6867370   0.5615781   0.3652696   0.2570871   0.0803742
      7:  -0.0913698  -0.1513450  -0.2930538
Ljung-Box Q-Statistics   Q(9)  =  70.8575.   Significance Level 0.00000000
```

While the residual errors are not white noise, there has been some decrease in the standard deviation as shown by the descriptive statistics below.

Series	Obs	Mean	Std Error	Minimum	Maximum
SERIESD	48	609.93750000	93.26681156	426.00000000	805.0000000
ERROR	36	-2.41666667	76.63098031	-129.00000000	124.0000000

2B-5. The Q-statistic is much lower for the residuals, however, we have not achieved white noise residuals. This pattern results from the strong autoregressive behavior of the residuals. We will model this behavior later in the book.

```
set error 2 48 = seriesb - seriesb(t-1)
```

Autocorrelations
```
      1:   0.4745085   0.3438836  -0.0117433  -0.1027072  -0.2773089  -0.2346506
      7:  -0.2687187  -0.2203532  -0.2257924  -0.1239967   0.0317659
Ljung-Box Q-Statistics   Q(11)  = 36.3425.   Significance Level 0.00014841
```

While the residual errors are not white noise there has been a great decrease in the standard deviation as shown by the descriptive statistics below.

Series	Obs	Mean	Std Error	Minimum	Maximum
SERIESB	48	750.2500000	184.1388814	426.0000000	1159.00000
ERROR	47	9.0851064	52.9580760	-87.0000000	98.000000

CHAPTER 3
INTRODUCTION TO REGRESSION ANALYSIS

I.   PROBLEMS

ESTIMATED DIFFICULTY

Elementary	Medium				Hard		Very Hard		Bad
1 E	2 E	3 M	4 M	5 E	6 M	7 E	8 E	9 E	10 E
11 M	12 M	13 M	14 E	15 E	16 M	17 M	18 M	19 M	20 M
21 **B**	22 H	23 M	24 M	25 H	26 V	27 V	28 V	29 **B**	

Minicases are all Hard.

3-1. The three general purpose of regression analysis are

1) To model the relationship between Y and X's. 2) To estimate the error in using that relationship. 3) To measure the degree of association (i.e., correlation) between Y and X's.

3-2. The method of least squares is a curve fitting method that minimizes the sum of the squared errors about the fitted curve while yielding a mean error of zero.

3-3. Automobile Tires at a tire shop = f(used cars on the road, gas prices, consumer income, weather)

3-4. Explain the difference between: a) correlation and causality - Correlation measures the degree of association without regard to causality, causality denotes that a variation in one variable causes a change in the other variable. b) A linear relationship denotes that a constant change in X is associated with a constant change in Y. A curvilinear relationships denotes that a constant change in X is associated with different changes in Y depending on the value or base of X. c) S_{yx} is the scatter of Y about its relationship with X, in other words, the value of Y given and X. S_y is the scatter of Y about its mean. d) The regression coefficient is the coefficient of correlation.

3-5. Define the two criteria used to select best fit linear relationships between Y and X. sum of $e = 0$, sum of e^2 = lowest possible.

3-6. Give a common English definition for the following regression concepts: R-bar^2 = percentage of original variance explained by the relationship. S_{yx} = scatter of Y values about it relationship with X. Durbin-Watson statistic measures the degree of association between adjacent residuals. t-value of the regression coefficient is the number of standard deviations that the regression coefficient is away from zero and its significance level is the probability of this t-value if the true, population coefficient was in fact zero.

3-7. See page 104 for R-bar^2 using explained, unexplained, and total variance.

3-8. Given Y=100, $\hat{Y}$=98, and Y=90, these values partition into: Total variation = 100 - 90 = 10 Explained variation = 98 - 90 = 8 Unexplained variation = 100 - 98 = 2

3-9. Given the variance about the regression line (S^2_{yx}) is 10 and the variance of Y (S^2_y) is 100, then R-bar^2 = 1 - 10/100 = .90

3-10. They are equal to each other for bivariate relationships.

3-11. See pages 110-114 for the 6 assumptions of regression analysis.

3-12. Serial correlation problems include important missing (i.e., excluded) independent variable, in correct S_{yx}, coefficient t-values, R^2, and F-test, and falsely inferring a strong association when there is none.

3-13. See pages 118-119 for definitions of S_r and S_f.

3-14. See page 459 for proving cause and effect.

3-15. See page 51 of Chapter 2 for the difference between fit and forecast errors, relate these to S_r and S_f.

3-16. The repeat the Big City Bookstore example is software dependent.

3-17. a) An F-test using the ANOVA of regression, b) b +/-2.58S_b c) Pages 119, 118, and 102 respectively.

3-18. a) Dependent Variable (vertical axis) is SAT scores versus hours of TV viewing.

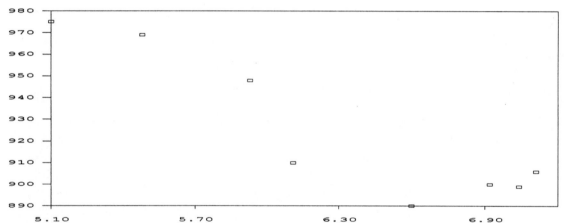

```
b)   Dependent Variable SAT - Estimation by Least Squares
Usable Observations        8              Degrees of Freedom       6
Centered R**2      0.824384                R Bar **2    0.795115
Uncentered R**2    0.999793                T x R**2        7.998
Mean of Dependent Variable              924.62500000
Std Error of Dependent Variable          33.96610706
Standard Error of Estimate               15.37450951
Sum of Squared Residuals               1418.2532567
Regression F(1,6)                         28.1654
Significance Level of F                    0.00181742
Durbin-Watson Statistic                    1.835681
     Variable   Coeff            Std Error         t-Stat              Signif
***********************************************************************************
1.   Constant   1182.313274      48.858583         24.19868         0.00000033
2.   TV          -40.992368       7.724044         -5.30711         0.00181742
```

c) As shown above, SAT scores and hours of TV viewing are negatively correlated. R^2 is almost 80%. TV viewing explains about 80% of the variance in SAT scores. The t-value on the regression coefficient of TV viewing is very significant because it equals -5.30711. The F-value is significant and because this is a bivariate relationship, $t^2 = F$. There is a nonlinear relationship between hours of TV viewing and SAT scores. That is, SAT scores are decreasing as TV viewing goes up, but then we see SAT scores actually increasing as TV viewing has increased. We suspect that there are interventions which are increasing SAT scores even as TV viewing has increased, also, we would like to think that there is more educational and child development TV watching taking place.

3-19. a) Dependent Variable (vertical axis) is suicide rate per 100,000 children versus percentage of children on welfare.

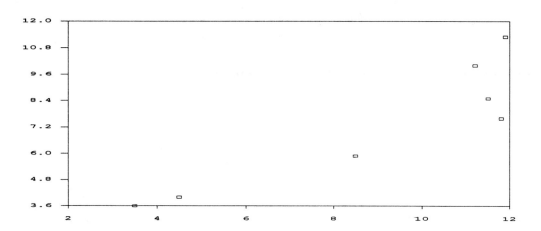

b) Dependent Variable SUI - Estimation by Least Squares
```
Usable Observations            7        Degrees of Freedom      5
Centered R**2       0.818085             R Bar **2    0.781702
Uncentered R**2     0.977834             T x R**2        6.845
Mean of Dependent Variable               7.2714285714
Std Error of Dependent Variable          2.9255850046
Standard Error of Estimate               1.3669020472
Sum of Squared Residuals                 9.3421060334
Regression F(1,5)                       22.4854
Significance Level of F                  0.00514150
Durbin-Watson Statistic                       0.699111
     Variable        Coeff             Std Error            t-Stat            Signif
*******************************************************************************
1.  Constant       0.6805019941      1.4828527782         0.45891         0.66555533
2.  TEEN-Welfare   0.7334894442      0.1546833806         4.74188         0.00514150
```

c) As shown above, suicide rate and percentage of children on welfare are positively correlated. R^2 is 78%. Teen suicides explain about 78% of the variance in suicide rate. The t-value on the regression coefficient of teen is significant because it equals 4.74188. The F-value is significant and because this is a bivariate relationship, $t^2 = F$. In viewing the graph, it appears that there is a linear relationship between teen welfare and suicide rates. Obviously, there are other factors which indirectly or directly influence each of these variables. In addition, the DW statistic is low denoting that there is a great deal of serial correlation within these two variables. This brings up the question of whether there is indeed a true association. As a preview of Chapter 10 consider the results of using a COILS procedure on this data. As shown, the welfare becomes insignificant.

```
Dependent Variable SUI - Estimation by Cochrane-Orcutt
Usable Observations       6        Degrees of Freedom      3
Centered R**2       0.971638       R Bar **2    0.952729
Mean of Dependent Variable         7.8833333333
Std Error of Dependent Variable  2.6693944382
Standard Error of Estimate         0.5803755871
Sum of Squared Residuals           1.0105074665
Durbin-Watson Statistic               1.449914
Q(1-1)                                0.049480
Significance Level of Q               0.00000000
    Variable                   Coeff      Std Error     T-Stat     Signif
***********************************************************************
1.   Constant            212.16446266  62.82620402     3.37701   0.04318670
2.   WELFARE               0.17822326   0.14248184     1.25085   0.29965977
3.   RHO                   0.99500761   0.16313200     6.09940   0.00885324
```

3-20. a) Dependent variable (vertical axis) is crime rate versus median prison sentence.

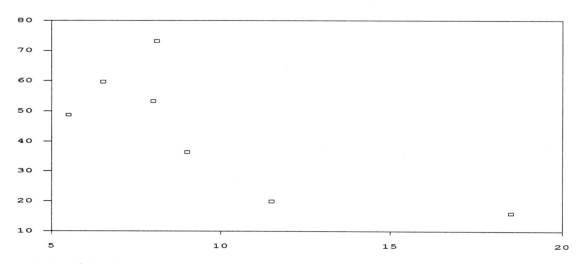

Figure P3-20. Crime Rate Vs. Median Prison Sentence

```
b) Linreg rate / res
#constant prison
Dependent Variable RATE - Estimation by Least Squares
Usable Observations       7        Degrees of Freedom      5
Centered R**2       0.578233       R Bar **2    0.493880
Uncentered R**2     0.931467       T x R**2        6.520
Mean of Dependent Variable         43.928571429
Std Error of Dependent Variable  20.899737980
Standard Error of Estimate         14.868514803
Sum of Squared Residuals         1105.3636622
Regression F(1,5)                     6.8549
Significance Level of F               0.04720099
Durbin-Watson Statistic               1.033027
    Variable                   Coeff      Std Error     T-Stat     Signif
***********************************************************************
1.   Constant             78.81553954  14.46145989     5.45004   0.00282591
2.   PRISON               -3.63947506   1.39007524    -2.61819   0.04720099
```

c) As shown above, median prison sentence and crime rate are negatively correlated. R^2 is almost 50%. The median of the prison sentence explains about 50% of the variance in crime rate. The t-value on the regression coefficient of median prison sentence is significant because it equals -2.61819. The F-value is barely significant and because this is a bivariate relationship, $t^2=F$. In viewing the graph, it appears that there is a nonlinear relationship between crime rate and median prison sentence. That is, the crime rate goes up as the median prison sentence decreases. We do not suggest that there is causality here, however, there is some relationship between the two variables. A one year decrease in the median prison sentence is associated with a 3.64 unit increase the crime rate. A one year increase in the median prison sentence is associated with 3.64 unit decrease in the crime rate.

A nonlinear relationship between the variables does not improve the fit enough to justify including the squared prison term. The Durbin-Watson statistic is low, however, this is such a small sample size that we cannot make strong inferences.

The interesting thing about this relationship is the considerable reduction in Median Prison Sentence as the Crime Rate increases. There is likely a complex mutual or simultaneous relationship between these two variables and other factors in our society and this simple linear regression oversimplifies the true relationship.

3-21. NOTE: USJAPAN.DAT contains 271 observations, thus, I would not assign this problem at this time, it is too complex because the wrong data file has been called out and the correct one is not on the data diskette. Also note that this problem is very difficult to solve because it requires knowledge of Chapter 13 before a really valid solution is possible. However, here are two solutions for those students who have studied the appendix of this chapter and Chapter 10 in order to know how to apply Cochrane Orcutt procedure to logarithmic values or this appendix and Chapter 13 in order to know how to apply MARIMA methods. This is a RATS program which is relatively self documenting.

```
set ljapan = log(japan)
set lus = log(us)
set dljapan 2 271 = log(japan) - log(japan(t-1))
set dlus 2 271 = log(us) - log(us(t-1))
```

The following is a Cochrane Orcutt estimation using logarithms of both variables and lags of 0 and 1 for the logs of the US stock index.

```
ar1 ljapan
#constant lus{0 1}
Dependent Variable LJAPAN - Estimation by Cochrane-Orcutt
Monthly Data From 1:03 To 23:07
Usable Observations      269        Degrees of Freedom    265
Centered R**2      0.998062      R Bar **2    0.998041
Uncentered R**2    0.999969      T x R**2     268.992
Mean of Dependent Variable       6.3633921254
Std Error of Dependent Variable 0.8160600019
Standard Error of Estimate       0.0361233967
Sum of Squared Residuals         0.3457984447
Durbin-Watson Statistic            1.390000
Q(36-1)                           46.710276
Significance Level of Q            0.08913036
    Variable                  Coeff        Std Error      T-Stat      Signif
*****************************************************************************
1.  Constant             3.5110687629 0.4843955105      7.24835    0.00000000
2.  LUS                  0.4062566255 0.0611872823      6.63956    0.00000000
3.  LUS{1}               0.2348998320 0.0610550708      3.84734    0.00014967
*****************************************************************************
4.  RHO                  0.9913086089 0.0042974440    230.67400    0.00000000
```

The following is a Cochrane Orcutt estimation using first differences of logarithms of both variables and lags of 0 and 1 for first differences of logs of the US stock index.

```
ar1 dljapan
#constant dlus{0 1}
Dependent Variable DLJAPAN - Estimation by Cochrane-Orcutt
Monthly Data From 1:04 To 23:07
Usable Observations    268        Degrees of Freedom    264
Centered R**2      0.301498        R Bar **2    0.293560
Uncentered R**2    0.322143        T x R**2         86.334
Mean of Dependent Variable        0.0071769975
Std Error of Dependent Variable 0.0412012372
Standard Error of Estimate        0.0346296303
Sum of Squared Residuals          0.3165917821
Durbin-Watson Statistic            1.979788
Q(36-1)                           16.892728
Significance Level of Q            0.99578508
    Variable                     Coeff      Std Error      T-Stat      Signif
*******************************************************************************
1.   Constant          0.0034313802 0.0030923158        1.10965    0.26816074
2.   DLUS              0.4090498759 0.0589292754        6.94137    0.00000000
3.   DLUS{1}           0.2155537768 0.0589077128        3.65918    0.00030548
*******************************************************************************
4.   RHO               0.3076140919 0.0586079082        5.24868    0.00000032
```

The following is a MARIMA model of first differences of logs for each variable and lags 0 and 1 for first differences of the US index in addition there is a noise model with a MA(1) component.

```
box(diff=1,apply,input=1,constant,ma=1) ljapan
#lus 1 0
Dependent Variable LJAPAN - Estimation by Box-Jenkins
Iterations Taken      6
Monthly Data From 1:03 To 23:07
Usable Observations    269        Degrees of Freedom    265
Centered R**2      0.998212        R Bar **2    0.998192
Uncentered R**2    0.999971        T x R**2        268.992
Mean of Dependent Variable        6.3633921254
Std Error of Dependent Variable 0.8160600019
Standard Error of Estimate        0.0347026304
Sum of Squared Residuals          0.3191322273
Durbin-Watson Statistic            1.965030
Q(36-1)                           19.797354
Significance Level of Q            0.98187441
    Variable                     Coeff      Std Error      T-Stat      Signif
*******************************************************************************
1.   CONSTANT          0.0037341494 0.0027992539        1.33398    0.18335562
2.   MA{1}             0.3053946971 0.0585987025        5.21163    0.00000038
3.   N_LUS{0}          0.4215944356 0.0594752535        7.08857    0.00000000
4.   N_LUS{1}          0.2076745826 0.0592461169        3.50529    0.00053540
```

3-22. There is a semilog relationship between MIPS and time as measured by the variable date which is the month of the integrated circuit/PC introduction and price. For this data there is no relationship between the cost or price and MIPS. Both have varied considerably over time.

```
linreg lmips
#constant date
Dependent Variable LMIPS - Estimation by Least Squares
Usable Observations      9        Degrees of Freedom      7
Centered R**2      0.550256        R Bar **2    0.486007
Uncentered R**2    0.681549        T x R**2         6.134
Mean of Dependent Variable        2.1996583077
Std Error of Dependent Variable 3.6335626687
```

```
Standard Error of Estimate        2.6050214115
Sum of Squared Residuals         47.502955879
Regression F(1,7)                      8.5644
Significance Level of F            0.02213420
Durbin-Watson Statistic              1.222026
     Variable                Coeff      Std Error     T-Stat    Signif
*********************************************************************************
1.  Constant            -2.713738967  1.890192582   -1.43569  0.19422851
2.  DATE                 0.252689003  0.086345077    2.92650  0.02213420
```

Explanation of the slope coefficient of Date is: exp(.2527)-1 = 0.28750

Each month results in a 28.7% increase in the MIPS. There is no easy interpretation of the constant.

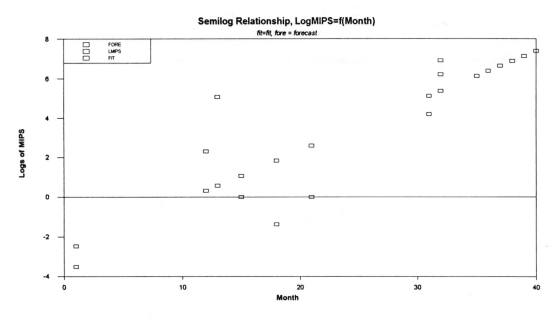

Semilog Relationship, LogMIPS=f(Month)
fit=fit, fore = forecast

The fit and forecast seem reasonable, however, this is a complex relationship and the forecast may have a slope which is lower than it should be.

3-23. CREDIT.DAT, credit charges versus income.   This appears to be a reasonably good fit. Residual analysis did not reveal any problems with the relationship.

```
linreg charge / res2
#constant income
Dependent Variable CHARGE - Estimation by Least Squares
Usable Observations      50      Degrees of Freedom      48
Centered R**2      0.738208      R Bar **2    0.732754
Mean of Dependent Variable     11337.755000
Std Error of Dependent Variable  1897.244275
Standard Error of Estimate       980.796621
Sum of Squared Residuals       46174176.544
Regression F(1,48)                 135.3516
Significance Level of F           0.00000000
Durbin-Watson Statistic            2.066085
     Variable                Coeff      Std Error     T-Stat    Signif
*********************************************************************************
1.  Constant            -65.0574811  989.8884586   -0.06572  0.94787210
2.  INCOME                0.2005654    0.0172395   11.63407  0.00000000
```

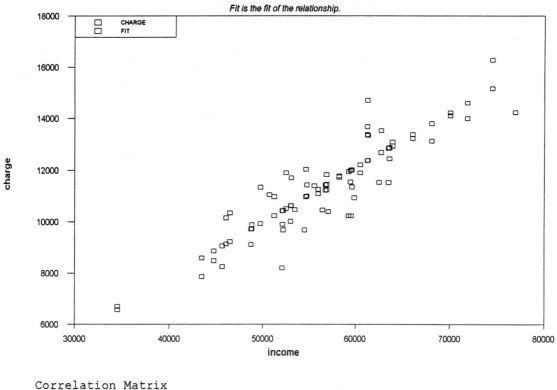

Figure 1: Scater Graph of Charge vs. Income

Fit is the fit of the relationship.

```
Correlation Matrix
            CHARGE          INCOME          RES2              FIT
CHARGE      1.0000000       0.8591902       0.5116563         0.8591902
INCOME      0.8591902       1.0000000 4.4393061e-014          1.0000000
RES2        0.5116563 4.4393061e-014        1.0000000 4.4402848e-014
FIT         0.8591902       1.0000000 4.4402848e-014          1.0000000
CHARGE      1.0000000       0.8591902       0.5116563         0.8591902
```

3-24. A total quality management program, TQM.DAT.   TQM training program and market share are positively correlated.

```
linreg share / res
#constant TQM
Dependent Variable SHARE - Estimation by Least Squares
Usable Observations      50      Degrees of Freedom    48
Centered R**2      0.929118      R Bar **2    0.927641
Uncentered R**2    0.998966      T x R**2       49.948
Mean of Dependent Variable       17.917000000
Std Error of Dependent Variable   2.202244912
Standard Error of Estimate        0.592393912
Sum of Squared Residuals         16.844666281
Regression F(1,48)                  629.1831
Significance Level of F              0.00000000
Durbin-Watson Statistic             1.899488
     Variable                 Coeff       Std Error      T-Stat      Signif
************************************************************************************
1.   Constant            1.7879647375 0.6484477770       2.75730    0.00821843
2.   TQM                 0.3603706088 0.0143668258      25.08352    0.00000000
```

TQM training program and market share are positively correlated. R^2 is about 93%. Thus, the TQM program explains about 93% of variance in the Market Share. The t-value on the regression coefficient of market share is very significant because it equals 25.08352. Thus, this appears to be a very successful program, assuming that there is at least mutual causality in the TQM and market share measures.

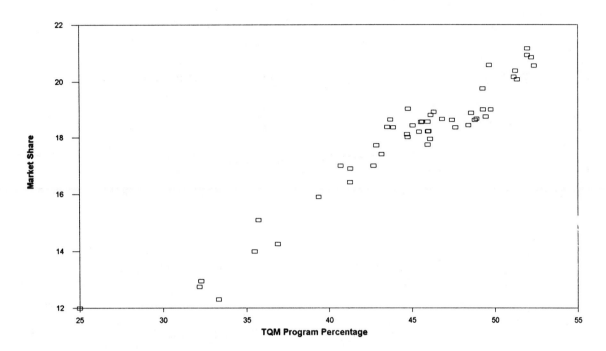

3-25. Continuous Quality Improvement, CQI.DAT.

```
linreg sat / res
#constant cqi
Dependent Variable SAT - Estimation by Least Squares
Usable Observations      50      Degrees of Freedom     48
Centered R**2     0.927794      R Bar **2    0.926289
Uncentered R**2   0.999961      T x R**2      49.998
Mean of Dependent Variable      90.363800000
Std Error of Dependent Variable  2.124099704
Standard Error of Estimate      0.576686901
Sum of Squared Residuals        15.963253536
Regression F(1,48)                616.7613
Significance Level of F           0.00000000
Durbin-Watson Statistic           1.949676
```

Variable	Coeff	Std Error	T-Stat	Signif
1. Constant	3.1971255356	3.5108246850	0.91065	0.36703143
2. CQI	0.0096399577	0.0003881652	24.83468	0.00000000

Patient satisfaction and continuous quality improvement expenditure are positively correlated. During these 50 months the hospital has been training and educating its health care providers on how to better relate to patients and their family. Adjusted R^2 is 93%. 93% of patient satisfaction variation is associated with CQI expenses. The t-value on the regression coefficient of satisfaction is very significant because it equals 24.83468. In viewing the graph, it appears that there is a linear relationship between the degree of patients satisfaction and continuous quality improvement expenditure. That is, as the hospital increases expenditures on training and educating programs its patient satisfaction has increased.

Problem 3A-9 continues this problem and as we shall see, there is a one period lag in the effect of CQI thus, the following relationship results. This is a logical result of lagged effects.

```
Dependent Variable SAT - Estimation by Least Squares
Annual Data From 2:01 To 50:01
Usable Observations      49      Degrees of Freedom      47
Centered R**2      0.983231      R Bar **2    0.982875
Uncentered R**2    0.999991      T x R**2       49.000
Mean of Dependent Variable        90.432448980
Std Error of Dependent Variable   2.089318600
Standard Error of Estimate         0.273417047
Sum of Squared Residuals           3.5135734390
Regression F(1,47)                   2755.8471
Significance Level of F            0.00000000
Durbin-Watson Statistic              1.680306
Q(12-0)                              6.762523
Significance Level of Q            0.87289971
     Variable                  Coeff       Std Error        T-Stat       Signif
*************************************************************************************
1.   Constant        0.7950999727 1.7079495823        0.46553    0.64370274
2.   CQI{1}          0.0099206780 0.0001889791       52.49616    0.00000000
```

Thus, SAT$_t$ is better related to CQI$_1$.

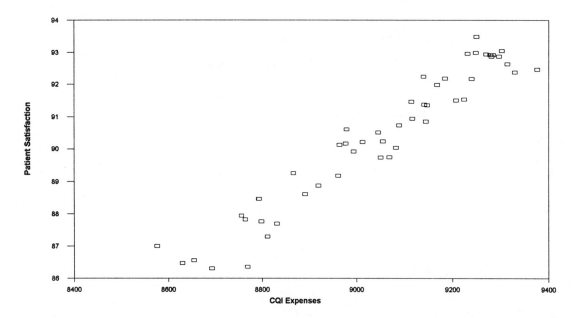

3-26. **Note: This may be a difficult problem for many students, so be cautious in assigning it.** As shown by the analyses here, the SP500 appears to react to interest rates more than anticipate them. There are some limitations to the inferences we can make using monthly data here. The dynamics of the market are complex and much more rapid than monthly data, nonetheless, this may provide some useful information and analysis.

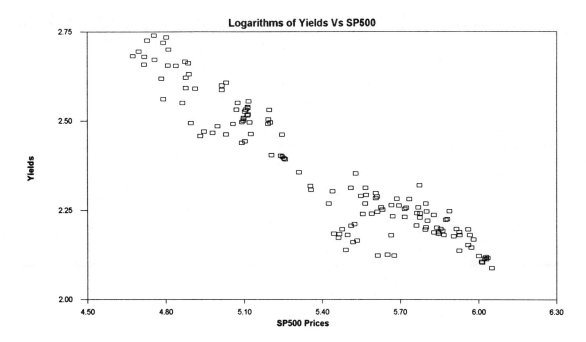

Logarithms of Yields Vs SP500

We should really analyze changes in these variables. Let's take first differences of the log values.

```
set lsp500 = log(sp500)          set lyield = log(yield)
```

As shown in the figure above, there is a very strong linear relationship, how much of this is serial correlation?

```
linreg lyield / res
#constant lsp500
Dependent Variable LYIELD - Estimation by Least Squares
Annual Data From 1981:01 To 2119:01
Usable Observations    139        Degrees of Freedom   137
Centered R**2      0.880599       R Bar **2   0.879727
Uncentered R**2    0.999279       T x R**2      138.900
Mean of Dependent Variable        2.3562150628
Std Error of Dependent Variable 0.1843770926
Standard Error of Estimate        0.0639425858
Sum of Squared Residuals          0.5601456360
Regression F(1,137)                 1010.3941
Significance Level of F             0.00000000
Durbin-Watson Statistic             0.187749
Q(34-0)                           532.161635
Significance Level of Q             0.00000000
    Variable              Coeff      Std Error     T-Stat      Signif
*******************************************************************************
1.   Constant         4.671801113  0.073049259    63.95412   0.00000000
2.   LSP500          -0.427140991  0.013437728   -31.78670   0.00000000
```

Note the very high serial correlation. Let us run an adjustment procedure, Cochrane-Orcutt. This relationship might be discussed in the context of this being somewhat of a "black box" that corrects for the problems with serial correlation.

```
ar1 lyield / res
#constant lsp500
Dependent Variable LYIELD - Estimation by Cochrane-Orcutt
Annual Data From 1982:01 To 2119:01
Usable Observations    138        Degrees of Freedom    135
Centered R**2       0.980760       R Bar **2    0.980475
Uncentered R**2     0.999884       T x R**2      137.984
Mean of Dependent Variable        2.3548091856
Std Error of Dependent Variable   0.1842995192
Standard Error of Estimate        0.0257525919
Sum of Squared Residuals          0.0895314584
Durbin-Watson Statistic              1.504128
Q(34-1)                             45.110622
Significance Level of Q              0.07787492
    Variable              Coeff       Std Error      T-Stat      Signif
***************************************************************************
1.  Constant           3.495807747  0.279240758    12.51897   0.00000000
2.  LSP500             -0.220333378  0.046338275    -4.75489   0.00000503
***************************************************************************
3.  RHO                0.973934002  0.022071460    44.12640   0.00000000
```

The relationship is still very strong. As shown below, adding a one period lag somewhat increases the OLS R^2, but does not improve the D-W. Consequently, a Cochrane-Orcutt estimation follows.

```
Dependent Variable LYIELD - Estimation by Least Squares
Annual Data From 1982:01 To 2119:01
Usable Observations    138        Degrees of Freedom    135
Centered R**2       0.881935       R Bar **2    0.880186
Uncentered R**2     0.999286       T x R**2      137.902
Mean of Dependent Variable        2.3548091856
Std Error of Dependent Variable   0.1842995192
Standard Error of Estimate        0.0637938112
Sum of Squared Residuals          0.5494027973
Regression F(2,135)                 504.2180
Significance Level of F              0.00000000
Durbin-Watson Statistic              0.273905
Q(34-0)                             511.077793
Significance Level of Q              0.00000000
    Variable              Coeff       Std Error      T-Stat      Signif
***************************************************************************
1.  Constant           4.671547455  0.073576430    63.49245   0.00000000
2.  LSP500             -0.598432264  0.116705829    -5.12770   0.00000100
3.  LSP500{1}           0.171668694  0.116931397     1.46811   0.14439920

ar1 lyield / res
#constant lsp500{0 1}
Dependent Variable LYIELD - Estimation by Cochrane-Orcutt
Annual Data From 1983:01 To 2119:01
Usable Observations    137        Degrees of Freedom    133
Centered R**2       0.981696       R Bar **2    0.981283
Uncentered R**2     0.999890       T x R**2      136.985
Mean of Dependent Variable        2.3530813958
Std Error of Dependent Variable   0.1838506741
Standard Error of Estimate        0.0251523959
Sum of Squared Residuals          0.0841415214
Durbin-Watson Statistic              1.441150
Q(34-1)                             48.375877
Significance Level of Q              0.04103646
```

```
      Variable                  Coeff        Std Error      T-Stat      Signif
******************************************************************************
1.  Constant                4.158630319    0.302153368     13.76331   0.00000000
2.  LSP500                 -0.227222611    0.043319589     -5.24526   0.00000069
3.  LSP500{1}              -0.108073358    0.043524042     -2.48307   0.01426964
******************************************************************************
4.  RHO                     0.944079592    0.033893345     27.85442   0.00000000
```

This is still very statistically significant, however, the strongest predictor variables are momentum as measured by RHO and the coincident time period of LSP500. Also, the use of monthly data may hide the true, underlying dynamics of the market. The following are the ACFs of the residuals of the AR1 model

```
Autocorrelations of AR1 residuals.
     1:   0.2699878 -0.1222753 -0.0352884  0.0637274  0.0545898 -0.1289008
     7:  -0.1342357  0.0260962  0.0317408  0.0881175  0.0747090 -0.0885913
    13:  -0.1500745 -0.0871826  0.0147624  0.0419626 -0.1822109 -0.1589606
    19:   0.0731519  0.0025806 -0.1125464 -0.0431728  0.0865085 -0.0389000
    25:  -0.0609574  0.0693648 -0.0249222 -0.1513419 -0.0624163 -0.0310512
    31:   0.0380324  0.0288801  0.0259333  0.0408591
```

The level of serial correlation is quite low, thus there is not much of a serial correlation problem. Let' try fi s in the opposite direction.

```
Dependent Variable LSP500 - Estimation by Least Squares
Annual Data From 1982:01 To 2119:01
Usable Observations     138        Degrees of Freedom    135
Centered R**2       0.890235       R Bar **2     0.888609
Uncentered R**2     0.999400       T x R**2       137.917
Mean of Dependent Variable       5.4251648269
Std Error of Dependent Variable 0.4037249870
Standard Error of Estimate       0.1347445420
Sum of Squared Residuals         2.4510723656
Regression F(2,135)                547.4495
Significance Level of F           0.00000000
Durbin-Watson Statistic           0.172612
Q(34-0)                          563.967124
Significance Level of Q           0.00000000
      Variable                  Coeff        Std Error      T-Stat      Signif
******************************************************************************
1.  Constant               10.32129303    0.14841145      69.54513   0.00000000
2.  LYIELD                 -0.58502238    0.42000566      -1.39289   0.16594211
3.  LYIELD{1}              -1.49205983    0.42156971      -3.53930   0.00055086

Dependent Variable LSP500 - Estimation by Cochrane-Orcutt
Annual Data From 1983:01 To 2119:01
Usable Observations     137        Degrees of Freedom    134
Centered R**2       0.987292       R Bar **2     0.987103
Uncentered R**2     0.999931       T x R**2       136.991
Standard Error of Estimate       0.0457052844
Sum of Squared Residuals         0.2799223849
Durbin-Watson Statistic           2.078351
Q(34-1)                           23.225764
Significance Level of Q           0.89679685
      Variable                  Coeff        Std Error      T-Stat      Signif
******************************************************************************
1.  Constant                7.344418520    0.566787528    12.95797   0.00000000
2.  LYIELD{1}              -0.431256592    0.142668299    -3.02279   0.00300163
******************************************************************************
3.  RHO                     0.992091772    0.011947991    83.03419   0.00000000
```

We would expect mutual causality and this provides some evidence of that. In summary, we see statistically significant relationships that have somewhat limited practical value. The utility of similar models might be increased by applying structural equations as developed in Chapter 11, however, that is doubtful. Problem 3A-10 furthers the analysis of these series further using first differences of logs in the calculation of CCFs and possible relationships.

3-27. Solution depends on chosen stock.

3-28. This is a very difficult problem. Students may find a number of different approaches which seem to work well in modeling this relationship. However, in all cases except those using Cochrane-Orcutt or MARIMA methods, the relationship will fall apart when the problems of autocorrelation are eliminated. This problem should be used to introduce the importance of graphing appropriately transformed variables, the devastating effects that very low D-W statistics can have on the validity of the relationship, and the great limitations of OLS procedures with this type of data. Find below several related graphs and models. None of these validly model the relationship other than those using Cochrane-Orcutt models of changes or ratios. The problem can be studied in much greater detail and requires the equivalent time and effort of a major case analysis. Comments on the validity of fitted relationships include the invalidity of the relationship after controlling for serial correlation, and even those relationships that might be valid will have such low explained variance that they will have very low practical significance. There is a lead-lag relationship between these two variables, but it is difficult to model until chapters 10 to 14 are studied.

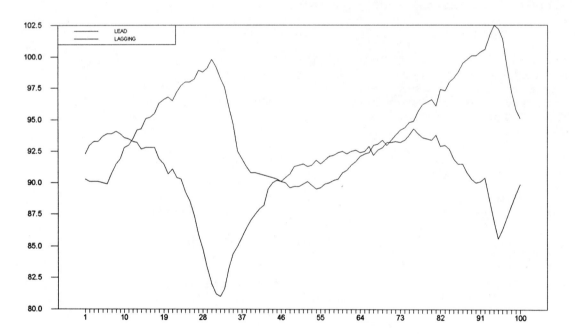

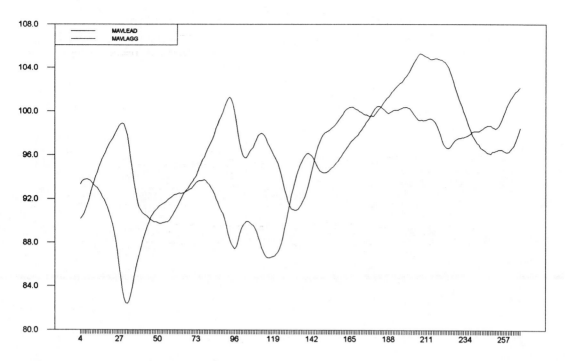

Fig. 3-28a. Seven Period Centered Moving Averages Leading and Lagging Indicators

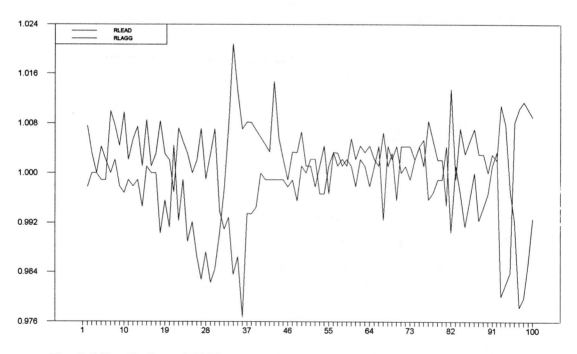

Fig. 3-28b. Ratios of Y_t/Y_{t-1} for both Leading and Lagging Indicators

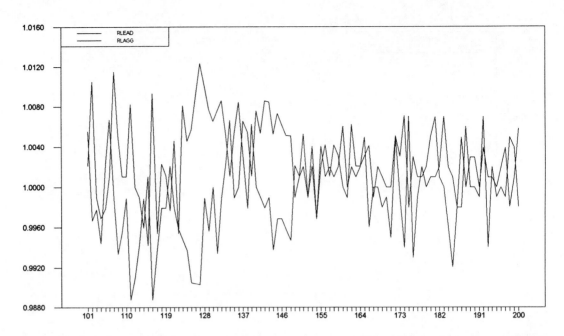

Fig. 3-28c. Ratios of Y_t/Y_{t-1} for both Leading and Lagging Indicators Continued.

Students may experiment with different lead-lag relationships, one of the stronger lags is of 16 months. The following relationship is for a lag of 16 months for the leading indicator on the lagging indicator. Unfortunately, the D-W is extremely low and much of the strength of the relationship is a result of serial correlation as shown by the Cochrane-Orcutt solution which follows. Unfortunately, the lead-lag relationship is not constant, the lag varies considerably and the slope coefficient will change greatly. This problem is revisited in the supplement to this chapter, problem 3A-7.

```
linreg lagging / res
#constant lead{16}
Dependent Variable LAGGING - Estimation by Least Squares
Annual Data From 17:01 To 270:01
Usable Observations    254        Degrees of Freedom    252
Centered R**2      0.673295       R Bar **2    0.671998
Uncentered R**2    0.999397       T x R**2      253.847
Mean of Dependent Variable       97.483464567
Std Error of Dependent Variable   4.201341095
Standard Error of Estimate        2.406168922
Sum of Squared Residuals       1458.9915178
Regression F(1,252)                 519.3370
Significance Level of F            0.00000000
Durbin-Watson Statistic             0.057356
Q(36-0)                          1570.043045
Significance Level of Q            0.00000000
     Variable                 Coeff        Std Error      T-Stat      Signif
*************************************************************************************
1.   Constant            27.907549465   3.056783267     9.12971    0.00000000
2.   LEAD{16}             0.741249704   0.032526691    22.78897    0.00000000
```

The following is a Cochrane-Orcutt fit of the above relationship.

```
Dependent Variable LAGGING - Estimation by Cochrane-Orcutt
Annual Data From 18:01 To 270:01
Usable Observations     253      Degrees of Freedom    250
Centered R**2       0.985650     R Bar **2    0.985536
Uncentered R**2     0.999973     T x R**2     252.993
Mean of Dependent Variable       97.491304348
Std Error of Dependent Variable  4.207806836
Standard Error of Estimate       0.506065361
Sum of Squared Residuals         64.025537360
Durbin-Watson Statistic           1.061217
Q(36-1)                          162.679095
Significance Level of Q           0.00000000

    Variable              Coeff        Std Error      T-Stat      Signif
******************************************************************************
1.  Constant          78.702323191  6.600203770     11.92423   0.0000000 ᴊ
2.  LEAD{16}           0.211973148   0.061574472      3.44255   0.00067539
******************************************************************************
3.  RHO               0.989119401   0.009274334    106.65125   0.00000000
```

3-29. THERE IS AN ERROR HERE, SKIP THIS PROBLEM. The data file JUNKMAIL.DAT does not contain the data identified in this question (one of the problems associated with printing the diskette before the book is completed). Instead this question should be reworded as follows: A direct marketing firm wants to estimate the time it takes to sort packages using the weight and length of packages. This information can be used to estimate the number of workers needed to sort packages each day. Thirty days of packages were randomly sampled for the weight and length of packages. The file JUNKMAIL.DAT lists the time of packages in seconds the weight in ounces, and the length in .10 inches. Using this data, complete the following:

a) Estimate the relationship between the time as a function of and the weight and length of packages.

b) What is the error in estimating the slope of this relationship.

```
linreg time / res
#constant weight length
Dependent Variable TIME - Estimation by Least Squares
Usable Observations     30       Degrees of Freedom     27
Centered R**2     0.892068       R Bar **2    0.884073
Mean of Dependent Variable       55.902333333
Std Error of Dependent Variable 25.145682934
Standard Error of Estimate        8.561620953
Sum of Squared Residuals       1979.1365404
Regression F(2,27)              111.5786
Significance Level of F           0.00000000
Durbin-Watson Statistic           1.700631
    Variable              Coeff        Std Error      T-Stat      Signif
******************************************************************************
1.  Constant          14.591546472  3.560714411      4.09793   0.0003414 ᴊ
2.  WEIGHT             0.151797023   0.060285531      2.51797   0.01803877
3.  LENGTH             0.182081060   0.031188668      5.83805   0.00000325
```

II. MINCASES

After some thought, write out an equation such as equation 3-1 which states the possible relationships between the dependent variable and important independent variables and influences. Be sure to be comprehensive in the identification of important causal influences. Include an estimate of the importance of these variables by designating these variables as somewhat important (S), important (I), or very important (V). Next identify the sign of the causality, that is, whether each variable positively (+) or negatively (-) influences the dependent variable and whether that influence is linear (L) or nonlinear (N). Now having defined a comprehensive causal model, identify potential sources of data which measure these causal variables.

MINICASE 3A-* Responses are added here using the following notation [C]=Coincident, [P]=Precedes, [F]=Follows the dependent variable; where [P] denotes all of the effect of the independent variable precedes the resulting change in the dependent variable, [C,P] denotes that there is both a coincident and lagged effect of the dependent variable. In some cases the lagged effect is the same as or opposite to that of the coincident effect. Other combinations of effects are possible. [F] denotes that the forthcoming event or influence effects the dependent variable before the actual event or influence occurs. Note that the assigning of the direction of causality is somewhat subjective, you might not agree with those noted here however, in general, we should emphasize the need to consider all possible combinations of F,C, and P that may influence a relationship. Finally, note that I did not discuss sources of these data in order to save space and time; in some cases sources are obvious, in others not. Students responsible for this completing these minicases should study book Appendix A and other sources of data.

MINICASE 3-1. Kansas Turnpike, Daily.

Traffic = f(Habits, Temperature, Rain, Snow, Ice, Holidays, College athletics, Major conventions, Major League sports)

Habits (V,+/-,L) [C]   Temperature (I,+/-,N)[C,P]   Rain(S,+/-,N)[C,P]   Snow(V,-,N)[C,P]
ICE(V,-,N)[C,P]   Holidays(V,+/-,L)[C,P] College Athletics(I,+,L)[C]   Conventions(I,+,L)[C,P]
MLS(I,+,L)[C,P]

MINICASE 3-2. Air Passengers by Quarter.

Revenues = f(Prices of Fares, Competitor Fares, Holidays, Weather, World Events, Olympics, Unemployment, Economic Conditions,Promotions)

Prices(V,-,N)[C,P]	Competitor Fares(V,+,N)[C,P]	Holidays(V,+,L)[C]
Extreme Weather(S,-,N)[C,P]	World Events(I,+/-,N)[C,P]	Olympics(I,+,L)[C]
Unemployment(V,-,N)[C,P]	Economic Conditions(V,+/-,N)[C,P]	Promotions(V,+,N)[C,P]

MINICASE 3-3. Hospital Census by Week.

Patients = f(Holidays, Physicians on Staff, Physician Work Schedules, Weather, Physician Conventions, Third Party Payers (Insurance Companies, HMO, using the facility), Costs)

Holidays(V,+,L)[C,P]	Physicians(V,+,N)[C,P]	Work Schedules(V,+,L)[C]
Extreme Weather(I,-,N)[C,P]	Physician Conventions(V,-,N)[C,P]	Third Party(V,+,L)[C,P]
Costs(V,-,N)[C,P]		

MINICASE 3-4. Henry Machler's Hideaway Orchids.

Sales = f(Seasons, Holidays, Advertising, Temperatures, Rain, Hurricanes)

Seasons(V,+/-,L)[C]   Holidays(V,+,L)[F,C,P] Advertising(I,+,L)[C,P] Temperatures(V,+/-,N)[C]
Rain(V,-,N)[C]   Hurricanes(V,-,L)[C,P]

MINICASE 3-6. Midwestern Building Materials

Sales = f(Seasons, Holidays, Promotions, Temperatures, Rain, Snow, Extreme Weather)

Seasons(V,+/-,L)[C]	Holidays(V,+/-,L)[C]	Promotions(V,+,N)[C,P]
Temperatures(V,+/-,N)[C]	Rain(V,-,N)[C,P]	Snow (V,-,N)[C,P]
Extreme Weather (V,-,N)[C,P]		

MINICASE 3-7. International Airline Passengers

Passengers = f(Prices of Fares, Competitor Fares, Holidays, Weather, World Events, Olympics,
Unemployment, Economic Conditions, Promotions)

Prices(V,-,N)[C,P]	Competitor Fares(V,+,N)[C,P]	Holidays(V,+,L)[C]
Extreme Weather(S,-,N)[C,P]	World Events(I,+/-,N)[C]	Olympics(I,+,L)[C]
Unemployment(V,-,N)[C,P]	Economic Conditions(V,+/-,N)[C,P]	Promotions(V,+,N)[C,P]

MINICASE 3-8. Automobile Sales

Sales = f(Prices, Competitor Prices, Holidays, Weather, Unemployment, Economic Conditions, Promotions)

Prices(V,-,N)[C,P]	Competitor Prices(V,+,N)[C,P] Holidays(V,+,L)[C]	
Extreme Weather(S,-,N)[C,P]	Unemployment(V,-,N)[C,P]	Economic Conditions(V,+/-,N)[C,P]
Promotions(V,+,N)[C,P]		

MINICASE 3-9. Consumption of Distilled Spirits

Sales = f(Prices, Competitor Prices, Holidays, World Events, Olympics, Unemployment,
Economic Conditions, Promotions, Societal View of Alcohol)

Prices(V,-,N)[C,P]	Competitor Fares(V,+,N)[C,P]	Holidays(V,+,L)[C]
World Events(I,+/-,N)[C]	Olympics(I,+,L)[C,P]	Unemployment(V,-,N)[C]
Economic Conditions(V,+/-,N)[C]	Promotions(V,+,N)[C,P]	Societal Views(V,+/-,N)[C,P]

MINICASE 3-10. Discount Consumer Electronics

Passengers = f(Prices, Competitor Prices, Holidays, Weather, World Events, Olympics, Unemployment,
Economic Conditions, Technological Improvements)[C]

Prices(V,-,N)[C,P]	Competitor Prices(V,+,N)[C,P]	Holidays(V,+,L)[C]
Extreme Weather(S,-,N)[C,P]	World Events(I,+/-,N)[C]	Olympics(I,+,L)[C]
Unemployment(V,-,N)[C,P]	Economic Conditions(V,+/-,N)[C,P]	Promotions(V,+,N)[C,P]
Technological Improvements(V,+,N)[C]		

APPENDIX 3A
CROSS-CORRELATION COEFFICIENTS

I. PROBLEMS

Note: In several of the following problems we will suggest using first differences to remove the high autocorrelation. However, be sure to point out to the student that as we shall study in Chapter 13, we may be overdifferencing some of these series. More importantly as discussed in Chapter 13, our goal is to transform the input series (i.e., the independent variable) to white noise and then to perform the same transformation on the output series (dependent variable) in order to better measure their cross correlations. In using indiscriminate differencing we risk over differencing one or more of the series, that may or may not be the case here depending on a student's approach.

ESTIMATED DIFFICULTY

| Elementary | Medium | | | | Hard | | Very Hard | | Bad |

1 M   2 M   3 M   4 M   5 M   6 M   7 V   8 V   9 V   10 V

11 H-V 12 H   13 V

Minicases are all Hard.

3A-1. See Pages 132 and 134. $t = CCF(k)/Se_{CCF}$

   H_0: There is no statistically significant cross correlation between Yt and Xt-k.

   H_1: There is a statistically significant cross correlation between Yt and Xt-k.

   The most appropriate with a small number of observations is the Pearson, also, remember the rule of using more than 50 observations and only n/4 observations for the CCF.

3A-2. The two standard errors for CCF(k)'s for 100 observations for k values of 1 and 36 is .2 for all lags, however, the values of n>25 are biased because of the small number of observations, in general the maximum k should be n/4.

3A-3. Procedure and results are software dependent.

3A-5. Using the TV-SAT of problem 3-18
a) Calculate ACF(k) for both series for k = 0 to 2.
b) Calculate CCFs for TV and SAT scores for k = 0 to 2.
c) Repeat a) and b) using first differences.
d) Comment on Your results by comparing the results of a), b), and c).
d) Fit a regression model to the original or first differences.

```
a) corr(num=2,qstat) tv
Correlations of Series TV, Autocorrelations    1: 0.63334966 0.28457545
Ljung-Box Q-Statistics  Q(2)   = 5.6641.  Significance Level 0.05889085
```

```
corr(num=2,qstat) SAT, Autocorrelations    1: 0.64039307 0.16363165
Ljung-Box Q-Statistics  Q(2)    =          5.0439.  Significance Level
0.08030291
```

b) These are extremely small numbers of observations, consequently, the results are unreliable, nonetheless, there is some serial correlation. Calculating the CCF for tv(t+k) vs sat(t) yields:

```
cross(qstat) tv sat 1 8 -2 2
Cross Correlations of Series TV(t+k) and SAT(t)
    -2: -0.1629850 -0.5732551 -0.9079559 -0.6933245 -0.3715586
Ljung-Box Q-Statistics
Q(1 to 2)   =          7.3344.  Significance Level 0.02554732
Q(-2 to -1) =          4.1099.  Significance Level 0.12810171
Q(-2 to 2)  =         19.6881.  Significance Level 0.00142979

Note that the lag is in the opposite direction, TV(t) = f(SAT(t-1))
```

c) set dtv 2 8 = tv- tv(t-1)   set dsat 2 8 = sat - sat(t-1)

```
Correlations of Series DTV,  Autocorrelations    1: -0.0140027 -0.3360451
Ljung-Box Q-Statistics  Q(2) = 1.4249.  Significance Level 0.49043369

Correlations of Series DSAT,  Autocorrelations  1:  0.2275082 -0.3062039
Ljung-Box Q-Statistics  Q(2) = 1.7249.  Significance Level 0.42213371

Calculating the CCF for dtv(t+k) vs dsat(t) yields:
-2: -0.1378526 -0.0982879  0.0706942 -0.7319475 -0.3359690
Ljung-Box Q-Statistics
Q(1 to 2)   =          7.0476.  Significance Level 0.02948757
Q(-2 to -1) =          0.3409.  Significance Level 0.84329482
Q(-2 to 2)  =          7.4334.  Significance Level 0.19034897
```

From the above and as before, it appears that dTV follows dSAT scores, lower changes in SAT scores yield greater TV watching. The most significant and valid of the relationships that can be fitted to this data is TV as a function of lagged SAT scores. Obviously, this is an extremely small data set with considerable mutual causality.

```
d)linreg tv / res
#constant sat{1}
Dependent Variable TV - Estimation by Least Squares
Annual Data From 2:01 To 8:01
Usable Observations        7        Degrees of Freedom        5
Centered R**2      0.955590      R Bar **2    0.946708
Uncentered R**2    0.999645      T x R**2      6.998
Mean of Dependent Variable       6.4557142857
Std Error of Dependent Variable 0.6263347652
Standard Error of Estimate       0.1445891749
Sum of Squared Residuals         0.1045301474
Regression F(1,5)                  107.5882
Significance Level of F           0.00014341
Durbin-Watson Statistic            2.095430
Q(1-0)                             0.434546
Significance Level of Q           0.50976692
    Variable             Coeff        Std Error      T-Stat      Signif
***********************************************************************
1.  Constant          22.72180428    1.56915006     14.48033   0.00002834
2.  SAT{1}            -0.01752272    0.00168935    -10.37247   0.00014341
```

3A-6. The cross correlation between PRISON(t+k) and CRIME(t) is:
```
Cross Correlations of Series PRISON and CRIME
 Lags   -2         -1          0          1          2
   -2: -0.3572759 -0.6763286 -0.7604166 -0.1140679  0.1938344
```

Thus, prison sentences in period t-1 affects crime rates in period t. Lower prison terms yield higher crime rates. This yields the following linear regression of Crime(t) = f(Prison(t-1)):

```
Dependent Variable CRIME - Estimation by Least Squares
Annual Data From 2:01 To 7:01
Usable Observations        6      Degrees of Freedom     4
Centered R**2       0.740976      R Bar **2    0.676220
Uncentered R**2     0.971970      T x R**2        5.832
Mean of Dependent Variable       48.566666667
Std Error of Dependent Variable  18.532637877
Standard Error of Estimate       10.545372482
Sum of Squared Residuals         444.81952310
Regression F(1,4)                   11.4426
Significance Level of F           0.02771640
Durbin-Watson Statistic            1.575304
Q(1-0)                             0.279890
Significance Level of Q           0.59677341
     Variable               Coeff     Std Error    T-Stat     Signif
********************************************************************************
1.   Constant            81.73621461  10.70911819   7.63239  0.0015826)
2.   PRISON{1}           -3.37317437   0.99718627  -3.38269  0.0277164U
```

The interpretation of this relationship is straightforward.

3A-7. Pearson Correlation Coefficient versus CCF.
```
Cross Correlations of Series PRISON(t+k) and CRIME(t)
 lags -2 to +2: -.3572759    -.6763286 -.7604166 -.1140679  .1938344
Pearson Cross Correlations
 lags -2 to + 2: -.806309    -.8607999 -.7604166 -.5648799  .2161947
```

The direction of causality is confirmed by these results.

3A-8. Determining whether there are significant lags between market Share and percentage of employees through a TQM program. As we see below, there is very high autocorrelation in these two series. This high degree of autocorrelation makes it difficult to measure the lead-lag relationship between the two variables as shown in the cross correlation function below.
```
Autcorrelations of Series TQM
1: 0.77635752 0.70811828 0.62303499 0.51221606 0.44198661 0.36743982
    7: 0.29027384 0.22316904 0.20380055 0.15462475 0.14656908 0.11535388
Ljung-Box Q-Statistics  Q(12)  =      129.4187  Significance Level 0.00000000

Autocorrelations of Series SHARE
1: 0.88770640 0.78237926 0.66016423 0.55048609 0.45366637 0.35105342
    7: 0.26085919 0.19512342 0.15232499 0.13247718 0.11740423 0.10771686
Ljung-Box Q-Statistics  Q(12)  =      146.1770  Significance Level 0.00000000

Cross Correlations of Series SHARE(t+k) and TQM(t)
  -12: 0.12060054 0.12562959 0.14543077 0.17710517 0.20691973 0.26147735
   -6: 0.35896589 0.44310646 0.53550562 0.63284845 0.71731487 0.81590380
    0: 0.96390774 0.85286999 0.76963617 0.64926515 0.52985891 0.45682618
    6: 0.36370490 0.29210261 0.21694382 0.18163925 0.15267251 0.12456029
   12: 0.11968954
```

```
Ljung-Box Q-Statistics
Q(1 to 12)  =        143.4379.  Significance Level 0.00000000
Q(-12 to -1)=        132.7117.  Significance Level 0.00000000
Q(-12 to 12)=        324.4637.  Significance Level 0.00000000
```

Let us remove the high autocorrelation by taking first differences of each. As we shall study in Chapter 13, we may be overdifferencing one of these series. More importantly as discussed in Chapter 13, our goal is to transform the input series (TQM) to white noise and then to perform the same transformation on the output series (SHARE) in order to better measure their cross correlations. In using indiscriminate differencing we risk over differencing one or more of the series, that is not the case here.

```
SET DSHARE 2 50 = SHARE - SHARE(T-1)    SET DTQM 2 50 = TQM - TQM(T-1)
Series              Obs        Mean        Std Error      Minimum         Maximum
SHARE               50   17.917000000   2.202244912   12.000000000   21.160000000
TQM                 50   44.756800000   5.890494051   25.000000000   52.380000000
DSHARE              49    0.171020408   0.475689171   -0.760000000    1.080000000
DTQM                49    0.536122449   2.556185974   -3.840000000    7.160000000

CROSS(QSTAT) DSHARE DTQM
Cross Correlations of Series DSHARE and DTQM
  -12:  0.1578071 -0.0778483  0.0856309  0.0763445 -0.0760780 -0.0180502
   -6: -0.1001511  0.0391884  0.1301840  0.0188214 -0.0622782  0.0733709
    0:  0.4664116 -0.1630080  0.1678143  0.1880030 -0.2571753  0.3457275
    6: -0.1088610  0.2862192 -0.2120324  0.0562678  0.2726446 -0.2097503
   12:  0.1248103
Ljung-Box Q-Statistics
Q(1 to 12)  =         32.4721.  Significance Level 0.00116957
Q(-12 to -1)=          5.4037.  Significance Level 0.94311875
Q(-12 to 12)=         48.9703.  Significance Level 0.00284858
```

Significant CCFs are greater than .283 as shown by the calculation below.

```
DISP 2/50**.5 = 0.28284
```

There are significant lags at 0 and 5, the lag at 5 may be spurious. To check whether the lag at 5 is statistically significant, the following regression is run. The results confirm that the relationship is significant, however, this relationships is inferior to that of problem 3-24. Thus, we choose to ignore the 5 period lag. However, as shown, the TQM training does precede the market SHARE variable as we had hoped.

```
linreg share / res
#constant TQM{0 5}
Dependent Variable SHARE - Estimation by Least Squares
Usable Observations        45        Degrees of Freedom      42
Centered R**2       0.903198        R Bar **2     0.898588
Uncentered R**2     0.999437        T x R**2        44.975
Mean of Dependent Variable        18.485333333
Std Error of Dependent Variable    1.429945326
Standard Error of Estimate         0.455369936
Sum of Squared Residuals           8.7091947166
Regression F(2,42)                  195.9366
Significance Level of F              0.00000000
Durbin-Watson Statistic             1.618728
     Variable             Coeff        Std Error     T-Stat      Signif
*****************************************************************************
1.  Constant        3.6898278608 0.8368967865     4.40894   0.00007068
2.  TQM             0.2431359340 0.0300514756     8.09065   0.00000000
3.  TQM{5}          0.0809388146 0.0208072510     3.88993   0.00035149
```

Finally, as shown by the descriptive statistics below, it does not appear that we have overdifferenced SHARE or TQM. However, a final determination of the best prewhitening model for TQM should be based on the methods of Chapter 13.

```
Series              Obs      Mean        Std Error      Minimum       Maximum
SHARE               50    17.917000000   2.202244912   12.000000000  21.160000000
TQM                 50    44.756800000   5.890494051   25.000000000  52.380000000
DSHARE              49     0.171020408   0.475689171   -0.760000000   1.080000000
DTQM                49     0.536122449   2.556185974   -3.840000000   7.160000000
```

3A-9. SATisfaction versus CQI training. As shown below, there is strong autocorrelations in each of these time series, thus, CCFs are overstated and we adjust for the problems of high ACFs by taking first differences as a means of better measuring the true CCF. There is a one-period lag in the effect of CQI training on SATisfaction. This is an excellent problem with which to introduce such relationships.

```
Autoorrelations of Series SAT
1: 0.93702815 0.86003151 0.78008350 0.70870803 0.62755152 0.56357262
 7: 0.51116747 0.45656780 0.40131657 0.34069289 0.27613592 0.21439488
Ljung-Box Q-Statistic  Q(12)  =     244.9178  Significance Level 0.00000000

Autocorrelations of Series CQI
1: 0.88846575 0.81996614 0.75691278 0.66513554 0.61227828 0.57513757
     7: 0.52072260 0.45563428 0.39703648 0.33390089 0.27494304 0.20983211
Ljung-Box Q-Statistics Q(12)  =     230.7511.  Significance Level 0.00000000

Cross Correlations of sat(t+k) vs CQI(t) or  sat(t) vs CQI(t-k)
  -12: 0.21057818 0.26541978 0.33196091 0.39564573 0.45732625 0.51468785
   -6: 0.58367347 0.63523869 0.68269397 0.74980416 0.83056160 0.89360290
    0: 0.96322045 0.93904940 0.86107710 0.78668985 0.70459838 0.62379377
    6: 0.55282191 0.49534598 0.45770350 0.41068543 0.34158940 0.28521541
   12: 0.21707558
Ljung-Box Q-Statistics
Q(1 to 12)  =        244.5224.  Significance Level 0.00000000
Q(-12 to -1)=        234.4110.  Significance Level 0.00000000
Q(-12 to 12)=        527.1787.  Significance Level 0.00000000
```

The above measures are greatly influenced by high degrees of autocorrelation. Let us remove the autocorrelation using first differences.

```
SET DCQI 2 50 = CQI - CQI(T-1)          SET DSAT 2 50 = sat - sat(T-1)

Series          Obs        Mean         Std Error       Minimum        Maximum
SAT             50      90.3638000      2.1240997      86.3100000     93.4900000
CQI             50    9042.2258000    212.2391322    8576.6400000   9376.4200000
DCQI            49      16.3220408     56.0603975     -80.4500000    138.9700000
DSAT            49       0.1114286      0.4900213      -0.8700000      1.1200000

Autocorrelations of Series DSAT
1: -0.0810060 -0.0432450 -0.0472746 -0.0199113 -0.1114230 -0.1623437
7:  0.2260308 -0.0617399 -0.0842449 -0.0287485 -0.0958044 -0.0226172
Ljung-Box Q-Statistics  Q(12)  =        7.2280.  Significance Level 0.84218608

Autocorrelations of Series DCQI
1: -0.1328978 -0.1877507  0.0834617  0.0200863 -0.2428661  0.0759595
7:  0.1242525 -0.0884083 -0.2287768 -0.0692627  0.1447681 -0.0172088
Ljung-Box Q-Statistics  Q(12)  =       13.2505.  Significance Level 0.35110098
```

```
Cross Correlations of Series DSAT(t+k) and DCQI(t)
  -12:   0.0614347 -0.0159956 -0.0151893 -0.1009138 -0.0258430 -0.2255842
   -6:   0.1674083  0.1207423 -0.1873705 -0.0749940 -0.0211941  0.0042830
    0:  -0.2153804  0.7347565  0.0185556 -0.1049411  0.0271179  0.0448467
    6:  -0.1724505 -0.1050761  0.1583088  0.0486738 -0.2897891  0.0291669
   12:   0.0516041
```

Note the very high CCF(1), thus CQI(t-1) influences SAT(t) more than other lags. This results in the following relationship.

```
Dependent Variable SAT - Estimation by Least Squares
Annual Data From 2:01 To 50:01
Usable Observations       49        Degrees of Freedom      47
Centered R**2        0.983231       R Bar **2      0.982875
Uncentered R**2      0.999991       T x R**2       49.000
Mean of Dependent Variable        90.432448980
Std Error of Dependent Variable    2.089318600
Standard Error of Estimate         0.273417047
Sum of Squared Residuals           3.5135734390
Regression F(1,47)                  2755.8471
Significance Level of F            0.00000000
Durbin-Watson Statistic            1.680306
Q(12-0)                            6.762523
Significance Level of Q            0.87289971
     Variable              Coeff       Std Error      T-Stat      Signif
*****************************************************************************
1.  Constant          0.7950999727 1.7079495823      0.46553   0.64370274
2.  CQI{1}            0.0099206780 0.0001889791     52.49616   0.00000000
```

The relationship between SAT(t) = f(CQI(t-1)) is quite strong and logical. This is a considerably better relationship than a coincident CQI.

3A-10. We should use logarithms and first differences of logs to model this relationship.
```
set lyield = log(yield)              set lsp500 = log(sp500)
set dlyield 2 139 = lyield - lyield(t-1)
set dlsp500 2 139 = lsp500 - lsp500(t-1)
Autocorrelations of Series DLYIELD
1:   0.3446303 -0.1099543 -0.0853705  0.0295208  0.1484334 -0.0011141
   7:  -0.0484405  0.0548726  0.0182131  0.0577107  0.0753832 -0.0701399
  13:  -0.2071448 -0.1455101 -0.0659242  0.0053339 -0.0824423 -0.1549408
  19:  -0.0696107 -0.1371880 -0.1622323 -0.0555841  0.0118446 -0.0565492
  25:  -0.0336496  0.0666343  0.0357819 -0.0981296 -0.0538739  0.0022328
  31:   0.0523569  0.0267568  0.0673545  0.1051242
Ljung-Box Q-Statistics          Q(34) =  57.5656.  Significance Level 0.00701179

Autocorrelations of Series DLSP500
1:   0.0360586 -0.0226431 -0.0975597 -0.0911829  0.1284525 -0.0316262
   7:   0.0004520 -0.1240868 -0.0925979  0.1023059 -0.0422666 -0.0572578
  13:  -0.0161622 -0.0353875 -0.0312251 -0.0554208 -0.0055946 -0.0887702
  19:  -0.0162130 -0.0378969 -0.0960156  0.0196040 -0.0713711  0.0903576
  25:   0.0109395  0.1228877  0.0394438  0.0095207  0.0823730 -0.0539667
  31:  -0.0148016 -0.0685756  0.0248033  0.0622174
Ljung-Box Q-Statistics          Q(34) =  23.9042.  Significance Level 0.90128875
```

Note that the series dlsp500 is prewhitened as necessary to achieve reliable cross correlations.

```
Cross Correlations of Series DLYIELD(t+k) and DLSP500(t)
  -28:   0.0244872 -0.0627201 -0.0397992 -0.0852984  0.0543862  0.2249953
  -22:   0.0804347  0.0205523  0.1452767  0.1465697  0.0509303 -0.0956141
```

```
-16: -0.0260207   0.1298060   0.0422349   0.0375344   0.0216820  -0.0970461
-10: -0.0700839   0.0840363   0.0390949  -0.0952604  -0.2302066  -0.2514209
 -4:  0.0027632   0.0267107  -0.0613600  -0.2481177  -0.3506034  -0.1581483
  2:  0.1150860   0.2011260   0.0977377  -0.1085916   0.0721591   0.0638853
  8:  0.0473213  -0.0613370  -0.0900602   0.1466152   0.0724079   0.0756932
 14:  0.0852909   0.0238150   0.1199589  -0.0262348  -0.0166222   0.0959154
 20:  0.0655125   0.0664746  -0.0144490  -0.0123966  -0.0833775  -0.0279939
 26:  0.0216622  -0.0699758  -0.0722558  -0.0069620   0.0018939   0.0001961
Ljung-Box Q-Statistics
Q(1 to 34)  =        36.2253.  Significance Level 0.36515393
Q(-34 to -1)=        56.4860.  Significance Level 0.00905443
Q(-34 to 34)=       109.9205.  Significance Level 0.00126682

disp 2/139**.5 = 0.16964
```

Changes in the YIELD preceded changes in the SP500. Refer to problem 3-26 for the fit a relationship between Yield and SP500. Again, the relationship between these two variables is better modeled using the MARIMA methods of Chapter 13.

3A-11. Dependent on the stock chosen by the student.

3A-12. Because of the loss of degrees of freedom in cross correlation calculations, CCF(k)'s are unreliable in detecting the date of the unknown specimen unless the number of observations are manipulated. The easiest way to detect the pattern is through graphs such as below or through the calculation of Pearson Correlation Coefficients.

```
linreg unknown
#constant known{5}
Dependent Variable UNKNOWN - Estimation by Least Squares
Usable Observations       8        Degrees of Freedom     6
Centered R**2       0.998680      R Bar **2    0.998460
Uncentered R**2     0.999649      T x R**2       7.997
Mean of Dependent Variable        4.2000000000
Std Error of Dependent Variable 2.7034369659
Standard Error of Estimate        0.1060807143
Sum of Squared Residuals          0.0675187077
Regression F(1,6)                 4540.2955
Significance Level of F           0.00000000
Durbin-Watson Statistic           2.577664
    Variable                    Coeff        Std Error      T-Stat      Signif
*********************************************************************************
1.  Constant              0.1229480936 0.0711878675      1.72709   0.13489571
2.  KNOWN{5}              0.9853901889 0.0146239998     67.38172   0.00000000
```

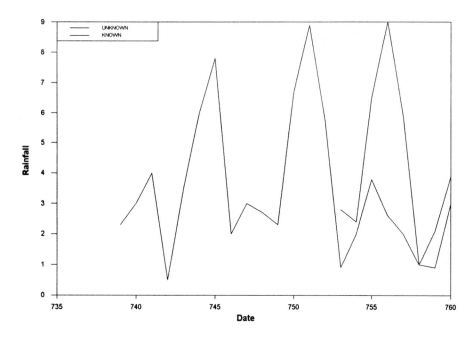

LUNKNOWN is UNKNOWN lagged for 5 periods as shown below.

ENTRY	DATE	KNOWN	UNKNOWN	LUNKNOWN	ERROR
10	748	2.7000	NA	2.8000	-0.100
11	749	2.3000	NA	2.4000	0.200
12	750	6.7000	NA	6.5000	-0.100
13	751	8.9000	NA	9.0000	-0.100
14	752	5.8000	NA	5.9000	-0.100
15	753	0.9000	2.8000	1.0000	-0.100
16	754	2.0000	2.4000	2.1000	-0.100
17	755	3.8000	6.5000	3.9000	-0.100
18	756	2.6000	9.0000	NA	
19	757	2.0000	5.9000	NA	
20	758	1.0000	1.0000	NA	
21	759	0.9000	2.1000	NA	
22	760	3.0000	3.9000	NA	

3A-13. As expected, the results are different than the non-logarithmic relationships. The first two CCF(k)
are statistically significant, thus, first differences of the logarithms of the German and US stock indexes are
related as follows:

$$dlgerm = f(dlus(t), dlus(t-1))$$

Unfortunately, the concepts of Chapter 10 to 14 must be studied in order to validly model this relationship.

```
Cross(qstat) lgerm lus / -24 24 dcross
Cross Correlations of Series LGERM and LUS
Monthly Data From 1:01 To 23:07
 -24: 0.72299407 0.73394258 0.74318694 0.75143509 0.75958900 0.76883504
 -18: 0.77739727 0.78701877 0.79677685 0.80684111 0.81737877 0.82834721
 -12: 0.83863911 0.84864642 0.85877538 0.86729727 0.87490539 0.88232141
  -6: 0.89111246 0.90069684 0.91069904 0.92067150 0.93089865 0.94076979
   0: 0.94918392 0.94158530 0.93147139 0.92020147 0.90934692 0.89757322
   6: 0.88483049 0.87174231 0.85972154 0.84782800 0.83596756 0.82378597
  12: 0.81140957 0.79999253 0.78924954 0.77849634 0.76800848 0.75772355
  18: 0.74785177 0.73922720 0.73125635 0.72408863 0.71757360 0.71059846
```

```
      24: 0.70410968
Ljung-Box Q-Statistics
Q(1 to 24)   =       4555.4397.   Significance Level 0.00000000
Q(-24 to -1)=        4763.3878.   Significance Level 0.00000000
Q(-24 to 24)=        9564.7869.   Significance Level 0.00000000


cor(num=36,qstat) lus
Correlations of Series LUS
Monthly Data From 1:01 To 23:07
Autocorrelations
       1: 0.98826936 0.97488436 0.96133324 0.94774939 0.93313989 0.91800902
       7: 0.90296519 0.88953079 0.87659339 0.86386497 0.85108457 0.83823864
      13: 0.82594240 0.81396610 0.80235410 0.79107835 0.77991799 0.76919326
      19: 0.75989119 0.75069224 0.74274540 0.73533903 0.72723016 0.71921240
      25: 0.71030399 0.70129904 0.69230553 0.68317095 0.67353689 0.66408953
      31: 0.65417944 0.64432213 0.63503295 0.62532303 0.61539866 0.60531783
Ljung-Box Q-Statistics  Q(36)  =   6476.9684.  Significance Level 0.00000000


cor(num=36,qstat) lgerm
Correlations of Series LGERM
Monthly Data From 1:01 To 23:07
Autocorrelations
       1: 0.99057641 0.97761143 0.96378943 0.94979898 0.93566311 0.92226842
       7: 0.91020361 0.89897401 0.88769232 0.87612484 0.86238656 0.84785030
      13: 0.83307145 0.81831731 0.80408166 0.79041957 0.77798245 0.76668757
      19: 0.75549064 0.74456960 0.73472603 0.72505946 0.71495114 0.70315682
      25: 0.68946885 0.67661074 0.66465232 0.65297550 0.64207953 0.63183758
      31: 0.62214739 0.61325038 0.60427268 0.59312069 0.58025845 0.56694418
Ljung-Box Q-Statistics  Q(36)  =   6350.5796.  Significance Level 0.00000000


cross(qstat) dlgerm dlus / -24 24 dcross
Cross Correlations of Series DLGERM and DLUS
Monthly Data From 1:02 To 23:07
     -24: -0.0097610 -0.0376214  0.0255869 -0.0496372 -0.0966872 -0.0835184
     -18:  0.0083970  0.0758657  0.0133382 -0.0384551  0.0204184  0.0237252
     -12:  0.0216118  0.0240533  0.1084615  0.1074049 -0.0591383 -0.0883930
      -6: -0.0362105 -0.0382406 -0.0503784 -0.0174369  0.0846082  0.0751444
       0:  0.4496902  0.3428469  0.1036626 -0.0470211  0.0054704  0.0480669
       6: -0.0002976 -0.0045341 -0.0739514 -0.0484552 -0.0286246 -0.0077346
      12: -0.0328684 -0.0225330  0.0004219 -0.0910508 -0.0159294 -0.0480913
      18: -0.0103138 -0.1199492 -0.1351466 -0.1115685 -0.0355831 -0.0742326
      24:  0.0556952
Ljung-Box Q-Statistics
Q(1 to 24)   =         58.5418.   Significance Level 0.00010231
Q(-24 to -1)=          23.6915.   Significance Level 0.47934719
Q(-24 to 24)=         137.2375.   Significance Level 0.00000000


corr(num=36,qstat) dlgerm
Correlations of Series DLGERM
Monthly Data From 1:02 To 23:07
Autocorrelations
       1:  0.3058047  0.1049270  0.0367712 -0.0198986 -0.0808623 -0.1040255
       7: -0.0169646 -0.0733826  0.0049991  0.1474687  0.0945178  0.0278969
      13: -0.0344255 -0.0093776 -0.0613373 -0.0981528 -0.0686392  0.0900175
      19: -0.1364551 -0.1066738 -0.0666468 -0.0256171  0.0208121  0.0278369
      25: -0.0451886 -0.1106696 -0.0663962 -0.0722099 -0.0410357 -0.0159806
      31:  0.0338553  0.1051042  0.1805632  0.1331615  0.0840688  0.1251122
Ljung-Box Q-Statistics  Q(36)  =     97.2707.  Significance Level 0.00000015
```

```
corr(num=36,qstat) dlus
Correlations of Series DLUS
Monthly Data From 1:02 To 23:07
Autocorrelations
     1:   0.2869867 -0.0119376 -0.0101889  0.0045831  0.0304016 -0.0617844
     7:  -0.1062312 -0.0229835 -0.0398542 -0.0177744  0.0635102 -0.0120219
    13:  -0.0177508 -0.0541767 -0.0498050 -0.0080598 -0.0555041 -0.0107697
    19:  -0.0895916 -0.1149359 -0.0793872 -0.0222634 -0.0748596 -0.0249068
    25:   0.0198862  0.0846460  0.1163255  0.0580350  0.0143786 -0.0184320
    31:  -0.0496389 -0.0819813  0.0058070  0.0867440  0.0448505 -0.0247036

Ljung-Box Q-Statistics  Q(36)  =    55.1337.  Significance Level 0.02157784
```

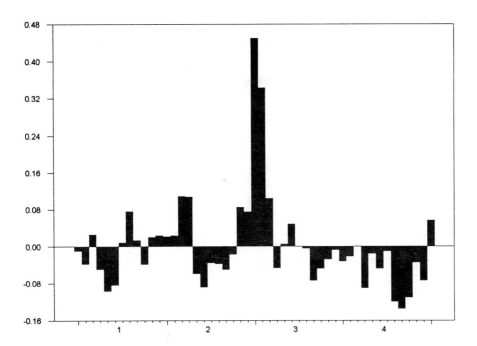

Fig. P3A-13. CCF(k) of dlGerman(t) = f(dlUS(t-k)), 2Se= 2/(270**.5) = .12172 (Lags are not shown correctly in the figure, 2.5 is 0.)

II. MINICASES

These answers are part of the previous answers given with Chapter 3 answers.

I. PROBLEMS

ESTIMATED DIFFICULTY

Elementary	Medium	Hard	Very Hard	Bad

1 E	2 E	3 E	4 E	5 M	6 E	7 M	8 E	9 M	10 M-H

11 M-H	12 M-H	13 M-H	14 M-H	15 M-H	16 M-H

17 E	18 M	19 M	20 M

Minicases are all hard to very hard.

4-1. Normally alpha and n are chosen to minimize the sum of e_t^2. There are exceptions, for example a very high alpha might be undesirable when unusual actual values might occur in the data, thus, some software constrain alpha to be less than some number such as .5.

4-2. The recent past is a better predictor of the immediate future than the distant past.

4-3. Neither method models trend or seasonality.

4-4. It is a versatile method for modeling random and seasonal components as $A_t = \alpha A_{t\text{-}s} + (1-\alpha)F_{t\text{-}s}$.

4-5. Low alpha or small n yield high smoothing, while a high alpha or low n yield little smoothing. A high alpha should be used for a random walk series like SERIESB.DAT.

4.6. More weight is given to the most recent past and this is advantageous as shown in 4-2 above.

4-7. See pages 157 to 159.

4-8. Smoothing and averaging are synonyms.

4-9. With ARRES high errors yield a high alpha, low errors a low alpha. In some actual applications, ARRES becomes unstable with erratic series having wide swings in actuals.

4-10. a) Forecasting the number of miles driven from 1982 to 1988 using a two-period moving average yields: set fore 3 9 = (driven(t-1)+driven(t-2))/2

```
Series      Obs       Mean          Std Dev       Minimum      Maximum
DRIVEN      9      1251.7777778   105.2779390   1122.0000000   1439
FORE        7      1226.2142857    72.9445321   1132.0000000   1338
ERROR       7        59.7857143    21.2462882     42.5000000    101
SERROR      7      3961.2500000  3040.4304040   1806.2500000  10201
RSE = 3961.25**.5 = 62.93846
```

b) While the RSE of the model (62.94) is somewhat lower than the standard deviation of the series (105.28), the model fits the data badly because it lags the trend.

c) Let's use an alpha of 1.0 in SES.

```
set fore2 3 9 = driven(t-1):
ERROR2      7       42.4285714     16.3997677     27.0000000     74
FORE2       7     1243.5714286     77.7835825   1142.0000000   1365
SERROR2     7     2030.7142857   1679.2708452    729.0000000   5476
RSE = 2039.7**.5 = 45.16304
```

d) The residual standard error of the SES is quite a bit better than that of the two-period moving average. However, this model lags the trend albeit less than the two period moving average. The out of sample forecast of the Simple Exponential Smoothing is poor because all future values equal the value of period 9 unless a trend component is added to the model.

e) The forecast for 1989 to 1992 is simply the most recent actual value of 1439. Later in chapter 6, we will learn how to use first differences to forecasts series such as this more accurately.

4-11. a) Forecasting ozone concentrations in the United States

```
set fit1 3 9 = (ozone(t-1) + ozone(t-2))/2
set error1 3 9 = ozone - fit1
set serror1 3 9 = error1**2
Series      Obs       Mean        Std Error      Minimum        Maximum
OZONE       9     0.1278889      0.0067905      0.1180000      0.1370000
FIT1        7     0.1263571      0.0046790      0.1205000      0.1315000
ERROR1      7     0.0005000      0.0093764     -0.0075000      0.0145000
SERROR1     7     0.0000756      0.0000677      0.0000203      0.0002103
RSE = .0000756**.5 = 0.00869.
```

b) The RSE for the two period moving average (.00869) is greater than the standard deviation of the original series, .00679, thus this is not a very good model. Consequently, we will use a low alpha value in fitting a exponential smoothing model.

c) The following is output of a RATS that optimizes the alpha value.

```
esm(est,smo=smo) ozone /
Model with TREND=None , SEASONAL=None
Estimated optimal coefficient: alpha =   0.403969

set fit2 3 9 = .404*ozone(t-1) + (1-.404)*fit2(t-1)
set error2 3 9 = ozone - fit2
set serror2 = error2**2
Series      Obs       Mean        Std Error      Minimum        Maximum
DATE        9  1984.0000000      2.7386128   1980.0000000         1988
OZONE       9     0.1278889      0.0067905      0.1180000      0.13700
FIT1        7     0.1263571      0.0046790      0.1205000      0.13150
ERROR1      7     0.0005000      0.0093764     -0.0075000      0.01450
SERROR1     7     0.0000756      0.0000677      0.0000203      0.000210
SMO         9     0.1290728      0.0041665      0.1231276      0.136000
ERROR       7     0.1281252      0.0037532      0.1231276      0.132464
FIT2        7     0.1281252      0.0037532      0.1231276      0.132464
ERROR2      7    -0.0012681      0.0084989     -0.0086028      0.012116
SERROR2     7     0.0000635      0.0000439      0.0000035      0.000147
RES = .0000635**.5 = 0.00797
```

d) The RSE of the exponential smoothing model is .00797. While this model fits the data better than the two-period moving average, it is not better than the mean of the series.

e) Neither model is better than the mean in forecasting ozone levels because this series is random about a mean of .12789, there are no discernible patterns other than randomness.

4-12. The robbery series appears to be a random walk series, thus a one or two-period moving average model should perform quite well.

Series	Obs	Mean	Std Error	Minimum	Maximum
DATE	10	1984.50000000	3.02765035	1980.00000000	1989.00000000
ROBS	10	228.20000000	20.13730645	205.00000000	269.00000000

a) Forecast using a two period moving average are:

```
SET FORE1 3 11 = (ROBS(T-1)+ROBS(T-2))/2
SET ERROR1 = ROBS-FORE1
SET SERROR1 = ERROR1**2
```

b) The two period moving average model yields a ME of -6.375 and a MSE of 367.9 or a RSE of 19.18 which is only slightly lower than the standard deviation of the original series. We had hoped that a better model would result, however, goodness must be determined in comparison to other methods. So let's see how well Simple Exponential Smoothing does. The following input and output is to RATS which optimizes the smoothing constant as 1.123. However, we will use 1 as the exponential smoothing constant.

```
ESM(EST,SMO=SMO) ROBS /
Model with TREND=None , SEASONAL=None
Estimated coefficients: alpha =  1.123009
```

OPTIMAL ALPHA > 1. LET'S USE 1 FOR DISCUSSION.

```
SET FORE2 3 11 = ROBS(T-1)
SET ERROR2 = ROBS-FORE2
SET SERROR2 = ERROR2**2
TAB
```

Series	Obs	Mean	Std Error	Minimum	Maximum
DATE	10	1984.5000000	3.0276504	1980.0000000	1989.0000000
ROBS	10	228.2000000	20.1373065	205.0000000	269.0000000
FORE1	9	226.6666667	18.5000000	207.0000000	260.0000000
ERROR1	8	-6.3750000	19.3386179	-37.0000000	18.0000000
SERROR1	8	367.8750000	453.0258389	4.0000000	1369.0000000
SMO	10	228.0173965	20.8107248	203.7968215	271.2141571
FORE2	9	225.6666667	19.5959179	205.0000000	269.0000000
SERROR2	8	269.0000000	292.1506461	16.0000000	900.0000000
ERROR2	8	-4.5000000	16.8607744	-30.0000000	16.0000000

c) The exponential smoothing model2 is the better of the two models having the lower MSE and RSE.

```
RSE1 =   MSE**.5 = 367.875**.5 = 19.18
RSE2 =   MSE**.5 = 269.000**.5 = 16.40
```

d) Neither of these residual standard errors are much lower than the standard deviation of robberies which is 20.137. Thus, the mean value of 228.2 performs almost as well as either of these models. Clearly though, the exponential smoothing model is the better of the two.

4-13. a) Because of the randomness in Series A, we anticipate that a long period moving average will be the best method and this is proven to be true. As shown below, the six-period moving average is the best of those tried.

b) The six-period moving average is best because it has the minimum mean squared error (4064.861111). Incidentally, exponential smoothing was used to determine the optimal smoothing constant, this yielded a smoothing constant of .167763 which corresponds to about an 11 period simple moving average model.

Series	Obs	Mean	Std Error	Minimum	Maximum
PAPER	48	850.083333333	64.557358080	682.000000000	993.0000000

```
set fore1 7 48 = paper(t-1)
set fore2 7 48 = (paper(t-4)+paper(t-3)+paper(t-2)+paper(t-1))/4
set fore3 7 48 = (paper(t-6)+paper(t-5)+paper(t-4)+paper(t-3)+paper(t-
2)+paper(t-1))/6
set error1 7 48 = paper - fore1        set error2 7 48 = paper - fore2
set error3 7 48 = paper - fore3        set serror1 = error1**2
set serror2 = error2**2                set serror3 = error3**2
```

Series	Obs	Mean	Std Error	Minimum	Maximum
PAPER	48	850.083333	64.557358	682.000000	993.000000
FORE1	42	848.285714	66.466308	682.000000	993.000000
FORE2	42	847.904762	41.862651	768.000000	905.250000
FORE3	42	847.880952	36.737668	768.833333	895.333333
ERRO1	42	4.404762	79.961899	-242.000000	133.000000
ERRO2	42	4.595238	81.995258	-134.000000	240.000000
ERRO3	42	5.380952	83.175674	-185.000000	221.000000
ERROR1	42	4.404762	79.961899	-242.000000	133.000000
ERROR2	42	4.785714	65.030049	-166.500000	151.500000
ERROR3	42	4.809524	64.345228	-166.166667	137.000000
SERROR1	42	6261.071429	9517.893635	25.000000	58564.000000
SERROR2	42	4151.122024	6147.455826	14.062500	27722.250000
SERROR3	42	4064.861111	5587.259684	0.027778	27611.361111

As shown by the MSE, the best model uses a six period moving average. Also, it has the lowest bias. Let's see what value of alpha is best. Using RATS exponential smoothing optimization.:

```
esm(est) paper 7 48
Model with TREND=None , SEASONAL=None
Estimated coefficients: alpha =  0.167763
```

This alpha value corresponds to about an 11 period moving average.

4-14. a) Exponential smoothing for Series A yields an alpha of .1 as the best of those tried.

```
set fore1 1 1 = paper                set fore2 1 1 = paper
set fore3 1 1 = paper                set fore4 1 1 = paper
set fore1 2 48 = .1*paper(t-1) + .9*fore1(t-1)
set fore2 2 48 = .3*paper(t-1) + .7*fore2(t-1)
set fore3 2 48 = .6*paper(t-1) + .4*fore3(t-1)
set fore4 2 48 = .9*paper(t-1) + .1*fore4(t-1)
set error1 2 48 = paper - fore1
set error2 2 48 = paper - fore2
set error3 2 48 = paper - fore3
set error4 2 48 = paper - fore4
set serror1 = error1**2
set serror2 = error2**2
```

```
set serror3 = error3**2
set serror4 = error4**2
```

Series	Obs	Mean	Std Error	Minimum	Maximum
PAPER	48	850.083333	64.557358	682.000000	993.000000
ERROR1	48	20.117028	61.191563	-147.483748	141.000000
ERROR2	48	7.325716	64.761501	-178.455431	141.000000
ERROR3	48	4.203409	69.698131	-205.897036	141.000000
ERROR4	48	3.045657	77.735638	-232.841441	141.000000
FORE1	48	829.966305	30.811706	779.000000	878.324570
FORE2	48	842.757618	37.590421	771.169537	911.390645
FORE3	48	845.879924	47.852625	746.320649	944.962615
FORE4	48	847.037676	59.882400	705.284144	980.142790
SERROR1	48	4071.093747	5439.457231	0.000000	21751.456071
SERROR2	48	4160.342079	6129.741861	0.000000	31846.340954
SERROR3	48	4774.293383	7350.585837	0.000000	42393.589609
SERROR4	48	5926.213108	8903.050521	0.000000	54215.136500

b) A low alpha is best for this series because it minimizes the sum of squared errors.

c) The optimal value for alpha is 0.151009. This is only slightly different than .1. Note also that this yields a mean error of 13.891 and a MSE of 3990.784 which is only slightly better than that of smoothing constant of .1.

4-15. For Series B, the best smoothing constant (i.e., having the lowest MSE and RSE) is .9. In addition, we have tried a smoothing constant of 1.0, it is the best value for alpha.

Series	Obs	Mean	Std Error	Minimum	Maximum
PRICE	48	750.25000000	184.13888144	426.00000000	1159.00000000

a) Calculating the appropriate forecasts, errors, squared errors, etc using RATS yields:

```
set fore1 1 1 = price                    set fore2 1 1 = price
set fore3 1 1 = price                    set fore4 1 1 = price
set fore1 2 48 = .1*price(t-1) + .9*fore1(t-1)
set fore2 2 48 = .3*price(t-1) + .7*fore2(t-1)
set fore3 2 48 = .6*price(t-1) + .4*fore3(t-1)
set fore4 2 48 = .9*price(t-1) + .1*fore4(t-1)
set error1 2 48 = price - fore1          set error2 2 48 = price - fore2
set error3 2 48 = price - fore3          set error4 2 48 = price - fore4
set serror1 = error1**2                  set serror2 = error2**2
set serror3 = error3**2                  set serror4 = error4**2
set fore5 1 1 = price
set fore5 2 48 = price(t-1)
set error5 2 48 = price - fore5
set serror5 = error5**2
```

Series	Obs	Mean	Std Error	Minimum	Maximum
PRICE	48	750.250000	184.138881	426.000000	1159.000000
FORE1	48	657.258731	120.590016	476.000000	924.508988
FORE2	48	715.276456	165.400263	476.000000	1054.008075
FORE3	48	734.266151	181.880597	452.286214	1122.355913
FORE4	48	740.216154	186.192593	433.587639	1152.907050
ERROR1	47	94.969806	117.285421	-198.199769	312.921831
ERROR2	47	35.717662	93.666524	-165.980049	164.065153
ERROR3	47	16.323931	69.633631	-104.288835	104.148665
ERROR4	47	10.247332	55.819835	-88.885521	98.000000
SERROR1	47	22482.455919	21779.251941	354.479706	97920.072607
SERROR2	47	9862.500702	7950.603409	1.016216	27549.376669

SERROR3	47	5012.146401	3347.878001	3.080582	10876.161094
SERROR4	47	3154.567064	2435.252242	70.767820	9604.000000
FORE5	48	741.354167	186.896090	426.000000	1159.000000
ERROR5	47	9.085106	52.958076	-87.000000	98.000000
SERROR5	47	2827.425532	2348.765085	144.000000	9604.000000

b) The best model is that with the minimum squared error or minimum mean squared error, which is shown to be an alpha value of 1.

c) Assuming that alpha is constrained to be less than or equal to 1, clearly an alpha of 1 is best of the five tried.

4-16. The following RATS program statements solve this problem.

Series	Obs	Mean	Std Error	Minimum	Maximum
UNITS	48	831.79166667	174.99883992	493.00000000	1166.00000000

```
set fore1 1 1 = units          set fore2 1 1 = units
set fore3 1 1 = units          set fore4 1 1 = units
set fore1 2 48 = .1*units(t-1) + .9*fore1(t-1)
set fore2 2 48 = .3*units(t-1) + .7*fore2(t-1)
set fore3 2 48 = .6*units(t-1) + .4*fore3(t-1)
set fore4 2 48 = .9*units(t-1) + .1*fore4(t-1)
set error1 2 48 = units - fore1          set error2 2 48 = units - fore2
set error3 2 48 = units - fore3          set error4 2 48 = units - fore4
set serror1 = error1**2            set serror2 = error2**2
set serror3 = error3**2            set serror4 = error4**2
set fore5 1 1 = units
set fore5 2 48 = .5*units(t-1) + .5*fore5(t-1)
set error5 2 48 = units - fore5
set serror5 = error5**2
```

Series	Obs	Mean	Std Error	Minimum	Maximum
UNITS	48	831.791667	174.998840	493.000000	1166.000000
FORE1	48	725.145529	157.633669	493.000000	987.001623
FORE2	48	790.414136	172.852576	493.000000	1055.766345
FORE3	48	809.742947	173.051844	493.000000	1083.798674
FORE4	48	816.413409	173.874907	493.000000	1110.723913
FORE5	48	805.791981	173.069605	493.000000	1073.939734
ERROR1	47	108.915204	41.674631	32.700000	198.198918
ERROR2	47	42.257904	41.895031	-39.279757	129.925679
ERROR3	47	22.517841	48.926732	-67.282177	125.174928
ERROR4	47	15.705454	58.409060	-84.174072	138.259281
ERROR5	47	26.552871	46.356542	-60.845213	123.625349
SERROR1	47	13562.343951	9415.320008	1069.290000	39282.810954
SERROR2	47	3503.579493	4027.658051	7.748841	16880.682180
SERROR3	47	2849.945847	2995.605421	1.511128	15668.762619
SERROR4	47	3585.691927	3295.677836	2.890000	19115.628748
SERROR5	47	2808.262024	3122.525466	0.232446	15283.226926

b) As measured by the MSE of 2849.9 an alpha of .6 is best for the four smoothing constants requested in the problem. In addition, a smoothing constant of .5 was tried. This is the best of the five smoothing constants because its MSE is only 2808.3. The best smoothing constant is that which minimizes the sum of squared errors (or MSE).

c) Smoothing constant optimization in RATS yields the best smoothing constant as .5034, this constant yields a MSE which is only slightly better than that of .6 or .5.

4-17. For SERIESD.DAT the following simple seasonal exponential smoothing model is quite effective:

$$F_t = \alpha A_{t-12} + 1 - \alpha F_{t-12}$$

4-18. Because the IBM stock price series behaves as a random walk, a SES model with an alpha of 1.0 is chosen as the best model of the closing price.

Series	Obs	Mean	Std Error	Minimum	Maximum
CLOSE	151	105.3700	30.1090	42.0000	168.3750

Setting alpha equal to 1.00 yields:

Mean Error = -.136, RSE = 7.056 as shown by the table values for ERROR and the square root of the mean squared error of 49.784.

```
set fore 1 1 = close              set fore 2 151 = close(t-1)
set error  = close - fore         set serror = error**2
```

Series	Obs	Mean	Std Error	Minimum	Maximum
CLOSE	151	105.370	30.109	42.000	168.375
SMO	151	105.355	30.235	41.515	169.303
FORE	150	105.793	29.757	44.500	168.375
ERROR	150	-0.136	7.078	-28.250	15.750
SERROR	150	49.784	88.451	0.000	798.062

RSE = 49.784**.5 = 7.05578

However, note that an alpha greater than one is possible, in fact an alpha of 1.1222 was found to minimize the sum of squared errors.

```
set fore2 1 1 = close
set fore2 2 151 = 1.1222*close(t-1) + (1-1.1222)*fore2(t-1)
set error2 = close - fore2
set serror2 = error2**2
```

Series	Obs	Mean	Std Error	Minimum	Maximum
FORE2	151	105.493	29.988	43.963	169.303
ERROR2	151	-0.123	7.001	-25.983	15.087
SERROR2	151	48.700	80.081	0.000	675.104

There is only a very slight advantage to an alpha of 1.1122 over that of 1.0. No univariate model fitted to this data will be particularly good in forecasting multiple periods ahead because of the random walk nature of this series.

4-19. The Birth series is a good example of a seasonal exponential smoothing model. The following illustrates a crude search for the best seasonal smoothing constant. No doubt students with good EXCEL™ or Lotus123™ skills can find the optimal solution using goal seeking. However, here we try out five values of the smoothing constant, the best being 1. Certainly, a zero smoothing with alpha of 1.0 is effective. There is a slight trend in the series that is statistically significant; that is, the mean error for the naïve model is 2.935 standard deviations away from zero using the simple t-test on the mean error:

t-value of mean error = 2.935 = Mean Error/Se/n$^{.5}$ = 11118.6/(20047.9/28**.5)

```
set fore 1 4 = births
set fore 5 32 = births(t-4) (This is the seasonally naïve model, but
nonetheless, the best model.)
set error = births - fore
set serror = error**2
set fore1 1 4 = births            set fore2 1 4 = births
set fore3 1 4 = births            set fore4 1 4 = births
set fore1 5 32 = .1*births(t-4) + .9*fore1(t-4)
set fore2 5 32 = .3*births(t-4) + .7*fore2(t-4)
set fore3 5 32 = .6*births(t-4) + .4*fore3(t-4)
set fore4 5 32 = .9*births(t-4) + .1*fore4(t-4)
set error1 5 32 = births - fore1  set error2 5 32 = births - fore2
set error3 5 32 = births - fore3  set error4 5 32 = births - fore4
set serror1 = error1**2           set serror2 = error2**2
set serror3 = error3**2           set serror4 = error4**2
```

Series	Obs	Mean	Std Error	Minimum	Maximum
BIRTHS	32	988380.7	53994.4	896013.0	1098868.)
FORE	28	980730.9	56907.9	896013.0	1098868.0
ERROR (naïve)	28	11118.6	20047.9	-29868.0	45647.0
SERROR (naïve)	28	511682689.1	596399791.5	0.0	2083648609.0
FORE1	32	948134.8	40091.9	896013.0	1026770.4
FORE2	32	960206.6	45505.3	896013.0	1058613.9
FORE3	32	971253.2	51981.9	896013.0	1083350.1
FORE4	32	977079.0	55042.8	896013.0	1096667.5
ERROR1	28	45995.3	31852.0	-10228.0	98453.5
ERROR2	28	32198.9	25328.8	-10228.0	79505.6
ERROR3	28	19574.3	22443.9	-15740.0	59604.7
ERROR4	28	12916.3	20780.1	-27667.5	46960.7
SERROR1	28	3093881387.5	2918966508.6	10816.0	9693098672.l
SERROR2	28	1655405224.7	1803247810.4	6336.2	6321143548.(
SERROR3	28	868893290.3	1021345999.2	10816.0	3552715207.(
SERROR4	28	583220879.7	659809509.2	10816.0	2205309185.)

Mean Error = 11118.6   RSE = 511682689**.5 = 22620.40426

4-20. Table 4-1 is a series with trend and randomness, thus a model should incorporate both trend and randomness. However, because we have not introduced trend adjusted methods of exponential smoothing, a simple naïve model may forecast this series well:

```
set fore 2 24 = sale(t-1)
set error = sale - fore
set serror = error**2
```

Series	Obs	Mean	Std Error	Minimum	Maximum
MONTH	24	12.50000000	7.07106781	1.00000000	24.0000000J
SALE	24	129.87500000	4.63739526	120.00000000	138.00000000
FORE	23	129.52173913	4.39906566	120.00000000	137.0000000)
ERROR	23	0.78260870	1.95300518	-3.00000000	4.0000000(
SERROR	23	4.26086957	4.39232172	0.00000000	16.0000000)

```
RSE = 4.26087**.5 = 2.06419
R-SQUARE = 1-4.26/4.6374**2 = .80191
```

II. MINICASES

Some Hints: The calculations for the minicases may be rather straight forward or very difficult depending on the software used by students. Thus, be careful in assigning these and in all situations be sure to give some suggestions to students. Here are a few to share. To calculate the DW and Q-statistics on errors it is suggested that a simple linear regression be performed with no explanatory (i.e., independent) variables other than the constant, for many statistical packages the needed statistics are standard outputs of least squares. Also, remind students that the Q-statistic should be used on 1/4 of the observations or about 24 lags, whichever is lower. To simplify the student analysis, some statistics may be eliminated from the table. However, it has been my experience that students, particularly when working in groups will learn quite a lot by struggling with the problem of how to calculate each statistic. Some common mistakes include not using the actual standard deviation of the period being fitted or forecasted when calculating the R^2.

The R^2 shown on the Master Forecasting Summary Table is actually an unadjusted R^2, this is suggested for this chapter. Note also that there can be minor roundoff errors in reported results, thus, it would not be unusual that student results are somewhat different than those reported here. When there was not enough data during the fitting process to choose the best alpha value, judgment was used based on the randomness of the time series. However, when there were a sufficient number of observations, then the optimal alpha was chosen to be that value of either .2, .5, .8, or 1 which minimized sum of squared errors in fit. Students will have a tendency to "cheat" and choose the best alpha in forecasting the out-of-sample values, point this mistake out when it occurs. Also, the ME added to the forecasts should be the ME realized during the fitting operation, not during the forecasting operation. Again, this is a common mistake made by students.

There is a website on the internet http://forecast.umkc.edu where I have left RATS programs used to solve each of these minicases. If you are an instructor and you leave your email address and regular phone number so that I can verify that you are an instructor, I will either send you the password to the instructor's directory of this website or mail a diskette with these programs and output.

MASTER FORECASTING SUMMARY TABLE
Time Series: TURNPIKM.DAT   Time Period Analyzed:36 MONTHS
Mean=1959.034   Standard Deviation=230.54   Transformations=TIMES .001

Method	Seasonal EXPOS ALPHA=1	Seasonal EXPOS & ME (a)	Seas. SMA (b)	Seas. SMA & ME (a)	Other	Comments Prob.
n	13 - 24		NA	NA		
ME	109.38					
RSE	139.18					
MPE	5.1					
F I MAPE	6.27					
T R-SQ	81.32					
D-W	.441					
Q-stat	7.23/.07					
(a)						

n	25 - 36	25 - 36	25 - 36	25 - 36		
ME	109.57	.1943	164.26	54.88		
F O RSE	119.05	46.56	168.43	66.33		
R MPE	5.51	.16	7.97	2.62		
E C MAPE	5.51	1.98	7.97	2.67		
A S R-SQ	71.0	95.5	41.65	90.95		
T D-W	.905	.905	1.838	1.838		
Q-stat	4.08/.25	4.08/.25	2.75/.43	2.75/.43		
(b)						

(a) Using the Mean Error of Fitted Seasonal Exponential Smoothing
(b) There are not enough observations to fit a Seasonal SMA2.

MASTER FORECASTING SUMMARY TABLE

Time Series: PASSAIR.DAT   Time Period Analyzed: 50 QUARTERS
Mean=11,916.59   Standard Deviation=2,921.16   Transformations = NONE

Method	Seasonal EXPOS $\alpha = 1$	Seasonal EXPOS & ME (e)	Seas. SMA	Seas. SMA & ME (e)	Other	Comments Prob.
n	5-42		9-42			
ME	752.49		1171.42			
RSE	968.95		1334.16			
F MPE	6.6		10.00			
I MAPE	7.3		10.01			
T R-SQ	84.10		27.69			
D-W	.880		.64			
a)Q-stat	22.30/.008		40.55/.000			
(a)	df=9					
n	43-50	43-50	43-50	43-50		
ME	627.06	-125.43	889.41	-272.01		
F RSE	777.58	476.62	1026.4	564.39		
O **R** MPE	3.93	-.9	5.66	-1.8		
E **C** MAPE	3.93	2.9	5.66	2.9		
A **S** R-SQ	24.0	71.4	5.47	59.95		
T D-W	1.085	1.085	1.209	1.209		
Q-stat	2.64/.267	2.64/.267	2.35/.308	2.35/.3085		
(b)						

(a) df=9.   (b) df=9.   (c) Using standard deviation of 9 to 42.
(d) df=2.   (e) Using mean errors of fit in the forecasting model.

MINICASE 4-3. HOSPITAL CENSUS BY WEEK

MASTER FORECASTING SUMMARY TABLE
Time Series: CENSUSW.DAT   Time Period Analyzed: 157 WEEKS

Mean =   Standard Deviation =   Transformations = NONE

Method	Seasonal EXPOS $\alpha = .5$	Seasonal EXPOS & ME	Seas. SMA	Seas. SMA & ME	Other	Comments Prob.
FIT						
n	53-105		N/A	N/A		
ME	-68.57					
RSE	167.33					
MPE	-2.77					
MAPE	4.93					
R-SQ	23.51					
D-W	.728					
Q-stat	52.59/.000					
(a)						
FORECAST						
n	106-157	106-157	106-157	106-157		
ME	-19.60	46.57	-20.99	45.20		
RSE	143.98	149.72	143.78	148.95		
MPE	-0.8	1.65	-0.8	1.60		
MAPE	3.89	4.14	3.86	4.09		
R-SQ	-26.9	-37.27	-26.9	-35.86		
D-W	1.46	1.46	1.46	1.46		
Q-stat	24.83/.024	24.83/.024	24.26/.029	24.26/.029		

(a) df=3. The trend does not persist in year 3.

MASTER FORECASTING SUMMARY TABLE

Time Series: MACHLERM.DAT   Time Period Analyzed: 96 MONTHS
Mean = 6077.99   Standard Deviation = 1650.43   Transformations = NONE

Method	Seasonal EXPOS $\alpha = .8$	Seasonal EXPOS & ME	Seas. SMA	Seas. SMA & ME	Other	Comments Prob.
n	13-84		25-84			
ME	195.81		258.22			
RSE	809.87		840.97			
MPE	2.78		3.56			
F I MAPE	11.33		11.49			
T R-SQ	76.41		74.57			
D-W	1.48		1.43			
Q-stat	20.98/.28		28.27/.02			
(a)						
n	85-96		85-96			
ME	253.85		253.57			
F RSE	562.20		664.72			
O R MPE	4.85		5.19			
E C MAPE	7.39		8.94			
A S R-SQ	72.70		61.84			
T D-W	1.57		1.18			
Q-stat	7.05/.071		6.30/.097			
(b)						

(a) df=18   (b) df=3

MASTER FORECASTING SUMMARY TABLE
Time Series: LUMBER.DAT   Time Period Analyzed: 120 MONTHS
Mean=86.794   Standard Deviation=23.374   Transformations=SCALED X.001

Method	Seasonal EXPOS $\alpha = 1$	Seasonl EXPOS & ME	Seas. SMA	Seas. SMA & ME	Other	Comments Prob.
n	13-108		25-108			
ME	4.79		6.96			
RSE	6.804		9.196			
MPE	5.93		8.11			
F I MAPE	7.17		9.11			
T R-SQ	91.53		84.06			
D-W	1.22		1.186			
Q-stat	37.77/.037		66.86/.000			
(a)						
n	109-120	109-120	109-120	109-120		
ME	5.419	.629	6.704	-.256		
F O RSE	6.230	3.138	7.655	3.705		
R E MPE	5.16	.403	6.46	-.456		
C A MAPE	5.28	2.163	6.46	2.984		
S T R-SQ	92.19	98.02	88.21	97.24		
D-W		1.680		1.233		
Q-stat		6.90/.075		3.49/.322		
(b)						

(a) df=24 for SES, df=21 for SMA2   (b) df=3

MASTER FORECASTING SUMMARY TABLE

Time Series: AIRLINE.DAT   Time Period Analyzed:
Mean =   Standard Deviation =   Transformations = NAT. LOG

Method	Seasonal EXPOS $\alpha = 1$	Seasonal EXPOS & ME	Seas. SMA	Seas. SMA & ME	Other	Comments Prob.
(a)						
n	13-108		25-108		13-108	
ME	.13277		.20595		-.1261	
RSE	.1458		.2130		12.823	
MPE	2.443		3.750		-.183	
F I MAPE	2.475		3.750		4.613	
T R-SQ	80.93		44.65		97.54	
D-W	.613		.615		.580	
Q-stat	212/.000		253/.000		281.36/.000	
(b)						
n	109-144	109-144	109-144	109-144	109-144	
ME	.0852	-.0475	.1293	-.0767	-19.83	
F O RSE	.0988	.0688	.1360	.0875	28.03	
R MPE	1.402	-.796	2.130	-1.280	-4.995	
E C MAPE	1.402	.911	2.130	1.290	5.676	
A S R-SQ	69.59	85.22	42.36	76.12	87.517	
T D-W		.6574		.8329	.8121	
Q-stat		63.84/.000		66.82/.000	51.531/.000	

(a) df=24   (b) df=9

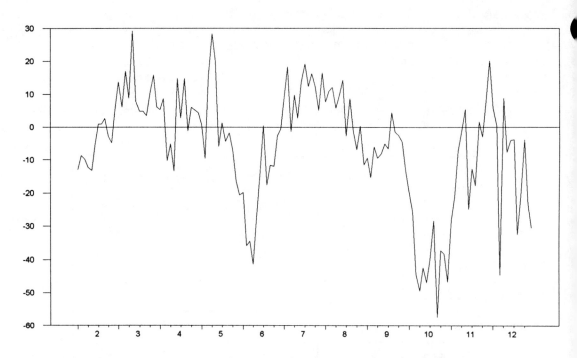

Fig. M4-7. Highly Autocorrelated Errors of the Transformed Seasonal EXPOS Model

---

MASTER FORECASTING SUMMARY TABLE

Time Series: AUTO.DAT   Time Period Analyzed: 185 MONTHS
Mean =   Standard Deviation =   Transformations = NONE

Method	Seasonal EXPOS	Seasonal EXPOS & ME	Seas. SMA	Seas. SMA & ME	Other	Comments Prob.
F I T n	13-173	13-173	25-173	13-173		
ME	-44.04		-60.58			
RSE	159.29		226.15			
MPE	-4.658		-6.867			
MAPE	10.063		14.711			
R-SQ	87.151		74.558			
D-W	.1112		0.0857			
Q-stat (a)	2046/.0000		2147/.0000			
F O R E C A S T n	174-185		174-185			
ME	-143.667	-94.187	-274.5	-199.87		
RSE	183.46	147.94	291.11	222.14		
MPE	-16.309	-9.575	-34.575	-24.60		
MAPE	16.456	13.224	34.757	24.60		
R-SQ	63.81	76.46	8.87	46.94		
D-W	.1546	.1546	.2493	.2493		
Q-stat (b)	17.046/.001		15.79/.001			

(a) df=36   (b) df=3
Series had a negative trend and models did not account for more rapid declines
at end of series.

MINICASE 4-9. CONSUMPTION OF DISTILLED SPIRITS

MASTER FORECASTING SUMMARY TABLE

Time Series: SPIRITS.DAT Time Period Analyzed: 132 MONTHS

Mean = Standard Deviation = Transformations = NONE

Method	Seasonal EXPOS α=1.0	Seasonal EXPOS & ME	Seas. SMA	Seas. SMA & ME	Other	Comments Prob.
FIT						
n	13-120	13-120	25-120	25-120		
ME	-674.81		-1031.41			
RSE	1526.15		1820.15			
MPE	-2.1		-3.3			
MAPE	3.5		4.5			
R-SQ	92.93		89.62			
D-W	2.083		2.214			
Q-stat (a)	85.865/.000		115.28/.000			
FORECAST						
n	121-132	121-132	121-132	121-132		
ME	-2342.5	-1667.69	-2218	-1187.34		
RSE	3265.17	2820.5	2938.6	2263.2		
MPE	-7.9	-5.5	-7.6	-4.0		
MAPE	7.9	6.0	7.8	5.9		
R-SQ	45.54	59.36	55.88	73.83		
D-W	1.054	1.054	1.429	1.429		
Q-stat (b)	1.50/.682	1.50/.682	2.16/.540	2.16/.540		

(a) df=27, df=24

(b) df=4

MASTER FORECASTING SUMMARY TABLE

Time Series: ELECT.DAT   Time Period Analyzed: 185 MONTHS
Mean = 73.6297 Standard Deviation = 16.3740 Transformations = NONE

Method	Seasonal EXPOS α=1.0	Seasonal EXPOS & ME	Seas. SMA	Seas. SMA & ME	Other	Comments Prob.
FIT						
n	13-173		25-173			
ME	3.326		4.912			
RSE	4.316		5.850			
MPE	4.736		6.744			
MAPE	5.146		6.942			
R-SQ	91.13		81.10			
D-W	1.902		1.826			
Q-stat	31.71/.673		87.55/.000			
(a)						

==

FORECAST						
n	174-185	174-185	174-185	174-185		
ME	2.722	-.604	4.3662	-.546		
RSE	3.781	2.694	5.440	3.291		
MPE	2.731	-.807	4.478	-.744		
MAPE	3.213	1.846	4.479	2.394		
R-SQ	89.74	94.79	78.76	92.22		
D-W	1.717	1.717	1.659	1.659		
Q-stat	.040/.998	.040/.998	.318/.957	.318/.957		
(b)						

(a) df=36
(b) df=3

MASTER FORECASTING SUMMARY TABLE

CHAPTERS 5 TO 8

INTRODUCTION

The following tables summarize the results of Minicases 1 to 10 for chapters 5, 6, 6a, and 8. These results are from models using RATS[tm], EXCEL[tm], and Forecast Pro[tm]. The results reported in these tables are presented as typical results; it is not anticipated that others will be able to exactly duplicate these results. Certainly, there are differences in software and approaches taken by students. In most cases, the programs used to complete these minicases are available to instructors using this instructor's manual (IM). Contact me via email so that I can provide you with the diskette of command language programs for most of these forecasts. As this IM goes to press, I am unsure of which programs are available and on which statistical package they were derived. I will share all that are available with you, but please excuse me if I am unable to find the program used to generate a specific forecast.

Most forecasts were generated using RATS[tm], however, in most cases the monthly and quarterly decomposition models were generated using ForecastPro[tm]. The ForecastPro[tm] forecasts were trend dampened, thus, they did not perform as well as other methods when the trend persists. No doubt other implementations of classical decomposition will perform better than some of these results; thus, do not be surprised if considerably better decomposition results are obtained by your students in Chapter 5's minicases. However, we do not expect significantly better results for Winters, FSA, or ARIMA implementations. In most cases Winters method was fitted using ForecastPro and this is an excellent implementation of Winters.

Reminder About R^2, DW, Q, RSE, MPE, MAPE

These tables specify that students are to record many statistics which may or may not be easily generated by their software. You should insure that your students know how to generate these statistics with the software of your class. Note that in RATS, the DW and Q statistics of residuals are very easily generated by running a simple linear regression of the errors as a function of the constant alone, no dependent variable is used in that regression. This works well in RATS, but may not work in some other software implementations. In addition, the table requests students to calculate the adjusted R^2 as well as RSE which is adjusted for degrees of freedom as is the usual case with the standard error of estimate. In all cases, the manner in which these statistics are calculated can be altered somewhat to achieve reasonable work loads on your students.

Omission of BIC or SBC

I have omitted the Schwarz Bayesian Information Criterion in these tables because it is not included in all statistical forecasting packages. If you are using ForecastPro or other software that routinely generates the BIC, then you should add this statistic to this table, possible replacing the DW or Q with the BIC.

Please feel free to contact me about any of the results of this table. In addition, please feel free to share with me, so that I can share with others, any forecasting results you or your students have generated as solutions to these minicases. As always, such material will be attributed to you.

MINICASE *-1.   Kansas Turnpikd, Daily Data, TURNPIKD.DAT

MASTER FORECASTING SUMMARY TABLE

Time Series: TURNPIKD.DAT   Time Period Analyzed: 91 Days
Mean=73171.9   Standard Deviation=6321.27   Transformations=None (a)

Method	DECOMP CHAP5	WINTERS CHAP6	FSA CHAP6A	ARIMA CHAP8		Comments Prob.
FIT						
n	77	77	77	77		
ME	0	N/A	0	627.243		
RSE	2042	2057	2172	1987.19		
MPE	-0.1	N/A	0.6	0.8		
MAPE	2.0	2.19	2.3	2.0		
R-SQ	89.8	89.12	88.3	90.0		
D-W	0.74	1.21	0.79	1.533		
Q-stat	58.6/.00	38/.004	54/.000	23.8/.07		
FORECAST						
n	14	14	14	14		
ME	-9497	-7781	-7593	-7896		
RSE	10707	9047	8822	9100		
MPE	-14	-11	-11	-12.0		
MAPE	14	11	11	12.00		
R-SQ	-193	-159	-99	-112		
D-W	0.18	0.30	0.21	1.71		
Q-stat	15.4/.002	5.5/.14	14/.002	24/.12		

MINICASE *-2.   Domestic Air Passengers by Quarter, PASSAIR.DAT

MASTER FORECASTING SUMMARY TABLE
Time Series: PASSAIR.DAT   Time Period Analyzed: 50
Mean=11,198.0   Standard Deviation=2,568.16   Transformations=None
----

Method	DECOMP CHAP5	WINTERS CHAP6	FSA CHAP6A	ARIMA CHAP8		Comments Prob.
n	42	42	42	42		
ME	26.9	N/A	−84.6	34.8		
RSE	475.0	404.6	521.1	345.1		
MPE	0.23	N/A	−1.3	0.31		
F I MAPE	3.38	2.65	3.92	2.11		
T R-SQ	96.7	97.4	96.0	97.8		
D-W	0.613	1.68	0.76	1.85		
Q-stat	47.3/.00	12.7/.81	58.6/.00	8.4/.30		
n	8	8	8	8		
ME	−645.6	269.8	−305.9	−446.6		
F O RSE	729.0	372.0	480.7	590		
R E MPE	−4.19	1.70	−2.03	−2.87		
C A MAPE	4.19	1.87	2.54	2.87		
S T R-SQ	33.2	82.6	71.0	56.2		
D-W	1.37	1.29	1.89	3.27		
Q-stat	1.05/.59	1.7/.42	.00/.997	3.3/.19		

MINICASE *-3. Hospital Census by Month, CENSUSM.DAT

MASTER FORECASTING SUMMARY TABLE

Time Series: CENSUSM.DAT Time Period Analyzed: 120 Months

Mean=10908.93 Standard Deviation=317.64 Transformations=None (a)

	Method (b)	MULT DECOMP CHAP5	WINTERS CHAP6	FSA CHAP6A	ARIMA CHAP8		Comments Prob.
FIT	n	84	84	84	84		
	ME	N/A	N/A	0.000	-34.456		
	RSE	167.8	233.6	227.8	229.82		
	MPE	N/A	N/A	-0.04	-0.33		
	MAPE	1.10	1.52	1.47	1.6		
	R-SQ	72.7	44.6	49.2	26.2		
	D-W	1.961	1.517	1.31	1.961		
	Q-stat	70/.000	35/.009	37/.015	19.31/.25		
FORECAST	n	36	36	36	36		
	ME	43.26	108.6	175.2	124.7		
	RSE	170	191.4	236.5	257.1		
	MPE	0.372	0.961	1.56	1.11		
	MAPE	1.18	1.36	1.69	1.96		
	R-SQ	59.0	48.0	20.5	6.1		
	D-W	1.72	1.69	1.69	1.87		
	Q-stat	5.5/.79	5.7/.77	4.12/.90	8.8/.45		

(a) Statistics for first 84 observations after adjusting outliers if any.
(b) No loss of degrees of freedom adjustment for RSE and R-Square.

MINICASE *-4. Henry Machler's Hideaway Orchids, MACHLERD.DAT

MASTER FORECASTING SUMMARY TABLE

Time Series: MACHLERD.DAT   Time Period Analyzed:
Mean=   Standard Deviation=   Transformations=

Method	(a) DECOMP CHAP5	WINTERS CHAP6	FSA CHAP6A	ARIMA CHAP8		Comments Prob.
n	133	133	133	133		
ME	0	N/A	-0.14	-0.0		
RSE	68.52	66.43	68.5	66.315		
F MPE	-14.2	N/A	-14.2	-12.68		
I MAPE T	34.1	28.9	34.2	31.5		
R-SQ	65.4	66.8	65.4	68.6		
D-W	2.16	1.75	2.16	1.736		
Q-stat	91/.000	27/.075	91/.000	26.78/.63		
n	7	7	7	7		
ME	1.56	15.56	4.21	17.7		
F RSE O	82.0	75.0	82.1	82.3		
R MPE E	-59	-31	-57	-37.2		
C MAPE A	80	57	80	63.5		
S R-SQ T	73.9	78.1	73.8	74		
D-W	1.63	2.61	1.63	2.37		
Q-stat	.06/.81	2.71/.10	.06/.81	1.5/.22		

(a) Statistics for first 84 observations after adjusting outliers if any.

MINICASE *-6.   Midwestern Building Materials, LUMBER.DAT

MASTER FORECASTING SUMMARY TABLE

Time Series: LUMBER.DAT   Time Period Analyzed: 120
Mean=83,964.99 Standard Deviation=23,985 (a) Transformations=None (a)

Method (b)	MULT DECOMP CHAP5	WINTERS CHAP6	FSA CHAP6A	ARIMA CHAP8		Comments Prob.
n	108	108	108	108		
ME	N/A	N/A	-199.6	2.05		
RSE	2664	4618	7375	4527.09		
MPE	N/A	N/A	-1.0	0.00		
F I MAPE T	2.61	4.3	8.0	4.0		
R-SQ	98.8	96.2	90.6	96.2		
D-W	1.66	1.24	1.85	1.856		
Q-stat	41/.000	35/.009	120/.000	22.5/.49		
n	12	12	12	12		
ME	13512	3007	-3044	958.54		
F O RSE	14860	4270	11786	2907.6		
R E MPE	13.0	2.8	-4.0	0.9		
C A MAPE	13.0	3.7	12.0	1.8		
S T R-SQ	56.0	96.3	72.0	98.3		
D-W	0.96	1.69	1.69	1.80		
Q-stat	2.68/.44	6.9/.07	.68/.88	6.9/.07		

(a) Statistics for first 108 observations after adjusting outliers if any.
(b) No loss of degrees of freedom adjustment for RSE and R-Square.

MINICASE *-7.   International Airline Passengers, AIRLINE.DAT

```
--------------------------------------------------------------------------
                    MASTER FORECASTING SUMMARY TABLE
Time Series: AIRLINE.DAT               Time Period Analyzed: 144
Mean=230.9      Standard Deviation=85.18    Transformations=None (a)
--------------------------------------------------------------------------
```

Method (b)	MULT DECOMP CHAP5	WINTERS CHAP6	FSA CHAP6A	ARIMA CHAP8		Comments Prob.
n	108	108	108	108		
ME	N/A	N/A	-0.88	0.65		
RSE	3.11	8.74	9.22	8.45		
MPE	N/A	N/A	-0.65	0.30		
MAPE	1.14	2.85	3.46	2.92		
R-SQ	99.8	98.9	98.8	99.0		
D-W	2.207	1.37	0.63	1.92		
Q-stat	51/.000	36.7/.00	167/.000	22/.51		
n	36	36	36	36		
ME	47.89	-17.8	-59.3	-31.7		
RSE	66.13	24.71	63.9	34.7		
MPE	10.1	-4.6	-14.3	-7.7		
MAPE	11.3	4.98	14.3	7.7		
R-SQ	30.5	90.3	35.1	81.0		
D-W	0.19	1.14	1.31	1.74		
Q-stat	109/.000	21/.013	10.7/.294	14/.12		

The first block is labelled "F I T" (FIT) and the second block is labelled "F O R E C A S T" (FORECAST) along the left margin.

```
--------------------------------------------------------------------------
```

(a) Statistics for first 108 observations after adjusting outliers if any.

(b) No loss of degrees of freedom adjustment for RSE and R-Square.

MINICASE *-8. Automobile Sales, AUTO.DAT

```
---------------------------------------------------------------------
                  MASTER FORECASTING SUMMARY TABLE
Time Series: AUTO.DAT                    Time Period Analyzed: 185
Mean=1,596.185      Standard Deviation=441.42    Transformations=None (a)
---------------------------------------------------------------------
```

Method (b)	ADD DECOMP CHAP5	WINTERS CHAP6	FSA CHAP6A	ARIMA CHAP8		Comments Prob.
FIT						
n	173	173	173	173		
ME	N/A	N/A	-20.3	-1.95		
RSE	25.33	80.59	108.6	48.22		
MPE	N/A	N/A	-2.47	-0.37		
MAPE	1.45	4.30	6.42	2.6		
R-SQ	99.7	96.6	94.0	98.82		
D-W	189	0.49	0.65	1.879		
Q-stat	91/.000	207/.000	514/.000	41.4/.18		
FORECAST						
n	12	12	12	12		
ME	-53.0	168	-144	148.37		
RSE	86.8	194	175	17.23		
MPE	-6.7	21.7	-18.1	22.79		
MAPE	10.6	21.7	19.0	22.79		
R-SQ	92	59.6	67.2	99.7		
D-W	0.935	0.61	0.89	0.207		
Q-stat	5.97/.11	6.4/.09	4.8/.19	15.6/.001		

(a) Statistics for first 108 observations after adjusting outliers if any.
(b) No loss of degrees of freedom adjustment for RSE and R-Square.

MINICASE *-9. Consumption of Distilled Spirits, SPIRITS.DAT

MASTER FORECASTING SUMMARY TABLE

Time Series: SPIRITS.DAT Time Period Analyzed: 132

Mean=33,847.4 Standard Deviation=5,833.80 Transformations=None (a)

	Method (b)	MULT DECOMP CHAP5	WINTERS CHAP6	FSA CHAP6A	ARIMA CHAP8		Comments Prob.
FIT	n	120	120	120	120		
	ME	N/A	N/A	28.5	-6.42		
	RSE	664.6	1207	1109	1212.91		
	MPE	N/A	N/A	-0.10	-0.00		
	MAPE	1.42	2.87	2.6	2.7		
	R-SQ	98.7	95.6	96.5	95.6		
	D-W	2.04	2.29	2.15	2.03		
	Q-stat	30/.04	97/.000	154/.000	32.2/.09		
FORECAST	n	12	12	12	12		
	ME	-2633	-2284	-1248	-1528.46		
	RSE	3258	2950	2295	2691		
	MPE	-9.1	-7.8	-4.2	-5.0		
	MAPE	9.1	7.9	5.6	5.6		
	R-SQ	45.8	55.6	73.3	63		
	D-W	1.32	1.40	1.37	1.10		
	Q-stat	1.6/.67	2.04/.56	1.65/.65	1.23/.75		

(a) Statistics for first 108 observations after adjusting outliers if any.

(b) No loss of degrees of freedom adjustment for RSE and R-Square.

MINICASE *-10.   Discount Consumer Electronics, ELECT.DAT

MASTER FORECASTING SUMMARY TABLE

Time Series: ELECT.DAT   Time Period Analyzed: 185
Mean=72.131   Standard Deviation=15.546   Transformations=None (a)

Method (b)	MULT DECOMP CHAP5	WINTERS CHAP6	FSA CHAP6A	ARIMA CHAP8		Comments Prob.
F I T						
n	173	173	173	173		
ME	N/A	N/A	-0.37	0.00		
RSE	1.474	2.706	5.40	2.76		
MPE	N/A	N/A	-6.7	0.05		
MAPE	1.70	2.95	5.97	3.20		
R-SQ	99.1	96.9	88.0	96.37		
D-W	2.44	1.97	1.22	1.902		
Q-stat	29/.046	17/.49	470/.000	31.6/.68		
F O R E C A S T						
n	12	12	12	12		
ME	0.21	-0.55	-8.8	-0.6044		
RSE	3.90	2.52	11.27	2.69		
MPE	0.11	-0.71	-9.7	-0.81		
MAPE	3.28	1.77	10.4	1.85		
R-SQ	89	95	8.8	95		
D-W	1.33	1.51	1.59	1.72		
Q-stat	2.0/.56	0.26/.97	2.3/.51	.04/.998		

(a) Statistics for first 173 observations after adjusting outliers if
any.
(b) No loss of degrees of freedom adjustment for RSE and R-Square.

CHAPTER 5
DECOMPOSITION METHODS AND SEASONAL INDEXES

I. PROBLEMS

ESTIMATED DIFFICULTY

Elementary	Medium	Hard			Very Hard	Bad

1 M	2 M	3 E	4 E	5 E	6 M	7 E	8 M	9 M	10 M
11 M	12 M	13 M	14 H	15 V	16 H	17 H	18 H	19 H	20 H
21 H	22 H	23 H	24 H						

Minicases	1 V	2 H	3 V	4 V	5 H-V	6 H	7 H	8 H	9 H	10 H

5-1. See pages 175 to 177.

5-2. Clearly the number of daylight hours vary by time of the year whether or not there are significant differences in temperature or precipitation, thus, human behavior will be affected. This is important in forecasting because seasonality will be more prevalent because of this behavior.

5-3. A seasonal index of 140 for an additive models denotes that sales are 140 units higher each July than the trend and cyclical value and a multiplicative index of 1.40 or 140%, denotes that sales are on average 40% higher in July than the trend and cyclical value of July.

5-4. Pronounced seasonality can makes it difficult to decompose a series into trend, cyclical and random variations.

5-5. a. The trend in soft drink sales is a function of long run movements in populations, including populations by age group, social custom, competing social drinks (e.g., tea, milk, beer, liquor etc.) and other habits of individuals. b. The cyclical causes of soft drink sales include personal income, cyclical prices of competing drinks, general business climate for the use of soft drinks, etc. c. Seasonal influences result from climatic conditions and man-made conventions and holidays. d. Irregular influences are small or large highly unpredictable occurrences such as wars, strikes, hurricanes, floods, etc. that significantly increase or decrease the demand for a product or service. Soft drink causes of a) Trend = f(long-run social and demographic habits or traditions, advertising, medical implications of product), b) Cyclical = f(economic, technological, and product life cycles), c) Seasonal = f(man-made conventions or traditions, climatic conditions, and promotions), d) Irregular = f(unexpected events like supply interruptions, sudden health concerns, etc.)

5-6. It can be inaccurate to simultaneously decompose the trend and seasonal components using dichotomous variables in regression analysis. The trend and seasonal components are not orthogonal, thus trend and seasonal affects are intermingled. The most likely result is that trend and seasonality will be over (under) and under (over) stated respectively in different periods. The classical decomposition and Fourier series models avoid this problem by estimating components separately.

5-7. If the average quarterly index is 100% then the sum of 4 quarterly indexes should be 4.00 or 400%.

5-8. In lieu of formal methods (i.e., Chapter 14) estimates of cyclical indexes can be multiplied times the projected trend-cycle, e.g., pessimistic, most likely, and optimistic cyclical values can be used to generate three scenarios.

5-9. See page 195.

For quarterly data: H_0: $S_I = S_{II} = S_{III} = S_{IV}$,
H_1: One or more Seasonal Indexes are Statistically Different

5-10. Trend-Cycle January = 10/.78 = 12.82 million

Trend-Cycle April = 15/1.01 = 14.851

Trend = (14.851 - 12.82)/3 = .6772

May   (14.851+.6772)*1.20   = 18.634 million

June   (14.851+2*.6772)*1.25 = 20.257 "   "

July   (14.851+3*.6772)*1.20 = 20.259 "   "

5-11. See Tables 5-3 and 5-4.

5-12. See Table 5-5.

5-13. See Table 5-7

5-14. Personal Computers Sold Over 24 Quarters.

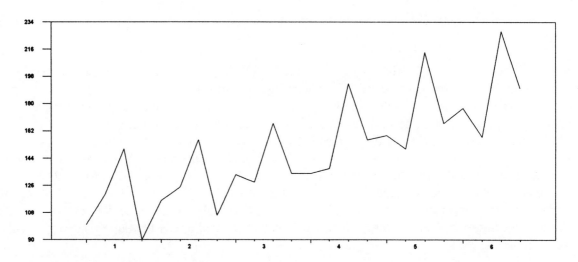

a) Clearly the series has trend and seasonality and likely cyclical behavior.

b) Since many students will use classical decomposition, we illustrate the regression method as developed on pages 192 through 194 and as shown below. These regression results can be compared to classical decomposition results.

```
Dependent Variable UNITS - Estimation by Least Squares
Quarterly Data From 1:01 To 4:04
Usable Observations        16        Degrees of Freedom      11
Centered R**2       0.906538        R Bar **2     0.872552
Uncentered R**2     0.996763        T x R**2        15.948
Mean of Dependent Variable        134.06250000
Std Error of Dependent Variable   26.22586192
Standard Error of Estimate         9.36258269
Sum of Squared Residuals         964.23750000
Regression F(4,11)                 26.6738
Significance Level of F            0.00001305
Durbin-Watson Statistic            1.832201
Q(4-0)                             7.387449
Significance Level of Q            0.11677593
    Variable            Coeff         Std Error      T-Stat     Signif
********************************************************************************
1.   Constant         97.16875000    5.94450275    16.34598   0.000
2.   TIME              3.36875000    0.52338428     6.43648   0.00004831
3.   QTR2              3.38125000    6.64100206     0.50915   0.62070659
4.   QTR3             39.01250000    6.70258918     5.82051   0.00011576
5.   QTR4             -9.35625000    6.80399568    -1.37511   0.19645636
```

c) A plot of the fitted values versus the actual values for these 16 observations is shown below. As shown, and discussed below, the regression decomposition fits this data quite well.

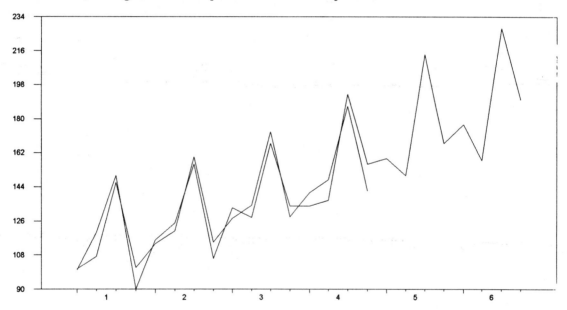

 The fit of the regression decomposition is quite good. As shown in the regression output above, the decomposition fit has a high R^2, low RSE, good DW, and F value. All of these statistics suggest the validity of this approach. While the t-statistics of the second and fourth quarter are not statistically significant, we retain them anyway.

d) Using the model fitted to the first 16 observations, the forecast of demands for periods 17 through 24 are shown in the following figure. Following this figure are appropriate error statistics.

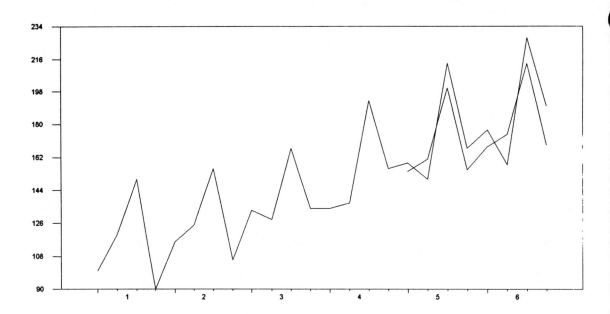

e) Using the forecasts of the above figure and the following RATS commands, we see that the mean forecast error for eight periods is 5.89 with a MSE and RSE of 187.17 and 13.68 respectively. These statistics compare favorably to the statistics of the actual series, mean = 180.375 and Standard Deviation of 28.1878. These statistics yield an R^2 of 0.76444, also as shown below the DW and Q-stat are indicative of white noise.

```
SET SERROR = ERROR*ERROR
SET PE 17 24 = ERROR/UNITS
SET APE 17 24 = ABS(PE)
```

Series	Obs	Mean	Std Error	Minimum	Maximum
ERROR	8	5.88750000	13.20211022	-16.66250000	21.33750000
SERROR	8	187.17140625	133.71083175	20.81640625	455.28890625
PE	8	0.02630736	0.07591581	-0.10545886	0.11230263
APE	8	0.97369264	0.07591581	0.88769737	1.10545886

```
RSE = 187.17**.5 = 13.68101
Durbin-Watson Statistic          2.096233
Q(2-0)                           2.870078
Significance Level of Q          0.23810609
```

5-15. This problem may be time consuming. The nonlinearity of the time series denotes that a nonlinear trend should be fit to the deseasonalized values. Below, we work this problem using the percent of centered moving average. In addition, it is worked using the percent of trend method in the file p5-15.prg which can be found on the website.

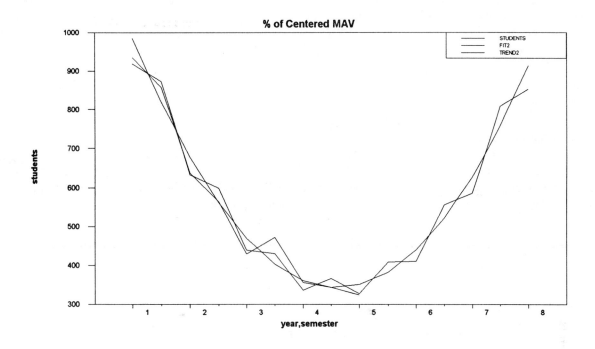

% of Centered MAV

a) The series has a nonlinear trend and is seasonal.

	STUDENTS	CRDHRS	CMAV2	%CMAV	SEAINDEX	DESEAS
FALL	935	7902			0.933412	1001.701
SPRG	858	7275	896.5	0.957055	1.066588	804.4344
FALL	638	6212	748	0.852941	0.933412	683.5138
SPRG	564	6047	601	0.938436	1.066588	528.789
FALL	429	5242	496.5	0.864048	0.933412	459.6041
SPRG	472	6047	450.5	1.047725	1.066588	442.5327
FALL	356	4578	414	0.859903	0.933412	381.3964
SPRG	344	4025	350	0.982857	1.066588	322.5238
FALL	324	3828	334		0.933412	347.1136
				0.981518	1.066588	
				0.858964	0.933412	
				1.840483	2	

b) Below we lists the forecast of the number of students for the Spring semester of year 5 and years 6 and 7, periods 10 to 14 and as shown, these forecasts are increasing instead of continuing their previous decline. The seasonal indexes for Fall and Spring are 0.933412 and 1.066588 respectively.

c) The model fits the data well. The RSE =50.21397 using 4 degrees of freedom (9-5) where 5 equals loss of degrees of freedom from estimating the three coefficients for the nonlinear trend and two seasonal indexes, Adjusted R^2 = .99, and ME = -0.426821884.

d) Comments about the validity of the forecast - The previous graph illustrates the percent of centered moving average method. Both the percent of centered moving average and percent of trend yield similar results, in general, the percent of trend method is not recommended because of the difficulties in estimating trends of highly seasonal data, however it works well here. In either case, this question illustrates the problems with using nonlinear functions such as the quadratic function of this problem. The student might explore another nonlinear relationship depending on your purpose in assigning this problem. The question of whether enrollments will continue to decline, level out, or increase as this model suggests, will not be known until sometime in the future. Those in charge of enrollment management may have more insights about the answer to this question. To be able to predict which will occur requires additional information not found in this problem. Finally, note to the student that at any point on the projected trend equation, management can select the current level as the level for several years into to the future, thus flattening the trend to a constant. That is, the trough of the nonlinear curve could be chosen as the trendless level for future years. Encourage students to explore alternative scenarios and to manipulate results based on valid considerations not included in the model.

Using the ratio to centered moving average method, the seasonal indexes for Fall and Spring are 0.933412 and 1.066588 respectively. These are used to deseasonalize the student series so that the following nonlinear, quadratic trend line using time (t) and squared time (t^2) results.

```
Dependent Variable DES - Estimation by Least Squares
Semi-Annual Data From 1:01 To 9:02
Usable Observations      18        Degrees of Freedom     15
Centered R**2       0.998015      R Bar **2     0.997750
Mean of Dependent Variable       696.87238509
Std Error of Dependent Variable 350.26092673
Standard Error of Estimate        16.61460318
Sum of Squared Residuals        4140.6755817
Regression F(2,15)                 3770.1556
Significance Level of F            0.000
Durbin-Watson Statistic            1.990863
Q(4-0)                             5.616804
Significance Level of Q            0.22965152
     Variable         Coeff       Std Error      T-Stat    Signif
*****************************************************************
1.  Constant       1175.434734    13.186406     89.13988   0.000
2.  TIME           -202.962496     3.195470    -63.51569   0.000
3.  STIME            12.371960     0.163423     75.70504   0.000
```

Multiplying the resulting trend line from the above relationship times the seasonal indexes and calculating the residuals yields:

```
YEAR  STUDENTS  TREND           FIT/FORE          RESID
1:01  935.0   984.8441978121  919.26539236814   15.73460763186
1:02  858.0   818.9975827625  873.53299380351  -15.53299380351
2:01  638.0   677.8948886364  632.75522379191    5.24477620809
2:02  564.0   561.5361154338  598.92768228831  -34.92768228831
3:01  429.0   469.9212631546  438.63014608367   -9.63014608367
3:02  472.0   403.0503317989  429.88864729269   42.11135270731
4:01  356.0   360.9233213666  336.89015924341   19.10984075659
4:02  344.0   343.5402318577  366.41588881666  -22.41588881666
5:01  324.0   350.9010632723  327.53526327113   -3.53526327113
5:02  NA      383.0058156103  408.50940686020    NA
6:01  NA      439.8544888718  410.56545816683    NA
6:02  NA      521.4470830568  556.16920142334    NA
7:01  NA      627.7835981651  585.98074393052    NA
7:02  NA      758.8640341970  809.39527250608    NA
8:01  NA      914.6883911522  853.78112056220    NA
```

```
Statistics on Series RESID
Semi-Annual Data From 1:01 To 5:01
Observations    9
Sample Mean      -0.426821884      Variance              560.115595
Standard Error  23.666761399       SE of Sample Mean       7.888920
t-Statistic       -0.05410         Signif Level (Mean=0) 0.95817905
Skewness           0.39860         Signif Level (Sk=0)   0.68480547
Kurtosis          -0.13245         Signif Level (Ku=0)   0.95833776
```

To calculate the residual standard error, we square the residuals.

```
set sres   = resid**2
Series     Obs      Mean      Std Error     Minimum      Maximum
STUDENTS    9    546.6666667   224.3886138    324.00       935.00
HOURS       9   5684.00       1396.8153063   3828.00      7902.00
SP         18      0.50          0.5144958      0.00         1.00
TIME       18      9.50          5.3385391      1.00        18.00
STIME      18    117.1666667   104.3863018      1.00       324.00
DES         9    552.4009996   231.3144437    322.5238    1001.701
RESD        9     -0.00         22.7504824    -32.7471      39.482
TREND       9    552.401       230.1929       343.5402     984.8442
RESID       9     -0.4268       23.66676      -34.9277      42.1114
SRES        9    498.06270     603.6711        12.49808   1773.366
```

RSE = 22.32

R-Square = $1-22.32**2/224.39**2 = 1-498/224.39**2 = 1-498/50351 = .99$

5-16. A northeastern university is facing declining enrollments because several new MBA programs entering the metropolitan area. The following is the number of students enrolled during the Fall (FA), Spring (SP), and Summer (SU) semesters over the last 4.3 years.

FA SP SU FA SP SU FA SP SU FA SP SU FA

632 612 355 585 542 292 464 429 233 392 369 210 356

Fit a classical decomposition model and answer the following:

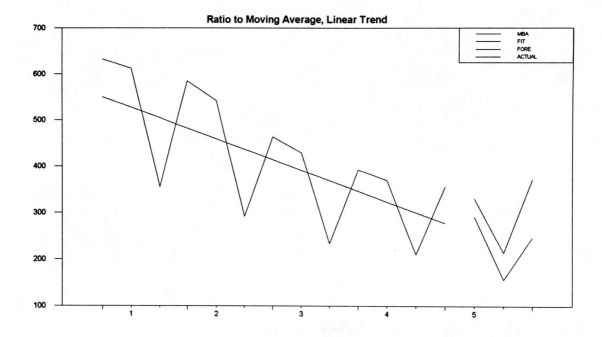

Ratio to Moving Average, Linear Trend

a) The annual trend for enrollments is -68.25 using deseasonalized data from the ratio-of-centered moving average method.

b) The seasonal indexes are Fall = 1.180664, Spring = 1.144285, and Summer = .67452 for a total of 2.99947.

c) When assuming linear trend, the forecast of the Fall, Spring, and Summer of the fifth year are all lower than the actual values because the trend was modeled linearly, when in fact it appears as a nonlinear trend where the negative slope is declining.

```
ENTRY   FIT/FORE   ACTUAL      ERROR   SERROR
 5:01   277.289   356.000     78.711   6195.422*  (*This is a fitted value.)
 5:02   291.266   330.000     38.734   1500.302
 5:03   156.348   214.000     57.652   3323.770
 6:01   246.809   372.000    125.191  15672.765
```

5-17. Fitting a classical decomposition model yields the graph below and that which follows:

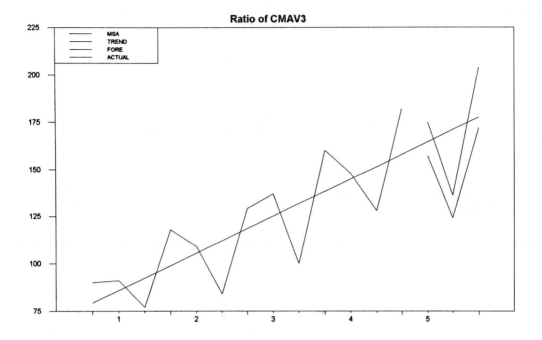

Ratio of CMAV3

a) The annual trend for enrollments is 19.6269 students per year.

b) The seasonal indexes are SPRING = 1.062721481, SUMMER = 0.796099114, and FALL = 1.14888\.6 using the ratio to centered moving average method.

c) Forecast the enrollments for the fifth year and comment on the validity of the model.

```
ENTRY      ACTUAL             FORE              ERROR              SERROR
   5:01    182 (*)    181.36630101020    0.63369898980       0.4015744097
   5:02    157        174.71676323469  -17.71676323469     313.8836995140
   5:03    124        136.09103342415  -12.09103342415     146.1930892638
   6:01    172        203.91542193999  -31.91542193999    1018.5941576075
(* This is a fitted value)
```

The linear trend seen in the in-sample data may not persist into the future because the errors in the Spring and Summer of year 5 and Fall year 6 are all negative, the forecast may be too high.

5-18. Fitting a classical decomposition model yields the graph below and the following answer:

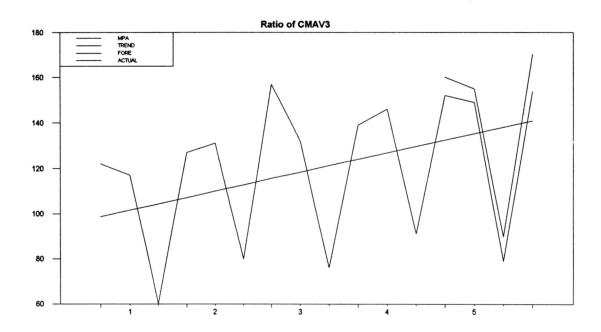

Ratio of CMAV3

a) The annual trend for enrollments is 8.40750 when using deseasonalized values to estimate a linear trend.

b) The seasonal indexes are SPRING=1.146615015, SUMMER=0.650784795, FALL= 1.20989, and the total is 3.007286686. (Because this was so close to 3.0, these were left unadjusted.)

c) The forecast the enrollments for the fifth year and beginning of the sixth year yield fairly accurate forecasts, but nonetheless, the error seems to be increasing as so often occurs as the length of the forecast horizon increases.

```
ENTRY      ACTUAL           FORE              ERROR             SERROR
  5:01    152.0 160.21108352871   -8.21108352871   67.42189271537
  5:02    149.0 155.04611287183   -6.04611287183   36.55548085891
  5:03     79.0  89.82340936743  -10.82340936743  117.14619033488
  6:01    154.0 170.38317177743  -16.38317177743  268.40831748870
```

5-19. Repeating problem 5-16 using **regression analysis** yields the following graph and answers. This method was applied to the logarithms of the dependent variable. The following is a graph of the fitted, actual, and forecasted values after converting them back to the original metric values.

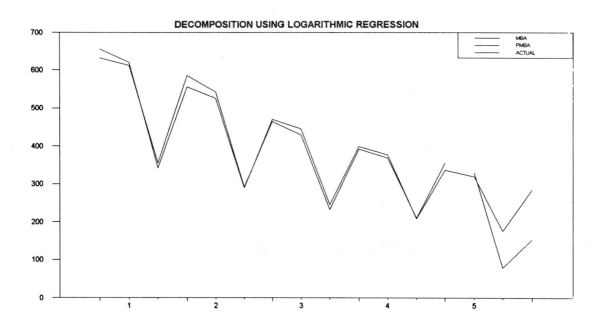

DECOMPOSITION USING LOGARITHMIC REGRESSION

```
SET LMBA = LOG(MBA)
LINREG LMBA / RES
#CONSTANT TIME WINTER SUMMER
Dependent Variable LMBA - Estimation by Least Squares
3/Year Data From 1:01 To 5:01
Usable Observations       13       Degrees of Freedom        9
Centered R**2      0.990744       R Bar **2    0.987658
Uncentered R**2    0.999970       T x R**2      13.000
Mean of Dependent Variable       5.9875267529
Std Error of Dependent Variable 0.3529237050
Standard Error of Estimate       0.0392071484
Sum of Squared Residuals         0.0138348043
Regression F(3,9)             321.1090
Significance Level of F          0.000
Durbin-Watson Statistic          0.633829
Q(3-0)                           7.286621
Significance Level of Q          0.06330215
     Variable          Coeff        Std Error       T-Stat      Signif
*********************************************************************
1.   Constant        6.549167986  0.026942536    243.07912   0.000
2.   TIME           -0.055407473  0.002922328    -18.96004   0.001
3.   WINTER         -0.017956448  0.026341511     -0.68168   0.51260032
4.   SUMMER         -0.546857542  0.026341511    -20.76029   0.001
```

```
LINREG LMBA / RES
#CONSTANT TIME SUMMER
Dependent Variable LMBA - Estimation by Least Squares
3/Year Data From 1:01 To 5:01
Usable Observations      13        Degrees of Freedom      10
Centered R**2        0.990266      R Bar **2    0.988319
Uncentered R**2      0.999969      T x R**2        13.000
Mean of Dependent Variable        5.9875267529
Std Error of Dependent Variable 0.3529237050
Standard Error of Estimate        0.0381433083
Sum of Squared Residuals          0.0145491197
Regression F(2,10)                  508.6605
Significance Level of F             0.000
Durbin-Watson Statistic            0.669988
Q(3-0)                             6.397862
Significance Level of Q            0.09377879
    Variable            Coeff       Std Error      T-Stat      Signif
*****************************************************************************
1.   Constant          6.540438390  0.023061359    283.61027   0.000
2.   TIME             -0.055296972  0.002838657    -19.47998   0.000
3.   SUMMER           -0.538956705  0.023012778    -23.41989   0.000

PRJ PLMBA 14 16
SET PLMBA = LMBA - RES
```

As the above regression shows, the Fall and Spring are not statistically significantly different than each other, which is likely for MBA students who are not so sensitive to the semester in which they start or end their programs. As shown below, Summer has an enrollment which is only about 40% of the Fall and Winter Semesters. Also shown below, the trend in enrollment has been a decline of about 5.4 percent.

```
DISP 1-EXP(-.5389567)= 0.41664
DISP TREND=1-EXP(-0.055296972) = 0.05380
SET PMBA = EXP(PLMBA)
```

Series	Obs	Mean	Std Error	Minimum	Maximum
YEAR	13	35.15384615	13.03742148	13.000	53.000
MBA	13	420.84615385	139.36872327	210.000	632.000
WINTER	16	0.31250000	0.47871355	0.000	1.000
SUMMER	16	0.31250000	0.47871355	0.000	1.000
LMBA	13	5.98752675	0.35292371	5.347107	6.448889
RES	13	-0.000	0.03481992	-0.05277	0.053353
TIME	16	8.500	4.76095229	1.000	16.000
PLMBA	16	5.90199016	0.38185125	5.17202710	6.48514
PMBA	16	390.71748659	143.55265074	176.27179678	655.3316

As shown below, in original metrics, the average trend in enrollments is a 22.64 decline per term. Not a good sign for enrollments.

```
DISP .0538*420.846 = 22.64151
```

Some additional actual values are now known and these are shown below.

```
set actual 14 14 = 330
set actual 15 15 = 79
set actual 16 16 = 154
set actual 1 13 = mba
set error = actual - pmba
```

```
print 1 16 actual pmba error
 ENTRY    ACTUAL          PMBA              ERROR
  1:01    632.0  655.33163303358   -23.3316330336
  1:02    612.0  620.07748462835    -8.0774846284
  1:03    355.0  342.26687471795    12.7331252820
  2:01    585.0  555.15674725353    29.8432527465
  2:02    542.0  525.29159597853    16.7084040215
  2:03    292.0  289.94749418927     2.0525058107
  3:01    464.0  470.29473092035    -6.2947309204
  3:02    429.0  444.99480733614   -15.9948073361
  3:03    233.0  245.62572541066   -12.6257254107
  4:01    392.0  398.40483795910    -6.4048379591
  4:02    369.0  376.97229514447    -7.9722951445
  4:03    210.0  208.07904255979     1.9209574402
  5:01    356.0  337.50413192722    18.4958680728
  5:02    330.0  319.34779679158    10.6522032084
  5:03     79.0  176.27179677622   -97.2717967762
  6:01    154.0  285.91279074688  -131.9127907469
```

As shown above the out-of-sample actuals are considerably lower than the forecasted and historic values.

5-20. Repeating problem 5-17 using **regression analysis** yields the following graph and answers. This is a graph of the fitted, actual, and forecasted values after converting them back to the original metric values.

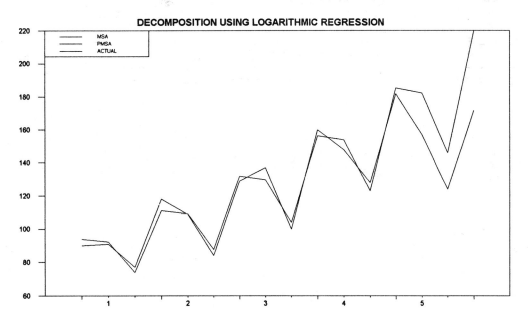

```
set lmsa = log(msa)
LINREG LMSA / RES
#CONSTANT TIME WINTER SUMMER
Dependent Variable LMSA - Estimation by Least Squares
3/Year Data From 1:01 To 5:01
Usable Observations      13        Degrees of Freedom      9
Centered R**2     0.978898        R Bar **2    0.971863
Uncentered R**2   0.999940        T x R**2       12.999
Mean of Dependent Variable        4.7508238816
Std Error of Dependent Variable 0.2639170557
Standard Error of Estimate        0.0442693169
Sum of Squared Residuals          0.0176379518
```

```
Regression F(3,9)                    139.1639
Significance Level of F          0.007
Durbin-Watson Statistic             2.327418
Q(3-0)                              5.643558
Significance Level of Q         0.13029997
     Variable           Coeff        Std Error      T-Stat      Signif
*************************************************************************
1.  Constant           4.484502441  0.030421178   147.41383   0.000
2.  TIME                0.056770714  0.003299640    17.20512   0.003
3.  WINTER             -0.073661936  0.029742554    -2.47665   0.03518422
4.  SUMMER             -0.352327130  0.029742554   -11.84589   0.086
```

Calculating the ratio of changes we see that Winter (i.e., Sprint) is typically about 93% of Fall and Summer is typically only about 70.3% of the Fall semester enrollment. In addition, the trend is about a 5.8% increase per semester.

```
DISP EXP(-0.073661936) = 0.92899 (Winter in proportion to Fall)
DISP EXP(-0.352327130) = 0.70305 (Summer in proportion to Fall)
DISP EXP(0.056770714)  = 1.05841 (Trend in enrollments)
SET PMSA 1 16 = EXP(PLMSA)
Series       Obs       Mean       Std Error       Minimum        Maximum
YEAR         13     35.15384615  13.03742148     13.000          53.000
MSA          13    119.46153846  31.71386496     77.000         182.000
WINTER       16      0.31250000   0.47871355      0.000           1.000
SUMMER       16      0.31250000   0.47871355      0.000           1.000
TIME         16      8.500        4.76095229      1.000          16.000
LMSA         13      4.75082388   0.26391706      4.34380542      5.20401
RES          13     -0.000        0.03833835     -0.04198280      0.0591
PLMSA        16      4.83393193   0.30341955      4.30248745      5.392834
PMSA         16    131.27232018  40.46119601     73.88334671    219.82546
```

Using the mean of enrollments, the average increase in students is about 7 students per term.

```
DISP .05841*119.46 = 6.97766
```

The Fall and Spring are statistically significantly different than each other. Again, additional values are known for terms 14 to 16 and are entered below.

```
set actual 14 14 = 157
set actual 15 15 = 124
set actual 16 16 = 172
set actual 1 13 = msa
set error = actual - pmsa
SET SERROR = ERROR*ERROR
```

```
ENTRY   ACTUAL           PMSA           ERROR            SERROR
  1:01    90.0   93.81015898890  -3.81015898890   14.5173115207
  1:02    91.0   92.23889839381  -1.23889839381    1.5348692302
  1:03    77.0   73.88334671420   3.11665328580    9.7135277039
  2:01   118.0  111.22835024994   6.77164975006   45.8552403375
  2:02   109.0  109.36534601150  -0.36534601150    0.1334777081
  2:03    84.0   87.60162923225  -3.60162923225   12.9717331266
  3:01   129.0  131.88066231491  -2.88066231491    8.2982153725
  3:02   137.0  129.67174496328   7.32825503672   53.7033218833
  3:03   100.0  103.86705239316  -3.86705239316   14.9540942114
  4:01   160.0  156.36759021901   3.63240978099   13.1944008170
  4:02   148.0  153.74853237380  -5.74853237380   33.0456244526
  4:03   128.0  123.15255626399   4.84744373601   23.4977107738
```

```
5:01   182.0 185.40112584903   -3.40112584903    11.5676570410
5:02   157.0 182.29577471785  -25.29577471785   639.8762185764
5:03   124.0 146.01889400835  -22.01889400835   484.8316933509
6:01   172.0 219.82546010938  -47.82546010938  2287.2746346738
```

As shown above, the out-of-sample actuals are lower than predicted.

5-21.   Repeating problem 5-18 using **regression analysis** yields the following graph and answers. Logarithms were used to fit the relationship. This is a graph of the fitted, actual, and forecasted values after converting them back to the original metric values.

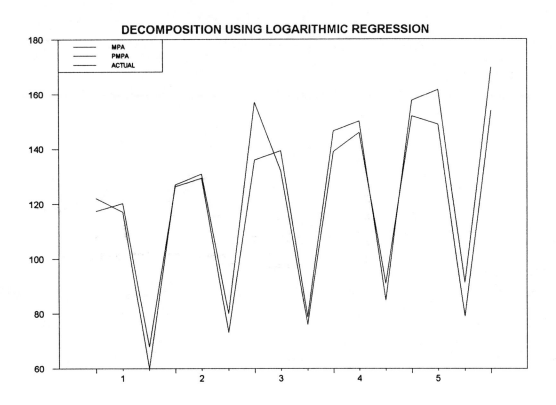

```
set lmpa = log(mpa)
LINREG LMPA / RES
#CONSTANT TIME WINTER SUMMER
Dependent Variable LMPA - Estimation by Least Squares
3/Year Data From 1:01 To 5:01
Usable Observations        13      Degrees of Freedom        9
Centered R**2       0.948715      R Bar **2    0.931620
Uncentered R**2    0.999808      T x R**2      12.997
Mean of Dependent Variable        4.7295809413
Std Error of Dependent Variable 0.3021436040
Standard Error of Estimate        0.0790093484
Sum of Squared Residuals          0.0561822942
Regression F(3,9)                    55.4965
Significance Level of F           0.397
Durbin-Watson Statistic            1.514777
Q(3-0)                             5.611991
Significance Level of Q           0.13209164
```

```
      Variable           Coeff       Std Error       T-Stat      Signif
**********************************************************************
1.  Constant           4.761635340  0.054293981     87.70098  0.000
2.  TIME               0.024418048  0.005889009      4.14638  0.00249781
3.  WINTER            -0.044407703  0.053082811     -0.83657  0.42448671
4.  SUMMER            -0.615279691  0.053082811    -11.59094  0.103

LINREG LMPA / RES
#CONSTANT TIME SUMMER
Dependent Variable LMPA - Estimation by Least Squares
3/Year Data From 1:01 To 5:01
Usable Observations     13      Degrees of Freedom     10
Centered R**2      0.944727      R Bar **2    0.933672
Uncentered R**2    0.999793      T x R**2        12.997
Mean of Dependent Variable       4.7295809413
Std Error of Dependent Variable  0.3021436040
Standard Error of Estimate       0.0778146068
Sum of Squared Residuals         0.0605511304
Regression F(2,10)                    85.4598
Significance Level of F              0.052
Durbin-Watson Statistic             1.671862
Q(3-0)                              3.461376
Significance Level of Q             0.32580620
      Variable           Coeff       Std Error       T-Stat      Signif
**********************************************************************
1.  Constant           4.740046364  0.047046538    100.75229  0.000
2.  TIME               0.024691326  0.005791028      4.26372  0.00165330
3.  SUMMER            -0.595740302  0.046947430    -12.68952  0.017

PRJ PLMPA 14 16
SET PLMPA 1 13 = LMPA - RES]
```

As shown below, summer enrollments are only about 45% of the Fall and Spring semesters. In addition the trend is an increase of about 2.4%.

```
DISP 1-EXP(-0.595740302) = 0.44885
DISP EXP(0.024691326)-1 = 0.02500
SET PMPA 1 16 = EXP(PLMPA)
Series     Obs      Mean          Std Error       Minimum        Maximum
YEAR       13    35.15384615    13.03742148     13.000         53.000
MPA        13   117.69230769    31.17794256     60.000        157.000
WINTER     16     0.31250000     0.47871355      0.000          1.000
SUMMER     16     0.31250000     0.47871355      0.000          1.000
TIME       16     8.500          4.76095229      1.000         16.000
LMPA       13     4.72958094     0.30214360      4.09434456     5.05624581
RES        13    -0.000          0.07103469     -0.12403548     0.14336016
PLMPA      13     4.72958094     0.29367470      4.21838004     5.06103361
PMPA       13   117.52719900    31.05490437     67.92336211   157.75348741
ACTUAL     16   119.500         32.04996100     60.000        157.000
ERROR      13     0.16510869     8.12344225     -7.92336211    20.96861250
```

As shown below, the typical trend is about 6.33 students per term, however, this is linearization of the percentage growth in trend.

```
DISP .0538*117.69 = 6.33172
set actual 14 14 = 149
set actual 15 15 = 79
set actual 16 16 = 154
```

```
set actual 1 13 = mpa
set error = actual - pmPa
SET SERROR = ERROR*ERROR
print 1 16 actual pmpa error SERROR
ENTRY           ACTUAL          PMPA            ERROR           SERROR
   1:01    122.0 117.30034427623    4.69965572377   22.08676392197
   1:02    117.0 120.23269825028   -3.23269825028   10.45033797737
   1:03     60.0  67.92336210762   -7.92336210762   62.77966708849
   2:01    127.0 126.31915367754    0.68084632246    0.46355171480
   2:02    131.0 129.47696599745    1.52303400255    2.31963257291
   2:03     80.0  73.14574965068    6.85425034932   46.98074785110
   3:01    157.0 136.03138749734   20.96861250266  439.68271028674
   3:02    132.0 139.43199285945   -7.43199285945   55.23451786297
   3:03     76.0  78.76966813691   -2.76966813691    7.67106158862
   4:01    139.0 146.49036069136   -7.49036069136   56.10550328673
   4:02    146.0 150.15242659564   -4.15242659564   17.24264663216
   4:03     91.0  84.82598986312    6.17401013688   38.11840117034
   5:01    152.0 157.75348741411   -5.75348741411   33.10261742436
   5:02    149.0 161.69711663868  -12.69711663868  161.21677093620
   5:03     79.0  91.34796078804  -12.34796078804  152.47213562303
   6:01    154.0 169.88259619175  -15.88259619175  252.25686179019
```

5-22. Repeating problem 5-15 using regression analysis on a nonlinear (i.e., quadratic) trend equation along with a graph of fitted and forecasted values given below.

a. This data requires a nonlinear curve. While certainly not the best choice, a quadratic is chosen to show the problems with the use of nonlinear curves. In contrast to this curve, an exponential curve might have been used so that it asymptotically approaches some lower bound.

```
open data c:\diskdata\ugdata.dat
data(org=obs) 1 9 students hours
Series     Obs      Mean        Std Error      Minimum         Maximum
STUDENTS    9   546.66666667   224.38861379   324.00000000   935.00000000
HOURS       9  5684.00000000  1396.81530633  3828.00000000  7902.00000000
SET TIME = T
```

The following creates a seasonal dummy variable for the Spring Semester.

```
seas SPRING 1 16 2 2
SET STIME = T*T
```

b. A nonlinear decomposition using regression analysis is chosen here.

```
LINREG STUDENTS / RES
#CONSTANT TIME STIME SPRING
Dependent Variable STUDENTS - Estimation by Least Squares
Semi-Annual Data From 1:01 To 5:01
Usable Observations        9        Degrees of Freedom       5
Centered R**2      0.990012        R Bar **2    0.984019
Uncentered R**2    0.998699        T x R**2        8.988
Mean of Dependent Variable         546.66666667
Std Error of Dependent Variable 224.38861379
Standard Error of Estimate          28.36633372
Sum of Squared Residuals          4023.2444444
Regression F(3,5)                    165.1978
Significance Level of F             0.00002024
Durbin-Watson Statistic                2.075161
```

```
Q(2-0)                            6.177636
Significance Level of Q           0.04555576
Variable              Coeff      Std Error      T-Stat      Signif
*****************************************************************
1.  Constant       1119.677778    36.105996     31.01085    0.00000065
2.  TIME           -192.922222    17.111481    -11.27443    0.00009592
3.  STIME            11.555556     1.671502      6.91328    0.00097082
4.  SPRING           57.766667    19.678345      2.93554    0.03242361
```

c. The graph below shows the requested values. While not shown, a linear model does not yield a statistically significant spring affect. In contrast to these results, I would have inferred that the Spring enrollment would be lower than the Fall Semester.

d. Only observations through period 16, the eighth year are shown in order to have a higher resolution on the points shown.

e. The usual error statistics are shown in the previous regression output. Because of the nonlinearity of this series and the likely inappropriateness of the quadratic relationship, all forecasts should be critically evaluated. It is not likely that the nonlinearity will continue; nor is it likely that enrollments will continue to drop. More likely, enrollments will start to increase because of the increasing number of high school graduates from the children of the Baby Boomers.

Series	Obs	Mean	Std Error	Minimum	Maximum
STUDENTS	9	546.6666667	224.3886138	324.0000000	935.0000000
HOURS	9	5684.0000000	1396.8153063	3828.0000000	7902.0000000
TIME	16	8.5000000	4.7609523	1.0000000	16.0000000
SPRINT	16	0.5000000	0.5163978	0.0000000	1.0000000
SPRING	16	0.5000000	0.5163978	0.0000000	1.0000000
RES	9	-0.0000000	22.4255559	-29.6222222	36.0888889
STIME	16	93.5000000	83.2554303	1.0000000	256.0000000
PSTUDENTS	16	589.1666667	228.3158690	319.3777778	1048.9111111

ENTRY	STUDENTS	PSTUDENTS	SPRING	RES
1:01	935.00000000000	938.3111111111	0.0000000000000	-3.31111111111
1:02	858.00000000000	837.8222222222	1.0000000000000	20.17777777778
2:01	638.00000000000	644.9111111111	0.0000000000000	-6.91111111111
2:02	564.00000000000	590.6444444444	1.0000000000000	-26.64444444444
3:01	429.00000000000	443.9555555556	0.0000000000000	-14.95555555556
3:02	472.00000000000	435.9111111111	1.0000000000000	36.08888888889
4:01	356.00000000000	335.4444444444	0.0000000000000	20.55555555555
4:02	344.00000000000	373.6222222222	1.0000000000000	-29.62222222222
5:01	324.00000000000	319.3777777778	0.0000000000000	4.62222222222
5:02	NA	403.7777777778	1.0000000000000	NA
6:01	NA	395.7555555556	0.0000000000000	NA
6:02	NA	526.3777777778	1.0000000000000	NA
7:01	NA	564.5777777778	0.0000000000000	NA
7:02	NA	741.4222222222	1.0000000000000	NA
8:01	NA	825.8444444444	0.0000000000000	NA
8:02	NA	1048.9111111111	1.0000000000000	NA

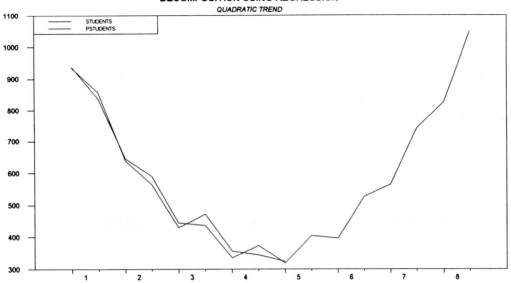

DECOMPOSITION USING REGRESSION

QUADRATIC TREND

5-23. The time series **BIRTHMAR.DAT** is the quarterly marriages in the United States which is fitted using regression decomposition.

```
open data c:\diskdata\birthmar.dat
data(org=obs) 1 32 date births marriages
cal 1985 1 4
tab
```

Series	Obs	Mean	Std Error	Minimum	Maximum
DATE	32	198852.50000	232.79785	198501.00000	199204.00000
BIRTHS	32	988380.68750	53994.42278	896013.00000	1098868.00000
MARRIAGES	32	599909.43750	116739.84222	402000.00000	724000.00000

The following creates seasonal dummy variables.

```
seas qtr2 1 32 4 2
seas qtr3 1 32 4 3
seas qtr4 1 32 4 4
set time = t
linreg marriages 1 24 res
#constant time qtr2 qtr3 qtr4
Dependent Variable MARRIAGES - Estimation by Least Squares
Quarterly Data From 1985:01 To 1990:04
Usable Observations      24      Degrees of Freedom      19
Centered R**2       0.994471      R Bar **2     0.993307
Uncentered R**2     0.999802      T x R**2      23.995
Mean of Dependent Variable       602670.91667
Std Error of Dependent Variable  118636.81608
Standard Error of Estimate         9706.12037
Sum of Squared Residuals        1789966678.7
Regression F(4,19)                  854.2941
Significance Level of F           0.00000000
Durbin-Watson Statistic             2.054098
Q(6-0)                              4.082347
Significance Level of Q           0.66553350
```

Variable	Coeff	Std Error	T-Stat	Signif
1. Constant	414507.83333	5087.17742	81.48091	0.00000000
2. TIME	270.00000	290.02582	0.93095	0.36355744
3. QTR2	278918.00000	5611.33132	49.70621	0.00000000
4. QTR3	286603.66667	5633.77175	50.87243	0.00000000
5. QTR4	173630.66667	5670.97513	30.61743	0.00000000

While the trend component is statistically insignificant, leaving it in the relationship has very little if any affect on the relationship. Obviously, it should be dropped, but is left in the relationship for explanatory purposes.

```
prj fore 1 32
set error = marriages - fore
set pe = error/marriages
set ape = abs(pe)
set serror = error*error/1000
```

Fit Statistics for periods 1 24.

Series	Obs	Mean	Std Error	Minimum	Maximum
DATE	24	198752.5000	174.4594	198501.0000	199004.
BIRTHS	24	976465.9167	55356.6005	896013.0000	1098868.
MARRIAGES	24	602670.9167	118636.8161	402000.0000	724000.
TIME	24	12.5000	7.0711	1.0000	24.
RES	24	-0.0000	8821.8274	-17097.8333	16678.5
FORE	24	602670.9167	118308.3661	414777.8333	707321.5
ERROR	24	-0.0000	8821.8274	-17097.8333	16678.5
PE	24	-0.0002	0.0156	-0.0425	0.023
APE	24	0.0122	0.0093	0.0004	0.043
SERROR	24	74581.9449	90805.2309	33.1847	292335.9047

Forecast statistics for periods 25 to 32.

Series	Obs	Mean	Std Error	Minimum	Maximum
DATE	8	199152.5000	53.4656	199101.0000	199204.0
BIRTHS	8	1024125.0000	29925.8011	983000.0000	1069000.0
MARRIAGES	8	591625.0000	118336.0077	411000.0000	709000.0
TIME	8	28.5000	2.4495	25.0000	32.0
RES	0				
FORE	8	606990.9167	123799.6363	421257.8333	709481.5
ERROR	8	-15365.9167	13437.1663	-39525.8333	662.17
PE	8	-0.0251	0.0203	-0.0597	0.002
APE	8	0.0257	0.0195	0.0008	0.06
SERROR	8	394099.1525	523823.8260	358.2022	1562291.50

Unadjusted R-square

```
disp 1-394099152.5/118336.0**2 = 0.97186
```

As shown above, the in-sample fit and out-of-sample forecasts differ somewhat, the in-sample fit being somewhat better, however, the out-of-sample values are quite good.

ENTRY	MARRIAGES	FORE	ERROR
1985:01	420240.00000000	414777.83333333	5462.16666667
1985:02	703900.00000000	693965.83333333	9934.16666667
1985:03	709010.00000000	701921.50000000	7088.50000000

```
1985:04   579475.00000000  589218.50000000   -9743.50000000
1986:01   416040.00000000  415857.83333333     182.16666667
1986:02   701072.00000000  695045.83333333    6026.16666667
1986:03   705020.00000000  703001.50000000    2018.50000000
1986:04   584967.00000000  590298.50000000   -5331.50000000
1987:01   425587.00000000  416937.83333333    8649.16666667
1987:02   692023.00000000  696125.83333333   -4102.83333333
1987:03   698699.00000000  704081.50000000   -5382.50000000
1987:04   587069.00000000  591378.50000000   -4309.50000000
1988:01   416000.00000000  418017.83333333   -2017.83333333
1988:02   681000.00000000  697205.83333333  -16205.83333333
1988:03   698000.00000000  705161.50000000   -7161.50000000
1988:04   594000.00000000  592458.50000000    1541.50000000
1989:01   402000.00000000  419097.83333333  -17097.83333333
1989:02   704000.00000000  698285.83333333    5714.16666667
1989:03   693000.00000000  706241.50000000  -13241.50000000
1989:04   606000.00000000  593538.50000000   12461.50000000
1990:01   425000.00000000  420177.83333333    4822.16666667
1990:02   698000.00000000  699365.83333333   -1365.83333333
1990:03   724000.00000000  707321.50000000   16678.50000000
1990:04   600000.00000000  594618.50000000    5381.50000000
1991:01   411000.00000000  421257.83333333  -10257.83333333
1991:02   674000.00000000  700445.83333333  -26445.83333333
1991:03   709000.00000000  708401.50000000     598.50000000
1991:04   578000.00000000  595698.50000000  -17698.50000000
1992:01   423000.00000000  422337.83333333     662.16666667
1992:02   662000.00000000  701525.83333333  -39525.83333333
1992:03   697000.00000000  709481.50000000  -12481.50000000
1992:04   579000.00000000  596778.50000000  -17778.50000000
ENTRY        MARRIAGES          FORE            ERROR
```

5-24. The time series **RETAIL.DAT** is the monthly retail sales in the United States. Repeating the analyses as in Problem 5-22 using the first eight years and forecasting the last two years of the this time series is illustrated below. Because logarithms are necessary to model this series as a percent of trend, this is a good problem with which to introduce variance nonstationarity.

The following creates seasonal dummy variables.

```
set lsales = log(sales)
seas feb 1 132 12 2
seas mar 1 132 12 3
seas apr 1 132 12 4
seas may 1 132 12 5
seas jun 1 132 12 6
seas jul 1 132 12 7
seas aug 1 132 12 8
seas sep 1 132 12 9
seas oct 1 132 12 10
seas nov 1 132 12 11
seas dec 1 132 12 12
set time = t
linreg lsales 1 120 res
#constant feb to time
Dependent Variable LSALES - Estimation by Least Squares
132/Year Data From 1:01 To 1:120
Usable Observations     120      Degrees of Freedom   107
Centered R**2      0.992216      R Bar **2     0.991343
Uncentered R**2    0.999958      T x R**2      119.995
```

```
Mean of Dependent Variable        3.6829009298
Std Error of Dependent Variable  0.2735980533
Standard Error of Estimate       0.0254570223
Sum of Squared Residuals         0.0693424186
Regression F(12,107)              1136.5343
Significance Level of F           0.00000000
Durbin-Watson Statistic           1.152170
Q(30-0)                          318.296035
Significance Level of Q           0.00000000
     Variable         Coeff        Std Error       T-Stat        Signif
************************************************************************
1.  Constant         3.127226182   0.008863254    352.83048    0.00000000
2.  FEB             -0.037431328   0.011384926     -3.28780    0.00136672
3.  MAR              0.089787338   0.011385525      7.88610    0.00000000
4.  APR              0.103995460   0.011386523      9.13321    0.00000000
5.  MAY              0.148858810   0.011387920     13.07164    0.00000000
6.  JUN              0.142329903   0.011389717     12.49635    0.00000000
7.  JUL              0.125457679   0.011391912     11.01287    0.00000000
8.  AUG              0.131565353   0.011394505     11.54639    0.00000000
9.  SEP              0.081749680   0.011397497      7.17260    0.00000000
10. OCT              0.130275693   0.011400887     11.42680    0.00000000
11. NOV              0.125176569   0.011404674     10.97590    0.00000000
12. DEC              0.286960841   0.011408858     25.15246    0.00000000
13. TIME             0.007354505   0.000067423    109.07990    0.00000000
prj plsales 1 132
```

The following statement takes antilogarithms of the logarithmic fits and forecasts.

```
set error = exp(lsales) - exp(plsales),   set fore = exp(plsales)
set serror = error**2,                    set pe = error/sales
set ape = abs(pe)
```

In-sample fitted statistics for periods 1 120.

Series	Obs	Mean	Std Error	Minimum	Maximum
SALES	120	41.26544167	11.37485803	23.05700000	75.59700
LSALES	120	3.68290093	0.27359805	3.13796941	4.325417
TIME	120	60.50000000	34.78505426	1.00000000	120.00000
RES	120	-0.00000000	0.02413937	-0.06545779	0.059772
PLSALES	120	3.68290093	0.27253107	3.10450386	4.296728
ERROR	120	0.02022442	0.99823043	-3.53559983	2.442832
FORE	120	41.24521724	11.23241653	22.29815333	73.459019
SERROR	120	0.98856915	1.64839509	0.00011734	12.500467
PE	120	-0.00028931	0.02419242	-0.06764767	0.05802
APE	120	0.01933953	0.01442904	0.00034298	0.067648

Out-of-sample forecast statistics for periods 121 132.

Series	Obs	Mean	Std Error	Minimum	Maximum
SALES	12	67.01750000	8.25506754	53.26900000	85.07500
LSALES	12	4.19792669	0.12443176	3.97535455	4.44353
TIME	12	126.50000000	3.60555128	121.00000000	132.0000
RES	0				
PLSALES	12	4.16829829	0.10124752	3.98704452	4.384982
ERROR	12	2.10684026	1.95873622	-2.27199211	4.838241
FORE	12	64.91065974	6.62621023	53.89536717	80.236759
SERROR	12	7.95570283	7.05702478	0.02321575	23.408581
PE	12	0.02880567	0.02901123	-0.04265130	0.058631
APE	12	0.03638674	0.01739235	0.00283511	0.058631

Unadjusted R-square equals:

disp 1-7.95570283/8.25506754**2 = 0.88326

As shown above, the in-sample fit and out-of-sample forecasts differ somewhat, the in-sample fit being somewhat better, however, the out-of-sample values are quite good.

5-25. The time series **SUPEROIL.DAT** is the sales of the Superoil Company in thousands of barrels during the last 79 months. Repeat the analysis of Problem 5-22 using the first six years and forecast the first seven months of the seventh year.

Creating seasonal dummies using the following RATS commands:

```
seas feb 1 108 12 2
    . . .
seas nov 1 108 12 11
seas dec 1 108 12 12
set time = t
linreg sales 1 96 res
#constant feb to time
Dependent Variable SALES - Estimation by Least Squares
Monthly Data From 1:01 To 8:12
Usable Observations        96      Degrees of Freedom     83
Centered R**2      0.968108      R Bar **2    0.963497
Uncentered R**2    0.999229      T x R**2        95.926
Mean of Dependent Variable       356.81250000
Std Error of Dependent Variable  56.43987252
Standard Error of Estimate       10.78330830
Sum of Squared Residuals         9651.2182540
Regression F(12,83)                 209.9588
Significance Level of F           0.00000000
Durbin-Watson Statistic             2.082605
Q(24-0)                            28.475669
Significance Level of Q           0.24048931
    Variable          Coeff        Std Error      T-Stat        Signif
************************************************************************
1.   Constant     232.20667989    4.18298889     55.51214    0.00000000
2.   FEB           15.23445767    5.39180273      2.82548    0.00591188
3.   MAR           15.96891534    5.39224844      2.96146    0.00399194
4.   APR           40.57837302    5.39299120      7.52428    0.00000000
5.   MAY           45.31283069    5.39403090      8.40055    0.00000000
6.   JUN           71.92228836    5.39536736     13.33038    0.00000000
7.   JUL           65.78174603    5.39700037     12.18858    0.00000000
8.   AUG           72.26620370    5.39892964     13.38528    0.00000000
9.   SEP           55.75066138    5.40115487     10.32199    0.00000000
10.  OCT           48.98511905    5.40367569      9.06515    0.00000000
11.  NOV           18.59457672    5.40649169      3.43931    0.00091474
12.  DEC           17.32903439    5.40960240      3.20338    0.00192716
13.  TIME           1.76554233    0.04002723     44.10853    0.00000000

prj psales 1 108
set error = sales - psales
set serror = error**2
set pe = error/sales
set ape = abs(pe)
```

In-sample fitted statistics for periods 1 to 96.

Series	Obs	Mean	Std Error	Minimum	Maximum
YRMO	96	456.50000000	230.35770811	101.00000000	812.00000
SALES	96	356.81250000	56.43987252	252.00000000	472.00000
TIME	96	48.50000000	27.85677655	1.00000000	96.00000
RES	96	0.00000000	10.07927433	-23.53174603	25.27778
PSALES	96	356.81250000	55.53257998	233.97222222	466.90278
ERROR	96	0.00000000	10.07927433	-23.53174603	25.27778
SERROR	96	100.53352348	139.91916882	0.00113772	638.96605
PE	96	-0.00060723	0.03087647	-0.08588228	0.08540
APE	96	0.02318385	0.02026277	0.00008288	0.08588

Out-of-sample forecast statistics for periods 97 108.

Series	Obs	Mean	Std Error	Minimum	Maximum
YRMO	12	906.50000000	3.60555128	901.00000000	912.00000000
SALES	12	451.91666667	30.43161733	391.00000000	489.00000000
TIME	12	102.50000000	3.60555128	97.00000000	108.00000000
RES	0				
PSALES	12	452.15178571	27.53878979	403.46428571	488.08928571
ERROR	12	-0.23511905	8.76213985	-12.46428571	15.53571429
SERROR	12	70.43245111	74.27103061	0.43654337	241.35841837
PE	12	-0.00113196	0.02046140	-0.03187797	0.03563237
APE	12	0.01637621	0.01129188	0.00139391	0.03563237

Unadjusted R-square equals:

disp 1-70.43245111/30.43161733**2 = 0.92395

As shown above, the in-sample fit and out-of-sample forecasts differ somewhat, the in-sample fit being somewhat better, however, the out-of-sample values are quite good.

II. MINICASES

FOR EACH OF THE FOLLOWING, SEE THE MASTER SUMMARY TABLE SECTION

MINICASE 5-1. Kansas Turnpike, Daily Data.

MINICASE 5-2. Domestic Air Passengers by Quarter.

MINICASE 5-3. Hospital Census by Month.

MINICASE 5-4. Henry Machler's Hideaway Orchids.

MINICASE 5-5. Your Forecasting Project.

MINICASE 5-6. Midwestern Building Materials.

MINICASE 5-7. International Airline Passengers.

MINICASE 5-8. Automobile Sales.

MINICASE 5-9. Consumption of Distilled Spirits.

MINICASE 5-10. Discount Consumer Electronics.

CHAPTER 6
TREND-SEASONAL AND HOLT-WINTERS SMOOTHING

I.   PROBLEMS

ESTIMATED DIFFICULTY

Elementary		Medium		Hard		Very Hard		Bad	
1 E	2 M	3 E	4 E	5 E	6 E	7 M	8 M	9 M	10 E
11 E	12 M	13 M	14 M	15 M	16 M	17 M	18 H	19 H	20 H
21 H	22 H	23 H	24 H	25 H	26 H	27 H	28 H	29 H	30 H
31 M	32 M	33 H	34 H	35 H	36 M	37 M	38 M	39 M	40 M
41 M	42 M	43 M							

Minicases are all hard.

6-1. First differences can be used to model series that drift (i.e., random walks) and trends depending on whether a constant (i.e., b) is not or is included respectively. The respective models and errors are:

Drift/Random Walk $\hat{Y}_t = Y_{t-1} + e_t$ $e_t = Y_t - Y_{t-1}$

Trend Model $\hat{Y}_t = Y_{t-1} + b + e_t$ $e_t = Y_t - Y_{t-1} - b$

6-2. First differences are a one-period moving average which will always lag the actual trend value. Double moving averages involve multiple-period moving averages which are adjusted to eliminate the lag with simple moving averages.

6-3. Brown's double smoothing method uses a single smoothing constant for the smoothed average (i.e., smoothed level) and smoothed trend. Holt added the flexibility of two smoothing constants, one for the smoothed constant and one for the trend.

6-4. A t-value is calculated assuming the null hypothesis is true (i.e., that there is no trend in the series). If the t-value is inconsistent with the no-trend assumption (that is, having a very high absolute value), then we infer that there is a trend.

6-5. The advantages include easily calculated trend value and simple statistical significance test on the trend. The disadvantages include, there is no smoothing of random variations in trend (b) and the base value (Y_{t-1}), if Y_{t-1} is a very unusual value, then all future forecasts will be biased by the unusual value. Finally, this is a very simple model of trend and at times the trend estimate or statistical significance test of b may be inaccurate when complex patterns exist in the time series.

6-6. The following relationships exist for seasonal time series.

Seasonal Drift/Random Walk $\hat{Y}_t = Y_{t-s} + e_t$ $e_t = Y_t - Y_{t-s}$

Seasonal Trend Model $\hat{Y}_t = Y_{t-s} + b + e_t$ $e_t = Y_t - Y_{t-s} - b$

Nonlinearity can be modeled using logarithms or second differences. However, these two types of models cannot represent all types of nonlinearity. Second differences are first differences of first differences and represent changes in changes, a nonlinear behavior. See also, pages 211 to 212.

6-7. First differences of logarithms result in the equivalent of a series with a constant percentage random walk or trend from period t-1 to t. Stated another way, if a series is modeled validly using first differences of logarithms, this denotes that the ratio of Y_t/Y_{t-1} is a constant as shown below:

Nonlinear Drift/Random Walk $\ln \hat{Y}_t = \ln Y_{t-s} + e_t$ $e_t = \ln Y_t - \ln Y_{t-s}$

Nonlinear Seasonal Trend Model $\ln \hat{Y}_t = \ln Y_{t-s} + b + e_t$ $e_t = \ln Y_t - \ln Y_{t-s} - b$

Now the first relationship denotes that with a random walk model, first differences of logarithms achieve white noise residuals. Also, it can be shown that first differences of logarithms are nearly perfectly correlated to Y_t/Y_{t-1}, that is, this ratio yields a white noise residual. When first differences of logarithms yields a nonzero b, then this denotes that there is constant percentage change in Y_t from period t-1 to t equal to e^b-1. See also, page 212.

6-8. See pages 215 to 218.

6-9. To the extent that double moving averages can use two different moving averages to measure a random level and trend, they resemble Holt's two parameter exponential smoothing. Double moving averages can be an effective method for modeling trends.

6-10. Through an iterative search procedure such as a gradient search, different smoothing constants are tried iteratively until one is found that minimizes the sum of squared errors. See also, Tables 6-9 and 6-11, on pages 221 and 223 respectively.

6-11. Winters' three parameter exponential smoothing is an enhanced Holt's two parameter exponential smoothing where a third equation and smoothing constant are added to model the seasonality of the time series. Thus, Winters' model includes Holt's model, consequently, a nonseasonal Winters' model is the equivalent of Holt's model.

6-12. Classical decomposition and Winters' method are very similar in forecasting form, compare equations 5-4 and 6-23. They differ in how trends and seasonal indexes are estimated.

6-13. To start the iterative process of searching for optimal smoothing constants, some initial values of smoothed level, trend, and seasonal values must be estimated. See also, pages 228 to 229.

6-14. Just as we do not expect that cyclical variations will persist indefinitely, trends do not continuously increase or decrease. The dampening tendency of trends is modeled using dampening relationships. See also, pages 231 to 232.

6-15. See equations 6-29 to 6-32.

6-16. See Table 6-1 of page 208 to 209.

6-17. See Table 6-1 of page 208 to 209.

6-18. a. The trend is nonlinear. The seasonality is not pronounced because of the strong nonlinear trend.

b. A nonlinear semilog model is used to model this series. Log(Students) = LSTUD= f(time)

```
linreg lstud
#constant time
Dependent Variable LSTUD - Estimation by Least Squares
Usable Observations        9      Degrees of Freedom      7
Centered R**2       0.943718      R Bar **2    0.935678
Uncentered R**2     0.999804      T x R**2        8.998
Mean of Dependent Variable        6.2336994414
Std Error of Dependent Variable   0.3911956755
Standard Error of Estimate        0.0992140760
Sum of Squared Residuals          0.0689040301
Regression F(1,7)                    117.3745
Significance Level of F             0.00001259
Durbin-Watson Statistic             2.011087
Q(2-0)                              0.283102
Significance Level of Q            0.86801076
     Variable           Coeff        Std Error      T-Stat      Signif
*********************************************************************
1.  Constant        6.927531921    0.072077355     96.11246   0.00000000
2.  TIME           -0.138766496    0.012808482    -10.83395   0.00001259
```

The following are the fit, forecast, and error of part a) where the exponentiation of the logarithmic values yielded the Metric values of fit (MFIT) and forecast (MFORE) shown below.

```
ENTRY        STUDENTS            MFIT                MFORE               ERROR
  1:01   935.00000000000   887.81680831302   887.81680831302    47.18319168698
  1:02   858.00000000000   772.78349781514   772.78349781514    85.21650218486
  2:01   638.00000000000   672.65490910244   672.65490910244   -34.65490910244
  2:02   564.00000000000   585.49985606427   585.49985606427   -21.49985606427
  3:01   429.00000000000   509.63737395258   509.63737395258   -80.63737395258
  3:02   472.00000000000   443.60429851374   443.60429851374    28.39570148626
  4:01   356.00000000000   386.12704585158   386.12704585158   -30.12704585158
  4:02   344.00000000000   336.09704873824   336.09704873824     7.90295126176
  5:01   324.00000000000   292.54937561141   292.54937561141    31.45062438859
  5:02   NA                NA                254.64411988122    NA
  6:01   NA                NA                221.65020060139    NA
  6:02   NA                NA                192.93126206705    NA
  7:01   NA                NA                167.93340038399    NA
  7:02   NA                NA                146.17448029095    NA
  8:01   NA                NA                127.23483618788    NA
```

c. As shown by the following error measures, this model fits the data quite well; also shown is a graph of the actual, mfit, and mfore.

Series	Obs	Mean	Std Error	Minimum	Maximum
STUDENTS	9	546.6666667	224.3886138	324.0000000	935.0000000
HOURS	9	5684.0000000	1396.8153063	3828.0000000	7902.0000000
TIME	15	8.0000000	4.4721360	1.0000000	15.0000000
MFIT	9	542.9744682	203.5472166	292.5493756	887.8168083
MFORE	15	399.8225676	239.6312868	127.2348362	887.8168083
ERROR	9	3.6921984	50.3693367	-80.6373740	85.2165022
SERROR	9	2268.8057338	2686.9278303	62.4566386	7261.8522446

RSE = 2268.8057338**.5 = 47.63198
R-SQUARE = 1-2268.8057338/224.3886138**2 = 0.95494

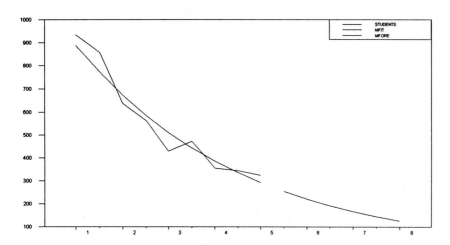

d. The annual and semester trends are not constant, with that in mind consider the following annual ratios of students/students(t-2) and students/students(t-1). The trend is not a constant number or constant percentage. As shown in the table of statistics, the average annual trend is about a .76-1.0 or a 24% decline, the average semester's trend is about one-half of the annual and equals .884-1.0 or 11.6% decline. However, these are not good representative numbers because as shown by the time series, R1 and R2 are both changing, thus the decline is decreasing back to no decline or possibly an increase.

```
set r1students 2 9 = students(t)/students(t-1)
set r2students 3 9 = students(t)/students(t-2)
print 1 9 students r1students r2students
ENTRY       STUDENTS          R1STUDENTS          R2STUDENTS
  1:01   935.00000000000        NA                  NA
  1:02   858.00000000000   0.9176470588235          NA
  2:01   638.00000000000   0.7435897435897     0.6823529411765
  2:02   564.00000000000   0.8840125391850     0.6573426573427
  3:01   429.00000000000   0.7606382978723     0.6724137931034
  3:02   472.00000000000   1.1002331002331     0.8368794326241
  4:01   356.00000000000   0.7542372881356     0.8298368298368
  4:02   344.00000000000   0.9662921348315     0.7288135593220
  5:01   324.00000000000   0.9418604651163     0.9101123595506
```

Series	Obs	Mean	Std Error	Minimum	Maximum
STUDENTS	9	546.6666667	224.3886138	324.0000000	935.0
TIME	15	8.0000000	4.4721360	1.0000000	15.00000
MFIT	9	542.9744682	203.5472166	292.5493756	887.81681
MFORE	15	399.8225676	239.6312868	127.2348362	887.81681
ERROR	9	3.6921984	50.3693367	-80.6373740	85.2165
SERROR	9	2268.8057338	2686.9278303	62.4566386	7261.8522
RSTUDENTS	7	0.7596788	0.0987692	0.6573427	0.9101
R2STUDENTS	7	0.7596788	0.0987692	0.6573427	0.9101
R1STUDENTS	8	0.8835638	0.1252305	0.7435897	1.10023

6-19. a. The trend is slightly nonlinear and seasonality is not pronounced because of the strong non-linear trend.

b. A nonlinear semilog model is used to model this series. Log(Hours) = LHOURS= f(time)

```
linreg lhours
#constant time
Dependent Variable LHOURS - Estimation by Least Squares
Semi-Annual Data From 1:01 To 5:01
Usable Observations        9        Degrees of Freedom      7
Centered R**2       0.918492        R Bar **2    0.906848
Uncentered R**2     0.999938        T x R**2        8.999
Mean of Dependent Variable        8.6177552661
Std Error of Dependent Variable 0.2517159201
Standard Error of Estimate        0.0768257966
Sum of Squared Residuals          0.0413154212
Regression F(1,7)                     78.8810
Significance Level of F           0.00004649
Durbin-Watson Statistic              2.523496
Q(2-0)                               1.111234
Significance Level of Q           0.57371816
    Variable           Coeff         Std Error       T-Stat     Signif
*******************************************************************
1.  Constant        9.058196245    0.055812647     162.29648   0.00000000
2.  TIME           -0.088088196    0.009918168      -8.88150   0.00004649
```

Following are the fit, forecast, and error of part a) where the exponentiation of the logarithmic values yielded the Metric fits, forecast, and errors shown below.

ENTRY	HOURS	MFIT	MFORE	ERROR
1:01	7902.0000000000	7864.4513076419	NA	37.5486923581
1:02	7275.0000000000	7201.3216701397	NA	73.6783298603
2:01	6212.0000000000	6594.1070480571	NA	-382.1070480571
2:02	6047.0000000000	6038.0926936698	NA	8.9073063302
3:01	5242.0000000000	5528.9614062439	NA	-286.9614062439
3:02	6047.0000000000	5062.7600109192	NA	984.2399890808
4:01	4578.0000000000	4635.8686640887	NA	-57.8686640887
4:02	4025.0000000000	4244.9727469460	NA	-219.9727469460
5:01	3828.0000000000	3887.0371289642	NA	-59.0371289642
5:02	NA	NA	3559.2826014763	NA
6:01	NA	NA	3259.1642983734	NA
6:02	NA	NA	2984.3519363666	NA
7:01	NA	NA	2732.7117213882	NA
7:02	NA	NA	2502.2897806431	NA
8:01	NA	NA	2291.2969916674	NA

c. As shown by the following error measures, this model fit the data quite well. Also, shown is a graph of the actual, mfit, and mfore.

Series	Obs	Mean	Std Error	Minimum	Maximum
STUDENTS	9	546.66667	224.38861	324.00000	935.00
HOURS	9	5684.00000	1396.81531	3828.00000	7902.00000
TIME	15	8.00000	4.47214	1.00000	15.00000
LHOURS	9	8.61776	0.25172	8.25010	8.97487
LFIT	9	8.61776	0.24124	8.26540	8.97011
LFORE	6	7.95709	0.16480	7.73687	8.17731
MFIT	9	5673.06363	1360.95846	3887.03713	7864.45131
MFORE	6	2888.18289	474.68054	2291.29699	3559.28260
ERROR	9	10.93637	396.57037	-382.10705	984.23999
SERROR	9	139913.43510	314791.12607	79.34011	968728.35611

RSE = 139913.43510**.5 = 374.05004

R^2= 1-139913.43510/1396.81531**2 = 0.92829

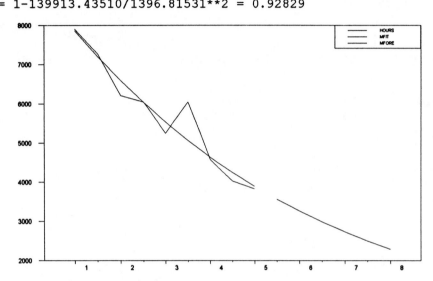

d. The annual and semester trends are not constant, with that in mind consider the following annual ratios of hours/hours(t-2) and students/students(t-1). The trend is not a constant number or constant percentage. As shown in the table of statistics, the average annual trend is about a 0.83376-1 or 16.62% decline, the average semester trend is about a 0.91947-1.0 or 8.1% decline. However, these are not good representative numbers because as shown by the time series, R1 and R2 are both changing, thus the decline is decreasing back to no decline or possibly an increase.

```
set r1hours 2 9 = hours(t)/hours(t-1)
set r2hours 3 9 = hours(t)/hours(t-2)
```

ENTRY	HOURS	R1HOURS	R2HOURS
1:01	7902.0000000000	NA	NA
1:02	7275.0000000000	0.9206529992407	NA
2:01	6212.0000000000	0.8538831615120	0.7861300936472
2:02	6047.0000000000	0.9734385061172	0.8312027491409
3:01	5242.0000000000	0.8668761369274	0.8438506117193
3:02	6047.0000000000	1.1535673407097	1.0000000000000
4:01	4578.0000000000	0.7570696212998	0.8733307897749
4:02	4025.0000000000	0.8792048929664	0.6656193153630
5:01	3828.0000000000	0.9510559006211	0.8361730013106

Series	Obs	Mean	Std Error	Minimum	Maximum
R1HOURS	8	0.91947	0.11574	0.75707	1.154
R2HOURS	7	0.83376	0.09988	0.66562	1.00

6-20. a. The trend is slightly nonlinear and positive. Seasonality is not pronounced at all because of the strong nonlinear trend; however, we would not expect there to be strong seasonality. The trend is positive as more full time students enter the undergraduate program.

ENTRY	STUDENTS	HOURS	SCRHRS
1:01	935.00000000000	7902.0000000000	8.451336898396
1:02	858.00000000000	7275.0000000000	8.479020979021
2:01	638.00000000000	6212.0000000000	9.736677115987
2:02	564.00000000000	6047.0000000000	10.721631205674
3:01	429.00000000000	5242.0000000000	12.219114219114
3:02	472.00000000000	6047.0000000000	12.811440677966
4:01	356.00000000000	4578.0000000000	12.859550561798
4:02	344.00000000000	4025.0000000000	11.700581395349
5:01	324.00000000000	3828.0000000000	11.814814814815

b. A nonlinear semilog model is used to model this series. Log(SCRHRS) = LSCRHRSS= f(time)

```
linreg lscrhrs
#constant ltime
Dependent Variable LSCRHRS - Estimation by Least Squares
Semi-Annual Data From 1:01 To 5:01
Usable Observations       9        Degrees of Freedom      7
Centered R**2      0.815101        R Bar **2    0.788687
Uncentered R**2    0.999213        T x R**2        8.993
Mean of Dependent Variable       2.3840558247
Std Error of Dependent Variable  0.1653188125
Standard Error of Estimate       0.0759950678
Sum of Squared Residuals         0.0404267523
Regression F(1,7)                      30.8585
Significance Level of F             0.00085536
Durbin-Watson Statistic               1.167373
Q(2-0)                                2.184263
Significance Level of Q             0.33550058
   Variable          Coeff        Std Error      T-Stat      Signif
*********************************************************************
1.  Constant     2.0888870879 0.0588646717      35.48626  0.00000000
2.  LTIME        0.2075108914 0.0373553914       5.55505  0.00085536
```

Following are the fit, forecast, and error of part a) where the exponentiation of the logarithmic values yielded the Metric values shown below.

ENTRY	SCRHRS	MFIT	MFORE	ERROR
1:01	8.451336898396	8.075922369360	NA	0.375414529036
1:02	8.479020979021	9.325221113726	NA	-0.846200134705
2:01	9.736677115987	10.143783990703	NA	-0.407106874716
2:02	10.721631205674	10.767779188889	NA	-0.046147983215
3:01	12.219114219114	11.278102160079	NA	0.941012059035
3:02	12.811440677966	11.712969035223	NA	1.098471642743
4:01	12.859550561798	12.093699777234	NA	0.765850784564
4:02	11.700581395349	12.433492701853	NA	-0.732911306504
5:01	11.814814814815	12.741127136194	NA	-0.926312321379
5:02	NA	NA	13.022759701721	NA
6:01	NA	NA	13.282886446703	NA
6:02	NA	NA	13.524897981448	NA
7:01	NA	NA	13.751418952850	NA
7:02	NA	NA	13.964525579592	NA
8:01	NA	NA	14.165890520564	NA

c. As shown by the following error measures, this model fits the data quite well; also shown is a graph of the actual, mfit, and mfore.

Series	Obs	Mean	Std Error	Minimum	Maximum
STUDENTS	9	546.6666667	224.3886138	324.0000000	935.0000000
HOURS	9	5684.0000000	1396.8153063	3828.0000000	7902.0000000
SCRHRS	9	10.9771298	1.7284389	8.4513369	12.8595506
LFIT	9	2.3840558	0.1492547	2.0888871	2.5448351
LFORE	6	2.6110344	0.0314546	2.5666986	2.6508370
MFIT	9	10.9524553	1.5407008	8.0759224	12.7411271
MFORE	6	13.6187299	0.4273971	13.0227597	14.1658905
ERROR	9	0.0246745	0.7979083	-0.9263123	1.0984716
SERROR	9	0.5665268	0.4000634	0.0021296	1.2066399

$RSE = 0.5665268**.5 = 0.75268$
$R^2 = 1 - 0.5665268/1.7284389**2 = 0.81037$

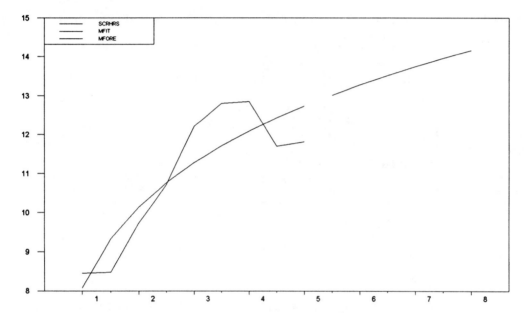

d. The annual and semester trends are not constant, with that in mind consider the following annual ratios of scrhrs/scrhrs(t-2) and scrhrs/scrhrs(t-1). The trend is not a constant number or constant percentage. As shown in the table of statistics, the average annual trend is about a 1.10727-1.0 or 10.7% increase, the average semester trend is about a 1.0455-1.0 or 4.6% increase. However, these are not good representative numbers because as shown by the time series, R1 and R2 are both changing, thus the increase is decreasing back to no increase or possibly a decrease.

```
set r1SCRHRS 2 9 = SCRHRS(t)/SCRHRS(t-1)
set r2SCRHRS 3 9 = SCRHRS(t)/SCRHRS(t-2)
```

ENTRY	HOURS	R1SCRHRS	R2SCRHRS
1:01	7902.0000000000	NA	NA
1:02	7275.0000000000	1.0032757043008	NA
2:01	6212.0000000000	1.1483256309989	1.1520872062071
2:02	6047.0000000000	1.1011591611751	1.2644892885867
3:01	5242.0000000000	1.1396693268696	1.2549573199927
3:02	6047.0000000000	1.0484754007721	1.1949152542373
4:01	4578.0000000000	1.0037552282402	1.0524126652063
4:02	4025.0000000000	0.9098748310931	0.9132916187539
5:01	3828.0000000000	1.0097630549804	0.9187579890944

Series	Obs	Mean	Std Error	Minimum	Maximum
R1SCRHRS	8	1.0455373	0.0808390	0.9098748	1.1483256
R2SCRHRS	7	1.1072730	0.1485449	0.9132916	1.2644893

6-21.   a. A nonlinear trend exists.

   b. We shall use a log-log model for this series.

```
linreg ldeaths
#constant ltime
Dependent Variable LDEATHS - Estimation by Least Squares
Usable Observations      8      Degrees of Freedom      6
Centered R**2     0.995674     R Bar **2    0.994953
Uncentered R**2   0.999906     T x R**2       7.999
Mean of Dependent Variable          8.6136535343
Std Error of Dependent Variable     1.3722589014
Standard Error of Estimate          0.0974853451
Sum of Squared Residuals            0.0570203550
Regression F(1,6)                    1381.0480
Significance Level of F             0.00000003
Durbin-Watson Statistic             1.293837
Q(2-0)                              3.283152
Significance Level of Q            0.19367452
      Variable       Coeff      Std Error    T-Stat     Signif
********************************************************************
1.  Constant     6.0331766037 0.0775211211    77.82623  0.00000000
2.  LTIME        1.9466844382 0.0523830972    37.16245  0.00000003
```

   Here is the fit and forecast using transformed values of the logarithmic fits and forecasts.

ENTRY	DEATHS	MFIT	MFORE	ERROR
1982:01	444.000000000	417.037690955	NA	26.962309
1983:01	1436.000000000	1607.628568798	NA	-171.628569
1984:01	3266.000000000	3539.808999423	NA	-273.808999
1985:01	6404.000000000	6197.208720626	NA	206.7912794
1986:01	10965.000000000	9568.620657595	NA	1396.3793424
1987:01	14612.000000000	13645.524610806	NA	966.4753892
1988:01	18248.000000000	18421.055482740	NA	-173.0554827
1989:01	21675.000000000	23889.470909138	NA	-2214.4709091
1990:01	NA	NA	30045.840038336	NA
1991:01	NA	NA	36885.845732348	NA
1992:01	NA	NA	44405.651030490	NA
1993:01	NA	NA	52601.804768137	NA
1994:01	NA	NA	61471.172418661	NA
1995:01	NA	NA	71010.883917116	NA
1996:01	NA	NA	81218.293335179	NA

Series	Obs	Mean	Std Error	Minimum	Maximum
DEATHS	8	9631.2500	8003.4483	444.0000	21675.0000
RDEATHS	7	1.8501	0.7297	1.1878	3.2342
LDEATHS	8	8.6137	1.3723	6.0958	9.9839
LTIME	15	1.8600	0.7820	0.0000	2.7081
TIME	15	8.0000	4.4721	1.0000	15.0000
LFIT	8	8.6137	1.3693	6.0332	10.0812
LFORE	7	10.8428	0.3573	10.3105	11.3049
MFIT	8	9660.7945	8407.8822	417.0377	23889.4709
MFORE	7	53948.4987	18469.3803	30045.8400	81218.2933
ERROR	8	-29.5445	1066.2829	-2214.4709	1396.3793
SERROR	8	995712.1108	1723792.9736	726.9661	4903881.4074

RSE=995712.1108**.5 = 997.85375 R^2 = 1-995712.1108/8003.4483**2 = 0.98446

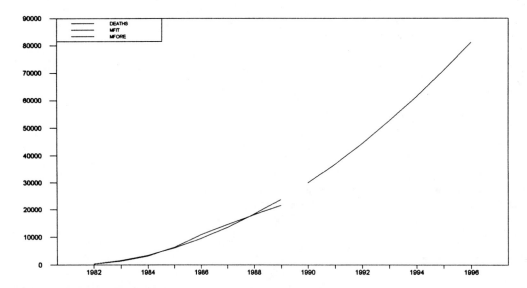

c. The trend or percentage growth is not constant as the ratios show below. This series can be modeled using S-growth curves developed in Chapter 15, until then, recognize that the trend will likely increase at a decreasing rate, despite the above graph and forecasts.

```
SET RDEATHS 2 8 = DEATHS(T)/DEATHS(T-1)
ENTRY          DATE            DEATHS         RDEATHS
   1:01   1982.0000000000    444.000000000       NA
   1:02   1983.0000000000   1436.000000000  3.2342342342342
   1:03   1984.0000000000   3266.000000000  2.2743732590529
   1:04   1985.0000000000   6404.000000000  1.9608083282303
   1:05   1986.0000000000  10965.000000000  1.7122111180512
   1:06   1987.0000000000  14612.000000000  1.3326037391701
   1:07   1988.0000000000  18248.000000000  1.2488365726800
   1:08   1989.0000000000  21675.000000000  1.1878014028935
```

6-22. a. There is a slight nonlinearity to the data. Let's model the series both linearly and nonlinearly.

```
SET TIME = T            SET STIME = T*T
Dependent Variable DOLLARS - Estimation by Least Squares
Usable Observations      7      Degrees of Freedom     5
Centered R**2      0.983517     R Bar **2     0.980221
Uncentered R**2    0.999597     T x R**2        6.997
Mean of Dependent Variable      1790.5714286
Std Error of Dependent Variable  306.2030139
Standard Error of Estimate        43.0640719
Sum of Squared Residuals        9272.5714286
Regression F(1,5)                298.3472
Significance Level of F            0.00001191
Durbin-Watson Statistic            0.921223
Q(1-0)                             0.685797
Significance Level of Q            0.40759752
   Variable          Coeff        Std Error      T-Stat      Signif
*******************************************************************
1.  Constant      1228.2857143    36.3957836    33.74802   0.00000043
2.  TIME           140.5714286     8.1383446    17.27273   0.00001191
```

```
LINREG DOLLARS
#CONSTANT TIME STIME
Dependent Variable DOLLARS - Estimation by Least Squares
Usable Observations      7     Degrees of Freedom      4
Centered R**2       0.998236     R Bar **2    0.997355
Uncentered R**2     0.999957     T x R**2     7.000
Mean of Dependent Variable     1790.5714286
Std Error of Dependent Variable  306.2030139
Standard Error of Estimate      15.7491496
Sum of Squared Residuals       992.14285714
Regression F(2,4)              1132.0337
Significance Level of F           0.00000311
Durbin-Watson Statistic           1.574689
Q(1-0)                            0.055298
Significance Level of Q           0.81408897
    Variable          Coeff        Std Error       T-Stat      Signif
*********************************************************************
1.  Constant      1347.4285714    24.5432771     54.90011   0.00000066
2.  TIME            61.1428571    14.0654900      4.34701   0.01218563
3.  STIME            9.9285714     1.7183731      5.77789   0.00445623
```

b. I have chosen the linear model because of the great concerns about increasing health care cost, thus, I believe that they will level out. Shown below are the actual, fitted, forecast, and RDOL, which is explained below. The fitted and forecast are those of the linear model which was chosen assuming there will be (or was) movement to reduce the increasing growth rate. Those more closely following this industry might not agree with the linear growth assumption. Finally, there is a graph of the fit and forecast following this data.

ENTRY	DOLLARS	FIT	FORE	RDOL
1983:01	1407.0000000000	1368.8571428571	NA	NA
1984:01	1518.0000000000	1509.4285714286	NA	1.078891258
1985:01	1638.0000000000	1650.0000000000	NA	1.079051383
1986:01	1749.0000000000	1790.5714285714	NA	1.067765568
1987:01	1887.0000000000	1931.1428571429	NA	1.078902230
1988:01	2061.0000000000	2071.7142857143	NA	1.092209857
1989:01	2274.0000000000	2212.2857142857	NA	1.103347889
1990:01	NA	NA	2352.8571428571	NA
1991:01	NA	NA	2493.4285714286	NA
1992:01	NA	NA	2634.0000000000	NA
1993:01	NA	NA	2774.5714285714	NA
1994:01	NA	NA	2915.1428571429	NA
1995:01	NA	NA	3055.7142857143	NA
1996:01	NA	NA	3196.2857142857	NA
1997:01	NA	NA	3336.8571428572	NA
1998:01	NA	NA	3477.4285714286	NA
1999:01	NA	NA	3618.0000000000	NA
2000:01	NA	NA	3758.5714285714	NA
2001:01	NA	NA	3899.1428571429	NA
2002:01	NA	NA	4039.7142857143	NA

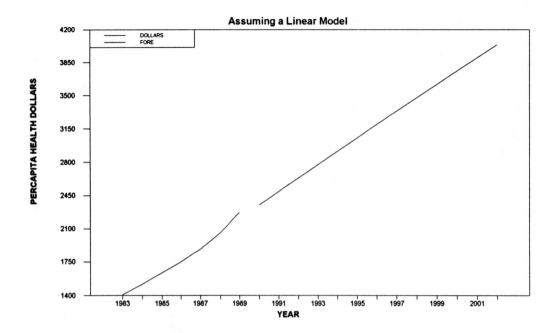

c. For percentage growth consider a semi-log relationship.

```
SET LDOL = LOG(DOLLARS)
LINREG LDOL
#CONSTANT TIME
Dependent Variable LDOL - Estimation by Least Squares
Usable Observations       7        Degrees of Freedom      5
Centered R**2       0.996259      R Bar **2    0.995511
Uncentered R**2     0.999998      T x R**2       7.000
Mean of Dependent Variable       7.4779115079
Std Error of Dependent Variable  0.1695379633
Standard Error of Estimate       0.0113587077
Sum of Squared Residuals         0.0006451012
Regression F(1,5)                   1331.6796
Significance Level of F            0.00000029
Durbin-Watson Statistic             1.050241
Q(1-0)                              0.585047
Significance Level of Q           0.44434086
    Variable          Coeff       Std Error      T-Stat     Signif
************************************************************************
1.  Constant      7.1645758824 0.0095998601     746.32086  0.00000000
2.  TIME          0.0783339064 0.0021465940      36.49219  0.00000029
```

%GROWTH = EXP(0.0783339064)-1 = 0.08148

This denotes that there is an annual increase of about 8.15%, however this is not reliable, because that increase is not constant. An alternative way of calculating the percentage growth is as follows:

```
set rdol 2 7 = dollars/dollars(t-1)
Statistics on Series RDOL
Observations     6
Sample Mean     1.08336136422      Variance                 0.000156
Standard Error  0.01248541182      SE of Sample Mean        0.005097
t-Statistic       212.54265        Signif Level (Mean=0)  0.00000000
```

6-23. This time series like several others, presents problems of extrapolating nonlinear function outside the area of experience. This series may or may not be best modeled using S-growth curves, but this must be left until chapter 15. The most easily defended model is a log-log model as defined below along with forecasts and a graph.

```
Set lcases = log(cases)  set ltime = log(time)
Dependent Variable LCASES - Estimation by Least Squares
Usable Observations        8        Degrees of Freedom      6
Centered R**2       0.991672      R Bar **2    0.990284
Uncentered R**2     0.999838      T x R**2       7.999
Mean of Dependent Variable       8.9869822140
Std Error of Dependent Variable 1.3546662559
Standard Error of Estimate       0.1335277012
Sum of Squared Residuals         0.1069778820
Regression F(1,6)                     714.4767
Significance Level of F             0.00000018
Durbin-Watson Statistic              1.309037
Q(2-0)                               1.141311
Significance Level of Q            0.56515492
    Variable        Coeff        Std Error      T-Stat      Signif
*****************************************************************
1.  Constant   6.4447122841 0.1061822891     60.69480   0.00000000
2.  LTIME      1.9178614820 0.0717502158     26.72970   0.00000018
```

The following graph illustrates the fit and the forecast after transforming them back to the original metric, thus, the term MFIT and MFORE are very descriptive.

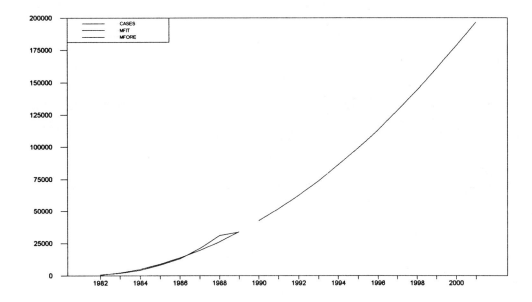

Here are the forecasts and fits of each year.

```
ENTRY          CASES            MFIT             ERROR            MFORE
 1982:01      744.000000000    629.365572414    114.634427586         NA
 1983:01     2117.000000000   2378.136705153   -261.136705153         NA
 1984:01     4445.000000000   5175.537493364   -730.537493364         NA
 1985:01     8249.000000000   8986.087635367   -737.087635367         NA
 1986:01    13166.000000000  13785.757376778   -619.757376778         NA
 1997:01    21070.000000000  19556.417162533   1513.582837467         NA
 1988:01    31001.000000000  26283.546300333   4717.453699667         NA
 1989:01    33722.000000000  33955.058519362   -233.058519362         NA
 1990:01         NA               NA               NA           42560.619010
 1991:01         NA               NA               NA           52091.2122668
 1992:01         NA               NA               NA           62538.8514442
 1993:01         NA               NA               NA           73896.3736086
 1994:01         NA               NA               NA           86157.2901610
 1995:01         NA               NA               NA           99315.6742887
 1996:01         NA               NA               NA          113366.0741948
 1997:01         NA               NA               NA          128303.4448179
 1998:01         NA               NA               NA          144123.0931563
 1999:01         NA               NA               NA          160820.6338207
 2000:01         NA               NA               NA          178391.9524258
 2001:01         NA               NA               NA          196833.1750854
```

The percentage growth is not constant as shown by the following ratios of CASE(t)/CASES(t-1)

```
set rcases 2 8 = cases/cases(t-1)
ENTRY          CASES            RCASES
 1982:01      744.000000000         NA
 1983:01     2117.000000000   2.8454301075269
 1984:01     4445.000000000   2.0996693434105
 1985:01     8249.000000000   1.8557930258718
 1986:01    13166.000000000   1.5960722511820
 1987:01    21070.000000000   1.6003341941364
 1988:01    31001.000000000   1.4713336497390
 1989:01    33722.000000000   1.0877713622141
```

6-24. This is not an easy time series to model, the relationship I choose is an inverse relationship between consumption and time. Thus, a new variable (itime) equal to 1/exp(time) is created. In addition, the first two years of data appear to be from another pattern, thus, they are dropped during the fitting process.

```
linreg pounds 3 7
#constant itime
Dependent Variable POUNDS - Estimation by Least Squares
Usable Observations        5       Degrees of Freedom       3
Centered R**2      0.943788       R Bar **2   0.925051
Uncentered R**2    0.999934       T x R**2        5.000
Mean of Dependent Variable        114.98000000
Std Error of Dependent Variable     4.40136343
Standard Error of Estimate          1.20495062
Sum of Squared Residuals          4.3557179589
Regression F(1,3)                     50.3698
Significance Level of F            0.00575459
Durbin-Watson Statistic              2.676725
Q(1-0)                               1.509009
Significance Level of Q           0.21929044
   Variable          Coeff        Std Error       T-Stat      Signif
*****************************************************************************
1.  Constant      102.63620451    1.82082156      56.36807   0.00001230
2.  ITIME          56.47488133    7.95737843       7.09717   0.00575459
```

```
ENTRY          POUNDS             FIT              FORE
 1983:01  120.30000000000         NA                NA
 1984:01  119.90000000000         NA                NA
 1985:01  120.90000000000  121.46116495253          NA
 1986:01  118.30000000000  116.75492484177          NA
 1987:01  113.30000000000  113.93118077532          NA
 1988:01  111.10000000000  112.04868473101          NA
 1989:01  111.30000000000  110.70404469937          NA
 1990:01        NA               NA         109.69556467563
 1991:01        NA               NA         108.91119132384
 1992:01        NA               NA         108.28369264240
 1993:01        NA               NA         107.77028463032
 1994:01        NA               NA         107.34244462025
 1995:01        NA               NA         106.98042615019
 1996:01        NA               NA         106.67012460443
 1997:01        NA               NA         106.40119659810
 1998:01        NA               NA         106.16588459256
 1999:01        NA               NA         105.95825635238
 2000:01        NA               NA         105.77369791667
 2001:01        NA               NA         105.60856668471
 2002:01        NA               NA         105.45994857595
```

The following illustrates that the percentage change is not constant, but has varied from a minus 5.2% to a plus .8%, the most recent being about a .18% increase.

```
set rpounds 2 7 = pounds(t)/pounds(t-1)
ENTRY          POUNDS           RPOUNDS
 1983:01  120.30000000000          NA
 1984:01  119.90000000000  0.9966749792186
 1985:01  120.90000000000  1.0083402835696
 1986:01  118.30000000000  0.9784946236559
 1987:01  113.30000000000  0.9577345731192
 1988:01  111.10000000000  0.9805825242718
 1989:01  111.30000000000  1.0018001800180
```

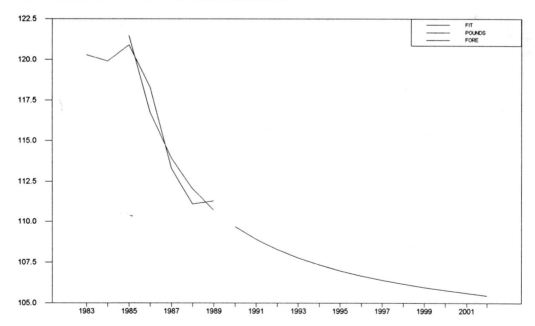

6-25. Both series seem to be random walks or have leveled out, thus, the previous actual seems to be a good way to forecast each.

```
set fitsat 2 8 = sat(t-1)         set fitact 2 8 = act(t-1)
set ressat = sat - fitsat         set resact = act - fitact
set foresat 9 20 = 1088           set foreact 9 20 = 18.6
```

ENTRY	SAT	FITSAT	FORESAT	RESSAT
1983:01	963.0000000000	NA	NA	NA
1984:01	965.0000000000	963.0000000000	NA	2.00000000
1985:01	977.0000000000	965.0000000000	NA	12.00000000
1986:01	1001.0000000000	977.0000000000	NA	24.00000000
1987:01	1080.0000000000	1001.0000000000	NA	79.00000000
1988:01	1134.0000000000	1080.0000000000	NA	54.00000000
1989:01	1088.0000000000	1134.0000000000	NA	-46.00000000
1990:01	NA	1088.0000000000	NA	NA
1991:01	NA	NA	1088.0000000000	NA
1992:01	NA	NA	1088.0000000000	NA
1993:01	NA	NA	1088.0000000000	NA
1994:01	NA	NA	1088.0000000000	NA
1995:01	NA	NA	1088.0000000000	NA
1996:01	NA	NA	1088.0000000000	NA
1997:01	NA	NA	1088.0000000000	NA
1998:01	NA	NA	1088.0000000000	NA
1999:01	NA	NA	1088.0000000000	NA
2000:01	NA	NA	1088.0000000000	NA
2001:01	NA	NA	1088.0000000000	NA
2002:01	NA	NA	1088.0000000000	NA

ENTRY	ACT	FITACT	FOREACT	RESACT
1983:01	18.000000000000	NA	NA	NA
1984:01	18.500000000000	18.000000000000	NA	0.50000000
1985:01	18.600000000000	18.500000000000	NA	0.10000000
1986:01	18.800000000000	18.600000000000	NA	0.20000000
1987:01	18.700000000000	18.800000000000	NA	-0.10000000
1988:01	18.800000000000	18.700000000000	NA	0.10000000
1989:01	18.600000000000	18.800000000000	NA	-0.20000000
1990:01	NA	18.600000000000	NA	NA
1991:01	NA	NA	18.600000000000	NA
1992:01	NA	NA	18.600000000000	NA
1993:01	NA	NA	18.600000000000	NA
1994:01	NA	NA	18.600000000000	NA
1995:01	NA	NA	18.600000000000	NA
1996:01	NA	NA	18.600000000000	NA
1997:01	NA	NA	18.600000000000	NA
1998:01	NA	NA	18.600000000000	NA
1999:01	NA	NA	18.600000000000	NA
2000:01	NA	NA	18.600000000000	NA
2001:01	NA	NA	18.600000000000	NA
2002:01	NA	NA	18.600000000000	NA

We see that both sets of residuals have means that are not statistically significantly different from zero as measured by the t-statistics in each table. Statistics on Series RESSAT

```
Annual Data From 1984:01 To 1989:01
Observations    6
Sample Mean     20.8333333333      Variance              1878.566667
Standard Error  43.3424349416      SE of Sample Mean       17.694475
t-Statistic      1.17739           Signif Level (Mean=0)  0.29202609
```

Statistics on Series RESACT
Annual Data From 1984:01 To 1989:01
Observations   6
Sample Mean   0.10000000000   Variance   0.060000
Standard Error 0.24494897428   SE of Sample Mean   0.100000
t-Statistic   1.00000   Signif Level (Mean=0) 0.36321747

6-26. The following illustrates a trend model using first differences. The model was fitted using RATS, however it is a simple deterministic trend model where:

Trend Model
$$\hat{Y}_t = Y_{t-1} + b + e_t \qquad e_t = Y_t - Y_{t-1} - b$$

Dependent Variable COST - Estimation by Box-Jenkins
Iterations Taken   2
1977/Year Data From 1:02 To 1:13
Usable Observations   12   Degrees of Freedom   11
Centered R**2   0.995572   R Bar **2   0.995572
Uncentered R**2   0.999805   T x R**2   11.998
Mean of Dependent Variable   100.55833333
Std Error of Dependent Variable 22.52705276
Standard Error of Estimate   1.49898956
Sum of Squared Residuals   24.716666667
Durbin-Watson Statistic   0.908294
Q(3-0)   5.972665
Significance Level of Q   0.11294775
   Variable   Coeff   Std Error   T-Stat   Signif
****
1. CONSTANT   6.0833333333 0.4327210125   14.05833   0.00000002

The statistics of the residuals of this model (res) are:

1977/Year Data From 1:02 To 1:13
Observations   12
Sample Mean   -0.0000000000   Variance   2.246970
Standard Error   1.4989895587   SE of Sample Mean   0.432721
t-Statistic   -0.00000   Signif Level (Mean=0) 1.00000000
Skewness   0.49276   Signif Level (Sk=0)   0.54248189
Kurtosis   -1.11728   Signif Level (Ku=0)   0.56561034

The following graph of actual, fitted, and forecast results.

ENTRY	COST	FIT	FORE	RES
1977:01	61.10000000000	NA	NA	NA
1978:01	65.20000000000	67.18333333333	NA	-1.9833333333
1979:01	70.20000000000	71.28333333333	NA	-1.0833333333
1980:01	77.20000000000	76.28333333333	NA	0.9166666667
1981:01	85.50000000000	83.28333333333	NA	2.2166666667
1982:01	94.00000000000	91.58333333333	NA	2.4166666667
1983:01	100.00000000000	100.08333333333	NA	-0.0833333333
1984:01	105.40000000000	106.08333333333	NA	-0.6833333333
1985:01	111.60000000000	111.48333333333	NA	0.1166666667
1986:01	116.30000000000	117.68333333333	NA	-1.3833333333
1987:01	120.90000000000	122.38333333333	NA	-1.4833333333
1988:01	126.30000000000	126.98333333333	NA	-0.6833333333
1989:01	134.10000000000	132.38333333333	132.38333333333	1.7166666667

ENTRY	COST	FIT	FORE	RES
1990:01	NA	NA	138.46666666667	NA
1991:01	NA	NA	144.55000000000	NA
1992:01	NA	NA	150.63333333333	NA
1993:01	NA	NA	156.71666666667	NA
1994:01	NA	NA	162.80000000000	NA
1995:01	NA	NA	168.88333333333	NA
1996:01	NA	NA	174.96666666667	NA
1997:01	NA	NA	181.05000000000	NA
1998:01	NA	NA	187.13333333333	NA
1999:01	NA	NA	193.21666666667	NA
2000:01	NA	NA	199.30000000000	NA
2001:01	NA	NA	205.38333333333	NA
ENTRY	COST	FIT	FORE	RES

The percent growth in this series is easily measured by the following ratio of COST(t)/COST(t-1).

ENTRY	COST	RCOST
1977:01	61.10000000000	NA
1978:01	65.20000000000	1.0671031096563
1979:01	70.20000000000	1.0766871165644
1980:01	77.20000000000	1.0997150997151
1981:01	85.50000000000	1.1075129533679
1982:01	94.00000000000	1.0994152046784
1983:01	100.00000000000	1.0638297872340
1984:01	105.40000000000	1.0540000000000
1985:01	111.60000000000	1.0588235294118
1986:01	116.30000000000	1.0421146953405
1987:01	120.90000000000	1.0395528804815
1988:01	126.30000000000	1.0446650124069
1989:01	134.10000000000	1.0617577197150

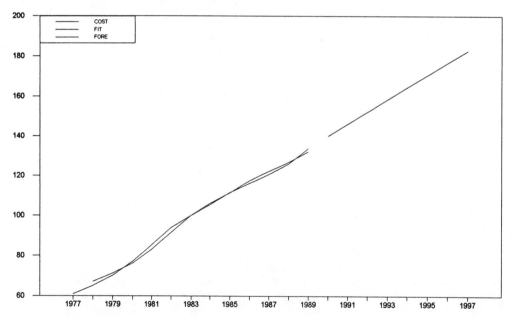

Because there is great concern about educational costs, there has been some movement to reduce these costs, however, I believe that momentum and the inherent lags in higher education will result in rather consistent growth in costs. As more students enter college in the late 1990s and early 2000s, per student cost will decline because of higher enrollments; this may result in a decrease in tuition per student.

6-27. We analyze this time series using logarithmic transformations of purchasing power (i.e., LPP).

```
set LPP = LOG(PP)
BOX(DEF=EQ1,DIFF=1,CONSTANT) LPP / RES
Dependent Variable LPP - Estimation by Box-Jenkins
Iterations Taken      2
Annual Data From 1981:01 To 1989:01
Usable Observations        9      Degrees of Freedom       8
Centered R**2      0.941114      R Bar **2    0.941114
Uncentered R**2    0.960414      T x R**2     8.644
Mean of Dependent Variable      -0.064904160
Std Error of Dependent Variable  0.098590518
Standard Error of Estimate       0.023924432
Sum of Squared Residuals         0.0045790277
Durbin-Watson Statistic            0.779861
Q(2-0)                             0.980113
Significance Level of Q            0.61259193
   Variable          Coeff        Std Error       T-Stat      Signif
***********************************************************************
1.  CONSTANT    -0.045463965  0.007974811    -5.70095   0.00045388


  ENTRY          PP              FIT              FORE
  1980:01   1.2150000000000        NA              NA
  1981:01   1.0980000000000   1.1609981526156     NA
  1982:01   1.0350000000000   1.0491983305119     NA
  1983:01   1.0030000000000   0.9889984263022     NA
  1984:01   0.9610000000000   0.9584206971798     NA
  1985:01   0.9280000000000   0.9182874277066     NA
  1986:01   0.9130000000000   0.8867541445492     NA
  1987:01   0.8800000000000   0.8724208340231     NA
  1988:01   0.8460000000000   0.8408875508656     NA
  1989:01   0.8070000000000   0.8083987136731     NA
  1990:01      NA                NA          0.7711321063052
  1991:01      NA                NA          0.7368583957554
  1992:01      NA                NA          0.7041080133427
  1993:01      NA                NA          0.6728132532779
  1994:01      NA                NA          0.6429094190213
  1995:01      NA                NA          0.6143346895333
  1996:01      NA                NA          0.5870299914698
  1997:01      NA                NA          0.5609388770587
  1998:01      NA                NA          0.5360074074037
  1999:01      NA                NA          0.5121840409744
  2000:01      NA                NA          0.4894195270539
  2001:01      NA                NA          0.4676668039206
```

The decline in the purchasing power of the US dollar is approximately 4.4% as calculated from the constant of the first differences model from above. That is:

```
%Growth =  exp(-0.045463965)-1 = -0.04445
```

Calculating this as a ratio of the original series, PP yields:

```
set rpp 2 10 = pp(t)/pp(t-1)          set pppd 2 10 = rpp - 1
ENTRY          PP                 RPP              PPPD
 1980:01   1.2150000000000        NA               NA
 1981:01   1.0980000000000   0.9037037037037  -0.096296296296
 1982:01   1.0350000000000   0.9426229508197  -0.057377049180
 1983:01   1.0030000000000   0.9690821256039  -0.030917874396
```

```
1984:01   0.9610000000000  0.9581256231306  -0.041874376869
1985:01   0.9280000000000  0.9656607700312  -0.034339229969
1986:01   0.9130000000000  0.9838362068966  -0.016163793103
1987:01   0.8800000000000  0.9638554216867  -0.036144578313
1988:01   0.8460000000000  0.9613636363636  -0.038636363636
1989:01   0.8070000000000  0.9539007092199  -0.046099290780
ENTRY            PP              RPP              PPPD
Statistics on Series PPPD
Annual Data From 1981:01 To 1989:01
Observations    9
Sample Mean     -0.0442054281      Variance              0.000507
Standard Error  0.0225061011       SE of Sample Mean     0.007502
t-Statistic     -5.89246           Signif Level (Mean=0) 0.00036483
Skewness        -1.65753           Signif Level (Sk=0)   0.09142250
Kurtosis         3.84027           Signif Level (Ku=0)   0.12986792
```

It is doubtful that this level of decline will persist, as we know, during the 1990s inflation has been below 3% as of November 1997. Thus, we are uncertain as to how accurate this projection will be into the year 2000, so far the decline has been too great.

6-28. By their nature, cyclical indexes are expected to rise and fall; thus, we do not think that this growth will continue indefinitely. There are at least three possible ways to model this series, assuming nonlinear, linear, or random walk behavior. We choose to model it with a linear trend and to generate intervals about this that include dampening and expansion at a rate of about 20 percent per year of the increase. Thus to dampen the trend, the index will increase with a constant of 5.0778 for 1990, .8*5.0778 for 1991, and so on. To expand the trend, the index will increase with a constant of 5.0778 for 1990, 1.2*5.0778 for 1991, and so on.

```
Dependent Variable INDEX - Estimation by Box-Jenkins
Iterations Taken     2
Annual Data From 1981:01 To 1989:01
Usable Observations      9       Degrees of Freedom      8
Centered R**2     0.907454       R Bar **2    0.907454
Uncentered R**2   0.998523       T x R**2        8.987
```

```
Mean of Dependent Variable        124.82222222
Std Error of Dependent Variable    16.86073677
Standard Error of Estimate          5.12927329
Sum of Squared Residuals          210.47555556
Durbin-Watson Statistic             2.348539
Q(2-0)                              2.980737
Significance Level of Q             0.22528957
     Variable          Coeff        Std Error      T-Stat      Signif
************************************************************************
1.  CONSTANT       5.0777777787 1.7097577617      2.96988  0.01787438

set fit = index - res
set dfore 11 22 = fore - ((1+.20)**(t-11))*5.0777777787
set ufore 11 22 = fore +((1+.20)**(t-11))*5.0777777787

ENTRY          INDEX            FORE          DFORE          UFORE
 1980:01   99.20000000000        NA            NA             NA
 1981:01  101.20000000000        NA            NA             NA
 1982:01  100.00000000000        NA            NA             NA
 1983:01  116.20000000000        NA            NA             NA
 1984:01  121.70000000000        NA            NA             NA
 1985:01  124.20000000000        NA            NA             NA
 1986:01  132.30000000000        NA            NA             NA
 1987:01  140.10000000000        NA            NA             NA
 1988:01  142.80000000000        NA            NA             NA
 1989:01  144.90000000000        NA            NA             NA
 1990:01       NA        149.97777777871 144.90000000001 155.05555556
 1991:01       NA        155.05555555743 148.96222222299 161.14888889
 1992:01       NA        160.13333333614 152.82133333481 167.44533334
 1993:01       NA        165.21111111485 156.43671111326 173.98551112
 1994:01       NA        170.28888889357 159.75960889165 180.81816890
 1995:01       NA        175.36666667228 162.73153066998 188.00180268
 1996:01       NA        180.44444445099 165.28228124824 195.60660765
 1997:01       NA        185.52222222970 167.32762638640 203.71681807
 1998:01       NA        190.60000000842 168.76648499645 212.43351502
 1999:01       NA        195.67777778713 169.47755977277 221.87799580
 2000:01       NA        200.75555556584 169.31529394861 232.19581718
 2001:01       NA        205.83333334456 168.10501940388 243.56164728
```

There is no objective rationale for using the trend dampening and expansion given here, only that these represent reasonable scenarios. Clearly, more objective information should be sought to confirm or deny the scenarios presented here.

6-29. Assuming that the number of miles driven increases and the new speed limit has some effect on accidents, then the following constant model is selected. The rationale is that accidents have decreased considerably because of technological improvements and lower speed limits, neither of the effects can remain indefinitely, thus, we choose a model that assumes that accidents will likely increase back towards the mean. This is very speculative, but we believe the trend will reverse, with the actual accidents being lower in the first two or three years, but higher thereafter, we hedge by using the mean. An alternative model might be a four year moving average.

```
Dependent Variable ACCIDENTS - Estimation by Box-Jenkins
Iterations Taken      2
Annual Data From 1984:01 To 1992:01
Usable Observations        9        Degrees of Freedom       8
Centered R**2       0.000000      R Bar **2   0.000000
Uncentered R**2    0.936264      T x R**2       8.426
Mean of Dependent Variable        15.866666667
Std Error of Dependent Variable   4.390899680
Standard Error of Estimate        4.390899680
Sum of Squared Residuals          154.24000000
Durbin-Watson Statistic             0.497407
Q(2-0)                              5.353114
Significance Level of Q             0.06879961
   Variable            Coeff        Std Error      T-Stat      Signif
************************************************************************
1.  CONSTANT       15.866666666  1.463633228      10.84060   0.00000463
ENTRY      ACCIDENTS          FIT              FORE
 1984:01  18.800000000000  15.866666666445      NA
 1985:01  19.300000000000  15.866666666445      NA
 1986:01  17.700000000000  15.866666666445      NA
 1987:01  20.800000000000  15.866666666445      NA
 1988:01  20.600000000000  15.866666666445      NA
 1989:01  12.800000000000  15.866666666445      NA
 1990:01  11.500000000000  15.866666666445      NA
 1991:01  11.300000000000  15.866666666445      NA
 1992:01  10.000000000000  15.866666666445      NA
 1993:01      NA              NA          15.866666666445
 1994:01      NA              NA          15.866666666445
 1995:01      NA              NA          15.866666666445
 1996:01      NA              NA          15.866666666445
 1997:01      NA              NA          15.866666666445
 1998:01      NA              NA          15.866666666445
 1999:01      NA              NA          15.866666666445
 2000:01      NA              NA          15.866666666445
 2001:01      NA              NA          15.866666666445
 2002:01      NA              NA          15.866666666445
 2003:01      NA              NA          15.866666666445
ENTRY      ACCIDENTS          FIT              FORE
```

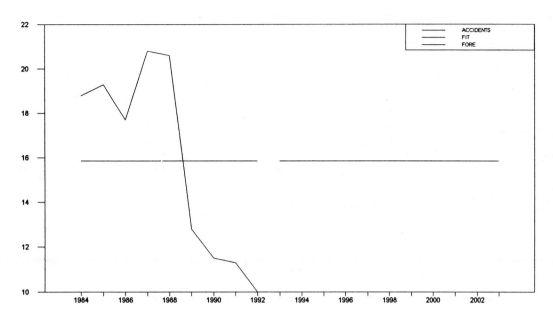

6-30. We choose the mean of this series as the forecast, not because it fits the past the best, but because it may fit the future the best. However, with several of these time series we are severely hampered in our analysis by not having more observations. We do not believe the historic rate of decline is operable in forecasting the future decline or growth.

```
set fit 1 8 = 3502
set fore 9 22 = 3502
set rships 2 8 = ships(t)/ships(t-1)
```

Series	Obs	Mean	Std Error	Minimum	Maximum
DATE	8	1986.50000000	2.44948974	1983.00000000	1990.000
SHIPS	8	3502.50000000	469.38957320	3003.00000000	4409.000
FIT	8	3502.00000000	0.00000000	3502.00000000	3502.000
FORE	14	3502.00000000	0.00000000	3502.00000000	3502.000
RSHIPS	7	0.95878737	0.08268539	0.89158539	1.108

ENTRY	SHIPS	RSHIPS
1983:01	4409.0000000000	NA
1984:01	3931.0000000000	0.8915853935133
1985:01	3597.0000000000	0.9150343424065
1986:01	3261.0000000000	0.9065888240200
1987:01	3003.0000000000	0.9208831646734
1988:01	3133.0000000000	1.0432900432900
1989:01	3471.0000000000	1.1078838174274
1990:01	3215.0000000000	0.9262460386056

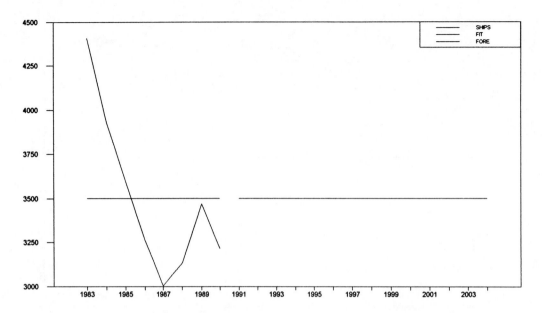

6-31. Percentage errors in President Lincoln's forecasts are shown in the following column.

```
set error = actual - lincoln        set perror = lincoln/actual
Series        Obs        Mean       Std Error      Minimum        Maximum
YEAR          20      1885.00          59.16       1790.00         1980.0
ACTUAL        20  77611197.55    70820827.85    3929827.00   226545805.0
LINCOLN        7 122394374.14    75619775.85   42323341.00   251680914.0
ERROR          7 -43912309.43    46385764.48 -128905868.00    -2504892.0
PERROR         7         1.44           0.36          1.06           2.05
```

The percent errors are listed below the following figure. Regarding the principle illustrated here, there are at lease two that relate to Lincoln's projections. First, he extrapolated outside his area of experience (i.e , the future). This is a tenuous proposition because the past behavior may not continue into the future. Second, population migration and other phenomena often follow a life cycle, better modeled using the S-growth curves of Chapter 15.

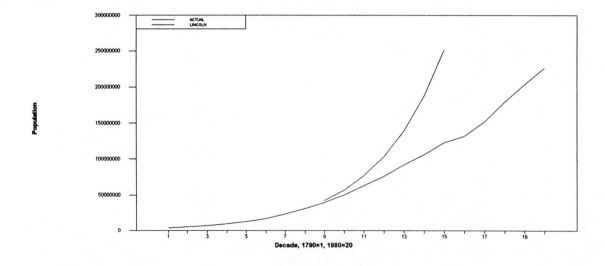

ENTRY	YEAR	ACTUAL	LINCOLN	PERROR
1	1790.0000000000	3929827.00000	NA	NA
2	1800.0000000000	5305937.00000	NA	NA
3	1810.0000000000	7239814.00000	NA	NA
4	1820.0000000000	9638131.00000	NA	NA
5	1830.0000000000	12866020.00000	NA	NA
6	1840.0000000000	17069020.00000	NA	NA
7	1850.0000000000	23191875.00000	NA	NA
8	1860.0000000000	31442790.00000	NA	NA
9	1870.0000000000	39818449.00000	42323341.00000	1.0629078244610
10	1880.0000000000	50155783.00000	56967216.00000	1.1358055361233
11	1890.0000000000	62947714.00000	76677872.00000	1.2181200416587
12	1900.0000000000	75994575.00000	103208415.00000	1.3581024040203
13	1910.0000000000	91972266.00000	138918526.00000	1.5104393100416
14	1920.0000000000	105710620.00000	186984335.00000	1.7688320719337
15	1930.0000000000	122775046.00000	251680914.00000	2.0499354078841
16	1940.0000000000	131669275.00000	NA	NA
17	1950.0000000000	151325798.00000	NA	NA
18	1960.0000000000	179323175.00000	NA	NA
19	1970.0000000000	203302031.00000	NA	NA
20	1980.0000000000	226545805.00000	NA	NA

6-32. Using Lincoln's method to forecast for 1940 to 1990: Obviously, the error for 1940 to 1980 is higher than through 1930. This extrapolation represents approximately a 500% error. While this is very notable, it is representative of the errors that can occur when nonlinear growth models are used incorrectly or when large secular shifts in trends occur.

```
set lincoln2 15 15 = lincoln
set lincoln2 16 20 = (1.346)*lincoln2(t-1)
set error2 16 20 = actual - lincoln2
set perror2 16 20 = lincoln2/actual
```

Series	Obs	Mean	Std Error	Minimum	Maximum
YEAR	20	1885.0	59.2	1790.0	1980.0
ACTUAL	20	77611197.6	70820827.8	3929827.0	226545805.0
LINCOLN	7	122394374.1	75619775.8	42323341.0	251680914.0
ERROR2	5	-490866690.6	269924107.8	-885379418.0	-207093235.2
PERROR2	5	3.3	1.0	2.6	4.9

ENTRY	YEAR	ACTUAL	LINCOLN2	PERROR2
16	1940.0000000000	131669275.00000	338762510.2440	2.5728288565727
17	1950.0000000000	151325798.00000	455974338.7884	3.0131963274922
18	1960.0000000000	179323175.00000	613741460.0092	3.4225440186926
19	1970.0000000000	203302031.00000	826096005.1724	4.0633927812182
20	1980.0000000000	226545805.00000	1111925222.9621	4.9081695552123

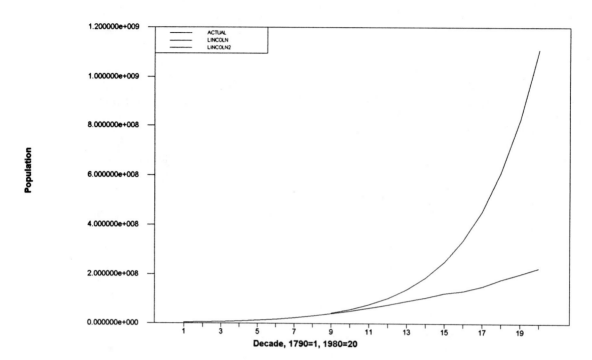

Population

Decade, 1790=1, 1980=20

6-33 and 6-34. Forecasting the population of the U.S. for 1940 to 1990: This is an extremely difficult problem to answer with objectivity (i.e., we know the right answer is). Originally, the actual population values were supposed to be at the very end of the chapter - some way they ended up in the problem. After trying not to cheat, I chose to use the last years percentage change (a 16.1 percent increase) as the percentage for the forecast.

```
set ractual = nactual/nactual(t-1)
ENTRY          YEAR              RACTUAL
   1:01   1790.0000000000         NA
   2:01   1800.0000000000   1.3501706309209
   3:01   1810.0000000000   1.3644741729877
   4:01   1820.0000000000   1.3312677646138
   5:01   1830.0000000000   1.3349081891500
   6:01   1840.0000000000   1.3266744494412
   7:01   1850.0000000000   1.3587115721934
   8:01   1860.0000000000   1.3557674832242
   9:01   1870.0000000000   1.2663777292028
  10:01   1880.0000000000   1.2596116689528
  11:01   1890.0000000000   1.2550439896432
  12:01   1900.0000000000   1.2072650485767
  13:01   1910.0000000000   1.2102477841346
  14:01   1920.0000000000   1.1493749648399
  15:01   1930.0000000000   1.1614258434961
```

The decline in percent growth during the 1920s and 1930 result social and economic influences such as the depression, World War I, and other social upheavals.

Series	Obs	Mean	Std Error	Minimum	Maximum
YEAR	20	1885.000	59.161	1790.000	1980.0
ACTUAL	20	77611197.550	70820827.846	3929827.000	226545805.000
LINCOLN	7	122394374.143	75619775.846	42323341.000	251680914.000
RACTUAL	13	1.290	0.070	1.149	1.364
TIME	20	10.500	5.916	1.000	20.000

```
set fore 15 15 = actual          set fore 16 20 = 1.1614258434961*fore(t-1)
set perror = fore/actual         set ractual 16 20 = actual(t)/actual(t-1)


ENTRY   YEAR  ACTUAL              FORE            PERROR           RACTUAL
16    1940  131669275.00000 142594111.36082 1.0829717970333 1.072443296
17    1950  151325798.00000 165612486.06482 1.0944101287001 1.149287091
18    1960  179323175.00000 192346621.32132 1.0726255617620 1.185013906
19    1970  203302031.00000 223396336.91174 1.0988396712659 1.133718667
20    1980  226545805.00000 259458279.03166 1.1452795562984 1.114331243
```

The decline in the growth during 1940 and 1950 are the result of World War II.

```
Statistics on Series RACTUAL
Annual Data From 16:01 To 20:01
Observations    5
Sample Mean     1.13095884076      Variance                    0.001742
Standard Error  0.04173139544      SE of Sample Mean           0.018663
t-Statistic        60.59948        Signif Level (Mean=0) 0.00000044
Skewness           -0.23411        Signif Level (Sk=0)   0.88229081
Kurtosis            0.42910        Signif Level (Ku=0)   0.93755590
```

6-35. TABLE6-7.DAT - The following illustrates the solution to this problem using RATS output. The BOX procedure is used to take first differences and to calculate the requested statistics.

```
Series      Obs      Mean        Std Error      Minimum        Maximum
DEMAND      30   82.600000000  13.387075599  63.000000000 105.000000000
```

The following illustrates the output from using first differences and the estimated trend constant. As shown below, the t-statistic for the mean of first differences yields a value of 2.826.

```
Dependent Variable DEMAND - Estimation by Box-Jenkins
Usable Observations       29       Degrees of Freedom     28
Centered R**2       0.955587       R Bar **2     0.955587
Uncentered R**2     0.998965       T x R**2       28.970
Mean of Dependent Variable        83.275862069
Std Error of Dependent Variable  13.092791233
Standard Error of Estimate        2.759220994
Sum of Squared Residuals        213.17241379
Durbin-Watson Statistic            2.894371
Q(7-0)                            27.000720
Significance Level of Q            0.00033318
   Variable        Coeff        Std Error      T-Stat      Signif
*******************************************************************
1.  CONSTANT    1.4482758615 0.5123744755     2.82660    0.00858590


Autocorrelations of Series RES
1: -0.44837 -0.36536  0.56139 -0.16860 -0.22277  0.24378 -0.0020694
```

The following is a graph of the first differences, as shown, the mean of first differences is nonzero, confirming that there is a trend in this data.

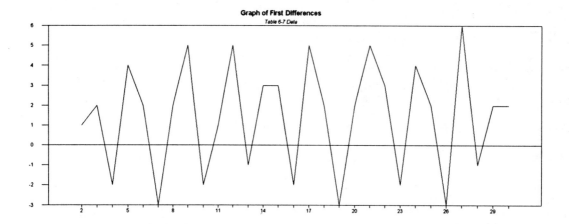

Graph of First Differences
Table 6-7 Data

6-36. SERIESB.DAT - a. The following output shows the statistics of the first differences of Series B for periods 1 to 36.

```
Dependent Variable PRICE - Estimation by Box-Jenkins
Usable Observations      35      Degrees of Freedom      35
Centered R**2      0.795317      R Bar **2      0.801165
Uncentered R**2    0.994116      T x R**2      34.794
Mean of Dependent Variable      672.45714286
Std Error of Dependent Variable 117.38256782
Standard Error of Estimate       52.34200717
Sum of Squared Residuals      95889.000000
Durbin-Watson Statistic           0.885628
Q(8-0)                           21.100270
Significance Level of Q           0.00688579
 NO ESTIMATED COEFFICIENTS
```

b. Because this is essentially a random walk model, the actual value of period 36 will be used to forecast periods 37 to 48. The actual for period 36 is 805.

```
set fore 37 48 = 805
set error = price - fore      set serror = error**2
set pe = error/price          set ape = abs(pe)
```

Series	Obs	Mean	Std Error	Minimum	Maximum
PRICE	48	750.25000	184.13888	426.00000	1159.00
RES	35	9.40000	52.24276	-87.00000	98.00

A table of forecasts and actuals for periods 37 to 48

Series	Obs	Mean	Std Error	Minimum	Maximum
PRICE	12	1000.000000	90.270301	864.000000	1159.00
FORE	12	805.000000	0.000000	805.000000	805.00
ERROR	12	195.000000	90.270301	59.000000	354.00
SERROR	12	45494.666667	37046.928744	3481.000000	125316.00
PE	12	0.188958	0.073304	0.068287	0.3054
APE	12	0.188958	0.073304	0.068287	0.3054

c. The following statistics result from the above table.

```
ME= 195                 MPE = 18.9
MAPE = 18.9             RSE = 45494.66667**.5 = 213.29479
R-SQUARE = 1-45494.66667/90.270301**2 = -4.58304
```

d. This model is valid, but nonetheless not a good forecast. A very negative R-square clearly illustrates inaccuracy of this forecast. However, good univariate forecasts with random walk series are nearly impossible.

6-37. SERIESC.DAT - a. As you may recall, series C has a strong trend. The following statistics show the fit of first differences with a trend constant. Because of the high negative autocorrelation in the residuals of this model, it appears that the mean of first differences is not statistically significantly different than zero, nonetheless, inclusion of a trend is warranted because of the strong trend in the graph. The trend is very significant when controlling for the high negative residual autocorrelation with ARIMA methods, a topic that is not discussed until Chapter 7.

```
Dependent Variable SALES - Estimation by Box-Jenkins
Usable Observations      35       Degrees of Freedom     34
Centered R**2        0.778145     R Bar **2     0.778145
Uncentered R**2      0.993582     T x R**2      34.775
Mean of Dependent Variable       769.31428571
Std Error of Dependent Variable 134.71686462
Standard Error of Estimate        63.45358921
Sum of Squared Residuals        136896.17143
Durbin-Watson Statistic             3.457014
Q(8-0)                             62.141401
Significance Level of Q            0.00000000
    Variable          Coeff        Std Error      T-Stat     Signif
********************************************************************
1.  CONSTANT       13.228571423 10.725614196     1.23336   0.22589957
```

b. The forecasts are made using a procedure in RATS software, these are shown in the following table:

```
ENTRY       SALES              FORE                ERROR               SERROR
 3:12    956.0000000000         NA                  NA                  NA
 4:01   1006.0000000000    969.2285714234    36.77142857664   1352.1379595671
 4:02    937.0000000000    982.4571428467   -45.45714284671   2066.3518357866
 4:03   1016.0000000000    995.6857142701    20.31428572993    412.6702047172
 4:04   1066.0000000000   1008.9142856934    57.08571430657   3258.7787778915
 4:05    999.0000000000   1022.1428571168   -23.14285711679    535.5918355280
 4:06   1026.0000000000   1035.3714285401    -9.37142854014     87.8236728830
 4:07   1020.0000000000   1048.5999999635   -28.59999996350    817.9599979122
 4:08   1038.0000000000   1061.8285713869   -23.82857138686    567.8008143386
 4:09   1119.0000000000   1075.0571428102    43.94285718979   1930.9746980019
 4:10   1030.0000000000   1088.2857142336   -58.28571423357   3397.2244837176
 4:11   1084.0000000000   1101.5142856569   -17.51428565693    306.7502020725
 4:12   1166.0000000000   1114.7428570803    51.25714291971   2627.2947002920
```

c. Calculate the ME, RSE, MPE, MAPE, and R-square.

```
set error = sales - fore        set serror = error**2
set pe = error/sales            set ape = abs(pe)
```

Table of Statistics for periods 37 to 48:

Series	Obs	Mean	Std Error	Minimum	Maximum
SALES	12	1042.2500000	59.8408875	937.0000000	1166.0
RES	0				
FORE	12	1041.9857143	47.6962926	969.2285714	1114.74
ERROR	12	0.2642857	39.7269327	-58.2857142	57.09

```
SERROR            12    1446.7799319   1180.2370824      87.8236729   3397.225
PE                12      -0.0009356      0.0379207      -0.0565881      0.054
APE               12       0.0331568      0.0154796       0.0091339      0.057
RSE = 1446.7799319**.5 = 38.03656
R-SQUARE 1-1446.7799319/59.8408875**2 = 0.59598
```

d. This is a reasonably good forecast as shown in the following graph. As mentioned, the t-test on the trend coefficient for this time series is somewhat misleading because of the high degree of negative correlation in the residuals.

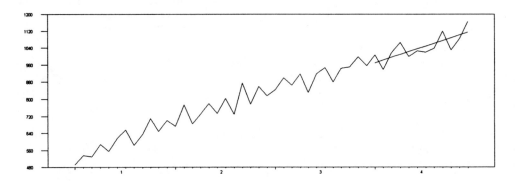

6-38. SERIESD.DAT - a. The fit of a seasonally differenced model ($Y_t = Y_{t-12} + e_t$) is shown below for periods 13 to 36.

```
Dependent Variable SALES - Estimation by Box-Jenkins
Monthly Data From 2:01 To 3:12
Usable Observations      24      Degrees of Freedom      24
Centered R**2       0.101245      R Bar**2      0.138693
Uncentered R**2     0.979916      T x R**2      23.518
Mean of Dependent Variable        621.00000000
Std Error of Dependent Variable    95.90665752
Standard Error of Estimate         89.00772438
Sum of Squared Residuals       190137.00000
Durbin-Watson Statistic             0.335022
Q(6-0)                             49.663540
Significance Level of Q             0.00000001
 NO ESTIMATED COEFFICIENTS
```

b. The forecasts of seasonal first differences are shown below in the following table and figure at the end of this problem.

```
ENTRY        SALES              FORE
 3:01    463.00000000000       NA
 3:02    497.00000000000       NA
 3:03    564.00000000000       NA
 3:04    582.00000000000       NA
 3:05    633.00000000000       NA
 3:06    686.00000000000       NA
 3:07    676.00000000000       NA
 3:08    657.00000000000       NA
 3:09    602.00000000000       NA
 3:10    534.00000000000       NA
 3:11    499.00000000000       NA
 3:12    472.00000000000       NA
 4:01    459.00000000000  463.00000000000
```

```
4:02    519.00000000000    497.00000000000
4:03    552.00000000000    564.00000000000
4:04    589.00000000000    582.00000000000
4:05    653.00000000000    633.00000000000
4:06    684.00000000000    686.00000000000
4:07    766.00000000000    676.00000000000
4:08    678.00000000000    657.00000000000
4:09    649.00000000000    602.00000000000
4:10    582.00000000000    534.00000000000
4:11    537.00000000000    499.00000000000
4:12    475.00000000000    472.00000000000
ENTRY        SALES             FORE
```

c. The error statistics are shown in the following table.

```
set error = sales - fore       set serror = error**2
set pe = error/sales      set ape = abs(pe)
Series     Obs       Mean        Std Error     Minimum        Maximum
SALES       12    595.2500000    92.6480388   459.0000000    766.0000000
FORE        12    572.0833333    79.8298854   463.0000000    686.0000000
ERROR       12     23.1666667    28.8627893   -12.0000000     90.0000000
SERROR      12  1300.3333333   2300.2975829     4.0000000   8100.0000000
PE          12      0.0359970     0.0423640    -0.0217391      0.1174935
APE         12      0.0415599     0.0363874     0.0029240      0.1174935
RSE = 1300.3333333**.5 = 36.06013
R-SQUARE = 1-1300.3333333/92.6480388**2 = 0.84851
```

d. This is a reasonably good forecast. While we may be disappointed in the R-square of the fit, the R-square of the forecast is quite good.

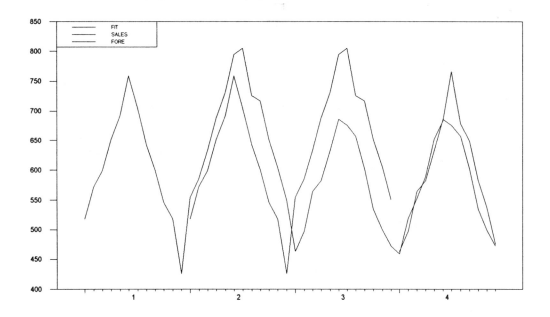

6-39. SERIESF.DAT -

Series	Obs	Mean	Std Error	Minimum	Maximum
SALES	48	827.43750000	130.96904072	546.00000000	1124.00000000

a. Seasonal differences with a trend parameter is the appropriate model. The following is RATS output of this model.

```
box(def=eq1,sdiff=1,constant) sales 13 36 res
Dependent Variable SALES - Estimation by Box-Jenkins
Iterations Taken     2
Monthly Data From 2:01 To 3:12
Usable Observations     24      Degrees of Freedom     23
Centered R**2      0.731005     R Bar **2    0.731005
Uncentered R**2    0.996744     T x R**2       23.922
Mean of Dependent Variable      831.08333333
Std Error of Dependent Variable  93.97821980
Standard Error of Estimate      48.74153587
Sum of Squared Residuals        54641.958333
Durbin-Watson Statistic          0.906410
Q(6-0)                          17.576051
Significance Level of Q          0.00738378
   Variable            Coeff       Std Error       T-Stat      Signif
**********************************************************************
1.  CONSTANT        83.541666667  9.949324372      8.39672   0.00000002
```

b. The following RATS command forecasts the 12 out-of-sample periods, 37 to 48.

```
fore 1 12 37
#eq1 fore
```

c. The ME RSE MPE MAPE R^2 are calculated by these RATS commands for both fit and forecast.

```
set fit = sales - res          set fitpe = res/sales
set fitape = abs(fitpe)        set error = sales - fore
set serror = error**2          set pe = error/sales
set ape = abs(pe)
```

Table of Fits for periods 13 to 24.

Series	Obs	Mean	Std Error	Minimum	Maximum
SALES	48	827.4375000	130.9690407	546.0000000	1124.0000000
RES	24	0.0000000	48.7415359	-100.5416667	60.4583333
FIT	24	831.0833333	108.2513095	629.5416667	1051.5416667
FITPE	24	0.0003244	0.0584196	-0.1192665	0.0782126
FITAPE	24	0.0443602	0.0368724	0.0005197	0.1192665

Table of Forecasts for periods 37 to 48.

Series	Obs	Mean	Std Error	Minimum	Maximum
SALES	12	951.0833333	103.4412071	787.0000000	1124.0000000
FORE	12	947.1250000	77.8255139	829.5416667	1062.5416667
ERROR	12	3.9583333	35.2819810	-86.5416667	61.4583333
SERROR	12	1156.7517361	2262.1837785	0.2100694	7489.4600694
PE	12	0.0011016	0.0402003	-0.1099640	0.0546782
APE	12	0.0242885	0.0312062	0.0005348	0.1099640

```
RSE = 1156.7517361**.5 = 34.01105
R-square =  1-1156.7517361/103.4412071**2 = 0.89189
```

ENTRY	SALES	FORE	ERROR
4:01	857.0000000000	856.5416666667	0.45833333333
4:02	876.0000000000	901.5416666667	-25.54166666667
4:03	959.0000000000	954.5416666667	4.45833333333
4:04	981.0000000000	965.5416666667	15.45833333333

```
4:05   1051.0000000000  1042.5416666667     8.45833333333
4:06   1124.0000000000  1062.5416666667    61.45833333333
4:07   1073.0000000000  1038.5416666667    34.45833333333
4:08   1020.0000000000  1008.5416666667    11.45833333333
4:09    933.0000000000   926.5416666667     6.45833333333
4:10    787.0000000000   873.5416666667   -86.54166666667
4:11    830.0000000000   829.5416666667     0.45833333333
4:12    922.0000000000   905.5416666667    16.45833333333
```

d. As shown above and by the graph below, this model is quite valid, all error statistics of the 12-period forecasts are very good in comparison to the fitted statistics. This is an excellent example for using a simple seasonal trend model.

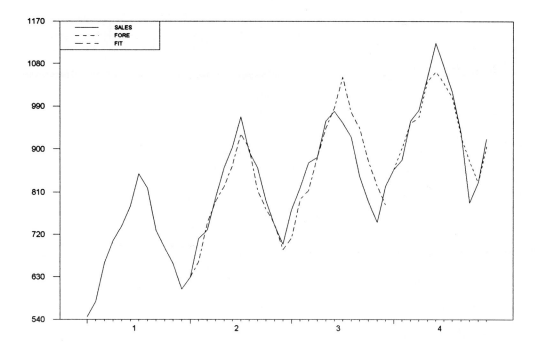

6-40   SERIESC.DAT - The following is output from using ForecastPro for Windows™ (FCP) where initially, we allow FCP to automatically select the model based on in-sample and out-of-sample forecasts for the first 36 observations. As shown below, it chose Winters' method, which yielded a very good fit and reasonable forecasts. Then I forced FCP to fit a Holt's trend adjusted exponential smoothing. Holt's did not fit the data as well, however, it did forecast the data better as shown by the rolling forecasts of the 12 observations that were withheld. This data was generated by the author to illustrate a trending series, not a seasonal series - it trends, but contains no seasonality. Now FCP is an excellent product, however, it did choose a more complex model in this case, even though there is little difference in the forecasts, Holt's, I believe, is the better method.

```
Forecast Pro for Windows Standard Edition Version 2.00
Oct 1997
FORECAST PRO OUTPUT
Expert data exploration of dependent variable DEMAND
----------------------------------------------------------------
Length 36  Minimum 493.0  Maximum 997.0
Mean 761.6 Standard deviation 138.6
Classical decomposition (multiplicative)
```

Trend-cycle: 82.14%   Seasonal: 6.96%   Irregular: 10.90%
There are no strongly significant regressors, so I will choose
a univariate method.
Exponential smoothing outperforms Box-Jenkins by 21.8 to 49.3
out-of-sample (MAD). I tried 21 forecasts up to a maximum horizon 6.
Series is trended and seasonal.
Recommended model: Exponential smoothing
Forecast Model for DEMAND
Automatic model selection
Multiplicative Winters: Linear trend, Multiplicative seasonality
Confidence limits proportional to indexes

Component	Smoothing Weight	Final Value
Level	0.08131	973.40
Trend	0.26222	10.193
Seasonal	0.19237	0.99764

Seasonal Indexes

January - March	0.97764	1.03029	0.97490
April - June	1.01398	0.97951	1.00033
July - September	1.03197	0.95442	1.02017
October - December	1.00909	1.01330	0.99764

Standard Diagnostics

Sample size 36	Number of parameters 3
Mean 761.6	Standard deviation 140.5
R-square 0.9482	Adjusted R-square 0.945
Durbin-Watson 2.876	** Ljung-Box(18)=44.89 P=0.9996
Forecast error 32.95	BIC 36.63 (Best so far)
MAPE 0.03618	RMSE 31.55
MAD 26.49	

Rolling simulation results

H	N	MAD	Cumulative Average	MAPE	Cumulative Average
1	12	43.2	43.2	0.042	0.042
2	11	42.3	42.8	0.041	0.041
3	10	33.2	39.9	0.031	0.038
4	9	33.9	38.6	0.032	0.037
5	8	35.7	38.1	0.033	0.036
6	7	43.7	38.8	0.041	0.037
7	6	45.3	39.4	0.042	0.037
8	5	34.3	39.0	0.031	0.037
9	4	44.2	39.3	0.040	0.037
10	3	57.3	40.1	0.052	0.038
11	2	36.9	40.0	0.032	0.038
12	1	72.9	40.4	0.062	0.038

Forecasts of DEMAND from base period 03-12

Period	Lower 2.5	Forecast	Upper 97.5	Actual
04-01	891.3	961.6	1031.9	1006.0
04-02	949.4	1023.9	1098.3	937.0
04-03	907.8	978.8	1049.8	1016.0
04-04	953.8	1028.4	1102.9	1066.0
04-05	930.4	1003.4	1076.4	999.0
04-06	959.1	1034.9	1110.7	1026.0
04-07	998.5	1078.2	1157.8	1020.0
04-08	931.5	1006.9	1082.3	1038.0
04-09	1004.0	1086.6	1169.3	1119.0

```
04-10          1001.0          1169.2          1030.0
               1085.1
04-11          1012.8          1187.1          1084.0
               1100.0
04-12          1004.4          1181.9          1166.0
               1093.1
```

Forecast Model for DEMAND
Holt exponential smoothing: Linear trend, No seasonality

Component	Smoothing Weight	Final Value
Level	0.06520	974.24
Trend	0.35872	9.7700

Standard Diagnostics

Sample size 36	Number of parameters 2
Mean 761.6	Standard deviation 140.5
R-square 0.929	Adjusted R-square 0.9269
Durbin-Watson 3.021	** Ljung-Box(18)=57.82 P=1
Forecast error 37.99	BIC 40.78
MAPE 0.04185	RMSE 36.92
MAD 30.79	

Rolling simulation results

H	N	MAD	Cumulative Average	MAPE	Cumulative Average
1	12	35.3	35.3	0.034	0.034
2	11	34.9	35.1	0.033	0.033
3	10	30.3	33.7	0.028	0.032
4	9	35.4	34.0	0.033	0.032
5	8	29.6	33.3	0.027	0.031
6	7	32.8	33.3	0.030	0.031
7	6	39.6	33.9	0.036	0.032
8	5	31.5	33.7	0.028	0.031
9	4	50.2	34.6	0.045	0.032
10	3	46.1	35.1	0.041	0.033
11	2	32.5	35.0	0.028	0.032
12	1	74.5	35.5	0.064	0.033

Forecasts of DEMAND from base period 03-12

Period	Lower 2.5	Holt's Forecast	Upper 97.5	Actual	Winters Forecast
04-01	904.1	+984.0	1063.9	1006.0	961.6
04-02	913.5	+993.8	1074.0	937.0	1023.9
04-03	922.8	+1003.5	1084.3	1016.0	978.8
04-04	931.9	1013.3	1094.8	1066.0	+1028.4
04-05	940.6	1023.1	1105.5	999.0	+1003.4
04-06	949.1	+1032.9	1116.6	1026.0	1034.9
04-07	957.3	+1042.6	1127.9	1020.0	1078.2
04-08	965.1	+1052.4	1139.6	1038.0	1006.9
04-09	972.6	1062.2	1151.7	1119.0	+1086.6
04-10	979.7	+1071.9	1164.2	1030.0	1085.1
04-11	986.4	+1081.7	1177.0	1084.0	1100.0
04-12	992.8	1091.5	1190.2	1166.0	+1093.1

In the above forecast table for Holt's method, we have included the forecasts of Winters' method in the last column for comparison purposes. As shown by the out-of-sample MAD and MAPE, Holt's method is better. Also, as shown, Holt's method outperformed Winters' 8 out of 12 times. Thus, Holt's method is the better of the two methods. This is an interesting example of overfitting to the past data and having the forecast suffer, albeit not by an extraordinary amount.

Answers to the original questions:

a. Holt's method is the better method.

b. Forecasts are shown above.

c. In and out of sample values are shown above, however, R^2 and RSE are not shown for both fit and forecast. The RMSE is the RSE unadjusted for degrees of freedom loss, other statistics are shown in the previous table.

d. The model is quite valid based on in and out-of-sample statistics.

6-41.   SERIESD.DAT - The following is output from using ForecastPro for Windows^{tm} (FCP) where initially, we allow FCP to automatically select the model based on in-sample and out-of-sample forecasts for the first 36 observations. As shown below, it chose Winters' method with a trend in it, this yielded a very good fit and reasonable forecasts. Then I forced FCP to fit Winters' without a trend. The trendless model did fit and forecast the data better as shown by the rolling forecasts of the 12 observations that were withheld. Now this data was generated by the author to illustrate a trendless seasonal series. Now FCP is an excellent product, however, it did choose a more complex model in this case, even though there is little difference in the forecasts, the trendless solution is, I believe, the better method.

```
Expert data exploration of dependent variable SALES
-------------------------------------------------------------------
Length 36  Minimum 426.0  Maximum 805.0
Mean 614.8 Standard deviation 92.9
Classical decomposition (multiplicative)
    Trend-cycle: 9.07%  Seasonal: 78.84%  Irregular: 12.09%
There are no strongly significant regressors, so I will choose
a univariate method.
Box-Jenkins outperforms exponential smoothing by 25.4 to 106.6
out-of-sample (MAD). I tried 21 forecasts up to a maximum horizon 6.
Series is trended and seasonal.
Recommended model: Box-Jenkins


Forecast Model for SALES
Automatic model selection
Multiplicative Winters: Linear trend, Multiplicative seasonality
Confidence limits proportional to indexes
                     Smoothing    Final
Component            Weight       Value
-----------------------------------------
Level                0.27713      559.08
Trend                0.00818      -1.3479
Seasonal             0.71139      0.83409
Seasonal Indexes
----------------------------------------------------------
January - March      0.79034    0.86684    0.97060
April - June         1.02738    1.11327    1.21595
July - September     1.20554    1.14083    1.07020
October - December   0.96632    0.91151    0.83409
Standard Diagnostics
----------------------------------------------------------
Sample size 36              Number of parameters 3
Mean 614.8                  Standard deviation 94.26
R-square 0.7412             Adjusted R-square 0.7256
Durbin-Watson 0.9509        ** Ljung-Box(18)=62.48 P=1
```

Forecast error 49.38   BIC 54.89 (Best so far)
MAPE 0.05968   RMSE 47.28
MAD 34.63
Rolling simulation results

H	N	MAD	Cumulative Average	MAPE	Cumulative Average
1	12	17.3	17.3	0.028	0.028
2	11	19.4	18.3	0.031	0.029
3	10	21.5	19.3	0.033	0.030
4	9	27.0	20.9	0.041	0.033
5	8	31.6	22.6	0.048	0.035
6	7	33.0	23.9	0.049	0.037
7	6	41.3	25.6	0.061	0.039
8	5	34.3	26.2	0.055	0.040
9	4	35.2	26.7	0.059	0.041
10	3	31.9	26.9	0.057	0.042
11	2	29.0	27.0	0.056	0.042
12	1	22.2	26.9	0.047	0.042

Forecasts of SALES from base period 03-12

Period	Lower 2.5	Forecast	Upper 97.5	Actual
04-01	347.2	440.8	534.4	459.0
04-02	375.7	482.3	588.9	519.0
04-03	415.1	538.7	662.3	552.0
04-04	433.5	568.8	704.2	589.0
04-05	463.5	614.9	766.3	653.0
04-06	499.5	670.0	840.5	684.0
04-07	488.5	662.6	836.7	766.0
04-08	456.1	625.5	794.9	678.0
04-09	422.1	585.3	748.6	649.0
04-10	375.9	527.2	678.5	582.0
04-11	349.7	496.1	642.4	537.0
04-12	315.6	452.8	590.0	475.0

Forecast Model for SALES
Exponential smoothing: No trend, Additive seasonality

Component	Smoothing Weight	Final Value
Level	0.29059	568.21
Seasonal	0.83807	-100.40

Seasonal Indexes

January - March	-144.92	-91.149	-23.570
April - June	9.8526	63.353	124.72
July - September	120.89	84.254	38.809
October - December	-24.155	-57.692	-100.40

Standard Diagnostics

Sample size 36   Number of parameters 2
Mean 614.8   Standard deviation 94.26
R-square 0.7398   Adjusted R-square 0.7322
Durbin-Watson 0.9091   ** Ljung-Box(18)=69.21 P=1
Forecast error 48.78   BIC 52.37 (Best so far)
MAPE 0.05966   RMSE 47.41
MAD 34.69

```
Rolling simulation results
                        Cumulative         Cumulative
  H   N       MAD       Average    MAPE     Average
-------------------------------------------------------------------
  1  12      19.6       19.6      0.033     0.033
  2  11      18.2       18.9      0.030     0.031
  3  10      16.0       18.0      0.024     0.029
  4   9      21.2       18.7      0.033     0.030
  5   8      23.4       19.5      0.037     0.031
  6   7      19.7       19.5      0.029     0.031
  7   6      25.9       20.1      0.039     0.032
  8   5      18.4       20.0      0.030     0.032
  9   4      21.2       20.0      0.036     0.032
 10   3      22.1       20.1      0.040     0.032
 11   2      14.9       20.0      0.028     0.032
 12   1       7.2       19.8      0.015     0.032
Forecasts of SALES from base period 03-12
  Period     Lower 2.5      Forecast     Upper 97.5        Actual
  04-01        320.7         423.3         525.9           459.0
  04-02        370.2         477.1         584.0           519.0
  04-03        433.7        +544.6         655.6           552.0
  04-04        463.2        +578.1         693.0           589.0
  04-05        512.8        +631.6         750.3           653.0
  04-06        570.5        +692.9         815.3           684.0
  04-07        563.1        +689.1         815.1           766.0
  04-08        523.0        +652.5         781.9           678.0
  04-09        474.2        +607.0         739.9           649.0
  04-10        407.9        +544.1         680.2           582.0
  04-11        371.1        +510.5         649.9           537.0
  04-12        325.3        +467.8         610.4           475.0
+ means trendless forecast better than Trending forecast.
```

In the above forecast table for trendless Winters' method, we have included a positive sign when the forecasts of trendless Winters' method outperformed the trend adjusted Winters' method. As shown by the out-sample MAD and MAPE, the trendless method is better. Also, as shown, the trendless method outperformed the trending method 10 out of 12 times. Thus, the trendless method is the better of the two methods. This is an interesting example of overfitting to the past data and having the forecast suffer, albeit not by an extraordinary amount.

Answer to the original questions:

a. Trendless Winters' method is the better method.

b. Forecasts are shown above.

c. In- and out-of-sample values are shown above, however, R^2 and RSE are not shown for both fit and forecast. The RMSE is the RSE unadjusted for degrees of freedom loss, other statistics are shown in the previous table.

d. The model is quite valid based on in- and out-of-sample statistics.

6-42. RETAIL.DAT - The following is output from using ForecastPro for Windows[tm] (FCP) where initially, we allow FCP to automatically select the model based on in-sample and out-of-sample forecasts for all but the last 12 observations. As shown below, it chose Winters' method with a trend in it, th.s yielded a very good fit and reasonable forecasts.

```
Forecast Pro for Windows Standard Edition Version 2.00
Oct 1997
Expert data exploration of dependent variable SALES
-------------------------------------------------------------------------
Length 120  Minimum 23.1  Maximum 75.6
Mean 41.3 Standard deviation 11.3
Classical decomposition (multiplicative)
    Trend-cycle: 90.45%  Seasonal: 8.96%  Irregular: 0.58%
There are no strongly significant regressors, so I will choose
a univariate method.
Exponential smoothing outperforms Box-Jenkins by 1.1 to 1.1
out-of-sample (MAD). I tried 78 forecasts up to a maximum horizon 12.
Series is trended and seasonal.
Recommended model: Exponential smoothing
Forecast Model for SALES
Automatic model selection
Multiplicative Winters: Linear trend, Multiplicative seasonality
Confidence limits proportional to indexes and level
                         Smoothing    Final
Component                Weight       Value
------------------------------------------------
Level                    0.29792      62.835
Trend                    0.06775      0.47410
Seasonal                 0.26770      1.1920

Seasonal Indexes
-----------------------------------------------------------
January - March          0.89473      0.86688      0.98622
April - June             0.99965      1.03509      1.03096
July - September         1.01655      1.01938      0.96810
October - December       1.01311      1.01160      1.19195

Standard Diagnostics
-----------------------------------------------------------
Sample size 120                  Number of parameters 3
Mean 41.27                       Standard deviation 11.37
R-square 0.992                   Adjusted R-square 0.9918
Durbin-Watson 1.991              ** Ljung-Box(18)=64.92 P=1
Forecast error 1.028             BIC 1.078 (Best so far)
MAPE 0.01901                     RMSE 1.015
MAD 0.785
Rolling simulation results
                       Cumulative         Cumulative
   H   N      MAD      Average    MAPE    Average
-----------------------------------------------------------
   1   12     1.4      1.4        0.022   0.022
   2   11     1.5      1.4        0.021   0.022
   3   10     1.6      1.5        0.022   0.022
   4    9     1.8      1.6        0.026   0.023
   5    8     2.2      1.7        0.030   0.024
   6    7     2.4      1.7        0.034   0.025
   7    6     2.7      1.8        0.038   0.026
   8    5     3.3      1.9        0.045   0.028
   9    4     3.5      2.0        0.048   0.029
  10    3     4.0      2.1        0.051   0.030
  11    2     4.4      2.2        0.055   0.030
  12    1     3.4      2.2        0.040   0.031
Forecasts of SALES from base period 1970-12
  Period      Lower 2.5       Forecast      Upper 97.5        Actual
 1971-01        53.9            56.6           59.4             53.3
```

1971-02	52.5	55.3	58.1	53.7
1971-03	60.0	63.4	66.7	65.0
1971-04	61.2	64.7	68.3	64.1
1971-05	63.6	67.5	71.4	68.4
1971-06	63.7	67.7	71.8	69.6
1971-07	63.0	67.2	71.5	67.1
1971-08	63.5	67.9	72.4	69.8
1971-09	60.5	65.0	69.4	66.9
1971-10	63.6	68.5	73.3	69.3
1971-11	63.7	68.8	73.9	72.0
1971-12	75.4	81.7	88.0	85.1

Answer to the original questions:

a. Winters' method with linear trend and multiplicative seasonality is a very good method for this data.

b. Forecasts are shown above.

c. In- and out-of-sample values are shown above, however, R^2 and RSE are not shown for both fit and forecast. The RMSE is the RSE unadjusted for degrees of freedom loss, other statistics are shown in the previous table.

d. The model is quite valid based on in- and out-of-sample statistics.

6-43. SUPEROIL.DAT - The following is output from using ForecastPro for Windows[tm] (FCP) where initially, we allow FCP to automatically select the model based on in-sample and out-of-sample forecasts for all but the last 12 observations. As shown below, it chose ARIMA model building as the best method, however, our assignment was to use Winters' method. Winter's method yielded a very good fit and reasonable forecasts.

```
Forecast Pro for Windows Standard Edition Version 2.00
Oct 1997
Expert data exploration of dependent variable BARRELS
------------------------------------------------------------------
Length 96  Minimum 252.0  Maximum 472.0
Mean 356.8 Standard deviation 56.1
Classical decomposition (multiplicative)
    Trend-cycle: 77.09%  Seasonal: 20.07%  Irregular: 2.84%
There are no strongly significant regressors, so I will choose
a univariate method.
Box-Jenkins outperforms exponential smoothing by 3.5 to 6.6
out-of-sample (MAD). I tried 78 forecasts up to a maximum horizon 12.
Series is trended and seasonal.
Recommended model: Box-Jenkins

Forecast Model for BARRELS
Automatic model selection
Multiplicative Winters: Linear trend, Multiplicative seasonality
Confidence limits proportional to indexes
                   Smoothing     Final
Component           Weight       Value
--------------------------------------
Level              0.08440      441.34
Trend              0.03995      1.7796
Seasonal           0.44069      0.94271
Seasonal Indexes
```

```
---------------------------------------------------------------
January - March          0.90216      0.95641      0.92762
April - June             1.00562      1.01130      1.08822
July - September         1.07771      1.09024      1.03496
October - December       1.05558      0.93293      0.94271
Standard Diagnostics
---------------------------------------------------------------
Sample size 96                    Number of parameters 3
Mean 356.8                        Standard deviation 56.44
R-square 0.9651                   Adjusted R-square 0.9643
Durbin-Watson 2.245               Ljung-Box(18)=15.22 P=0.3532
Forecast error 10.66              BIC 11.27 (Best so far)
MAPE 0.02264                      RMSE 10.49
MAD 7.982
Rolling simulation results
                    Cumulative          Cumulative
  H    N      MAD    Average    MAPE     Average
---------------------------------------------------------------
  1   12      7.7      7.7      0.017     0.017
  2   11      7.4      7.6      0.016     0.017
  3   10      7.4      7.5      0.016     0.016
  4    9      7.6      7.5      0.016     0.016
  5    8      7.5      7.5      0.016     0.016
  6    7      7.5      7.5      0.016     0.016
  7    6      6.2      7.4      0.013     0.016
  8    5      6.8      7.4      0.015     0.016
  9    4      6.0      7.3      0.013     0.016
 10    3      8.4      7.3      0.019     0.016
 11    2      7.5      7.3      0.017     0.016
 12    1     10.8      7.4      0.024     0.016
Forecasts of BARRELS from base period 08-12
  Period      Lower 2.5      Forecast      Upper 97.5        Actual
  09-01         379.5          399.8          420.1          391.0
  09-02         403.9          425.5          447.1          436.0
  09-03         393.3          414.4          435.4          411.0
  09-04         428.1          451.0          473.9          458.0
  09-05         432.2          455.3          478.5          447.0
  09-06         466.9          491.9          516.9          480.0
  09-07         464.2          489.1          514.0          483.0
  09-08         471.4          496.7          522.0          489.0
  09-09         449.2          473.3          497.5          474.0
  09-10         459.8          484.7          509.5          474.0
  09-11         407.9          430.0          452.1          433.0
  09-12         413.7          436.2          458.6          447.0
  Period      Lower 2.5      Forecast      Upper 97.5        Actual
```

Answer to the original questions:

a. Winters' method with linear trend and multiplicative seasonality is a good method.

b. Forecasts are shown above.

c. In- and out-of-sample values are shown above, however, R^2 and RSE are not shown for both fit and forecast. The RMSE is the RSE unadjusted for degrees of freedom loss, other statistics are shown in the previous table.

d. The model is quite valid based on in- and out-of-sample statistics.

II.   MINICASE

See the Master Forecasting Summary Table Section

PROBLEMS

ESTIMATED DIFFICULTY

Elementary	Medium	Hard	Very Hard	Bad

1 E   2 M   3 M   4 M   5 M   6 M   7 H   8 M   9 H   10 H

11 M   12 M   13 H   14 H   15 H   16 M

Minicases are all hard.

6A-1. Elementary question with answers on pages 241 to 245.

6A-2. (n-1)/2=3, Frequencies of 1, 2, and 3 cycles every 7 periods, 1/7, 2/7, 3/7.

6A-3. If A greater than or equal to .5*RSE, see page 246 for A formula.

6A-4. n/2=24/2=12 frequencies of 1, 2, ... , 12 cycles every 24 periods, 1/24, 2/24, 3/24, ..., 12/24.

6A-5. The line spectrum equals the total series sums of squares explained by a specific frequency. The sum of the intensities of all frequencies equals the series total sums of squares, see page 255 and 256.

6A-6. As shown on page 244, the frequency of interest is approximately 70/700 or 10. Other frequencies such as 9 and 11 should be included because of some random variations about a wavelength of 70 years.

6A-7. There is no trend in this series, so we center the data on 609.9375. The regression results of centered Series D are:

```
Usable Observations        48      Degrees of Freedom      37
R Bar **2                           0.739482
Mean of Dependent Variable          0.000000000
Std Error of Dependent Variable    93.266811559
Standard Error of Estimate         47.604282094
Sum of Squared Residuals        83848.203925
Regression F(10,37)                14.3410
Significance Level of F             0.00000000
Durbin-Watson Statistic             0.522181
Q(12-0)                            92.411377
Significance Level of Q             0.00000000
```

	Variable	Coeff	Std Error	T-Stat	Signif
1.	S1	-29.6827020	9.7171832	-3.05466	0.00416269
2.	C1	-111.2694594	9.7171836	-11.45079	0.00000000
3.	S2	4.7270572	9.7171832	0.48646	0.62950754
4.	C2	-0.5624923	9.7171835	-0.05789	0.95415065
5.	S3	-7.8333204	9.7171834	-0.80613	0.42531854
6.	C3	-11.2916860	9.7171834	-1.16203	0.25266325
7.	S4	0.9021076	9.7171837	0.09284	0.92653447

```
 8.  C4         0.1875019   9.7171831       0.01930  0.98470873
 9.  S5        -5.6505742   9.7171845      -0.58150  0.56442749
10.  C5        -2.4389206   9.7171823      -0.25099  0.80321012
11.  C6        -3.8124995   6.8710863      -0.55486  0.58232859
Variable          Coeff    Std Error      T-Stat    Signif
```

All frequencies above 1 cycle in 12 are statistically insignificant. The amplitude for a frequency of 2 is A2 = SQRT(22.32*22.32 + 6.741*6.741) = 4.69347. This is much less than .5*RSE, therefore, it and all frequencies above it are dropped. The analysis with a partial model of only S1 to C1 is:

```
Dependent Variable CENTERED - Estimation by Least Squares
Monthly Data From 1:01 To 4:12
Usable Observations      48    Degrees of Freedom      46
R Bar** 2                       0.773699
Standard Error of Estimate     44.368004154
Sum of Squared Residuals    90551.910459
Regression F(1,46)            161.6884
Significance Level of F          0.00000000
Durbin-Watson Statistic          0.645287
Q(12-0)                         77.411423
Significance Level of Q          0.00000000
     Variable      Coeff     Std Error     T-Stat     Signif
**********************************************************************
1.  S1         -29.6827014   9.0565807     -3.27747  0.00199785
2.  C1        -111.2694575   9.0565811    -12.28603  0.00000000
```

Note how much R^2 has improved with the partial model also, because of orthogonality, the coefficient values have not changed. Clearly the other frequencies were insignificant. A graph of Series D confirms that there is only one peak and trough every 12 periods.

6A-8. See the discussion in the Advantages section of p. 255.

6A-9. MARRIAGES - Marriages is not trending, so we center the series.

```
set center = marriage - 599909.4375,
set trd = t, set tpi = 6.283185.
```

Let's create sinusoidal functions for a full model.

```
SET S1 = SIN((1*TRD/4)*TPI)        SET C1 = COS((1*TRD/4)*TPI)
SET S2 = SIN((2*TRD/4)*TPI)        SET C2 = COS((2*TRD/4)*TPI),
```

Note that s2 is all zeros, so it should not be included.

```
Dependent Variable CENTER - Estimation by Least Squares
Usable Observations      32    Degrees of Freedom      29
R Bar **2                        0.990904
Mean of Dependent Variable       0.00000
Std Error of Dependent Variable 116739.84222
Standard Error of Estimate     11134.07661
Sum of Squared Residuals    3595062194.5
Regression F(2,29)            1689.4682
Significance Level of F          0.00000000
Durbin-Watson Statistic          1.988771
Q(12-0)                         17.328236
Significance Level of Q          0.13766174
```

```
      Variable              Coeff        Std Error      T-Stat       Signif
*****************************************************************************
1.  S1                -143428.8168      2783.5192      -51.52787    0.00000000
2.  C1                 -50467.9375      2783.5192      -18.13098    0.00000000
3.  C2                  39122.1839      1968.2453       19.87668    0.00000000
```

All frequencies are statistically significant, note that the coefficient for C2>.5*11134.07661, thus both frequencies are statistically significant.

The forecast of two seasonal cycles are very plausible.

6A-10. BIRTHS - The series is trending and the following trend line is used to estimate the seasonal component.

Trend = 942317.97321 + 2878.91964*t, this series is called sbirths = births - ptrend.

```
SET TRD = T,                      SET TPI = 6.283185,
SET S1 = SIN((1*TRD/4)*TPI),      SET C1 = COS((1*TRD/4)*TPI)
SET S2 = SIN((2*TRD/4)*TPI),      SET C2 = COS((2*TRD/4)*TPI),
```

Note that S2 is all zeros, so it should not be included in the model.

A full model yields a C2 frequency that is statistically insignificant. It should be eliminated. The final model of sbirths is:

```
Quarterly Data From 1985:01 To 1996:04
Usable Observations         32      Degrees of Freedom      30
R Bar **2                          0.689579
Mean of Dependent Variable       -1439.45977
Std Error of Dependent Variable  39922.92239
Standard Error of Estimate       22243.23829
Sum of Squared Residuals         14842849483
Durbin-Watson Statistic           1.047456
Q(12-0)                          65.166591
Significance Level of Q           0.00000000
      Variable           Coeff        Std Error      T-Stat       Signif
*****************************************************************************
1.  S1              -46289.82072      5560.80957      -8.32430     0.00000000
2.  C1               -4667.22709      5560.80957      -0.83931     0.40793567

set fit = sbirths - res,   set ffit = fit + ptrend
```

The forecast of two seasonal cycles are very plausible.

6A-11. The terms cyclical and seasonal are sometimes, but nonetheless, inappropriately used interchangeably when the period of a phenomena is quite long, such as every 22 years, thus, this question can be interpreted two ways. If the cyclical phenomena is really seasonal such as sunspot activity, then a seasonal FSA model can be fitted as shown here, when the activity in question is truly cyclical, having recurrence but no constant period, then a full Fourier Series model can be built with n/2 frequencies in an exploration of the dominant period of recurrence.

6A-12. When a time series has a nonstationary variance proportionate to the level of the series, then a logarithmic transformation can be made prior to FSA.

6A-13. ELECT.DAT - This series is variance nonstationary, so we take natural logarithms of the time series and estimate a trend. The trend line using the seasonal differencing model of the chapter is (PTREND) = .90492+ 0.00400*t

TPI = 6.283185, two Π and let's create a trendless series, SSALES. The usual seasonal monthly trig functions are created for S1 to C6. The resulting model is:

```
Usable Observations        185      Degrees of Freedom     174
R Bar **2                           0.595659
Mean of Dependent Variable         -0.003996008
Std Error of Dependent Variable    0.126141885
Standard Error of Estimate          0.080210910
Sum of Squared Residuals            1.1194794684
Durbin-Watson Statistic             1.342761
Q(36-0)                             427.611923
Significance Level of Q             0.00000000
Variable       Coeff        Std Error      T-Stat      Signif
*************************************************************
1.  S1     0.018454718  0.008318482      2.21852   0.02781315
2.  C1    -0.050262471  0.008366436     -6.00763   0.00000001
3.  S2    -0.009613576  0.008321815     -1.15523   0.24958188
4.  C2     0.050387883  0.008366198      6.02279   0.00000001
5.  S3    -0.009059837  0.008321576     -1.08872   0.27778453
6.  C3     0.044354145  0.008366436      5.30144   0.00000035
7.  S4     0.010143462  0.008321815      1.21890   0.22453198
8.  C4     0.030504584  0.008366198      3.64617   0.00035136
9.  S5     0.003689394  0.008321799      0.44334   0.65806991
10. C5     0.050109346  0.008366435      5.98933   0.00000001
11. C6     0.065725418  0.005900124     11.13967   0.00000000
```

Clearly all amplitudes are greater than .5*RSE, thus, we keep all frequencies in the model.

```
ENTRY        SALES            FULFITT            FSALES
 15:02  4.5106287106548  4.5614441613447        NA
 16:05  4.5376405291945  4.6776144314124        NA
 16:06      NA               NA           4.7513368091293
        . . .
 19:04      NA               NA           4.8845260869837
 19:05      NA               NA           4.8216144960807
```

Reversing the Logarithmic process yields:

```
set fasales = exp(fsales)
ENTRY         ASALES         FASALES
 16:06         NA       115.73890197793
 16:07         NA       108.04063448797
 16:08         NA       109.58868004255
 16:09         NA        94.07635309812
 16:10         NA       104.59467217591
 16:11         NA        92.17958054659
 . . .
 17:03         NA       102.56689994404
 17:04         NA       120.12419923170
 17:05         NA       112.79978724862
 17:06         NA       121.42985920085
 . . .
 19:04         NA       132.22778601429
```

These forecasts are very plausible.

6A-14. RETAIL.DAT - The retail series appears to be variance nonstationary, thus, we will analyze natural logarithms of the series. The resulting trend line is:

$$PTREND = 3.24670 + 0.00727*t.$$

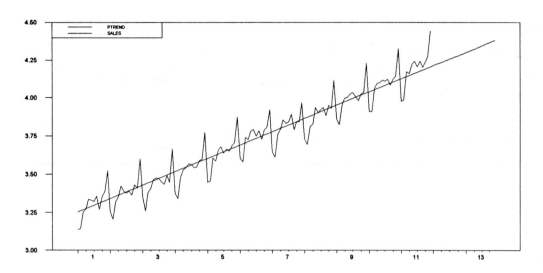

Running a full model on the seasonal series yields:

```
Usable Observations        120      Degrees of Freedom    109
R Bar **2                           0.898943
Mean of Dependent Variable         -0.003634070
Std Error of Dependent Variable     0.080817447
Standard Error of Estimate          0.025691415
Sum of Squared Residuals           0.0719453180
Durbin-Watson Statistic             1.111329
Q(30-0)                             303.357801
Significance Level of Q             0.00000000
     Variable          Coeff        Std Error       T-Stat       Signif
**********************************************************************
 1.  S1          -0.035642835    0.003316747     -10.74632    0.00000000
 2.  C1          -0.009229912    0.003316747      -2.78282    0.00635309
 3.  S2          -0.041818908    0.003316747     -12.60841    0.00000000
 4.  C2           0.048967333    0.003316747      14.76366    0.00000000
 5.  S3          -0.018386909    0.003316747      -5.54366    0.00000021
 6.  C3           0.047975647    0.003316747      14.46467    0.00000000
 7.  S4          -0.001267318    0.003316747      -0.38210    0.70313353
 8.  C4           0.039564267    0.003316747      11.92863    0.00000000
 9.  S5           0.021021219    0.003316748       6.33790    0.00000001
10.  C5           0.033823252    0.003316747      10.19772    0.00000000
11.  C6           0.015597725    0.002345295       6.65065    0.00000000
```

Clearly C6 is greater than .5*RSE, this confirms the compound seasonality of this series, note the high t-values at all frequencies.

Here are the fit and forecast error statistics. SET ERROR = SALES - FULFITT

SET SERROR = ERROR**2,   SET PE = ERROR/SALES,   SET APE = ABS(PE)

In fitting the first 120 observations using logarithms:

```
SET FULLFIT = EXP(FULFITT)
SET AERROR = ASALES - FULLFIT
SET SAERROR = AERROR**2
SET PAE = AERROR/ASALES
SET AAPE = ABS(PAE)
TAB
```

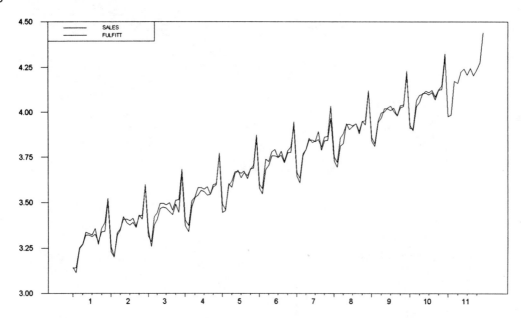

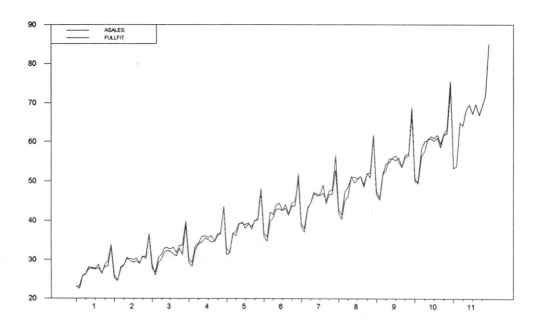

Series	Obs	Mean	Std Error	Minimum	Maximum
ASALES	132	43.60653788	13.35975303	23.05700000	85.0750000
SALES	132	3.72972145	0.30230439	3.13796941	4.4435332
DSALES	108	0.08722201	0.03196831	0.01898072	0.1708557
PTREND	156	3.81739500	0.32843990	3.25397000	4.3808200
TRD	156	78.50000000	45.17742799	1.00000000	156.000000
RES	120	-0.00363407	0.02431594	-0.07162725	0.0566446
TPI	156	6.28318500	0.00000000	6.28318500	6.2831850
SSALES	132	-0.00043355	0.08321262	-0.18190194	0.2371932
FITT	120	-0.00000000	0.07707266	-0.14853923	0.1766985
FULFITT	120	3.68653500	0.26980114	3.11270171	4.2957985
FSSALES	156	-0.00000000	0.07699804	-0.14853954	0.1766986
FSALES	36	4.25359500	0.12200052	3.98510067	4.5575186

Fitted Error for 1 to 120

ERROR	120	-0.09994557	1.01455962	-3.65483836	2.3916700
SERROR	120	1.03074257	1.72422502	0.00003123	13.3578435
PE	120	-0.03147095	0.26937319	-0.92126563	0.6199318
APE	120	0.01977468	0.01482752	0.00016135	0.0742548

Forecasted Error for 121 to 132

FULLFIT	120	41.36538723	11.15408667	22.48170153	73.3907966
AERROR	12	2.23285852	1.96887252	-2.16422098	4.9940047
SAERROR	12	8.53907790	7.49618962	0.00227568	24.9400831
PAE	12	0.03069115	0.02895511	-0.04062815	0.0604592
AAPE	12	0.03761045	0.01796764	0.00088763	0.0604592
FASALES	36	70.86976470	8.70399408	53.79070409	95.3465939

```
DISP FIT RSE  = 1.0307**.5 = 1.015
DISP FIT R-SQ = 1-1.0307/11.3748**2 = .992
DISP FORE RSE = 8.53907790**.5 = 2.922
DISP  1-2.922/8.2550675401**2 = .875

SET FASALES = EXP(FSALES)
```

ENTRY	ASALES	FULLFIT	FASALES
10:12	75.597000000000	73.390796590558	NA
11:01	53.269000000000	NA	55.433220982860
11:02	53.743000000000	NA	53.790704089074
11:03	65.007000000000	NA	61.539196044243
11:04	64.118000000000	NA	62.880551454119
11:05	68.360000000000	NA	66.251276509018
11:06	69.557000000000	NA	66.306018566127
11:07	67.117000000000	NA	65.677908222392
11:08	69.782000000000	NA	66.568080350848
11:09	66.872000000000	NA	63.800664383329
11:10	69.339000000000	NA	67.467392405230
11:11	71.971000000000	NA	67.619689484838
11:12	85.075000000000	NA	80.080995284885
12:01	NA	NA	60.486442994734
12:02	NA	NA	58.694179257736
12:03	NA	NA	67.149017176430
12:04	NA	NA	68.612648665789
12:05	NA	NA	72.290643453864
12:06	NA	NA	72.350379795538
12:07	NA	NA	71.665007686580
12:08	NA	NA	72.636331753656

```
12:09        NA          NA          69.616636906733
12:10        NA          NA          73.617622111260
12:11        NA          NA          73.783794280509
12:12        NA          NA          87.381062799927
```

These forecasts appear to be very plausible.

6A-15. SUPEROIL.DAT

```
TAB 1 96
Series     Obs      Mean      Std Error     Minimum       Maximum
DATE       96   456.50000000  230.35770811  101.00000000  812.00000000
SALES      96   356.81250000   56.43987252  252.00000000  472.00000000
```

There is a very significant trend in this time series.

Let's define a trend line using one-twelfth of the mean of the 12th order differences.

```
COMPUTE B = 20.5833333333/12 = 1.71528
COMPUTE A = 356.81250000 - 1.71528*(96/2) = 274.47906
```

The trend equation for this series is:

```
SET PTREND = 274.47906+ 1.71528*TRD
```

Let's compare this robust line to a regression line.

```
LINREG SALES 1 96 RES
#CONSTANT TRD
Dependent Variable SALES - Estimation by Least Squares
Monthly Data From 1:01 To 8:12
Usable Observations      96      Degrees of Freedom      94
Centered R**2       0.787741     R Bar **2    0.785483
Uncentered R**2     0.994872     T x R**2       95.508
Mean of Dependent Variable     356.81250000
Std Error of Dependent Variable  56.43987252
Standard Error of Estimate      26.14069863
Sum of Squared Residuals     64233.595754
Regression F(1,94)             348.8547
Significance Level of F          0.00000000
Durbin-Watson Statistic          0.716678
Q(24-0)                        706.456535
Significance Level of Q          0.00000000
    Variable         Coeff      Std Error     T-Stat      Signif
*******************************************************************
1.  Constant      269.59802632   5.37790868   50.13064   0.00000000
2.  TRD             1.79823657   0.09627744   18.67765   0.00000000
```

Note that both trend lines are nearly equal, we choose the robust line because it is not influenced heavily by the seasonality of the series.

Let's create the sinusoidal functions for modeling seasonality, also, we shall calculate the value of two pie and the detrened, seasonalized values of the series.

```
SET TPI = 6.283185
SET SSALES = SALES - PTREND
```

```
SET S1 = SIN((4*TRD/48)*TPI)
SET C1 = COS((4*TRD/48)*TPI)
SET S2 = SIN((8*TRD/48)*TPI)
SET C2 = COS((8*TRD/48)*TPI)
SET S3 = SIN((12*TRD/48)*TPI)
SET C3 = COS((12*TRD/48)*TPI)
SET S4 = SIN((16*TRD/48)*TPI)
SET C4 = COS((16*TRD/48)*TPI)
SET S5 = SIN((20*TRD/48)*TPI)
SET C5 = COS((20*TRD/48)*TPI)
SET S6 = SIN((24*TRD/48)*TPI)
SET C6 = COS((24*TRD/48)*TPI)
```

S6 is dropped because each term equals zero. Now. let's run a full model.

```
LINREG SSALES 1 96 RES1
#S1 C1 S2 C2 S3 C3 S4 C4 S5 C5 C6
Dependent Variable SSALES - Estimation by Least Squares
Monthly Data From 1:01 To 8:12
Usable Observations        96      Degrees of Freedom     85
Centered R**2       0.847003      R Bar **2    0.829003
Uncentered R**2     0.847170      T x R**2       81.328
Mean of Dependent Variable       -0.85764000
Std Error of Dependent Variable  26.10523672
Standard Error of Estimate       10.79497560
Sum of Squared Residuals       9905.1773493
Durbin-Watson Statistic           2.027023
Q(24-0)                           34.549701
Significance Level of Q           0.07536279
    Variable           Coeff        Std Error     T-Stat      Signif
***********************************************************************
1.  S1             -19.51836174    1.55812048    -12.52686   0.00000000
2.  C1             -26.45194822    1.55812055    -16.97683   0.00000000
3.  S2              -0.11425824    1.55812049     -0.07333   0.94171516
4.  C2              -0.97569533    1.55812054     -0.62620   0.53286170
5.  S3               0.06945769    1.55812052      0.04458   0.96454834
6.  C3              -0.94444592    1.55812052     -0.60614   0.54603428
7.  S4               0.53926580    1.55812056      0.34610   0.73012265
8.  C4               1.31597992    1.55812047      0.84459   0.40070826
9.  S5              -0.45382715    1.55812069     -0.29127   0.77155768
10. C5               0.25052885    1.55812034      0.16079   0.87264100
11. C6               5.43402638    1.10175758      4.93214   0.00000399
    Variable           Coeff        Std Error     T-Stat      Signif
```

A6 is greater than .5*RSE, thus, it is statistically significant, we will keep all frequencies. Let's create a fitted value called FIT for the seasonal component and FULFITT for the full series.

```
SET FIT 1 96 = SSALES - RES1
SET FULFITT = FIT + PTREND
```

While not shown here, there is a very good fit during the first eight years. Let's create a forecast value called FSSALES for the seasonal sales series.

```
PRJ FSSALES 97 132
```

Now let's create the full model with trend and seasonality.

```
SET FSALES 97 132 = PTREND + FSSALES
```

The fit looks quite good graphically.

F* ARE FITTED ERROR STATISTICS

```
SET FERROR = SALES - FULFITT
SET SFERROR = FERROR*FERROR
SET FPE = FERROR/SALES
SET FAPE = ABS(FERROR/SALES)
TAB   1 96
```

Series	Obs	Mean	Std Error	Minimum	Maximum
DATE	96	456.50000000	230.35770811	101.00000000	812.00000000
SALES	96	356.81250000	56.43987252	252.00000000	472.00000000
FERROR	96	-0.85764155	10.17456304	-24.69096648	23.10055820
SFERROR	96	103.17893072	142.10487818	0.01159371	609.64382575
FPE	96	-0.00361292	0.03083401	-0.09011302	0.07536868
FAPE	96	0.02379332	0.01979508	0.00028637	0.09011302

```
DISPLAY FIT RSE = 103.1789**.5 = 10.15770
DISPLAY FIT R-SQ = 1-103.17893072/56.43987252**2 = 0.96761
```

The following are the actual forecast error statistics.

```
SET ERROR = SALES - FSALES
SET SERROR = ERROR*ERROR
SET PE = ERROR/SALES
SET APE = ABS(ERROR/SALES)
```

Series	Obs	Mean	Std Error	Minimum	Maximum
DATE	12	906.50000000	3.60555128	901.00000000	912.00000000
SALES	12	451.91666667	30.43161733	391.00000000	489.00000000
ERROR	12	1.62140512	8.76213190	-10.60777196	17.39226496
SERROR	12	73.00599703	82.76261229	5.55891374	302.49088031
PE	12	0.00299408	0.02031411	-0.02712985	0.03989052
APE	12	0.01690658	0.01051786	0.00491195	0.03989052

```
DISPLAY FORECAST RSE = 73.006**.5 = 8.54435
DISPLAY FORECAST R-SQ = 1-73.006/30.43161733**2 = .92
```

MINICASES

MINICASE 6A-1. Kansas Turnpike, Daily Data.
MINICASE 6A-2. Domestic Air Passengers by Quarter.
MINICASE 6A-3. Hospital Census by Month.
MINICASE 6A-4. Henry Machler's Hideaway Orchids, Daily.
MINICASE 6A-5. Your Forecasting Project.
MINICASE 6A-6. Midwestern Building Materials.
MINICASE 6A-7. International Airline Passengers.
MINICASE 6A-8. Automobile Sales.
MINICASE 6A-9. Consumption of Distilled Spirits.
MINICASE 6A-10. Discount Consumer Electronics.

Each of these minicase results are shown in the Master Forecast Summary Table section which precedes Chapter 5.

PROBLEMS

ESTIMATED DIFFICULTY

Elementary	Medium	Hard	Very Hard	Bad

1 E   2 M   3 M   4 E   5 E   6 E   7 M   8 E   9 E   10 M

11 H   12 E   13 E   14 E   15 E   16 E   17 E   18 E   19 M   20 M

21 M   22 M   23 M   24 M   25 H   26 H   27 M   28 M   29 M   30 H

31 H   32 H   33 H   34 H

Minicases are all hard.

7-1. See page 268.

7-2. Level and variance nonstationarity - pages 273 and 290 respectively.

7-3. I(1), p. 277, AR(1), p.277, AR(2), p. 306, MA(1), p. 277, and MA(2), p.307.

7-4. White noise is completely patternless data centered on zero and having a constant variance.

7-5. See appendix 7-B, page 322.

7-6. a) $Y_{t-1} = BY_t$
      b) $Y_{t-5} = B^5 Y_t$
      c) $Y_{t-12} = B^{12} Y_t$
      d) $Y_t - 2Y_{t-1} + Y_{t-2} = (1-B)^2 Y_t$
      d) $Y_t - Y_{t-12} = (1-B^{12})Y_t$
      e) $Y_t - Y_{t-1} - Y_{t-12} + Y_{t-13} = (1-B)(1-B^{12})Y_t$

7-7. ACFs and PACFs for a monthly seasonal $I(1)^{12}$, an $AR(1)^{12}$, $AR(2)^{12}$, and $MA(2)^{12}$ on pages 309, 306, and 307 but change significant lags to 12, 24, 36 instead of the lags of 4, 8, 12.

7-8. Use example 7-4 of page 274 to review the meaning of fitted and forecast errors, particularly out-of-sample error.

7-9. The attributes of a good forecasting model are in Table 7-2, p.281.

7-10. A common English definition of the concept of the partial autocorrelation is given in the third sentence of page 326.

7-11. In statistical terms, there are two theoretical partial autocorrelations for an AR(2) process, ϕ_1 and ϕ_2. ϕ_1 is the direct association between Y_t and Y_{t-1} that is independent of their mutual correlation with other lags of Y_t, similarly, ϕ_2 is the direct association between Y_t and Y_{t-2} that is independent of their mutual correlation with other lags of Y_t.

7-12. $\hat{Y}_7 = 17$

7-13. $\hat{Y}_6 = 17 + 1.75 = 18.75$

7-14. $\hat{Y}_6 = 4 + .8 * 17 = 17.6$

7-15.

t	1	2	3	4	5	6	Mean	StdDev
Actual	17	15	13	12	10		13.4	2.701851
Fitted/Forecast		17.6	16	14.4	13.6	12	15.4	
Error		-2.6	-3	-2.4	-3.6		-2.9	0.52915
Mean Error =		-2.9						
RSE =		4.152 With 4-2 = 2 degrees of freedom.						

Note how much the RSE of 2.93598 is greater than the StdDev of the errors, .52915.

There is bias in the forecast because all errors are negative. The adjusted R-square will be negative because RSE of the errors is > StdDev of Y_t.

7-16.

t	1	2	3	4	5	6	Mean	StdDev
Actual	17	15	13	12	10		13.4	2.701851
First Differences		-2	-2	-1	-2		-1.75	0.5
Fitted/Forecast		15.25	13.25	11.25	10.25	8.25	12.5	
Error		-0.25	-0.25	0.75	-0.25		0	0.5
Mean Error =		0						
RSE =		0.612372 With 4-2 = 2 degrees of freedom.						

This model has a much better fit of the data than that of Problem 7-15. It has a reasonably good adjusted R-sq. of about 95%.

7-17.

t	1	2	3	4	5	6	Mean	StdDev
Actual	17	15	13	12	10			13.4	2.7019
Fitted/Forecast	10	15.6	9.52	12.784	9.3728	10.50176	11.455	
Error	7	-0.6	3.48	-0.784	0.6272		0.6808	1.9685
Mean Error =		0.6808						
RSE =		2.596 With 4-2 = 2 degrees of freedom.						

This model will have a negative R-square and doesn't fit the data very well.
The error in Period 1 is not included in the Fit statistics. The mean denotes that there is little bias.

7-18. $\hat{Y}_{90}(10)$

7-19. Actual values for one-period ahead forecasts are known through period t-1, however, actual values for n-period ahead forecasts are only known through period t-n, where in both cases t is the period being forecasted.

7-20. Health care prices (costs) have not been increasing linearly, thus linear projections have a nonlinearly increasing negative bias or error.

7-21. Using your software analyze IBM stock prices for March 1981 through September 1993 (IBMMN. DAT) as was done for USIND.DAT in the chapter. a) Is this series trending or drifting? b) Confirm your results with appropriate statistics. c) Write out this model using backshift notation.

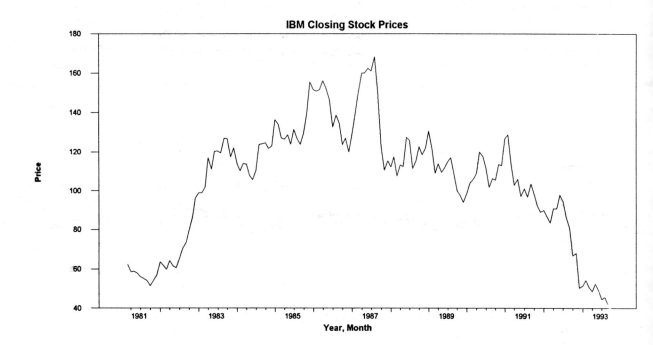

a) As shown above, the closing price series of IBM stock is drifting and as discussed below, requires logarithms to achieve variance stationarity. The following analysis is used to generate the table which follows.

Taking first differences of the series results in a variance nonstationary series. Thus, logarithms are necessary. As shown below, first differences of the logs yield the following statistics.

```
Dependent Variable LPRICE - Estimation by Box-Jenkins
Monthly Data From 1981:04 To 1993:09
Usable Observations     150        Degrees of Freedom    150
Centered R**2      0.957672        R Bar **2    0.957954
Uncentered R**2    0.999787        T x R**2     149.968
Mean of Dependent Variable        4.6118277283
Std Error of Dependent Variable 0.3292300933
Standard Error of Estimate        0.0675088748
Sum of Squared Residuals          0.6836172275
Durbin-Watson Statistic             1.824608
Q(36-0)                            33.663777
Significance Level of Q            0.58020494
```

```
corr(par=par) res
Correlations of Series RES
Monthly Data From 1981:04 To 1993:09
Autocorrelations
     1:   0.0786881   0.0808561   0.0827650   0.0289416  -0.0653254   0.0048607
     7:  -0.0394034  -0.0407797   0.0813475   0.1045404   0.0633441  -0.0190559
    13:  -0.0453442  -0.0005832  -0.0157153   0.2339332   0.0886677  -0.0065320
    19:   0.0332902   0.0691694  -0.0383474  -0.0899743  -0.1484689   0.0435276
    25:   0.1214383  -0.0117349   0.0226015   0.0196342   0.0023183  -0.0442171
    31:   0.0238272  -0.0105555   0.0057855  -0.0382460   0.0737796   0.1207481
Partial Autocorrelations
     1:   0.0786881   0.0751295   0.0718163   0.0122690  -0.0810515   0.0058539
     7:  -0.0331382  -0.0261599   0.0963270   0.1011637   0.0468099  -0.0617863
    13:  -0.0800763   0.0080209   0.0082363   0.2763729   0.0898075  -0.0653291
    19:  -0.0579054  -0.0028967  -0.0179687  -0.0589442  -0.1081042   0.1334227
    25:   0.1485674  -0.0983023  -0.0904806  -0.0252895   0.0598015  -0.0244007
    31:   0.0424051   0.0082962   0.0072216  -0.0914677   0.0101316   0.1087460
disp 2/150**.5 = 0.16330
```

None of the above ACFs or PACFs for first differences of logs are statistically significant, thus, there are consistent with white noise.

b) Defining Y_t = IBM Closing Price and $\ln Y_t = \log(Y_t)$:

		Obs	Mean	Std Error	Minimum	Maximum	Stationarity Level	White Var.	Noise
PRICE	Y_t	151	105.370	30.109	42.000	168.375	No	No	No
LPRICE	$\ln Y_t$	151	4.609	0.330	3.738	5.126	No	Yes	No
DPRICE	$(1-B)Y_t$	150	-0.136	7.078	-28.250	15.750	Yes	No	No
DLPRICE	$(1-B)\ln Y_t$	150	-0.003	0.068	-0.304	0.140	Yes	Yes	Yes

c) $(1-B)\ln Y_t = e_t$ This is an ARIMA(0,1,0)0,1 model where the last 0,1 denotes no trend with logarithmic transformations.

7-22. a) The series has a statistically significant trend as shown by the t-value of 9.48 on the mean of first differences.

b) t-value = 9.48.

c) $(1-B)Y_t = \Theta_0 + e_t$ d) See the forecasts in the following table.

t	1	2	3	4	5	6	7	8	9	10	11	MEAN	12	13	14	15
Yt	10	12	13	15	17	19	21	22	24	27	28		30	32	33	35
Yt-Yt-1		2	1	2	2	2	2	1	2	3	1	1.8				
										STDEV		0.63				
										t-VALUE		9.48				

7-23. a) The trend is not statistically significant. b) The t-value of the mean of first differences is not statistically significant. c) $(1-B)Y_t = e_t$ d) See the forecasts in the following table.

t	1	2	3	4	5	6	7	8	9	10	11	MEAN	12	13	14	15
Yt	10	12	11	10	9	11	13	14	15	13	12		12	12	12	12
Yt-Yt-1		2	-1	-1	-1	2	2	1	1	-2	-1	0.2				
										STDEV		1.55				
										t-VALUE		0.43				

7-24. a) The series has a very significant nonlinear trend. Thus, the series will be transformed to natural logarithms as shown in the fourth row of the following table.

b) The t-statistic of the mean of first differences is very statistically significant.

c) $(1-B)\ln Y_t = \Theta_0 + e_t$

d) See the forecasts in the table below.

e) The forecasts in logs and original metric are shown below.

t	1	2	3	4	5	6	7	8	9	10	11	MEAN	12	13	14	15
Yt	10	16	23	36	53	81	122	181	274	409	615		928	1402	2116	3195
Yt-Yt-1		6	7	13	17	28	41	59	93	135	206	60.5	FORECAST ABOVE			
Yt-Yt-1	2.3	2.8	3.1	3.6	4	4.4	4.8	5.2	5.6	6	6.4		6.8	7.25	7.657	8.069
		0.5	0.4	0.4	0.4	0.4	0.4	0.4	0.4	0.4	0.4	0.41				
											STDEV	0.03				
											t-VALUE	44.9				

7-25. a) The first 11 observations are drifting however, for the full time series of 271 observations, the determination of whether there is a trend or not is dependent on whether logarithms are used to achieve variance stationarity.

b) Statistical t-tests are shown below.

c) The random walk model $(1-B)Y_t = e_t$, with or without logarithmic transformations, a trend model is:

$(1-B)\ln Y_t = \Theta_0 + e_t$.

Statistics for all 271 observations.

Series	Obs	Mean	Std Error	Minimum	Maximum
DATE	271	1980.8614022	6.5331741	1970.0100000	1992.07
PRICE	271	804.4343173	674.1106869	134.5000000	2589.40
DPRICE	270	3.5929630	51.4560930	-286.1000000	183.20
LPRICE	271	6.3538500	0.8205567	4.9015642	7.859181
DLPRICE	270	0.0072284	0.0411395	-0.1479819	0.102768

Statistics for the first 11 observations.

Series	Obs	Mean	Std Error	Minimum	Maximum
DATE	11	1970.0600000	0.0331662	1970.0100000	1970.11
PRICE	11	149.2454545	10.3643971	139.9000000	165.20
DPRICE	10	-2.0700000	7.7621661	-22.6000000	7.30
LPRICE	11	5.0034523	0.0681951	4.9409279	5.11
DLPRICE	10	-0.0137989	0.0505447	-0.1479819	0.045194

A t-test of the mean of first differences of the first 11 observations is not statistically significantly different than zero.

Observations	10		
Sample Mean	-2.0700000000	Variance	60.251222
Standard Error	7.7621660780	SE of Sample Mean	2.454612
t-Statistic	-0.84331	Signif Level (Mean=0)	0.42090211

A t-test of the mean of the first differences of the first 11 logarithmic observations is not statistically significantly different than zero.

```
Observations    10
Sample Mean     -0.0137988920        Variance                 0.002555
Standard Error  0.0505447004         SE of Sample Mean        0.015984
t-Statistic     -0.86331             Signif Level (Mean=0) 0.41038093
```

A t-test on the mean of first differences of all observations is not statistically significantly different than zero.

```
Observations    270
Sample Mean     3.5929629630         Variance              2647.729504
Standard Error  51.4560929745        SE of Sample Mean        3.131518
t-Statistic     1.14736              Signif Level (Mean=0) 0.25225435
```

A t-test on the mean of the first differences of all logarithmic observations is statistically significantly different than zero.

```
Observations    270
Sample Mean     0.00722842736        Variance                 0.001692
Standard Error  0.04113947162        SE of Sample Mean        0.002504
t-Statistic     2.88713              Signif Level (Mean=0) 0.00420338
```

e) If a transformation is used to forecast Y_t from t=12 through t=15 show the forecasts in the original metric scale.

```
ENTRY      PRICE       DPRICE    LPRICE              DLPRICE
 1970:10   139.9000    -1.8000 4.9409278816714     -0.012785
 1970:11   139.9000     0.0000 4.9409278816714      0.000000
```

7-26. a. Statistics for the first half of Japan.dat where price is the original time series and lprice is the natural logarithms.

```
Series           Obs        Mean      Std Error       Minimum        Maximum
DATE             135 1975.19733333  3.26009276 1970.01000000 1981.03000000
PRICE            135  305.69777778 90.70531955  134.50000000  467.50000000
LPRICE           135    5.66988532  0.34332962    4.90156420    6.14739935
```

Statistics for the second half of Japan.dat.

```
Series           Obs        Mean      Std Error       Minimum        Maximum
DATE             136 1986.48382353  3.29966554 1981.04000000 1992.07000000
PRICE            136 1299.50367647 636.42486641  473.80000000 2589.40000000
LPRICE           136    7.03278560  0.54538857    6.16078529    7.85918147
```

b. Note that the variance increases for both time series, original and logarithmic time series as t increases. In addition, consider the F-ratios of the variances calculated below:

```
PRICE:   636.42486641**2/90.70531955**2 = 49.22988
LPRICE:    0.54538857**2/0.34332962**2 = 2.52342
```

c. The process of taking logarithms dramatically reduces the change in variances between the first half of the time series and the second half. Also, when a time series is nonstationary, we are interested in the change in the variances of first differences. The use of logarithmic transformation is effective when the variance is proportionate to the level of series. This is the situation in for the JAPAN.DAT time series.

7-27. Software dependent answer. This is a good exercise for the student, forcing them to understand these concepts.

7-28. $(1-\phi_1 B)y_t = e_t$

$(1-\phi_1 B)(Y_t - \mu) = e_t$ therefore, $(1-\phi_1 B)Yt = (1-\phi_1 B)\mu + e_t$
$Yt = (1-\phi_1)\mu + \phi_1 Y_{t-1} + e_t = 50 + .5Y_{t-1} + e_t$

7-29. The following is a cross-listing of the actual time series which have been named SERIESA*.DAT with the actual time series. The file names are descriptive of the ARIMA process that should be fitted to these models. The page number or table illustrating the final fitted model of some of these series is given in parentheses. For others, the model is specified in the name of the time series (e.g., AR1P.DAT).

```
SERIESAA = SERIESB.DAT(Table 8-5) SERIESAK = I12.DAT
SERIESAB = AR1P.DAT(Eq. 9-26)     SERIESAL = MA1N.DAT
SERIESAC = SERIESA.DAT(Table 7-15)SERIESAM = FAD.DAT (Table 7-8)
SERIESAD = AR2NP.DAT              SERIESAN = MA2NN.DAT
SERIESAE = SERIESD.DAT            SERIESAO = PHARMDEM.DAT (Table 8-8)
SERIESAF = AR2PP.DAT              SERIESAP = MA2PN.DAT
SERIESAG = USIND.DAT(Table 7-15)  SERIESAQ = DAIRY.DAT (Table 7-6)
SERIESAH = I4.DAT                 SERIESAR = I1T.DAT
SERIESAI = AR1N.DAT               SERIESAS = STOCKA.DAT (Table 7-3)
SERIESAJ = ARMAPN.DAT             SERIESAT = I4T.DAT

I*.DAT=INTEGRATED SERIES, RANDOM WALK      I*T.DAT=INTEGRATED SERIES, TREND
```

7-30. While there are not a large number of observations in this time series, its trend (nonstationarity) is quite obvious. First differences do not yield white noise, however, adding an AR1 to the model significantly improves the results. The following is RATS output. Note that RATS outputs the constant assuming that the dependent variable is deviations, thus the constant reported in other software may be (1-0.631045549)*68.5283381 = 25.28384.

```
box(diff=1,constant,ar=1,def=eq1) surge / res
Dependent Variable SURGE - Estimation by Box-Jenkins
Iterations Taken       3
Usable Observations    10       Degrees of Freedom     8
R Bar **2                         0.990211
Mean of Dependent Variable        530.3
Std Error of Dependent Variable   220.3205
Standard Error of Estimate         21.79799515
Sum of Squared Res.              3801.221
Durbin-Watson Statistic            1.593473
Q(2-1)                             0.547657
Sign. Level of Q                   0.45928
    Variable            Coeff        Std Error      T-Stat    Signif
************************************************************************
1.  CONSTANT      68.528338138 19.712388495       3.47641  0.00836361
2.  AR{1}          0.631045549  0.231311829       2.72812  0.02592121
```

```
Autocorrelations of Surge
      1: 0.79031844 0.55600714 0.31102956
set PRED2 3 12 = surge(t-1) + 0.631045549*(surge(t-1)-surge(t-2)) + 25.28384
```

ENTRY	PRED	PRED2	FORE
1980:01	NA	NA	NA
1981:01	NA	NA	NA
1982:01	255.53579189813	255.53579652900	NA
1983:01	284.69101964380	284.69102427400	NA
1984:01	320.47729293860	320.47729756800	NA
1985:01	363.89461178254	363.89461641100	NA
1986:01	445.30179606001	445.30180068500	NA
1987:01	585.32989132015	585.32989593900	NA
1988:01	676.75734473055	676.75734935100	NA
1989:01	752.92270704268	752.92271166500	NA
1990:01	772.68088507734	772.68088970500	NA
1991:01	845.40865941261	845.40866403800	NA
1992:01	NA	NA	900.8844772161
1993:01	NA	NA	965.2202364901
1994:01	NA	NA	1031.1028663964
1995:01	NA	NA	1097.9616421303

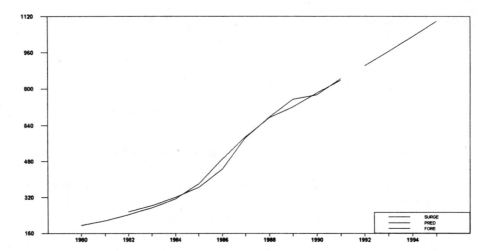

7-31. An IMA(1,1) is the equivalent of an exponential smoothing model as shown below.

$$(1-B)Y_t = (1-\Theta B)e_t$$

$$\hat{Y}_t = Y_{t-1} - \Theta_1 e_t$$

$$\hat{Y}_t = Y_{t-1} - \Theta_1(Y_{t-1} - \hat{Y}_{t-1}) = Y_{t-1} - \Theta_1 Y_{t-1} + \Theta_1 \hat{Y}_{t-1} = (1-\Theta_1)Y_{t-1} + \Theta_1 \hat{Y}_{t-1}$$

7-32. The time series **BIRTHMAR.DAT** is the quarterly marriages in the United States. Completing the common minicase forecasting assignment:

```
set dmar 2 32 = marriage - marriage(t-1)
set d4mar 5 32 = marriage - marriage(t-4)
set d14mar 6 32 = d4mar - d4mar(t-1)
```

```
AutoCorrelations of Series MARRIAGE
1: -0.1249580 -0.7113432 -0.1088449  0.8753146 -0.1027594 -0.6130366
7: -0.1067595  0.7433771
Partial Autocorrelations
1: -0.1249580 -0.7384889 -0.7946991  0.2447736 -0.2501486  0.0991728
7: -0.1067620 -0.1058799
Ljung-Box Q-Statistics
Q(8)    =        90.8147.  Significance Level 0.00000000
Note that the MARRIAGE series is seasonally nonstationary.

AutoCorrelations of First Differences of MARRIAGE (dmar)
1:  0.0026670  0.2458110  0.1350704 -0.2033804 -0.0759279 -0.1054829
7: -0.2506138
Partial Autocorrelations
1:  0.0026670  0.2458056  0.1425333 -0.2820809 -0.1758389  0.0050019
7: -0.1336555
Ljung-Box Q-Statistics  Q(7) = 7.1607.   Significance Level 0.41233695

AutoCorrelations of Series D4MAR
1:  0.0026670  0.2458110  0.1350704 -0.2033804 -0.0759279 -0.1054829
7: -0.2506138 -0.1889910
Partial Autocorrelations
1:  0.0026670  0.2458056  0.1425333 -0.2820809 -0.1758389  0.0050019
7: -0.1336555 -0.2341171
Ljung-Box Q-Statistics Q(8) = 8.6609.  Significance Level 0.37170527

AutoCorrelations of Series D14MAR
1: -0.6184818  0.1775536  0.1094151 -0.2222599  0.0723036  0.0616935
Partial Autocorrelations
1: -0.6184818 -0.3319395  0.0916958 -0.0609718 -0.2181648 -0.0591664
Ljung-Box Q-Statistics Q(6) = 14.9074.  Significance Level 0.02098946
```

Note that fourth-order seasonal differences of MARRIAGE appears to be white noise as measured by the Q-statistic; also, none of the first 7 ACFs are statistically significant(approx. $2Se = 2/32^{**}.5 = .35355$). Thus, this appears to be seasonal random walk series. Note also that first and fourth differences combined result in a higher standard deviation than fourth difference alone. Nonetheless, one might explore low-order and seasonal differencing later during the estimation of ARIMA models.

Series	Obs	Mean	Std Error	Minimum	Maximum	Stationary Level	White Noise Var.	
MARRIAGE	32	599909.4375	116739.8422	402000	724000	No	Yes	No
DMAR	31	5121.2903	174833.2036	-192000	302000	No	Yes	No
D4MAR	28	-1843.7500	13369.2345	-24000	31000	Yes	Yes	Yes
D14MAR	27	192.5926	19226.7703	-37000	37000	Yes	Yes	No

7-33. The time series **RETAIL.DAT** is the monthly retail sales in the United States. Completing the common minicase forecasting assignment: This series is variance nonstationary, so logarithms of this series are taken:

```
set lsales = log(sales)
AutoCorrelations of Series LSALES
    1: 0.90026816 0.84917444 0.83061202 0.81720407 0.80827232 0.78779978
    7: 0.76609157 0.73470023 0.70434666 0.67736508 0.68978414 0.74389395
```

```
13:  0.65509876 0.61017046 0.58988333 0.57824477 0.57089284 0.54953838
19:  0.52934390 0.49953067 0.46884459 0.44569496 0.45421949 0.49778778
25:  0.41743997 0.37614751 0.35520814 0.34469415 0.33590884 0.31532134
31:  0.29861422 0.26974037 0.24133660
Partial Autocorrelations
 1:  0.9002682  0.2041592  0.2114652  0.1318183  0.1172374  0.0137611
 7:  0.0055583 -0.0730443 -0.0583549 -0.0496817  0.1935805  0.4081182
13: -0.5878152  0.0010937  0.0189777  0.0482891 -0.0000152 -0.0279362
19:  0.0039396 -0.0207560  0.0073902  0.0852616 -0.0286665  0.0419852
25: -0.1964888 -0.0225575  0.0044667  0.0059658 -0.0321199  0.0089778
31:  0.0182949 -0.0165171  0.0169309
Ljung-Box Q-Statistics  Q(33) = 1735.4392.  Significance Level 0.00000000
```

Note the extremely high ACFS at lags 1, 12, 24, etc. So let's explore first, and seasonal twelfth-order differences.

```
set dlsales 2 132 = lsales - lsales(t-1)
set d12sales 13 132 = lsales - lsales(t-12)
set d112sales 14 132 = d12sales - d12sales(t-1)
```

Series	Obs	Mean	Std Error	Minimum	Maximum	Stationarity Level	Var	WN
SALES	132	43.60653	13.35975	23.057000000	85.075000000	No	No	No
LSALES	132	3.72972	0.30230	3.137969411	4.443533220	No	Yes	No
DLSALES	131	0.00997	0.10796	-0.350062051	0.220567046	No	Yes	No
D12SALES	120	0.08905	0.03162	0.018980721	0.170855719	Maybe	Yes	No
D112SALE	119	-0.00002	0.03275	-0.105386725	0.063333562	Yes	Yes	No

Clearly, twelfth-order differences has the lowest standard deviation. Let's see if DLSALES, D12SALES, and D112SALES are stationary:

```
AutoCorrelations of Series DLSALES
 1: -0.3113745 -0.2029153 -0.0223342 -0.0364539  0.1007745 -0.0167628
 7:  0.0927517 -0.0185777 -0.0059055 -0.2131301 -0.2771438  0.8533886
13: -0.2897426 -0.1462435 -0.0436145 -0.0294178  0.0989667 -0.0247237
19:  0.0842386 -0.0075578 -0.0243656 -0.1903691 -0.2057580  0.7235001
25: -0.2586843 -0.1171982 -0.0546203 -0.0084922  0.0783002 -0.0334104
31:  0.0929258 -0.0142362
Partial Autocorrelations
 1: -0.3113745 -0.3320643 -0.2612342 -0.2916811 -0.1554930 -0.1704546
 7:  0.0213618  0.0603851  0.1577325 -0.1394367 -0.6575976  0.5947696
13:  0.0131297  0.0825115 -0.0471307  0.0462515 -0.0155479 -0.0140435
19: -0.0211120 -0.0256451 -0.1749398 -0.0334764  0.0771729  0.0289360
25:  0.0558957 -0.0254785  0.0285370  0.0441884 -0.0416765 -0.0478255
31: -0.0115804 -0.1065738
Ljung-Box Q-Statistics  Q(32) = 279.0547.  Significance Level 0.00000000
```

First-order differences are not stationary.

```
AutoCorrelations of Series D12SALES
 1:  0.4605708  0.3731116  0.4939797  0.2854936  0.2503803  0.2670202
 7:  0.1006361  0.1230514  0.1883190 -0.0322698  0.0110386 -0.0207350
13: -0.0606903  0.0857709 -0.0017663 -0.0813426  0.0333425 -0.0385008
19: -0.1510760 -0.0859708 -0.2095203 -0.2949440 -0.1080285 -0.4002793
25: -0.3316476 -0.1694971 -0.3242828 -0.2598208 -0.0849902 -0.1475410
```

```
Partial Autocorrelations
     1:   0.4605708   0.2043297   0.3485389  -0.0745706   0.0213676   0.0050278
     7:  -0.1187665   0.0242561   0.0993484  -0.1760503   0.0023164  -0.1244932
    13:   0.0747765   0.1835738  -0.0342368  -0.0703813  -0.0101751  -0.0754561
    19:  -0.1015791  -0.0592605  -0.1311007  -0.1797520   0.1145230  -0.3277116
    25:   0.1289101   0.0589078  -0.0126861   0.0197920   0.1473551   0.0803278
Ljung-Box Q-Statistics   Q(30) = 215.8274.   Significance Level 0.00000000


AutoCorrelations of Series D112SALE, First and 12th Differences
Autocorrelations
     1:  -0.4136738  -0.1932650   0.3063735  -0.1658375  -0.0367425   0.1672077
     7:  -0.1723430  -0.0414290   0.2628527  -0.2263934   0.0581888  -0.0028006
    13:  -0.1694551   0.2223825  -0.0088848  -0.1821455   0.1747917   0.0318133
    19:  -0.1593705   0.1749795  -0.0373912  -0.2433985   0.4518158  -0.3434206
    25:  -0.1007141   0.3001964  -0.2165691  -0.0859971   0.2089631
Partial Autocorrelations
     1:  -0.4136738  -0.4396218   0.0140839  -0.0939276  -0.0551748   0.0608109
     7:  -0.0759398  -0.1455645   0.1258508  -0.0413544   0.0689334  -0.1433323
    13:  -0.2342985   0.0003106   0.0450764  -0.0272026   0.0427228   0.0548699
    19:  -0.0029649   0.0637563   0.0986798  -0.1739316   0.2649293  -0.2354826
    25:  -0.1662918  -0.0799970  -0.1012165  -0.1981673  -0.1132806
Ljung-Box Q-Statistics   Q(29) = 181.0111.   Significance Level 0.00000000
```

Note that d12sales appears to be autoregressive while dlsales is seasonally nonstationary. First and 12th differences may or may not be required depending on the results of further modeling. Thus, we conclude that seasonal differences alone or first and 12th differences may be necessary to model this time series. The results of that analysis are shown in the solution of problem 8-16.

7-34.   Superoil.dat Analysis - This series appears to be variance stationary. Let's consider first and twelfth-order differences.

```
set d12bar 13 108 = barrels - barrels(t-12)
set d1bar 2 108 = barrels - barrels(t-1)
AutoCorrelations of Series D12BAR
     1:  -0.0750593   0.2018157  -0.0295959   0.1540913   0.0357003   0.0408258
     7:   0.0167370  -0.0242547   0.1312766  -0.0124666   0.0882717  -0.3295260
    13:   0.1113371  -0.0240070   0.0976027   0.0089246  -0.0541929   0.0877697
    19:  -0.1013289   0.1768065  -0.1007770   0.1035505   0.0589218   0.0772358
Partial Autocorrelations
     1:  -0.0750593   0.1972933  -0.0027496   0.1175471   0.0615003  -0.0038287
     7:   0.0055206  -0.0488606   0.1165487   0.0096084   0.0423876  -0.3341491
    13:   0.0289476   0.1058421   0.0707312   0.0958817  -0.0891971   0.0571453
    19:  -0.1257834   0.1381421   0.0370850   0.0490228   0.1472938  -0.1655680
Ljung-Box Q-Statistics Q(24) = 35.3086.   Significance Level 0.06395355
```

Clearly, seasonal differences are stationary and very nearly equal to white noise. Thus, this appears to be the best transformation for achieving stationarity, however, before accepting this conclusion, consider first differences.

```
AutoCorrelations of Series D1BAR
     1:  -0.3092470   0.5095490  -0.3410968   0.2287300  -0.6269343   0.1129723
     7:  -0.6060360   0.1799709  -0.2666507   0.3856779  -0.0642876   0.6072868
    13:  -0.0910982   0.3674517  -0.2094279   0.1061322  -0.4854979   0.0412504
```

```
   19: -0.5007486  0.1666897 -0.2600378  0.3403117 -0.0295190  0.5138019
   25: -0.0931905  0.3548433
Partial Autocorrelations
    1: -0.3092470  0.4576854 -0.1596016 -0.1040449 -0.5586984 -0.2860708
    7: -0.4288985 -0.3157744 -0.1303626 -0.0856158 -0.1217486  0.1652921
   13:  0.0616960 -0.0853875 -0.0430099  0.0180102 -0.0748887  0.0587323
   19: -0.0397306  0.1071287  0.0014123 -0.0720374 -0.0302496  0.0561713
   25: -0.0003102 -0.0412828
Ljung-Box Q-Statistics Q(26) =  397.8623.  Significance Level 0.00000000
```

First differences appear to have seasonal nonstationarity. However, because seasonal differences are stationary, we do not believe that it is not necessary to take first and twelfth differences. The tentative model shown below confirms that seasonal differences are sufficient to achieve stationarity.

Series	Obs	Mean	Std Error	Minimum	Maximum	Stationarity Level	WN Var.	
BARRELS	108	367.37962963	61.84722171	252.00	489.00	No	Yes	No
D12BAR	96	20.35416667	12.00962699	-8.00	56.00	Yes	Yes	Maybe
D1BAR	107	1.82242991	22.74917087	-61.00	49.00	No	Yes	No
RES(a)	96	-0.36473840	11.27512534	-28.63	34.47	Yes	Yes	Yes

(a) These are residuals from the following tentative model.

```
Tentative Model
box(sma=1,sdiff=1,constant) barrels / res
Dependent Variable BARRELS - Estimation by Box-Jenkins
Iterations Taken      9
Monthly Data From 2:01 To 9:12
Usable Observations      96        Degrees of Freedom     94
Centered R**2       0.962433       R Bar **2    0.962033
Uncentered R**2     0.999135       T x R**2       95.917
Mean of Dependent Variable        377.16666667
Std Error of Dependent Variable    58.20303242
Standard Error of Estimate         11.34093235
Sum of Squared Residuals        12089.974168
Durbin-Watson Statistic             2.003986
Q(24-1)                             30.372855
Significance Level of Q             0.13899473
     Variable              Coeff        Std Error     T-Stat      Signif
******************************************************************************
1.  CONSTANT           20.63078771    0.77635080    26.57405    0.00000000
2.  SMA{12}            -0.37479137    0.09790075    -3.82828    0.00023251
```

MINICASES

MINICASE 7-1. Kansas Turnpike, Daily Data, TURNPIKD.DAT.

```
Adjusting the Fourth of July values.
Extreme Values of Series VEHICLES
Minimum Value is 56242.000000000 at 5:06  Entry 34
Maximum Value is 95411.000000000 at 5:04  Entry 32
ENTRY        DAY              DATE          VEHICLES
  5:04   6.0000000000000   7293.000000000 95411.000000000
  5:05   7.0000000000000   7393.000000000 73128.000000000
  5:06   1.0000000000000   7493.000000000 56242.000000000
set sales = vehicles
set sales 31 37 = (sales(t-7)+sales(t+7))/2
Having adjusted the Fourth of July, consider the following three differences.
set d7sales 8 91 = sales - sales(t-7)
set d1sales 2 91 = sales - sales(t-1)
set d17sales 9 91 = d7sales - d7sales(t-1)
```

Series	Obs	Mean	Std Error	Minimum	Maximum	Stationary Level	White Noise Var.	
Unadjusted	91	72706.373	6972.597	56242	95411	No	Yes	No
Adjusted	91	72571.676	6468.238	59900	91665	No	Yes	No
$Y_t - Y_{t-7}$	84	-285.000	3845.008	-8939	8299	Maybe	Yes	No
$Y_t - Y_{t-1}$	90	-109.122	6668.524	-12681	15609	No	Yes	No
$(1-B)(1-B^7)$	83	10.157	2349.498	-10805	5946	Yes	Yes	No

As a tentative identification consider the analysis completed by ForecastPro for Windows using the series adjusted for the 4th of July called ASALES in Forecast Pro.

```
Expert data exploration of dependent variable ASALES
----------------------------------------------------------------------
Length 91  Minimum 59900.0  Maximum 91665.0
Mean 72571.7 Standard deviation 6432.6

Classical decomposition (multiplicative)
Trend-cycle: 32.91%  Seasonal: 60.72%  Irregular: 6.36%

Exponential smoothing outperforms Box-Jenkins by 7240.4 to 7689.6
out-of-sample (MAD). I tried 105 forecasts up to a maximum horizon 14.

Series is trended and seasonal.  Recommended model: Exponential smoothing
However, ForecastPro is asked to automatically fit an ARIMA model.
Forecast Model for ASALES, Automatic ARIMA model selection
```
$ARIMA(0,1,0)*(0,1,1)^7$

Term	Coefficient	Std. Error	t-Statistic	Significance
B[7]	0.8791	0.0403	21.8394	1.0000

```
Standard Diagnostics
----------------------------------------------------------------------
Sample size 83                 Number of parameters 1
Mean 7.297e+004                Standard deviation 6467
```

```
R-square 0.9126                    Adjusted R-square 0.9126
Durbin-Watson 1.876                ** Ljung-Box(18)=36.5 P=0.9939
Forecast error 1912                BIC 1952 (Best so far)
MAPE 0.02059                       RMSE 1901
MAD 1505
```

As an alternate to this model, we fit a custom ARIMA model.
Forecast Model for ASALES, Custom model selection
ARIMA(1,0,0)*(0,1,1)^7

Term	Coefficient	Std. Error	t-Statistic	Significance
a[1]	0.9131	0.0495	18.4574	1.0000
B[7]	0.8814	0.0413	21.3673	1.0000

Standard Diagnostics

```
Sample size 84                     Number of parameters 2
Mean 7.286e+004                    Standard deviation 6508
R-square 0.9184                    Adjusted R-square 0.9174
Durbin-Watson 1.81                 * Ljung-Box(18)=32.51 P=0.9809
Forecast error 1870                BIC 1948 (Best so far)
MAPE 0.02                          RMSE 1848
MAD 1465
```

Note that the model with only seasonal differences has a lower BIC, and thus is chosen as the preferred model.

MINICASE 7-2. Domestic Air Passengers by Quarter, PASSAIR.DAT.

Series	Obs	Mean	Std Error	Minimum	Maximum	Stationarity Level	Var.	WhiteNoise
APASS	50	11916.592	2921.163	7025.431	17164.4227	No	No	No
LPASS	50	9.354	0.257	8.857	9.7506	No	Yes	No
SPASS	50	108.328	13.611	83.818	131.0131	No	Yes	No
$(1-B^4)$	46	0.065	0.053	-0.050	0.1616	Maybe	Yes	No
$(1-B)$	49	0.017	0.083	-0.153	0.1366	No	Yes	No
$(1-B)(1-B^4)$	45	0.000	0.045	-0.145	0.1384	Yes	Yes	No

Where APASS=original time series, LPASS=logs(APASS), SPASS=SPASS$^{.5}$,
$(1-B^4)$LPASS,$(1-B)$LPASS,$(1-B)(1-B^4)$LPASS

As a tentative identification consider the analysis completed by Forecast Pro using the series adjusted for the 4th of July called ASALES in Forecast Pro.

Expert data exploration of dependent variable APASS
```
-----------------------------------------------------------------
Length 50  Minimum 7025.4  Maximum 17164.4
Mean 11916.6 Standard deviation 2891.8
```

Classical decomposition (multiplicative)
    Trend-cycle: 95.12% Seasonal: 4.44% Irregular: 0.44%
Square root transform recommended for Box-Jenkins.
Exponential smoothing outperforms Box-Jenkins by 321.3 to 486.4
out-of-sample (MAD). I tried 36 forecasts up to a maximum horizon 8.
For Box-Jenkins, I used a square root transform.

```
Series is trended and seasonal. Recommended model: Exponential smoothing
Tentative Models with Square Roots and Logarithms:
```

Forecast Model for APASS with Square root transforms
```
Automatic model selection              ARIMA(0,1,0)*(0,1,1)⁴
Custom model selection                 ARIMA(1,0,0)*(0,1,1)⁴
```
Forecast Model for APASS with log transforms
```
Automatic model selection              ARIMA(0,1,0)*(0,1,1)⁴
Custom model selection                 ARIMA(1,0,0)*(0,1,1)⁴
```

Automatic model selection $\quad$ ARIMA$(0,1,0)*(0,1,1)^4$
Custom model selection $\quad$ ARIMA$(1,0,0)*(0,1,1)^4$
Automatic model selection $\quad$ ARIMA$(0,1,0)*(0,1,1)^4$
Custom model selection $\quad$ ARIMA$(1,0,0)*(0,1,1)^4$

```
See the file M7-2.TRL for more output and discussion.
```

MINICASE 7-3. Hospital Census by Month, CENSUSM.DAT.

This series has two outliers in periods 15 and 16 which are equated to adjacent seasonal sales (sales(t-12)+sales(t-12))/2. In addition, the actual series (aseries) has a repeating pattern of 4, 4, and 5 week months, thus every third month is adjusted to by the multiplier 4/5. This yields the final series designated as sales shown below.

Series	Obs	Mean	Std Error	Min	Max	Stationary Level	Var	White Noise
ASALES	120	11861.467	1209.621	10161	14398.	NO	YES	NO
SALES	120	10982.583	306.020	10042.4	11668.	NO	YES	NO
$(1-B^{12})$	108	-1.702	237.631	-756.8	682.	YES	YES	NO
$(1-B)$	119	-0.634	389.267	-992.6	1189.4	NO	YES	NO
$(1-B^{12})(1-B)$	107	-4.83551	310.968	-860.0	824.0	YES	YES	NO

As a tentative identification consider the analysis completed by Forecast Pro using the series adjusted for the 4th of July called ASALES in Forecast Pro.

```
Automatic model selection        ARIMA(0,0,0)*(1,0,0)¹²   BIC= 209.6
Custom forecast Model            ARIMA(1,0,0)*(0,1,1)¹²   BIC= 193.2
```

Automatic model selection $\quad$ ARIMA$(0,0,0)*(1,0,0)^{12}$ $\quad$ BIC= 209.6
Custom forecast Model $\quad$ ARIMA$(1,0,0)*(0,1,1)^{12}$ $\quad$ BIC= 193.2

```
Refer to M7-3.TRL for more information about these two FCP models.
```

MINICASE 7-4. Henry Machler's Hideaway Orchids, MACHLERD.DAT.

This series has considerable day of the year variation which is not evident when looking at just one years worth of 140 observations, nonetheless, this series can be modeled. After modeling this series here and in other chapters, it is good to emphasize the limitation of not having last years values to model this years values. There is such a large effect from Mother's Day week that we adjust the sales as shown below.

```
set asales = sales
set asales 36 42 = (sales(t-7)+sales(t+7))/2
set d1sales 2 140 = asales - asales(t-1)
set d7sales 8 140 = asales - asales(t-7)
set d17sales 9 140 = d7sales - d7sales(t-1)
```

Series	Obs	Mean	Std Error	Min	Max	Stationary	White	Noise
						Level	Var.	
SALES	140	227.510	145.738	37.07	1057.96	NO	YES	NO
ASALES	140	216.886	118.734	37.07	559.31	NO	YES	NO
D1SALES	139	-0.542	162.748	-375.47	422.48	NO	YES	NO
D7SALES	133	2.755	68.938	-238.35	161.89	YES	YES	MAYBE
D17SALES	132	-0.553	93.351	-205.14	190.55	YE	YES	NO

As a tentative identification consider the analysis completed by Forecast Pro using the series adjusted for Mother's Day called ASALES in Forecast Pro.

```
Forecast Pro for Windows Standard Edition Version 2.00
Sun Jul 20 09:40:27 1997
Expert data exploration of dependent variable ASALES
-----------------------------------------------------------------------
Length 140  Minimum 37.1  Maximum 559.3
Mean 216.9 Standard deviation 118.3
Classical decomposition (multiplicative)
    Trend-cycle: 10.92%   Seasonal: 41.93%   Irregular: 47.15%
Series is too volatile to support Box-Jenkins.
Series is trended and seasonal.  Recommended model: Exponential smoothing
```

Automatic model selection $\quad\quad\quad$ ARIMA$(0,0,0)*(1,1,2)^7$
BIC 66.08 (Best so far)   MAPE 0.3178   RMSE 62.53   MAD 51.22
Custom model selection $\quad\quad\quad$ ARIMA$(0,0,0)*(1,1,1)^7$
BIC 66.84   MAPE 0.3217   RMSE 64.42   MAD 52.01
Custom model selection $\quad\quad\quad$ ARIMA$(0,0,0)*(0,1,2)^7$
BIC 66.24   MAPE 0.3255   RMSE 63.85   MAD 51.87

```
A more detailed output exists in M7-4.TRL.
```

MINICASE 7-6. Midwestern Building Materials, LUMBER.DAT.

```
set d1sales 2 120 = sales - sales(t-1)
set d12sales 13 120 = sales - sales(t-12)
set d112sales 14 120 = d12sales - d12sales(t-1)
```

Series	Obs	Mean	Std Error	Min	Max	Stationary		
						Level	Var	WN
SALES	120	86075.34	24666.706	31984.	145752.	NO	YES	NO
D1SALES	119	245.33	21112.290	-49005.	40956.	NO	YES	NO
D12SALES	108	4859.47	4696.063	-6384.	15200.	YES	YES	NO
D112SALES	107	4.46	5287.801	-13110.	13502.	YES	YES	NO

Tentative Model: $(0,0,1)1,0(0,1,0)^{12}$
A more detailed output exists in M7-6.TRL.

MINICASE 7-7. International Airline Passengers, AIRLINE.DAT.

The is the famous nonstationary level and variance series popularized by the original Box Jenkins text of 1970.

```
set lpass = log(pass)
set dllpass 2 144 = lpass - lpass(t-1)
set d12lpass 13 144 = lpass - lpass(t-12)
set d112lpass 14 144 = d12lpass - d12lpass(t-1)
```

Series	Obs	Mean	Std Error	Min	Max	Stationary Level	Var	WN
PASS	144	280.299	119.966	104.000	622.000	NO	NO	NO
LPASS	144	5.542	0.441	4.644	6.433	NO	YES	NO
D1LPASS	143	0.009	0.107	-0.223	0.223	NO	YES	NO
D12LPASS	132	0.120	0.062	-0.042	0.319	MAYBE	YES	NO
D112LPASS	131	0.000	0.046	-0.141	0.141	YES	YES	NO

Tentative Model $(1,0,0)1,1(0,1,1)^{12}$ or $(0,1,1)0,1(0,1,1)^{12}$

MINICASE 7-8. Automobile Sales, AUTO.DAT.

```
LET'S ADJUST THE OUTLIERS FIRST.
SET SALES 1 1 = SALES(T+12)
SET SALES 55 55 = (SALES(T-12)+SALES(T+12))/2
SET D12SALES 13 185 = SALES - SALES(T-12)
SET D1SALES 2 185 = SALES - SALES(T-1)
SET D112SALES 14 185 = D12SALES - D12SALES(T-1)
```

Series	Obs	Mean	Std Error	Min	Max	Stationary Level	Var	WN
SALES	185	1546.938	473.194	446.000	2558.000	NO	YES	NO
D12SALES	173	-49.480	152.526	-340.000	286.000	NO	YES	NO
D1SALES	184	0.130	242.020	-482.000	467.000	NO	YES	NO
D112SALES	172	-0.570	51.085	-144.000	148.000	YES	YES	NO

Tentative Models $(1,0,0)(0,1,1)^{12}$ and $(0,1,0)(0,1,1)^{12}$

MINICASE 7-9. Consumption of Distilled Spirits, SPIRITS.DAT

```
THE SERIES APPEARS VARIANCE STATIONARY
SET D12SALES 13 132 = SALES - SALES(T-12)
SET D1SALES 2 132 = SALES - SALES(T-1)
SET D112SALES 14 132 = D12SALES - D12SALES(T-1)
The last observation, 132 is a seasonal outlier.
```

Series	Obs	Mean	Std Error	Min	Max	Stationary Level	Var	WN
SALES	132	33393.902	5906.877	21960.000	54090.000	NO	YES	NO
D12SALES	120	-841.583	1573.125	-8510.000	4650.000	YES	YES	NO
D1SALES	131	51.832	7064.852	-23410.000	12090.000	NO	YES	NO
D112SALES	119	-53.529	2093.439	-5520.000	5450.000	YES	YES	NO

```
AutoCorrelations of Series D12SALES
      1:   0.0187082  -0.1030098   0.1000960  -0.0844604   0.0407744   0.1430770
      7:  -0.0633017  -0.0354068   0.2121068   0.0183849   0.0833820  -0.1833591
     13:  -0.2500726   0.1332028   0.0236651  -0.0841686   0.0525087  -0.0430547
     19:  -0.1026349   0.0853090   0.0349296  -0.1610238   0.1271553  -0.2331629
     25:  -0.0096449   0.1362879  -0.1294105   0.0109364  -0.0058683  -0.1018934
Partial Autocorrelations
      1:   0.0187082  -0.1033960   0.1053191  -0.1027223   0.0714169   0.1107636
      7:  -0.0441572  -0.0230840   0.1965363   0.0256793   0.1152292  -0.2637349
     13:  -0.1874774   0.0918228  -0.0204196  -0.0682052   0.0176762  -0.0065456
     19:  -0.0543665  -0.0267474   0.1289626  -0.0404045   0.1541499  -0.3652257
     25:   0.0311173   0.0443998  -0.0150798  -0.0109660  -0.0835203  -0.0285328
```

Tentative Models $(0,0,0)1,0(0,1,2)^{12}$ and $(0,0,0)1,0(0,1,1)^{12}$

MINICASE 7-10. Discount Consumer Electronics, ELECT.DAT.

This series has some strange behavior in variance, however, logarithmic or other power transformations yield models that are not any more effective than a simple trend model with the original series.

```
SET D12SALES 13 185 = SALES - SALES(T-12)
SET D1SALES 2 185 = SALES - SALES(T-1)
SET D112SALES 14 185 = D12SALES - D12SALES(T-1)
```

Series	Obs	Mean	Std Error	Minimum	Maximum	Stationary Level	Var	WN
SALES	185	73.630	16.374	35.496	124.869	NO	YES	NO
D12SALES	173	3.284	2.755	-3.523	11.249	YES	YES	YES
D1SALES	184	0.298	13.716	-43.258	38.061	NO	YES	NO
D112SALES	172	-0.032	3.797	-10.390	12.745	YES	YES	NO

Despite some minor problems with strangely behaving variances, 12th-order seasonal differences yields white noise as shown by the following ACFs and PACFs.

```
AutoCorrelations of Series D12SALES
      1:   0.0474874   0.0920964   0.0227904  -0.0463284   0.0263726  -0.0093671
      7:  -0.0164174  -0.0050755   0.0383565   0.0783542   0.1129697   0.0774220
     13:  -0.0163937   0.1508453   0.1263217   0.0242080  -0.0275109  -0.0945926
     19:   0.0023172   0.0800022  -0.0249303   0.0539746   0.0223822   0.0531594
Partial Autocorrelations
      1:   0.0474874   0.0900444   0.0146868  -0.0568147   0.0277057  -0.0025198
      7:  -0.0192110  -0.0061806   0.0459060   0.0762704   0.0993401   0.0553858
     13:  -0.0402482   0.1470773   0.1336168  -0.0046696  -0.0607462  -0.0795196
     19:   0.0229387   0.0889561  -0.0533413   0.0167189   0.0168860   0.0350474
```

Note that logarithmic or other power transformations yield models that are not any more effective than a simple trend model. Thus, the tentative model is:

$(0,0,0)1,0(0,1,0)^{12}$

PROBLEMS

ESTIMATED DIFFICULTY

Elementary	Medium	Hard		Very Hard	Bad

1 M   2 M   3 M   4 M   5 M   6 M   7 H   8 M   9 M   10 M

11 H   12 M   13 H   14 M   15 H   16 H   17 H

Minicases are Hard to Very hard.

8-1. The four steps of ARIMA model building are identification, estimation, diagnosis, and forecasting as defined in Figure 8-1 page 332.

8-2. Seasonal level nonstationarity is normally detectable through study of the plots of the series, ACF, and PACFs. For series of sufficient length, the ACFs and PACFs will remain very high at seasonal lags and decline in a linear as opposed to exponential decline. When in doubt a seasonal autoregressive model can be fitted and the phi value assessed as either being stationary or not, however, this procedure is not infallible. When in doubt, two models can be entertained, one a seasonal autoregressive the other a seasonal differenced model.

8-3. Seasonal variance nonstationarity is normally detectable through study of the plots of the series which will have diverging (increasing variance) values as the series increases. When this is very pronounced it will be obvious from this time series plot. When less pronounced, variance nonstationarity will be obvious in taking differences on in the residuals of the resulting model. There is no difference between the concepts of nonseasonal versus seasonal nonstationarity except we have noted that students have difficulty in remembering to model both the seasonality and the variance nonstationarity.

8-4. The number of required observations is dependent on the strength of the pattern in the time series. In some cases series with as few as 48 observations can be successfully analyzed. However, one general rule of thumb is to have at least 5 to 8 seasonal cycles in order to successfully identify an ARIMA model.

8-5. Theory should drive the choice when the empirical evidence is some what sketchy. However, when there is not strong theory, either hedge by developing and presenting both models or by developing the one which is most empirically correct.

8-6. The 2 Se limits are approximately the same for lags of 1, 10 and 24, they equal $2/\sqrt{100} = .2$

8-7. Variance nonstationarity confounds the ACFs and PACFs. This is so because on average the numerator of the ACF function, the covariance is lower while the denominator, the variance is higher, thus, on average, ACFs are lower and the patterns are less pronounced. This can happen to such an extent that a series will appear as having white ACFs without logarithmic transformations and very strong discernible patterns with appropriate logarithmic transformations.

8-8. The RSE of a logarithmic time series denotes that the residual standard errors of the original series are a constant percentage of the level of the series. See pages 351 to 352 for examples.

8-9. Level stationarity is achieved when the series has a constant mean with ACFs that decline rapidly. Unfortunately, highly autocorrelated series appear as near random walks when plotted, however, typically, the ACFs patterns of autocorrelated series decline exponentially, while those of a random walk decline linearly.

8-10. a. High and significant peaks in the ACFs at 4, 8, 12, etc. that linearly decline while there is a single PACF peak a 4.

b. High and significant peaks in the ACFs at 4, 8, 12, etc. that exponentially decline while there is a single PACF peak a 4.

c. High and significant peaks in the PACFs at 4, 8, 12, etc. that exponentially decline while there is a single ACF peak a 4.

d. High and significant peaks in both the ACFs and PACFs at 4, 8, 12, etc that exponentially decline.

8-11. Outliers decrease the numerator (i.e., crosscovariance) of the ACF formula while increasing the denominator (i.e., the variance), thus ACFs are understated and typically ambiguous, this is very nearly the same as the situation discussed in problem 8-7.

8-12. The simple transformation is the exponentiation of the logarithmic forecast e^{Ft} or in spreadsheet or software format $\exp(F_t)$.

8-13. An ARIMA $(0,1,1)^{12}$ is

$$(1 - B^{12})Y_t = (1 - \theta_{12}B^{12})e_{t-12}$$

$$\hat{Y}_t = Y_{t-12} - \theta_{12}e_{t-12}$$

$$\hat{Y}_t = Y_{t-12} - \theta_{12}(Y_{t-12} - \hat{Y}_{t-12}) = Y_{t-12} - \theta_{12}Y_{t-12} + \theta_{12}\hat{Y}_{t-12} = (1 - \theta_{12})Y_{t-12} + \theta_{12}\hat{Y}_{t-12}$$

8-14. Refering to page 338 which illustrates all three forms of model expressions.

$ARIMA(1,1,0)$

$$(1 - \phi B)(1 - B)Y_t = e_t$$
$$Y_t = Y_{t-1} + \phi_1 Y_{t-1} - \phi_1 Y_{t-2} + e_t$$
$$\hat{Y}_t = Y_{t-1} + \phi_1 Y_{t-1} - \phi_1 Y_{t-2}$$

8-15. BIRTHMAR.DAT, refer to Problem 7-32 for Table 8-15 of the marriage time series.

```
BOX(SDIFF=1,diff=1,ma=1) MARRIAGE / RES
Dependent Variable MARRIAGE - Estimation by Box-Jenkins
Iterations Taken    10
```

```
Quarterly Data From 2:02 To 8:04
Usable Observations      27        Degrees of Freedom    26
Centered R**2       0.893073        R Bar **2    0.893073
Uncentered R**2     0.999744        T x R**2       26.993
Mean of Dependent Variable        998759.92593
Std Error of Dependent Variable   49875.18838
Standard Error of Estimate        16309.07094
Sum of Squared Residuals          6915630671.4
Durbin-Watson Statistic              2.170445
Q(6-1)                               5.145223
Significance Level of Q              0.39841543
    Variable      Coeff       Std Error      T-Stat     Signif
*******************************************************************
1.  MA{1}     -0.459975018  0.177096325     -2.59732  0.01526320


AutoCorrelations of Series RES
     1: -0.0975030  0.2111882   0.0967571 -0.2640670
Partial Autocorrelations
     1: -0.0975030  0.2036172   0.1400940 -0.3066557
Ljung-Box Q-Statistics Q(4)= 4.4919.  Significance Level 0.34351301
2 Se(acf) = 2/27**.5 = 0.38490
```

8-16. The time series **RETAIL.DAT** is the monthly retail sales in the United States. Refer to Problem 7-33 for Table 8-15 of this time series.

```
box(def=eq1,sdiff=1,ar=1,sma=2,vcv,constant) lsales / res3
Dependent Variable LSALES - Estimation by Box-Jenkins
Iterations Taken     16
Monthly Data From 2:02 To 11:12
Usable Observations      119       Degrees of Freedom   115
Centered R**2       0.992561        R Bar **2    0.992367
Uncentered R**2     0.999960        T x R**2      118.995
Mean of Dependent Variable        3.7762680466
Std Error of Dependent Variable   0.2796933504
Standard Error of Estimate        0.0244357593
Sum of Squared Residuals          0.0686672285
Durbin-Watson Statistic              2.061419
Q(29-3)                             78.681680
Significance Level of Q              0.00000033
    Variable      Coeff       Std Error       T-Stat     Signif
*******************************************************************
1.  CONSTANT   0.087566079  0.002046765      42.78268  0.00000000
2.  AR{1}      0.485084071  0.083461024       5.81210  0.00000006
3.  SMA{12}   -0.133972262  0.083778621      -1.59912  0.11253734
4.  SMA{24}   -0.626453376  0.088870609      -7.04905  0.00000000
Covariance\Correlation Matrix of Coefficients
            CONSTANT          AR{1}          SMA{12}          SMA{24}
CONSTANT   0.00000418925  -0.0492866923    0.2770856086    0.35060404
AR{1}     -0.00000841940   0.00696574255  -0.0179745514   -0.08877298
SMA{12}    0.00004751329  -0.00012568255   0.00701885739  -0.12948460
SMA{24}    0.00006377391  -0.00065844984  -0.00096407209   0.007897985


AutoCorrelations of Series RES3
  1: -0.0548761 -0.0418568   0.3169090 -0.0602523   0.0580570   0.24318
  7: -0.0650471  0.0681676   0.2966658 -0.1116095  -0.0071684  -0.03058
 13: -0.1256974  0.1408394   0.1459599 -0.0784003   0.0682278   0.05254
 19: -0.1515117  0.0460625  -0.0217867 -0.2104565   0.2433010  -0.00651
```

```
Partial Autocorrelations
  1: -0.0548761 -0.0450037  0.3136168 -0.0339676  0.0849808  0.16333
  7: -0.0184073  0.0444084  0.2176902 -0.0648077 -0.0618222 -0.23382
 13: -0.1009374  0.0924768  0.1840440  0.0509869  0.0163299 -0.03092
 19: -0.1118006 -0.0193320  0.0064234 -0.1794932  0.1352091 -0.07662
Ljung-Box Q-Stat  Q(24) = 64.7804.  Significance Level 0.00001311

set sres = res3*res3          set pe = res3/sales
set ape = abs(pe)

Series   Obs       Mean      Std Error      Minimum        Maximum
SALES    132  43.606537879  13.359753029  23.057000000  85.07500
LSALES   132   3.729721454   0.302304387   3.137969411   4.44353
RES3     119  -0.002329562   0.024009432  -0.062796263   0.04538
SRES     119   0.000577036   0.000730271   0.000000100   0.00394
PE       119  -0.000109918   0.000625679  -0.002078658   0.00123
APE      119   0.000481115   0.000412583   0.000008843   0.00208
```

8-17. SUPEROIL.DAT - Refer to Problem 7-34 for Table 8-15 of this time series.

```
box(sma=1,sdiff=1,constant) barrels / res
Dependent Variable BARRELS - Estimation by Box-Jenkins
Iterations Taken      9
Monthly Data From 2:01 To 9:12
Usable Observations       96      Degrees of Freedom     94
Centered R**2       0.962433     R Bar **2    0.962033
Uncentered R**2     0.999135     T x R**2       95.917
Mean of Dependent Variable      377.16666667
Std Error of Dependent Variable  58.20303242
Standard Error of Estimate       11.34093235
Sum of Squared Residuals      12089.974168
Durbin-Watson Statistic           2.003986
Q(24-1)                          30.372855
Significance Level of Q           0.13899473
    Variable    Coeff      Std Error      T-Stat      Signif
*******************************************************************
1.  CONSTANT   20.63078771   0.77635080    26.57405   0.00000000
2.  SMA{12}    -0.37479137   0.09790075    -3.82828   0.00023251

Series   Obs       Mean      Std Error      Minimum        Maximum
DATE     108  506.50000000  259.42580377  101.00000000  912.0000
BARRELS  108  367.37962963   61.84722171  252.00000000  489.0000
D12BAR    96   20.35416667   12.00962699   -8.00000000   56.0000
D1BAR    107    1.82242991   22.74917087  -61.00000000   49.0000
RES       96   -0.36473840   11.27512534  -28.63078771   34.4717
```

MINICASES

MINICASE 8-1. Kansas Turnpike, Daily Data, TURNPIKD.DAT.

Refer to Minicase 7-1 for Table 8-15.
Adjusting the Fourth of July values as shown in Minicase 7-1.

```
box(sdiff=1,ar=1,sma=1,vcv,def=eq1) sales 9 77 res2
Dependent Variable SALES - Estimation by Box-Jenkins
Iterations Taken      8
7/Year Data From 2:02 To 11:07
Usable Observations       69      Degrees of Freedom      67
Centered R**2       0.901683      R Bar **2    0.900215
Uncentered R**2     0.999299      T x R**2        68.952
Mean of Dependent Variable       73716.007246
Std Error of Dependent Variable   6290.832040
Standard Error of Estimate        1987.193115
Sum of Squared Residuals         264578743.92
Durbin-Watson Statistic             1.533603
Q(17-2)                            23.877179
Significance Level of Q             0.06720876
    Variable        Coeff        Std Error      T-Stat      Signif
**************************************************************
1.  AR{1}       0.739101638  0.081177882       9.10472   0.00000000
2.  SMA{7}     -0.532378457  0.113241920      -4.70125   0.00001333
Covariance\Correlation Matrix of Coefficients
              AR{1}          SMA{7}
AR{1}     0.00658984856  -0.2034105169
SMA{7} -0.00186989985   0.01282373251
```

FORE is the out-of-sample forecast, and FERROR is the out-of-sample forecast error.

```
set sres = res2*res2
set pe2 = res2/sales
set ape2 = abs(pe2)
set ferror = sales - fore
set sferror = ferror**2
set fpe = ferror/sales
set afpe = abs(fpe)
```

Series	Obs	Mean	Std Error	Minimum	Maximum
DAY	91	4.000	2.011	1.000	7.000
DATE	91	52967.725	30420.248	6193.000	83093.000
VEHICLES	91	72706.374	6972.597	56242.000	95411.000
SALES	91	72571.676	6468.238	59900.000	91665.000
D7SALES	70	796.357	3031.592	-6069.000	8299.000
RES2	69	627.243	1868.594	-6742.959	4643.416
FORE	12	77452.206	5298.983	72391.915	87765.580
SRES	69	3834474.550	6978309.097	993.994	45467490.535
PE	69	0.008	0.025	-0.095	0.066
PE2	69	0.008	0.025	-0.095	0.066
APE2	69	0.020	0.017	0.000	0.095
FERROR	12	-6811.873	4087.558	-15208.156	-810.179
SFERROR	12	61717398.90	64470715.00	656389.55	231288012.33
FPE	12	-0.099	0.063	-0.238	-0.011
AFPE	12	0.099	0.063	0.011	0.238

As we have seen previously, this series is not accurately forecasted because the daily data does not include day of the year affects.

MINICASE 8-2. Domestic Air Passengers by Quarter, PASSAIR.DAT.

Refer to Minicase 7-2 for Table 8-15. seasonal trending series. Analyses of the logarithms of passenger revenue (simply notated as pass below) yields the following model, fits, and forecasts.

```
box(def=eq1,sdiff=1,sma=1,ar=1,vcv,constant) pass 6 42 res1
Dependent Variable PASS - Estimation by Box-Jenkins
Iterations Taken     18
Quarterly Data From 1983:02 To 1992:02
Usable Observations      37      Degrees of Freedom     34
Centered R**2       0.967895     R Bar **2    0.966006
Uncentered R**2     0.999985     T x R**2       36.999
Mean of Dependent Variable       9.3472522101
Std Error of Dependent Variable 0.2037555330
Standard Error of Estimate       0.0375672679
Sum of Squared Residuals         0.0479841871
Durbin-Watson Statistic             1.710398
Q(9-2)                              5.045297
Significance Level of Q             0.65443531
     Variable         Coeff       Std Error      T-Stat      Signif
**********************************************************************
1.   CONSTANT     0.075300098  0.012191286      6.17655  0.00000051
2.   AR{1}        0.791975438  0.136574551      5.79885  0.00000157
3.   SMA{4}      -0.732573244  0.160559797     -4.56262  0.00006293
Covariance\Correlation Matrix of Coefficients
            CONSTANT          AR{1}           SMA{4}
CONSTANT  0.00014862745   0.0893564059   -0.4999320388
AR{1}     0.00014878015   0.01865260803  -0.2352766712
SMA{4}   -0.00097858217  -0.00515923678   0.02577944850

AutoCorrelations of Series RES1
1:   0.0222743   0.0617949   0.0485331  -0.0296100
Partial Autocorrelations
1:   0.0222743   0.0613291   0.0460711  -0.0354700
Ljung-Box Q-Statistics Q(4) = 0.3156.   Significance Level 0.98878
```

FORE is the out-of-sample forecast, and FERROR is the out-of-sample forecast error.

```
set sres = res1*res1          set pe2 = res1/pass
set ape2 = abs(pe2)           set ferror = pass - fore
set sferror = ferror**2       set fpe = ferror/pass
set afpe = abs(fpe)
```

Series	Obs	Mean	Std Error	Minimum	Maximum
DATE	50	880.060000	36.456521	821.000000	942.0000
APASS	50	11916.592375	2921.162808	7025.431137	17164.4227
PASS	50	9.354418	0.256781	8.857292	9.7506
SPASS	50	108.328365	13.611138	83.817845	131.0131
RES1	37	0.003698	0.036316	-0.113664	0.0673
FORE	8	9.701635	0.070466	9.604237	9.8005
SRES	37	0.001297	0.002630	0.000017	0.0129
PE2	37	0.000420	0.003872	-0.012015	0.0075
APE2	37	0.002933	0.002517	0.000427	0.0120
FERROR	8	-0.042313	0.036622	-0.096942	0.0001
SFERROR	8	0.002964	0.003693	0.000000	0.0094
FPE	8	-0.004379	0.003789	-0.009990	0.0000
AFPE	8	0.004382	0.003785	0.000012	0.0100

MINICASE 8-3. Hospital Census by Month, CENSUSM.DAT.

Refer to Minicase 7-3 for Table 8-15. Remember we need to adjust the 3,3,4 week artificial seasonality out of this data before analysis. The following two RATS commands eliminate the 3,3,4 influence; then we need to adjuste the outliers in observations in periods 15 and 16 as shown below.

```
seas s3 1 120 3 3
set sales = asales*(1-s3) + asales*s3*4/5
* outlier adjustment as developed below.
set sales 15 16 = (sales(t-12)+sales(t+12))/2
CORR(PAR=PAR,NUM=24,QSTAT) SALES 1 84
Correlations of Series SALES
Monthly Data From 1:01 To 7:12
Autocorrelations
  1:   0.1911186 -0.0296157  0.0722925 -0.0017976  0.0333620  0.1637441
  7:   0.0194524 -0.0460732  0.0393665 -0.0112514  0.1237176  0.5304603
 13:   0.0789548 -0.0613669  0.0192159 -0.0572984 -0.0739961  0.0716404
 19:   0.0270080 -0.0858528 -0.0202148 -0.0087029 -0.0001480  0.2746923
Partial Autocorrelations
  1:   0.1911186 -0.0686496  0.0953783 -0.0398591  0.0538253  0.1444789
  7:  -0.0387008 -0.0305592  0.0335558 -0.0274301  0.1459147  0.4889803
 13:  -0.1135924 -0.0175147 -0.0577913 -0.0797752 -0.1195490 -0.0262585
 19:   0.0577774 -0.0417945 -0.0170416  0.0197612 -0.0946281  0.0323053
Ljung-Box Q-Statistics  Q(24) = 49.0700.  Significance Level 0.00185626


BOX(DEF=EQ1,SDIFF=1,MA=1) SALES 14 84 RES1
Dependent Variable SALES - Estimation by Box-Jenkins
Iterations Taken      5
Monthly Data From 2:02 To 7:12
Usable Observations      71      Degrees of Freedom    70
Centered R**2       0.262055     R Bar **2    0.262055
Uncentered R**2     0.999561     T x R**2        70.969
Mean of Dependent Variable      10886.207042
Std Error of Dependent Variable   267.535182
Standard Error of Estimate        229.822719
Sum of Squared Residuals         3697293.7582
Durbin-Watson Statistic             1.961036
Q(17-1)                            19.310541
Significance Level of Q             0.25288888
 Variable      Coeff       Std Error     T-Stat     Signif
**********************************************************************
1.  MA{1}   0.1409030935 0.1185334200     1.18872   0.23856682


AutoCorrelations of Series RES1
  1:   0.1368561  0.0835049  0.1324470  0.2184692  0.2207480  0.1053361
  7:   0.0291332  0.0122808  0.0653958  0.1088857  0.1445324 -0.1068721
 13:   0.1600446  0.1053823  0.2185287  0.0283580  0.0670722
Partial Autocorrelations
  1:   0.1368561  0.0660116  0.1153938  0.1892928  0.1722675  0.0398500
  7:  -0.0460307 -0.0781681 -0.0215958  0.0515434  0.1331123 -0.1332170
 13:   0.1830894  0.0374352  0.1747926 -0.0589032  0.0308722
Ljung-Box Q-Statistics Q(17) = 24.1315.  Significance Level 0.11590584
```

FORE is the out-of-sample forecast, and FERROR is the out-of-sample forecast error.

```
set srse = res1*res1
set pe = res1/sales
set ape = abs(pe)
set ferror = sales - fore
set sferror = ferror**2
set fpe = ferror/sales
set afpe = abs(fpe)
```

```
Series        Obs      Mean      Std Error    Minimum        Maximum
ASALES        120   11861.46667   1209.62066   10161.00000    14398.00000
SALES         120   10978.36083    300.93062   10042.40000    11668.00000
RES1           71     -34.45655    227.18774    -747.89477       454.03656
SRSE           71   52074.55997  86313.95350      2.89440    559346.58348
PE             71      -0.00330      0.02093     -0.07125         0.04090
APE            71       0.01612      0.01363      0.00016         0.07125
FORE           12   10959.43982    324.24311   10042.40000     11364.00000
FERROR         12      37.04352     204.57118    -346.00000       329.72222
SFERROR        12   39734.14183   38810.36250     144.00000    119716.00000
FPE            12       0.00330       0.01855     -0.03140         0.02920
AFPE           12       0.01576       0.00921      0.00109         0.03140
```

```
LINREG RES1
#CONSTANT
Dependent Variable RES1 - Estimation by Least Squares
Monthly Data From 2:02 To 7:12
Usable Observations       71      Degrees of Freedom      70
Centered R**2      0.000000      R Bar **2    0.000000
Uncentered R**2    0.022799      T x R**2        1.619
Mean of Dependent Variable        -34.4565466
Std Error of Dependent Variable   227.1877371
Standard Error of Estimate        227.1877371
Sum of Squared Residuals         3612998.7526
Durbin-Watson Statistic             2.006789
Q(17-0)                            19.310541
Significance Level of Q            0.31100134
   Variable      Coeff      Std Error      T-Stat      Signif
*************************************************************************
1.  Constant     -34.45654655  26.96222394    -1.27796  0.20548649
```

Refer to M7-3.TRL for more information about these two FCPro models.

MINICASE 8-4. Henry Machler's Hideaway Orchids, MACHLERD.DAT.

Refer to Minicase 7-4 for Table 8-15. This series, while having some strange behavior in its variance is a simple seasonal trending series.

This series has considerable day of the year variation which is not evident when looking at just one years worth of 140 observations, nonetheless, this series can be modeled. After modeling this series here and in other chapters, it is good to emphasize the limitation of not having last years values to model this years values. There is such a large effect from Mother's Day week that we adjust the sales as shown below.

```
set asales = sales
set asales 36 42 = (sales(t-7)+sales(t+7))/2
set d1sales 2 140 = asales - asales(t-1)
set d7sales 8 140 = asales - asales(t-7)
set d17sales 9 140 = d7sales - d7sales(t-1)

box(def=eq1,sar=1,constant,vcv) asales 8 133 res1
Dependent Variable ASALES - Estimation by Box-Jenkins
Iterations Taken      3
7/Year Data From 2:01 To 19:07
Usable Observations      126      Degrees of Freedom      124
Centered R**2      0.688580      R Bar **2    0.686069
Uncentered R**2    0.928197      T x R**2      116.953
Mean of Dependent Variable        215.35305556
Std Error of Dependent Variable   118.35729376
Standard Error of Estimate         66.31505544
Sum of Squared Residuals          545313.13564
Durbin-Watson Statistic             1.737807
```

```
Q(31-1)                               26.777743
Significance Level of Q                0.63491644
     Variable       Coeff      Std Error     T-Stat      Signif
***********************************************************************
1.  CONSTANT     226.22597823  37.31352051    6.06284   0.00000001
2.  SAR{7}         0.84069593   0.05077193   16.55828   0.00000000
Covariance\Correlation Matrix of Coefficients
              CONSTANT         SAR{7}
CONSTANT  1392.298812932    0.1104682655
SAR{7}       0.209279878    0.002577789


corr(par=par,qstat,num=21) res1
Correlations of Series RES1
7/Year Data From 2:01 To 19:07
Autocorrelations
 1:   0.1241156  0.0136959 -0.0186775   0.0482044 -0.0640172  0.0756320
 7:   0.0677629 -0.0545034 -0.0836170   0.0837744  0.0759645  0.0531699
13:   0.0115844 -0.1004861 -0.1440737   0.0008877 -0.0034478 -0.0582375
19:   0.0220492 -0.0155424 -0.1588815
Partial Autocorrelations
 1:   0.1241156 -0.0017355 -0.0204805   0.0539096 -0.0778202  0.0946029
 7:   0.0504837 -0.0801739 -0.0565308   0.0960501  0.0587039  0.0410957
13:  -0.0105742 -0.1209705 -0.0944495   0.0362616 -0.0327206 -0.0632614
19:   0.0542370 -0.0220654 -0.1394497
Ljung-Box Q-Statistics, Q(21) = 16.8420.  Significance Level 0.72063872
```

FORE is the out-of-sample forecast, and FERROR is the out-of-sample forecast error.

```
set srse = res1*res1          set pe = res1/asales
set ape = abs(pe)             set ferror = asales - fore
set sferror = ferror**2       set fpe = ferror/asales
set afpe = abs(fpe)
```

Series	Obs	Mean	Std Error	Minimum	Maximum
DAY	140	70.500000	40.558600	1.000000	140.000000
SALES	140	227.510143	145.737967	37.070000	1057.960000
ASALES	140	216.885607	118.734057	37.070000	559.310000
D1SALES	139	-0.542014	162.747764	-375.470000	422.480000
D7SALES	133	2.754737	68.937688	-238.350000	161.890000
D17SALES	132	-0.552500	93.350690	-205.140000	190.550000
SRSE	126	4327.882029	6328.108183	1.315795	39456.438803
PE	126	-0.126829	0.461781	-2.788334	0.577185
APE	126	0.315023	0.359754	0.003223	2.788334
FORE	12	251.950206	102.156551	136.443034	459.816725
FERROR	12	5.713960	79.141096	-104.869230	142.713203
SFERROR	12	5774.019696	6214.295963	97.838861	20367.058288
FPE	12	-0.307128	0.882286	-2.788334	0.385077
AFPE	12	0.489918	0.787078	0.044533	2.788334
RES2	126	-0.000000	66.049263	-198.636449	172.384233

To calculate the DW and Q-statistics for the forecast errors, the following linear regression was run.

```
linreg ferror
#constant
Dependent Variable FERROR - Estimation by Least Squares
7/Year Data From 16:04 To 18:01
Usable Observations      12        Degrees of Freedom     11
Centered R**2     0.000000        R Bar **2    0.000000
Uncentered R**2   0.005655        T x R**2        0.068
Mean of Dependent Variable        5.713960256
Std Error of Dependent Variable  79.141096234
Standard Error of Estimate       79.141096234
```

```
Sum of Squared Residuals          68896.444245
Durbin-Watson Statistic               1.910811
Q(3-0)                                1.495595
Significance Level of Q             0.68328728
    Variable       Coeff      Std Error     T-Stat     Signif
**************************************************************
1.  Constant     5.713960256 22.846066607    0.25011  0.80711418
```

MINICASE 8-6. Midwestern Building Materials, LUMBER.DAT.

Refer to Minicase 7-6 for Table 8-15. Tentative Model: $(0,0,1)1,0(0,1,0)^{12}$

```
box(def=eq1,sdiff=1,constant,ma=1) sales 13 108 res1
Dependent Variable SALES - Estimation by Box-Jenkins
Iterations Taken    14
Monthly Data From 2:01 To 9:12
Usable Observations     96      Degrees of Freedom    94
Centered R**2     0.962883      R Bar **2    0.962488
Uncentered R**2   0.997514      T x R**2     95.761
Mean of Dependent Variable       86793.958333
Std Error of Dependent Variable 23374.015707
Standard Error of Estimate        4527.087723
Sum of Squared Residuals       1926485185.7
Durbin-Watson Statistic             1.856289
Q(24-1)                            22.501125
Significance Level of Q          0.49019691
    Variable       Coeff      Std Error     t-Stat     Signif
**************************************************************
1.  CONSTANT    4750.4835    629.37308     7.54796  0.000000
2.  MA{1}          0.3669      0.09847     3.72548  0.000333
```

FORE is the out-of-sample forecast, and FERROR is the out-of-sample forecast error.

```
set srse = res1*res1          set pe = res1/sales
set ape = abs(pe)             set ferror = sales - fore
set sferror = ferror**2       set fpe = ferror/sales
set afpe = abs(fpe)
Series    Obs       Mean      Std Error       Minimum       Maximum
DATE      120      556.50       288.45        101.00       1012.00
SALES     120    86075.34     24666.71      31984.00     145752.00
RES2      108        2.17      4340.20     -10639.22       9094.35
RES1      108       94.41      4379.38     -10604.36       9154.68
D12SALES  108     4859.47      4696.06      -6384.00      15200.00
SRSE      108 19010323.94  25592334.46         63.62  112452521.66
PE        108        0.00         0.06         -0.21          0.16
APE       108        0.04         0.04          0.00          0.21
FORE       12   104109.96     22054.48      71647.25     144133.48
FERROR     12      958.54      2867.11      -5593.48       7003.52
SFERROR    12  8454108.98  15450960.20        380.89   49049243.33
FPE        12        0.01         0.02         -0.04          0.06
AFPE       12        0.02         0.02          0.00          0.06
```

MINICASE 8-7. International Airline Passengers, AIRLINE.DAT.

Refer to Minicase 7-7 for Table 8-15. We fit two different ARIMA models to this data. Not surprisingly, the classical $(0,1,1)0,1$ $(0,1,1)12$ of Box and Jenkins fits and forecasts the out-of-sample data the best. Both models are illustrated below.

```
box(def=eq1,diff=1,sdiff=1,sma=1,ma=1) lpass 14 108 res2
Dependent Variable LPASS - Estimation by Box-Jenkins
Iterations Taken      7
Monthly Data From 1950:02 To 1957:12
Usable Observations        95        Degrees of Freedom    93
Centered R**2        0.986422        R Bar **2    0.986276
Uncentered R**2      0.999952        T x R**2      94.995
Mean of Dependent Variable          5.4494345706
Std Error of Dependent Variable 0.3278291639
Standard Error of Estimate          0.0384053215
Sum of Squared Residuals            0.1371720909
Durbin-Watson Statistic                1.958257
Q(23-2)                               16.785071
Significance Level of Q              0.72404973
    Variable       Coeff        Std Error      T-Stat      Signif
**********************************************************************
1.   MA{1}      -0.351678902  0.098084014      -3.58549   0.00053846
2.   SMA{12}    -0.609708211  0.089046649      -6.84707   0.00000000

box(def=eq2,ar=1,sdiff=1,constant,sma=1) lpass 14 108 res3
Dependent Variable LPASS - Estimation by Box-Jenkins
Iterations Taken      8
Monthly Data From 1950:02 To 1957:12
Usable Observations        95        Degrees of Freedom    92
Centered R**2        0.987058        R Bar **2    0.986777
Uncentered R**2      0.999954        T x R**2      94.996
Mean of Dependent Variable          5.4494345706
Std Error of Dependent Variable 0.3278291639
Standard Error of Estimate          0.0376982146
Sum of Squared Residuals            0.1307462951
Durbin-Watson Statistic                2.290179
Q(23-2)                               18.572234
Significance Level of Q              0.61255986
    Variable       Coeff        Std Error      T-Stat      Signif
**********************************************************************
1.   CONSTANT    0.135723933  0.005979076      22.69982   0.00000000
2.   AR{1}       0.701140843  0.076251365       9.19513   0.00000000
3.   SMA{12}    -0.626744332  0.087999463      -7.12214   0.00000000
```

FORE is the out-of-sample forecast, and FERROR is the out-of-sample forecast error.

```
fore 1 36 109
#eq1 fore1
fore 1 36 109
#eq2 fore2
set pe1 = res2/lpass,       set ape1 = abs(pe1)
set pe2 = res3/lpass,       set ape2 = abs(pe2)
set ferror1=lpass-fore1,    set ferror2 = lpass-fore2
set fpe1 = fore1/lpass,     set fpe2 = fore2/lpass
set afpe1 = abs(fpe1),      set afpe2 = abs(fpe2)
set sferror1 = ferror1**2,  set sferror2 = ferror2**2
```

Series	Obs	Mean	Std Error	Minimum	Maximum
PASS	144	280.2986	119.96631694	104.000	622.000
LPASS	144	5.5422	0.44145642	4.644	6.433
RES2	95	0.0038	0.03801153	-0.118	0.110
RES3	95	0.0013	0.03727066	-0.138	0.121
FORE1	36	6.1177	0.16833989	5.824	6.469
FORE2	36	6.1739	0.18186065	5.842	6.548
PE1	95	0.0007	0.00716247	-0.022	0.021
APE1	95	0.0055	0.00464716	0.000	0.022
PE2	95	0.0003	0.00705037	-0.026	0.024
APE2	95	0.0053	0.00466607	0.000	0.026
FERROR1	36	-0.0734	0.03309783	-0.178	-0.0008
FERROR2	36	-0.1296	0.04086830	-0.252	-0.0315
FPE1	36	1.0122	0.00560308	1.000	1.0295
FPE2	36	1.0215	0.00681919	1.005	1.0418
AFPE1	36	1.0122	0.00560308	1.000	1.0295
AFPE2	36	1.0215	0.00681919	1.005	1.0418
SFERROR1	36	0.0064	0.00574155	0.000	0.0318
SFERROR2	36	0.0184	0.01124503	0.001	0.0637

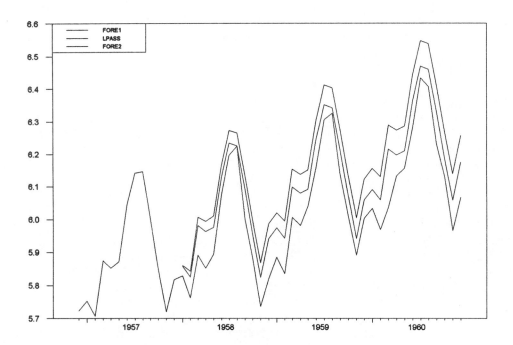

The following illustrate the DW and Q-stat for the each error.

```
Dependent Variable FERROR1 - Estimation by Least Squares
Usable Observations       36        Degrees of Freedom    35
Centered R**2    -0.000000       R Bar **2  -0.000000
Mean of Dependent Variable      -0.073352294
Std Error of Dependent Variable  0.033097834
Standard Error of Estimate       0.033097834
Sum of Squared Residuals         0.0383413309
Durbin-Watson Statistic            1.523621
Q(9-0)                            14.402843
Significance Level of Q            0.10869960
```

```
Variable        Coeff        Std Error       T-Stat      Signif
****************************************************************
1.  Constant  -0.073352294  0.005516306    -13.29736   0.00000000

Dependent Variable FERROR2 - Estimation by Least Squares
Usable Observations      36      Degrees of Freedom    35
Centered R**2      0.000000      R Bar **2    0.000000
Mean of Dependent Variable        -0.129558560
Std Error of Dependent Variable   0.040868296
Standard Error of Estimate        0.040868296
Sum of Squared Residuals          0.0584576177
Durbin-Watson Statistic           1.040384
Q(9-0)                            10.574965
Significance Level of Q           0.30597081
Variable        Coeff        Std Error       T-Stat      Signif
****************************************************************
1.  Constant  -0.129558560  0.006811383    -19.02089   0.00000000
```

MINICASE 8-8. Automobile Sales, AUTO.DAT.

Refer to Minicase 7-8 for Table 8-15.
Tentative Models $(1,0,0)(0,1,1)^{12}$ and $(0,1,0)(0,1,1)^{12}$

```
BOX(DEF=EQ1,AR=1,SDIFF=1,SMA=1,VCV) SALES 14 173 RES1
Dependent Variable SALES - Estimation by Box-Jenkins
Iterations Taken      8
Monthly Data From 2:02 To 15:05
Usable Observations     160      Degrees of Freedom   158
Centered R**2      0.988246      R Bar **2    0.988171
Mean of Dependent Variable        1603.9281250
Std Error of Dependent Variable   443.3577812
Standard Error of Estimate        48.2198101
Sum of Squared Residuals          367373.71391
Durbin-Watson Statistic           1.879002
Q(36-2)                           41.413077
Significance Level of Q           0.17866945
    Variable        Coeff        Std Error      T-Stat      Signif
****************************************************************************
1.  AR{1}    0.9460255177  0.0301420125     31.38561   0.00000000
2.  SMA{12}  0.3580955127  0.0790095186      4.53231   0.00001146
Covariance\Correlation Matrix of Coefficients
             AR{1}         SMA{12}
AR{1}     0.00090854092  -0.0644271631
SMA{12}  -0.00015343367   0.00624250403

CORR(PAR=PAR) RES1
Correlations of Series RES
Monthly Data From 2:02 To 15:05
Autocorrelations
 1:  0.0512249 -0.1318700 -0.0851502  0.0369227 -0.0913331 -0.1486698
 7:  0.1011794  0.0831812 -0.0165678  0.0404545  0.0253181  0.0137857
13: -0.1318505  0.0195562 -0.0154822  0.0861730  0.0328747  0.0344141
19:  0.0945051  0.1206502 -0.0583116 -0.0317718  0.0700084  0.0111131
25: -0.0553048 -0.0119895  0.0993558 -0.0221213  0.0291235  0.0881302
31: -0.0502744 -0.1569107 -0.0426639  0.1528857  0.0466991 -0.0899612
37:  0.0622450  0.1142443  0.0830027 -0.1318302
```

```
Partial Autocorrelations
  1:    0.0512249 -0.1348479 -0.0720730   0.0282370 -0.1182875 -0.1414012
  7:    0.0982346  0.0187087 -0.0196121   0.0784320 -0.0084662  0.0181359
 13:   -0.0850925  0.0371529 -0.0511151   0.1012391  0.0248990  0.0252989
 19:    0.1011510  0.1528022 -0.0401511   0.0586605  0.1086793 -0.0106732
 25:    0.0217679  0.0034589  0.0575372  -0.0438994  0.1148604  0.0570562
 31:   -0.0670939 -0.1055082 -0.0023588   0.0718913  0.0313955 -0.0905929
 37:    0.0208826  0.0630981  0.0769585  -0.0913000
```

FORE is the out-of-sample forecast, and FERROR is the out-of-sample forecast error.

```
set srse = res1**2              set pe = res1/sales
set ape = abs(pe)               set srse = res1**2
set ferror = sales - fore       set sferror = ferror*2
set fpe = ferror/sales          set afpe = abs(fpe)
tab
Series     Obs       Mean    Std Error     Minimum       Maximum
DATE       185   93.000000   53.549043    1.000000      185.000
SALES      185 1546.937838  473.194099  446.000000     2558.000
D12SALES   173  -49.479769  152.526412 -340.000000      286.000
D1SALES    184    0.130435  242.019931 -482.000000      467.000
D112SALES  172   -0.569767   51.085020 -144.000000      148.000
RES        160   -3.753492   47.920238 -152.547773      131.969
PAR         41    0.032666    0.171619   -0.141401        1.000
FORE        12  688.629775  375.654045  185.256378     1341.077
SRSE       160 2296.085712 3524.252126    0.723192    23270.823
RES2       160   -1.950512   48.513948 -154.771645      137.563
RES1       160   -3.753492   47.920238 -152.547773      131.968583
PE         160   -0.003722    0.034869   -0.140996        0.107978
APE        160    0.026090    0.023342    0.000738        0.140996
FERROR      12  148.370225   95.638201   14.171837      264.743627
SFERROR     12  296.740449  191.276402   28.343674      529.487253
FPE         12    0.227936    0.180854    0.010860        0.584627
AFPE        12    0.227936    0.180854    0.010860        0.584627
```

To calculate the DW and Q-statistics for the forecast errors, the following linear regression was run.

```
Dependent Variable FERROR - Estimation by Least Squares
Monthly Data From 15:06 To 16:05
Usable Observations       12      Degrees of Freedom     11
Centered R**2      0.000000      R Bar **2    0.000000
Uncentered R**2    0.724179      T x R**2        8.690
Mean of Dependent Variable      148.37022469
Std Error of Dependent Variable  95.63820076
Standard Error of Estimate       95.63820076
Sum of Squared Residuals        100613.31989
Durbin-Watson Statistic            0.207532
Q(3-0)                            15.607353
Significance Level of Q            0.00136475
    Variable        Coeff       Std Error     T-Stat     Signif
************************************************************************
1.  Constant    148.37022469   27.60837048    5.37410   0.00022537
```

MINICASE 8-9. Consumption of Distilled Spirits, SPIRITS.DAT

Refer to Minicase 7-9 for Table 8-15.

```
BOX(def=eq1,SDIFF=1,ar=||3||,SMA=2,CONSTANT) SALES 16 120 RES1
Dependent Variable SALES - Estimation by Box-Jenkins
Iterations Taken    10
Monthly Data From 2:04 To 10:12
```

```
Usable Observations    105        Degrees of Freedom   101
Centered R**2       0.957553      R Bar **2    0.956292
Uncentered R**2     0.998776      T x R**2      104.871
Mean of Dependent Variable        33502.619048
Std Error of Dependent Variable   5801.594654
Standard Error of Estimate        1212.910079
Sum of Squared Residuals          148586236.94
Durbin-Watson Statistic              2.028972
Q(26-3)                             32.230043
Significance Level of Q              0.09545305
    Variable         Coeff         Std Error      T-Stat      Signif
***********************************************************************
1.   CONSTANT     -722.7023272    65.0367312    -11.11222   0.00000000
2.   AR{3}           0.2679964     0.1032956      2.59446   0.01088249
3.   SMA{12}        -0.3455211     0.0993612     -3.47742   0.00074811
4.   SMA{24}        -0.4266202     0.1071430     -3.98178   0.00012909

corr(par=par) res1
Correlations of Series RES1
Monthly Data From 2:01 To 10:12
Autocorrelations
 1: -0.0626422 -0.0801365 -0.0647699 -0.1193899  0.0483687  0.11095
 7: -0.0264684 -0.0848240  0.1921032 -0.0005794  0.0957604 -0.01092
13: -0.2743247  0.1157623  0.0518043 -0.0131387  0.0461766  0.02753
19: -0.0453756  0.0086955  0.1457680 -0.1800682  0.1298079 -0.08289
25: -0.0245327  0.0261669 -0.0677936
Partial Autocorrelations
 1: -0.0626422 -0.0843917 -0.0763411 -0.1384917  0.0165947  0.09076
 7: -0.0238071 -0.0856515  0.2083138  0.0391552  0.1120441  0.01007
13: -0.2145025  0.1148603  0.0099491 -0.0537882  0.0226979  0.04402
19:  0.0186207 -0.0597186  0.1363033 -0.0763816  0.1124209 -0.06361
25: -0.0251098 -0.0686747 -0.0491448
```

Calculating Fitted Error (Residual) Errors

```
set srse = res1*res1
set pe = res1/sales
set ape = abs(pe)
```

FORE is the out-of-sample forecast, and FERROR is the out-of-sample forecast error.
Calculating Forecast Errors for Observations 174 to 185

```
set ferror = sales - fore
set sferror = ferror**2
set fpe = ferror/sales
set afpe = abs(fpe)
Series    Obs      Mean        Std Error      Minimum      Maximum
SALES     132    33393.902      5906.877      21960.000     54090.
RES1      105       -6.420      1195.271      -2707.732      3834.5
SRSE      105  1415107.018   2293530.614         40.205  14703281.2
PE        105       -0.000         0.034         -0.065       0.095
APE       105        0.027         0.021          0.000       0.095
FORE       12    30387.627      5969.819      24694.102     46955.6
FERROR     12    -1528.460      2313.219      -7325.612       467.7
SFERROR    12  7241255.552  15150160.272        816.341  53664588.9
FPE        12       -0.050         0.069         -0.185       0.016
AFPE       12        0.056         0.064          0.001       0.185
```

To calculate the DW and Q-statistics for the forecast errors, the following linear regression was run.

```
linreg ferror
#constant
Dependent Variable FERROR - Estimation by Least Squares
Monthly Data From 11:01 To 11:12
Usable Observations      12        Degrees of Freedom     11
Centered R**2      0.000000      R Bar **2   0.000000
Uncentered R**2    0.322622      T x R**2        3.871
Mean of Dependent Variable        -1528.459962
Std Error of Dependent Variable  2313.218701
Standard Error of Estimate        2313.218701
Sum of Squared Residuals          58860788.339
Durbin-Watson Statistic              1.103976
Q(3-0)                               1.229265
Significance Level of Q            0.74599425
    Variable        Coeff        Std Error       T-Stat      Signif
*******************************************************************
1.  Constant     -1528.459962   667.768720     -2.28891   0.04286002
```

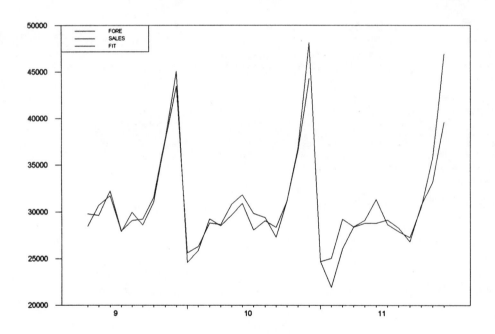

MINICASE 8-10. Discount Consumer Electronics, ELECT.DAT.

Refer to Minicase 7-10 for Table 8-15. This series, while have some strange behavior in its variance is a simple seasonal trending series.

```
BOX(def=eq1,SDIFF=1,CONSTANT) SALES 13 173 RES1
Dependent Variable SALES - Estimation by Box-Jenkins
Iterations Taken      2
Monthly Data From 2:01 To 15:05
Usable Observations    161      Degrees of Freedom   160
Centered R**2      0.963742     R Bar **2    0.963742
Uncentered R**2    0.998666     T x R**2     160.785
Mean of Dependent Variable      73.938534161
Std Error of Dependent Variable 14.494233021
Standard Error of Estimate       2.759923750
Sum of Squared Residuals      1218.7486571
Durbin-Watson Statistic          1.902174
Q(36-0)                         31.621715
Significance Level of Q          0.67689502
    Variable     Coeff      Std Error     T-Stat     Signif
***************************************************************
1.  CONSTANT  3.3263602484 0.2175124628    15.29273  0.00000000
```

FORE is the out-of-sample forecast, and FERROR is the out-of-sample forecast error.

```
set srse = res1**2
set pe = res1/sales
set ape = abs(pe)
set srse = res1**2
set ferror = sales - fore
set sferror = ferror*2
set fpe = ferror/sales
set afpe = abs(fpe)
```

Series	Obs	Mean	Std Error	Minimum	Maximum
SALES	185	73.6297	16.3740	35.4960	124.8690
RES1	161	0.0000	2.7599	-6.8494	7.9226
FORE	12	95.8379	10.2924	80.3174	118.7894
SRSE	161	7.5699	10.1802	0.0001	62.7682
PE	161	0.0005	0.0403	-0.0946	0.1117
APE	161	0.0320	0.0244	0.0001	0.1117
FERROR	12	-0.6044	2.7418	-4.6694	6.0796
SFERROR	12	-1.2087	5.4835	-9.3387	12.1593
FPE	12	-0.0081	0.0262	-0.0525	0.0487
AFPE	12	0.0185	0.0197	0.0018	0.0525

```
print 174 185 sales fore ferror fpe
```

ENTRY	SALES	FORE	FERROR	FPE
15:06	100.869	100.623	0.2456	0.0024
15:07	94.274	95.973	-1.6994	-0.0180
15:08	89.017	93.686	-4.6694	-0.0525
15:09	94.379	95.157	-0.7784	-0.0082
15:10	97.175	96.588	0.5866	0.0060

```
15:11    86.808   87.812  -1.0044  -0.0116
15:12   124.869  118.789   6.0796   0.0487
16:01    81.611   82.254  -0.6434  -0.0079
16:02    94.631   94.305   0.3256   0.0034
16:03    80.459   80.317   0.1416   0.0018
16:04   105.241  106.452  -1.2114  -0.0115
16:05    93.470   98.095  -4.6254  -0.0495
```

The following simple regression analysis is used to calculate the DW and Qstatistic of forecast errors.

```
linreg ferror
#constant
Dependent Variable FERROR - Estimation by Least Squares
Monthly Data From 15:06 To 16:05
Usable Observations       12        Degrees of Freedom    11
Centered R**2       0.000000       R Bar **2    0.000000
Uncentered R**2     0.050337       T x R**2        0.604
Mean of Dependent Variable        -0.604360248
Std Error of Dependent Variable   2.741767678
Standard Error of Estimate        2.741767678
Sum of Squared Residuals          82.690190000
Durbin-Watson Statistic            1.716998
Q(3-0)                             0.039855
Significance Level of Q            0.99790902
   Variable        Coeff       Std Error      T-Stat     Signif
**********************************************************************
1.  Constant    -0.604360248  0.791480153    -0.76358  0.46118014
```

PROBLEMS

ESTIMATED DIFFICULTY

Elementary	Medium	Hard	Very Hard	Bad

1 M   2 M   3 E   4 E   5 M   6 M   7 H   8 H   9 H   10 H

11 M-V[a]   12 M-V[a]   13 M-V[a]   14 M-V[a]

Minicases are all Hard to Very hard[a].

Note a. Concerning Problems 9-11 through Minicases:

These problems can be of Medium difficulty to Very Hard depending on the software used in the class. If the software generates prediction intervals as SAS and ForecastPro for Windows[tm], then these are not difficult problems. In contrast, these are extremely difficult if intervals have to be generated manually.

9-1   a. Fig. 9-1(a) and Fig. 9-2,   b. Similar to Fig. 9-1 (c) and see equation 9-25,

c. Similar to Fig. 9-1(d) but having a finite maximum and minimum limits, see equation 9-25

d. See Fig. 9-4,   e. See Fig. 9-5,   f. Similar to Fig. 9-1(d),

g. See Fig. 9-7,   h. See Fig. 9-13,   i. See Fig. 9-10,

j. Similar to Fig. 9-10 but with changes at 12 instead of 4,

k. Similar to Fig. 9-8 with an MA(1) component.

9-2.   a. (0,0,0)   b. (0,0,0)   c. (0,1,0)1

d. $(0,1,0)^4 1$ e. $(0,1,0)^4$ f. $(0,1,0)^4 1$

9-3. A conditional forecast uses all known actual values through period t, while an unconditional forecast does not use any actual information other than the nature of the stochastic process that generates the output series, the unconditional forecast is the equivalent of an extremely long-period conditional forecast.

9-4. See Table 9-1.   9-5. See Table 9-1.

9-6. The analyst may want to choose the (0,1,0)1 model because the deterministic trend reduces the width of the prediction intervals. However, if theory dictated that the series is actually a random walk with a stochastic trend, then that model should be chosen. If both models are equally plausible, then both might be used in planning purposes.

9-7. From the spreadsheet P8-7.wk1 the following results:

```
phi=      0.75343 sigma=    1.9248
m         EMSE(m) EFSE(m)
     1  3.70486   1.9248
     2  5.80794   2.40997
     3  7.00177   2.64609
     4  7.67946   2.77118
```

9-8. Prediction intervals are useful when they confirm the theory of the series. The width of prediction intervals can be very sobering. It is important to present these intervals to avoid greater disappointment when the actual values fall at the extreme of the intervals. To keep the reality of the prediction intervals in perspective, it is useful to present 68% (1 sigma), 95% (2 sigma) and 99.73 (3 sigma) intervals in many planning processes.

9-9.   a. See page 379.   b. See page 383.   c. See pages 380.

        d. See page 383.   e. See page 386 except with psi values of zero at 2, 3, and 4 only.

        f. See page 386 except with psi values of zero at 2, 3, and 4 only.

9-10. The actual error in forecasting will deviate greater the further in the future projections are made because of the cumulative effects from minor or fundamental shifts in the time series. Tracking signals which are discussed in Chapter 17 are designed to detect such fundamental changes.

Note Concerning Problems 9-11 through Minicases:

These problems can be of Medium to Very Hard depending on the software used in the class. If the software generates prediction intervals as SAS^{tm} and ForecastPro^{tm}, then these are not difficult problems. In contrast, these are quite difficult if intervals have to be generated manually. The remaining problems use output from ForecastPro^{tm} which is easily interpreted.

9-11. BIRTHMAR.DAT - The following is the output of ForecastPro for Windows^{tm}.

```
Forecast Model for MARR
Automatic model selection
ARIMA(1,1,1)*(0,1,0)
Term            Coefficient  Std. Error  t-Statistic  Significance
-------------------------------------------------------------------
a[1]               -0.6886      0.2205      -3.1237       0.9938
b[1]                0.5502      0.2258       2.4366       0.9739
Standard Diagnostics
-------------------------------------------------------------

Sample size 19                  Number of parameters 2
Mean 6.124e+005                 Standard deviation 1.135e+005
R-square 0.9902                 Adjusted R-square 0.9896
Durbin-Watson 2.214             Ljung-Box(7)=3.893 P=0.208
Forecast error 1.157e+004       BIC 1.278e+004
MAPE 0.01577                    RMSE 1.095e+004
MAD 8975
```

Rolling simulation results

H	N	Cumulative MAD	Average	Cumulative MAPE	Average
1	8	19034.1	19034.1	0.035	0.035
2	7	13880.6	16629.1	0.024	0.030
3	6	15654.0	16350.5	0.027	0.029
4	5	12594.3	15628.2	0.024	0.028
5	4	28656.0	17365.2	0.051	0.031
6	3	24246.3	17990.8	0.036	0.032
7	2	41941.2	19359.4	0.064	0.034
8	1	37643.4	19867.2	0.065	0.034

Prediction Intervals for Forecasts of MARR from base period 1990-Q4

Period	Lower 2.5	Forecast	Upper 97.5	Actual
1991-Q1	421993.5	447047.3	472101.2	411000.0
1991-Q2	674974.1	700732.8	726491.5	674000.0
1991-Q3	710027.7	740033.6	770039.4	709000.0
1991-Q4	576860.8	606874.1	636887.5	578000.0
1992-Q1	413465.8	460229.0	506992.1	423000.0
1992-Q2	662757.9	709570.8	756383.7	662000.0
1992-Q3	699245.6	751862.8	804479.9	697000.0
1992-Q4	563686.1	616643.4	669600.8	579000.0

These are reasonably tight 95% prediction intervals for two year ahead forecasts, however, in all cases these intervals yielded forecasts which were higher than the actual values. The fact that 8 observations were withheld out of only 32 has adversely affected the accuracy of the final results.

9-12. RETAIL.DAT - The following is the output of ForecastPro for Windows[tm].
Forecast Model for SALES (Log transform)
ARIMA(1,0,0)*(0,1,2)

Term	Coefficient	Std. Error	t-Statistic	Significance
a[1]	0.4374	0.0910	4.8074	1.0000
B[12]	0.1055	0.0580	1.8187	0.9278
B[24]	0.7689	0.0562	13.6725	1.0000
_CONST	0.0493	0.0081	6.0894	1.0000

Standard Diagnostics

Sample size 96	Number of parameters 3
Mean 3.679	Standard deviation 0.2283
R-square 0.9914	Adjusted R-square 0.9912
Durbin-Watson 2.062	Ljung-Box(18)=27.76 P=0.9341
Forecast error 0.02143	BIC 0.8969 (Best so far)
MAPE 0.01713	RMSE 0.8936
MAD 0.7023	

Rolling simulation results

H	N	MAD	Cumulative Average	MAPE	Cumulative Average
1	24	1.1	1.1	0.017	0.017
2	23	1.3	1.2	0.020	0.019
3	22	1.4	1.3	0.021	0.019
4	21	1.4	1.3	0.021	0.020
5	20	1.5	1.3	0.022	0.020
6	19	1.5	1.4	0.023	0.021
7	18	1.6	1.4	0.024	0.021
8	17	1.7	1.4	0.024	0.021
9	16	1.7	1.4	0.025	0.022
10	15	1.7	1.5	0.026	0.022
11	14	1.7	1.5	0.025	0.022
12	13	1.8	1.5	0.026	0.022
13	12	2.4	1.6	0.035	0.023
14	11	2.6	1.6	0.038	0.024
15	10	3.0	1.7	0.042	0.024
16	9	2.9	1.7	0.041	0.025
17	8	3.2	1.7	0.044	0.026
18	7	3.3	1.8	0.045	0.026
19	6	3.3	1.8	0.045	0.026
20	5	3.7	1.8	0.051	0.027
21	4	3.8	1.9	0.051	0.027
22	3	3.9	1.9	0.052	0.027
23	2	4.7	1.9	0.061	0.028
24	1	5.5	1.9	0.065	0.028

Prediction Intervals for Forecasts of SALES from base period 1976-12

Period	Lower 2.5	Forecast	Upper 97.5	Actual
1977-01	49.1	51.3	53.6	49.9
1977-02	47.3	49.7	52.1	49.8
1977-03	54.2	57.0	59.8	58.3
1977-04	57.0	59.9	62.9	60.0
1977-05	56.5	59.3	62.4	60.4
1977-06	58.2	61.2	64.3	61.4
1977-07	58.6	61.6	64.7	60.8
1977-08	58.2	61.1	64.2	61.8
1977-09	55.3	58.1	61.0	59.4
1977-10	57.0	59.9	62.9	62.0
1977-11	57.8	60.8	63.8	63.2
1977-12	69.5	73.0	76.7	75.6
1978-01	52.3	55.8	59.4	53.3
1978-02	50.5	53.9	57.6	53.7
1978-03	57.5	61.5	65.7	65.0
1978-04	59.2	63.2	67.5	64.1
1978-05	61.6	65.8	70.3	68.4
1978-06	62.1	66.3	70.9	69.6
1978-07	61.9	66.1	70.7	67.1
1978-08	62.1	66.3	70.9	69.8
1978-09	59.4	63.5	67.8	66.9
1978-10	62.6	66.9	71.5	69.3
1978-11	62.8	67.1	71.7	72.0
1978-12	74.5	79.6	85.0	85.1

These are reasonably tight and accurate 95% prediction intervals for two year ahead forecasts. Note that the actuals value do not deviate greatly from the forecast.

9-13 SUPEROIL.DAT - The following is the output of ForecastPro for Windows[tm].

```
Forecast Pro for Windows Standard Edition Version 2.00
Sat Jul 26 15:48:02 1997
Forecast Model for BARRELS
ARIMA(0,0,0)*(0,1,1)
Term          Coefficient  Std. Error  t-Statistic  Significance
----------------------------------------------------------------
B[12]              0.8140      0.0511      15.9158       1.0000
_CONST            20.8700      0.6322      33.0136       1.0000
Standard Diagnostics
----------------------------------------------------------------
Sample size 72              Number of parameters 1
Mean 355.4                  Standard deviation 47.84
R-square 0.9469             Adjusted R-square 0.9469
Durbin-Watson 2.14          Ljung-Box(18)=25.89 P=0.8977
Forecast error 11.02        BIC 11.27
MAPE 0.02584                RMSE 10.94
MAD 8.933
```

Rolling simulation results

H	N	MAD	Cumulative Average	MAPE	Cumulative Average
1	24	6.7	6.7	0.015	0.015
2	23	6.6	6.7	0.015	0.015
3	22	6.4	6.6	0.014	0.015
4	21	6.2	6.5	0.014	0.015
5	20	6.4	6.5	0.014	0.015
6	19	6.7	6.5	0.015	0.015
7	18	6.8	6.5	0.015	0.015
8	17	6.8	6.6	0.015	0.015
9	16	6.8	6.6	0.015	0.015
10	15	7.0	6.6	0.016	0.015
11	14	6.0	6.6	0.014	0.015
12	13	5.8	6.5	0.013	0.015
13	12	7.1	6.6	0.016	0.015
14	11	6.9	6.6	0.016	0.015
15	10	6.0	6.6	0.013	0.015
16	9	5.5	6.5	0.012	0.015
17	8	4.9	6.5	0.011	0.015
18	7	4.6	6.4	0.010	0.015
19	6	4.8	6.4	0.010	0.014
20	5	4.9	6.4	0.011	0.014
21	4	5.6	6.4	0.012	0.014
22	3	6.6	6.4	0.015	0.014
23	2	6.6	6.4	0.015	0.014
24	1	9.2	6.4	0.021	0.014

Prediction Intervals for Forecasts of BARRELS from base period 16-12

Period	Lower 2.5	Forecast	Upper 97.5	Actual
17-01	357.5	379.6	401.7	388.0
17-02	377.0	399.1	421.2	411.0
17-03	379.0	401.1	423.2	392.0
17-04	405.0	427.1	449.2	430.0
17-05	411.2	433.3	455.4	432.0
17-06	440.3	462.4	484.5	467.0
17-07	435.9	458.0	480.1	465.0
17-08	443.8	465.9	488.0	472.0
17-09	428.5	450.6	472.7	447.0
17-10	424.5	446.6	468.7	469.0
17-11	394.2	416.3	438.4	408.0
17-12	394.9	417.0	439.1	417.0
18-01	378.0	400.5	422.9	391.0
18-02	397.5	419.9	442.4	436.0
18-03	399.5	422.0	444.4	411.0
18-04	425.5	447.9	470.4	458.0
18-05	431.7	454.2	476.7	447.0
18-06	460.8	483.3	505.7	480.0
18-07	456.4	478.9	501.4	483.0
18-08	464.3	486.8	509.2	489.0
18-09	449.0	471.5	493.9	474.0
18-10	445.0	467.5	489.9	474.0
18-11	414.7	437.1	459.6	433.0
18-12	415.4	437.8	460.3	447.0

These are reasonably tight and accurate 95% prediction intervals for two year ahead forecasts. Note that the actual value do not deviate greatly from the forecast.

9-14 MILK.DAT - The following is the output of ForecastPro for Windows[tm].

```
Forecast Model for MILK
Automatic model selection
ARIMA(1,1,0)*(0,1,1)
Term         Coefficient  Std. Error  t-Statistic  Significance
------------------------------------------------------------------
a[1]            0.3538      0.0916       3.8636        0.9998
B[12]           0.2928      0.0962       3.0427        0.9970

Standard Diagnostics
------------------------------------------------------------------
Sample size 104              Number of parameters 2
Mean 1.031e+004              Standard deviation 804.3
R-square 0.9956              Adjusted R-square 0.9955
Durbin-Watson 2.02           Ljung-Box(18)=15.47 P=0.3708
Forecast error 53.81         BIC 55.72
MAPE 0.004295                RMSE 53.29
MAD 44.26
```

Rolling simulation results

H	N	MAD	Cumulative Average	MAPE	Cumulative Average
1	24	60.5	60.5	0.005	0.005
2	23	107.1	83.3	0.009	0.007
3	22	143.8	102.6	0.013	0.009
4	21	177.9	120.2	0.015	0.011
5	20	213.1	137.1	0.018	0.012
6	19	264.8	155.9	0.023	0.014
7	18	323.4	176.4	0.028	0.015
8	17	375.4	197.0	0.033	0.017
9	16	421.6	217.0	0.037	0.019
10	15	449.8	234.9	0.039	0.020
11	14	476.2	251.1	0.042	0.022
12	13	502.5	265.8	0.044	0.023
13	12	525.2	279.1	0.046	0.024
14	11	574.6	292.4	0.050	0.025
15	10	603.5	304.6	0.053	0.027
16	9	622.1	315.4	0.054	0.027
17	8	646.5	325.1	0.056	0.028
18	7	678.0	334.0	0.059	0.029
19	6	683.5	341.3	0.060	0.030
20	5	682.7	347.2	0.060	0.030
21	4	625.1	351.0	0.055	0.031
22	3	675.6	354.3	0.060	0.031
23	2	698.8	356.6	0.063	0.031
24	1	631.4	357.5	0.058	0.031

Prediction Intervals for Forecasts of MILK from base period 1982-09

Period	Lower 2.5	Forecast	Upper 97.5	Actual
1982-10	10905.7	11014.9	11124.1	11055.0
1982-11	10451.8	10635.6	10819.4	10661.0
1982-12	10848.2	11092.9	11337.6	11088.0
1983-01	11018.6	11314.4	11610.3	11473.0
1983-02	10258.8	10599.0	10939.3	10725.0
1983-03	11561.6	11941.3	12321.1	12049.0
1983-04	11482.7	11898.3	12314.0	11966.0
1983-05	12046.3	12494.9	12943.6	12642.0
1983-06	11584.7	12064.1	12543.5	12273.0
1983-07	11383.1	11891.4	12399.7	12061.0
1983-08	11089.4	11625.1	12160.8	11692.0
1983-09	10618.6	11180.3	11742.0	11262.0
1983-10	10680.8	11294.1	11907.4	11430.0
1983-11	10242.5	10914.1	11585.6	11000.0
1983-12	10642.3	11371.1	12099.9	11395.0
1984-01	10809.4	11592.6	12375.7	11490.0
1984-02	10042.8	10877.1	11711.5	10529.0
1984-03	11336.7	12219.4	13102.2	11741.0
1984-04	11247.7	12176.4	13105.1	11674.0
1984-05	11800.5	12773.0	13745.5	12283.0
1984-06	11327.9	12342.2	13356.6	11832.0
1984-07	11114.9	12169.5	13224.1	11570.0
1984-08	10809.8	11903.2	12996.5	11243.0
1984-09	10327.6	11458.4	12589.1	10827.0

These are reasonably tight and accurate 95% prediction intervals for two year ahead forecasts. Note that the actual value did not deviate greatly from the forecast.

MINICASES (See Note on Page 9-10 Below)

MINICASE 9-1. Kansas Turnpike, Daily Data, TURNPIKD.DAT.

The following output from ForecastPro™, is used to answer Minicase I and II.

Using the same model as in Minicase 8-1, but now estimated by Forecast Pro(tm):

```
Forecast Model for ASALES
ARIMA(1,0,0)*(0,1,1)
Term          Coefficient   Std. Error   t-Statistic   Significance
-----------------------------------------------------------------------
a[1]            0.8590         0.0640       13.4165        1.0000
B[7]            0.8662         0.0484       17.9044        1.0000

Standard Diagnostics
-----------------------------------------------------------------------
Sample size 70                  Number of parameters 2
Mean 7.357e+004                 Standard deviation 6360
R-square 0.9217                 Adjusted R-square 0.9205
Durbin-Watson 1.878             ** Ljung-Box(18)=35.63 P=0.9921
Forecast error 1793             BIC 1878 (Best so far)
MAPE 0.01932                    RMSE 1767
MAD 1426
```

Prediction Intervals for Forecasts of ASALES from base period 12-02

Period	Lower 2.5	Forecast	Upper 97.5	Actual
12-03	69395.2	73075.6	76755.9	72360.0
12-04	68876.3	73728.1	78580.0	72518.0
12-05	70497.5	76057.7	81617.9	73568.0
12-06	82199.1	88229.0	94258.8	82842.0
12-07	71760.6	78114.8	84469.0	71992.0
13-01	69405.4	75988.7	82572.0	71136.0
13-02	64899.6	71647.0	78394.3	65126.0
13-03	64024.6	70998.4	77972.2	64534.0
13-04	64807.4	71943.8	79080.1	64741.0
13-05	67271.0	74524.9	81778.8	68890.0
13-06	79572.7	86912.2	94251.7	76135.0
13-07	69581.7	76983.7	84385.7	63842.0
14-01	67569.2	75017.0	82464.8	62200.0
14-02	63330.8	70812.3	78293.7	59900.0

Approximate EFSE(3) = (81617.9-76057.7)/1.96 = 2836.84

EFSE(7) = (78394.3-70998.4)/1.96 = 3773.42

EFSE(14) = (78293.7-70812.3)/1.96 = 3817.04

Minicase 9-1-I

From the statistics above we see that the fitted RSE of 1767 is lower than those of the approximate EFSE at horizons of 3, 7, and 14. However, there is not a great difference. The EFSE(14) is about 2.16 times that of RSE(1). This reflects the relatively good fit of in-sample data and the relatively good fit of the out-of-sample data. Unfortunately, as shown below, this good fit is not realized in actual out-of-sample results. Again, this reflects the fact that this series has a strong annual seasonality that would be reflected in the model if more than one year of data were used in the analyses. A much larger data set exists in TURNPIKT.DAT. This data can be used as needed for other case analyses.

Minicase 9-1-II

The following is the results of a rolling out-of-sample simulation using ForecastPro™. The last fourteen observations of the time series were used in a simulated out-of-sample validation.

H	N	MAD	Cumulative Average	MAPE	Cumulative Average
1	14	1752.1	1752.1	0.025	0.025
2	13	3064.1	2383.8	0.045	0.034
3	12	4473.3	3026.7	0.066	0.044
4	11	5619.6	3597.1	0.084	0.053
5	10	6255.8	4040.2	0.095	0.060
6	9	6878.8	4410.5	0.105	0.066
7	8	7628.3	4744.8	0.117	0.071
8	7	8440.5	5052.8	0.129	0.076
9	6	9251.5	5332.7	0.142	0.080
10	5	10170.9	5587.3	0.156	0.084
11	4	11735.9	5835.8	0.181	0.088
12	3	12255.5	6024.6	0.197	0.091
13	2	11876.3	6137.1	0.194	0.093
14	1	10912.3	6182.6	0.182	0.094

Approximate: Expected   Actual: 1.25*ForecastMAD

$EFSE(3) = (81617.9-76057.7)/1.96 = 2836.8$ $FSE(3) = 1.25*4473.3 = 5591.6$
$EFSE(7) = (78394.3-70998.4)/1.96 = 3773.4$ $FSE(7) = 1.25*7628.3 = 9535.4$
$EFSE(14)= (78293.7-70812.3)/1.96 = 3817.0$ $FSE(14) = 1.25*10912.3= 13640.$

There is such a large difference between expected and actual FSE because the model does not adequately model day of the year effects as we have seen before. The prediction intervals are quite useful if the future is reflected in the past patterns. However, as this example shows, this is not always true, particularly when a fundamental pattern of the data (i.e., day of the year pattern) is not modeled.

Note Concerning Minicase 9-2 to 9-10. The following are the results of a rolling out-of-sample simulation using ForecastPro™. The last two seasons of observations of the time series were used in a simulated out-of-sample validation. In completing Minicase assignments I and II, the student should repeat the analysis of as done in Minicase 9-1.

MINICASE 9-2. Domestic Air Passengers by Quarter, PASSAIR.DAT.

```
Forecast Model for PASS (Log transform)
ARIMA(1,0,0)*(0,1,1)
```

Term	Coefficient	Std. Error	t-Statistic	Significance
a[1]	0.7720	0.1210	6.3797	1.0000
B[4]	0.8596	0.0541	15.8792	1.0000
_CONST	0.0160	0.0091	1.7568	0.9123

```
Constant term is not significant.
Standard Diagnostics
```

Sample size 38	Number of parameters 2
Mean 9.335	Standard deviation 0.2155
R-square 0.9783	Adjusted R-square 0.9777
Durbin-Watson 1.82	Ljung-Box(18)=11.95 P=0.1502
Forecast error 0.03217	BIC 390.2
MAPE 0.02366	RMSE 407.2
MAD 278.7	

Rolling simulation results

H	N	MAD	Cumulative Average	MAPE	Cumulative Average
1	8	378.1	378.1	0.024	0.024
2	7	554.5	460.4	0.035	0.029
3	6	695.4	527.5	0.044	0.033
4	5	914.4	601.9	0.058	0.038
5	4	1109.9	669.7	0.070	0.042
6	3	1260.7	723.4	0.080	0.046
7	2	1497.2	767.6	0.095	0.049
8	1	1708.7	793.8	0.104	0.050

Prediction Intervals for Forecasts of PASS from base period 1992-Q2

Period	Lower 2.5	Forecast	Upper 97.5	Actual
1992-Q3	14988.4	16035.8	17156.3	15983.1
1992-Q4	13572.6	14781.6	16098.3	14404.8
1993-Q1	13600.1	14945.8	16424.6	14986.1
1993-Q2	15006.7	16574.1	18305.1	16152.2
1993-Q3	16069.2	17845.1	19817.4	17164.4
1993-Q4	14643.5	16313.1	18173.0	15370.7
1994-Q1	14684.4	16388.5	18290.5	15077.1
1994-Q2	16186.1	18084.0	20204.4	16375.3

MINICASE 9-3. Hospital Census by Month, CENSUSM.DAT.

```
Forecast Model for ACENSUS
ARIMA(0,0,1)*(0,1,0)
Term          Coefficient  Std. Error  t-Statistic  Significance
----------------------------------------------------------------------
b[1]              -0.1155     0.1055      -1.0943       0.7230
Try alternative model ARIMA(0,0,0)*(0,1,0)
Standard Diagnostics
----------------------------------------------------------------
Sample size 84              Number of parameters 1
Mean 1.091e+004             Standard deviation 281.3
R-square 0.3255             Adjusted R-square 0.3255
Durbin-Watson 1.947         Ljung-Box(18)=26.91 P=0.9194
Forecast error 231          BIC 235.8
MAPE 0.01643                RMSE 229.6
MAD 179.2
```

Rolling simulation results

H	N	MAD	Cumulative Average	MAPE	Cumulative Average
1	24	154.3	154.3	0.014	0.014
2	23	165.3	159.7	0.015	0.014
3	22	171.8	163.5	0.015	0.015
4	21	179.6	167.3	0.016	0.015
5	20	177.2	169.1	0.016	0.015
6	19	173.5	169.7	0.016	0.015
7	18	174.2	170.3	0.016	0.015
8	17	144.3	167.6	0.013	0.015
9	16	141.5	165.3	0.013	0.015
10	15	148.7	164.0	0.013	0.015
11	14	152.2	163.2	0.014	0.015
12	13	158.7	162.9	0.014	0.015
13	12	148.1	162.2	0.013	0.015
14	11	160.3	162.1	0.014	0.015
15	10	158.8	162.0	0.014	0.015
16	9	156.5	161.8	0.014	0.015
17	8	149.6	161.4	0.014	0.015
18	7	117.0	160.3	0.011	0.014
19	6	57.5	158.1	0.005	0.014
20	5	42.2	156.1	0.004	0.014
21	4	51.3	154.7	0.005	0.014
22	3	50.5	153.7	0.004	0.014
23	2	23.8	152.8	0.002	0.014
24	1	29.6	152.4	0.003	0.014

Prediction Intervals for Forecasts of ACENSUS from base period 1986-06

Period	Lower 2.5	Forecast	Upper 97.5	Actual
1986-07	10847.7	11309.8	11772.0	11404.0
1986-08	10622.8	11088.0	11553.2	11066.0
1986-09	10502.0	10967.2	11432.4	10959.2
1986-10	10536.8	11002.0	11467.2	11229.0
1986-11	10419.8	10885.0	11350.2	11133.0
1986-12	9754.8	10220.0	10685.2	10381.6
1987-01	10423.8	10889.0	11354.2	11571.0
1987-02	10552.8	11018.0	11483.2	11207.0

Period	Lower 2.5	Forecast	Upper 97.5	Actual
1987-03	10629.2	11094.4	11559.6	11128.0
1987-04	10945.8	11411.0	11876.2	11311.0
1987-05	10521.8	10987.0	11452.2	10920.0
1987-06	10638.0	11103.2	11568.4	11116.0
1987-07	10654.1	11309.8	11965.6	11289.0
1987-08	10430.1	11088.0	11745.9	11263.0
1987-09	10309.3	10967.2	11625.1	11146.4
1987-10	10344.1	11002.0	11659.9	11214.0
1987-11	10227.1	10885.0	11542.9	11263.0
1987-12	9562.1	10220.0	10877.9	10693.6
1988-01	10231.1	10889.0	11546.9	11023.0
1988-02	10360.1	11018.0	11675.9	11012.0
1988-03	10436.5	11094.4	11752.3	11148.0
1988-04	10753.1	11411.0	12068.9	11515.0
1988-05	10329.1	10987.0	11644.9	11005.0
1988-06	10445.3	11103.2	11761.1	11073.6

MINICASE 8-3. Hospital Census by Month, CENSUSM.DAT.

```
Forecast Model for ACENSUS
ARIMA(0,0,1)*(0,1,0)
```

Term	Coefficient	Std. Error	t-Statistic	Significance
b[1]	-0.1155	0.1055	-1.0943	0.7230

```
The alternative ARIMA(0,0,0)*(0,1,0) model results are:
Standard Diagnostics
```

Sample size 84	Number of parameters 1
Mean 1.091e+004	Standard deviation 281.3
R-square 0.3255	Adjusted R-square 0.3255
Durbin-Watson 1.947	Ljung-Box(18)=26.91 P=0.9194
Forecast error 231	BIC 235.8
MAPE 0.01643	RMSE 229.6
MAD 179.2	

Rolling simulation results

H	N	MAD	Cumulative Average	MAPE	Cumulative Average
1	24	154.3	154.3	0.014	0.014
2	23	165.3	159.7	0.015	0.014
3	22	171.8	163.5	0.015	0.015
4	21	179.6	167.3	0.016	0.015
5	20	177.2	169.1	0.016	0.015
6	19	173.5	169.7	0.016	0.015
7	18	174.2	170.3	0.016	0.015
8	17	144.3	167.6	0.013	0.015
9	16	141.5	165.3	0.013	0.015
10	15	148.7	164.0	0.013	0.015
11	14	152.2	163.2	0.014	0.015
12	13	158.7	162.9	0.014	0.015
13	12	148.1	162.2	0.013	0.015
14	11	160.3	162.1	0.014	0.015

15	10	158.8	162.0	0.014	0.015
16	9	156.5	161.8	0.014	0.015
17	8	149.6	161.4	0.014	0.015
18	7	117.0	160.3	0.011	0.014
19	6	57.5	158.1	0.005	0.014
20	5	42.2	156.1	0.004	0.014
21	4	51.3	154.7	0.005	0.014
22	3	50.5	153.7	0.004	0.014
23	2	23.8	152.8	0.002	0.014
24	1	29.6	152.4	0.003	0.014
Cumulative			Cumulative		
H	N	MAD	Average	MAPE	Average

Prediction Intervals for Forecasts of ACENSUS from base period 1986-06

Period	Lower 2.5	Forecast	Upper 97.5	Actual
1986-07	10847.7	11309.8	11772.0	11404.0
1986-08	10622.8	11088.0	11553.2	11066.0
1986-09	10502.0	10967.2	11432.4	10959.2
1986-10	10536.8	11002.0	11467.2	11229.0
1986-11	10419.8	10885.0	11350.2	11133.0
1986-12	9754.8	10220.0	10685.2	10381.6
1987-01	10423.8	10889.0	11354.2	11571.0
1987-02	10552.8	11018.0	11483.2	11207.0
1987-03	10629.2	11094.4	11559.6	11128.0
1987-04	10945.8	11411.0	11876.2	11311.0
1987-05	10521.8	10987.0	11452.2	10920.0
1987-06	10638.0	11103.2	11568.4	11116.0
1987-07	10654.1	11309.8	11965.6	11289.0
1987-08	10430.1	11088.0	11745.9	11263.0
1987-09	10309.3	10967.2	11625.1	11146.4
1987-10	10344.1	11002.0	11659.9	11214.0
1987-11	10227.1	10885.0	11542.9	11263.0
1987-12	9562.1	10220.0	10877.9	10693.6
1988-01	10231.1	10889.0	11546.9	11023.0
1988-02	10360.1	11018.0	11675.9	11012.0
1988-03	10436.5	11094.4	11752.3	11148.0
1988-04	10753.1	11411.0	12068.9	11515.0
1988-05	10329.1	10987.0	11644.9	11005.0

MINICASE 9-4. Henry Machler's Hideaway Orchids, MACHLERD.DAT.

```
Forecast Pro for Windows Standard Edition Version 2.00
Sat Jul 26 12:43:42 1997
Forecast Model for ASALES
ARIMA(0,0,0)*(1,0,0)
```

Term	Coefficient	Std. Error	t-Statistic	Significance
A[7]	0.8793	0.0486	18.0791	1.0000
_CONST	25.7489			

Standard Diagnostics

Sample size 126	Number of parameters 1
Mean 213.3	Standard deviation 116.8
R-square 0.6861	Adjusted R-square 0.6861
Durbin-Watson 1.706	Ljung-Box(18)=16.92 P=0.4712

```
Forecast error 65.45          BIC 66.45
MAPE 0.3012                   RMSE 65.19     MAD 50.65
```
Rolling simulation results

H	N	MAD	Cumulative Average	MAPE	Cumulative Average
1	14	52.8	52.8	0.410	0.410
2	13	56.8	54.7	0.440	0.424
3	12	59.4	56.2	0.469	0.438
4	11	62.6	57.6	0.499	0.451
5	10	63.6	58.6	0.535	0.465
6	9	70.1	60.1	0.593	0.482
7	8	70.2	61.1	0.614	0.496
8	7	81.9	62.9	0.886	0.528
9	6	82.3	64.2	0.982	0.559
10	5	93.9	65.7	1.158	0.590
11	4	103.8	67.3	1.320	0.620
12	3	110.0	68.5	1.704	0.652
13	2	154.7	70.2	2.530	0.688
14	1	166.4	71.1	4.489	0.724

Prediction Intervals for Forecasts of ASALES from base period 98-07

Period	Lower 2.5	Forecast	Upper 97.5	Actual
99-01	40.1	170.3	300.6	172.0
99-02	140.7	271.0	401.2	246.3
99-03	23.8	154.1	284.3	178.7
99-04	319.2	449.4	579.7	397.1
99-05	275.3	405.5	535.8	411.0
99-06	-37.2	93.1	223.3	162.7
99-07	71.9	202.1	332.4	123.3
100-01	2.1	175.5	348.9	254.9
100-02	90.6	264.0	437.5	239.8
100-03	-12.2	161.2	334.7	106.7
100-04	247.5	420.9	594.3	506.0
100-05	208.9	382.3	555.7	402.9
100-06	-65.9	107.6	281.0	250.5
100-07	30.0	203.5	376.9	37.1

MINICASE 9-6. Midwestern Building Materials, LUMBER.DAT.

```
Forecast Model for SALES
ARIMA(0,0,1)*(0,1,0)
```

Term	Coefficient	Std. Error	t-Statistic	Significance
b[1]	-0.3469	0.1036	-3.3470	0.9988
_CONST	5083.9602	654.6285	7.7662	1.0000

Standard Diagnostics

```
Sample size 84                Number of parameters 1
Mean 8.496e+004               Standard deviation 2.315e+004
R-square 0.9617               Adjusted R-square 0.9617
Durbin-Watson 1.933           Ljung-Box(18)=15.02 P=0.3395
Forecast error 4529           BIC 4622 (Best so far)
MAPE 0.04487                  RMSE 4502
MAD 3614
```

Rolling simulation results

H	N	MAD	Cumulative Average	MAPE	Cumulative Average
1	24	2711.6	2711.6	0.028	0.028
2	23	3260.4	2980.2	0.034	0.031
3	22	3225.8	3058.5	0.033	0.031
4	21	3280.3	3110.3	0.033	0.032
5	20	3386.5	3160.5	0.035	0.032
6	19	3479.6	3207.5	0.035	0.033
7	18	3612.5	3257.1	0.037	0.033
8	17	3430.6	3275.1	0.036	0.034
9	16	3063.7	3256.3	0.032	0.033
10	15	2952.3	3232.9	0.031	0.033
11	14	2786.1	3203.0	0.030	0.033
12	13	2812.2	3180.1	0.031	0.033
13	12	4224.5	3233.6	0.042	0.033
14	11	5289.8	3326.0	0.052	0.034
15	10	5296.8	3403.3	0.051	0.035
16	9	5480.8	3474.1	0.053	0.035
17	8	5187.7	3524.5	0.051	0.036
18	7	5735.9	3580.0	0.057	0.036
19	6	5522.9	3620.9	0.057	0.037
20	5	5424.9	3652.0	0.058	0.037
21	4	5078.7	3671.4	0.056	0.037
22	3	5654.3	3691.4	0.064	0.038
23	2	6484.4	3710.1	0.083	0.038
24	1	10206.9	3731.7	0.138	0.038

Prediction Intervals for Forecasts of SALES from base period 08-12

Period	Lower 2.5	Forecast	Upper 97.5	Actual
09-01	59117.6	68176.7	77235.9	70377.0
09-02	71106.2	80695.0	90283.7	84717.0
09-03	82583.2	92172.0	101760.7	94253.0
09-04	101948.2	111537.0	121125.7	112693.0
09-05	76021.2	85610.0	95198.7	87229.0
09-06	116977.2	126566.0	136154.7	125479.0
09-07	115633.2	125222.0	134810.7	118518.0
09-08	91343.2	100932.0	110520.7	91630.0
09-09	103474.2	113063.0	122651.7	108329.0
09-10	135073.2	144662.0	154250.7	139383.0
09-11	86872.2	96461.0	106049.7	94013.0
09-12	69608.2	79197.0	88785.7	69173.0
10-01	60069.4	73260.7	86452.0	70897.0
10-02	72218.4	85778.9	99339.4	90999.0
10-03	83695.4	97255.9	110816.4	100896.0
10-04	103060.4	116620.9	130181.4	124447.0
10-05	77133.4	90693.9	104254.4	92044.0
10-06	118089.4	131649.9	145210.4	124636.0
10-07	116745.4	130305.9	143866.4	124293.0
10-08	92455.4	106015.9	119576.4	99206.0
10-09	104586.4	118146.9	131707.4	114795.0
10-10	136185.4	149745.9	163306.4	145752.0
10-11	87984.4	101544.9	115105.4	98783.0
10-12	70720.4	84280.9	97841.4	74074.0

MINICASE 9-7. International Airline Passengers, AIRLINE.DAT.

```
Forecast Model for SALES (Log transform)
Automatic model selection
ARIMA(0,1,1)*(0,1,1)
```

Term	Coefficient	Std. Error	t-Statistic	Significance
b[1]	0.3345	0.0912	3.6678	0.9996
B[12]	0.6238	0.0794	7.8520	1.0000
_CONST	-0.0006	0.0011	-0.4863	0.3722

```
Constant term is not significant.
Standard Diagnostics
```

```
Sample size 107                   Number of parameters 2
Mean 5.503                        Standard deviation 0.3482
R-square 0.9888                   Adjusted R-square 0.9887
Durbin-Watson 1.961              Ljung-Box(18)=13.4 P=0.2326
Forecast error 0.03709           BIC 9.424 (Best so far)
MAPE 0.029                        RMSE 9.406
MAD 7.261
```

Rolling simulation results

H	N	MAD	Cumulative Average	MAPE	Cumulative Average
1	24	11.7	11.7	0.026	0.026
2	23	11.9	11.8	0.027	0.026
3	22	13.0	12.2	0.028	0.027
4	21	14.7	12.8	0.031	0.028
5	20	15.5	13.3	0.033	0.029
6	19	16.6	13.8	0.035	0.030
7	18	19.2	14.4	0.041	0.031
8	17	18.9	14.9	0.042	0.032
9	16	17.5	15.1	0.040	0.033
10	15	18.4	15.4	0.043	0.034
11	14	18.4	15.6	0.043	0.034
12	13	20.0	15.8	0.044	0.035
13	12	20.7	16.1	0.044	0.035
14	11	21.6	16.3	0.045	0.036
15	10	25.6	16.7	0.051	0.036
16	9	33.7	17.3	0.066	0.037
17	8	37.1	17.9	0.071	0.038
18	7	40.4	18.4	0.075	0.039
19	6	43.6	19.0	0.081	0.040
20	5	44.0	19.4	0.089	0.041
21	4	44.0	19.7	0.097	0.042
22	3	47.4	20.0	0.110	0.042
23	2	43.7	20.2	0.107	0.043
24	1	51.8	20.3	0.120	0.043

Prediction Intervals for Forecasts of SALES from base period 1958-12

Period	Lower 2.5	Forecast	Upper 97.5	Actual
1959-01	323.2	348.4	375.6	360.0
1959-02	304.0	332.8	364.2	342.0
1959-03	346.8	384.6	426.5	406.0
1959-04	333.3	373.8	419.3	396.0
1959-05	337.2	382.2	433.2	420.0
1959-06	392.6	449.2	514.1	472.0
1959-07	434.5	501.7	579.4	548.0
1959-08	432.3	503.4	586.3	559.0
1959-09	363.0	426.2	500.3	463.0
1959-10	315.2	372.9	441.1	407.0
1959-11	272.8	325.0	387.3	362.0
1959-12	300.5	360.6	432.8	405.0
1960-01	303.1	369.6	450.7	417.0
1960-02	286.0	352.8	435.3	391.0
1960-03	326.7	407.5	508.4	419.0
1960-04	314.1	395.9	499.1	461.0
1960-05	317.7	404.6	515.2	472.0
1960-06	369.7	475.3	611.0	535.0
1960-07	408.8	530.5	688.3	622.0
1960-08	406.3	532.0	696.5	606.0
1960-09	340.8	450.1	594.4	508.0
1960-10	295.6	393.6	524.3	461.0
1960-11	255.4	342.9	460.4	390.0
1960-12	280.9	380.2	514.7	432.0

MINICASE 9-8. Automobile Sales, AUTO.DAT.

```
Forecast Model for ASALES
ARIMA(1,0,0)*(0,1,1)
Term        Coefficient  Std. Error  t-Statistic  Significance
--------------------------------------------------------------
a[1]            0.9142      0.0334     27.3702      1.0000
B[12]          -0.4513      0.0756     -5.9677      1.0000
Standard Diagnostics
--------------------------------------------------------------
Sample size 149              Number of parameters 2
Mean 1649                    Standard deviation 411.5
R-square 0.987               Adjusted R-square 0.9869
Durbin-Watson 1.826          Ljung-Box(18)=20.1 P=0.6728
Forecast error 47.12         BIC 48.4 (Best so far)
MAPE 0.02481                 RMSE 46.8
MAD 37.63
```

Rolling simulation results

H	N	MAD	Cumulative Average	MAPE	Cumulative Average
1	24	36.5	36.5	0.047	0.047
2	23	63.1	49.6	0.080	0.063
3	22	88.2	61.9	0.114	0.079
4	21	111.4	73.4	0.150	0.096
5	20	129.8	83.7	0.175	0.110

H	N	MAD	Average	MAPE	Average
6	19	143.9	92.5	0.200	0.123
7	18	151.2	99.7	0.213	0.134
8	17	157.5	105.7	0.219	0.143
9	16	161.5	110.7	0.214	0.149
10	15	161.7	114.6	0.198	0.153
11	14	160.6	117.7	0.191	0.156
12	13	150.9	119.6	0.176	0.157
13	12	133.2	120.3	0.154	0.157
14	11	144.0	121.4	0.172	0.157
15	10	149.9	122.5	0.196	0.159
16	9	155.4	123.6	0.219	0.161
17	8	144.3	124.2	0.202	0.162
18	7	143.8	124.7	0.220	0.164
19	6	159.0	125.4	0.261	0.166
20	5	179.1	126.4	0.276	0.168
21	4	208.0	127.5	0.276	0.169
22	3	253.5	128.8	0.290	0.170
23	2	335.6	130.1	0.383	0.172
24	1	380.4	131.0	0.409	0.172
Cumulative			Cumulative		
H	N	MAD	Average	MAPE	Average

Prediction Intervals for Forecasts of ASALES from base period 14-05

Period	Lower 2.5	Forecast	Upper 97.5	Actual
14-06	1557.8	1652.7	1747.6	1658.0
14-07	1563.7	1692.2	1820.8	1617.0
14-08	1303.2	1454.2	1605.2	1371.0
14-09	860.5	1028.0	1195.4	889.0
14-10	911.6	1091.7	1271.8	947.0
14-11	968.6	1158.6	1348.7	982.0
14-12	526.8	724.8	922.7	576.0
15-01	483.1	687.4	891.7	541.0
15-02	398.3	607.8	817.3	446.0
15-03	841.7	1055.4	1269.1	886.0
15-04	898.1	1115.3	1332.4	826.0
15-05	1106.0	1326.0	1546.1	1029.0
15-06	1335.4	1613.4	1891.5	1359.0
15-07	1337.8	1656.3	1974.9	1305.0
15-08	1072.6	1421.4	1770.1	1083.0
15-09	625.8	997.9	1370.1	644.0
15-10	673.6	1064.3	1454.9	759.0
15-11	728.1	1133.6	1539.0	860.0
15-12	284.5	701.9	1119.3	481.0
16-01	239.3	666.4	1093.6	470.0
16-02	153.5	588.6	1023.7	446.0
16-03	596.2	1037.9	1479.6	894.0
16-04	652.2	1099.3	1546.3	812.0
16-05	859.9	1311.4	1762.9	931.0

MINICASE 9-9. Consumption of Distilled Spirits, SPIRITS.DAT

```
Forecast Model for GALLONS
Automatic model selection
ARIMA(0,0,0)*(0,1,2)
Term            Coefficient   Std. Error   t-Statistic  Significance
-----------------------------------------------------------------------
B[12]               0.3575       0.0837        4.2732       1.0000
B[24]               0.4961       0.0816        6.0813       1.0000
_CONST           -805.6352      52.9091      -15.2268       1.0000
Standard Diagnostics
-----------------------------------------------------------------------
Sample size 96                  Number of parameters 2
Mean 3.375e+004                 Standard deviation 5665
R-square 0.9693                 Adjusted R-square 0.9689
Durbin-Watson 2.164             ** Ljung-Box(18)=38.39 P=0.9966
Forecast error 998.4            BIC 1036
MAPE 0.02269                    RMSE 988
MAD 758.3
```

Rolling simulation results

H	N	MAD	Cumulative Average	MAPE	Cumulative Average
1	24	1379.1	1379.1	0.043	0.043
2	23	1396.0	1387.4	0.044	0.043
3	22	1433.8	1402.2	0.045	0.044
4	21	1472.1	1418.5	0.046	0.044
5	20	1505.6	1434.3	0.046	0.045
6	19	1515.9	1446.4	0.047	0.045
7	18	1548.8	1458.9	0.048	0.045
8	17	1506.2	1463.8	0.046	0.045
9	16	1559.8	1472.3	0.047	0.046
10	15	1622.7	1483.9	0.049	0.046
11	14	1674.7	1496.7	0.051	0.046
12	13	1758.5	1512.0	0.053	0.047
13	12	1648.1	1519.0	0.056	0.047
14	11	1706.4	1527.4	0.058	0.048
15	10	1646.5	1532.1	0.053	0.048
16	9	1577.0	1533.6	0.049	0.048
17	8	1662.2	1537.4	0.052	0.048
18	7	1787.6	1543.7	0.055	0.048
19	6	1844.3	1550.0	0.056	0.048
20	5	1735.8	1553.2	0.051	0.048
21	4	1949.6	1558.6	0.055	0.048
22	3	2432.2	1567.4	0.068	0.049
23	2	3057.9	1577.4	0.082	0.049
24	1	4011.9	1585.5	0.101	0.049

Prediction Intervals for Forecasts of GALLONS from base period 1983-12

Period	Lower 2.5	Forecast	Upper 97.5	Actual
1984-01	22578.7	24609.4	26640.1	25600.0
1984-02	23703.6	25734.3	27765.0	26300.0
1984-03	27418.5	29449.2	31479.9	28820.0

Period	Lower 2.5	Forecast	Upper 97.5	Actual
1984-04	25818.3	27848.9	29879.6	28650.0
1984-05	27467.8	29498.4	31529.1	30810.0
1984-06	28876.9	30907.6	32938.3	31830.0
1984-07	25506.2	27536.9	29567.5	29810.0
1984-08	26710.0	28740.7	30771.4	29390.0
1984-09	25845.1	27875.8	29906.5	27260.0
1984-10	28174.8	30205.5	32236.2	31100.0
1984-11	34094.1	36124.8	38155.5	36710.0
1984-12	41931.4	43962.1	45992.8	48140.0
1985-01	21309.8	23723.5	26137.2	24730.0
1985-02	21852.3	24265.9	26679.6	21960.0
1985-03	25918.5	28332.2	30745.8	26060.0
1985-04	25051.5	27465.2	29878.8	28360.0
1985-05	25591.7	28005.4	30419.0	28790.0
1985-06	27803.7	30217.4	32631.0	28770.0
1985-07	24299.8	26713.4	29127.1	29100.0
1985-08	24955.7	27369.4	29783.0	28250.0
1985-09	24888.4	27302.1	29715.8	26800.0
1985-10	27105.6	29519.3	31933.0	30700.0
1985-11	32850.2	35263.9	37677.6	33160.0
1985-12	41228.2	43641.9	46055.6	39630.0

MINICASE 9-10. Discount Consumer Electronics, ELECT.DAT.

```
Forecast Model for SALES
ARIMA(0,0,0)*(0,1,0)
```

Term	Coefficient	Std. Error	t-Statistic	Significance
_CONST	3.3294	0.2305	14.4456	1.0000

```
Standard Diagnostics
```

Sample size 149		Number of parameters 0
Mean 72.44		Standard deviation 13.75
R-square 0.9578		Adjusted R-square 0.9581
Durbin-Watson 1.908		Ljung-Box(18)=17.46 P=0.5083
Forecast error 2.813		BIC 2.813 (Best so far)
MAPE 0.03314		RMSE 2.813
MAD 2.278		

Rolling simulation results

H	N	MAD	Cumulative Average	MAPE	Cumulative Average
1	24	1.7	1.7	0.018	0.018
2	23	1.8	1.7	0.019	0.018
3	22	1.8	1.8	0.019	0.019
4	21	1.8	1.8	0.019	0.019
5	20	1.8	1.8	0.019	0.019
6	19	1.8	1.8	0.019	0.019
7	18	1.9	1.8	0.019	0.019
8	17	1.9	1.8	0.020	0.019
9	16	1.9	1.8	0.019	0.019
10	15	1.9	1.8	0.020	0.019
11	14	1.8	1.8	0.018	0.019

12	13	1.8	1.8	0.019	0.019
13	12	3.0	1.9	0.032	0.020
14	11	3.3	1.9	0.034	0.020
15	10	3.4	2.0	0.035	0.021
16	9	2.9	2.0	0.030	0.021
17	8	2.9	2.0	0.030	0.021
18	7	3.2	2.1	0.033	0.022
19	6	3.3	2.1	0.033	0.022
20	5	2.4	2.1	0.028	0.022
21	4	2.7	2.1	0.031	0.022
22	3	3.5	2.1	0.039	0.022
23	2	3.4	2.1	0.036	0.022
24	1	6.6	2.2	0.071	0.023
Cumulative			Cumulative		
H	N	MAD	Average	MAPE	Average

Prediction Intervals for Forecasts of SALES from base period 14-05

Period	Lower 2.5	Forecast	Upper 97.5	Actual
14-06	91.6	97.1	102.6	97.3
14-07	87.9	93.4	98.9	92.6
14-08	87.6	93.1	98.6	90.4
14-09	88.0	93.5	99.1	91.8
14-10	87.3	92.8	98.3	93.3
14-11	80.6	86.1	91.6	84.5
14-12	108.3	113.8	119.3	115.5
15-01	71.5	77.0	82.5	78.9
15-02	86.3	91.8	97.3	91.0
15-03	67.9	73.5	79.0	77.0
15-04	96.3	101.8	107.3	103.1
15-05	91.2	96.7	102.3	94.8
15-06	92.6	100.4	108.2	100.9
15-07	88.9	96.7	104.5	94.3
15-08	88.7	96.5	104.3	89.0
15-09	89.1	96.9	104.7	94.4
15-10	88.4	96.2	104.0	97.2
15-11	81.6	89.4	97.2	86.8
15-12	109.3	117.1	124.9	124.9
16-01	72.5	80.3	88.1	81.6
16-02	87.3	95.1	102.9	94.6
16-03	69.0	76.8	84.6	80.5
16-04	97.3	105.1	112.9	105.2
16-05	92.3	100.1	107.9	93.5

CHAPTER 10
MULTIPLE REGRESSION OF TIME SERIES

PROBLEMS

ESTIMATED DIFFICULTY

Elementary	Medium	Hard	Very Hard	Bad

1 E	2 E	3 M	4 M	5 M	6 M	7 M	8 M	9 M	10 M
11 E	12 E	13 M	14 M	15 H	16 M	17 E	18 M	19 E	20 M
21 M	22 M	23 M	24 M	25 M	26 M	27 M	28 H	29 M	30 M
31 **B**	32 H	33 H	34 M	35 M	36 H	37 H	38 H	39 H	40 V

Minicases are all hard.

10-1. Software dependent, however a good question to emphasize the difference between adjusted and unadjusted R-square.

10-2. See page 406.

10-3. See page 410, the logical four steps are the identification, estimation, diagnostics, and out-of-sample (forecasting) steps defined for ARIMA.

10-4. The flowchart on page 410 emphasizes theory in several ways, the first step after starting is planning the model based on theory, then including or excluding variables based on theory, ignoring insignificance and including a variable based on theory, looking for missing variables based on theory, judging model validity based on theory.

10-5. See Figures 3-7 and 3-8 of Chapter 3, see also page 409.

10-6. Multicollinearity is correlation among two or more independent variables. a. It is a problem when the estimation technique cannot distinguish between the individual affects on Y. b. Perfect multicollineariy will result in an indeterminate solution, while partial multicollinearity results in dramatic changes in t-values and regression coefficients as variables are included or excluded. c. With perfect multicollinearity one or more variables can be dropped if they are redundant, otherwise structural equation models can be employed, factor analysis, or ridge regression. d. The signs of coefficients may change as variables are added to or removed from the relationship, see pages 413 and 414 for further discussion.

10-7. This is most easily explained in the context of dummy variables as shown on page 412. Perfect multicollinearity will result in an indeterminate solution.

10-8. Prior to fitting models, the correlation matrix assists in understanding the simple linear relationships between variables and can therefore be very helpful in theory and model building, anticipation of multicollinearity. During and after models are fitted, the correlation matrix assists in determining what variables should be added to a relationship. However, remind the student that the correlation matrix measures only linear affects in the presence of influence from other variables, thus, there is always the possibility of confounding and intervening variables which increase or decrease the correlation coefficient.

10-9. See pages 414 to 416 for a full discussion of the partial F-test and pages 108 to 110 of Chapter 3 for the test of significance for the overall relationship using the F-test..

10-10. Calculating beta coefficients from Table 10-2c) and page 434 yields:

beta(advert)=2.52481084*(7.6633721512/18.122478926) = 1.06766

beta(comp)=-0.54492346*(8.0716488496/18.122478926) = -0.24271

The usual interpretation of these standardized coefficients pertains to these coefficients; that is, a one standard deviation change in advertising results in a 1.06766 standard deviation change in sales. However as pointed out on page 457, it is not possible to uncouple the mutual influences between advertising and competition when interpreting these beta coefficients because no single measure of influence is satisfactory when there is multicollinearity between independent variables. For example, in this situation, a one standard deviation change in advertising is accompanied by a .426 standard deviation change in competition. To better understand the mutual relationship between requires introducing path coefficients as developed for this example in Chapter 11 on page 456.

10-11. Dichotomous variables take on only two values, typically zero and one, they are effectively used to model events. See pages 434 to 437 for further discussion.

10-12. See pages 414-416 for a discussion of the partial F-test.

10-13. See page 416 for a discussion of the purpose of COILS.

10-14. See page 417 for a discussion of the steps of COILS.

10-15. See pages 425-426 for a discussion of elasticities. The use of logarithmic dependent and independent variables result in regression coefficient that can be interpreted as elasticities.

10-16. The use of first differences can be interpreted as the use of a rho value of 1.0 in the COILS procedure, however, in general, forcing rho to equal 1.0 is not recommended.

10-17. See pages 426-428 for a discussion of heteroscedasticity. Unequal variances in the scatter of the dependent variables denotes a misspecification of the model as well as a RSE or SEE that is not constant. The structure of the model should be changed to eliminate heteroscedasticity while modeling the true functional relationship between variables.

10-18. See pages 430 to 433 for a discussion of purpose and steps of weighted least squares.

10-19. See pages 428 to 430 for a discussion of the Goldfeld-Quandt test.

10-20. See page 429 for a discussion of the steps of the Goldfeld-Quandt test.

10-21. See pages 416 for a discussion of the causes of first-order serial correlation.

10-22. With one period ahead forecasts, e_{t-1} is known and therefore, typically, more accurate forecasts result, however with more than one-period ahead forecasts, e_{t-1} is unknown and therefore, typically, less accurate forecasts result because the first order correlation is no longer operating.

10-23. See pages 438 to 441 for a discussion of parsimony in regression analysis.

10-24. See middle of page 441 for a discussion of automated regression analysis.

10-25. $3^4 = 81$, see pages for a discussion of this data requirement.

10-26. See problem 10-10 for this answer.

10-27. See page 416 for the partial F-test for Big City Bookstore

10-28. Elasticities in Table 10-16 are as follows:

A one percent change in the price of the U.S. Stock Index in period t yields a 1.561 change in the U.K. Stock Index in period t, a one percent change in the price of the U.S. Stock Index in period t-1 yields a .004 percent change in the price of the U.K. Stock Index. Now the regression coefficient for period t-1 is statistically insignificant. More important, the results of Table 10-16 have such high serial correlation that all results may be invalid. In that context, Table 10-17 illustrates a COILS analysis of this relationship.

No doubt the models in Tables 10-16 and 10-17 will stimulate questions about the use of nonstationary series and whether first differences should have been used here. To shed some more light on this matter we have included the MARIMA models below. We recognize that this is an advanced area, probably too advanced for most uses of this textbook. However as Enders (1995, Applied Econometric Time Series, Walter Enders, John Wiley and Sons) notes about cointegration models and unit root test, the usual procedure of relating first differences of nonstationary time series may at times be misleading. In that context, consider the following two models of LUK as a function of LUS. In one model the relationship between LUS$_{t-1}$ and LUK$_t$ appears spurious when first differences are used and the other where the relationship between LUS$_{t-1}$ and LUK$_t$ appears correct. The resolution of this problem may or may not be easily resolved easily here. I contemplated on whether to delete this example, however, these series past muster in MARIMA terms if one uses nonstationary LUK and LUS in appropriate MARIMA models. Thus, it appears that these are cointegrated and this example is appropriate to introduce these concepts in more advanced classes. Finally, we have not addressed the problems with feedforward and feedback, that is mutual causality, that is addressed in the next chapter, but this is a rather advanced topic in the context of this book. Whether theoretically correct or not, the COILS model of Table 10-17 provides a useful forecast. More may be forthcoming about this on the Website, http:// forecast.umkc.edu.

Below, I illustrate alternative MARIMA models with and without the assumption of cointegration. First we achieve white noise residuals for both variables so that valid cross correlations can be measured.

```
BOX(DIFF=1,MA=1) LUK / RESU
Dependent Variable LUK - Estimation by Box-Jenkins
Iterations Taken     5
Usable Observations    270      Degrees of Freedom    269
Centered R**2        0.996165   R Bar **2    0.996165
Uncentered R**2      0.999923   T x R**2      269.979
Mean of Dependent Variable      5.8126803893
Std Error of Dependent Variable 0.8313005675
Standard Error of Estimate      0.0514786132
Sum of Squared Residuals        0.7128628100
Durbin-Watson Statistic            2.001859
Q(36-1)                           30.942473
Significance Level of Q            0.66440125
   Variable          Coeff        Std Error      T-Stat     Signif
***********************************************************************
1.  MA{1}         0.4266164260 0.0551552508      7.73483  0.00000000


BOX(DIFF=1,MA=1) LUS / RESS
Dependent Variable LUS - Estimation by Box-Jenkins
Iterations Taken     3
Usable Observations    270      Degrees of Freedom    269
Centered R**2        0.995120   R Bar **2    0.995120
Uncentered R**2      0.999951   T x R**2      269.987
Mean of Dependent Variable      5.0969420403
Std Error of Dependent Variable 0.5151246368
Standard Error of Estimate      0.0359839213
Sum of Squared Residuals        0.3483126575
Durbin-Watson Statistic            1.992408
Q(36-1)                           25.383162
Significance Level of Q            0.88374005
   Variable          Coeff        Std Error      T-Stat     Signif
***********************************************************************
1.  MA{1}         0.3335863269 0.0575692998      5.79452  0.00000002
```

Measuring Cross Correlations between Output and Input Variables.

```
CROSS RESU RESS / -25 25
Cross Correlations of Series RESU and RESS
 -25:   0.0006200 -0.0058584 -0.0267370  0.0246140 -0.1177470 -0.0460928
 -19: -0.0294965 -0.0364740  0.0566120 -0.0118009  0.0256716 -0.0267776
 -13: -0.0614188  0.0726421  0.0166138 -0.0497285  0.1025857  0.0518704
  -7: -0.1245787 -0.0763867  0.0181369  0.0801781 -0.0154449 -0.0101635
  -1:  0.0455372  0.5060561  0.1546690 -0.0985317  0.0609505  0.0968007
   5: -0.1296904 -0.0769517  0.0424366 -0.0562359 -0.0273091  0.0521715
  11:  0.0548440 -0.0222886 -0.0135330 -0.0143293 -0.0614932  0.0017012
  17: -0.1130321  0.0863333 -0.0596886 -0.0141730 -0.1614413  0.0720201
  23:  0.0137971 -0.0198078  0.0486588
DISP 2/269**.5 = 0.12194
```

There are statistically significant correlations between LUK_t and LUS_t and LUS_{t-1}:

Using first differences between these variables yields a model which implies that the coefficients of LUS_t and LUS_{t-1} are redundant and while not shown, for the relationship with only LUS_t in it yield a statistically insignificant coefficient.

```
BOX(MA=1,DIFF=1,INPUT=1,VCV) LUK / RES
#LUS 1
Dependent Variable LUK - Estimation by Box-Jenkins
Iterations Taken      9
Usable Observations   270        Degrees of Freedom   267
Centered R**2       0.997176     R Bar **2    0.997155
Uncentered R**2     0.999944     T x R**2      269.985
Mean of Dependent Variable       5.8126803893
Std Error of Dependent Variable 0.8313005675
Standard Error of Estimate       0.0443403453
Sum of Squared Residuals         0.5249396802
Durbin-Watson Statistic             2.005881
Q(36-1)                            32.381953
Significance Level of Q            0.59513879
     Variable            Coeff       Std Error       T-Stat       Signif
****************************************************************************
1.  MA{1}             0.258228986  0.059524872       4.33817   0.00002039
2.  N_LUS{0}          0.761884781  0.075607248      10.07687   0.00000000
3.  N_LUS{1}         -0.761267227  0.075693807     -10.05719   0.00000000
Covariance\Correlation Matrix of Coefficients
                 MA{1}         N_LUS{0}        N_LUS{1}
MA{1}         0.00354321043  -0.0534976335   0.0534468868
N_LUS{0}     -0.00024076673   0.00571645591  -0.9999616492
N_LUS{1}      0.00024081372  -0.00572278090   0.00572955235
```

Using nonstationary LUK and LUS in a MARIMA model and assuming cointegration yields results which are consistent with the cross correlations generated previously.

```
BOX(MA=1,AR=1,INPUT=1,VCV) LUK / RES
#LUS 1
Dependent Variable LUK - Estimation by Box-Jenkins
Iterations Taken      9
Usable Observations   269        Degrees of Freedom   265
Centered R**2       0.997334     R Bar **2    0.997303
Uncentered R**2     0.999947     T x R**2      268.986
Mean of Dependent Variable       5.8160563991
Std Error of Dependent Variable 0.8309936379
Standard Error of Estimate       0.0431527497
Sum of Squared Residuals         0.4934723497
Durbin-Watson Statistic             2.011668
Q(36-2)                            30.333113
Significance Level of Q            0.64804433
     Variable            Coeff       Std Error       T-Stat       Signif
****************************************************************************
1.  AR{1}             0.9805826880  0.0115600835     84.82488   0.00000000
2.  MA{1}             0.3024822559  0.0595346225      5.08078   0.00000071
3.  N_LUS{0}          0.7953814859  0.0555234429     14.32515   0.00000000
4.  N_LUS{1}          0.3488521819  0.0556543040      6.26820   0.00000000
Covariance\Correlation Matrix of Coefficients
                 AR{1}          MA{1}          N_LUS{0}        N_LUS{1}
AR{1}         0.00013363553  -0.1358194822  -0.0060870895  -0.0221103029
MA{1}        -0.00009347439   0.00354437127  -0.0879748958   0.0812620286
N_LUS{0}     -0.00000390703  -0.00029080693   0.00308285271  -0.8435059675
N_LUS{1}     -0.00001422507   0.00026925019  -0.00260653345   0.00309740156
```

A first-order transfer function is inferior to that of the previous zero-order transfer function.

```
BOX(MA=1,ar=1,INPUT=1,VCV) LUK / RES
#LUS 0 1 0
Dependent Variable LUK - Estimation by Box-Jenkins
Iterations Taken    15
Usable Observations     270      Degrees of Freedom    266
Centered R**2       0.997311     R Bar **2    0.997281
Uncentered R**2     0.999946     T x R**2      269.986
Mean of Dependent Variable      5.8126803893
Std Error of Dependent Variable 0.8313005675
Standard Error of Estimate      0.0433466854
Sum of Squared Residuals        0.4997967467
Durbin-Watson Statistic            2.013346
Q(36-2)                            30.922626
Significance Level of Q            0.61924576
    Variable           Coeff       Std Error     T-Stat     Signif
*****************************************************************************
1.   AR{1}        0.9806639908 0.0113861942     86.12746   0.00000000
2.   MA{1}        0.2862034494 0.0597253816      4.79199   0.00000275
3.   N_LUS{0}     0.7868383553 0.0664579185     11.83965   0.00000000
4.   D_LUS{1}     0.3152461703 0.0588544432      5.35637   0.00000018
Covariance\Correlation Matrix of Coefficients
                   AR{1}          MA{1}         N_LUS{0}        D_LUS{1}
AR{1}        0.00012964542  -0.1375020376  -0.0006274717    0.0101794638
MA{1}       -0.00009350754   0.00356712120 -0.0754186667    0.0698516619
N_LUS{0}    -0.00000047481  -0.00029935362  0.00441665493  -0.9480190582
D_LUS{1}     0.00000682154   0.00024553586 -0.00370802846   0.00346384548
```

10-29. a. True.

b. False, this may or may not be true.

c. Because there are no t-values, it is not possible to know if one, two, or none are statistically significant.

d. True, the high R^2 denotes this as true.

e. This again is a question which cannot be answered from the statistics alone, the relationship only denotes that there is a strong association.

f. May true or false, R^2 measures the explained variance, we have seen forecasting situations in which a R^2 is associated with SEE and forecast errors which were considered to be too large from a practical value, thus, a high R^2 does not assure a practically useful or desirable model.

g. false, one or more regression assumptions can be violated even though the R^2 is quite high, this is a common situation with high first-order serial correlation.

h. it is unknown whether b1 and b2 are statistically significant, however, if either of these, but not both are very low (less than 1), then dropping the least significant coefficient will not adversely affect R^2.

10-30 a. unknown, because this is dependent on the value of the Beta coefficient and there is insufficient information with which to calculate the Beta coefficients.

b. In general it is not recommended that the constant be dropped from the relationship. If adequate theory exists that it should be zero, then it can be dropped, otherwise retain it.

c. True.

d. True, this can be calculated from the R^2.

e. False, the DW is essentially 2.

f. Unknown, this again is a Beta coefficient issue.

g. True, the F-value is very statistically significant.

10-31. A BAD problem because the data of this problem is incorrectly labeled. However, the following relationship results after correcting the names of the variables.

Series	Obs	Mean	Std Error	Minimum	Maximum
UNIT	48	77.30937500	13.01224553	47.50000000	101.88000000
COST	48	965.00000000	163.92434685	640.00000000	1200.00000000

A scatter diagram of each variable with the dependent variable yields what appears to be a nonlinear relationship between them, thus squared terms and an interactive term are created. There appears to be a nonlinear function between cost and time.

```
set stime = time*time
set sunit = unit*unit
linreg(vcv) cost / res
#constant time unit stime sunit
```

Dependent Variable COST - Estimation by Least Squares
Usable Observations   48   Degrees of Freedom   43
Centered R**2   0.927384   R Bar **2   0.920629
Uncentered R**2   0.998005   T x R**2   47.904
Mean of Dependent Variable   965.00000000
Std Error of Dependent Variable 163.92434685
Standard Error of Estimate   46.18223232
Sum of Squared Residuals   91710.339021
Regression F(4,43)   137.2886
Significance Level of F   0.00000000
Durbin-Watson Statistic   1.697482
Q(12-0)   12.858756
Significance Level of Q   0.37939002

Variable	Coeff	Std Error	T-Stat	Signif
1. Constant	-3337.953011	296.018481	-11.27616	0.00000000
2. TIME	13.505571	13.352177	1.01149	0.31744081
3. UNIT	70.762343	8.854820	7.99139	0.00000000
4. STIME	0.212683	0.145305	1.46371	0.15054698
5. SUNIT	-0.383375	0.052506	-7.30153	0.00000000

Covariance\Correlation Matrix of Coefficients

	Constant	TIME	UNIT	STIME
Constant	87626.9412662	-0.1511091848	-0.6104486784	0.0648103459
TIME	-597.2577347	178.2806414	-0.6768449863	-0.9937067082
UNIT	-1600.1022307	-80.0241476	78.4078406	0.7253780277
STIME	2.7876813	-1.9279256	0.9333061	0.0211135
SUNIT	9.5287566	0.4556717	-0.4624347	-0.0052913

	SUNIT
Constant	0.6130657271
TIME	0.6499644457
UNIT	-0.9946271372
STIME	-0.6935449418
SUNIT	0.0027569

10-32 EXPRESS.DAT

Series	Obs	Mean	Std Error	Minimum	Maximum
TIME	25	54.997600000	25.801993670	14.700000000	102.900000000
WEIGHT	25	57.024000000	49.824524082	4.800000000	178.560000000
LENGTH	25	175.220800000	97.595482004	33.950000000	382.180000000

Answer to the requested questions:
a. The relationship below was chosen.

b. The usual interpretation of the regression are obvious.
c. Graphs of residuals versus the independent variables follow.

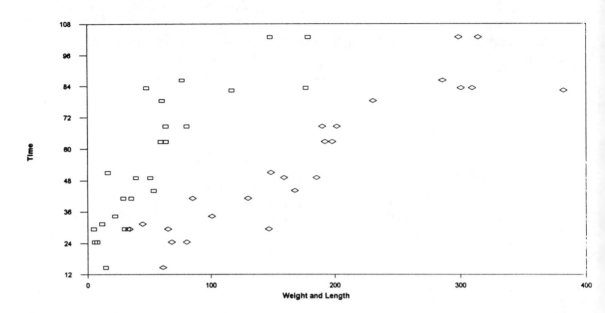

```
linreg time / res
#constant length weight
Dependent Variable TIME - Estimation by Least Squares
Usable Observations      25      Degrees of Freedom      22
Centered R**2      0.877637      R Bar **2      0.866513
Uncentered R**2    0.978655      T x R**2        24.466
Mean of Dependent Variable        54.997600000
Std Error of Dependent Variable  25.801993670
Standard Error of Estimate         9.426974819
Sum of Squared Residuals        1955.0927933
Regression F(2,22)                   78.8966
Significance Level of F            0.00000000
Durbin-Watson Statistic             1.693883
Q(6-0)                              2.702356
Significance Level of Q            0.84516891
     Variable              Coeff        Std Error        T-Stat        Signif
***************************************************************************
1.   Constant          14.691079373  4.127384702      3.55942      0.00175485
2.   LENGTH             0.183658398  0.035860440      5.12148      0.00003928
3.   WEIGHT             0.142497006  0.070242857      2.02863      0.05477050
corr(par=par) res
Correlations of Series RES
Annual Data From 1:01 To 25:01
Autocorrelations
    1:  0.0427626  0.1696939  0.0694562 -0.0332270 -0.1297628 -0.1722468
Partial Autocorrelations
    1:  0.0427626  0.1681728  0.0579711 -0.0679515 -0.1541487 -0.1620766
```

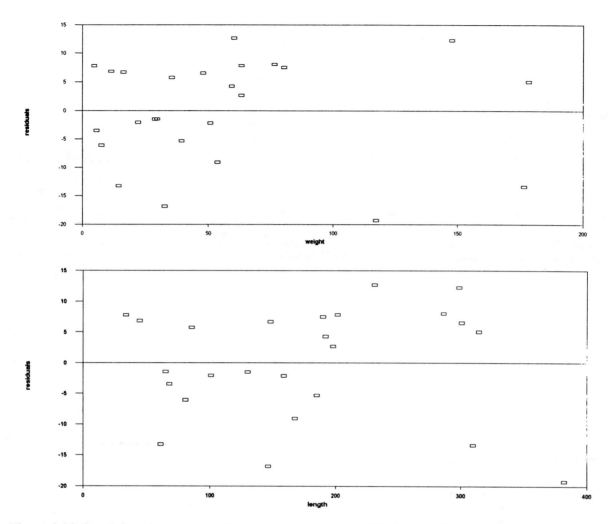

d. The variable length has the greatest influence on time because, if its Beta coefficient is the greater of the two.

```
Beta(Weight) = 0.142497006*49.824524082/25.801993670 = 0.27517
Beta(Length) = 0.183658398*97.595482004/25.801993670 = 0.69468
```

e. The assumptions of regression appear to be achieved, however, we have taken this relationship quite far considering the small number of observations. From a practical standpoint we have some confidence in the relationship, from a theoretical standpoint, the small sample size makes inferences tenuous. Note that the coefficient on the weight variable is marginally insignificant. The interaction between length and weight might be investigated further.

10-33. REALTOR.DAT

a. The best relationship is shown below:

```
linreg price / res
#constant area elevation
Dependent Variable PRICE - Estimation by Least Squares
Usable Observations      20        Degrees of Freedom      17
Centered R**2       0.700070      R Bar **2    0.664784
```

```
Uncentered R**2     0.984926      T x R**2      19.699
Mean of Dependent Variable       101.60000000
Std Error of Dependent Variable   23.97893813
Standard Error of Estimate        13.88328254
Sum of Squared Residuals        3276.6740812
Regression F(2,17)                  19.8400
Significance Level of F            0.00003586
Durbin-Watson Statistic            1.174384
Q(5-0)                            13.078982
Significance Level of Q            0.02264976
    Variable         Coeff        Std Error       T-Stat      Signif
*****************************************************************************
1.  Constant      -77.30575456   28.85370081     -2.67923   0.01584677
2.  AREA            4.14576413    1.03225314      4.01623   0.00089517
3.  ELEVATION       0.63193571    0.13864180      4.55805   0.00027893
```

b) The usual interpretations of this model are possible.

c) Graphs of the residuals versus all independent variables are shown below. These relationships appear random.

d) Based on Beta coefficients the elevation affects the price the most:

```
Beta(Area)     = 4.14576413*3.093199623/23.97893813 = 0.53479
Beta(Elevation) = 0.63193571*23.030319712/23.97893813 = 0.60694
```

```
Series       Obs      Mean      Std Error      Minimum       Maximum
PRICE         20    101.600000   23.978938     58.000000    140.000000
AREA          20     16.204300    3.093200     11.858000     22.540000
ELEVATION     20    176.800500   23.030320    126.250000    217.150000
RES           20     -0.000000   13.132271    -21.605860     30.511264
```

```
corr(par=par,qstat) res
Correlations of Series RES
ACFS (k)      1:   0.3876234   0.0120398 -0.1093771 -0.2084173 -0.5252189
PACFS(k)      1:   0.3876234  -0.1626507 -0.0625624 -0.1630618 -0.4856480
Ljung-Box Q-Statistics   Q(5) = 13.0790.  Significance Level 0.02264976
2Se(ACF) = 2/20**.5 = .45
```

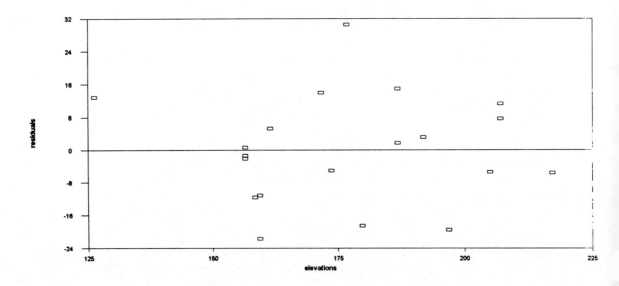

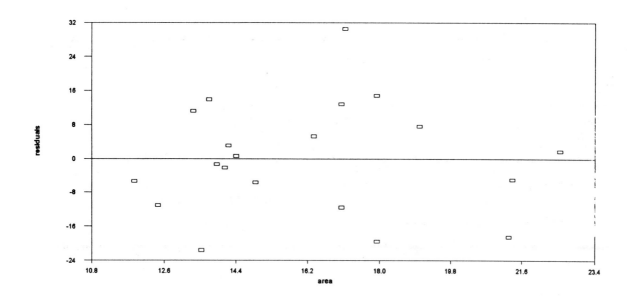

e) Assumptions of Regression. Any discussion of violation or compliance with the assumptions of regression analysis must take into consideration the small number of observations. There is marginally insignificant autocorrelation in the residuals of this relationship, however, no other modeling structure other than COILS eliminated this problem. Several different linear and nonlinear relationships were tried, but none were successful. Because of this we have two alternative models, the previous regression of parts a) to d) or the autoregressive result below. I would choose the following relationship and explore possible causes of the serial correlation problem.

```
ar1 price / res
#constant elevation area
Dependent Variable PRICE - Estimation by Cochrane-Orcutt
Usable Observations      19        Degrees of Freedom     15
Centered R**2      0.774532        R Bar **2     0.729439
Uncentered R**2    0.988740        T x R**2       18.786
Mean of Dependent Variable        102.63157895
Std Error of Dependent Variable    24.17576961
Standard Error of Estimate         12.57514800
Sum of Squared Residuals         2372.0152096
Durbin-Watson Statistic              1.811936
Q(4-1)                               0.992005
Significance Level of Q              0.80318655
     Variable          Coeff        Std Error      T-Stat     Signif
****************************************************************************
1.   Constant        -15.80727423   33.47017206    -0.47228   0.64352499
2.   ELEVATION         0.42056802    0.14075704     2.98790   0.00919650
3.   AREA              2.73355191    0.95041666     2.87616   0.01153893
****************************************************************************
4.   RHO               0.64765422    0.21718577     2.98203   0.00930705
```

10-34. MULT1.DAT

Series	Obs	Mean	Std Error	Minimum	Maximum
SALES	40	267.45000000	28.76157515	222.00000000	333.000000
X1	40	981.85000000	210.33191718	222.00000000	1375.00000
X2	40	6047.90000000	625.53311827	4774.00000000	7356.000000
X3	40	115.02500000	39.26405513	27.00000000	194.000000

```
X4                    40    8.71575000    1.04853961    5.84000000   10.600000
X5                    40 2991.50000000  425.21608383 2210.00000000 3775.000000
```

a) The expected direction of the relationship between Sales and the other variables is confirmed in the first column of the following correlation matrix except for the last variable, average traffic count at the intersection. We would expect that variable to be positive.

```
Correlation Matrix
SALES          X1             X2             X3
SALES  1.00000000000  0.50981603686  0.93502051814 -0.15951507136
X1     0.50981603686  1.00000000000  0.21502640145 -0.19717982280
X2     0.93502051814  0.21502640145  1.00000000000 -0.08415886435
X3    -0.15951507136 -0.19717982280 -0.08415886435  1.00000000000
X4    -0.03976836649  0.36507306313 -0.13150559274 -0.18575035963
X5    -0.04969122612  0.10425243481 -0.17426229984 -0.06666000109
               X4             X5
SALES -0.03976836649 -0.04969122612
X1     0.36507306313  0.10425243481
X2    -0.13150559274 -0.17426229984
X3    -0.18575035963 -0.06666000109
X4     1.00000000000  0.09170117986
X5     0.09170117986  1.00000000000
```

b) All signs in the following relationship are as expected.   The expression of this equation form is quite straightforward.

```
linreg sales / res1
#constant x1 to x5
Dependent Variable SALES - Estimation by Least Squares
Usable Observations      40      Degrees of Freedom      34
Centered R**2      0.982161     R Bar **2      0.979537
Uncentered R**2    0.999801     T x R**2       39.992
Mean of Dependent Variable       267.45000000
Std Error of Dependent Variable   28.76157515
Standard Error of Estimate         4.11428941
Sum of Squared Residuals         575.53082907
Regression F(5,34)                 374.3801
Significance Level of F              0.00000000
Durbin-Watson Statistic             2.383783
Q(10-0)                            19.304604
Significance Level of Q             0.03656003
     Variable            Coeff       Std Error      T-Stat      Signif
************************************************************************
1.   Constant         -15.74040790  11.39598813    -1.38122   0.17622119
2.   X1                 0.04545707   0.00356072    12.76627   0.00000000
3.   X2                 0.03980518   0.00113409    35.09881   0.00000000
4.   X3                -0.02004020   0.01732578    -1.15667   0.25546998
5.   X4                -1.61259735   0.70041970    -2.30233   0.02756651
6.   X5                 0.00474036   0.00159344     2.97492   0.00536157
```

c) The usual interpretation of the results are obvious.

d) Unless there is some strong theoretical reason for including X3 in the relationship it can be dropped, however, the sign of this variable is correct. Often the competitor variable is one which is confounded by the fact that more competitors move into high demand areas, thus, sometimes without proper structure of the model (i.e., correct independent variables and form) this variable will have an insignificant or even positive sign. Little predictive power will be lost by dropping X3 - however, explanatory power or the search for a better causal model may be sacrificed.

e) As shown below, X3 should be removed from the relationship. While stepwise regression is shown below, some backward elimination process will yield the same list of variables and relationship. Finally, the interpretation of this relationship is obvious.

```
stw sales / res
#constant x1 to x5
 Stepping In with P= 0.000000 Variable X2
 Stepping In with P= 0.000000 Variable X1
 Stepping In with P= 0.005174 Variable X4
 Stepping In with P= 0.027329 Variable X5
 Stepping In with P= 0.064371 Variable Constant

Dependent Variable SALES - Estimation by Stepwise
Usable Observations      40      Degrees of Freedom    35
Centered R**2      0.981459     R Bar **2   0.979340
Uncentered R**2    0.999793     T x R**2      39.992
Mean of Dependent Variable        267.45000000
Std Error of Dependent Variable   28.76157515
Standard Error of Estimate         4.13410103
Sum of Squared Residuals         598.17769578
Durbin-Watson Statistic            2.337279

      Variable      Coeff      Std Error     T-Stat     Signif
*****************************************************************************
1.  Constant     -20.43545329  10.69985323   -1.90988  0.06437106
2.  X1             0.04589821   0.00355728   12.90262  0.00000000
3.  X2             0.03991611   0.00113547   35.15388  0.00000000
4.  X4            -1.50066451   0.69704278   -2.15290  0.03829982
5.  X5             0.00484409   0.00159858    3.03025  0.00457333

Correlation Matrix
SALES           X1              X2              X3
SALES      1.000000        0.509816        0.935021       -0.159515
X1         0.509816        1.000000        0.215026       -0.197180
X2         0.935021        0.215026        1.000000       -0.084159
X3        -0.159515       -0.197180       -0.084159        1.000000
X4        -0.039768        0.365073       -0.131506       -0.185750
X5        -0.049691        0.104252       -0.174262       -0.066660
RES1       0.133564  -7.354229e-014  -2.976508e-013  -3.729823e-014
RES        0.136166   4.667615e-014  -5.848820e-014       -0.188436
                X4              X5             RES1            RES
SALES     -0.039768       -0.049691        0.133564        0.136166
X1         0.365073        0.104252  -7.354229e-014   4.667615e-014
X2        -0.131506       -0.174262  -2.976508e-013  -5.848820e-014
X3        -0.185750       -0.066660  -3.729823e-014       -0.188436
X4         1.000000        0.091701   1.473427e-013   1.089306e-013
X5         0.091701        1.000000  -1.671856e-014  -1.567499e-014
RES1   1.473427e-013  -1.671856e-014        1.000000        0.980887
RES    1.089306e-013  -1.567499e-014        0.980887        1.000000
```

10-35 a) An intervention variable is created with values of 0.0 for all observations except 1.0 for the first observation and the sales of the first store was set to 180, not 281. The RATS statements used to make these changes are:

```
set sales 1 1 = 180           set inter = 0
set inter 1 1 = 1
```

Series	Obs	Mean	Std Error	Minimum	Maximum
SALES	40	264.92500000	31.81306577	180.00000000	333.00000000
X1	40	981.85000000	210.33191718	222.00000000	1375.00000000
X2	40	6047.90000000	625.53311827	4774.00000000	7356.00000000
X3	40	115.02500000	39.26405513	27.00000000	194.00000000
X4	40	8.71575000	1.04853961	5.84000000	10.60000000
X5	40	2991.50000000	425.21608383	2210.00000000	3775.00000000
INTER	40	0.02500000	0.15811388	0.00000000	1.00000000

b) I discourage students from using stepwise regression, thus do not infer that these results were generated solely this way, but instead through a manual stepwise process, the results of which were identical to those of the stepwise procedure. The interpretation of the intervention is simply that poor management has reduced mean sales of this store by approximately $102,060 per month.

```
stw sales / res
#constant x1 x2 x3 sx3 x4 x5 inter
 Stepping In with P= 0.000000 Variable X2
 Stepping In with P= 0.000000 Variable INTER
 Stepping In with P= 0.000000 Variable X1
 Stepping In with P= 0.004648 Variable X4
 Stepping In with P= 0.037226 Variable X5
 Stepping In with P= 0.072194 Variable Constant
```

```
Dependent Variable SALES - Estimation by Stepwise
Usable Observations     40      Degrees of Freedom    34
Centered R**2      0.984871     R Bar **2    0.982646
Uncentered R**2    0.999790     T x R**2        39.992
Mean of Dependent Variable       264.92500000
Std Error of Dependent Variable   31.81306577
Standard Error of Estimate         4.19088544
Sum of Squared Residuals         597.15970659
Durbin-Watson Statistic            2.353330
```

	Variable	Coeff	Std Error	T-Stat	Signif
1.	Constant	-20.2054716	10.8888062	-1.85562	0.07219398
2.	X1	0.0458523	0.0036112	12.69737	0.00000000
3.	X2	0.0399444	0.0011570	34.52299	0.00000000
4.	X4	-1.5113540	0.7080107	-2.13465	0.04008171
5.	X5	0.0047651	0.0016534	2.88204	0.00680029
6.	INTER	-102.0613573	4.4085505	-23.15077	0.00000000

c. The annual effect is 12*102.06 = $1,224,720.

10-36 BLOOD.DAT - This time series includes the variable INTERVENTION which is zero until period 135. The actual demand and the regression fit are shown below. The interpretation of the relationship and confirmation of regression assumptions are quite obvious to the instructor.

Series	Obs	Mean	Std Error	Minimum	Maximum
DATE	187	94.000000000	54.126395286	1.000000000	187.000000000
DEMAND	187	52.841050267	6.036729606	37.556400000	67.114400000
INTERVENTION	187	0.283422460	0.451869531	0.000000000	1.000000000

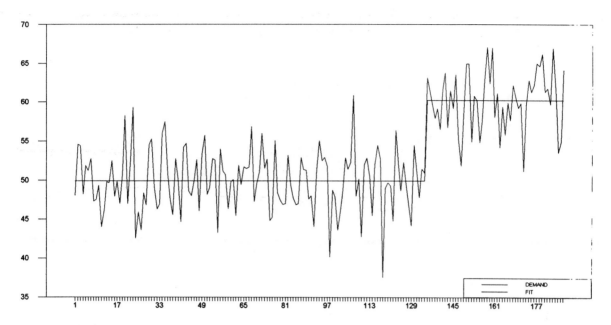

```
linreg demand / res
#constant intervention
Dependent Variable DEMAND - Estimation by Least Squares
Usable Observations      187      Degrees of Freedom    185
Centered R**2      0.595488      R Bar **2    0.593301
Uncentered R**2    0.994816      T x R**2      186.031
Mean of Dependent Variable       52.841050267
Std Error of Dependent Variable  6.036729606
Standard Error of Estimate       3.849800758
Sum of Squared Residuals         2741.8786877
Regression F(1,185)                272.3407
Significance Level of F            0.00000000
Durbin-Watson Statistic            1.834871
Q(36-0)                           47.296817
Significance Level of Q            0.09854677
    Variable         Coeff        Std Error      T-Stat      Signif
************************************************************************
1.  Constant       49.919191045  0.332572132   150.10034   0.00000000
2.  INTERVENTION   10.309201408  0.624695997    16.50275   0.00000000
```

10-37. WATER.DAT - Demand for water before, during, and after a flood. The original intervention variable turns on in period 75 but stays on, thus, to solve this problem the student must create a dummy variable that turns on after period 84 which turns the flood's effect off in period 85.

Series	Obs	Mean	Std Error	Minimum	Maximum
DATE	110	55.500000000	31.898275815	1.000000000	110.000000000
SALES	110	124.898323636	19.266710024	89.546000000	167.083600000
INTER	110	0.327272727	0.471365203	0.000000000	1.000000000

The following creates the second intervention variable.

```
set inter2 = 0
set inter2 85 110 = 1
```

We create a trend variable to model the trend.

```
set trend = t
linreg sales / res
#constant inter inter2 trend
Dependent Variable SALES - Estimation by Least Squares
Usable Observations    110      Degrees of Freedom    106
Centered R**2      0.963919     R Bar **2    0.962898
Uncentered R**2    0.999169     T x R**2     109.909
Mean of Dependent Variable      124.89832364
Std Error of Dependent Variable 19.26671002
Standard Error of Estimate       3.71113709
Sum of Squared Residuals      1459.8890797
Regression F(3,106)                943.9455
Significance Level of F            0.00000000
Durbin-Watson Statistic            1.846608
Q(27-0)                           20.429837
Significance Level of Q            0.81224229
     Variable            Coeff        Std Error       T-Stat       Signif
*************************************************************************
1.   Constant        94.62953526     0.85712133     110.40390    0.00000000
2.   INTER           24.07943754     1.50048652      16.04775    0.00000000
3.   INTER2         -25.20652807     1.42595612     -17.67693    0.00000000
4.   TREND            0.51074147     0.01975029      25.85995    0.00000000
```

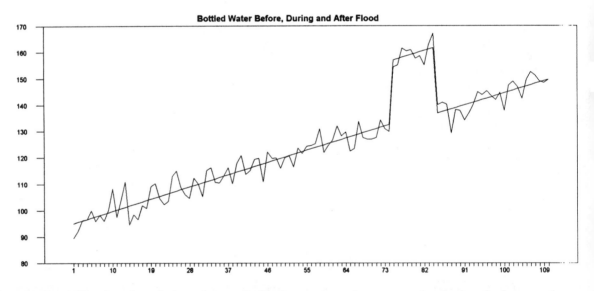

Bottled Water Before, During and After Flood

The intervention affect is rather obvious, interestingly, the company lost some sales during the intervention period because of increased competition during the flood. This is seen when we compare the peri and post intervention coefficients. The post negative intervention coefficient is greater than the peri intervention coefficient. No assumptions of regression analysis are violated by this relationship.

10-38. SP500MN.DAT - This should be an interesting problem for most students, modeling the effect of the stock market crash of October 1987. The decline in the market persist from the closing price in October and November 1987. To simplify things in the context of this chapter, we will use a time variable to model the trend, obviously there are many other approaches, some of which are developed in Chapter 12. As is usual, we model the closing prices of the S&P 500 using logarithms. Below, we create logs of the index, create two dummy variables that are step functions turning on in October and November 1987 respectively.

```
cal 1981 3 12
set lclose = log(close)        set trend = t
set inter1 = 0                 set inter1 1987:10 1993:02 = 1
set inter2 = 0                 set inter2 1987:11 1993:02 = 1
ar1 lclose / res1
#constant trend inter1 inter2
Dependent Variable LCLOSE - Estimation by Cochrane-Orcutt
Usable Observations     143      Degrees of Freedom    138
Centered R**2      0.991298      R Bar **2    0.991046
Uncentered R**2    0.999951      T x R**2      142.993
Mean of Dependent Variable       5.4636617928
Std Error of Dependent Variable 0.4143701390
Standard Error of Estimate       0.0392099140
Sum of Squared Residuals         0.2121635949
Durbin-Watson Statistic             2.073581
Q(35-1)                            34.330127
Significance Level of Q            0.45192604
    Variable        Coeff        Std Error      T-Stat      Signif
*******************************************************************
1.  Constant      4.598966905   0.077771808    59.13411   0.00000000
2.  TREND         0.013526285   0.001001218    13.50984   0.00000000
3.  INTER1       -0.243391664   0.039753018    -6.12260   0.00000001
4.  INTER2       -0.088127161   0.039756256    -2.21669   0.02828140
5.  RHO           0.902824623   0.034580563    26.10786   0.00000000
set pred1 = lclose - res1
```

The following converts the logarithmic coefficients of this relationship to ratios. As shown, October 1987 was only .784 or 78.4 percent of the expected value, also, November 1987 was only .916 or 91.6 percent of the expected value for that month. This interpretation is clarified on page 522, Table 12-14.

```
October's Intervention  =  exp(-0.243391664) = 0.78396
November's Intervention =  exp(-0.088127161) = 0.91564
```

There are no serious violations of the assumptions of regression in this analysis, however, there are better methods for modeling this time series as discussed in Chapter 12. As a double check on the residuals of this model, the following ACFs and PACFs denote that the residuals are white noise.

```
corr(par=par,qstat) res1
Correlations of Series RES1
Autocorrelations
 1: -0.0374428   0.0970084  -0.0051005  -0.0193847   0.1680396  -0.0286903
 7:  0.0387132  -0.1021723   0.0016478   0.1050842   0.0223129  -0.0025775
13: -0.1303650   0.0329222  -0.0180783  -0.0914403   0.0604080  -0.0628649
19:  0.0265861   0.0401819  -0.0263975   0.0647164  -0.0428292   0.1526253
25: -0.0184104   0.0976974  -0.0874077   0.0197528   0.1399994  -0.0842790
31:  0.0244445  -0.1478286   0.0142653  -0.0439838   0.0671232  -0.1053868
Partial Autocorrelations
 1: -0.0374428   0.0957407   0.0017877  -0.0290920   0.1686390  -0.0139479
 7:  0.0043649  -0.0976056  -0.0013884   0.1005708   0.0356537  -0.0345532
13: -0.1101336   0.0328084  -0.0188130  -0.1245317   0.0602528   0.0216601
19:  0.0074039   0.0403658  -0.0293153   0.0488350   0.0011466   0.1253295
25: -0.0150135   0.0952979  -0.1023778   0.0062298   0.1044496  -0.0642726
31: -0.0603334  -0.1011073   0.0307634  -0.0886023   0.0866030  -0.1294755
Ljung-Box Q-Statistics
Q(36)  =        36.6888.  Significance Level 0.43675297
```

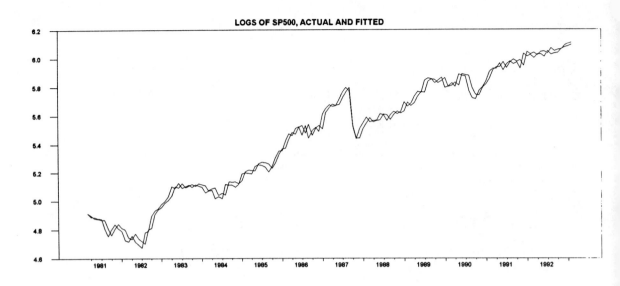

LOGS OF SP500, ACTUAL AND FITTED

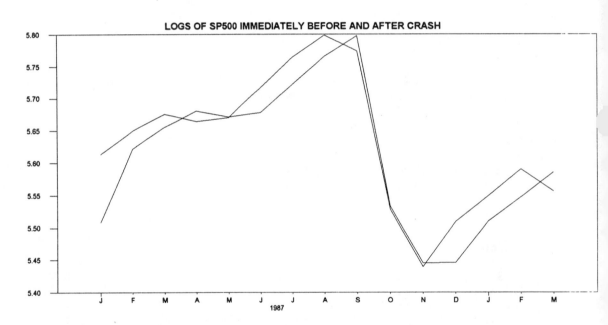

LOGS OF SP500 IMMEDIATELY BEFORE AND AFTER CRASH

10-39. AIRLINI.DAT - The data of this problem has been contrived using the famous Bob Brown, George Box, and Gwilym Jenkins International Airline Passengers data. The analysis parallels that of the previous problem fairly closely. As before the intervention variable included here is a step function in period 121. The logarithms of the time series are analyzed.

Series	Obs	Mean	Std Error	Minimum	Maximum
DATE	144	195456.500000	346.427482	194901.000000	196012.000000
PASS	144	327.239817	209.773549	104.000000	1025.503600
LPASS	144	5.622032	0.564604	4.644390	6.932930
INTER	144	0.166667	0.373979	0.000000	1.000000

We create trend variable and dummy variables for each month of the year next by using December as the base month (i.e., that month is embedded in the constant).

```
set trend = t
```

```
seas jan / 12 1    seas feb / 12 2
seas mar / 12 3    seas apr / 12 4
seas may / 12 5    seas jun / 12 6
seas jul / 12 7    seas aug / 12 8
seas sep / 12 9    seas oct / 12 10
seas nov / 12 11
```

Running a full model yields the following model with serially correlated errors.

```
linreg lpass / res
#constant trend inter jan feb mar apr may jun jul aug sep oct nov
Dependent Variable LPASS - Estimation by Least Squares
Monthly Data From 1949:01 To 1960:12
Usable Observations     144        Degrees of Freedom    130
Centered R**2       0.990180       R Bar **2    0.989198
Uncentered R**2     0.999903       T x R**2       143.986
Mean of Dependent Variable         5.6220323611
Std Error of Dependent Variable 0.5646040610
Standard Error of Estimate         0.0586815202
Sum of Squared Residuals           0.4476577062
Regression F(13,130)                 1008.3052
Significance Level of F               0.00000000
Durbin-Watson Statistic              0.481802
Q(36-0)                            349.630229
Significance Level of Q              0.00000000
    Variable        Coeff        Std Error      T-Stat       Signif
***********************************************************************
1.  Constant     4.680746316   0.019907978    235.11912    0.00000000
2.  TREND        0.010632039   0.000154950     68.61611    0.00000000
3.  INTER        0.384597859   0.017223259     22.33014    0.00000000
4.  JAN          0.006687429   0.024017187      0.27844    0.78111436
5.  FEB         -0.005510443   0.024006688     -0.22954    0.81881166
6.  MAR          0.129363351   0.023997185      5.39077    0.00000032
7.  APR          0.100137145   0.023988679      4.17435    0.00005435
8.  MAY          0.098502606   0.023981172      4.10750    0.00007030
9.  JUN          0.220735567   0.023974663      9.20704    0.00000000
10. JUL          0.324438528   0.023969155     13.53567    0.00000000
11. AUG          0.314743989   0.023964647     13.13368    0.00000000
12. SEP          0.169629450   0.023961140      7.07936    0.00000000
13. OCT          0.030947411   0.023958635      1.29170    0.19875222
14. NOV         -0.113312128   0.023957131     -4.72979    0.00000577
```

Because there is a serious problem with serial correlation, we will fit a COILS estimation procedure.

```
ar1 lpass / res
#constant trend inter jan feb mar apr may jun jul aug sep oct nov
Dependent Variable LPASS - Estimation by Cochrane-Orcutt
Monthly Data From 1949:02 To 1960:12
Usable Observations     143        Degrees of Freedom    128
Centered R**2       0.995838       R Bar **2    0.995383
Uncentered R**2     0.999959       T x R**2       142.994
Mean of Dependent Variable         5.6283508392
Std Error of Dependent Variable 0.5614563546
Standard Error of Estimate         0.0381509286
Sum of Squared Residuals           0.1863031492
Durbin-Watson Statistic              2.038125
Q(35-1)                             40.113831
Significance Level of Q              0.21742059
```

Variable	Coeff	Std Error	T-Stat	Signif
1. Constant	4.662575954	0.035359757	131.86109	0.00000000
2. TREND	0.010972805	0.000416448	26.34859	0.00000000
3. INTER	0.332648674	0.033597692	9.90094	0.00000000
4. JAN	0.006870055	0.012308717	0.55815	0.57772002
5. FEB	-0.004830196	0.015694022	-0.30777	0.75875533
6. MAR	0.130356955	0.017752839	7.34288	0.00000000
7. APR	0.101300339	0.019014124	5.32764	0.00000043
8. MAY	0.099723221	0.019695227	5.06332	0.00000140
9. JUN	0.221926087	0.019893156	11.15590	0.00000000
10. JUL	0.325530672	0.019634318	16.57968	0.00000000
11. AUG	0.315684483	0.018884322	16.71675	0.00000000
12. SEP	0.170376729	0.017531478	9.71833	0.00000000
13. OCT	0.031469046	0.015321117	2.05397	0.04201491
14. NOV	-0.113041440	0.011590531	-9.75291	0.00000000
15. RHO	0.780214632	0.055154524	14.14598	0.00000000

We rerun this relationship without the insignificant months of January and February which are assumed to be the same as December, these three months all being embodied in the constant term. These results are nearly identical to the previous relationship.

```
ar1 lpass / res
#constant trend inter mar apr may jun jul aug sep oct nov
Dependent Variable LPASS - Estimation by Cochrane-Orcutt
Monthly Data From 1949:02 To 1960:12
Usable Observations      143         Degrees of Freedom    130
Centered R**2       0.995800       R Bar **2     0.995412
Uncentered R**2     0.999959       T x R**2      142.994
Mean of Dependent Variable        5.6283508392
Std Error of Dependent Variable 0.5614563546
Standard Error of Estimate      0.0380307115
Sum of Squared Residuals        0.1880235526
Durbin-Watson Statistic           2.047547
Q(35-1)                          37.913569
Significance Level of Q           0.29538327
```

Variable	Coeff	Std Error	T-Stat	Signif
1. Constant	4.661483395	0.032941395	141.50838	0.00000000
2. TREND	0.010953702	0.000403431	27.15134	0.00000000
3. INTER	0.337332760	0.032491742	10.38211	0.00000000
4. MAR	0.134413543	0.011397057	11.79371	0.00000000
5. APR	0.104733912	0.014826223	7.06410	0.00000000
6. MAY	0.102644170	0.016690297	6.14993	0.00000001
7. JUN	0.224411426	0.017655269	12.71073	0.00000000
8. JUL	0.327628774	0.017953896	18.24834	0.00000000
9. AUG	0.317418005	0.017649158	17.98488	0.00000000
10. SEP	0.171743913	0.016680154	10.29630	0.00000000
11. OCT	0.032443459	0.014815870	2.18978	0.03032479
12. NOV	-0.112512737	0.011391046	-9.87730	0.00000000
13. RHO	0.775015676	0.055231553	14.03212	0.00000000

The COILS procedure has eliminated all of the serious problems with first order serial correlation.
```
corr(par=par,qstat) res
Correlations of Series RES
Monthly Data From 1949:01 To 1960:12
```

```
Autocorrelations
  1: -0.0260813   0.0880285   0.0028232  -0.1026451   0.0209264   0.0386541
  7: -0.0919384  -0.0507391   0.1102655  -0.0238115   0.0426983   0.1003260
 13:  0.0062481   0.0461781  -0.0189237  -0.2291080  -0.0066038  -0.0707528
 19: -0.1177440  -0.0780648  -0.0822225  -0.0627939   0.1807907   0.0378873
 25:  0.0071618   0.0121209  -0.0626917  -0.0799567  -0.1075770  -0.0741553
 31: -0.0452072   0.0882237  -0.1052602   0.0625966  -0.0404214  -0.0137395
Partial Autocorrelations
  1: -0.0260813   0.0874077   0.0072585  -0.1110254   0.0152442   0.0604837
  7: -0.0947997  -0.0784378   0.1362029   0.0043013  -0.0106344   0.0995817
 13:  0.0504433   0.0099346  -0.0431885  -0.2053033  -0.0000676  -0.0431372
 19: -0.1285770  -0.1225089  -0.0648078  -0.0550402   0.1276820   0.0283592
 25:  0.0169987  -0.0113279  -0.0234850  -0.0483624  -0.1204495  -0.0280701
 31:  0.0042941   0.0355562  -0.1168553   0.0278712  -0.0966093  -0.1050742
Ljung-Box Q-Statistics
Q(36)  =          39.7683.  Significance Level 0.30590240
```

The intervention effect is a 40% increase:
$$\exp(0.337332760)-1 = 0.40121$$

The monthly trend in passengers is 1.11% increase:
$$\exp(0.010953702)-1 = 0.01101$$

July passengers are on average 38.8% higher than December's:
$$\exp(0.327628774)-1 = 0.38767$$

There are no serious violations of the assumptions of regression analysis that were not corrected by the COILS estimation procedure.

10-40. IBMNYLN.DAT -

```
Series       Obs        Mean      Std Error      Minimum        Maximum
DATE         242  45910.111570  37071.539708  1394.000000  123193.000000
LONP         242     40.493058      3.459584    34.750000      46.875000
NYP          242     62.104483      6.881452    52.000000      76.125000
```

Considerable theory supports using logarithms.
```
set llonp = log(lonp)
set lnyp = log(nyp)
set dllonp 2 242 = llonp - llonp(t-1)
set dlnyp 2 242 = lnyp - lnyp(t-1)
```

As a double check that first differences are white noise, consider the following ACFs and PACFS.
```
corr(par=par,qstat,num=14) dlnyp
Correlations of Series DLNYP
Autocorrelations
  1: -0.0633064  -0.0654602  -0.0077548  -0.0606923   0.0864428   0.0200550
  7:  0.0771084  -0.0848920  -0.1164253   0.0182076  -0.0086991   0.0256797
 13: -0.0304346  -0.0996342
Partial Autocorrelations
  1: -0.0633064  -0.0697474  -0.0167516  -0.0675437   0.0769800   0.0222843
  7:  0.0917051  -0.0745333  -0.1074874  -0.0119673  -0.0193352   0.0005949
 13: -0.0344048  -0.0901656
Ljung-Box Q-Statistics
Q(14)  =          14.6993.  Significance Level 0.39901554
Correlations of Series DLLONP
Autocorrelations
  1: -0.1210107  -0.0785832  -0.0220076  -0.0698551   0.1094547   0.0059297
  7:  0.0563289  -0.0916890  -0.0960625   0.0476982  -0.0336316   0.0318329
 13:  0.0113070  -0.0529461
Partial Autocorrelations
  1: -0.1210107  -0.0946123  -0.0449199  -0.0884517   0.0848393   0.0170855
  7:  0.0754684  -0.0738545  -0.0951749   0.0023168  -0.0462218  -0.0021815
```

```
  13:  0.0134172 -0.0292155
Ljung-Box Q-Statistics
Q(14)  =          16.5095.  Significance Level 0.28326035
```

First differences of the New York Stock Exchange price is white noise, while first difference of the London exchange price may not be. Nonetheless, we can still achieve valid CCFs with a prewhitened input variable.

Using first differences we explore cross correlations.
```
cross  dllonp dlnyp
Cross Correlations of Series DLLONP and DLNYP
 -30:   0.0150898 -0.0261199 -0.0331999  0.0000232 -0.0456000 -0.0082816
 -24:   0.0189865 -0.0542485  0.0507405 -0.0967118  0.1328965  0.0201598
 -18:  -0.1710802  0.0817881 -0.0069284 -0.0021595  0.0468970 -0.0645271
 -12:   0.0192877  0.0158199 -0.0204609  0.0151210 -0.1087735 -0.0894083
  -6:   0.0859159  0.0173518  0.0823662 -0.0323010 -0.0563955 -0.0328379
   0:  -0.0459778  0.8791011 -0.0472586 -0.0937849  0.0153299 -0.0936779
   6:   0.0838653  0.0487297  0.0336375 -0.0993089 -0.0998622  0.0428230
  12:  -0.0009418  0.0320179 -0.0301321 -0.1052640  0.0401393 -0.0025003
  18:  -0.0036431  0.0789280 -0.1078851  0.0268851  0.0766192 -0.1374756
  24:   0.0963931 -0.0793338 -0.0225520  0.0307780 -0.0050821 -0.0277304
  30:  -0.0951080  0.0073929  0.0083667  0.0299165  0.0126121 -0.0703218
Ljung-Box Q-Statistics
Q(1 to 25)   =        221.2153.  Significance Level 0.00000000
Q(-25 to -1)=         30.1447.  Significance Level 0.21891584
Q(-25 to 25)=        251.8737.  Significance Level 0.00000000
```

Thus, $dLLONP_t = f(dLNYP_{t-1})$

After fitting an OLS there was considerable serial correlation in the residuals, thus a COILS procedure was used.

```
ar1 dllonp / res3
# dlnyp{1}
Dependent Variable DLLONP - Estimation by Cochrane-Orcutt
Usable Observations    239       Degrees of Freedom    237
Centered R**2      0.808026      R Bar **2    0.807216
Uncentered R**2    0.808230      T x R**2     193.167
Mean of Dependent Variable      0.0006545194
Std Error of Dependent Variable 0.0201094641
Standard Error of Estimate      0.0088294929
Sum of Squared Residuals        0.0184765068
Durbin-Watson Statistic          2.205184
Q(36-1)                         45.758166
Significance Level of Q          0.10536660
    Variable           Coeff        Std Error      T-Stat      Signif
*********************************************************************
1.  DLNYP{1}       0.952434780  0.029175731     32.64476    0.00000000
*********************************************************************
2.  RHO           -0.384629350  0.059734468     -6.43899    0.00000000
corr(par=par,num=21,qstat) res3
Correlations of Series RES3
Autocorrelations
  1: -0.1026834 -0.2588324  0.0015233  0.0408969  0.0954426 -0.1379804
  7:  0.0078061  0.0683994  0.0248642  0.0178046 -0.0863842  0.0075583
 13:  0.0368527  0.0730814 -0.0625735  0.0094688  0.0450528 -0.0970967
 19:  0.0035535 -0.0450160 -0.0740831
Partial Autocorrelations
  1: -0.1026834 -0.2722468 -0.0657616 -0.0420096  0.0868996 -0.1224472
```

```
 7:   0.0270139   0.0095418   0.0454854   0.0429450  -0.0405794  -0.0098066
13:   0.0009004   0.0889374  -0.0384320   0.0633338   0.0112963  -0.0844138
19:  -0.0132339  -0.0758723  -0.1262380
Ljung-Box Q-Statistics
Q(21)  =          37.3722.  Significance Level 0.01525092
```

Unfortunately, there is no easy way to remove the low order serial correlation at lag 2 until we learn MARIMA concepts in Chapter 13. A MARIMA model is developed below. In this example, we have sidestepped the issue of whether this is a cointegration model by going directly to first differences.

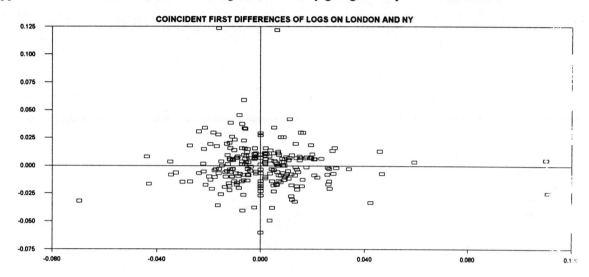

COINCIDENT FIRST DIFFERENCES OF LOGS ON LONDON AND NY

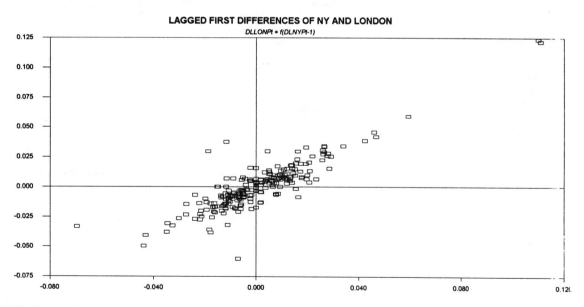

LAGGED FIRST DIFFERENCES OF NY AND LONDON
DLLONPt = f(DLNYPt-1)

```
box(diff=1,ma=1,input=1,apply) llonp / res1
#lnyp 0 0 1
Dependent Variable LLONP - Estimation by Box-Jenkins
Iterations Taken      8
Usable Observations    240      Degrees of Freedom    238
Centered R**2      0.990221     R Bar **2    0.990180
Uncentered R**2    0.999995     T x R**2      239.999
Mean of Dependent Variable      3.6978423279
Std Error of Dependent Variable 0.0855391828
```

```
Standard Error of Estimate        0.0084764148
Sum of Squared Residuals          0.0171002065
Durbin-Watson Statistic             1.956020
Q(36-1)                            26.282362
Significance Level of Q            0.85591691
    Variable        Coeff       Std Error      T-Stat      Signif
**********************************************************************
1.  MA{1}        -0.545163641  0.054370543   -10.02682   0.00000000
2.  N_LNYP{1}     0.942493965  0.026010614    36.23498   0.00000000
corr(par=par,num=21,qstat) res1
Correlations of Series RES1
Autocorrelations
  1:   0.0131353 -0.0619563  0.0159049  0.0202832  0.0956718 -0.1101024
  7:   0.0236854  0.0572887  0.0269046  0.0300924 -0.0700809  0.0246084
 13:   0.0285309  0.0764361 -0.0483763 -0.0053090  0.0152777 -0.1195909
 19:  -0.0329116 -0.0773979 -0.0790997
Partial Autocorrelations
  1:   0.0131353 -0.0621396  0.0176567  0.0160162  0.0976664 -0.1124226
  7:   0.0402686  0.0387289  0.0311662  0.0274763 -0.0507349  0.0108906
 13:   0.0164941  0.0867407 -0.0543050  0.0203866 -0.0176111 -0.1224318
 19:  -0.0342451 -0.0694799 -0.0960541
Ljung-Box Q-Statistics
Q(21)   =          18.8341.  Significance Level 0.59578000
cross res1 dlnyp
Cross Correlations of Series RES1 and DLNYP
-24:   0.0118074  0.0662533  0.0016549  0.0341195  0.0787960  0.0371261
-18:  -0.0365868 -0.0768631  0.0124201 -0.0554970 -0.0170390  0.0474252
-12:   0.1385702  0.0605763  0.0055079  0.0012726 -0.0168012 -0.0432962
 -6:   0.0216861  0.0102953  0.0204030  0.0637930 -0.0847850  0.0088268
  0:   0.0247961  0.0247266  0.0385696 -0.0686756  0.0158088 -0.0855788
  6:  -0.0266452  0.0589618 -0.0509981 -0.0863343 -0.0322380  0.0443702
 12:   0.0418521  0.0406102  0.0181834 -0.0346761 -0.0245848 -0.0675657
 18:   0.0280122 -0.0512329  0.0641191  0.0470333 -0.0517789 -0.0872705
 24:   0.0367891  0.0036328 -0.1030277  0.0627428  0.1109624 -0.0457923
disp 2/242**.5 = 0.12856
```

MINICASES

The solutions to these Minicases are available from the author's website. However, you will have to call the author or email him to get permission or copies of these Minicase solutions. He is available at delurgio@cctr.umkc.edu, sad@forecast.umkc.edu, 1-816-235-2311.

PROBLEMS

ESTIMATED DIFFICULTY

Elementary		Medium		Hard		Very Hard		Bad	
1 E	2 E	3 M	4 E	5 M	6 M	7 M	8 M	9 E	10 E
11 M	12 M	13 M	14 M	15 V	16 M	17 M	18 M	19 M	20 H
21 H	22 H	23 M	24 M	25 M	26 H	27 H	28 H		

Minicases	1 H	2 H	3 H	4 H	5 H-V	6 H	7 H	8 H	9 H	10 H

11-1. A system of equations consists of two or more equations with interrelated variables, sometimes recursively determined equations (i.e., having recursive relationships) and other times nonrecursively (i.e., simultaneously) determined equations.

11-2. Time precedence, lagged correlation, and ceteris paribus, all other things held constant or controlled for. This last requirement is the most difficult to achieve.

11-3. A recursive relationship is one where an endogenous variable may exist in two or more equations once as a dependent variable and one or more times as an independent or predetermined variable as in equations 11-2 to 11-4. However, in no case are equations and variables simultaneously determined. Simultaneous equations have two or more variables that are simultaneously determined as in equations 11-15 and 11-16 where two or more variables are mutually related, $Y=f(X)$ and $X=f(Y)$.

11-4. A path coefficient is a standardized regression coefficient (i.e., Beta coefficient) expressing the relationship between two variables in a system of equations.

11-5. A partial correlation coefficient measures the association between two variables (e.g., Y and X) while controlling for their individual correlation with another variable (e.g., Z). This correlation is designated as $r_{YX.Z}$, where the dot denotes that the correlation is between Y and X net of or after partialing out the correlation with Z. Partial correlation coefficients are important in measuring causality because they control for the influence of other variables which may make the two variables seem correlated, when they are not (e.g., see 11-6 a.). See also pages 461-463.

11-6. a. there is no correlation between X_1 and X_2 other than through their individual correlation with X_3. Thus, the partial correlation between X_1 and X_2 is zero when controlling for X_3. b. The partial correlation coefficient between X_1 and X_2 after controlling for X_3 is positive. c. The partial correlation coefficient between X_1 and X_2 after controlling for X_3 is negative.

Causality is neither implied nor proven through partial correlation coefficients. This may provide evidence of causality, however, note that we have not defined the direction of influence as either being from X_1 to X_2 or X_2 to X_1.

11-7. A total influence is the total correlation between two variables with out regard to whether there are intervening or confounding influences from other variables. Direct influences are path (beta) coefficients that measure the influence between two variables net or partial of other influences. Indirect influences are the difference between total correlations and direct influences as measured by the path coefficients.

11-8. See pages 456-461 for this explanation.

11-9. This denotes that there is no correlation between X_1 and X_2 after controlling for other influences for example X_3.

11-10. Weak causal ordering denotes that X_1 may cause X_2 but that X_2 can not cause X_1. This is important in proving causality, otherwise, the direction of causality is more difficult to prove.

11-11. Specification errors are the inclusion of the wrong variable, variables, or variable forms (e.g., squared variables) in a relationship or the exclusion of important variables.

11-12. See pages 469 to 472.

11-13. See page 472.

11-14. See page 474

11-15. The term instrumental variable must has been mistakenly deleted, why or how, I do not know. However, the term instrumental variable applies to the method of obtaining consistent OLS parameter estimates by replacing an explanatory or predictor variable which has measurement errors with another variable (referred to as an instrumental variable) that is highly correlated with the original predictor variable but is independent of the error term. The terms $\hat{S}_t$ and $\hat{A}_t$ in equations 11-19 to 11-22 are instrumental variables, thus instrumental variables make it possible to estimate simultaneous relationships using OLS in procedures such as 2SLS.

11-16. See page 473.

11-17. See page 479

11-18. 2SLS should be used when there is simultaneity in two or more relationships and none of the limitations discussed on page 478 apply. See page 474 for an explanations of process steps.

11-19. ILS cannot be used for overidentified equations and does not provide estimates of the standard error of the structural coefficients.

11-20. a. $r_{12} \neq 0$, $r_{23} \neq 0$, $r_{13.2} \neq 0.0$, as denoted by the lack of path between 1 and 3.
Note also that $r_{13} \neq 0$.
b. $r_{21} \neq 0$, $r_{23} \neq 0$, $r_{13} \neq 0$, $r_{13.2} \neq ?$, note also that $r_{32.1} = 0$
c. $r_{21} \neq 0$, $r_{23} = 0$, $r_{32} = r_{23} = 0$, $r_{21.3} \neq ?$
d. $r_{12} \neq 0$, $r_{23} \neq 0$, $r_{13.2} = 0$

11-21. a. $r_{21.3}=0$, $r_{32}\neq 0$, $r_{31}\neq 0$

      b. $r_{21.3}=0$, $r_{31}\neq 0$, $r_{23}\neq 0$

      c. $r_{31}\neq$, $r_{23}=0$, $r_{21}=0$ $r_{31.2}=$?

      d. $r_{32}\neq 0$, $r_{21}\neq 0$, $r_{31}\neq 0$, $r_{31.2}=0$

11-22. See pages 456 to 458.

11-23. See pages 478 and 479.

11-24. a. R_t and Y_t are simultaneously determined.

      b. If OLS is used to estimate the above two relationships, then the regression coefficients will be biased because of the simultaneity and errors that are correlated with independent variables.

      c. Exogenous variables are M_t, endogenous variables are Y_t and R_t.

      d. Reduced form equations express each endogenous variable in the system only as a function of all exogenous variables in that system as in equations 11-23 and 11-24 see also there derivations on page 475. The predicted dependent variables of the reduced form equations become instrumental variables in the second stage of 2SLS.

      e. The first equation is exactly identified and the second equation is underidentified.

11-25. Exogenous are X2 and X1 and Y1, Y2, and Y3 are endogenous. Equations 1 and 2 are exactly identified while equation 3 is overidentified.

11-26. a. Two stage least squares should be used to model each of these. Equations 1 and 2 are exactly identified.

      b. Fitting OLS to each Relationship.

```
Correlation Matrix
              EN1                 EN2                 EX1                 EX2
EN1 1.000000000000 0.192820307248 0.223362755171 0.997545265515
EN2 0.192820307248 1.000000000000 0.997248637755 0.173778375523
EX1 0.223362755171 0.997248637755 1.000000000000 0.204242947939
EX2 0.997545265515 0.173778375523 0.204242947939 1.000000000000

LINREG EN1 / OLS1
#CONSTANT EN2 EX1
Dependent Variable EN1 - Estimation by Least Squares
Usable Observations      100        Degrees of Freedom      97
Centered R**2      0.212885        R Bar **2     0.196656
Uncentered R**2    0.769984        T x R**2       76.998
Mean of Dependent Variable      470.02000000
Std Error of Dependent Variable 303.53702718
Standard Error of Estimate      272.05858503
Sum of Squared Residuals        7179539.7476
Regression F(2,97)                 13.1174
Significance Level of F           0.00000907
Durbin-Watson Statistic            2.186442
     Variable              Coeff        Std Error       T-Stat      Signif
**************************************************************************
1.   Constant           506.0984511    62.2065221        8.13578   0.00000000
2.   EN2                 -5.6701225     1.2651423       -4.48181   0.00002028
3.   EX1                 58.2448469    12.5169324        4.65328   0.00001035
PRJ FOLS1 (Saving Fitted values as FOLS1 (fitted values OLS1)
```

```
LINREG EN2 / OLS2
#CONSTANT EN1 EX2
Dependent Variable EN2 - Estimation by Least Squares
Usable Observations     100        Degrees of Freedom     97
Centered R**2      0.107496     R Bar **2    0.089094
Uncentered R**2    0.779359     T x R**2        77.936
Mean of Dependent Variable      506.21000000
Std Error of Dependent Variable 291.55165854
Standard Error of Estimate      278.26095854
Sum of Squared Residuals        7510628.6217
Regression F(2,97)                    5.8415
Significance Level of F           0.00402335
Durbin-Watson Statistic           1.721830
    Variable            Coeff        Std Error       T-Stat      Signif
*******************************************************************************
1.  Constant          480.3040887    56.0253771     8.57297   0.00000000
2.  EN1                  3.8136026     1.3157471     2.89843   0.00463734
3.  EX2                -36.4465356    13.1839826    -2.76446   0.00682476
PRJ FOLS2 (Saving Fitted values as FOLS2 (fitted values OLS2)
```

These are rather low R-squares.

c. Now let's generate the Instrumental Variables Using the Reduced Form Equations.

```
LINREG EN1 / RED1
#CONSTANT EX1 EX2
Dependent Variable EN1 - Estimation by Least Squares
Usable Observations     100        Degrees of Freedom     97
Centered R**2      0.995498     R Bar **2    0.995405
Uncentered R**2    0.998684     T x R**2        99.868
Mean of Dependent Variable      470.02000000
Std Error of Dependent Variable 303.53702718
Standard Error of Estimate       20.57459938
Sum of Squared Residuals        41061.471563
Regression F(2,97)              10725.2223
Significance Level of F           0.00000000
Durbin-Watson Statistic           1.652907
    Variable            Coeff        Std Error       T-Stat      Signif
*******************************************************************************
1.  Constant          -22.69595456    4.79661202    -4.73166   0.00000757
2.  EX1                 0.21090408     0.07168190     2.94222   0.00407607
3.  EX2                 9.95364890     0.06973150   142.74250   0.00000000
```

Let's call the Instrumental Variable for EN1, INEN1, remember that these are the fitted values from the reduced form equation. Also, note how much higher the R-squares are here in comparison to those of the previous OLS.

```
PRJ INEN1

LINREG EN2 / RED2
#CONSTANT EX1 EX2
Dependent Variable EN2 - Estimation by Least Squares
Usable Observations     100        Degrees of Freedom     97
Centered R**2      0.995438     R Bar **2    0.995344
Uncentered R**2    0.998872     T x R**2        99.887
Mean of Dependent Variable      506.21000000
Std Error of Dependent Variable 291.55165854
Standard Error of Estimate       19.89426525
Sum of Squared Residuals        38390.833598
```

```
Regression F(2,97)                    10582.6544
Significance Level of F                0.00000000
Durbin-Watson Statistic               2.090165
      Variable          Coeff       Std Error      T-Stat      Signif
*****************************************************************************
1.   Constant        37.59589212    4.63800389       8.10605   0.00000000
2.   EX1              9.92952945    0.06931162     143.25924   0.00000000
3.   EX2             -0.30032588    0.06742571      -4.45417   0.00002257
```

Again, let's call the Instrumental Variable for EN2, INEN2 and as before, note how much higher R-square is here. RED1 and RED2 are the errors from the first and second REDuced form relationships.

```
PRJ INEN2
LINREG EN1 / TSLS1
#CONSTANT INEN2 EX1
Dependent Variable EN1 - Estimation by Least Squares
Usable Observations    100      Degrees of Freedom     97
Centered R**2      0.995498      R Bar **2   0.995405
Uncentered R**2    0.998684      T x R**2       99.868
Mean of Dependent Variable       470.02000000
Std Error of Dependent Variable 303.53702718
Standard Error of Estimate        20.57459938
Sum of Squared Residuals       41061.471563
Regression F(2,97)                10725.2223
Significance Level of F            0.00000000
Durbin-Watson Statistic            1.652907
      Variable          Coeff       Std Error      T-Stat      Signif
*****************************************************************************
1.   Constant       1223.338228     7.255140      168.61676   0.00000000
2.   INEN2           -33.142828     0.232186     -142.74250   0.00000000
3.   EX1             329.303590     2.291933      143.67943   0.00000000
PRJ F12SLS
LINREG EN2 / TSLS2
#CONSTANT INEN1 EX2
Dependent Variable EN2 - Estimation by Least Squares
Usable Observations    100      Degrees of Freedom     97
Centered R**2      0.995438      R Bar **2   0.995344
Uncentered R**2    0.998872      T x R**2       99.887
Mean of Dependent Variable       506.21000000
Std Error of Dependent Variable 291.55165854
Standard Error of Estimate        19.89426525
Sum of Squared Residuals       38390.833598
Regression F(2,97)                10582.6544
Significance Level of F            0.00000000
Durbin-Watson Statistic            2.090165
      Variable          Coeff       Std Error      T-Stat      Signif
*****************************************************************************
1.   Constant       1106.139234     6.065443      182.36744   0.00000000
2.   INEN1            47.080784     0.328640      143.25924   0.00000000
3.   EX2            -468.925923     3.285606     -142.72128   0.00000000
PRJ F22SLS
```

The residuals of both 2SLS equations are notated as TSLS1 and TSLS2

d. The usual interpretation of these relationships can be made through inspection.

e. A Hausman test for simultaneity is used to show that the residuals are uncorrelated as developed on pages 479 to 480. As shown by the following four regression, the OLS residuals of one equation are highly correlated with the dependent variable of the other equation. This confirms that IN1 and IN2 are simultaneously determined.

The following OLS estimations use the two residuals (OLS1 and OLS2) from the original OLS estimation of EN1 = f(EX1,EN2) + OLS1 and EN2 = f(EX2,EN1) + OLS2 in the following OLS estimations to show that there is simultaneity bias in the original OLS estimations. Note how highly associated each residual (OLS*) is associated with the dependent variable in the other relationships.

```
Dependent Variable EN1 - Estimation by Least Squares
Variable          Coeff         Std Error         T-Stat        Signif
*****************************************************************************
1.   Constant     -260.9255596  139.9122056       -1.86492      0.06524679
2.   EN2            -2.4347792    1.2168623        -2.00087      0.04823052
3.   EX1            40.3504964   11.1772869         3.61004      0.00048885
4.   OLS2           -1.6040914    0.2703748        -5.93284      0.00000005

Dependent Variable EN2 - Estimation by Least Squares
Variable          Coeff         Std Error         T-Stat        Signif
*****************************************************************************
1.   Constant      173.5473962   97.1901690         1.78565      0.07731402
2.   EN1             3.8108945    1.2350703          3.08557      0.00265452
3.   EX2           -30.0914801   12.4908857         -2.40907      0.01790061
4.   OLS1           -0.8003441    0.2132445         -3.75318      0.00029902
```

The following OLS estimations use the two residuals (TSLS1 and TSLS2) from the 2SLS estimation that used instrumental variables (INEN2 and INEN1) in the following relationships EN1 = f(EX1,INEN2) + TSLS1 and EN2 = f(EX2,INEN1) + TSLS1. These OLS estimations show that there is **no** simultaneity bias in these models. Note now how each residual (TSLS*) is **NOT** associated with the dependent variable in each of the following relationships that use instrumental variables to control for simultaneity.

```
Dependent Variable EN1 - Estimation by Least Squares
Variable          Coeff        Std Error         T-Stat        Signif
*****************************************************************************
1.   Constant     1223.338228    7.283937        167.95014      0.00000000
2.   INEN2         -33.142828     0.233108       -142.17818      0.00000000
3.   EX1           329.303590     2.301030        143.11139      0.00000000
4.   TSLS2          -0.051056     0.105424         -0.48429      0.62928024

Dependent Variable EN2 - Estimation by Least Squares
Variable          Coeff        Std Error         T-Stat        Signif
*****************************************************************************
1.   Constant     1106.139234    6.089518        181.64645      0.00000000
2.   INEN1          47.080784     0.329945        142.69287      0.00000000
3.   EX2          -468.925923     3.298647       -142.15704      0.00000000
4.   TSLS1          -0.047735     0.098567         -0.48429      0.62928024
```

f. The fits of the reduced form and second stage relationships are nearly identical. Note also how much better the R^2s are for the reduced form and second stage relationships than the relationship of the simple OLS solution. Herein lies the importance of methods such as 2SLS using instrumental variables.

11-27. a. Two stage least squares should be used to model each of these. Equations 1 and 2 are exactly identified.

```
Correlation Matrix
Annual Data From 1:01 To 100:01
             EN1                EN2                EX1                EX2
EN1   1.00000000000  -0.06241702850  -0.03858073846   0.93734742269
EN2  -0.06241702850   1.00000000000   0.95258666158  -0.10571677936
EX1  -0.03858073846   0.95258666158   1.00000000000  -0.08288154981
EX2   0.93734742269  -0.10571677936  -0.08288154981   1.00000000000
```

b. Fitting OLS models to each of these relationships.

```
LINREG EN1 / OLS1
#CONSTANT EN2 EX1
Dependent Variable EN1 - Estimation by Least Squares
Annual Data From 1:01 To 100:01
Usable Observations    100       Degrees of Freedom    97
Centered R**2      0.008604      R Bar **2  -0.011837
Uncentered R**2    0.776462      T x R**2       77.646
Mean of Dependent Variable        524.25000000
Std Error of Dependent Variable 284.28646724
Standard Error of Estimate        285.96412976
Sum of Squared Residuals         7932221.9005
Regression F(2,97)                      0.4209
Significance Level of F            0.65764787
Durbin-Watson Statistic             2.134843
Q(25-0)                            21.790916
Significance Level of Q            0.64778707
    Variable           Coeff        Std Error      T-Stat     Signif
****************************************************************************
1.   Constant        543.2273343   57.3710883      9.46866   0.00000000
2.   EN2              -0.2439265    0.2923492      -0.83437   0.40612441
3.   EX1               2.1289648    3.1368653       0.67869   0.49894923
PRJ FOLS1
LINREG EN2 / OLS2
#CONSTANT EN1 EX2
Dependent Variable EN2 - Estimation by Least Squares
Annual Data From 1:01 To 100:01
Usable Observations    100       Degrees of Freedom    97
Centered R**2      0.022258      R Bar **2   0.002099
Uncentered R**2    0.738907      T x R**2       73.891
Mean of Dependent Variable        532.61000000
Std Error of Dependent Variable 323.09975615
Standard Error of Estimate        322.76055103
Sum of Squared Residuals         10104914.210
Regression F(2,97)                      1.1041
Significance Level of F            0.33563908
Durbin-Watson Statistic             1.629283
Q(25-0)                            28.441910
Significance Level of Q            0.28791503
    Variable           Coeff        Std Error      T-Stat     Signif
****************************************************************************
1.   Constant        603.7211804   72.4693287      8.33071   0.00000000
2.   EN1               0.3434154    0.3275167       1.04854   0.29699397
3.   EX2              -4.6183653    3.4217684      -1.34970   0.18025332
PRJ FOLS2
```

These are rather low R-squares. OLS1 and OLS2 are the errors from the first and second OLS relationships.

c. Now let's generate the Instrumental Variables Using the Reduced Form Equations.

```
LINREG EN1 / RED1
#CONSTANT EX1 EX2
Dependent Variable EN1 - Estimation by Least Squares
Annual Data From 1:01 To 100:01
Usable Observations     100        Degrees of Freedom      97
Centered R**2       0.880160       R Bar **2     0.877689
Uncentered R**2     0.972979       T x R**2       97.298
Mean of Dependent Variable        524.25000000
Std Error of Dependent Variable 284.28646724
Standard Error of Estimate         99.42335978
Sum of Squared Residuals       958845.43364
Regression F(2,97)                 356.2070
Significance Level of F              0.00000000
Durbin-Watson Statistic              2.199619
Q(25-0)                             16.343799
Significance Level of Q              0.90420509
     Variable          Coeff        Std Error       T-Stat     Signif
*****************************************************************
1.   Constant      -29.52297775  29.31075745    -1.00724  0.31632531
2.   EX1             0.37176928   0.33298523     1.11647  0.26697742
3.   EX2             9.82714381   0.36849248    26.66851  0.00000000
```

Let's call the Instrumental Variable for EN1, INEN1, note how much higher the R-squares are here.
```
PRJ INEN1
LINREG EN2 / RED2
#CONSTANT EX1 EX2
Dependent Variable EN2 - Estimation by Least Squares
Annual Data From 1:01 To 100:01
Usable Observations     100        Degrees of Freedom      97
Centered R**2       0.908143       R Bar **2     0.906249
Uncentered R**2     0.975471       T x R**2       97.547
Mean of Dependent Variable        532.61000000
Std Error of Dependent Variable 323.09975615
Standard Error of Estimate         98.92937924
Sum of Squared Residuals       949341.14148
Regression F(2,97)                 479.4927
Significance Level of F              0.00000000
Durbin-Watson Statistic              2.043945
Q(25-0)                             27.128170
Significance Level of Q              0.34951193
     Variable          Coeff        Std Error       T-Stat     Signif
*******************************************************************
1.   Constant       18.63827666  29.16512826     0.63906  0.52428991
2.   EX1            10.19715242   0.33133081    30.77635  0.00000000
3.   EX2            -0.32000532   0.36666165    -0.87275  0.38495267
PRJ INEN2
```
Let's call the Instrumental Variable for EN2, INEN2. RED1 and RED2 are the errors from the first and second REDuced form relationships.

```
PRJ INEN2
```

```
LINREG EN1 / TSLS1
#CONSTANT INEN2 EX1
Dependent Variable EN1 - Estimation by Least Squares
Annual Data From 1:01 To 100:01
Usable Observations      100       Degrees of Freedom      97
Centered R**2       0.880160       R Bar **2    0.877689
Uncentered R**2     0.972979       T x R**2        97.298
Mean of Dependent Variable        524.25000000
Std Error of Dependent Variable 284.28646724
Standard Error of Estimate         99.42335978
Sum of Squared Residuals          958845.43364
Regression F(2,97)                   356.2070
Significance Level of F              0.00000000
Durbin-Watson Statistic              2.199619
Q(25-0)                             16.343799
Significance Level of Q             0.90420509
     Variable          Coeff        Std Error      T-Stat      Signif
***********************************************************************
1.   Constant        542.8457185    19.9466550     27.21487   0.00000000
2.   INEN2           -30.7093143     1.1515199    -26.66851   0.00000000
3.   EX1             313.5193280    11.7744991     26.62698   0.00000000
PRJ F12SLS
LINREG EN2 / TSLS2
#CONSTANT INEN1 EX2
Dependent Variable EN2 - Estimation by Least Squares
Annual Data From 1:01 To 100:01
Usable Observations      100       Degrees of Freedom      97
Centered R**2       0.908143       R Bar **2    0.906249
Uncentered R**2     0.975471       T x R**2        97.547
Mean of Dependent Variable        532.61000000
Std Error of Dependent Variable 323.09975615
Standard Error of Estimate         98.92937924
Sum of Squared Residuals          949341.14148
Regression F(2,97)                   479.4927
Significance Level of F              0.00000000
Durbin-Watson Statistic              2.043945
Q(25-0)                             27.128170
Significance Level of Q             0.34951193
     Variable          Coeff        Std Error      T-Stat      Signif
***********************************************************************
1.   Constant        828.4155211    23.3959047     35.40857   0.00000000
2.   INEN1            27.4287117     0.8912270     30.77635   0.00000000
3.   EX2            -269.8658995     8.7354718    -30.89311   0.00000000
PRJ F22SLS
```

d. The usual interpretations of the regressions coefficients are obvious here.

e. A Hausman test for simultaneity is used to show that the residuals are uncorrelated as developed on pages 479 to 480. As shown by the following four regression, the OLS residuals of one equation are highly correlated with the dependent variable of the other equation. This confirms that IN1 and IN2 are simultaneously determined.

The following OLS estimations use the two residuals (OLS1 and OLS2) from the original OLS estimation of EN1 = f(EX1,EN2) + OLS1 and EN2 = f(EX2,EN1) + OLS2 in the following OLS estimations to show that there is simultaneity bias in the original OLS estimations. Note how highly associated each residual (OLS*) is associated with the dependent variable in each of the following relationships.

```
Dependent Variable EN1 - Estimation by Least Squares
Variable          Coeff         Std Error      T-Stat      Signif
*****************************************************************
1.   Constant     1826.261428   292.205716     6.24992     0.00000001
2.   EN2            -2.635462      0.598836    -4.40097     0.00002794
3.   EX1             1.950913      2.869725     0.67983     0.49825089
4.   OLS2            2.462146      0.551626     4.46344     0.00002197
Dependent Variable EN2 - Estimation by Least Squares
Variable          Coeff         Std Error      T-Stat      Signif
*****************************************************************
1.   Constant     4833.810672   482.919528    10.00956     0.00000000
2.   EN1            -7.911520      0.967917    -8.17376     0.00000000
3.   EX2            -2.824319      2.565089    -1.10106     0.27362330
4.   OLS1            8.164218      0.926172     8.81501     0.00000000
```

The following OLS estimations use the two residuals (TSLS1 and TSLS2) from the 2SLS estimation that used instrumental variables (INEN2 and INEN1) in the following relationships EN1 = f(EX1,INEN2) + TSLS1 and EN2 = f(EX2,INEN1) + TSLS1. These OLS estimations show that there is **no** simultaneity bias in these models. Note now how each residual (TSLS*) is **NOT** associated with the dependent variable in each of the following relationships that use instrumental variables to control for simultaneity.

```
Dependent Variable EN1 - Estimation by Least Squares
Variable          Coeff         Std Error      T-Stat      Signif
*****************************************************************
1.   Constant      542.8457185    20.0500559    27.07452    0.00000000
2.   INEN2         -30.7093143     1.1574892   -26.53097    0.00000000
3.   EX1           313.5193280    11.8355366    26.48966    0.00000000
4.   TSLS2          -0.0046950     0.1025706    -0.04577    0.96358618
Dependent Variable EN2 - Estimation by Least Squares
Variable          Coeff         Std Error      T-Stat      Signif
*****************************************************************
1.   Constant      828.4155211    23.5171861    35.22596    0.00000000
2.   INEN1          27.4287117     0.8958470    30.61763    0.00000000
3.   EX2          -269.8658995     8.7807553   -30.73379    0.00000000
4.   TSLS1          -0.0046484     0.1015539    -0.04577    0.96358618
```

f. The fits of the reduced form and second stage relationships are nearly identical. Note also how much better the R^2 are for the reduced form and second stage relationships than the relationship of the simple OLS solution. Herein lies the importance of methods such as 2SLS using instrumental variables.

11-28. a. Two stage least squares should be used to model each of these. Equations 1 and 2 are exactly identified.

```
TAB
Series        Obs      Mean          Std Error        Minimum        Maximum
EN1           100   857847.310000  18930.982494   806477.000000  901971.000000
EN2           100    74644.510000   4270.903482    66352.000000   82927.000000
EX1           100      929.570000    569.860168        3.000000    1933.000000
EX2           100      524.370000    270.466513       42.000000     996.000000
Correlation Matrix
EN1              EN2              EX1              EX2
EN1  1.00000000000   0.83064806829   0.32574114467    0.82957996251
EN2  0.83064806829   1.00000000000   0.07618570392    0.96286838730
EX1  0.32574114467   0.07618570392   1.00000000000   -0.03789345125
EX2  0.82957996251   0.96286838730  -0.03789345125    1.00000000000
```

b. Fitting OLS models to each of these relationships.

```
LINREG EN1 / OLS1
#CONSTANT EN2 EX1
Dependent Variable EN1 - Estimation by Least Squares
Annual Data From 1:01 To 100:01
Usable Observations     100      Degrees of Freedom     97
Centered R**2       0.759262     R Bar **2     0.754299
Uncentered R**2     0.999884     T x R**2        99.988
Mean of Dependent Variable        857847.31000
Std Error of Dependent Variable   18930.98249
Standard Error of Estimate         9383.75944
Sum of Squared Residuals         8541329299.5
Regression F(2,97)                    152.9641
Significance Level of F              0.00000000
Durbin-Watson Statistic               2.114348
Q(25-0)                              20.162817
Significance Level of Q              0.73823316
    Variable          Coeff        Std Error      T-Stat       Signif
***************************************************************************
1.   Constant     581516.91749  16512.16514    35.21748   0.00000000
2.   EN2               3.59274       0.22146    16.22266   0.00000000
3.   EX1               8.76985       1.65980     5.28369   0.00000078

PRJ FOLS1
LINREG EN2 / OLS2
#CONSTANT EN1 EX2
Dependent Variable EN2 - Estimation by Least Squares
Annual Data From 1:01 To 100:01
Usable Observations     100      Degrees of Freedom     97
Centered R**2       0.930373     R Bar **2     0.928938
Uncentered R**2     0.999775     T x R**2        99.978
Mean of Dependent Variable         74644.510000
Std Error of Dependent Variable     4270.903482
Standard Error of Estimate          1138.515475
Sum of Squared Residuals         125733096.22
Regression F(2,97)                    648.0733
Significance Level of F              0.00000000
Durbin-Watson Statistic               2.088817
Q(25-0)                              26.233541
Significance Level of Q              0.39522099
    Variable          Coeff        Std Error      T-Stat       Signif
***************************************************************************
1.   Constant      47590.946063  8959.745580     5.31164   0.00000069
2.   EN1               0.023061      0.010825     2.13043   0.03566507
3.   EX2              13.865482      0.757656    18.30051   0.00000000

PRJ FOLS2
```

These are rather low R-squares. Let's illustrate how the error terms of these two relationships are correlated with the endogenous variables EN1 and EN2, where OLS1 and OLS2 are the errors from the first and second OLS relationships.

c. Now let's generate the Instrumental Variables Using the Reduced Form Equations.

```
LINREG EN1 / RED1
#CONSTANT EX1 EX2
Dependent Variable EN1 - Estimation by Least Squares
Annual Data From 1:01 To 100:01
Usable Observations    100       Degrees of Freedom    97
Centered R**2     0.815962       R Bar **2   0.812167
Uncentered R**2   0.999911       T x R**2      99.991
Mean of Dependent Variable       857847.31000
Std Error of Dependent Variable  18930.98249
Standard Error of Estimate        8204.63146
Sum of Squared Residuals         6529649810.5
Regression F(2,97)                215.0320
Significance Level of F            0.00000000
Durbin-Watson Statistic            1.988490
Q(25-0)                           13.678379
Significance Level of Q            0.96705314
     Variable          Coeff       Std Error      T-Stat      Signif
*****************************************************************************
1.   Constant        815856.32453  2282.05431   357.50960   0.00000000
2.   EX1                 11.88262     1.44806     8.20591   0.00000000
3.   EX2                 59.01417     3.05098    19.34266   0.00000000
```

Let's call the Instrumental Variable for EN1, INEN1. Note how much higher the R-squares are here.

```
PRJ INEN1
LINREG EN2 / RED2
#CONSTANT EX1 EX2
Dependent Variable EN2 - Estimation by Least Squares
Annual Data From 1:01 To 100:01
Usable Observations    100       Degrees of Freedom    97
Centered R**2     0.939829       R Bar **2   0.938588
Uncentered R**2   0.999806       T x R**2      99.981
Mean of Dependent Variable       74644.510000
Std Error of Dependent Variable  4270.903482
Standard Error of Estimate       1058.390314
Sum of Squared Residuals         108658435.47
Regression F(2,97)                757.5333
Significance Level of F            0.00000000
Durbin-Watson Statistic            1.991767
Q(25-0)                           24.050222
Significance Level of Q            0.51647316
     Variable          Coeff       Std Error      T-Stat      Signif
*****************************************************************************
1.   Constant        65850.210316   294.383019   223.68889   0.00000000
2.   EX1                 0.845653     0.186798     4.52710   0.00001700
3.   EX2                15.272053     0.393574    38.80348   0.00000000
PRJ INEN2
```

Let's call the Instrumental Variable for EN2, INEN2. Note how much higher R-square is here. RED1 and RED2 are the errors from the first and second REDuced form relationships.

```
PRJ INEN2
LINREG EN1 / TSLS1
#CONSTANT INEN2 EX1
Dependent Variable EN1 - Estimation by Least Squares
Annual Data From 1:01 To 100:01
Usable Observations    100       Degrees of Freedom    97
Centered R**2     0.815962       R Bar **2   0.812167
Uncentered R**2   0.999911       T x R**2      99.991
```

11-12

```
Mean of Dependent Variable        857847.31000
Std Error of Dependent Variable   18930.98249
Standard Error of Estimate         8204.63146
Sum of Squared Residuals          6529649810.5
Regression F(2,97)                  215.0320
Significance Level of F             0.00000000
Durbin-Watson Statistic             1.988490
Q(25-0)                            13.678379
Significance Level of Q             0.96705314
     Variable          Coeff       Std Error      T-Stat     Signif
********************************************************************
1.  Constant      561398.36457   14889.71767    37.70376   0.00000000
2.  INEN2              3.86419        0.19978    19.34266   0.00000000
3.  EX1                8.61485        1.45150     5.93512   0.00000005
PRJ F12SLS


LINREG EN2 / TSLS2
#CONSTANT INEN1 EX2
Dependent Variable EN2 - Estimation by Least Squares
Annual Data From 1:01 To 100:01
Usable Observations      100      Degrees of Freedom      97
Centered R**2        0.939829     R Bar **2    0.938588
Uncentered R**2      0.999806     T x R**2       99.981
Mean of Dependent Variable        74644.510000
Std Error of Dependent Variable    4270.903482
Standard Error of Estimate         1058.390314
Sum of Squared Residuals          108658435.47
Regression F(2,97)                  757.5333
Significance Level of F             0.00000000
Durbin-Watson Statistic             1.991767
Q(25-0)                            24.050222
Significance Level of Q             0.51647316
     Variable         Coeff      Std Error       T-Stat     Signif
********************************************************************
1.  Constant      7788.010923  13009.004562     0.59866   0.55079305
2.  INEN1            0.071167       0.015720     4.52710   0.00001700
3.  EX2             11.072181       0.993927    11.13984   0.00000000
PRJ F22SLS
```

d. The usual interpretations of the regressions coefficients are obvious here.

e. A Hausman test for simultaneity is used to show that the residuals are uncorrelated as developed on pages 479 to 480. As shown by the following four regression, the OLS residuals of one equation are highly correlated with the dependent variable of the other equation. This confirms that IN1 and IN2 are simultaneously determined.

The following OLS estimations use the two residuals (OLS1 and OLS2) from the original OLS estimation of EN1 = f(EX1,EN2) + OLS1 and EN2 = f(EX2,EN1) + OLS2 in the following OLS estimations to show that there is simultaneity bias in the original OLS estimations. Note how highly associated each residual (OLS*) is associated with the dependent variable in each of the following relationships.

```
Dependent Variable EN1 - Estimation by Least Squares
Variable          Coeff       Std Error      T-Stat      Signif
**************************************************************************
1.  Constant   551477.4114   13301.0316     41.46125   0.00000000
2.  EN2             3.9574        0.1771     22.33982   0.00000000
3.  EX1            11.8039        1.3375      8.82528   0.00000000
4.  OLS2           -5.6802        0.6991     -8.12451   0.00000000
Dependent Variable EN2 - Estimation by Least Squares
Variable          Coeff       Std Error      T-Stat      Signif
**************************************************************************
1.  Constant   -26275.38638   6912.45934    -3.80116   0.00025290
2.  EN1             0.11196       0.00834    13.43195   0.00000000
3.  EX2             9.30234       0.51209    18.16543   0.00000000
4.  OLS1           -0.14461       0.00956   -15.13347   0.00000000
```

The following OLS estimations use the two residuals (TSLS1 and TSLS2) from the 2SLS estimation that used instrumental variables (INEN2 and INEN1) in the following relationships EN1 = f(EX1,INEN2) + TSLS1 and EN2 = f(EX2,INEN1) + TSLS1. These OLS estimations show that there is **no** simultaneity bias in these models. Note now how each residual (TSLS*) is **NOT** associated with the dependent variable in each of the following relationships that use instrumental variables to control for simultaneity.

```
Dependent Variable EN1 - Estimation by Least Squares
Variable          Coeff       Std Error      T-Stat      Signif
**************************************************************************
1.  Constant   561398.3646   14918.9655     37.62985   0.00000000
2.  INEN2           3.8642        0.2002     19.30474   0.00000000
3.  EX1             8.6149        1.4544      5.92348   0.00000005
4.  TSLS2          -0.6210        0.7886     -0.78743   0.43297011
Dependent Variable EN2 - Estimation by Least Squares
Variable          Coeff       Std Error      T-Stat      Signif
**************************************************************************
1.  Constant     7788.01092  13034.55815     0.59749   0.55158741
2.  INEN1           0.07117       0.01575     4.51822   0.00001777
3.  EX2            11.07218       0.99588    11.11800   0.00000000
4.  TSLS1          -0.01033       0.01312    -0.78743   0.43297011
```

f. The fits of the reduced form and second stage relationships are nearly identical. Note also how much better the R^2 are for the reduced form and second stage relationships than the relationship of the simple OLS solution. Herein lies the importance of methods such as 2SLS using instrumental variables.

Minicases

The use of Granger Causality tests on this data is rather routine. To save space in the Instructor's Manual, the solutions to these Minicases can be found on Irwin/McGraw-Hill's or the Author's WEBSITE. If you do not have access to that site, then contact the author at delurgio@ cctr.umkc.edu, sad@forecast.umkc.edu, 1-816-235-2311, fax, 1-816-235-2312. If for some reason the author cannot be reached at these numbers, then call McGraw-Hill for this information or my address, phone number, or WEBSITE.

Summary of Granger Causality Statistics:

```
n=total number of observations
m=number of lags in the variables
r=number of variables restricted when calculating ESSr
k=number of unrestricted coefficients
n-m-k=Degree of freedom for unrestricted model
```

The Granger F-test first is based on the following formula:
$$F = [(ESSr-ESSu)/r]/[ESSu/(n-m-k)]$$

MINICASE 11-1. Kansas Turnpike, Daily Data.

1. Granger for Lags 1 to 4

```
Index 1 Granger Causality
F = ((3496290035.1-481520418.59)/4)/(481520418.59/(91-4-9))
F(4,78)=    122.08830 with Significance Level 0.00000000

Index 2 Granger Causality
F = ((3496290035.1-3345052462.5)/4)/(3345052462.5/(91-4-9))
F(4,78)=      0.88164 with Significance Level 0.47895271
```

2. Granger for Lags 1 to 7

```
Index 1 Granger Causality
F =  ((1706288948.2-345659462.72)/7)/(345659462.72/(91-7-15))
F(7,69)=     38.80096 with Significance Level 0.00000000

Index 2 Granger Causality
F =  ((1706288948.2-1509952856.4)/7)/(1509952856.4/(91-7-15))
F(7,69)=      1.28170 with Significance Level 0.27232335
```

MINICASE 11-2. Domestic Air Passengers by Quarter.

1. Granger for Lags 1 to 2

```
Index 1 Granger Causality
F =  ((44253163.365-40093461.625)/2)/(40093461.625/(50-2-5))
F(2,43)=       2.23063 with Significance Level 0.11975058
```

```
Index 2 Granger Causality
F =  ((44253163.365-41178569.174)/2)/(41178569.174/(50-2-5))
F(2,43)=       1.60530 with Significance Level 0.21263132
```

```
Index 3 Granger Causality
F =  ((44253163.365-1925674.1015)/2)/(1925674.1015/(50-2-5))
F(2,5)=    472.58309 with Significance Level 0.00000201
```

2. Granger for Lags 1 to 4

```
Index 1 Granger Causality
F =  ((12016215.508-10907341.100)/4)/(10907341.100/(50-4-9))
F(4,37)=       0.94038 with Significance Level 0.45146137
```

```
Index 2 Granger Causality
F =  ((12016215.508-11737763.422)/4)/(11737763.422/(50-4-9))
F(4,37)=       0.21944 with Significance Level 0.92590523
```

```
Index 3 Granger Causality
F =  ((12016215.508-1492772.0210)/4)/(1492772.0210/(50-4-9))
F(4,37)=      65.20879 with Significance Level 0.00000000
```

MINICASE 11-3. Hospital Census by Month.

1. Granger for Lags 1 to 6

```
Index 1 Granger Causality
F =  ((16947062.060-3506784.1388)/6)/(3506784.1388/(120-6-13))
F(6,101)=      64.51628 with Significance Level 0.00000000
```

```
Index 2 Granger Causality
F =  ((16947062.060-16159317.943)/6)/(16159317.943/(120-6-13))
F(6,101)=       0.82060 with Significance Level 0.55650013
```

2. Granger for Lags 1 to 12

```
Index 1 Granger Causality
F =  ((8021771.6438-2315992.1976)/12)/(2315992.1976/(120-12-25))
F(12,83)=      64.51628 with Significance Level 0.00000000
```

```
Index 2 Granger Causality
F =  ((8021771.6438-7141675.6360)/12)/(7141675.6360/(120-12-25))
F(12,83)=       0.82060 with Significance Level 0.62881987
```

MINICASE 11-4. Henry Machler's Hideaway Orchids.

1. Granger for Lags 1 to 6

```
Man 1 Granger Causality
F =  ((134287949.91-125448858.89)/6)/(125448858.89/(96-6-13))
F(6,77)=       0.90423 with Significance Level 0.49644230

Man 2 Granger Causality
F =  ((134287949.91-125282843.07)/6)/(125282843.07/(96-6-13))
F(6,77)=       0.92244 with Significance Level 0.48368027

Man 3 Granger Causality
F =  ((134287949.91-1907180.2997)/6)/(1907180.2997/(96-6-13))
F(6,77)=       890.78444 with Significance Level 0.00000000
```

2. Granger for Lags 1 to 12

```
Man 1 Granger Causality
F =  ((37533736.382-31321175.317)/12)/(31321175.317/(96-12-25))
F(12,59)=       0.97522 with Significance Level 0.48243248

Man 2 Granger Causality
F =  ((37533736.382-31258899.278)/12)/(31258899.278/(96-12-25))
F(12,59)=       0.98696 with Significance Level 0.47193448

Man 3 Granger Causality
F =  ((37533736.382-1183090.8489)/12)/(1183090.8489/(96-12-25))
F(12,59)=       151.06533 with Significance Level 0.00000000
```

MINICASE 11-5. Your Forecasting Project.

1. Granger for Lags 1 to S/2

2. Granger for Lags 1 to S

MINICASE 11-6. Midwestern Building Materials.

1. Granger for Lags 1 to 6

```
Index 1 Granger Causality
F =  ((34948406417-581886051.03)/6)/(581886051.03/(120-6-13))
F(6,101)=       994.18622 with Significance Level 0.00000000

Index 2 Granger Causality
F =  ((34948406417-34242375786)/6)/(34242375786/(120-6-13))
F(6,101)=       0.34708 with Significance Level 0.91010325
```

2. Granger for Lags 1 to 12

```
Index 1 Granger Causality
F =  ((1864572110.0-335022811.89)/12)/(335022811.89/(120-12-25))
F(12,83)=       31.57810 with Significance Level 0.00000000

Index 2 Granger Causality
F =  ((1864572110.0-1564287723.3)/12)/(1564287723.3/(120-12-25))
F(12,83)=       1.32774 with Significance Level 0.21884029
```

MINICASE 11-7. International Airline Passengers.

1. Granger for Lags 1 to 6

```
Index 1 Granger Causality
F =  ((124971.92271-122368.87608)/6)/(122368.87608/(144-6-13))
F(6,125)=      0.44317 with Significance Level 0.84863344

Index 2 Granger Causality
F =  ((124971.92271-9749.5830193)/6)/(9749.5830193/(144-6-13))
F(6,125)=      246.21211 with Significance Level 0.00000000
```

2. Granger for Lags 1 to 12

```
Index 1 Granger Causality
F =  ((24094.957928-22329.189767)/12)/(22329.189767/(144-12-25))
F(12,107)=      0.70512 with Significance Level 0.74347987

Index 2 Granger Causality
F =  ((24094.957928-4392.8349733)/12)/(4392.8349733/(144-12-25))
F(12,107)=      39.99177 with Significance Level 0.00000000
```

MINICASE 11-8. Automobile Sales.

1. Granger for Lags 1 to 6

```
Index 1 Granger Causality
F =  ((846318897.76-176893043.42)/6)/(176893043.42/(185-6-13))
F(6,166)=      104.70045 with Significance Level 0.00000000

Index 2 Granger Causality
F =  ((846318897.76-822789327.63)/6)/(822789327.63/(185-6-13))
F(6,166)=      0.79119 with Significance Level 0.57801695
```

2. Granger for Lags 1 to 12

```
Index 1 Granger Causality
F =  ((210563976.27-100215603.55)/12)/(100215603.55/(185-12-25))
F(12,148)=      13.58035 with Significance Level 0.00000000

Index 2 Granger Causality
F =  ((210563976.27-200335402.97)/12)/(200335402.97/(185-12-25))
F(12,148)=      0.62971 with Significance Level 0.81437396
```

MINICASE 11-9. Consumption of Distilled Spirits.

1. Granger for Lags 1 to 6

```
Index 1 Granger Causality
F =  ((3721945291.4-3174287067.2)/6)/(3174287067.2/(132-6-13))
F(6,113)=       3.24931 with Significance Level 0.00552964

Index 2 Granger Causality
F =  ((3721945291.4-150769273.76)/6)/(150769273.76/(132-6-13))
F(6,113)=       446.09320 with Significance Level 0.00000000
```

2. Granger for Lags 1 to 12

```
Index 1 Granger Causality
F =  ((270481480.47-240163026.46)/12)/(240163026.46/(132-12-25))
F(12,95)=       0.99941 with Significance Level 0.45570936

Index 2 Granger Causality
F =  ((270481480.47-84736607.617)/12)/(84736607.617/(132-12-25))
F(12,95)=       17.35354 with Significance Level 0.00000000
```

MINICASE 11-10. Discount Consumer Electronics.

1. Granger for Lags 1 to 6

```
Index 1 Granger Causality
F =  ((13268.134702-13108.836348)/6)/(13108.836348/(185-6-13))
F(6,166)=       0.33620 with Significance Level 0.91700486

Index 2 Granger Causality
F =  ((13268.134702-291.71988849)/6)/(291.71988849/(185-6-13))
F(6,166)=       1230.68107 with Significance Level 0.00000000
```

2. Granger for Lags 1 to 12

```
Index 1 Granger Causality
F =  ((1187.7549958-1065.6523002)/12)/(1065.6523002/(185-12-25))
F(12,148)=       1.41316 with Significance Level 0.16575876

Index 2 Granger Causality
F =  ((1187.7549958-217.26070062)/12)/(217.26070062/(185-12-25))
F(12,148)=       55.09247 with Significance Level 0.00000000
```

PROBLEMS

ESTIMATED DIFFICULTY

Elementary	Medium	Hard	Very Hard	Bad

1 M   2 H   3 M   4 M   5 H   6 H   7 H   8 M   9 M   10 M

11 M   12 V   13 H   14 M   15 **V-B** 16 V

Minicases are all hard.

12-1. See Figure 12-6, pages 502 to 504.

12-2. Differencing is almost always applied to both Yt and It. To determine how to handle differences, plot and print the differences of the output series and the intervention and observe the behavior of the relationship between these two. Also, see the examples on pages 500 to 501. Differencing is applied to both series in order to preserve the intervention effect when the output series is nonstationary. If differencing is applied solely to the intervention term then this denotes that the intervention effect includes a change in the slope or trend of the output series.

12-3. A pulse function is one which yields a single very high intervention effect while a step function provides a permanent shift of a series to a higher or lower value. A simple pulse function might result from a product stock out while a step function might result from a product improvement which permanently increases the demand for a product.

12-4. Referring to Figure 12-3 we see that r is the level of autoregression in the intervention effect much as in ARIMA modeling, s is the number of omega terms minus one in the numerator, and b is the delay or lag in the impact of the intervention.

12-5.

		a. STEP FUNCTIONS				b. PULSE FUNCTIONS		
OMEGA		10	10	10		10	10	10
DELTA		0.3	0.6	1.2		0.3	0.6	1.2
TIME	I(t)				I(t)			
1	0	0	0	0	0	0	0	0
2	1	10	10	10	1	10	10	10
3	1	13	16	22	0	3	6	12
4	1	13.9	19.6	36.4	0	0.9	3.6	14.4
5	1	14.17	21.76	53.68	0	0.27	2.16	17.28
6	1	14.251	23.056	74.416	0	0.081	1.296	20.736
7	1	14.2753	23.8336	99.2992	0	0.0243	0.7776	24.8832
8	1	14.2825	24.3001	129.159	0	0.00729	0.46656	29.8598
9	1	14.2847	24.5801	164.990	0	0.00218	0.27993	35.8318
10	1	14.2854	24.7480	207.989	0	0.00065	0.16796	42.9981

11	1	14.2856	24.8488	259.586	0	0.00019	0.10077	51.5978
12	1	14.2856	24.9093	321.504	0	5.9E-05	0.06046	61.9173
13	1	14.2857	24.9455	395.805	0	1.77E-05	0.03628	74.3008
14	1	14.2857	24.9673	484.966	0	5.31E-06	0.02176	89.161
15	1	14.2857	24.9804	591.959	0	1.59E-06	0.01306	106.993
16	1	14.2857	24.9882	720.351	0	4.78E-07	0.00783	128.391
17	1	14.2857	24.9929	874.421	0	1.43E-07	0.00470	154.070
18	1	14.2857	24.9957	1059.300	0	4.3E-08	0.00282	184.884
19	1	14.2857	24.9974	1281.160	0	1.29E-08	0.00169	221.861
20	1	14.2857	24.9984	1547.400	0	3.87E-09	0.00101	266.233

c. The impact of the nonstationary value of delta is quite clear in the spreadsheet values above, both for the step and pulse functions.

12-6.a, b, c, and e are given in Figure 12-3. d. is profile b. but the exponential decline starts at lag 1.

12-7. While there is great versatility in the way that intervention models can be expressed with different values of r, pulses, and step functions, the following are common models:

a. Abrupt, temporary impacts include pulses with r=0 as in Figures 12-1 a) and b), and a step function as in Figure 12-1 d), however, some would refer to this as a sustained pulse.

b. Abrupt, permanent impacts include step functions with r=0 as in Figures 12-1 c)

c. Gradual, temporary impact include values of r=1 with step functions as in Figures 12-2 b) and d).

d. Gradual, permanent impact include values of r=1 with step functions as in Figures a: and c).

12-8. As t approaches infinity the intervention affect reaches its limit as shown on page 496.

12-9. We should know the date of the intervention and have a substantive basis for believing that an intervention occurred.

12-10. The intervention component should have statistically significant, parsimonious, nonredundant coefficients that are in the bounds of stability, the intervention profile should be intuitively and theoretically appealing, the ARIMA (i.e., noise) model should pass muster on all ARIMA criteria as discussed in Chapter 8, parsimonious structure, invertible, stationary, and nonredundant coefficients and white noise residuals. Finally, the overall models should have intuitive and theoretical appeal and provide one of the lowest BICs.

12-11. An invalid model may result, particularly when the intervention effect is strong. The results might be meaningless and misleading as the intervention effect is either adjusted as an outlier or an inappropriate univariate model is accepted.

12-12. If sufficient preintervention observations exist, then a univariate model can be fitted to the preintervention series and then the intervention and post intervention series can be forecasted using the preintervention model. The residuals of the intervention and post intervention series can be plotted and then used in regression analysis to model the intervention component. However, with this procedure it may be quite difficult to objectively model the rate parameter delta. Alternatively for simple models, linear regression can be used to fit the intervention portion and then univariate ARIMA modeling can be used to fit the noise component using the residuals of the regression model.

12-13. When logarithms are used, then coefficients represent ratios. An omega of 10 is extremely high value representing that there is an e^{omega} ratio between Y_t and Y_{t-1} at time of intervention as shown below:

```
omega   10
delta   0.3
time-t  I_t   lnY_t       Y_t
    1   0        0           1
    2   0        0           1
    3   0        0           1
    4   1       10       22026
    5   1       13      442413
    6   1     13.9     1088161
    7   1    14.17     1425453
    8   1   14.251     1545719
    9   1  14.2753     1583740
   10   1 14.28259     1595328
```

12-14. Because interventions may appear as outliers, shifts, or ramp functions depending on their profiles, the ACFS and PACFs will look considerably different for preintervention, intervention, and post intervention periods. When these different behaviors are assumed to be the same, then the ACFs and PACFs of the total series are tainted. They may appear to be white noise or have significant peaks at strange lags. In some cases have extraordinary behavior.

12-15. This series is so short and the intervention so pronounced that students may find it particularly difficult to analyze, thus, do not assign this as a first problem.

Let's view seasonal differences in order to understand the intervention affect.

```
SET SDMARR 5 32 = MARR - MARR(T-4)
PRINT 1 32 MARR SDMARR LAW
  ENTRY          MARR              SDMARR              LAW
   1:01      420240.00000000         NA           0.0000000000000
   1:02      703900.00000000         NA           0.0000000000000
   1:03      709010.00000000         NA           0.0000000000000
   1:04      579475.00000000         NA           0.0000000000000
   2:01      416040.00000000     -4200.00000000   0.0000000000000
   2:02      701072.00000000     -2828.00000000   0.0000000000000
   2:03      705020.00000000     -3990.00000000   0.0000000000000
   2:04      584967.00000000      5492.00000000   0.0000000000000
   3:01      425587.00000000      9547.00000000   0.0000000000000
   3:02      692023.00000000     -9049.00000000   0.0000000000000
   3:03      698699.00000000     -6321.00000000   0.0000000000000
   3:04      587069.00000000      2102.00000000   0.0000000000000
   4:01      416000.00000000     -9587.00000000   0.0000000000000
   4:02      681000.00000000    -11023.00000000   0.0000000000000
   4:03      698000.00000000      -699.00000000   0.0000000000000
   4:04      594000.00000000      6931.00000000   0.0000000000000
   5:01      402000.00000000    -14000.00000000   0.0000000000000
   5:02      704000.00000000     23000.00000000   0.0000000000000
   5:03      693000.00000000     -5000.00000000   0.0000000000000
   5:04      606000.00000000     12000.00000000   0.0000000000000
   6:01      445000.00000000     43000.00000000   1.0000000000000
   6:02      728000.00000000     24000.00000000   1.0000000000000
   6:03      759000.00000000     66000.00000000   1.0000000000000
```

```
6:04   637500.00000000   31500.00000000  1.0000000000000
7:01   449750.00000000    4750.00000000  1.0000000000000
7:02   713375.00000000  -14625.00000000  1.0000000000000
7:03   748687.00000000  -10313.00000000  1.0000000000000
7:04   617843.00000000  -19657.00000000  1.0000000000000
8:01   462921.00000000   13171.00000000  1.0000000000000
8:02   701960.00000000  -11415.00000000  1.0000000000000
8:03   736980.00000000  -11707.00000000  1.0000000000000
8:04   618990.00000000    1147.00000000  1.0000000000000
```

Modeling the preintervention behavior of the time series.

```
BOX(SDIFF=1) MARR 5 20 RES
Dependent Variable MARR - Estimation by Box-Jenkins
Iterations Taken      2
Quarterly Data From 2:01 To 5:04
Usable Observations       16      Degrees of Freedom      16
Centered R**2      0.993211       R Bar **2     0.993636
Uncentered R**2    0.999758       T x R**2       15.996
Mean of Dependent Variable       600279.81250
Std Error of Dependent Variable  119127.27088
Standard Error of Estimate         9503.51009
Sum of Squared Residuals        1445067263.0
Durbin-Watson Statistic            2.572467
Q(4-0)                             3.302487
Significance Level of Q            0.50853837
 NO ESTIMATED COEFFICIENTS
```

The preintervention series is a seasonal random walk process. Now let's model the full intervention effect as a zero order model.

```
BOX(SDIFF=1,APPLY,INPUT=1) MARR / RES3
#LAW 0  0
Dependent Variable MARR - Estimation by Box-Jenkins
Iterations Taken      2
Quarterly Data From 2:01 To 8:04
Usable Observations       28      Degrees of Freedom      27
Centered R**2      0.990454       R Bar **2     0.990454
Uncentered R**2    0.999670       T x R**2       27.991
Mean of Dependent Variable       615160.10714
Std Error of Dependent Variable  118587.00183
Standard Error of Estimate        11586.40715
Sum of Squared Residuals        3624610430.0
Durbin-Watson Statistic            2.668024
Q(7-0)                             6.043580
Significance Level of Q            0.53467011
    Variable                    Coeff      Std Error      T-Stat      Signif
*****************************************************************************
1.  N_LAW{0}               41125.000000  5793.201616     7.09884   0.00000012
```

This appears to be a good model. A plot of the residuals reveals some variance nonstationarity before and after the intervention. Below, we perform an F-test on the pre and post residuals of the above model as a check for variance nonstationarity.

```
PREINTERVENTION STATISTICS: TAB 1 19
Series          Obs      Mean          Std Error       Minimum         Maximum
DATE            19   198691.89474      140.88723    198501.00000    198903.00000
MARR            19   600584.31579   122075.04272    402000.00000    709010.00000
LAW             19        0.00000        0.00000         0.00000         0.00000
RES3            15    -1308.33333     9544.59915    -14000.00000     23000.00000
SDMARR          15    -1308.33333     9544.59915    -14000.00000     23000.00000

PERI-POST INTERVENTION STATISTICS: TAB 20 32
Series          Obs      Mean          Std Error       Minimum         Maximum
DATE            13   199087.23077       98.48279    198904.00000    199204.00000
MARR            13   632769.69231   115230.90895    445000.00000    759000.00000
LAW             13        0.92308        0.27735         0.00000         1.00000
RES3            13    -2819.15385    13602.15668    -19657.00000     24875.00000
SDMARR          13     9834.69231    25546.08649    -19657.00000     66000.00000

STAT RES3 20 32
Statistics on Series RES3
Quarterly Data From 5:04 To 8:04
Observations    13
Sample Mean        -2819.153846        Variance             1.850187e+008
Standard Error     13602.156685        SE of Sample Mean    3772.559491
t-Statistic           -0.74728         Signif Level (Mean=0) 0.46928563
Skewness               0.69510         Signif Level (Sk=0)   0.36586208
Kurtosis              -0.44508         Signif Level (Ku=0)   0.80671267

STAT RES3 1 19
Statistics on Series RES3
Quarterly Data From 1:01 To 5:03
Observations    15    (19 Total - 4 Skipped/Missing)
Sample Mean        -1308.3333333       Variance             91099372.952381
Standard Error     9544.5991510        SE of Sample Mean    2464.404904
t-Statistic           -0.53089         Signif Level (Mean=0) 0.60381414
Skewness               1.16976         Signif Level (Sk=0)   0.09622228
Kurtosis               1.71276         Signif Level (Ku=0)   0.29158174

F-TEST = 1.850187e+008/91099372.952381 = 2.03095
CDF FTEST 2.03095 13 15
F(13,15)=      2.03095 with Significance Level 0.09523398
```

Thus, there is not a statistically significant difference between residual variances pre, peri, and post intervention. Consequently, we accept the above model. While not shown here, several other intervention models were tried, but none was better than the above.

12-16. There are three alternative modeling approaches to this series, either the original metric, logarithms, or square root transformations. That which seems to yield the best model is the square root transformation however, this is not certain.

The following is a zero-order intervention model using logarithms.

```
BOX(SDIFF=1,MA=1,AR=1,SMA=1,INPUT=1,APPLY,ITER=40,VCV,CONSTANT) LSALES / RESI
#INTER
Dependent Variable LSALES - Estimation by Box-Jenkins
Iterations Taken     10
Quarterly Data From 1971:01 To 1992:04
Usable Observations       88       Degrees of Freedom     83
Centered R**2       0.994996       R Bar **2     0.994755
Uncentered R**2     0.999974       T x R**2        87.998
Mean of Dependent Variable        6.1002659760
Std Error of Dependent Variable 0.4396695268
Standard Error of Estimate        0.0318415185
Sum of Squared Residuals          0.0841522310
Durbin-Watson Statistic              1.970136
Q(22-3)                             12.809558
Significance Level of Q             0.84817591
    Variable             Coeff        Std Error       T-Stat      Signif
***********************************************************************************
1.  CONSTANT          0.069812629  0.016676751       4.18622   0.00007020
2.  AR{1}             0.916228458  0.059048029      15.51666   0.00000000
3.  MA{1}             0.345265834  0.110366902       3.12835   0.00242515
4.  SMA{4}           -0.740493970  0.093959522      -7.88099   0.00000000
5.  N_INTER{0}        0.079086808  0.029548460       2.67651   0.00896244
Covariance\Correlation Matrix of Coefficients
               CONSTANT         AR{1}          MA{1}          SMA{4}
CONSTANT      0.00027811404   0.2155772156  -0.0760672259  -0.2942684457
AR{1}         0.00021228520   0.00348666977 -0.3531925631  -0.5570080568
MA{1}        -0.00014000640  -0.00230173759  0.01218085308  0.1826208163
SMA{4}       -0.00046110088  -0.00309035010  0.00189378176  0.00882839171
N_INTER{0}   -0.00004827411   0.00012110958  0.00000613064  0.00004569254
                N_INTER{0}
CONSTANT      -0.0979643192
AR{1}          0.0694125854
MA{1}          0.0018798892
SMA{4}         0.0164577192
N_INTER{0}     0.00087311150
```

```
CORR(NUM=20,QSTAT) RESI
Correlations of Series RESI
Quarterly Data From 1971:01 To 1992:04
Autocorrelations
     1: -0.0037390  0.0117752  0.0284647 -0.0021690  0.2109268  0.0834784
     7:  0.0280429 -0.0755565 -0.0441411  0.1175121  0.0316203  0.0987406
    13: -0.0498819  0.0898893  0.0680978 -0.0159853  0.0988926 -0.0213533
    19:  0.0761355  0.0335140
Ljung-Box Q-Statistics
Q(20)  =         11.9642.  Significance Level 0.91730144
```

The following is a zero-order intervention model using the original series.

```
BOX(SDIFF=1,MA=1,AR=1,SMA=1,INPUT=1,APPLY,ITER=40,VCV,CONSTANT) SALES / RESO
```

```
#INTER
Dependent Variable SALES - Estimation by Box-Jenkins
Iterations Taken    17
Quarterly Data From 1971:01 To 1992:04
Usable Observations      88      Degrees of Freedom     83
Centered R**2       0.995331     R Bar **2    0.995106
Uncentered R**2     0.999381     T x R**2        87.946
Mean of Dependent Variable       486.98659091
Std Error of Dependent Variable 191.49211783
Standard Error of Estimate        13.39568457
Sum of Squared Residuals       14893.882294
Durbin-Watson Statistic            1.935171
Q(22-3)                           13.944852
Significance Level of Q            0.78689658
    Variable               Coeff       Std Error      T-Stat     Signif
*****************************************************************************
1.  CONSTANT              27.96409000   3.76446240     7.42844   0.00000000
2.  AR{1}                  0.80409303   0.07492688    10.73170   0.00000000
3.  MA{1}                  0.33518909   0.12316664     2.72143   0.00791828
4.  SMA{4}                -0.64736204   0.09806500    -6.60136   0.00000000
5.  N_INTER{0}            60.66370815  12.26573065     4.94579   0.00000390

Covariance\Correlation Matrix of Coefficients
              CONSTANT         AR{1}           MA{1}          SMA{4}
CONSTANT     14.171177159  0.1458624433  -0.0767675234  -0.0653487789
AR{1}         0.041141878  0.005614038   -0.5077002408  -0.4004257741
MA{1}        -0.035593736 -0.004685308    0.015170020    0.3801270934
SMA{4}       -0.024124286 -0.002942210    0.004591303    0.009616744
N_INTER{0}   -6.793985035  0.026339497   -0.024283434   -0.037059549
              N_INTER{0}
CONSTANT     -0.1471391350
AR{1}         0.0286600133
MA{1}        -0.0160739864
SMA{4}       -0.0308100702
N_INTER{0}  150.448148447

SET SSALES = SALES**.5
```

The following is a zero-order intervention model using the square root of sales.

```
BOX(SDIFF=1,MA=1,AR=1,SMA=1,INPUT=1,APPLY,ITER=40,VCV,CONSTANT) SSALES / RESN
#INTER
Dependent Variable SSALES - Estimation by Box-Jenkins
Iterations Taken    13
Quarterly Data From 1971:01 To 1992:04
Usable Observations      88      Degrees of Freedom     83
Centered R**2       0.995630     R Bar **2    0.995420
Uncentered R**2     0.999820     T x R**2        87.984
Mean of Dependent Variable       21.609447624
Std Error of Dependent Variable   4.499828934
Standard Error of Estimate        0.304537500
Sum of Squared Residuals          7.6976763683
Durbin-Watson Statistic           1.960140
Q(22-3)                           7.122948
Significance Level of Q           0.99352833
    Variable               Coeff       Std Error      T-Stat     Signif
*****************************************************************************
1.  CONSTANT               0.688211487  0.094302477    7.29792   0.00000000
2.  AR{1}                  0.850316976  0.068859562   12.34857   0.00000000
```

3. MA{1}	0.373442105	0.113959732	3.27697	0.00153307
4. SMA{4}	-0.727998163	0.092790993	-7.84557	0.00000000
5. N_INTER{0}	1.025182514	0.282632626	3.62726	0.00049343

Covariance\Correlation Matrix of Coefficients

	CONSTANT	AR{1}	MA{1}	SMA{4}
CONSTANT	0.00889295708	0.2114467525	-0.1114990804	-0.2452595207
AR{1}	0.00137305639	0.00474163931	-0.4389374342	-0.4736315755
MA{1}	-0.00119824549	-0.00344443742	0.01298682060	0.2829158464
SMA{4}	-0.00214612393	-0.00302629129	0.00299167572	0.00861016842
N_INTER{0}	-0.00394209887	0.00074675432	0.00024144157	0.00217562089

	N_INTER{0}
CONSTANT	-0.1479047497
AR{1}	0.0383699465
MA{1}	0.0074961512
SMA{4}	0.0829573947
N_INTER{0}	0.07988120116

While not shown here, graphs of the residuals show some variance nonstationarity for all models with only slight differences between these different models. To help answer the question of which is best, we perform a simple F-test on the residuals..

```
* RESJ = Original Metric Values
* RESI = Logarithms Values
* RESN = Square Root Values
```

First Half of Data

Series	Obs	Mean	Std Error	Minimum	Maximum
RESI	43	0.01255	0.03597	-0.10419	0.08555
RESJ	43	2.58486	11.33987	-32.35016	35.60027
RESN	43	0.10619	0.29751	-0.83559	0.77702

Second Half Data

Series	Obs	Mean	Std Error	Minimum	Maximum
RESI	43	-0.00711	0.01995	-0.07032	0.02402
RESJ	43	-1.51514	13.94532	-42.94130	22.93615
RESN	43	-0.06700	0.26321	-0.87586	0.31200

F-test on the Residuals of each model. It appears that either the original series or square foot series should be accepted, only the logarithmic model had significant variance differences between pre and post intervention.

```
F-test of original series:    13.945**2/11.33987**2 = 1.51224
cdf ftest 1.51224 43 43
F(43,43)=      1.51224 with Significance Level 0.08956143

F-test of logarithms:         0.03597**2/0.01995**2 = 3.25084
cdf ftest 3.25084 43 43
F(43,43)=      3.25084 with Significance Level 0.00009194

F-test of square roots:       0.29751**2/0.26321**2 = 1.27761
cdf ftest 1.27761 43 43
F(43,43)=      1.27761 with Significance Level 0.21254794
```

MINICASES

Solutions to each of the Minicases are available from the author by contacting him at either delurgio@cctr.umkc.edu or sad@forecast.umkc.edu. He will supply this in one of several formats.

PROBLEMS

ESTIMATED DIFFICULTY

Elementary	Medium	Hard	Very Hard	Bad

1 M   2 M   3 M   4 M   5 M   6 M   7 H   8 H   9 H   10 M

11 M   12 M   13 M   14 H   15 V   16 V

Minicases are Very Hard.

13-1. Simple linear regression is the equivalent of a MARIMA model where r, s, and b all equal 0 and there is one input variable. The general multiple regression model is an MARIMA model with r and s equal to 0 and there are multiple input variables.

13-2. COILS or similar models are MARIMA models where r and s equal 0 and the noise model is a first-order moving average model.

13-3. See Figure 13-5 for each step.

13-4. The first step in MARIMA analysis is to achieve stationarity to facilitate the identification of r, s, b, p, and q. Also, as mentioned previously, stationarity is an important process in its own right and should be modeled.

13-5. A pulse function has a duration of a single period, while a step function steps to a new level; thus yielding a permanent change. In actual applications there is great versatility in modeling the relationships between input series and output series, thus there are many possible relationships that can be modeled with pulses and step functions.

13-6. See Figure 13-13 which illustrates the affect of r, s, and b. Clearly, r is the level of autoregressive behavior that results from the input series, s is one less than the number of omega coefficients in the numerator, and b is the delay or lag in the effect of the input series.

13-7.

		a. STEP FUNCTIONS				b. PULSE FUNCTIONS		
OMEGA		10	10	10		10	10	10
DELTA		0.3	0.6	1.2		0.3	0.6	1.2
TIME	X(t)				X(t)			
1	0	0	0	0	0	0	0	0
2	1	10	10	10	1	10	10	10
3	1	13	16	22	0	3	6	12
4	1	13.9	19.6	36.4	0	0.9	3.6	14.4
5	1	14.17	21.76	53.68	0	0.27	2.16	17.28
6	1	14.251	23.056	74.416	0	0.081	1.296	20.736
7	1	14.2753	23.8336	99.2992	0	0.0243	0.7776	24.8832
8	1	14.2825	24.3001	129.159	0	0.00729	0.46656	29.8598
9	1	14.2847	24.5801	164.990	0	0.00218	0.27993	35.8318
10	1	14.2854	24.7480	207.989	0	0.00065	0.16796	42.9981
11	1	14.2856	24.8488	259.586	0	0.00019	0.10077	51.5978
12	1	14.2856	24.9093	321.504	0	5.9E-05	0.06046	61.9173
13	1	14.2857	24.9455	395.805	0	1.77E-05	0.03628	74.3008
14	1	14.2857	24.9673	484.966	0	5.31E-06	0.02176	89.161
15	1	14.2857	24.9804	591.959	0	1.59E-06	0.01306	106.993
16	1	14.2857	24.9882	720.351	0	4.78E-07	0.00783	128.391
17	1	14.2857	24.9929	874.421	0	1.43E-07	0.00470	154.070
18	1	14.2857	24.9957	1059.300	0	4.3E-08	0.00282	184.884
19	1	14.2857	24.9974	1281.160	0	1.29E-08	0.00169	221.861
20	1	14.2857	24.9984	1547.400	0	3.87E-09	0.00101	266.233

c. The impact of the nonstationary value of delta is quite clear in the spreadsheet values above, both for the step and pulse functions, the series continues to increase indefinitely to infinity.

13-8.   a, b, c, and e are given in Figure 13-13.

d. is profile b, but the exponential decline starts at lag 1.

13-9. As t approaches infinity the affect of a change reaches its limit as shown on page 496 of Chapter 12.

13-10. First, there is a substantive basis for believing that one variable, the input variable influences the output variable, next, sufficient observations exist to apply the procedures summarized in Figure 13-5.

13-11. The transfer function should have statistically significant, parsimonious, nonredundant coefficients which are in the bounds of stability, the structure should be intuitively and theoretically appealing, the ARIMA (i.e., noise) model should pass muster on all ARIMA criteria as discussed in Chapter 8, having parsimonious structure, invertible, stationary, and nonredundant coefficients and white noise residuals. Finally, the overall models should have intuitive and theoretical appeal and provide a low BIC.

13-12. Depending on the complexity and regularity of the transfer function there might be little or great impact on the quality of the final model and its forecasts when a TF is ignored. That is, at times there can be a tremendous amount of explained variance that is lost when a univariate model is fitted instead of a transfer function. It is possible to have a very good and significant MARIMA transfer function and a completely random ARIMA model, a (0,0,0) model with zero explained variance. In such cases, there is great utility in the transfer function component, that is, there is a very significant decrease in the RSE. In all cases, but to varying degrees, there may be an incomplete understanding of the determinants of the output series if input series are not included in the model. As mentioned, the univariate results might be meaningless and misleading depending on the type of pattern in the output series that is generated by the transfer function.

13-13. For simple models, linear regression can be used to fit the transfer function portion and then univariate ARIMA modeling can be used on the errors of the regression model to fit the noise component. However, there may be significant violations of the assumptions of OLS that might make the regression model less then appropriate. Also, with this procedure it may be difficult to objectively model the rate parameter, delta. When your software supports autoregressive models on the residuals of regression models, then these can be used to simultaneously fit a linear regression model and an autoregressive noise model on the residuals such as Cochrane-Orcutt or Prais Winsten when, for example, using software such as AUTOREG in SAS/ETS.

13-14. When logarithms are used, then coefficients represent ratios and the omega coefficient is an elasticity measure. An omega of 10 is extremely high value denoting that there is an e^{omega} ratio affect between Y_t and Y_{t-1} caused by X_t at the time of intervention as shown below:

omega	10		
delta	0.3		
time-t	X_t	lnY_t	Y_t
1	0	0	1
2	0	0	1
3	0	0	1
4	1	10	22026
5	1	13	442413
6	1	13.9	1088161
7	1	14.17	1425453
8	1	14.251	1545719
9	1	14.2753	1583740
10	1	14.2825	1595328

13-15. a) Analyzing the GERMUS.DAT using logarithms.

```
SET LUS = LOG(US)
SET LGERM = LOG(GERM)
```

PREWHITENING THE INPUT SERIES:

```
BOX(CONSTANT,DIFF=1,MA=1) LUS / PWUS
Dependent Variable LUS - Estimation by Box-Jenkins
Iterations Taken    5
Monthly Data From 1970:02 To 1992:07
Usable Observations    270      Degrees of Freedom    268
Centered R**2      0.995188     R Bar **2    0.995170
Mean of Dependent Variable      5.0969420403
Std Error of Dependent Variable 0.5151246368
Standard Error of Estimate      0.0358018529
Sum of Squared Residuals        0.3435150763
Durbin-Watson Statistic            2.001029
Q(36-1)                            25.401221
Significance Level of Q             0.88321557
    Variable           Coeff        Std Error      T-Stat      Signif
***********************************************************************
1.  CONSTANT      0.0055954194 0.0028806267      1.94243   0.05313236
2.  MA{1}         0.3235828669 0.0578702942      5.59152   0.00000006
CORR(QSTAT,NUM=24) PWUS
Correlations of Series PWUS
Monthly Data From 1970:02 To 1992:07
Autocorrelations
     1: -0.0034875 -0.0098207 -0.0048693 -0.0076170  0.0461403 -0.0474150
     7: -0.0955796  0.0153208 -0.0349864 -0.0321188  0.0837059 -0.0379344
    13:  0.0058690 -0.0425975 -0.0452676  0.0269184 -0.0733055  0.0354768
    19: -0.0788101 -0.0724737 -0.0632750  0.0192205 -0.0799680 -0.0041876
Ljung-Box Q-Statistics
Q(24)   =        16.7305.  Significance Level 0.85992785
```

PWUS IS THE PREWHITENED INPUT SERIES

PRETREATING THE OUTPUT SERIES:

```
SET PWGERM1 1 1 = LGERM
SET PWGERM1 2 271 = 0.0055954194 + LGERM(T-1) + .323583*(LGERM(T-1) -
PWGERM1(T-1))
SET PWOUT = LGERM - PWGERM1
```

PRETREATED OUTPUT SERIES IS PWOUT

```
CORR(QSTAT,NUM=24) PWOUT
Correlations of Series PWOUT
Monthly Data From 1970:01 To 1992:07
Autocorrelations
     1: -0.0208678  0.1072222  0.0065720 -0.0075008 -0.0491137 -0.0994339
     7:  0.0337295 -0.0773626 -0.0124422  0.1378088  0.0441569  0.0288680
    13: -0.0462432  0.0180855 -0.0507167 -0.0530043 -0.1023521  0.1657369
    19: -0.1681270 -0.0430571 -0.0479448 -0.0157630  0.0197896  0.0344062
Ljung-Box Q-Statistics
Q(24)   =        38.3824.  Significance Level 0.03166928

CROSS(QSTAT) PWOUT PWUS / -4 4
Cross Correlations of Series PWOUT and PWUS
Monthly Data From 1970:02 To 1992:07
    -4: -0.0294198 -0.0437474  0.1211115 -0.0821807  0.4115997  0.2001095
     2:  0.0654793 -0.0695466  0.0109684
```

```
Ljung-Box Q-Statistics
Q(1 to 4)   =          13.4709.  Significance Level 0.00919001
Q(-4 to -1) =           6.6287.  Significance Level 0.15686131
Q(-4 to 4)  =          66.1803.  Significance Level 0.00000000
```

These cross correlations suggest the following model with r=1, s=0, and b=0:

PWOUT = f(PWUS(t), PWUS(t-1))

```
BOX(DIFF=1,INPUT=1,APPLY,MA=1,VCV) LGERM / RESL
#LUS  0 1 0
Dependent Variable LGERM - Estimation by Box-Jenkins
Iterations Taken    11
Monthly Data From 1970:02 To 1992:07
Usable Observations    270      Degrees of Freedom    267
Centered R**2       0.993455    R Bar **2    0.993406
Uncentered R**2     0.999955    T x R**2       269.988
Mean of Dependent Variable      5.1215956169
Std Error of Dependent Variable 0.4267709606
Standard Error of Estimate      0.0346563119
Sum of Squared Residuals        0.3206830075
Durbin-Watson Statistic            1.979580
Q(36-1)                           56.373494
Significance Level of Q            0.01247538
    Variable             Coeff         Std Error       T-Stat      Signif
*******************************************************************************
1.  MA{1}             0.2211740630 0.0603057762      3.66754   0.00029552
2.  N_LUS{0}          0.4514536078 0.0574608833      7.85671   0.00000000
3.  D_LUS{1}          0.3921949470 0.0971153231      4.03845   0.00007037
Covariance\Correlation Matrix of Coefficients
                 MA{1}          N_LUS{0}          D_LUS{1}
MA{1}        0.00363678664   0.1002987404    -0.0567172977
N_LUS{0}     0.00034755752   0.00330175311   -0.4353829843
D_LUS{1}    -0.00033217137  -0.00242958171    0.00943138598

corr(qstat,num=24) res2
Correlations of Series RES2
Monthly Data From 1970:02 To 1992:07
Autocorrelations
    1:   0.0047375   0.0359298   0.0554800  -0.0099306  -0.0761264  -0.1189341
    7:   0.0517195  -0.0113737  -0.0384815   0.1310373   0.0729180   0.0300519
   13:  -0.0623324  -0.0193392  -0.0078895  -0.0960337  -0.1316496   0.1711405
   19:  -0.1156206  -0.0000906   0.0037406  -0.0403542   0.0568813  -0.0071457
Ljung-Box Q-Statistics
Q(24)  =          37.4331.  Significance Level 0.03959333

disp 2/271**.5 = 0.12149
```

```
CROS(QSTAT) RES2 PWUS / -12 12
Cross Correlations of Series RES2 and PWUS
Monthly Data From 1970:02 To 1992:07
   -12:   0.0443354 -0.0317427  0.0861430  0.1461979 -0.0693983 -0.0382163
    -6:   0.0290134 -0.0329133 -0.0364240 -0.0493263  0.1383814 -0.0735529
     0:  -0.0127903  0.0485887  0.0110582 -0.1022151 -0.0039562  0.0370995
     6:  -0.0087879  0.0730483 -0.0636542 -0.0091665 -0.0031074 -0.0219189
    12:  -0.0272591
Ljung-Box Q-Statistics
Q(1 to 12)   =            6.9590.  Significance Level 0.86031343
Q(-12 to -1)=           19.0076.  Significance Level 0.08834428
Q(-12 to 12)=           26.0111.  Significance Level 0.40700656
```

While the residuals of this model are not strictly white noise, we choose it anyway because of the very good statistics of other diagnostics. Also, we choose to ignore the possibility of mutual causality, implied by the marginally significant CCF value at -2 albeit this should be investigated. Thus, we accept the above transfer function model. However, when graphing the residuals, there is a large intervention at the time of the 1987 stock market crash, an intervention model of the October 1987 crash might be fitted to this data. For now we accept the previously fitted MARIMA model. The affect of the market crash can be modeled if so desired.

b) USJAPAN.DAT - Analyzing Logarithms:

```
SET LUS = LOG(US)
SET LJAPAN = LOG(JAPAN)
```

PREWHITENING THE INPUT SERIES

```
BOX(CONSTANT,DIFF=1,MA=1) LUS / PWUS
Dependent Variable LUS - Estimation by Box-Jenkins
Iterations Taken    5
Monthly Data From 1970:02 To 1992:07
Usable Observations     270        Degrees of Freedom    268
Centered R**2       0.995188       R Bar **2    0.995170
Uncentered R**2     0.999952       T x R**2      269.987
Mean of Dependent Variable      5.0969420403
Std Error of Dependent Variable 0.5151246368
Standard Error of Estimate      0.0358018529
Sum of Squared Residuals        0.3435150763
Durbin-Watson Statistic            2.001029
Q(36-1)                           25.401221
Significance Level of Q            0.88321557
    Variable            Coeff        Std Error      T-Stat      Signif
******************************************************************************
1.  CONSTANT       0.0055954194 0.0028806267       1.94243   0.05313236
2.  MA{1}          0.3235828669 0.0578702942       5.59152   0.00000006

CORR(QSTAT,NUM=24) PWUS
Correlations of Series PWUS
Monthly Data From 1970:02 To 1992:07
Autocorrelations
    1: -0.0034875 -0.0098207 -0.0048693 -0.0076170  0.0461403 -0.0474150
    7: -0.0955796  0.0153208 -0.0349864 -0.0321188  0.0837059 -0.0379344
   13:  0.0058690 -0.0425975 -0.0452676  0.0269184 -0.0733055  0.0354768
   19: -0.0788101 -0.0724737 -0.0632750  0.0192205 -0.0799680 -0.0041876
Ljung-Box Q-Statistics
Q(24)    =           16.7305.  Significance Level 0.85992785
```

PWUS IS THE PREWHITENED INPUT SERIES

PRETREATING THE OUTPUT SERIES.

```
SET PWJAPAN1 1 1 = LJAPAN
SET PWJAPAN1 2 271 = 0.0055954194 + LJAPAN(T-1) + .323583*(LJAPAN(T-1) -
PWJAPAN1(T-1))
SET PWOUT = LJAPAN - PWJAPAN1
```

PRETREATED OUTPUT SERIES IS PWOUT

```
CORR(QSTAT,NUM=24) PWOUT
Correlations of Series PWOUT
Monthly Data From 1970:01 To 1992:07
Autocorrelations
     1:   0.0701902   0.0847100   0.0221639   0.0248598   0.0299910  -0.0306326
     7:   0.0551247   0.0088682   0.0892686   0.1004818   0.0063743   0.0284335
    13:  -0.0122870  -0.0436417   0.0106530   0.0057425  -0.0051001   0.0859027
    19:  -0.0287083   0.0123375  -0.0408790  -0.0076795   0.0176520   0.0528733
Ljung-Box Q-Statistics
Q(24)  =          14.8995.  Significance Level 0.92366532

CROSS(QSTAT) PWOUT PWUS / -4 4
Cross Correlations of Series PWOUT and PWUS
Monthly Data From 1970:02 To 1992:07
    -4:  -0.0044917  -0.0661696   0.0360691  -0.0370548   0.3955332   0.1898559
     2:   0.0660930  -0.0074980   0.0576599
Ljung-Box Q-Statistics
Q(1 to 4)   =          11.9712.  Significance Level 0.01756690
Q(-4 to -1) =           1.9412.  Significance Level 0.74656445
Q(-4 to 4)  =          56.4659.  Significance Level 0.00000001
```

These cross correlations suggest the following model with r=1, s=0, and b=0.
THUS PWOUT = f(PWUS(t), PWUS(t-1))

The following first-order model results with r=1, s=0, b=0:

```
BOX(DIFF=1,INPUT=1,APPLY,MA=1,VCV) LJAPAN / RESL
#LUS  0 1 0
Dependent Variable LJAPAN - Estimation by Box-Jenkins
Iterations Taken    6
Monthly Data From 1970:02 To 1992:07
Usable Observations    270       Degrees of Freedom   267
Centered R**2      0.998230      R Bar **2    0.998216
Uncentered R**2    0.999971      T x R**2     269.992
Mean of Dependent Variable     6.3585720135
Std Error of Dependent Variable 0.8183833458
Standard Error of Estimate     0.0345621449
Sum of Squared Residuals       0.3189426766
Durbin-Watson Statistic          1.973317
Q(36-1)                         21.498844
Significance Level of Q          0.96430974
    Variable          Coeff        Std Error      T-Stat      Signif
*******************************************************************************
1.  MA{1}       0.3098908860 0.0582632930        5.31880    0.00000022
2.  N_LUS{0}    0.4369343499 0.0573225592        7.62238    0.00000000
3.  D_LUS{1}    0.4502522798 0.0942348352        4.77798    0.00000293
```

```
Covariance\Correlation Matrix of Coefficients
                    MA{1}         N_LUS{0}         D_LUS{1}
MA{1}        0.00339461131    0.0452836043    -0.0261015396
N_LUS{0}     0.00015123823    0.00328587580   -0.4336270501
D_LUS{1}    -0.00014330872   -0.00234235876    0.00888020416


corr(qstat,num=24) resL
Monthly Data From 1970:02 To 1992:07
Autocorrelations
     1:   0.0088361   0.0541398   0.0523415   0.0277859   0.0931271  -0.0017786
     7:   0.0835579   0.0347396   0.0668924   0.1189313   0.0051771   0.0486384
    13:   0.0097039  -0.0510692   0.0268732   0.0013564  -0.0177496   0.0735349
    19:  -0.0144072   0.0643080   0.0299669  -0.0245059   0.0340096   0.0535321
Ljung-Box Q-Statistics
Q(24)   =           17.9875.   Significance Level 0.80361374


disp 2/271**.5 = 0.12149
CROS(QSTAT) RESL PWUS / -12 12
Cross Correlations of Series RESL and PWUS
Monthly Data From 1970:02 To 1992:07
   -12:   0.0416752  -0.0341305  -0.0150743   0.0719210  -0.0418864  -0.0632650
    -6:  -0.0226806  -0.0502040  -0.0032399  -0.0706074   0.0451210  -0.0361330
     0:  -0.0117842   0.0100127  -0.0127495  -0.0453089   0.0507179  -0.0750475
     6:  -0.0408350   0.0847090   0.0179172   0.0808761   0.0194695   0.0421285
    12:  -0.0198544
Ljung-Box Q-Statistics
Q(1 to 12)   =         8.0282.   Significance Level 0.78292318
Q(-12 to -1)=         7.0839.   Significance Level 0.85202053
Q(-12 to 12)=        15.1499.   Significance Level 0.93780958
```

We accept the above transfer function model even though there is a large intervention at the time of the 1987 stock market crash which might be investigated, but is ignored at this time.

c) UKUSIND.DAT - Analyzing the logarithms of these series.

PREWHITENING THE INPUT SERIES

```
BOX(CONSTANT,DIFF=1,MA=1) LUS / PWUS
Dependent Variable LUS - Estimation by Box-Jenkins
Iterations Taken      5
Monthly Data From 1970:02 To 1992:07
Usable Observations      270       Degrees of Freedom    268
Centered R**2       0.995188       R Bar **2    0.995170
Uncentered R**2     0.999952       T x R**2      269.987
Mean of Dependent Variable        5.0969420403
Std Error of Dependent Variable   0.5151246368
Standard Error of Estimate        0.0358018529
Sum of Squared Residuals          0.3435150763
Durbin-Watson Statistic              2.001029
Q(36-1)                             25.401221
Significance Level of Q             0.88321557
   Variable        Coeff        Std Error      T-Stat      Signif
*****************************************************************************
1.  CONSTANT    0.0055954194 0.0028806267      1.94243    0.05313236
2.  MA{1}       0.3235828669 0.0578702942      5.59152    0.00000006
```

```
CORR(QSTAT,NUM=24) PWUS
Correlations of Series PWUS
Monthly Data From 1970:02 To 1992:07
Autocorrelations
     1: -0.0034875 -0.0098207 -0.0048693 -0.0076170  0.0461403 -0.0474150
     7: -0.0955796  0.0153208 -0.0349864 -0.0321188  0.0837059 -0.0379344
    13:  0.0058690 -0.0425975 -0.0452676  0.0269184 -0.0733055  0.0354768
    19: -0.0788101 -0.0724737 -0.0632750  0.0192205 -0.0799680 -0.0041876
Ljung-Box Q-Statistics
Q(24)  =           16.7305.  Significance Level 0.85992785
```

PWUS IS THE PREWHITENED INPUT SERIES

PRETREATING THE OUTPUT SERIES.

```
SET PWUKIND1 1 1 = LUKIND
SET PWUKIND1 2 271 = 0.0055954194 + LUKIND(T-1) + .323583*(LUKIND(T-1) -
PWUKIND1(T-1))
SET PWOUT = LUKIND - PWUKIND1
```

PRETREATED OUTPUT SERIES IS PWOUT

```
CORR(QSTAT,NUM=24) PWOUT
Correlations of Series PWOUT
Monthly Data From 1970:01 To 1992:07
Autocorrelations
     1:  0.0801044 -0.0691448  0.0324228  0.0870813 -0.1055453 -0.1094588
     7:  0.0357758 -0.0321766  0.0514770  0.0470343 -0.0304839  0.0125982
    13: -0.0448090 -0.0927045 -0.0044671 -0.0193253 -0.0646976  0.0095795
    19: -0.0148738 -0.0798419 -0.0684113  0.0617456  0.1089369  0.0441405
Ljung-Box Q-Statistics
Q(24)  =           27.2383.  Significance Level 0.29346846

CROSS(QSTAT) PWOUT PWUS / -4 4
Cross Correlations of Series PWOUT and PWUS
Monthly Data From 1970:02 To 1992:07
    -4:  0.0825146 -0.0075511 -0.0149237  0.0497621  0.5105609  0.2033601
     2: -0.0986225  0.0524733  0.1048123
Ljung-Box Q-Statistics
Q(1 to 4)   =        17.7462.  Significance Level 0.00138332
Q(-4 to -1) =         2.6326.  Significance Level 0.62106486
Q(-4 to 4)  =        91.2816.  Significance Level 0.00000000
```

These cross correlations suggest the following model with r=1, s=0, b=0.

THUS PWOUT = f(PWUS(t), PWUS(t-1))

```
BOX(DIFF=1,INPUT=1,APPLY,MA=1,VCV) LUKIND / RESL
#LUS  0 1 0
Dependent Variable LUKIND - Estimation by Box-Jenkins
Iterations Taken     8
Monthly Data From 1970:02 To 1992:07
Usable Observations    270      Degrees of Freedom   267
Centered R**2     0.997287      R Bar **2   0.997267
Uncentered R**2   0.999946      T x R**2      269.985
Mean of Dependent Variable      5.8126803893
Std Error of Dependent Variable 0.8313005675
Standard Error of Estimate      0.0434580464
```

```
Sum of Squared Residuals          0.5042566789
Durbin-Watson Statistic                2.017636
Q(36-1)                               32.417268
Significance Level of Q             0.59341809
     Variable           Coeff        Std Error      T-Stat      Signif
************************************************************************
1.  MA{1}          0.2773661002 0.0591634890        4.68813  0.00000440
2.  N_LUS{0}       0.7610755259 0.0733687987       10.37329  0.00000000
3.  D_LUS{1}       0.2772587115 0.0845252789        3.28019  0.00117528
Covariance\Correlation Matrix of Coefficients
                   MA{1}          N_LUS{0}        D_LUS{1}
MA{1}        0.00350031843  -0.0618049100    0.0296284501
N_LUS{0}    -0.00026827992   0.00538298062  -0.3132357189
D_LUS{1}     0.00014816626  -0.00194253700   0.00714452277


corr(qstat,num=24) resL
Correlations of Series RESL
Monthly Data From 1970:02 To 1992:07
Autocorrelations
     1: -0.0168380 -0.0592508 -0.0002078  0.0116396 -0.0611204 -0.0566651
     7:  0.0939838 -0.0276264 -0.0128577  0.0197394 -0.0710878 -0.0292170
    13: -0.0215222 -0.1016470  0.0107322 -0.0084033 -0.0917350 -0.0180784
    19:  0.0089710 -0.0566853  0.0673709  0.0507963  0.1298830  0.0706704
Ljung-Box Q-Statistics
Q(24)  =         22.7833.  Significance Level 0.53261924


disp 2/271**.5 = 0.12149


CROS(QSTAT) RESL PWUS / -12 12
Cross Correlations of Series RESL and PWUS
Monthly Data From 1970:02 To 1992:07
   -12:  0.1027581 -0.0102238 -0.0545113  0.1393263  0.0785817 -0.0862612
    -6: -0.0645073  0.0006118  0.0989593 -0.0014711 -0.0122200  0.0632420
     0: -0.0171981  0.0686170 -0.1553531  0.0457983  0.1318489 -0.1704639
     6: -0.0970534  0.1125339 -0.0468457 -0.0201335  0.0892397  0.0297148
    12: -0.0101295
Ljung-Box Q-Statistics
Q(1 to 12)  =       30.7432.  Significance Level 0.00215559
Q(-12 to -1)=       18.1403.  Significance Level 0.11149595
Q(-12 to 12)=       48.9639.  Significance Level 0.00285367
```

There appears to be some unexplained structure in the above model. This suggests fitting alternative models with r=0,s=1,b=0.

```
BOX(DIFF=1,INPUT=1,APPLY,VCV,MA=1) LUKIND / RES2
#LUS 1 0
Dependent Variable LUKIND - Estimation by Box-Jenkins
Iterations Taken      7
Monthly Data From 1970:03 To 1992:07
Usable Observations    269       Degrees of Freedom    266
Centered R**2      0.997315      R Bar **2    0.997295
Uncentered R**2    0.999946      T x R**2     268.986
Mean of Dependent Variable       5.8160563991
Std Error of Dependent Variable 0.8309936379
Standard Error of Estimate       0.0432198428
Sum of Squared Residuals         0.4968759796
Durbin-Watson Statistic                2.017488
Q(36-1)                               32.092857
Significance Level of Q             0.60919990
```

```
     Variable            Coeff      Std Error     T-Stat     Signif
**********************************************************************
1.  MA{1}           0.2926797433 0.0589718821      4.96304  0.00000124
2.  N_LUS{0}         0.7450252563 0.0735702311     10.12672  0.00000000
3.  N_LUS{1}         0.2955227658 0.0733008732      4.03164  0.00007239
Covariance\Correlation Matrix of Coefficients
                    MA{1}           N_LUS{0}          N_LUS{1}
MA{1}         0.00347768287  -0.0654807075    0.0195206471
N_LUS{0}     -0.00028409296   0.00541257891   -0.0442016256
N_LUS{1}      0.00008438171  -0.00023836886    0.00537301802


corr(qstat,num=24) res2
Correlations of Series RES2
Monthly Data From 1970:03 To 1992:07
Autocorrelations
     1: -0.0172507 -0.0627576 -0.0151325  0.0256620 -0.0584426 -0.0659198
     7:  0.1054562 -0.0182892 -0.0279689  0.0100211 -0.0601688 -0.0266740
    13: -0.0326085 -0.0918489  0.0093060 -0.0024269 -0.0943769 -0.0234087
    19:  0.0121523 -0.0481113  0.0676761  0.0516865  0.1279112  0.0658977
Ljung-Box Q-Statistics
Q(24)  =        22.6808.  Significance Level 0.53870130

CROS(QSTAT) RES2 PWUS / -12 12
Cross Correlations of Series RES2 and PWUS
Monthly Data From 1970:03 To 1992:07
   -12:  0.1016817 -0.0089706 -0.0614670  0.1459195  0.0794611 -0.0912048
    -6: -0.0571933  0.0004685  0.0932133 -0.0036072 -0.0118868  0.0647385
     0: -0.0060945 -0.0034113 -0.1111452  0.0640908  0.1364666 -0.1703716
     6: -0.0993734  0.1154810 -0.0401486 -0.0337922  0.0889274  0.0278543
    12: -0.0235894
Ljung-Box Q-Statistics
Q(1 to 12)  =        27.4610.  Significance Level 0.00662839
Q(-12 to -1)=        18.5461.  Significance Level 0.10008826
Q(-12 to 12)=        46.0171.  Significance Level 0.00638861

cross res2 lus / -12 12
Cross Correlations of Series RES2 and LUS
Monthly Data From 1970:03 To 1992:07
   -12: -0.0148872 -0.0209455 -0.0171564 -0.0188309 -0.0343371 -0.0449322
    -6: -0.0377712 -0.0338705 -0.0365880 -0.0392777 -0.0308799 -0.0411357
     0: -0.0592839 -0.0617363 -0.0584066 -0.0532402 -0.0592713 -0.0635579
     6: -0.0497490 -0.0484899 -0.0521444 -0.0562603 -0.0580991 -0.0671579
    12: -0.0732932
```

While the zero-order model fits better, there are still some significant CCFs at lags 4 and 5 for both models, however, other models did not eliminate these. Thus, we will accept either of these transfer function models with a decided preference for the second, zero order model.

13-16a. British Airways Stock Prices - analyzing the logs of these series:

```
SET LLONP = LOG(LONP)
SET LNYP = LOG(NYP)
```

Our first step is to find a prewhitening model for LNYP.

```
CORR(PAR=PAR,NUM=30,QSTAT) LNYP
Correlations of Series LNYP
Autocorrelations
```

```
    1:  0.96092355 0.91466341 0.87067189 0.82917406 0.79111132 0.75370262
    7:  0.71403382 0.68134263 0.65105415 0.62528069 0.60529771 0.58820191
   13:  0.56756321 0.53874272 0.50477183 0.47370615 0.43989771 0.40340295
   19:  0.36650459 0.33568205 0.30727537 0.28222509 0.25837733 0.24033191
   25:  0.22248442 0.20268774 0.17952628 0.15744138 0.13839941 0.12380022
Partial Autocorrelations
    1:  0.9609235 -0.1136777  0.0141742  0.0032318  0.0182947 -0.0188368
    7: -0.0490236  0.0772307 -0.0056916  0.0415561  0.0527979  0.0227961
   13: -0.0552023 -0.1112603 -0.0569088  0.0223805 -0.0705007 -0.0477755
   19: -0.0149702  0.0652629 -0.0157688  0.0064589 -0.0102028  0.0416498
   25: -0.0399731 -0.0402665 -0.0359265  0.0073185  0.0231633  0.0487707
Ljung-Box Q-Statistics
Q(30)  =        2458.2407.  Significance Level 0.00000000


CORR(PAR=PAR,NUM=30,QSTAT) LLONP
Correlations of Series LLONP
Autocorrelations
    1:  0.9545851  0.9004247  0.8436584  0.7882237  0.7354803  0.6878690
    7:  0.6378068  0.5904959  0.5513917  0.5178071  0.4914525  0.4679712
   13:  0.4428295  0.4080471  0.3641929  0.3281671  0.2942145  0.2599716
   19:  0.2287277  0.2048355  0.1798154  0.1567656  0.1375067  0.1201275
   25:  0.0984291  0.0773700  0.0497104  0.0205261  0.0050500 -0.0056603
Partial Autocorrelations
    1:  0.9545851 -0.1217565 -0.0491726 -0.0110543 -0.0027394  0.0222745
    7: -0.0676883  0.0050522  0.0624425  0.0207879  0.0469247 -0.0036830
   13: -0.0364756 -0.1177924 -0.1096579  0.0915851 -0.0110446 -0.0376263
   19:  0.0133009  0.0692213 -0.0341846 -0.0312603  0.0018306 -0.0026280
   25: -0.0832172 -0.0025243 -0.0656029 -0.0006680  0.1367370 -0.0039560
Ljung-Box Q-Statistics
Q(30)  =        1833.0815.  Significance Level 0.00000000
```

Both series appear to be random walk models, so let's prewhiten LNYP.

```
BOX(DIFF=1,CONSTANT) LNYP / RES
Dependent Variable LNYP - Estimation by Box-Jenkins
Iterations Taken     2
Usable Observations   259      Degrees of Freedom   258
Centered R**2     0.926230     R Bar **2    0.926230
Uncentered R**2   0.999798     T x R**2     258.948
Mean of Dependent Variable       1.5476637262
Std Error of Dependent Variable  0.0813051133
Standard Error of Estimate       0.0220830495
Sum of Squared Residuals         0.1258165568
Durbin-Watson Statistic             1.828088
Q(36-0)                            27.640588
Significance Level of Q             0.83976124
    Variable          Coeff       Std Error     T-Stat     Signif
***************************************************************************
1.  CONSTANT      0.0003098054 0.0013721739     0.22578   0.82155355
```

This model appears to have white noise residuals, however, the constant is not significant and will be dropped.

```
BOX(DIFF=1) LNYP / ALPHA
Dependent Variable LNYP - Estimation by Box-Jenkins
Iterations Taken     4
Usable Observations   259      Degrees of Freedom   259
Centered R**2     0.926215     R Bar **2    0.926500
Uncentered R**2   0.999798     T x R**2     258.948
```

```
Mean of Dependent Variable       1.5476637262
Std Error of Dependent Variable  0.0813051133
Standard Error of Estimate       0.0220425541
Sum of Squared Residuals         0.1258414155
Durbin-Watson Statistic             1.827726
Q(36-0)                            27.640588
Significance Level of Q           0.83976124
 NO ESTIMATED COEFFICIENTS
```

A CHECK FOR WHITE NOISE RESIDUALS:

```
CORR(PAR=PAR,NUM=21,qstat) ALPHA
Correlations of Series ALPHA
Autocorrelations
     1:   0.0845767  -0.0313685  -0.0394577  -0.0469034  -0.0196447   0.0279395
     7:  -0.0735290  -0.0173393  -0.0734153  -0.0693076  -0.0427567   0.0517770
    13:   0.1187055   0.0756763  -0.0288621   0.0199546   0.0098823   0.0117516
    19:  -0.0789199  -0.0347889  -0.0339070
Partial Autocorrelations
     1:   0.0845767  -0.0387992  -0.0337118  -0.0421735  -0.0146709   0.0268924
     7:  -0.0834396  -0.0052743  -0.0778884  -0.0620837  -0.0453491   0.0444389
    13:   0.1034760   0.0461303  -0.0315149   0.0317749   0.0104543   0.0038547
    19:  -0.0911424  -0.0165508  -0.0202231
Ljung-Box Q-Statistics
Q(21)  =          17.2463.  Significance Level 0.69607085

DISP 2/260**.5 = 0.12403
```

ALPHA is the prewhitened input series of LNYP. Now let's pretreat LONP.

```
BOX(DIFF=1) LONP / BETA
Dependent Variable LONP - Estimation by Box-Jenkins
Iterations Taken      4
Usable Observations     259       Degrees of Freedom    259
Centered R**2       0.932362      R Bar **2    0.932623
Uncentered R**2     0.999546      T x R**2      258.882
Mean of Dependent Variable       2.6881544402
Std Error of Dependent Variable  0.2214281676
Standard Error of Estimate       0.0574763003
Sum of Squared Residuals         0.8556130000
Durbin-Watson Statistic             1.755255
Q(36-0)                            34.990570
Significance Level of Q           0.51644741
 NO ESTIMATED COEFFICIENTS
```

Further diagnostics confirm that the first differences model is a "best" model. Also, as a benchmark of how well the MARIMA model improves the fit and hopefully, the forecast, we fit an ARIMA model to LLONP.

```
BOX(DIFF=1,MA=1) LLONP / RES5
Dependent Variable LLONP - Estimation by Box-Jenkins
Iterations Taken      4
Usable Observations     259       Degrees of Freedom    258
Centered R**2       0.933138      R Bar **2    0.933138
Uncentered R**2     0.999528      T x R**2      258.878
Mean of Dependent Variable       0.9854295435
Std Error of Dependent Variable  0.0832470445
Standard Error of Estimate       0.0215257628
Sum of Squared Residuals         0.1195464842
```

```
Durbin-Watson Statistic                 1.994241
Q(36-1)                                 29.174352
Significance Level of Q                  0.74480526
     Variable          Coeff       Std Error      T-Stat      Signif
******************************************************************************
1.  MA{1}       0.1197055843 0.0618097360        1.93668   0.05387653
```

Thus the "best" univariate model of British Airways in London is shown above. Now let's fit the MARIMA model. The prewhitening model for NY and London seems to be the first differenced model of logarithms. Thus, we can cross correlate Beta and Alpha as shown below.

```
CROSS(QSTAT) BETA ALPHA / -21 21
Cross Correlations of Series BETA and ALPHA
-15: -0.0648961  0.1122820  0.1103581  0.0458947 -0.0791645 -0.0504942
  -9: -0.0878687 -0.0527315 -0.1177569  0.0440302 -0.0756507 -0.0697332
  -3: -0.0014092  0.0240862  0.0486981  0.7925756  0.1995190  0.0548780
   3: -0.1105698 -0.0529814 -0.0191317  0.0608273  0.0025707 -0.0058607
   9: -0.0682743 -0.0239997 -0.0161950  0.0477547  0.1158468  0.0903380
  15: -0.0067354  0.0121871 -0.0286638  0.0215106 -0.1112848  0.0082393
Ljung-Box Q-Statistics
Q(1 to 21)  =       28.2824.  Significance Level 0.13232164
Q(-21 to -1)=       28.4031.  Significance Level 0.12908365
Q(-21 to 21)=      220.6395.  Significance Level 0.00000000
```

These cross correlations suggest the following zero-order model with r=0, s=1, b=0.

```
BOX(DIFF=1,INPUT=1,VCV,APPLY,CONSTANT) LONP / RES4
#NYP 1 0 0
Dependent Variable LONP - Estimation by Box-Jenkins
Iterations Taken     2
Usable Observations    258      Degrees of Freedom    255
Centered R**2     0.975863      R Bar **2    0.975674
Uncentered R**2   0.999840      T x R**2     257.959
Mean of Dependent Variable        2.6896976744
Std Error of Dependent Variable 0.2204585813
Standard Error of Estimate        0.0343844124
Sum of Squared Residuals          0.3014833924
Durbin-Watson Statistic           2.155493
Q(36-0)                          58.917128
Significance Level of Q           0.00934141
     Variable          Coeff       Std Error      T-Stat      Signif
******************************************************************************
1.  CONSTANT       0.0022439359 0.0021411254        1.04802   0.29562306
2.  N_NYP{0}       0.4371155516 0.0208567520       20.95799   0.00000000
3.  N_NYP{1}       0.0697633793 0.0208327164        3.34874   0.00093449
Covariance\Correlation Matrix of Coefficients
             CONSTANT        N_NYP{0}         N_NYP{1}
CONSTANT   0.00000458442  -0.0153006438   -0.0120779409
N_NYP{0}  -0.00000068328   0.00043500410  -0.0885374384
N_NYP{1}  -0.00000053874  -0.00003846976   0.00043400207
```

```
CORR(NUM=21,QSTAT,PAR=PAR) RES4
Correlations of Series RES4
Autocorrelations
   1: -0.0810442 -0.1186483  0.1004438  0.0638093 -0.0603775 -0.0519418
   7:  0.0619036 -0.1084760  0.0641254 -0.0003168  0.0284087  0.0085604
  13:  0.0187326  0.0798750 -0.0969802  0.0639348 -0.0423263 -0.0870652
  19:  0.0238605 -0.0094986  0.0172627
```

```
Partial Autocorrelations
      1: -0.0810442 -0.1260444  0.0812161  0.0663653 -0.0290466 -0.0551575
      7:  0.0324056 -0.1117238  0.0753120 -0.0174905  0.0550140  0.0133152
     13:  0.0202480  0.0732201 -0.0764255  0.0521410 -0.0529206 -0.0865096
     19:  0.0207037 -0.0299821  0.0369458
Ljung-Box Q-Statistics
Q(21)  =          24.9039.  Significance Level 0.25134841

CROSS(QSTAT) RES4 ALPHA / -21 21
Cross Correlations of Series RES4 and ALPHA
    -21: -0.0595345  0.0529395 -0.0657638 -0.0165019  0.0347951 -0.1684171
    -15: -0.0769635  0.0973316  0.0191200 -0.0237778 -0.0882211  0.0058894
     -9: -0.0329882 -0.0520053 -0.0973463  0.0522251 -0.0994306 -0.0443122
     -3:  0.0648418  0.0804898 -0.0266929  0.0010543  0.0114528  0.1038988
      3: -0.1272169 -0.0163906  0.0148414  0.0724050  0.0846106  0.0302272
      9: -0.0025542  0.0642774  0.0471829  0.0077744  0.0244236  0.0325553
     15:  0.0088937 -0.0064239 -0.0626889  0.0154492 -0.0850791  0.0912325
Ljung-Box Q-Statistics
Q(1 to 21)  =          20.3481.  Significance Level 0.49931606
Q(-21 to -1)=          28.4097.  Significance Level 0.12891016
Q(-21 to 21)=          48.7581.  Significance Level 0.25258431

CROSS(QSTAT) RES4 LNYP / -21 21
Cross Correlations of Series RES4 and LNYP
-21: -0.1078328 -0.0927797 -0.1078642 -0.0904274 -0.0866368 -0.0984494
    -15: -0.0525447 -0.0313487 -0.0570320 -0.0625948 -0.0544091 -0.0275439
     -9: -0.0282355 -0.0201960 -0.0079223  0.0165902  0.0024253  0.0272338
     -3:  0.0398292  0.0212561 -0.0017405  0.0046833  0.0071617  0.0003118
      3: -0.0031214  0.0351017  0.0436096  0.0435072  0.0246265  0.0018137
      9: -0.0024269 -0.0015688 -0.0242697 -0.0437863 -0.0471698 -0.0578668
     15: -0.0611753 -0.0645037 -0.0584958 -0.0431102 -0.0483804 -0.0211692
     21: -0.0462729
Ljung-Box Q-Statistics
Q(1 to 21)  =           8.8066.  Significance Level 0.99065596
Q(-21 to -1)=          21.2685.  Significance Level 0.44265207
Q(-21 to 21)=          30.0808.  Significance Level 0.93185872
```

The MARIMA model appears to past muster on all diagnostics checks, albeit we are concerned about the large CCF(3). However, alternative models did not eliminate these near significant peak at CCF(2) and the significant peak at CCF(3) .

13-16b. General Motors Stock Prices, GM.DAT - Analyzing logarithms.

Based on a graph of the residuals of these variables, let's analyze logarithms.

```
SET LLONP = LOG(LONP)
SET LNYP = LOG(NYP)
```

Our first step is to find a prewhitening model for the NYP.

```
CORR(PAR=PAR,NUM=30,QSTAT) LNYP
Correlations of Series LNYP
Autocorrelations
      1: 0.97658738 0.95364212 0.93397363 0.91758413 0.90343528 0.89034177
      7: 0.87789195 0.86078377 0.84211635 0.82560744 0.81210940 0.79900095
     13: 0.78578027 0.77039115 0.75443614 0.73786589 0.72331798 0.71037007
     19: 0.69981756 0.68969001 0.67920478 0.66720498 0.65731240 0.64640281
     25: 0.63335773 0.61728778 0.59961131 0.58366930 0.57046007 0.55486273
```

```
Partial Autocorrelations
     1:   0.9765874 -0.0017457  0.0591612  0.0622603  0.0466722  0.0269597
     7:   0.0204300 -0.0961331 -0.0369065  0.0282952  0.0437550 -0.0034708
    13:  -0.0031637 -0.0480019 -0.0067165 -0.0176279  0.0248820  0.0094377
    19:   0.0449320  0.0142789  0.0112337 -0.0234491  0.0483344 -0.0359263
    25:  -0.0560886 -0.0857448 -0.0533292  0.0138600  0.0485503 -0.0784480
Ljung-Box Q-Statistics
Q(30)  =        4848.8425.  Significance Level 0.00000000


CORR(PAR=PAR,NUM=30,QSTAT) LLONP
Correlations of Series LLONP
Autocorrelations
     1: 0.95143546 0.90696364 0.86678779 0.83737322 0.80835333 0.77950750
     7: 0.75044665 0.71934087 0.68359009 0.65221452 0.62528244 0.60751535
    13: 0.58441772 0.56048273 0.53261058 0.50257795 0.47790287 0.45823666
    19: 0.44784414 0.44312453 0.43638191 0.42794492 0.41251609 0.39750048
    25: 0.38362707 0.36443528 0.34574012 0.31804076 0.29538754 0.27563036
Partial Autocorrelations
     1:   0.9514355  0.0182990  0.0237562  0.0958325 -0.0003760 -0.0032326
     7:  -0.0043099 -0.0349971 -0.0671378  0.0207852  0.0234892  0.0779219
    13:  -0.0484047 -0.0096322 -0.0406534 -0.0501627  0.0334889  0.0278408
    19:   0.0832359  0.0740703  0.0118817  0.0073586 -0.0610065 -0.0247679
    25:  -0.0146509 -0.0929274 -0.0193649 -0.1010573  0.0312123  0.0353490
Ljung-Box Q-Statistics
Q(30)  =        2882.6381.  Significance Level 0.00000000
```

Both series appear to be Random Walks, let's prewhiten LNYP.

```
BOX(DIFF=1,CONSTANT) LNYP / RES
Dependent Variable LNYP - Estimation by Box-Jenkins
Iterations Taken     2
Usable Observations    259        Degrees of Freedom    258
Centered R**2       0.963616      R Bar **2    0.963616
Uncentered R**2     0.999965      T x R**2      258.991
Mean of Dependent Variable       3.5868606323
Std Error of Dependent Variable 0.1109175015
Standard Error of Estimate       0.0211570845
Sum of Squared Residuals         0.1154865342
Durbin-Watson Statistic             1.882075
Q(36-0)                             35.414953
Significance Level of Q              0.49622989
    Variable          Coeff        Std Error      T-Stat      Signif
*********************************************************************************
1.  CONSTANT      0.0001824436 0.0013146373      0.13878   0.88973333
```

This model appears to have white noise residuals, however, the constant is not significant.
Let's drop the constant.

```
BOX(DIFF=1) LNYP / ALPHA
Dependent Variable LNYP - Estimation by Box-Jenkins
Iterations Taken     2
Usable Observations    259        Degrees of Freedom    259
Centered R**2       0.963613      R Bar **2    0.963754
Uncentered R**2     0.999965      T x R**2      258.991
Mean of Dependent Variable       3.5868606323
Std Error of Dependent Variable 0.1109175015
Standard Error of Estimate       0.0211169894
Sum of Squared Residuals         0.1154951551
Durbin-Watson Statistic             1.881934
```

```
Q(36-0)                              35.414953
Significance Level of Q              0.49622989
 NO ESTIMATED COEFFICIENTS
```

A check for white noise:

```
CORR(PAR=PAR,NUM=21,qstat) ALPHA
Correlations of Series ALPHA
Autocorrelations
    1:  0.0493699 -0.0334178 -0.0971525 -0.1144429 -0.0292622 -0.0472286
    7:  0.1146662  0.0849777 -0.0719646  0.0164077 -0.0404791  0.0170308
   13:  0.0291363  0.0222733  0.0320220 -0.0444798  0.0000500 -0.0666583
   19: -0.1096947  0.0098966  0.0162665
Partial Autocorrelations
    1:  0.0493699 -0.0359428 -0.0940192 -0.1075490 -0.0266009 -0.0629503
    7:  0.0985573  0.0578250 -0.0884528  0.0357136 -0.0165594  0.0240640
   13:  0.0313884  0.0156295  0.0081965 -0.0235535  0.0178350 -0.0667523
   19: -0.1034258 -0.0020421 -0.0039108
Ljung-Box Q-Statistics
Q(21)  =        21.1349.  Significance Level 0.45073328
DISP 2/261**.5 = 0.12380
```

Thus, ALPHA is the prewhitened input series.

```
BOX(DIFF=1) LONP / BETA
Dependent Variable LONP - Estimation by Box-Jenkins
Iterations Taken     2
Usable Observations     259       Degrees of Freedom    259
Centered R**2      0.935422       R Bar **2    0.935671
Uncentered R**2    0.999472       T x R**2      258.863
Mean of Dependent Variable        20.551077220
Std Error of Dependent Variable   1.870312125
Standard Error of Estimate        0.474368790
Sum of Squared Residuals          58.281669000
Durbin-Watson Statistic            1.869935
Q(36-0)                           29.105824
Significance Level of Q           0.78554356
 NO ESTIMATED COEFFICIENTS
```

BETA is the prewhitened output series.

As a benchmark of how well the MARIMA model improves a model of London Prices, let's fit an ARIMA model to LLONP as a benchmark.

```
BOX(DIFF=1) LLONP / RES5
Dependent Variable LLONP - Estimation by Box-Jenkins
Iterations Taken     6
Usable Observations     259       Degrees of Freedom    259
Centered R**2      0.937042       R Bar **2    0.937285
Uncentered R**2    0.999941       T x R**2      258.985
Mean of Dependent Variable        3.0186877414
Std Error of Dependent Variable   0.0927080101
Standard Error of Estimate        0.0232168532
Sum of Squared Residuals          0.1396067685
Durbin-Watson Statistic            1.823736
Q(36-0)                           30.449072
Significance Level of Q           0.72955714
 NO ESTIMATED COEFFICIENTS
```

```
CORR(PAR=PAR,NUM=21,QSTAT) RES5
Correlations of Series RES5
Autocorrelations
     1:  0.0659039  0.0434133 -0.1399829 -0.0273692 -0.0373992  0.0446970
     7:  0.0122181  0.0603353 -0.0042419 -0.0277949 -0.0165215  0.0059619
    13: -0.0022443 -0.0104077  0.0598445 -0.0851846 -0.0801608 -0.0609812
    19: -0.1159229 -0.0495206  0.0393429
Partial Autocorrelations
     1:  0.0659039  0.0392404 -0.1461768 -0.0104582 -0.0222946  0.0309740
     7:  0.0047747  0.0482421 -0.0028574 -0.0306305  0.0049884  0.0097371
    13: -0.0084843 -0.0177202  0.0644184 -0.0978374 -0.0795526 -0.0239411
    19: -0.1316021 -0.0563127  0.0360879
Ljung-Box Q-Statistics
Q(21)  =          20.0302.  Significance Level 0.51934933
```

This a "best" univariate model of British Airways, now let's fit the MARIMA model.

```
CROSS(QSTAT) BETA ALPHA / -21 21
Cross Correlations of Series BETA and ALPHA
   -21:  0.0156291  0.0264731  0.0069393 -0.0904721 -0.0602107 -0.0342255
   -15: -0.0460029  0.0446499 -0.0112316  0.0096709  0.0479755 -0.0217252
    -9: -0.0385670 -0.0948908  0.0790038  0.0674325  0.0533171 -0.0902315
    -3: -0.0823670 -0.1539493  0.0049655  0.1209363  0.7685362  0.0794746
     3:  0.0229032 -0.0549638 -0.0892905 -0.0157105 -0.0591638  0.0689507
     9:  0.0513516  0.0004157 -0.0108648 -0.0225510  0.0202161 -0.0122255
    15:  0.0422409 -0.0099391 -0.0392013 -0.0610216 -0.0554319 -0.1150903
    21: -0.0425736
Ljung-Box Q-Statistics
Q(1 to 21)  =         169.9247.  Significance Level 0.00000000
Q(-21 to -1)=          22.5309.  Significance Level 0.36948752
Q(-21 to 21)=         196.2730.  Significance Level 0.00000000
```

These correlations confirm that the direction of influence is from BETA(t) to ALPHA(t+k). BETA (NY) influences ALPHA (LONDON) prices. These cross correlations suggest the following zero-order model with r=0, s=1, b=0:

```
BOX(DIFF=1,INPUT=1,VCV,APPLY,MA=1) LONP / RES4
#NYP 1 0 0
Dependent Variable LONP - Estimation by Box-Jenkins
Iterations Taken     8
Usable Observations    258      Degrees of Freedom    255
Centered R**2      0.976064     R Bar **2    0.975876
Uncentered R**2    0.999807     T x R**2      257.950
Mean of Dependent Variable    20.566779070
Std Error of Dependent Variable  1.856764439
Standard Error of Estimate      0.288391689
Sum of Squared Residuals       21.208290420
Durbin-Watson Statistic         1.987912
Q(36-1)                        40.165883
Significance Level of Q         0.25197295
   Variable          Coeff        Std Error      T-Stat      Signif
*******************************************************************
1.  MA{1}        -0.236476681  0.060863088    -3.88539   0.00013028
2.  N_NYP{0}      0.043236901  0.023703681     1.82406   0.06931355
3.  N_NYP{1}      0.484373395  0.023479199    20.62989   0.00000000
```

```
Covariance\Correlation Matrix of Coefficients
                   MA{1}          N_NYP{0}          N_NYP{1}
MA{1}        0.00370431549    0.0226718975    -0.0017849818
N_NYP{0}     0.00003270828    0.00056186450   -0.2664926582
N_NYP{1}    -0.00000255077   -0.00014831474    0.00055127279


CORR(NUM=21,QSTAT,PAR=PAR) RES4
Correlations of Series RES4
Autocorrelations
      1: -0.0005372 -0.0146099 -0.0901351  0.1091049  0.0438002  0.0535574
      7: -0.0831110 -0.0453223  0.0777710  0.0503121  0.0396076 -0.1091355
     13:  0.0386129 -0.0130834  0.0836134 -0.1003127 -0.0567947 -0.0113861
Partial Autocorrelations
      1: -0.0005372 -0.0146102 -0.0901702  0.1095887  0.0413302  0.0490565
      7: -0.0643120 -0.0493402  0.0781599  0.0247036  0.0462976 -0.0868114
     13:  0.0422730 -0.0230528  0.0461137 -0.0769810 -0.0546499  0.0138931
Ljung-Box Q-Statistics
Q(21) =           24.5558.  Significance Level 0.26691356


CROSS(QSTAT) RES4 ALPHA / -21 21
Cross Correlations of Series RES4 and ALPHA
   -21:  0.0058561  0.0274393  0.0243202  0.0429849 -0.0073601 -0.0721056
   -15: -0.0438479  0.0414838 -0.0570500 -0.0196230  0.0580618 -0.0035628
    -9: -0.1298781 -0.1026140 -0.0065156 -0.0003415  0.1682795 -0.0579226
    -3: -0.0012621 -0.1311649 -0.0002460 -0.0078342 -0.0237995  0.0713763
     3:  0.1096165  0.0553821 -0.0198264  0.0185868 -0.0452048 -0.0474051
     9: -0.0034071  0.0824433 -0.0016436 -0.0155069  0.0148698 -0.0666088
    15:  0.0116548 -0.0214945 -0.0179729 -0.0905541 -0.0103878 -0.0606098
    21: -0.0957421
Ljung-Box Q-Statistics
Q(1 to 21)  =         16.1946.  Significance Level 0.75861711
Q(-21 to -1)=         25.5632.  Significance Level 0.22359417
Q(-21 to 21)=         41.7738.  Significance Level 0.52446368
```

The model appears to past muster on these diagnostics checks.

MINICASES

These Minicase solutions will be available directly from the authors or you will be given directions to finding them on the author's website, http://forecast.umkc.edu. You can email the author at either delurgio@cctr.umkc.edu or sad@forecast.umkc.edu, at that time we can determine the best format for forwarding these.

CHAPTER 14
CYCLICAL FORECASTING METHODS

PROBLEMS

ESTIMATED DIFFICULTY

Elementary	Medium	Hard	Very Hard	Bad

1 M   2 M   3 M   4 M   5 M   6 M   7 M   8 M   9 E   10 M

11 E   12 E   13 E   14 M   15 E   16 H   17 V   18 M   19 <u>V-B</u> 20 H-V

21 V   22 H   23 H   24 H   25 V   26 V

Minicase difficulty depends on which part of the minicase is assigned, thus as explained below with the minicases, they can be Medium to Very hard.

14-1. In summary, the reasons for studying cyclical influences include the desire to better understand, analyze, predict, and control the cyclical influences on a company, industry, or economy; also, see pages 584 to 585 for a more in depth presentation of reasons.

14-2. They are recurrent but not periodic.

14-3. See pages 585 to 586 - prosperity, liquidation, recession (depression), and recovery as defined by Wesley Mitchell, others have defined six phases: growth prosperity, warning, recession, depression, and recovery.

14-4. The bottom-up approach is simply the use of regional economics to understand and predict the relationship among and between regional economies and there relationship to the national economy, see for example, the special interest box on page 591.

14-5. Because of the sinusoidal-like behavior of X_t, RX_t tends to lead X_t as shown in Table 14-7. Similarly, X_t might lead Y_t because of the lead-lag relationship of two sinusoidal-like series. Remind the student that these types of behavior do occur in composite indexes, but unfortunately, the length of the lead-lag can vary significantly and make it difficult to predict the turning points. When RX_t leads X_t and X_t leads Y_t, the RX_t will lead Y_t even more than X_t does.

14-6. A pressure cycle is the ratio of two moving totals, for example the most recent three-month total to the 12-month moving total of last year. In some cases these ratios lead actual movements in the time series using the same mechanism as ratio analysis. Also see pages 608 to 611.

14-7. RX and RY are defined in equations 14-2 and 14-3, they are the ratios of $100*X_t/X_{t-1}$ and $100*Y_t/Y_{t-1}$, the rate of change in each of these respectively. RXY_t is the rate of change ratio for $100*X_t/Y_t$. $RXRY_t$ is the ratio of the ratios $100*RX_t/Y_t$.

14-8. See page 604. These ratios may behave this way because cyclical indicators may behave with a sinusoidal pattern. When lead-lag relationships exist between the indicators, then the ratios of indicators may lead or lag the original cyclical indicator by a greater number of periods.

14-9. A diffusion index is the percentage or proportion of the components of an index, for example, the composite index of leading economic indicators that show an increase (decrease). Thus, if 6 out of 10 series in an index all show an increase, then the diffusion index is 60 percent.

14-10. A cyclical index is an index that reflects recurrent movement of a time series from it seasonal and trend values that are caused by business expansions and contractions. Cyclical indexes can be projected by the methods discussed on page 596, decomposition, isolation using seasonal differences, Fourier Series Analysis, MARIMA, paired indexes, company composite indexes, and pressure cycles.

14-11. Harvey's rule is "expect a recession two to five quarters (i.e., 6 to 15 months) after inversion of the term structure of interest rates from the normal upward sloping structure to a downward-sloping structure." The rule's use in forecasting is clear, however, the variation in the number of months between inversion and recession makes can vary greatly, 6 to 15 months; thus, Harvey's rule is a relatively crude rule of thumb that may or may not be effective in contingency planning.

14-12. The term structure of interest rates is the relationship between the yield of relatively equal risk debt instruments versus maturity dates; see Figure 14-3. The TSIR is used in Harvey's rule as well as other rules of thumb and models.

14-13. Sunspots affect weather, agriculture, and in modern times, telecommunications. Those economies that dependent on agricultural productivity can be adversely affected by sunspots.

14-14. Answers to this question are contingent on the pair of indicators chosen. See pages 587 and 588 for several explanations.

14-15. Because of the smooth transitions from growth to decline shown in Figure 14-6 a and b certain patterns exist in the ratio of X_t/X_{t-1}. For example, here the original series, X_t is increasing at an increasing rate and thus the ratio of X_t/X_{t-1} is increasing, however, as X_t increases at a decreasing rate, then the ratio of X_t/X_{t-1} start decreasing, and so on as shown in the middle of page 604 and Figure 14-6. Cyclical indicators may behave this way, but not assuredly.

14-16. Assuming no trend in this series, the fitted cyclical indexes are shown in the table below; note the cyclical downturn in year 3. The fit of cyclical indexes provide historical variations from trend-seasonal patterns of a time series, and to the extent that they reflect cyclical influences, they assist in understanding past variations and to a much less extent they assist in predicting future cyclical impacts. That is, these indexes are independent variables which must be forecast into the future in order to predict future values of the dependent variable (i.e., SeriesD). However, cyclical indexes have neither persistent trends or seasonality and thus are very difficult to forecast. The smoothed cyclical indexes below are three-period centered moving averages.

Trend Calculation

Period (t)	Actual (Yt)	Seasonal Index (S)	Deseasonalized (Yt/S)	(X*X)	(X*Y)	No Trend	Fit (S*T)	CYCLICAL-IRREGULAR Y/T*S
1	518	0.81747	633.6618	1	633.66	609.940	498.61	1.04
2	572	0.88500	646.3274	4	1,292.65	609.940	539.80	1.06
3	599	0.96456	621.0061	9	1,863.02	609.940	588.33	1.02
4	652	1.02264	637.5635	16	2,550.25	609.940	623.75	1.05
5	692	1.10920	623.8727	25	3,119.36	609.940	676.55	1.02
6	759	1.18836	638.6945	36	3,832.17	609.940	724.83	1.05
7	705	1.19561	589.6575	49	4,127.60	609.940	729.25	0.97
8	643	1.11253	577.9626	64	4,623.70	609.940	678.58	0.95
9	600	1.05416	569.1749	81	5,122.57	609.940	642.97	0.93
10	546	0.95289	572.9948	100	5,729.95	609.940	581.20	0.94
11	518	0.89517	578.6624	121	6,365.29	609.940	546.00	0.95
12	426	0.80241	530.9020	144	6,370.82	609.940	489.42	0.87
13	554	0.81747	677.7000	169	8,810.10	609.940	498.61	1.11
14	585	0.88500	661.0167	196	9,254.23	609.940	539.80	1.08
15	633	0.96456	656.2552	225	9,843.83	609.940	588.33	1.08
16	688	1.02264	672.7664	256	10,764.26	609.940	623.75	1.10
17	731	1.10920	659.0332	289	11,203.56	609.940	676.55	1.08
18	794	1.18836	668.1468	324	12,026.64	609.940	724.83	1.10
19	805	1.19561	673.2969	361	12,792.64	609.940	729.25	1.10
20	726	1.11253	652.5674	400	13,051.35	609.940	678.58	1.07
21	717	1.05416	680.1640	441	14,283.44	609.940	642.97	1.12
22	651	0.95289	683.1862	484	15,030.10	609.940	581.20	1.12
23	605	0.89517	675.8509	529	15,544.57	609.940	546.00	1.11
24	550	0.80241	685.4368	576	16,450.48	609.940	489.42	1.12
25	463	0.81747	566.3811	625	14,159.53	609.940	498.61	0.93
26	497	0.88500	561.5817	676	14,601.12	609.940	539.80	0.92
27	564	0.96456	584.7202	729	15,787.45	609.940	588.33	0.96
28	582	1.02264	569.1135	784	15,935.18	609.940	623.75	0.93
29	633	1.10920	570.6813	841	16,549.76	609.940	676.55	0.94
30	686	1.18836	577.2653	900	17,317.96	609.940	724.83	0.95
31	676	1.19561	565.4021	961	17,527.47	609.940	729.25	0.93
32	657	1.11253	590.5465	1,024	18,897.49	609.940	678.58	0.97
33	602	1.05416	571.0722	1,089	18,845.38	609.940	642.97	0.94
34	534	0.95289	560.4015	1,156	19,053.65	609.940	581.20	0.92
35	499	0.89517	557.4373	1,225	19,510.31	609.940	546.00	0.91
36	472	0.80241	588.2294	1,296	21,176.26	609.940	489.42	0.96
37	459	0.81747	561.4879	1,369	20,775.05	609.940	498.61	0.92
38	519	0.88500	586.4404	1,444	22,284.74	609.940	539.80	0.96
39	552	0.96456	572.2794	1,521	22,318.90	609.940	588.33	0.94
40	589	1.02264	575.9585	1,600	23,038.34	609.940	623.75	0.94
41	653	1.10920	588.7123	1,681	24,137.20	609.940	676.55	0.97

14-3

42	684	1.18836	575.5824	1,764	24,174.46	609.940	724.83	0.94
43	766	1.19561	640.6775	1,849	27,549.13	609.940	729.25	1.05
44	678	1.11253	609.4224	1,936	26,814.59	609.940	678.58	1.00
45	649	1.05416	615.6576	2,025	27,704.59	609.940	642.97	1.01
46	582	0.95289	610.7747	2,116	28,095.64	609.940	581.20	1.00
47	537	0.89517	599.8875	2,209	28,194.71	609.940	546.00	0.98
48	475	0.80241	591.9682	2,304	28,414.47	609.940	489.42	0.97
SUM			48	29,257.6	38,024	707,550		0.07018

Forecast Error

Fit (S*T)	CYCLICAL IRREGULAR Y/T*S	SMOOTHED CYCLICAL 3CMAV	FITTED VALUES TCS	ERROR Y-TCS ERROR	SQUARED ERRORS
498.61	1.04	1.04	518.00	-2.71E-03	7.3314E-06
539.80	1.06	1.04	560.79	1.12E+01	125.578091
588.33	1.02	1.04	612.46	-1.35E+01	181.304087
623.75	1.05	1.03	641.69	1.03E+01	106.317772
676.55	1.02	1.04	702.54	-1.05E+01	111.134463
724.83	1.05	1.01	733.70	2.53E+01	639.873694
729.25	0.97	0.99	719.88	-1.49E+01	221.477828
678.58	0.95	0.95	644.08	-1.08E+00	1.16243807
642.97	0.93	0.94	604.43	-4.43E+00	19.6258981
581.20	0.94	0.94	546.59	-5.87E-01	0.34440965
546.00	0.95	0.92	502.06	1.59E+01	254.157889
489.42	0.87	0.98	478.04	-5.20E+01	2707.99736
498.61	1.11	1.02	509.45	4.45E+01	1984.44401
539.80	1.08	1.09	588.52	-3.52E+00	12.3689518
588.33	1.08	1.09	639.84	-6.84E+00	46.7807133
623.75	1.10	1.09	677.69	1.03E+01	106.291325
676.55	1.08	1.09	739.45	-8.45E+00	71.3557139
724.83	1.10	1.09	792.43	1.57E+00	2.46492109
729.25	1.10	1.09	794.69	1.03E+01	106.37823
678.58	1.07	1.10	743.92	-1.79E+01	321.177534
642.97	1.12	1.10	708.36	8.64E+00	74.5657988
581.20	1.12	1.11	647.71	3.29E+00	10.822902
546.00	1.11	1.12	610.05	-5.05E+00	25.4936705
489.42	1.12	1.05	515.59	3.44E+01	1183.89101
498.61	0.93	0.99	494.13	-3.11E+01	969.310054
539.80	0.92	0.94	505.24	-8.24E+00	67.925626
588.33	0.96	0.94	551.54	1.25E+01	155.188185
623.75	0.93	0.94	587.85	-5.85E+00	34.2751813
676.55	0.94	0.94	634.85	-1.85E+00	3.43983038
724.83	0.95	0.94	678.69	7.31E+00	53.3974784
729.25	0.93	0.95	690.75	-1.47E+01	217.529651

678.58	0.97	0.94	640.45	1.65E+01	273.787892
642.97	0.94	0.94	605.09	-3.09E+00	9.56970558
581.20	0.92	0.92	536.45	-2.45E+00	5.99163215
546.00	0.91	0.93	509.07	-1.01E+01	101.455836
489.42	0.96	0.93	456.61	1.54E+01	236.805096
498.61	0.92	0.95	473.09	-1.41E+01	198.418374
539.80	0.96	0.94	507.46	1.15E+01	133.136927
588.33	0.94	0.95	557.74	-5.74E+00	32.9014258
623.75	0.94	0.95	592.09	-3.09E+00	9.56918376
676.55	0.97	0.95	643.43	9.57E+00	91.5865136
724.83	0.94	0.99	714.99	-3.10E+01	960.167593
729.25	1.05	1.00	727.60	3.84E+01	1474.49136
678.58	1.00	1.02	691.90	-1.39E+01	193.293223
642.97	1.01	1.00	645.09	3.91E+00	15.2622376
581.20	1.00	1.00	580.09	1.91E+00	3.63735252
546.00	0.98	0.99	537.89	-8.86E-01	0.78431074
489.42	0.97	0.99	482.15	-7.15E+00	51.0987382

SUM	0.07018	47.97	29276.24	7.64E-01	13608.03

Sum of squared errors	13608.03
Residual Standar Error	19.718
Standard deviation of series	93.27
R-square	95.53%

14-17. This problem can be solved different ways depending on what previous chapters were covered. Three different, but essentially identical solutions are shown below, using Cochrane-Orcutt, OLS, and MARIMA estimation procedures. Students may struggle to achieve models with white noise residuals because the exact lag between Y_t and X_t is some place between 7 to 9 periods. Nonetheless, the peak cross correlation occurs at lag 8, $Y_t = f(X_{t-8})$ as shown below. The relationship is very valid because this is the way in which the data was contrived.

```
Correlation Matrix
          X                Y
X 1.000000000000 0.042083018479
Y 0.042083018479 1.000000000000

Cross Correlations of Series X and Y
  -25: -0.6890271 -0.7336703 -0.7492566 -0.7343660 -0.6888180 -0.6136951
  -19: -0.5113422 -0.3852897 -0.2401417 -0.0814023  0.0847241  0.2515882
  -13:  0.4123425  0.5602427  0.6889124  0.7926332  0.8665836  0.9070636
   -7:  0.9116738  0.8794356  0.8108705  0.7079998  0.5743062  0.4146075
   -1:  0.2348914  0.0420830 -0.1586658 -0.3493670 -0.5226556 -0.6720041
    5: -0.7919734 -0.8784036 -0.9285608 -0.9412133 -0.9166515 -0.8566451
   11: -0.7643402 -0.6441052 -0.5013278 -0.3421768 -0.1733379 -0.0017353
   17:  0.1657566  0.3225843  0.4627734  0.5811549  0.6735569  0.7369447
   23:  0.7695183  0.7707566  0.7414053
```
The peak correlation appears at lag = 8
```
Autocorrelations of Series X
    1:  0.9705095  0.9031099  0.8012388  0.6696496  0.5141893  0.3415454
    7:  0.1589571 -0.0260869 -0.2061561 -0.3741740 -0.5236982 -0.6491693
   13: -0.7461122 -0.8112920 -0.8428249 -0.8402227 -0.8043755 -0.7374925
```

```
 19: -0.6429807 -0.5252798 -0.3896550 -0.2419641 -0.0884158  0.0647022
 25:  0.2112726
Autcorrelations of Series Y
  1:  0.9717416  0.9055435  0.8048069  0.6742558  0.5197038  0.3478163
  7:  0.1658061 -0.0188569 -0.1987541 -0.3668196 -0.5166118 -0.6425667
 13: -0.7401992 -0.8062605 -0.8388412 -0.8374277 -0.8028779 -0.7373639
 19: -0.6442500 -0.5279331 -0.3936304 -0.2471610 -0.0946896  0.0575371
 25:  0.2034410
```

A Cochrane-Orcutt Solution with lags at 7, 8, and 9.

```
ar1 y / res2
#constant x{7 8 9}
Dependent Variable Y - Estimation by Cochrane-Orcutt
Annual Data From 11:01 To 100:01
Usable Observations       90      Degrees of Freedom      85
Centered R**2       1.000000     R Bar **2    1.000000
Uncentered R**2     1.000000     T x R**2       90.000
Mean of Dependent Variable       97.719111111
Std Error of Dependent Variable 34.740028968
Standard Error of Estimate        0.003502530
Sum of Squared Residuals          0.0010427561
Durbin-Watson Statistic           2.039579
Q(22-1)                          18.462599
Significance Level of Q           0.61957116
```

Variable	Coeff	Std Error	T-Stat	Signif
1. Constant	-1.068137575	0.184161968	-5.79999	0.00000011
2. X{7}	0.351781295	0.046190615	7.61586	0.00000000
3. X{8}	0.454172671	0.090540096	5.01626	0.00000285
4. X{9}	0.204724716	0.046191091	4.43213	0.00002768
5. RHO	0.274308290	0.104852390	2.61614	0.01052251

A OLS Regression Solution with lags at 7, 8, and 9.

```
Dependent Variable Y - Estimation by Least Squares
Annual Data From 10:01 To 100:01
Usable Observations       91      Degrees of Freedom      87
Centered R**2       1.000000     R Bar **2    1.000000
Uncentered R**2     1.000000     T x R**2       91.000
Mean of Dependent Variable       98.243736264
Std Error of Dependent Variable 34.907105601
Standard Error of Estimate        0.003620644
Sum of Squared Residuals          0.0011404887
Durbin-Watson Statistic           1.449992
Q(22-0)                          32.416620
Significance Level of Q           0.07056535
```

Variable	Coeff	Std Error	T-Stat	Signif
1. Constant	-1.144100021	0.228025985	-5.01741	0.00000275
2. X{7}	0.370887876	0.057196464	6.48445	0.00000001
3. X{8}	0.416723121	0.112112783	3.71700	0.00035595
4. X{9}	0.223826575	0.057196551	3.91329	0.00018029

```
Autocorrelations of Series RES2
  1:  0.2647005  0.1690819  0.1655022  0.1262225 -0.1613454 -0.0775473
  7: -0.1308003 -0.1987140 -0.1175836 -0.0724951  0.0512810  0.0573595
 13:  0.1753192  0.0249826  0.1084633  0.0487786  0.0981996  0.0319236
 19:  0.0615086 -0.0180589 -0.0385549 -0.0664781
```

A MARIMA Solution with lags at 7, 8, and 9.

```
box(input=1,diff=1,apply,ma=1,iter=40) y / res1
#x 2 0 7
Dependent Variable Y - Estimation by Box-Jenkins
Iterations Taken    25
Annual Data From 11:01 To 100:01
Usable Observations      90     Degrees of Freedom      86
Centered R**2     1.000000     R Bar **2    1.000000
Uncentered R**2   1.000000     T x R**2      90.000
Mean of Dependent Variable      97.719111111
Std Error of Dependent Variable 34.740028968
Standard Error of Estimate       0.003644311
Sum of Squared Residuals         0.0011421663
Durbin-Watson Statistic          1.808832
Q(22-1)                          23.931904
Significance Level of Q          0.29636970
   Variable          Coeff        Std Error      T-Stat      Signif
*****************************************************************************
1.   MA{1}        -0.758458722   0.070640839    -10.73683   0.00000000
2.   N_X{7}        0.365940048   0.050483819      7.24866   0.00000000
3.   N_X{8}        0.426406484   0.098956091      4.30905   0.00004341
4.   N_X{9}        0.218889694   0.050484615      4.33577   0.00003930

Autocorrelations of Series RES1
    1:   0.0710375   0.0154574   0.0845575   0.0850729  -0.2469274  -0.1066325
    7:  -0.1377082  -0.2098253  -0.0997437  -0.0870584   0.0471522   0.0490142
   13:   0.1822125  -0.0371200   0.0853956   0.0258555   0.0737164   0.0073914
   19:   0.0676708  -0.0184918  -0.0250841  -0.0642462
```

14-18. See the discussion on the bottom of page 607 and top of page 608.

14-19. **Without some direction, this is an extremely difficult** and time consuming problem to solve unless the student is directed to estimate a model using a specific method and cautioned not to expect a statistically significant model. There is no easy and effective way to model the lead-lag between these two variables. Models which pass muster on statistical significance and valid diagnostics do not yield a model of practical value. That is, significant lags can be found at several lags including those between 12 to 14, however, in all cases the independent variable leadi910.dat does not explain much variance, thus, any resulting model has very limited forecasting significance. Methods that can be tried include, OLS, Cochrane-Orcutt, MARIMA, Fourier Series Analysis, and while not developed in this text, Vector AutoRegression models. The first four approaches did not yield models that were useful in predicting $Lagg_t = f(Lead_{t-k})$. The analyst has the age-old problem of modeling a time series where shifts in the lead-lag relationship occur during different time periods. Also, these time series are extremely long, and thus may require different models for different time segments. Also, GARCH and ARCH models may be necessary to validly model some time segments. These problem persists whether logs are used or not.

14-20. As shown it the figure and the table that follow, the lag between the pressure cycles of the leading and lagging indicators varies considerably between 12 to 18 months. This lead-lag relationship can be used to better predict the movement of the lagging indicator or the industries that lag the economy. Unfortunately, these indicators are not synonymous with economic conditions in commodity, product, and financial markets, thus, to judge the significance of these in a specific forecasting setting we must see how strong the relationship is between the market and changes in these indicators.

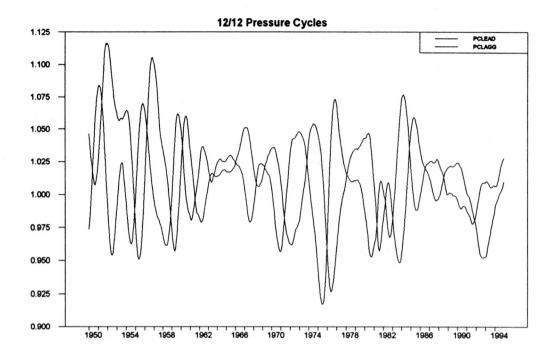

12/12 Pressure Cycles

```
set tlead 12 564 = lead(t-11)+lead(t-10)+lead(t-9)+lead(t-8)+lead(t-7)+lead(t-
6)+lead(t-5) + lead(t-4)+lead(t-3)+lead(t-2)+lead(t-1)+lead
set tlagg 12 564 = lagg(t-11)+lagg(t-10)+lagg(t-9)+lagg(t-8)+lagg(t-7)+lagg(t-
6)+lagg(t-5)+ lagg(t-4)+lagg(t-3)+lagg(t-2)+lagg(t-1)+lagg
set pclead 24 564 = tlead/tlead(t-12)
set pclagg 24 564 = tlagg/tlagg(t-12)
cross pclagg pclead
Cross Correlations of Series PCLAGG and PCLEAD
Monthly Data From 3:01 To 47:12
    -21: -0.0232464 -0.0580113 -0.0973929 -0.1413922 -0.1896311 -0.2414065
    -15: -0.2958209 -0.3516794 -0.4074728 -0.4614365 -0.5114241 -0.5552010
     -9: -0.5905641 -0.6153296 -0.6278831 -0.6267249 -0.6108370 -0.5795866
     -3: -0.5329165 -0.4712420 -0.3955573 -0.3075186 -0.2071999 -0.1000602
      3:  0.0105992  0.1213731  0.2290212  0.3303393  0.4225181  0.5031689
      9:  0.5706451  0.6238605  0.6619920  0.6850441  0.6933306  0.6879992
     15:  0.6705964  0.6430578  0.6073792  0.5657303  0.5203138  0.4732508
     21:  0.4262579  0.3805368  0.3371569  0.2967889  0.2602716  0.2278500
```

```
print 200 360 pclead pclagg
 ENTRY          PCLEAD          PCLAGG
 1964:07  1.0251732572360  1.0186574942673
 1964:08  1.0252109382942  1.0187402394586
 1964:09  1.0250430903376  1.0187168555683
 1964:10  1.0248761249874  1.0188992731049
 1964:11  1.0254288597376  1.0182459050384
 1964:12  1.0263873501863  1.0172824174687
 1965:01  1.0274454609430  1.0172574144880
 1965:02  1.0280983442047  1.0172307057367
 1965:03  1.0290552048893  1.0169927909372
```

```
1965:04    1.0293029302930    1.0169613486842
1965:05    1.0297523961661    1.0174466338259
1965:06    1.0297957149975    1.0176229508197    ** Peak in Leading Indicator
1965:07    1.0291281439507    1.0183157679321
1965:08    1.0279623202776    1.0191108840061
1965:09    1.0268051434224    1.0200061243238
1965:10    1.0261470152935    1.0205870362821
1965:11    1.0253887030112    1.0221950722867
1965:12    1.0244333235208    1.0249237029502
1966:01    1.0232876712329    1.0267167817960
1966:02    1.0226451927770    1.0286033066234
1966:03    1.0221010612404    1.0303797468354
1966:04    1.0219588029538    1.0322450217325
1966:05    1.0209424083770    1.0342949364535
1966:06    1.0198374298432    1.0370519532823
1966:07    1.0184505409583    1.0400924437299
1966:08    1.0168804861580    1.0431207380666
1966:09    1.0150274540025    1.0458320824577
1966:10    1.0116346153846    1.0483323347314
1966:11    1.0075815738964    1.0504980079681
1966:12    1.0032567049808    1.0508188585608
1967:01    0.9993306559572    1.0513505491244    ** Peak in the Lagging I., 19
1967:02    0.9950367471604    1.0511783847747    periods after the Leading I.
1967:03    0.9899028386359    1.0510073710074
1967:04    0.9851682829435    1.0498433215825
1967:05    0.9819563152896    1.0472986151746
1967:06    0.9798842394914    1.0443689320388
1967:07    0.9790382244143    1.0404791807555    ** Leading Indicator Trough
1967:08    0.9797951052931    1.0359546241107
1967:09    0.9812090727911    1.0318629796192
1967:10    0.9842220321262    1.0279100781101
1967:11    0.9880941042004    1.0229449132455
1967:12    0.9928394118770    1.0189855483140
1968:01    0.9969380920486    1.0149632975720
1968:02    1.0020143884892    1.0119136960600
1968:03    1.0081793687452    1.0089769964466
1968:04    1.0135109052307    1.0071821658427
1968:05    1.0179883945841    1.0067045348729
1968:06    1.0211097124044    1.0062285023705
1968:07    1.0231544274365    1.0061281337047    ** Lagging Trough, 12 periods
1968:08    1.0232355503921    1.0075167037862    after the Leading Indicator
1968:19    1.0234065190057    1.0085311572700
1968:10    1.0235634958957    1.0095449911964    ** Leading Indicator Peak
1968:11    1.0234239444766    1.0118639354899
1968:12    1.0224060005770    1.0141824249166
1969:01    1.0224589691909    1.0173388966157
1969:02    1.0213478843576    1.0198386947251
1969:03    1.0194712226782    1.0220574606117
1969:04    1.0187583317463    1.0239859233191
1969:05    1.0177655329660    1.0256220516141
1969:06    1.0167852062589    1.0275314116778
1969:07    1.0155288324969    1.0296234772979
1969:08    1.0151386129246    1.0305793497283
1969:09    1.0139873357906    1.0319051121736
1969:10    1.0111331257666    1.0335964751239
1969:11    1.0077234623717    1.0346248969497
1969:12    1.0041384499624    1.0354629375743
1970:01    0.9989674270159    1.0355450236967
1970:02    0.9937201237229    1.0356331242614
1970:03    0.9885778485161    1.0360899528473    ** Lagging Peak, 17 periods
```

```
1970:04    0.9822413309655    1.0353622139821    after Leading Indicator
1970:05    0.9764771772613    1.0337301587302
1970:06    0.9717403469502    1.0311994245639
1970:07    0.9678321678322    1.0283230259030
1970:08    0.9640227421008    1.0255608186612
1970:19    0.9602945288470    1.0220974783926
1970:10    0.9580106373052    1.0180284191829
1970:11    0.9568183942425    1.0138114209827    ** Leading Indicator Trough
1970:12    0.9572873735481    1.0088269044046
1971:01    0.9599699304642    1.0032564689315
1971:02    0.9644406715714    0.9975423505661
1971:03    0.9703570413865    0.9909854717311
1971:04    0.9779236844609    0.9852375960867
1971:05    0.9854698403594    0.9803699179899
1971:06    0.9924176984356    0.9756735547999
1971:07    0.9992292870906    0.9720212673233
1971:08    1.0058977085952    0.9690631808279
1971:09    1.0132970979326    0.9668729840467
1971:10    1.0206486802377    0.9647561720318
1971:11    1.0276448178177    0.9628853375251
1971:12    1.0333659491194    0.9625514043223
1972:01    1.0377838684417    0.9621019387666
1972:02    1.0407823960880    0.9619005719314    ** Lagging Trough, 15 periods
1972:03    1.0423579933633    0.9630839883423    after Leading Indicator
1972:04    1.0426194414712    0.9652451458463
1972:05    1.0427781550102    0.9676070125478
1972:06    1.0433268858801    0.9712243074173
1972:07    1.0442537601234    0.9735473457676
1972:08    1.0457516339869    0.9746402877698
1972:09    1.0469348659004    0.9755657740510
1972:10    1.0476190476190    0.9772131295777
1972:11    1.0481939163498    0.9793216034827    ** Leading Indicator Peak
1972:12    1.0480068175362    0.9806381238069
1973:01    1.0472552348613    0.9847724993161
1973:02    1.0463258785942    0.9900292718624
1973:03    1.0450374531835    0.9946813388354
1973:04    1.0436770881941    0.9991733259851
1973:05    1.0421395348837    1.0032189828014
1973:06    1.0398591027067    1.0066249539934
1973:07    1.0365617209861    1.0112369899604
1973:08    1.0316176470588    1.0168850341391
1973:09    1.0264409881061    1.0231977818854
1973:10    1.0214975405356    1.0291477745905
1973:11    1.0161421964270    1.0350990924245
1973:12    1.0105710155403    1.0419911012236
1974:01    1.0052238133838    1.0462037037037
1974:02    0.9992815446789    1.0488773907419
1974:03    0.9944449422095    1.0507974555177
1974:04    0.9896271125816    1.0518477661335
1974:05    0.9850040167812    1.0532636596993
1974:06    0.9801212337315    1.0542961608775    ** Lagging Peak, 19 periods
1974:07    0.9752382648971    1.0540122051189       after the Leading Indicator
1974:08    0.9707769066287    1.0535341620543
1974:09    0.9650592744451    1.0522084725860
1974:10    0.9583556268950    1.0506203920158
1974:11    0.9506470325747    1.0486713787242
1974:12    0.9434957532409    1.0458144293212
1975:01    0.9362960308216    1.0427471457651
1975:02    0.9304394715557    1.0392001409443
1975:03    0.9242274078746    1.0359712230216
```

```
1975:04    0.9204843227614  1.0309386470897
1975:05    0.9178069777979  1.0241100182784
1975:06    0.9172351068668  1.0153459337611  ** Leading Indicator Trough
1975:07    0.9184400401863  1.0067404078811
1975:08    0.9219897209985  0.9974162432176
1975:09    0.9288814999538  0.9872092025067
1975:10    0.9383083651252  0.9773213521609
1975:11    0.9509951182876  0.9671529732958
1975:12    0.9657917179949  0.9564477713508
1976:01    0.9832535885167  0.9469529791207
1976:02    1.0011590843234  0.9390523014326
1976:03    1.0188145837395  0.9319952574526
1976:04    1.0325905565917  0.9279416751441
1976:05    1.0445300157978  0.9263131055584  ** Lagging Trough, 11 periods
1976:06    1.0546355974219  0.9281871744514   after Leading Indicator.
1976:07    1.0632458233890  0.9311587982833
1976:08    1.0692813059924  0.9353251014593
1976:09    1.0725862583275  0.9411304347826
1976:10    1.0734827449425  0.9471103327496
1976:11    1.0720631786772  0.9533345095272
1976:12    1.0690737833595  0.9601565279260
1977:01    1.0623844282238  0.9668369633414
1977:02    1.0548962855765  0.9732803755190
1977:03    1.0480336809875  0.9794638800545
1977:04    1.0432550622683  0.9848346427919
1977:05    1.0392286605539  0.9893568217268
1977:06    1.0353516359534  0.9931002759890
1977:07    1.0308641975309  0.9963126843658
1977:08    1.0270899273878  0.9993537666174
1977:09    1.0238249745063  1.0018479164742
1977:10    1.0212471131640  1.0043454142012
1977:11    1.0189686924494  1.0074951420376
```

14-21 a. As shown by the following graph, the leading economic indicator normally leads its pressure cycle but sometimes appears to lag it, thus, the pressure cycle is not always useful in predicting changes in the Leading Economic Indicator. The top trace in the following figure is the PCLEAD, the series with the pronounced trend is LEAD.

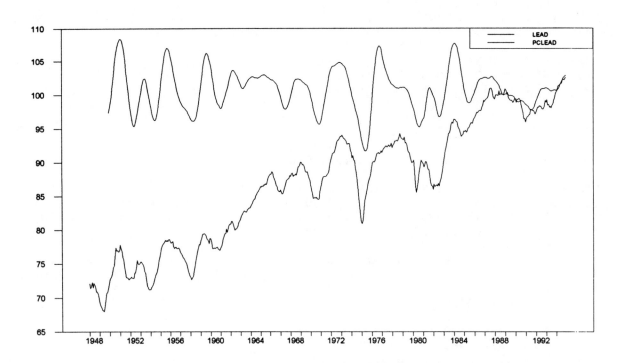

b. a. As shown by the following graph, the lagging economic indicator (the trending series) normally leads its pressure cycle, thus, the pressure cycle is not useful in predicting changes in the Lagging Economic Indicator.

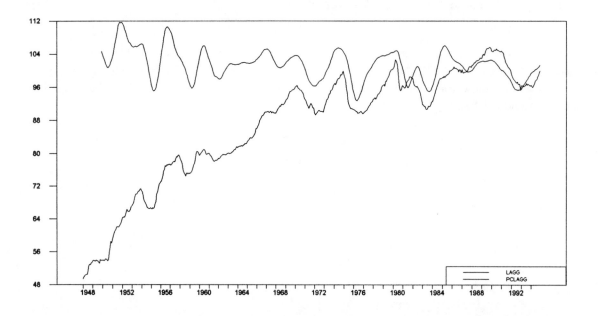

c. As shown in the figure below, the PC of the Leading Indicator (the top series) leads the lagging indicator by many months. You might ask the students to verify the lead-lag using actual numbers for 1978 onward as shown in the listing of actual values following the figure.

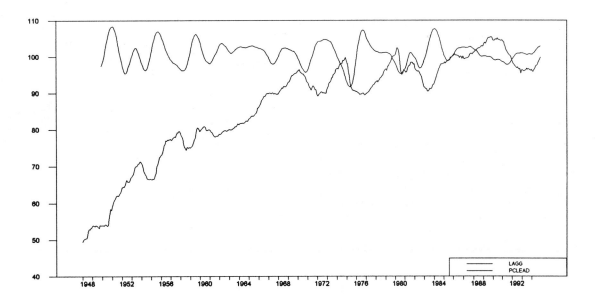

ENTRY	LAGG	PCLEAD	
1964:08	82.00000000000	102.52109382942	
1964:09	82.10000000000	102.50430903376	
1964:10	82.40000000000	102.48761249874	
1964:11	82.30000000000	102.54288597376	
1964:12	82.40000000000	102.63873501863	
1965:01	82.80000000000	102.74454609430	
1965:02	83.10000000000	102.80983442047	
1965:03	83.30000000000	102.90552048893	
1965:04	83.60000000000	102.93029302930	
1965:05	83.80000000000	102.97523961661	
1965:06	83.70000000000	102.97957149975	** Peak in PCLEAD
1965:07	83.70000000000	102.91281439507	
1965:08	84.00000000000	102.79623202776	
1965:09	84.20000000000	102.68051434224	
1965:10	84.50000000000	102.61470152935	
1965:11	84.90000000000	102.53887030112	
1965:12	85.90000000000	102.44333235208	
1966:01	86.00000000000	102.32876712329	
1966:02	86.50000000000	102.26451927770	
1966:03	86.70000000000	102.21010612404	
1966:04	87.30000000000	102.19588029538	
1966:05	88.00000000000	102.09424083770	
1966:06	88.30000000000	101.98374298432	
1966:07	88.80000000000	101.84505409583	
1966:08	89.10000000000	101.68804861580	
1966:09	89.10000000000	101.50274540025	
1966:10	89.20000000000	101.16346153846	
1966:11	89.80000000000	100.75815738964	
1966:12	89.90000000000	100.32567049808	
1967:01	89.90000000000	99.93306559572	
1967:02	89.90000000000	99.50367471604	
1967:03	90.10000000000	98.99028386359	** Peak in Lagging Indicator
1967:04	90.00000000000	98.51682829435	21 months after PCLEAD peak.
1967:05	89.80000000000	98.19563152896	
1967:06	90.10000000000	97.98842394914	
1967:07	90.10000000000	97.90382244143	** Trough in PCLEAD

```
1967:08    89.70000000000    97.97951052931
1967:09    89.90000000000    98.12090727911
1967:10    89.90000000000    98.42220321262
1967:11    89.60000000000    98.80941042004
1967:12    89.80000000000    99.28394118770
1968:01    89.60000000000    99.69380920486   ** Trough in Lagging Indicator
1968:02    90.10000000000   100.20143884892      6 mos. after PCLEAD trough.
1968:03    90.40000000000   100.81793687452
1968:04    90.80000000000   101.35109052307
1968:05    91.10000000000   101.79883945841
1968:06    91.40000000000   102.11097124044
1968:07    91.30000000000   102.31544274365
1968:08    91.80000000000   102.32355503921
1968:09    91.80000000000   102.34065190057
1968:10    91.70000000000   102.35634958957   ** Peak in PCLEAD
1968:11    91.90000000000   102.34239444766
1968:12    92.20000000000   102.24060005770
1969:01    92.70000000000   102.24589691909
1969:02    93.00000000000   102.13478843576
1969:03    93.10000000000   101.94712226782
1969:04    93.70000000000   101.87583317463
1969:05    94.20000000000   101.77655329660
1969:06    94.80000000000   101.67852062589
1969:07    94.80000000000   101.55288324969
1969:08    95.00000000000   101.51386129246
1969:09    95.20000000000   101.39873357906
1969:10    95.40000000000   101.11331257666
1969:11    95.40000000000   100.77234623717
1969:12    95.60000000000   100.41384499624
1970:01    96.00000000000    99.89674270159
1970:02    96.10000000000    99.37201237229
1970:03    96.40000000000    98.85778485161   ** Peak in Lagging Indicator
1970:04    95.90000000000    98.22413309655      17 months after PCLEAD peak.
1970:05    95.60000000000    97.64771772613
1970:06    95.50000000000    97.17403469502
1970:07    95.20000000000    96.78321678322
1970:08    95.20000000000    96.40227421008
1970:09    94.80000000000    96.02945288471
1970:10    94.60000000000    95.80106373052
1970:11    94.20000000000    95.68183942425   ** Trough in PCLEAD
1970:12    93.40000000000    95.72873735481
1971:01    93.00000000000    95.99699304642
1971:02    92.70000000000    96.44406715714
1971:03    92.20000000000    97.03570413865
1971:04    91.50000000000    97.79236844609
1971:05    91.40000000000    98.54698403594
1971:06    90.80000000000    99.24176984356
1971:07    91.40000000000    99.92292870906
1971:08    92.00000000000   100.58977085952
1971:09    91.90000000000   101.32970979326
1971:10    91.40000000000   102.06486802377
1971:11    90.90000000000   102.76448178177
1971:12    90.90000000000   103.33659491194
1972:01    89.60000000000   103.77838684417
1972:02    89.20000000000   104.07823960880   ** Trough in Lagging Indicator
1972:03    89.50000000000   104.23579933633      16 mos. after PCLEAD trough.
1972:04    89.70000000000   104.26194414712
1972:05    90.00000000000   104.27781550102
1972:06    90.30000000000   104.33268858801
1972:07    90.30000000000   104.42537601234
```

```
1972:08     90.10000000000  104.57516339869
1972:09     90.10000000000  104.69348659004
1972:10     90.10000000000  104.76190476190
1972:11     90.00000000000  104.81939163498  ** Peak in PCLEAD
1972:12     89.90000000000  104.80068175362
1973:01     90.80000000000  104.72552348613
1973:02     91.50000000000  104.63258785942
1973:03     91.90000000000  104.50374531835
1973:04     92.80000000000  104.36770881941
1973:05     93.00000000000  104.21395348837
1973:06     93.50000000000  103.98591027067
1973:07     94.20000000000  103.65617209861
1973:08     94.30000000000  103.16176470588
1973:09     95.10000000000  102.64409881061
1973:10     95.20000000000  102.14975405356
1973:11     95.50000000000  101.61421964270
1973:12     96.30000000000  101.05710155403
1974:01     96.60000000000  100.52238133838
1974:02     96.80000000000   99.92815446789
1974:03     96.50000000000   99.44449422095
1974:04     97.20000000000   98.96271125816
1974:05     97.70000000000   98.50040167812
1974:06     98.00000000000   98.01212337315
1974:07     98.00000000000   97.52382648971
1974:08     98.20000000000   97.07769066287
1974:09     98.90000000000   96.50592744451  ** Peak in Lagging Indicator
1974:10     98.80000000000   95.83556268950     22 months after PCLEAD peak.
1974:11     99.10000000000   95.06470325747
1974:12     99.80000000000   94.34957532409
1975:01     99.20000000000   93.62960308216
1975:02     98.30000000000   93.04394715557
1975:03     97.60000000000   92.42274078746
1975:04     96.00000000000   92.04843227614
1975:05     94.70000000000   91.78069777979
1975:06     92.50000000000   91.72351068668  ** Trough in PCLEAD
1975:07     91.90000000000   91.84400401863
1975:08     91.30000000000   92.19897209985
1975:09     90.80000000000   92.88814999538
1975:10     90.80000000000   93.83083651252
1975:11     90.70000000000   95.09951182876
1975:12     90.60000000000   96.57917179949
1976:01     90.50000000000   98.32535885167
1976:02     90.40000000000  100.11590843234
1976:03     90.30000000000  101.88145837395
1976:04     90.10000000000  103.25905565917
1976:05     90.00000000000  104.45300157978
1976:06     89.60000000000  105.46355974219
1976:07     89.70000000000  106.32458233890
1976:08     89.70000000000  106.92813059924
1976:09     89.90000000000  107.25862583275
1976:10     90.10000000000  107.34827449425
1976:11     89.80000000000  107.20631786772
1976:12     89.50000000000  106.90737833595  ** Trough in Lagging Indicator
1977:01     89.60000000000  106.23844282238     18 mos. after PCLEAD trough.
1977:02     89.90000000000  105.48962855765
1977:03     90.00000000000  104.80336809875
1977:04     90.20000000000  104.32550622683
1977:05     90.30000000000  103.92286605539
1977:06     90.80000000000  103.53516359534
1977:07     91.00000000000  103.08641975309
```

```
1977:08    91.40000000000  102.70899273878
1977:09    91.70000000000  102.38249745063
1977:10    92.10000000000  102.12471131640
1977:11    92.30000000000  101.89686924494
1977:12    92.40000000000  101.66116005874
1977:12    92.40000000000  101.66116005874
```

d. See the answer to question 14-20 for this solution. The most useful relationships are between the PCLAGG and PCLEAD and PCLEAD and LAGG. However, these relationships are only useful in an actual application when the variable we want to forecast is related to these indicators with a sufficiently long and consistent lag so that turning points can be anticipated with some useful precision.

14-22. Answers to this question are contingent on the indicators chosen. When assigning this question, recognize that students can generate their own spreadsheets solutions to these problems fairly easily.

14-23. As shown in the figure below, the ratio of the coincident to lagging economic indicators (RCL) is often, but not always leading or coincident with the index of leading economic indicators (LEAD). The RCL is the series with the lower slope, while that of LEAD is has the higher slope and ends in the upper right hand corner.

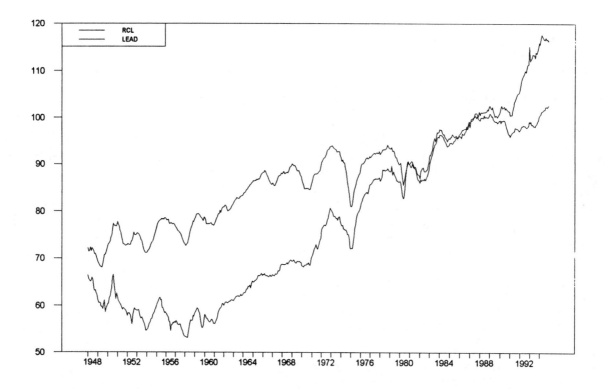

14-24. As shown in the figure above and below, the ratio of the coincident to lagging economic indicators (RCL) is often, but not always leading or coincident with the index of leading economic indicators (LEAD) and thus, RCL (the middle series at first, then top figure after the intersection) is most often a better leading indicator than LEAD (the top series at first then the bottom series after the intersection).

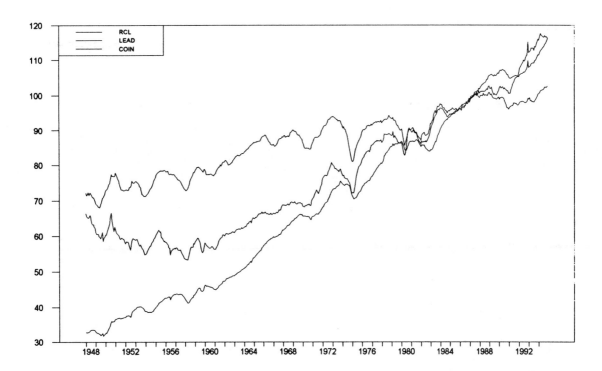

14-25   a. For retail.dat, the composite index of leading indicators would seem to be useful in predicting changes in retail sales.   In particular the average weekly hours worked WORKHR1.DAT, UCLAIM5.DAT, MANFIL92.DAT, PLTEQP20.DAT, and PRIHOU29.DAT would seem to be likely candidates for specific leading indicators of retail sales. However, the ratio of the coincident to lagging indicator may be a better leading indicator as shown in the graph below.

b. As shown in the following figure, the Ratio of the Coincident to Lagging indicator appears to predict the turning points of the rather erratic three period moving average of deseasonalized logarithmic retail sales (smodsale). Also, shown in the figure are the PC for sales and the index of Composite Leading Economic Indicators.

c. The MFSTable is very much dependent on what models have been fitted in previous chapters.

```
set lsales = log(sales)
```
Deseasonalize the sales
```
set dlsales 1969:01 1978:12 = lsales - lsales(t-12)
```
Scaling deseasonalized sales for a better comparison.
```
set sdlsales = 1000*dlsales
```
There is too much randomness in deseasonalized sales, let's using a 3-month mavg.
```
set smodsale = (sdlsales+sdlsales(t-1)+sdlsales(t-2))/3
```

Let create PCs for Sales and the Leading Indicator
```
set tlead 12 564 = lead(t-11)+lead(t-10)+lead(t-9)+lead(t-8)+lead(t-7)+lead(t-
6)+lead(t-5)$
+ lead(t-4)+lead(t-3)+lead(t-2)+lead(t-1)+lead
set tsales 1969:01 1978:12 = sales(t-11)+sales(t-10)+sales(t-9)+sales(t-
8)+sales(t-7)+sales(t-6)+sales(t-5)$
+ sales(t-4)+sales(t-3)+sales(t-2)+sales(t-1)+sales
set pclead 24 564 = 100*tlead/tlead(t-12)
```

```
set pcsales 1970:01 1978:12 = 100*tsales/tsales(t-12)
```

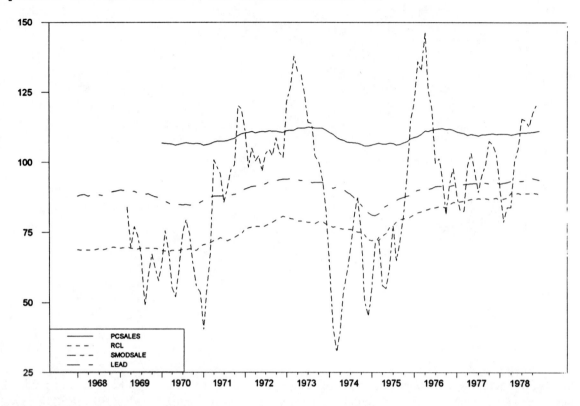

14-26. a. For superoil.dat, the composite index of leading indicators would seem to be useful in predicting changes in sales, however, sales of crude oil and other oil products should itself be a leading economic indicator, thus it would seem that the ratio of the coincident to lagging indicator would be a better leading indicator. Let's see if there is any cyclical pattern in the series by analyzing smoothed deseasonalized values, asales. As shown in the following figure, there appears to be some cyclical pattern in the time series. However, as discussed in b. we can not relate this pattern to the composite indexes.

```
set ssales 13 108 = sales - sales(t-12)
set asales 16 108 = (ssales + ssales(t-1) + ssales(t-2) + ssales(t+1) +
ssales(t+2))/5
```

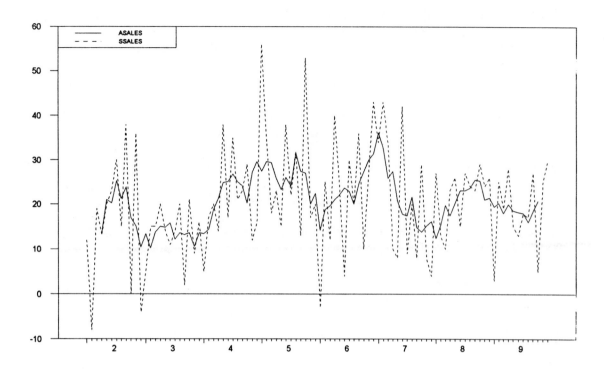

b. Unfortunately, in absolute terms, this series is not dated, so it is not possible to relate it to other economic variables; thus, we cannot answer parts b. and c.

MINICASES

The list of minicases in the textbook has an error in it. The listing of minicases below is the correct designation and the same order as other chapter. As always, be cautious in assigning minicase exercises, depending on your purpose, you may want to assign only part a) (speculation) or b) (fitting a cyclical model), and possibly not part c) (filling out the Master Forecasting Summary Table). Because the solutions to this assignment are very much dependent on the data bases available to the students and your purpose in assigning these minicases, no solutions are provided here. In addition, recognize that some minicases are time series that are undated in absolute terms, thus, it is not possible to fit cyclical relationships of these undated series to national, regional, or local economic indicators like the composite indicators shown before problem 14-19; nonetheless, the student can speculate on leading indicators in answering part a).

MINICASE 14-1. Kansas Turnpike, Monthly Data.

This series is dated, but only three years of data exist. Nonetheless, the student can speculate on leading indicators in answering part a).

MINICASE 14-2. Domestic Air Passengers by Quarter.

This series is dated and offers a very good example for using quarterly economic data as leading indicators in answering part a).

MINICASE 14-3. Hospital Census by Month.

This series is dated, but reflects regional economic influences more than the previous time series.

MINICASE 14-4. Henry Machler's Hideaway Orchids.

While this series is dated, there is not good prospects of finding regional or national leading economic indicators, nonetheless, the student can speculate on possible relationships in answering part a).

MINICASE 14-5. Your Forecasting Project.

MINICASE 14-6. Midwestern Building Materials.

To maintain confidentiality of the company that supplied this data, this data is undated, nonetheless, the student can speculate on possible relationships in answering part a).

MINICASE 14-7. International Airline Passengers.

This widely used time series can be used very successfully in this exercise if economic data can be found as far back as 1949. Nonetheless, the student can speculate on possible relationships in answering part a).

MINICASE 14-8. Automobile Sales.

This data is undated, nonetheless, the student can speculate on possible relationships in answering part a).

MINICASE 14-9. Consumption of Distilled Spirits.

This series is dated and offers a very good example for using quarterly economic data as leading indicators. Questions a), b), and c) of this assignment can be completed using this data.

MINICASE 14-10. Discount Consumer Electronics.

This data is undated, nonetheless, the student can speculate on possible relationships in answering part a).

CHAPTER 15
TECHNOLOGICAL AND QUALITATIVE FORECASTING METHODS

PROBLEMS

ESTIMATED DIFFICULTY

Elementary		Medium		Hard		Very Hard		Bad		
1 M	2 M	3 M	4 E	5 E	6 E	7 M	8 E	9 E	10 E	
11 M	12 H	13 E	14 H	15 H	16 M	17 H	18 M	19 M	20 M	
21 M	22 M	23 H	24 H	25 H	26 H	27 H	28 H	29 H	30 H	
31 H	32 H	33 H	34 H	35 M	36 M	37 M	38 M	39 M	40 M	41 H

15-1. The four different general approaches to long-term forecasting methods surveyed here are subjective methods, exploratory methods, normative methods, and S-growth curves, these are defined on pages 628, 632, 641, and 643 respectively.

15-2. Same response as question 15-1.

15-3 As discussed on page 625, subjective judgment is the primary input to these methods because there is little relevant numeric data because the past data may not exist or the forecasts are so far into the future that past data is irrelevant.

15-4. As discussed on page 625, the term technology is meant in its broadest meaning, the technology of products, services, processes, systems, market behavior, scientific developments, and sociological phenomena.

15-5. Page 629 discusses the characteristics including face to face discussion, diversity of the jury, simplicity, biased discussions when those of authority are present during discussions, and that there may possibly be no easy way to reach a consensus or convergence of ideas.

15-6. Page 630 discusses the advantages and disadvantages of the sales force composite method including: advantages; surveys of those close to the market in a timely fashion, the diversity of a bottom-up projection, the use of aggregating methods for combining the bottom and top down estimates: disadvantages; the optimism or pessimism of the sales force, the biases introduced by sales commission and compensation plans, the microeconomic focus of the sales force which might result in overlooking important macroeconomic trends and cyclical influences.

15-7. Page 631 very briefly discusses marketing research and survey methods. Marketing research is not a subjective method, but instead is characterized by objective, scientific methods for researching questions about marketing matters such as the affects of changes in prices, products, places (i.e., distribution channels), and promotions. It differs primarily in its use of the scientific method and objectivity.

15-8. Page 633 and 634 discuss the steps of scenario analysis.

15-9. The advantages of scenario analysis are discussed on pages 634 and 635.

15-10. The bottom of page 636 and the top of page 638 discuss the Delphi method.

15-11. Figure 15-1 can be viewed as stacked S-curves as shown in Figure 15-4 except each position of the stacked S-curves is projected onto a single "standardized" curve showing the maturity of each of the identified technologies, thus CIM is the most immature technology while automated materials handling is the most mature.

15-12. A contrast of the characteristics of the logistics and Gompertz curves is discussed on the bottom of pages 651 and top of page 652.

15-13. The biggest difference between the Delphi and Jury of Executive Opinion approaches is in the possible biases that result from open, real-time discussion between participants in the Jury of Executive Opinion method. Thus, there is a tendency with the Jury of Executive Opinion to have less than objective, unbiased, and free thinking/input. In addition, there is a tendency to have more tolerance of differences of opinion in the final "write-up" of results with the Delphi methodology.

15-14. The answers to problems 15-14 and 15-15 are very similar. Video Telephones have been around for more than a decade but have not been successful. It seems this product has not been successful for a number of reasons including the initial fixed cost of the product (you need two video telephones to communicate), the variable cost of long distance service, and the limited number of people with which you can use these phones (i.e., there has not been a "bandwagon" effect as yet). Clearly, the demand, price elasticity of demand, and best promotional strategy should be estimated using some combination of subjective, exploratory, normative, S-curves, and market research methods. Consumer focus groups can be used for subjective and exploratory estimates of desired product costs and features. Clearly, complementary and competing technologies such as the internet and web-TVs have to be considered in estimating market issues. A variety of market research methods can be used to estimate the demand, price, product features, place, and promotional methods that should be used to have a successful product. Just as was true for the Cellular mobile telephone, cross impact analysis of related technologies can have dramatic impacts on the success of video telephones. It seems likely, because of web-TV, that video telephones may have a very small, if non-existent life cycles. The video telephone/web-TV relationship may be analogous to the fate of the standalone word processors that have lingered at discount stores for years because of the declining cost and increasing capabilities of PCs. In contrast, some might argue that web-TVs provide a market for the CCD device of image capturing devices we see in inexpensive camcorders. These CCDs are the image capturing transducers placed on the web-TV or PC. Now we have to consider that Cable TV companies and even our local electric utility company into the competitive market, and these may dramatically alter the way in which telecommunications takes place in our homes.

15-15. Cellular mobile telephones have been around for more than two decades and have been successful. Clearly, price elasticity of demand should be estimated using some combination of subjective, exploratory, normative, S-curves, and market research methods. Consumer focus groups can be used for subjective and exploratory estimates of desired product costs and features. Clearly, complementary and competing technologies such as the wide acceptance of inexpensive electronic gadgets have to be considered in estimating market issues. The advent of micro- electronics, improvements in design and capabilities of communications devices suggest that cross impact analysis is important in estimating the demand for cellular phones; that cross impact analysis of related technologies have had dramatic impacts on the success of cellular phones. Also, there has been a heightened concern about personal safety as the number of random murders has increased dramatically in the 1980s and early 1990s. These suggest the need for greater security in the lives of wives and daughters. A variety of market research methods can be used to estimate the demand, price, product features, place, and promotional methods that should be used to have a successful product. Many did not anticipate the extraordinary demand for cellular phones because they did not anticipate the cross impact of crime, technological improvements, deregulation of the telecommunications industry, and other important causal trends.

15-16. Survey research, focus groups, other survey methods, and sociological and political references and research can be used to estimate the acceptability of a party's platform. Obviously, a survey of existing party members can be used to measure the acceptability of the platform. However, this survey will be biased, thus survey's of competing party members and the general voting population should be considered. Obviously, we must assure that a SIRS (a simple independent random sample) has been taken of the target population.

15-17. While on the market in some geographic areas, the global mobile phone system will soon be available in a many more areas. This system makes it possible to send and receive phone calls at any site on the face of the earth using direct satellite connections. This product must compete with other telecommunications methods primarily traditional long distance service and cellular mobile phones. Thus, issues such as prices of competing products, price elasticity of demand, consumer surveys, customer demands for specific technological capabilities. Initially, the Delphi, survey of executives, surveys of consumers, focus groups, and other surveys can be used to estimate the price elasticity of demand. In addition, forecasting of this product's technological capabilities as well as the capabilities of competing technologies and products should be estimated. Thus, subjective, exploratory, normative, and S-curves might be used to estimate different aspects of this product's demand relationship. In addition, the costs and product features of other products such as cellular mobile radios can be used with analogy methods to better estimate the profile of market demands.

15-18. See page 638 for a definition of forecasting using analogies. Video phones and standalone word processors may be an analogy, Web-TVs and color TV adoption rates, High Definition TVs and color TV adoption. Still Digital Camera and Camcorder adoptions.

15-19. Relevance trees are a hierarchical representation of events and decisions that are necessary to achieve some desired future. This method is used to identify the relative importance (i.e., importance weight) of different decisions and events in achieving some desired future. Martino illustrates two relevance trees. One relevance tree is used to manage the development of the major components needed to produce a new type of automobile, the components of the automobile are the branches of the tree and weights can be assigned to the branches in proportion to their importance in achieving the desired type of automobile. Another tree illustrates the components and events needed to produce an electric automobile

15-20. The series NUPOWER.DAT is a time series of the world wide nuclear electricity generating capacity measured in gigawatts. The accurate assessment of an S-curse was and still is difficult because of the very complex problems of nuclear power plants. The regulatory, environment, and economic consequences of nuclear power plants are complex. For example, the following have made S-curve estimation difficult: the control problems (e.g., Chernobyl), environment consequences of accidents (Chernobyl and Three-Mile Island diasters) and waste disposal, and the recently developed lower cost electricity sources (e.g., the efficiency of smaller plants has increased dramatically lately) including new developments in solar and turbine powered peak electricity providers.

15-21. The answer to this and several questions of this chapter are highly subjective, thus, all may not agree with the following answer, lower case x of secondary source, upper case X for primary.

	Expert Opinions	Quantitative Methods	Both
a. Technological Success of New Drug	X	X	X
b. Sales of a new Drug	X	X	X
c. Federal Judge's response to patent	X		
d. A New Product Line	X	X	X
e. A New Market (geographic)	X	X	X

15-22. The greater the sharing of information in earlier discussions the better, thus a setting which fosters debate and differing opinions will yield a more objective discussion. Thus, initially there should be no push for an immediate consensus and therefore forecasts and rationales from each member should be encouraged. Then, a final forecast can be generated, hopefully consisting of an objective composite forecast.

NOTE CONCERNING PROBLEMS 15-23 TO 15-34

To help you choose which of the following series to analyze, each problem has a graph to illustrate the fit of the selected method. Note that several of these time series have maximum levels that are difficult to estimate, thus, student solutions will vary. These problems can be used several different ways to illustrate:
1) how difficult it is to apply S-curves when accurate estimates of the maximum level L is unknown,
2) how difficult it is to apply S-curves when the form of the relationship (i.e., Gompertz vs logistics vs other curvilinear relationships) is unknown,
3) that many markets and technologies develop as a series of S-curves.

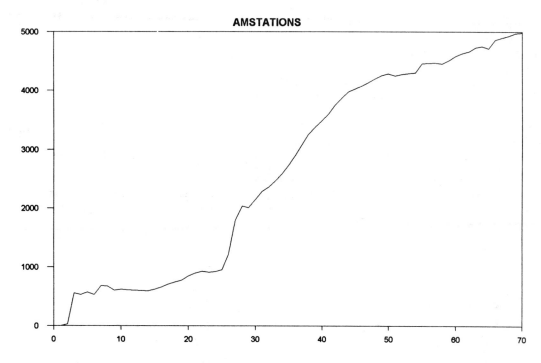

AMSTATIONS

This series seems to consist of a series of S-curves. Obviously this complicates the analysis.
Extreme Values of Series **STATIONS**:

```
Minimum Value is      1.0000000000 at 1921:01   Entry 1
Maximum Value is 4987.0000000000 at 1990:01   Entry 70
```

A value of 6000 will be chosen as the maximum level of the Gompertz and Logistics curves.

```
set gy = log(log(6000/stations))
set ly = log(stations/(6000-stations))
```

As shown below, the curves fit fairly well when using 1928 onward.

```
linreg gy 1928:01 1990:01 resg
#constant time
Dependent Variable GY - Estimation by Least Squares
Usable Observations      63      Degrees of Freedom    61
Centered R**2       0.969051     R Bar **2    0.968544
Uncentered R**2     0.974362     T x R**2       61.385
Mean of Dependent Variable       -0.395751542
Std Error of Dependent Variable   0.876484496
Standard Error of Estimate        0.155452306
Sum of Squared Residuals          1.4740905807
Regression F(1,61)                  1909.9964
Significance Level of F             0.00000000
Durbin-Watson Statistic             0.100443
Q(15-0)                           238.759348
Significance Level of Q             0.00000000
   Variable           Coeff       Std Error      T-Stat      Signif
*********************************************************************
1.  Constant        1.439994352  0.046346089    31.07046   0.00000000
2.  TIME           -0.047070408  0.001077040   -43.70351   0.00000000
```

```
linreg ly 1928:01 1990:01 resl
#constant time
Dependent Variable LY - Estimation by Least Squares
Usable Observations      63      Degrees of Freedom      61
Centered R**2      0.947621      R Bar **2    0.946762
Uncentered R**2    0.948283      T x R**2        59.742
Mean of Dependent Variable    -0.149888648
Std Error of Dependent Variable  1.335068136
Standard Error of Estimate     0.308044493
Sum of Squared Residuals       5.7883759911
Regression F(1,61)             1103.5862
Significance Level of F        0.00000000
Durbin-Watson Statistic        0.075942
Q(15-0)                        273.338403
Significance Level of Q        0.00000000
   Variable          Coeff        Std Error      T-Stat      Signif
***************************************************************************
1.  Constant      -2.915019642  0.091839470    -31.74038  0.00000000
2.  TIME           0.070900795  0.002134263     33.22027  0.00000000

set ply = ly - resl
set pgy = gy - resg
```

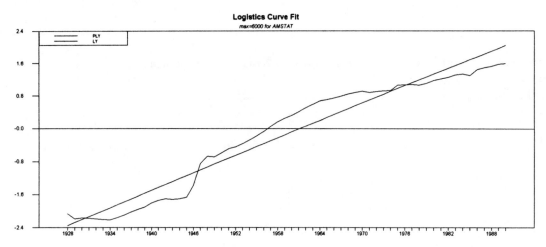

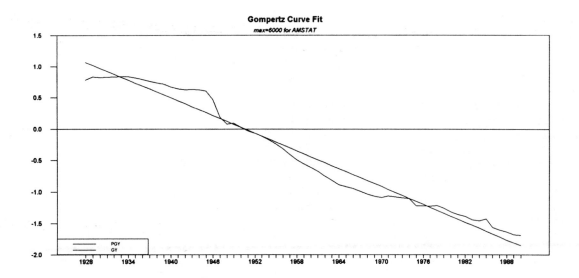

Gompertz Curve Fit
max=6000 for AMSTAT

15-24. FMSTAT.DAT

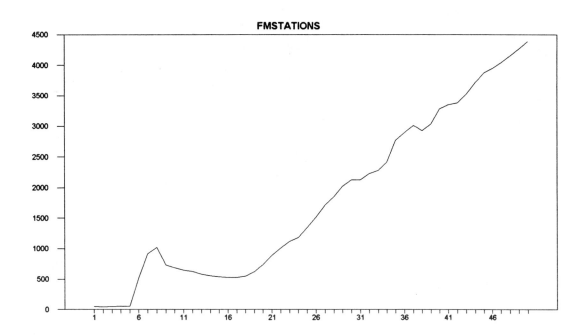

FMSTATIONS

This series seems to consist of a series of S-curves. Obviously this complicates the analysis.
```
Extreme Values of Series STATIONS
Minimum Value is    42.0000000000 at 2:01   Entry 2
Maximum Value is 4392.0000000000 at 50:01   Entry 50
```

A value of 6000 will be chosen as the maximum level.

```
set gy = log(log(6000/stations))
set ly = log(stations/(6000-stations))
```

As shown below, both curves have approximately the same fit when using observation 15 onward.

```
linreg gy 15 50   resg
#constant time
Dependent Variable GY - Estimation by Least Squares
Usable Observations     36      Degrees of Freedom     34
Centered R**2       0.994802    R Bar **2   0.994649
Uncentered R**2     0.994845    T x R**2        35.814
Mean of Dependent Variable      -0.056680382
Std Error of Dependent Variable  0.632344990
Standard Error of Estimate       0.046254324
Sum of Squared Residuals         0.0727417258
Regression F(1,34)                  6507.4123
Significance Level of F             0.00000000
Durbin-Watson Statistic              0.719216
Q(9-0)                              17.829449
Significance Level of Q             0.03720459
     Variable           Coeff        Std Error      T-Stat      Signif
*************************************************************************
1.  Constant          1.888878386  0.025320041     74.60013  0.00000000
2.  TIME             -0.059863347  0.000742090    -80.66853  0.00000000

linreg ly 15 50 resl
#constant time
Dependent Variable LY - Estimation by Least Squares
Annual Data From 15:01 To 50:01
Usable Observations     36      Degrees of Freedom     34
Centered R**2       0.982123    R Bar **2   0.981598
Uncentered R**2     0.986491    T x R**2        35.514
Mean of Dependent Variable      -0.583680807
Std Error of Dependent Variable  1.041077226
Standard Error of Estimate       0.141227802
Sum of Squared Residuals         0.6781399288
Regression F(1,34)                  1867.9257
Significance Level of F             0.00000000
Durbin-Watson Statistic              0.218084
Q(9-0)                              69.513458
Significance Level of Q             0.00000000
     Variable           Coeff        Std Error      T-Stat      Signif
*************************************************************************
1.  Constant         -3.766323196  0.077309394    -48.71754  0.00000000
2.  TIME              0.097927458  0.002265816     43.21951  0.00000000

set ply = ly - resl
set pgy = gy - resg
```

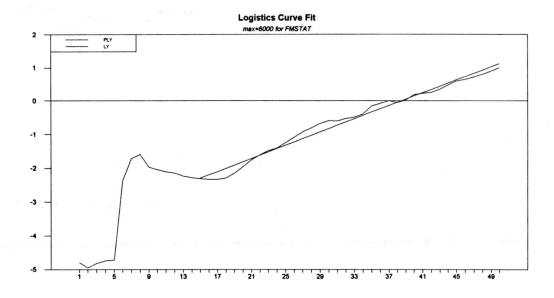

Logistics Curve Fit
max=6000 for FMSTAT

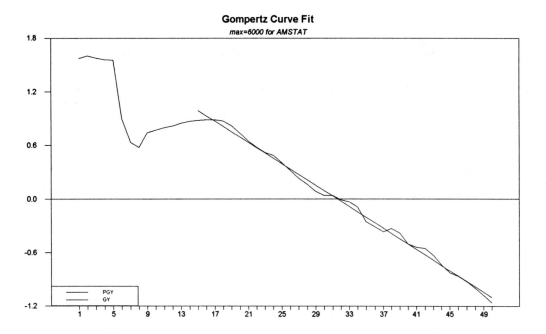

Gompertz Curve Fit
max=6000 for AMSTAT

15-25. TVSTAT.DAT

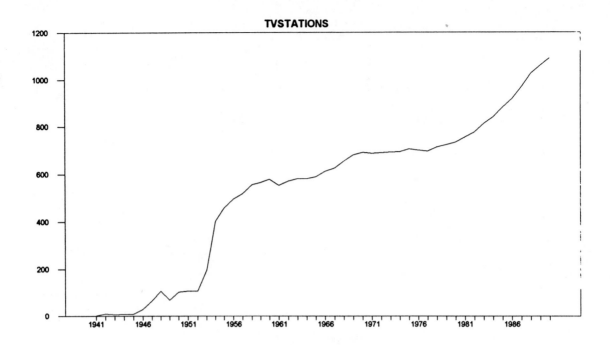

TVSTATIONS

Based on full series analysis and graphs, we will analyze 1970 onward. This series seems to consist of a series of S-curves. Obviously this complexes the analysis.

```
Extreme Values of Series STATIONS
Annual Data From 1941:01 To 1990:01
Minimum Value is    2.0000000000 at 1941:01  Entry 1
Maximum Value is 1092.0000000000 at 1990:01  Entry 50
```

A value of 1300 will be chosen as the maximum level.

```
set gy = log(log(1300/stations))
set ly = log(stations/(1300-stations))
```

The Gompertz curves appears somewhat.

```
set time = t
linreg gy / resg
#constant time
Dependent Variable GY - Estimation by Least Squares
Annual Data From 1941:01 To 1990:01
Usable Observations      50      Degrees of Freedom     48
Centered R**2      0.883728      R Bar **2    0.881306
Uncentered R**2    0.884296      T x R**2      44.215
Mean of Dependent Variable      -0.061257142
Std Error of Dependent Variable  0.883325868
Standard Error of Estimate       0.304323534
Sum of Squared Residuals         4.4454150394
Regression F(1,48)                 364.8259
Significance Level of F            0.00000000
Durbin-Watson Statistic            0.127159
Q(12-0)                          144.654790
Significance Level of Q            0.00000000
    Variable        Coeff        Std Error      T-Stat       Signif
********************************************************************
1.  Constant     1.391326078   0.087383248     15.92211   0.00000000
2.  TIME        -0.056964048   0.002982346    -19.10042   0.00000000
```

```
PRJ FGY
linreg ly / resl
#constant time
Dependent Variable LY - Estimation by Least Squares
Annual Data From 1941:01 To 1990:01
Usable Observations      50      Degrees of Freedom      48
Centered R**2       0.759261     R Bar **2    0.754246
Uncentered R**2     0.797346     T x R**2      39.867
Mean of Dependent Variable       -0.815592505
Std Error of Dependent Variable   1.900475850
Standard Error of Estimate        0.942133746
Sum of Squared Residuals         42.605567810
Regression F(1,48)                    151.3865
Significance Level of F            0.00000000
Durbin-Watson Statistic              0.139966
Q(12-0)                            131.090348
Significance Level of Q            0.00000000
    Variable           Coeff       Std Error      T-Stat      Signif
***********************************************************************
1.  Constant        -3.712394129  0.270523628   -13.72299  0.00000000
2.  TIME             0.113600064  0.009232835    12.30392  0.00000000
```

PRJ FLY
```
set pgy = gy - resg
set pgy = exp(exp(fgy))
```
The following is the logistics constant a. a = exp(-a')
```
disp exp(3.71239413) = 40.95173
```
The logistics slope b equals b'
```
set plog = 1300/(1+40.95173*exp(-0.113600064*time))
```
"a" for Gompertz = exp(a) from gy, b = -b'
```
disp exp(1.391326078) = 4.02018
set pgom = 1300*exp(-4.02018*exp(-0.056964048*time))
```

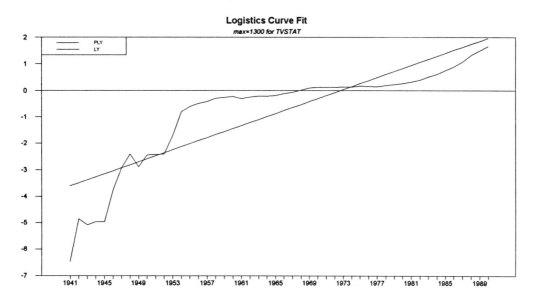

Logistics Curve Fit
max=1300 for TVSTAT

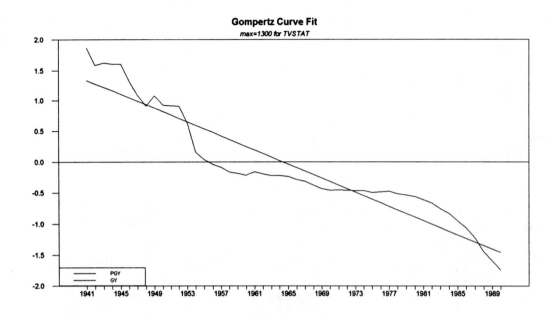

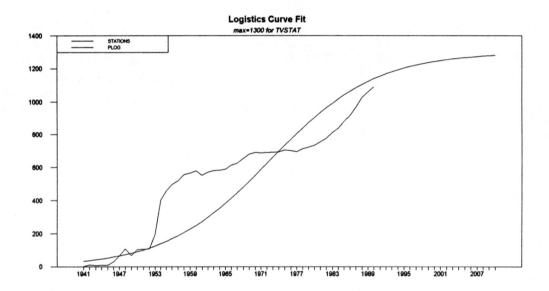

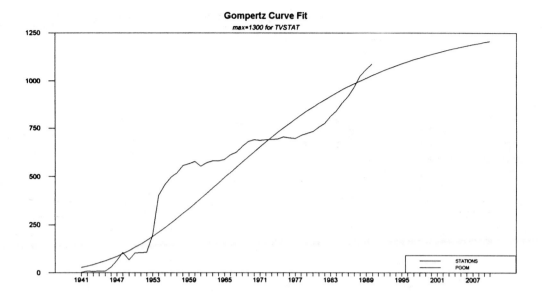

Gompertz Curve Fit

max=1300 for TVSTAT

15-26.   RADIOHH.DAT   The maximum level L was chosen to be 100,000(000), however, from these results this number is likely too low. This illustrates the problem in choosing L and its effect on forecasts. As formulated, neither model will ever have a forecast of more than 100,000,000. This problem might better be approached as a saturation   problem where the number of households is modeled and the saturation rate (i.e., estimate of the proportion of households with one or more radios) is modeled as an S-growth curve. From the following graphs and fit statistics, the   curve fits the data better than the   curve.

```
ext househ
Extreme Values of Series HOUSEH
Annual Data From 1921:01 To 1989:01
Minimum Value is    60.000000000 at 1921:01   Entry 1
Maximum Value is 94400.000000000 at 1989:01   Entry 69
```

A value of 100,000 will be chosen as the maximum level.

```
set gy = log(log(100000/househ))
set ly = log(househ/(100000-househ))
set time = t
linreg gy /  resg
#constant time
Dependent Variable GY - Estimation by Least Squares
Annual Data From 1921:01 To 1989:01
Usable Observations       69       Degrees of Freedom     67
Centered R**2       0.938971     R Bar **2    0.938060
Uncentered R**2     0.944924     T x R**2      65.200
Mean of Dependent Variable       -0.335044042
Std Error of Dependent Variable   1.026573505
Standard Error of Estimate        0.255491381
Sum of Squared Residuals          4.3734816712
Regression F(1,67)                  1030.8336
Significance Level of F             0.00000000
Durbin-Watson Statistic             0.066592
Q(17-0)                           183.834973
Significance Level of Q            0.00000000
   Variable          Coeff       Std Error      T-Stat      Signif
**********************************************************************
```

```
1.  Constant        1.400362285  0.062189870     22.51753  0.00000000
2.  TIME           -0.049583038  0.001544326    -32.10660  0.00000000
```

```
PRJ FGY
linreg ly / resl
#constant time
Dependent Variable LY - Estimation by Least Squares
Annual Data From 1921:01 To 1989:01
Usable Observations       69      Degrees of Freedom       67
Centered R**2      0.828377     R Bar **2     0.825816
Uncentered R**2    0.834556     T x R**2         57.584
Mean of Dependent Variable      -0.343014443
Std Error of Dependent Variable  1.788007893
Standard Error of Estimate       0.746232249
Sum of Squared Residuals        37.309792123
Regression F(1,67)                 323.3910
Significance Level of F           0.00000000
Durbin-Watson Statistic            0.147699
Q(17-0)                           70.812834
Significance Level of Q           0.00000002
   Variable          Coeff        Std Error      T-Stat      Signif
***********************************************************************
1.  Constant      -3.182035376  0.181642474    -17.51812  0.00000000
2.  TIME           0.081114884  0.004510624     17.98307  0.00000000
PRJ FLY
set ply = ly - resl
set pgy = gy - resg
```

The following is the logistics constant a = exp(-a).

```
disp exp(3.182035376) = 24.09575
```

The logistics slope b equals 0.081114884

```
set plog = 100000/(1+24.09575*exp(-0.081114884*time))
graph(head="Logistics Curve Fit", sub="max=100,000 for HHRADIO") 2
#househ
#plog
```

The Gompertz constant a = exp(a') and the slope b equals -b'

```
disp exp(1.400362285) = 4.05667
set pgom = 100000*exp(-4.05667*exp(-0.049583038*time))
```

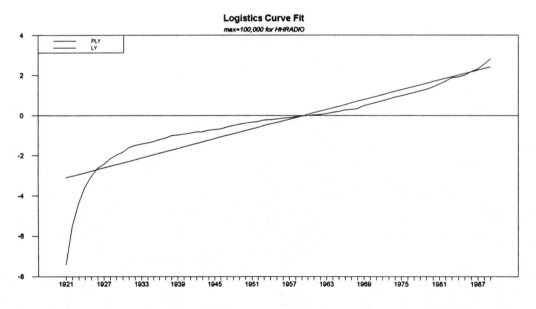

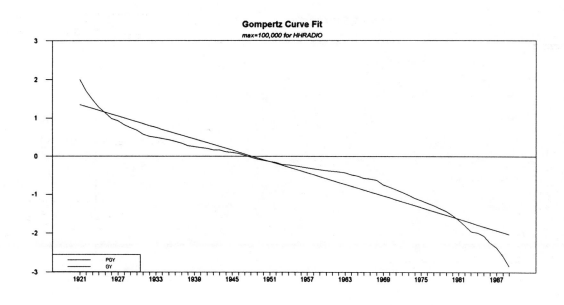

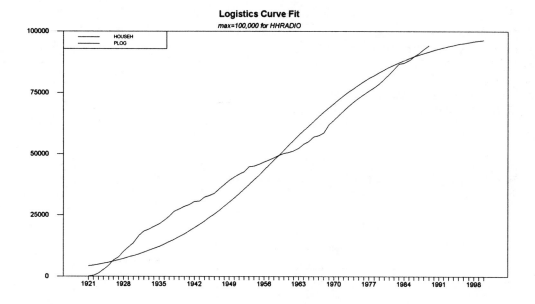

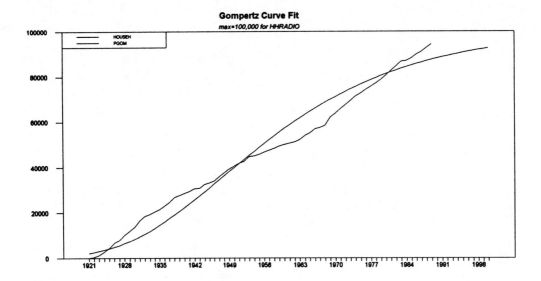

Gompertz Curve Fit

max=100,000 for HHRADIO

HOUSEH
PGOM

15-27. TVSETSH.DAT

```
ext househ
Extreme Values of Series HOUSEH
Annual Data From 1946:01 To 1992:01
Minimum Value is      8.000000000 at 1946:01   Entry 1
Maximum Value is 93000.000000000 at 1992:01   Entry 47
```

A value of 100000 will be chosen as the maximum level.

```
set gy = log(log(100000/househ))
set ly = log(househ/(100000-househ))
set time = t
linreg gy /  resg
#constant time
Dependent Variable GY - Estimation by Least Squares
Annual Data From 1946:01 To 1992:01
Usable Observations      47        Degrees of Freedom     45
Centered R**2       0.934758       R Bar **2     0.933308
Uncentered R**2     0.945669       T x R**2        44.446
Mean of Dependent Variable        -0.522079800
Std Error of Dependent Variable    1.177566511
Standard Error of Estimate         0.304104558
Sum of Squared Residuals           4.1615812120
Regression F(1,45)                    644.7360
Significance Level of F              0.00000000
Durbin-Watson Statistic               0.109521
Q(11-0)                              96.349312
Significance Level of Q              0.00000000
   Variable            Coeff        Std Error       T-Stat      Signif
*********************************************************************
1.  Constant         1.470736540  0.090151278      16.31410   0.00000000
2.  TIME            -0.083034014  0.003270131     -25.39165   0.00000000
PRJ FGY 48 80

linreg ly / resl
#constant time
Dependent Variable LY - Estimation by Least Squares
Annual Data From 1946:01 To 1992:01
Usable Observations      47        Degrees of Freedom     45
```

```
Centered R**2        0.678311      R Bar **2    0.671163
Uncentered R**2      0.682663      T x R**2      32.085
Mean of Dependent Variable        -0.298462989
Std Error of Dependent Variable    2.576328695
Standard Error of Estimate         1.477378889
Sum of Squared Residuals          98.219177187
Regression F(1,45)                        94.8868
Significance Level of F            0.00000000
Durbin-Watson Statistic                  0.121473
Q(11-0)                                  55.832792
Significance Level of Q            0.00000005
    Variable              Coeff        Std Error       T-Stat      Signif
************************************************************************
1.  Constant        -4.012515904  0.437966452    -9.16170   0.00000000
2.  TIME             0.154752205  0.015886713     9.74098   0.00000000
PRJ FLY 48 80

set ply = ly - resl
set pgy = gy - resg
************************************************************************
*   LOGISTICS   a = exp(-a')    b=b'     yt = 1/(1+a*exp(-bt))        *
*   GOMPERTZ    a = exp(a')    -b=b'     yt = L*exp(-a*exp(-b*t))     *
************************************************************************
```

The following is the logistics constant a.
```
disp exp(4.012515904) = 55.28579
```
The logistics slope b equals 0.154752205
```
set plog = 100000/(1+55.28579*exp(-0.154752205*time))
disp exp(1.470736540) = 4.35244
set pgom = 100000*exp(-4.35244*exp(-0.083034014*time))
```

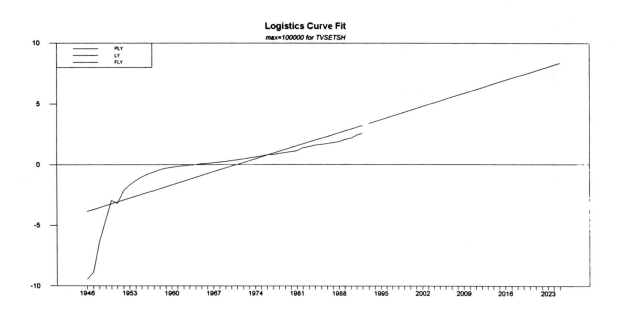

Logistics Curve Fit
max=100000 for TVSETSH

Gompertz Curve Fit
max=100000 for TVSETSH

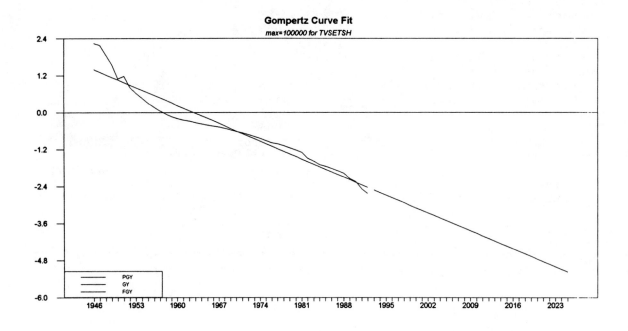

Logistics Curve Fit
max=100000 for TVSETSH

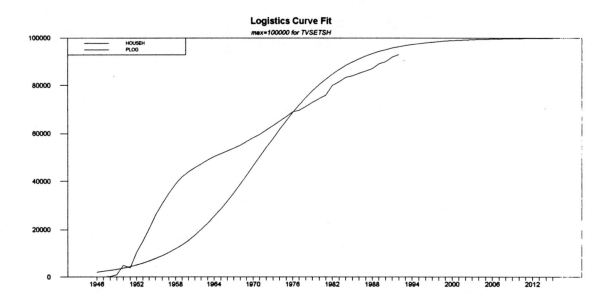

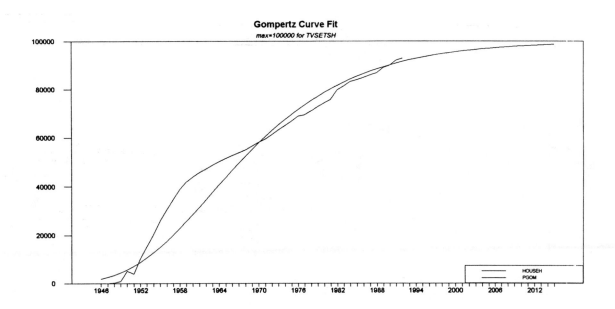

15-28. CARBON.DAT

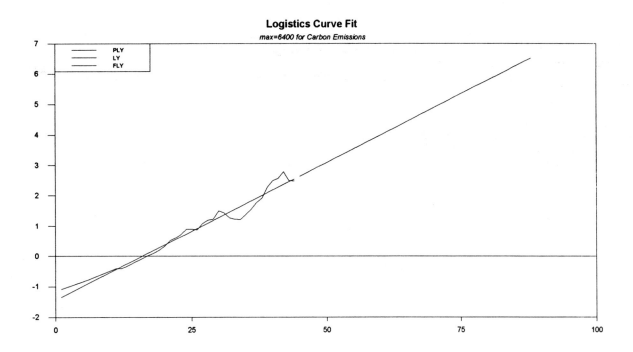

Gompertz Curve Fit

max=6400 for Carbon Emissions

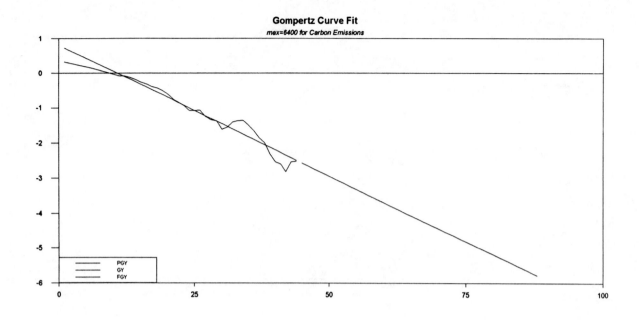

Logistics Curve Fit

max=6400 for Carbon Emissions

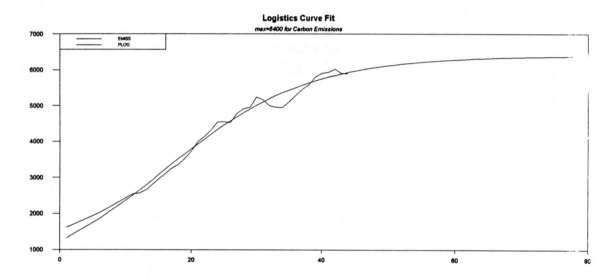

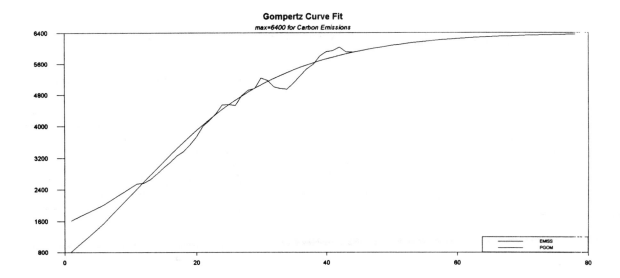

Gompertz Curve Fit
max=6400 for Carbon Emissions

```
ext emiss
Extreme Values of Series EMISS
Annual Data From 1:01 To 36:01
Minimum Value is 1620.0000000000 at 1:01   Entry 1
Maximum Value is 6026.0000000000 at 34:01   Entry 34
set gy = log(log(6400/emiss))
set ly = log(emiss/(6400-emiss))
linreg gy / resg
#constant time
Dependent Variable GY - Estimation by Least Squares
Annual Data From 1:01 To 36:01
Usable Observations      36        Degrees of Freedom    34
Centered R**2       0.950632       R Bar **2    0.949181
Uncentered R**2     0.982913       T x R**2       35.385
Mean of Dependent Variable       -1.161362567
Std Error of Dependent Variable   0.856948859
Standard Error of Estimate        0.193183522
Sum of Squared Residuals          1.2688756822
Regression F(1,34)                   654.7121
Significance Level of F              0.00000000
Durbin-Watson Statistic              0.382699
Q(9-0)                              59.266321
Significance Level of Q              0.00000000
     Variable          Coeff       Std Error      T-Stat      Signif
***********************************************************************
1.  Constant      0.794570176  0.082945486       9.57943   0.00000000
2.  TIME         -0.074749022  0.002921328     -25.58734   0.00000000
PRJ FGY 37 80
linreg ly / resl
#constant time
Dependent Variable LY - Estimation by Least Squares
Annual Data From 1:01 To 36:01
Usable Observations      36        Degrees of Freedom    34
Centered R**2       0.968148       R Bar **2    0.967211
Uncentered R**2     0.982784       T x R**2       35.380
Mean of Dependent Variable       0.9336822913
Std Error of Dependent Variable  1.0270122910
Standard Error of Estimate       0.1859687001
Sum of Squared Residuals         1.1758681517
```

```
Regression F(1,34)                 1033.4305
Significance Level of F            0.00000000
Durbin-Watson Statistic             0.447440
Q(9-0)                             68.584716
Significance Level of Q            0.00000000
    Variable           Coeff      Std Error     T-Stat      Signif
*******************************************************************
1.  Constant         -1.431905991  0.079847723   -17.93296  0.00000000
2.  TIME              0.090404648  0.002812225    32.14701  0.00000000
PRJ FLY 37 80
set ply = ly - resl
set pgy = gy - resg
*******************************************************************
*   LOGISTICS   a = exp(-a')   b=b'    yt = 1/(1+a*exp(-bt))      *
*   GOMPERTZ    a = exp(a')   -b=b'    yt = L*exp(-a*exp(-b*t))   *
*******************************************************************
```

The following is the logistics constant a.
```
disp exp(1.431905991) = 4.18667
* The logistics slope b equals 0.090404648
set plog = 6400/(1+4.18667*exp(-0.090404648*time))
scat(head="Logistics Curve Fit", sub="max=6400 for Carbon
Emissions",key=upl,sty=line) 2
#time emiss
#time plog 1 70
disp exp(0.794570176) = 2.21349
set pgom = 6400*exp(-2.21349*exp(-0.074749022*time))
scat(head="Gompertz Curve Fit", sub="max=6400 for Carbon
Emissions",key=lor,sty=line) 2
#time emiss
#time pgom 1 70
```

15-29. PAPER.DAT

```
ext prod
Extreme Values of Series PROD
Annual Data From 1:01 To 36:01
Minimum Value is  38.00000000000 at 1:01   Entry 1
Maximum Value is 247.00000000000 at 36:01  Entry 36
set gy = log(log(300/prod))
set ly = log(prod/(300-prod))
linreg gy / resg
#constant time
Dependent Variable GY - Estimation by Least Squares
Annual Data From 1:01 To 36:01
Usable Observations     36      Degrees of Freedom    34
Centered R**2      0.947954      R Bar **2    0.946423
Uncentered R**2    0.965044      T x R**2        34.742
Mean of Dependent Variable      -0.432247952
Std Error of Dependent Variable  0.626967631
Standard Error of Estimate       0.145121872
Sum of Squared Residuals         0.7160521669
Regression F(1,34)                 619.2697
Significance Level of F           0.00000000
Durbin-Watson Statistic            0.217237
Q(9-0)                            61.314503
Significance Level of Q           0.00000000
    Variable           Coeff      Std Error     T-Stat      Signif
*******************************************************************
1.  Constant          0.996749531  0.062309685    15.99670  0.00000000
```

```
2.  TIME        -0.054611369  0.002194538    -24.88513   0.00000000
PRJ FGY 37 80
linreg ly / resl
#constant time
Dependent Variable LY - Estimation by Least Squares
Annual Data From 1:01 To 36:01
Usable Observations      36     Degrees of Freedom     34
Centered R**2      0.975347    R Bar **2    0.974622
Uncentered R**2    0.975354    T x R**2       35.113
Mean of Dependent Variable     0.0140118710
Std Error of Dependent Variable 0.8691464965
Standard Error of Estimate     0.1384582884
Sum of Squared Residuals       0.6518037197
Regression F(1,34)               1345.1646
Significance Level of F          0.00000000
Durbin-Watson Statistic           0.394144
Q(9-0)                           59.936035
Significance Level of Q          0.00000000
   Variable          Coeff        Std Error      T-Stat      Signif
**********************************************************************
1.  Constant      -1.995383204  0.059448601    -33.56485   0.00000000
2.  TIME           0.076792168  0.002093771     36.67649   0.00000000
PRJ FLY 37 80
set ply = ly - resl
set pgy = gy - resg
**********************************************************************
*   LOGISTICS   a = exp(-a')   b=b'    yt = 1/(1+a*exp(-bt))        *
*   GOMPERTZ    a = exp(a')   -b=b'    yt = L*exp(-a*exp(-b*t))     *
**********************************************************************
```

The following is the logistics constant a.
```
disp exp(1.995383204) = 7.35502
```
The logistics slope b equals 0.076792168
```
set plog = 300/(1+7.35502*exp(-0.076792168*time))
disp exp(0.996749531) = 2.70946
set pgom = 300*exp(-2.70946*exp(-0.054611369*time))
```

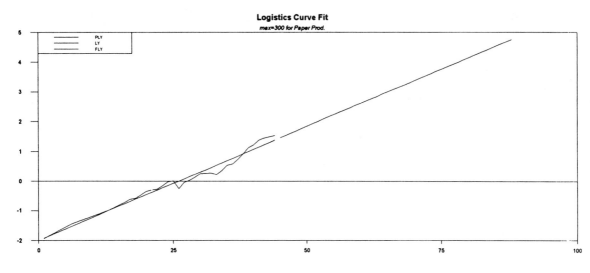

Logistics Curve Fit
max=300 for Paper Prod.

15-23

Gompertz Curve Fit
max=300 for Paper Prod.

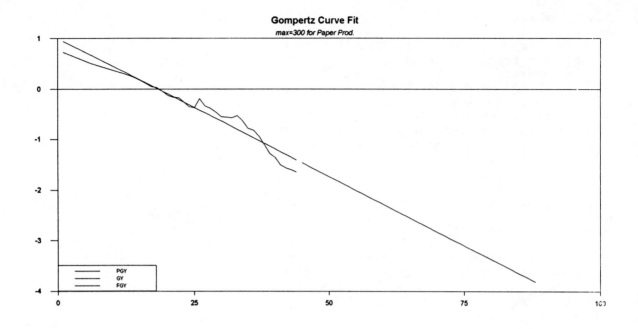

Logistics Curve Fit
max=300 for Paper Prod.

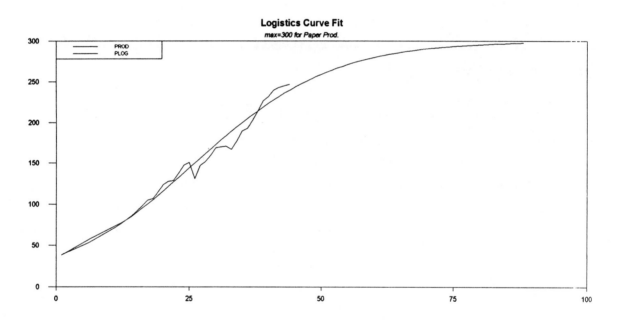

15-24

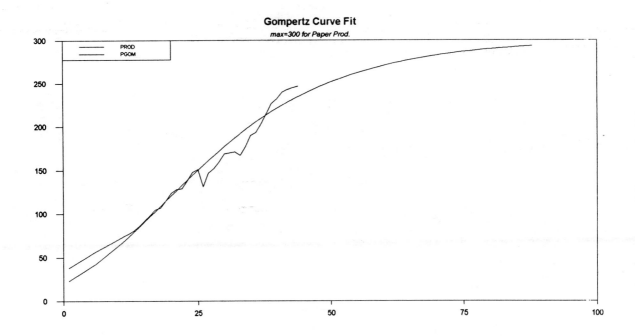

Gompertz Curve Fit

max=300 for Paper Prod.

15-30. **OIL.DAT**

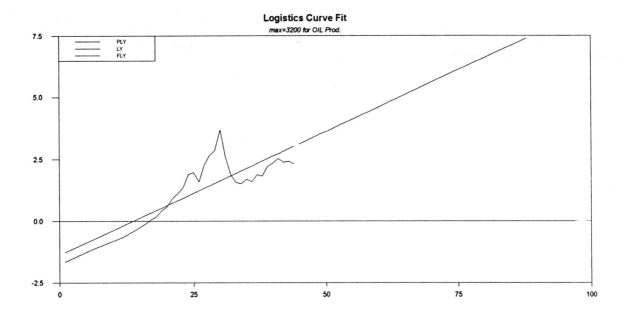

Logistics Curve Fit

max=3200 for OIL Prod.

Gompertz Curve Fit
max=3200 for OIL Prod.

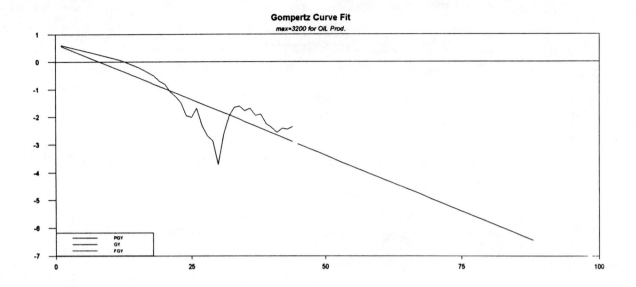

Logistics Curve Fit
max=3200 for OIL Prod.

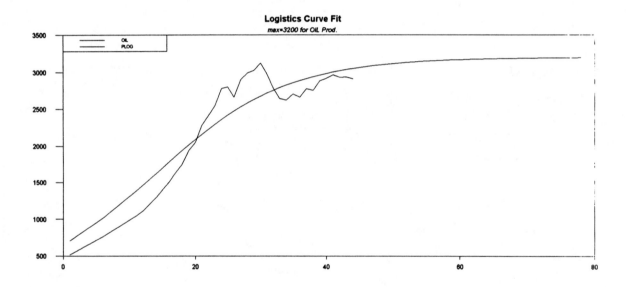

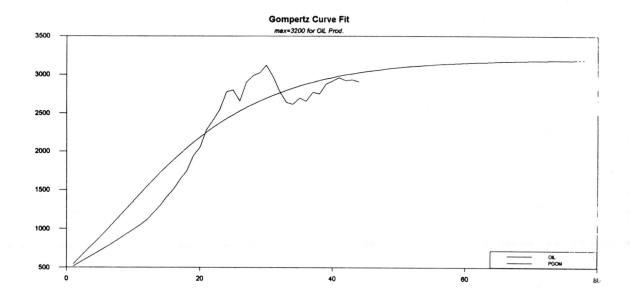

Gompertz Curve Fit

max=3200 for OIL Prod.

```
ext oil
Extreme Values of Series OIL
Annual Data From 1:01 To 36:01
Minimum Value is   518.0000000000 at 1:01   Entry 1
Maximum Value is 3122.0000000000 at 22:01   Entry 22
set gy = log(log(3200/oil))
set ly = log(oil/(3200-oil))
linreg gy /  resg
#constant time
Dependent Variable GY - Estimation by Least Squares
Annual Data From 1:01 To 36:01
Usable Observations       36      Degrees of Freedom    34
Centered R**2      0.711459      R Bar **2   0.702972
Uncentered R**2    0.901220      T x R**2       32.444
Mean of Dependent Variable       -1.459163886
Std Error of Dependent Variable   1.067710400
Standard Error of Estimate        0.581905058
Sum of Squared Residuals         11.512858889
Regression F(1,34)                   83.8340
Significance Level of F            0.00000000
Durbin-Watson Statistic            0.325918
Q(9-0)                            59.705532
Significance Level of Q            0.00000000
    Variable          Coeff         Std Error       T-Stat     Signif
*******************************************************************************
1.  Constant       0.649080554  0.249847387      2.59791  0.01376516
2.  TIME          -0.080569851  0.008799589     -9.15609  0.00000000

PRJ FGY 37 80
linreg ly / resl
#constant time
Dependent Variable LY - Estimation by Least Squares
Annual Data From 1:01 To 36:01
Usable Observations       36      Degrees of Freedom    34
Centered R**2      0.740405      R Bar **2   0.732770
Uncentered R**2    0.867041      T x R**2       31.213
Mean of Dependent Variable        1.2442046229
```

```
Std Error of Dependent Variable 1.2929709114
Standard Error of Estimate      0.6683921914
Sum of Squared Residuals       15.189436133
Regression F(1,34)                 96.9733
Significance Level of F          0.00000000
Durbin-Watson Statistic           0.269494
Q(9-0)                           66.261094
Significance Level of Q          0.00000000
    Variable            Coeff      Std Error      T-Stat      Signif
*******************************************************************
1.  Constant       -1.360246136  0.286981597   -4.73984   0.00003725
2.  TIME            0.099533150  0.010107451    9.84750   0.00000000

PRJ FLY 37 80
set ply = ly - resl
set pgy = gy - resg
*******************************************************************
*   LOGISTICS   a = exp(-a')   b=b'    yt = 1/(1+a*exp(-bt))       *
*   GOMPERTZ    a = exp(a')   -b=b'    yt = L*exp(-a*exp(-b*t))     *
*******************************************************************
```

The following is the logistics constant a.
```
disp exp(1.360246136) = 3.89715
```
The logistics slope b equals 0.099533150
```
set plog = 3200/(1+3.89715*exp(-0.099533150*time))
disp exp(0.649080554) = 1.91378
set pgom = 3200*exp(-1.91378*exp(-0.080569851*time))
```

15-31. NATGAS.DAT

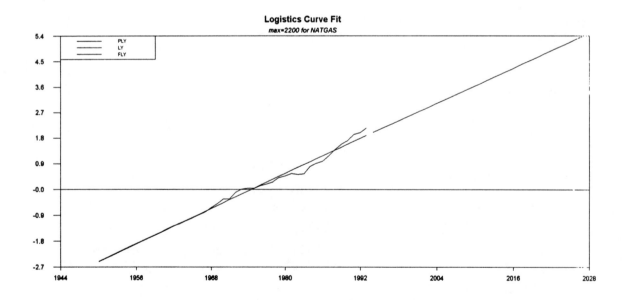

Gompertz Curve Fit

max=2200 for NATGAS

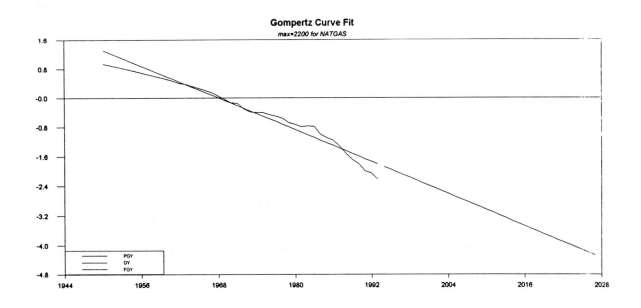

Logistics Curve Fit

max=2200 for NATGAS

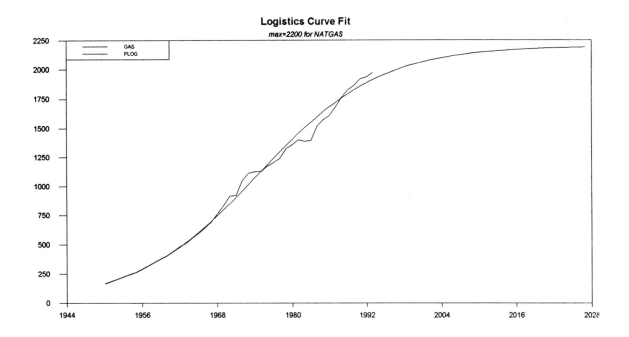

15-29

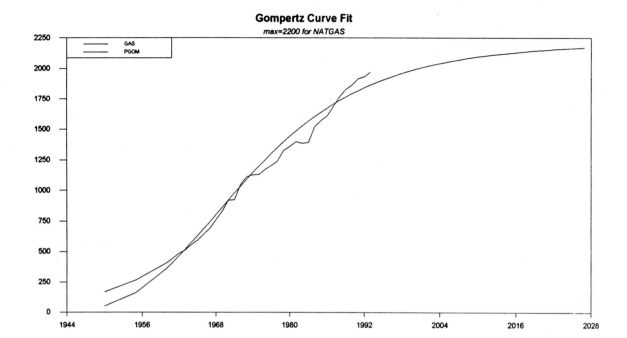

Gompertz Curve Fit

max=2200 for NATGAS

```
ext gas
Extreme Values of Series GAS
Annual Data From 1:01 To 36:01
Minimum Value is  168.0000000000 at 1:01  Entry 1
Maximum Value is 1974.0000000000 at 36:01   Entry 36
set gy = log(log(2200/gas))
set ly = log(gas/(2200-gas))
linreg gy /  resg
#constant time
Dependent Variable GY - Estimation by Least Squares
Annual Data From 1:01 To 36:01
Usable Observations     36      Degrees of Freedom    34
Centered R**2     0.958319      R Bar **2   0.957093
Uncentered R**2   0.970086      T x R**2      34.923
Mean of Dependent Variable      -0.512637291
Std Error of Dependent Variable  0.828937921
Standard Error of Estimate       0.171706078
Sum of Squared Residuals         1.0024212289
Regression F(1,34)                 781.7193
Significance Level of F            0.00000000
Durbin-Watson Statistic            0.164616
Q(9-0)                            51.951906
Significance Level of Q            0.00000005
Variable            Coeff       Std Error      T-Stat      Signif
*****************************************************************
1.  Constant      1.386995863  0.073723908    18.81338  0.00000000
2.  TIME         -0.072597445  0.002596545   -27.95924  0.00000000
PRJ FGY 37 80
linreg ly / resl
#constant time
Dependent Variable LY - Estimation by Least Squares
Annual Data From 1:01 To 36:01
Usable Observations     36      Degrees of Freedom    34
Centered R**2     0.987448      R Bar **2   0.987079
```

```
Uncentered R**2      0.987496        T x R**2        35.550
Mean of Dependent Variable       0.0706829578
Std Error of Dependent Variable 1.1536797212
Standard Error of Estimate       0.1311402390
Sum of Squared Residuals         0.5847239181
Regression F(1,34)                   2674.7356
Significance Level of F          0.00000000
Durbin-Watson Statistic            0.266875
Q(9-0)                              76.763423
Significance Level of Q          0.00000000
   Variable          Coeff        Std Error       T-Stat      Signif
**************************************************************************
1.  Constant       -2.613023837  0.056306515    -46.40713   0.00000000
2.  TIME            0.102562043  0.001983107     51.71785   0.00000000
PRJ FLY 37 80
set ply = ly - resl
set pgy = gy - resg
**************************************************************************
*   LOGISTICS   a = exp(-a')    b=b'     yt = 1/(1+a*exp(-bt))          *
*   GOMPERTZ    a = exp(a')    -b=b'     yt = L*exp(-a*exp(-b*t))       *
**************************************************************************
```

The following is the logistics constant a.
```
disp exp(2.613023837) = 13.64023
* The logistics slope b equals 0.102562043
set plog = 2200/(1+13.64023*exp(-0.102562043*time))
disp exp(1.386995863) = 4.00281
set pgom = 2200*exp(-4.00281*exp(-0.072597445*time))
```

15-32. GRAIN.DAT

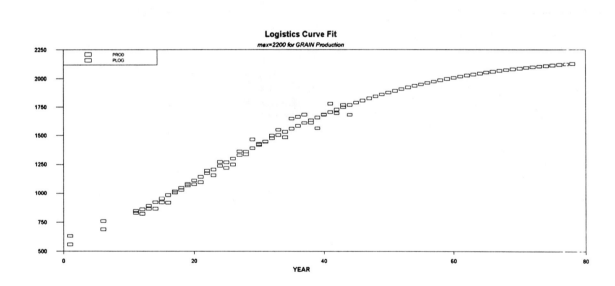

```
ext prod
Extreme Values of Series PROD
Annual Data From 1:01 To 36:01
Minimum Value is   631.0000000000 at 1:01   Entry 1
Maximum Value is 1780.0000000000 at 33:01   Entry 33
set gy = log(log(2200/prod))
set ly = log(prod/(2200-prod))
linreg gy / resg
#constant time
```

15-31

```
Dependent Variable GY - Estimation by Least Squares
Annual Data From 1:01 To 36:01
Usable Observations       36        Degrees of Freedom      34
Centered R**2        0.960272      R Bar **2    0.959104
Uncentered R**2      0.986091      T x R**2       35.499
Mean of Dependent Variable        -0.680204695
Std Error of Dependent Variable   0.506319304
Standard Error of Estimate        0.102392172
Sum of Squared Residuals          0.3564613322
Regression F(1,34)                     821.8221
Significance Level of F              0.00000000
Durbin-Watson Statistic                1.430432
Q(9-0)                                 6.634172
Significance Level of Q             0.67514711
     Variable            Coeff         Std Error      T-Stat      Signif
*************************************************************************
1.   Constant        0.481282246  0.043963214      10.94739   0.00000000
2.   TIME           -0.044388036  0.001548378     -28.66744   0.00000000
PRJ FGY 37 80
linreg ly / resl
#constant time
Dependent Variable LY - Estimation by Least Squares
Annual Data From 1:01 To 36:01
Usable Observations       36        Degrees of Freedom      34
Centered R**2        0.970179      R Bar **2    0.969302
Uncentered R**2      0.977741      T x R**2       35.199
Mean of Dependent Variable        0.3778301986
Std Error of Dependent Variable   0.6574251976
Standard Error of Estimate        0.1151866086
Sum of Squared Residuals          0.4511104631
Regression F(1,34)                    1106.1362
Significance Level of F              0.00000000
Durbin-Watson Statistic                1.589840
Q(9-0)                                 6.590568
Significance Level of Q             0.67966186
     Variable            Coeff         Std Error      T-Stat      Signif
*************************************************************************
1.   Constant       -1.138050302  0.049456647     -23.01107   0.00000000
2.   TIME            0.057931739  0.001741856      33.25863   0.00000000
PRJ FLY 37 80
*************************************************************************
**   LOGISTICS  a = exp(-a')    b=b'     yt = 1/(1+a*exp(-bt))
**   GOMPERTZ   a = exp(a')    -b=b'     yt = L*exp(-a*exp(-b*t))
*************************************************************************
```

The following is the logistics constant a.
compute a=exp(1.138050302) = 3.12068
The logistics slope b equals 0.104314136
set plog = 2200/(1+a*exp(-0.057931739*time))

15-33. FISH.DAT

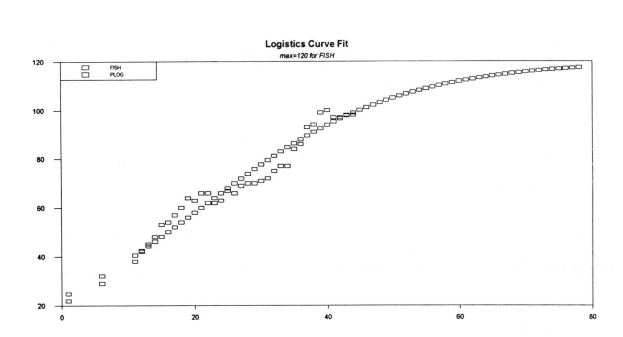

Logistics Curve Fit
max=120 for FISH

The maximum value of this time series is chosen as 120, again, empirically chosen based on the shape of the graph. In an actual application, more time and effort should be spent in determining the maximum possible, sustainable fish harvest. From this 120, the following two transformed variables were generated.
```
set gy = log(log(120/fish))     set ly = log(fish/(120-fish))
```

The Logistics curve fit is the better of the two and is shown below.

```
Dependent Variable LY - Estimation by Least Squares
Annual Data From 1:01 To 36:01
Usable Observations        36        Degrees of Freedom     34
Centered R**2      0.949792        R Bar **2    0.948315
Uncentered R**2    0.958460        T x R**2       34.505
Mean of Dependent Variable       0.3475235155
Std Error of Dependent Variable  0.7715667459
Standard Error of Estimate       0.1754107961
Sum of Squared Residuals         1.0461442110
Regression F(1,34)                  643.1773
Significance Level of F           0.00000000
Durbin-Watson Statistic              0.305836
Q(9-0)                              77.212591
Significance Level of Q           0.00000000
      Variable          Coeff        Std Error      T-Stat      Signif
*************************************************************************
1.   Constant      -1.412750774   0.075314570    -18.75800   0.00000000
2.   TIME           0.067271629   0.002652568     25.36094   0.00000000
PRJ FLY 37 80
set ply = ly - resl
```

The logistics constant is exp(1.412750774) = 4.10724
The fitted logistics function is flog = 120/(1+a*exp(-0.067271629*time))

15-34. MICROPRO.DAT, number of transistors on Intel ICs.

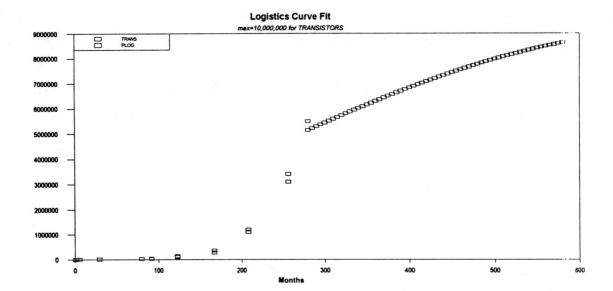

Logistics Curve Fit
max=10,000,000 for TRANSISTORS

Months

```
Extreme Values of Series TRANS
Minimum Value is      2300.0000000 at 1:01   Entry 1
Maximum Value is 5500000.0000000 at 10:01  Entry 10
```

Transformations for the Gompertz and Logistics curves are:

```
set gy = log(log(10000000/trans))
set ly = log(trans/(10000000-trans))
linreg gy /  resg
#constant time
Dependent Variable GY - Estimation by Least Squares
Annual Data From 1:01 To 10:01
Usable Observations     10        Degrees of Freedom      8
Centered R**2      0.921080       R Bar **2    0.911215
Uncentered R**2    0.976248       T x R**2        9.762
Mean of Dependent Variable        1.2869939138
Std Error of Dependent Variable 0.8901471601
Standard Error of Estimate        0.2652353576
Sum of Squared Residuals          0.5627983593
Regression F(1,8)                      93.3686
Significance Level of F            0.00001096
Durbin-Watson Statistic             0.688927
Q(2-0)                              2.274557
Significance Level of Q            0.32069061
    Variable       Coeff       Std Error      T-Stat      Signif
************************************************************************
1.  Constant      2.333363900  0.136972694      17.03525   0.00000014
2.  TIME         -0.008445278  0.000874004      -9.66274   0.00001096
linreg ly / resl
#constant time
Dependent Variable LY - Estimation by Least Squares
Annual Data From 1:01 To 10:01
Usable Observations     10        Degrees of Freedom      8
Centered R**2      0.995796       R Bar **2    0.995270
Uncentered R**2    0.998822       T x R**2        9.988
Mean of Dependent Variable       -4.588926277
Std Error of Dependent Variable 3.018448221
Standard Error of Estimate        0.207591190
Sum of Squared Residuals          0.3447528171
```

```
Regression F(1,8)                    1894.7956
Significance Level of F              0.00000000
Durbin-Watson Statistic               3.474769
Q(2-0)                               13.070632
Significance Level of Q              0.00145127
    Variable          Coeff        Std Error       T-Stat       Signif
*******************************************************************************
1.  Constant        -8.278223251   0.107204125    -77.21926    0.00000000
2.  TIME             0.029776408   0.000684055     43.52925    0.00000000
PRJ FLY 11 70
*******************************************************************************
*   LOGISTICS   a = exp(-a')   b=b'    yt = 1/(1+a*exp(-bt))              *
*   GOMPERTZ    a = exp(a')   -b=b'    yt = L*exp(-a*exp(-b*t))           *
*******************************************************************************
```

The following is the logistics constant a.
```
COMPUTE      a=EXP(8.278223251) = 3937.19276
set plog = 10000000/(1+a*exp(-0.029776408*time))
```

15-35. Per a 1994 Almanac, in 1993, 78% are high school graduates.

15-36. Per a 1994 Almanac, in 1993, the average monthly earnings without a high school diploma is \$452.[*]

15-37. Per a 1994 Almanac, in 1993, the average monthly earnings with a high school diploma is \$921.[*]

15-38. Per a 1994 Almanac, in 1993, the average monthly earnings with a college diploma is \$1829.[*]

15-39. Per a 1994 Almanac, in 1993, the average monthly earnings with a doctorate is \$3537.[*]

[*]No doubt these numbers are low, however, they can be updated through use of an approximate CPI of 3%. Here are the recent estimates from a class of 20 students in 1996:

15-35. Mean=72% and median=70%,
15-36. Mean=972 and median=1000,
15-37. Mean=1632 and median=1500,
15-38. Mean=2404 and median=2250,
15-39. Mean=3727 and median=3000. It is interesting that all but the doctorate levels were greatly overestimated by the students.
14-40. The problem in fitting a S-curve to this data, as in many other cases relates to the estimation of the maximum market (penetration) for steel frame buildings as well as the determination of the type of S-curve. Clearly, we need additional information with which to estimate L and the specific type of S-curve.

15-41. This project will vary depending on the choice of trip.

CHAPTER 16

ARTIFICIAL NEURAL NETWORKS, EXPERT SYSTEMS, AND GENETIC ALGORITHMS

PROBLEMS

ESTIMATED DIFFICULTY

Elementary	Medium	Hard		Very Hard	Bad

1 E	2 E	3 E	4 E	5 M	6 E	7 M	8 E	9 M	10 E
11 M	12 M	13 M	14 M	15 E	16 M	17 M	18 M	19 M	20 M
21 H	22 H	23 H	24 H	25 V	26 E	27 H	28 V	29 V	

Minicases are all Hard to Very hard depending on software used in the class.

16-1. CPS are programs that we use everyday including spreadsheets and word processors. A task needs to be completed and code is written to accomplish that task. An expert system consist of a system which 's acts and reacts more like a human analyst. See also pages 664, 3rd paragraph, see also problem 16-3.

16-2. See Table 16-10, page 698.

16-3. CPS - Used when a computational or IT job needs to be done quickly and inexpensively. Expert Systems - Used when it is effective to prompt and guide the user for information and judgment about the problem at hand. ANNs - Used when there are unknown, complex mathematical and logical relationships between several input and several output variables. CPS - A forecasting "engine" (i.e., a program which forecasts with several different methods on in-sample data as it chooses a best method for out-of-sample forecasts. An expert system might be used to weight the RSE or SSE for selecting from one model or another in the CPS program listed above. A user is prompted for information such as is the series seasonal, trending, cyclical, and the probability of such patterns. ANN applications are most effective when the logic and interactions of the system are complex.

16-4. The transfer function operates as a logic element which varies between 0 and 1 depending on the value of the Input. The sigmoid or negative exponential function is the most common.

16-5. See page 685, Table 16-4. The first derivative of the sigmoid is $O_j(1-O_j)$ which is the product of the output and one minus that output. The first derivative is used in a gradient search of the optimal (i.e., minimum SSE) weights to be applied to a node.

16-6. Training a ANN is analogous to the process of fitting model coefficients except in this case network weights are being fitted using an iterative process such as the back propagation method. Learning takes place during the training process.

16-7. The generalized delta rule is described starting on page 694 and appendix 16A. The process involves adjusting weights in proportion to the negative of the change in the sum of squared errors with respect to the change in the weights. Thus, the changes in the weights of a ANN are proportionate to the negative of the rate of change of the sum squared errors with respect to the weights as shown in Figure 16-11.

16-8. A 4x4x1 ANN has 4 input nodes, 4 hidden nodes, and 1 output node.

16-9. Training involves a programmed iterative process of adjusting weights so as to achieve minimum sum of squared errors or RMS. Programming a computer involves writing code to achieve some desired output. Training involves using a preprogrammed set of procedures like back propagation, however, before training the network, we may have to design the network which is analogous to programming. In fact some advanced ANN has already had this feature designed into the software.

16-10. Running a network is the process of using a previously trained (i.e., fitted) ANN to actually forecast, training is defined in problem 16-9.

16-11. The number of neurodes in the input layer is determined by the total number of input variables. The number of output nodes is determined by the number of different variables that are to be predicted. The number of hidden nodes and layers is not so easily determined. Some suggest using 50% of the number of input nodes as the number of hidden nodes. Typically, the number of hidden nodes should be less than the number of inputs nodes. With too few hidden nodes, the ANN model is not rich enough to represent the logic and mathematical relationships of the system and the RMS will remain too high. With too many hidden nodes, the ANN model is not parsimonious and it will memorize the input data and the RMS in fit will be much less than that of testing. Some ANN software will iterate to the maximum number of nodes trying to balance network complexity with out-of-sample representativeness.

16-12. There are only one input and one output layer in ANN. However, the number of hidden layers is a much more complex problem. Typically only one hidden layer is necessary, however when there are complex interactions between the input variables, then more than one hidden layer may be necessary.

16-13. If the output of the network is greater (less) than the actual or desired output than the weights to that node and the other nodes feeding the output node should be reduced (increased). Thus, it is the negative of the deviation or error which is fed back through the network to adjust the weights at each node. This negative of the output error results in a negative feedback loop which often, but not always dampens to that value of error which is approximately zero.

16-14. Page 690 discusses out-of-sample validation. This is the same process as other forecasting model validation schemes. Data is withheld from the model fitting process in order to judge the out-of-sample accuracy of the model. Hopefully, the out-of-sample data is indicative of future value of input and output data. Thus, the representativeness of the in-sample and out-of-sample data is a key in the validation process. If this data is not representative of the future, then the network may not be generalizable. In some situations we may have confidence in the representativeness of the data, at least for the immediate or intermediate term, but in other cases, it may be difficult to assess how representative the current data base will be of future values. Clearly, validation requires an ongoing process of control and assessment using control and validation methods discussed in Chapter 17.

16-15. The function of the bias weight is clearly shown on page 684, it positions the sigmoid function so as to yield the correct output on the vertical or output axis.

16-16. The temperature tomorrow = f(Some moving average of recent temperatures, barometric pressure, cloud cover, humidity, pre5cipitation, wind speed, wind direction, and temperature of air feeding the area). (Incidentally, this is a laymen's answer, we will likely get a much more precise model from a meteorologist.)

16-17. The variables shown on page 691 used to forecast the S&P 500 are important inputs. However, one of the most important input variables may or may not be included, the expectations of the buyers and sellers of investment securities. Thus, consumer sentiment, optimism, pessimism, or expectations are not shown here. These measures can be gotten through interviews collected just for this purpose or from sources such as the University of Michigan's Survey Research Center or the Conference Board's survey of consumer sentiments. These may be extremely important inputs.

16-18. See pages 699 and 700

16-19. See Figure 16-10 of page 693.

16-20. The following is the output of the spreadsheet, THREE.WK1 when the weights of Figure 16-5 input as fixed values. Note that the optimal weights of a ANN can vary considerably based on the initial or starting values of the weights, also round-off errors can make weights appear different, when differences are actually very minor numerically. Finally, when a network is more complex than necessary, then there are a number of optimal combination of weights.

SIMPLE 2X1X1 NEURAL RMS= 0.000967
NETWORK
          RANDOMLY INITIALIZE WEIGHTS WITH A 1 IN C3, THEN USE 0.0
et   1   0   BIAS BIAS
a=
I0 I1 D4   w03   d03   w13   d13   I3   O3   I2   w24
   0 0 0.5 1.94636   0 -2.00113   0   0   0.5   1 -1.44568
   0 1 0.25 1.94636   0 -2.00113 2E-06 -2.00113 0.11908433   1 -1.44568
   1 0 0.75 1.94636   0 -2.00113   0   1.94636 0.87504919   1 -1.44568

BIAS
d24   d34   w34   I4   O4   E4   d4   RMS   D4
-7.1E-05 -3.5E-05 2.90041   0.004525 0.501131 -0.00113 -1E-04 1.3E-06   0.5
1.47E-05 1.75E-06 2.90041 -1.1002866 0.249686 0.000314   3E-05 9.8E-08   0.25
5.56E-05 4.86E-05 2.90041 1.09232143 0.748819 0.001181 0.0001 1.4E-06   0.75

16-21 a) Validating MARRIAGE.WK1 with weights equal to those of Table 16-7, yields:

I1	I2	D6	I0	w04	d04	w14	d14	w24	d24	I4	O4
0.122	0.456	0.146	1	-1.78847	2E-04	4.77881	2E-05	0.05415	7E-05	-1.181	0.2349
0.648	0.146	0.624	1	-1.78847	-0	4.77881	-0	0.05415	-0	1.3161	0.7885
0.718	0.624	0.694	1	-1.78847	-0	4.77881	-0	0.05415	-0	1.6765	0.8424
0.456	0.694	0.458	1	-1.78847	4E-04	4.77881	2E-04	0.05415	3E-04	0.4282	0.6055

I3	w35	d35	d45	w45	I5	O5	e5	d5	RMS = D5
1	-3.0419	0.0009	0.0002	4.61689	-1.957	0.123757	0.0222	0.001	0.00049 0.146
1	-3.0419	-0.002	-0.0014	4.61689	0.5987	0.645352	-0.021	-0	0.00046 0.624
1	-3.0419	-5E-04	-0.0004	4.61689	0.8476	0.700055	-0.006	-0	3.7E-05 0.694
1	-3.0419	0.0017	0.00104	4.61689	-0.247	0.438665	0.0193	0.003	0.00037 0.458
									0.01845

b) As shown here, the RMS value for out-of-sample observations, 29, 30, 31, and 32 is only .01845 which is considerably better than the in-sample training RMS.

c) We infer that this is a very good ANN because it models the repeating pattern of this time series well, however, remind the student that this ANN is an overkill for such a simple pattern.

16-22. The following are the weights trained in P16-22.WK1 found on the website or diskette.

```
2.790189 0.000188 -0.63621
w14      d14      w24
```

As shown, the weight from advertising is quite high at 2.790189 denoting a strong positive relationship between sales and advertising, in contrast, there is a lower negative value from competition to sales as shown by the -.63621. So as advertising increases sales increase and as competition increases sales decline. This is the same interpretation as in Chapter 10. The R^2 for this model is approximately 96% from an RMS value of .0495.

16-23. a) See Figure 16-5. b) After 400 epochs, RMS = .0127, R^2 is .99+,

c) w_{03} = .8521 w_{13} = .4643 w_{24} = -6.1547 w_{34} = 9.4144. The first input variable has a greater influence than the second input variable. This can be confirmed using regression analysis as shown below:

```
Dependent Variable D - Estimation by Least Squares
Usable Observations        8       Degrees of Freedom      5
R Bar **2                          0.999972
Mean of Dependent Variable         0.5000000000
Std Error of Dependent Variable 0.2390481123
Standard Error of Estimate         0.0012649111
Sum of Squared Residuals           0.0000080000
Regression F(2,5)                  125000.0000
Significance Level of F            0.00000000
Variable            Coeff        Std Error       T-Stat      Signif
***********************************************************************
1.  Constant      0.2000000000 0.0007745967     258.19889   0.00000000
2.  I0            0.4000000000 0.0008944272     447.21360   0.00000000
3.  I1            0.2000000000 0.0008944272     223.60680   0.00000000
```

Series	Obs	Mean	Std Error	Minimum	Maximum
I0	8	0.50000000000	0.53452248382	0.00000000000	1.00000000000
I1	8	0.50000000000	0.53452248382	0.00000000000	1.00000000000
D	8	0.50000000000	0.23904811231	0.19900000000	0.80100000000

Because the standard deviations of the input variables are the same, their beta coefficients will be in proportion to their regression coefficients, thus I0 has twice the influence that I1 has.

d) The usual forecasting error statistics can and should be used to select from ANN models or any other models given that everything else is equal.

16-24. The RMS of the validation data is only, .02852, thus this ANN fit training and validation data quite well. The following figure illustrates the fit of the 25 validation (i.e., out-of-sample) observations.

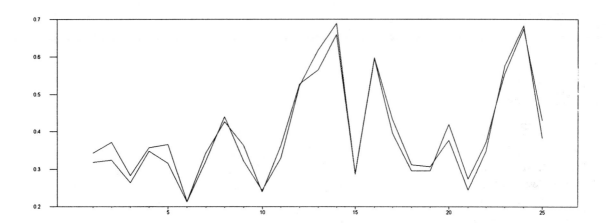

NETWORK STRUCTURE
==================

RMS error = 0.0319383   Eta = 0.95   Momentum = 0
Output delta = 0.0765043

network[0] is a type bias node on layer 0 with value 1 delta 0
network[1] is a type input node on layer 0 with value 0.331885 delta 0
network[2] is a type input node on layer 0 with value 0.535111 delta 0
network[3] is a type input node on layer 0 with value 0.499694 delta 0
network[4] is a type input node on layer 0 with value 0.29446 delta 0
network[5] is a type bias node on layer 1 with value 1 delta 0
network[6] is a type hidden node on layer 1 with value 0.557759 delta -0.00619843
  weight[0], source node[0], destination node [6], value = -1.58704
  weight[1], source node[1], destination node [6], value = 0.651647
  weight[2], source node[2], destination node [6], value = 1.96813
  weight[3], source node[3], destination node [6], value = 0.81656
  weight[4], source node[4], destination node [6], value = 0.446371
network[7] is a type hidden node on layer 1 with value 0.557759 delta -0.00619843
  weight[5], source node[0], destination node [7], value = -1.58704
  weight[6], source node[1], destination node [7], value = 0.651647
  weight[7], source node[2], destination node [7], value = 1.96813

weight[8], source node[3], destination node [7], value = 0.81656
weight[9], source node[4], destination node [7], value = 0.446371
network[8] is an output node on layer 2 with a 0.48286 delta -0.00579 and target value of 0.459665
weight[10], source node[5], destination node [8], value = -4.91732
weight[11], source node[6], destination node [8], value = 4.33862
weight[12], source node[7], destination node [8], value = 4.33862

The RMS of the validation data is .02852

16-25. Warn the student that depending on round-off error, results of these calculations will vary, in some cases considerably. Using a spreadsheet, the following values resulted. O_4 = .20409, O_5 = .7979, O_6= .07539. These are considerably different than those of Figure 16-10; we assume the differences are round-off error.

16-26. There are 2^4 = 16 combinations:
0000, 0001, 0010, 0011, 0100, 0101, 0110, 0111, 1000, 1001, 1010 ,1011, 1100, 1101, 1110, 1111

16-27. a. 0110, 1001   b. 0000, 1111   c. 0111, 1101   d. 0110, 1111

16-28. Minicase Assignment I for Retail Sales. For a univariate model the most logical inputs for forecasting monthly Retail Sales are the value last month, last year, and some form of trend, finally, if four inputs can be used, then some form of moving average of the last several periods can be used as an input, this being a surrogate for cyclical variations. For a multivariate model, the noise components could include the univariate components while the causal component could include, inflation rate, unemployment rates, interest rates, consumer sentiment, GDP, or disposable income, consumer sentiment or confidence, among other variables.

Minicase Assignment II for Retail Sales. The three input variables for retail sales are the value of last month, last year, and a trend. The mean error and RMS values of the fitted and forecasted values are calculated as shown below.

FIT   RMS =   .0232   FIT R-SQ.   = .977
FORECAST RMS =   .0699   FORECAST R-SQ. = .617

The details of ANN are shown in P16-28.WK1 and P16-28A.WK1, following are the weights, RMS in fit and forecast.

I1	I2	I0	D6	w04	w05	w14	w24	w15
0.7942	0.7942	0.88	0.929643	0.6174726	0.0204065	2.19822	0.098592	2.964801

w25	I4	O4	I5	O5	I3	w36	w46	w56
−0.15278	2.367602	0.91432	2.251382	0.90477	1	−6.77743	3.68605	4.9696639

I6	O6	E6	RMS	D6
1.08920661	0.748232	0.181411	0.03290979	0.929643

16-29. Minicase Assignment I Super Oil. For a univariate model the most logical inputs for forecasting Super Oil are the value last month, last year, and some form of trend, finally, if four inputs can be used, then some form of moving average of the last several periods can be used as an input, this being a surrogate for cyclical variations. For a multivariate model, the noise components could include the univariate components while the causal component could include, oil prices, unemployment rates, consumer sentiment, GDP, or disposable income, and consumer confidence among other variables.

Minicase Assignment II for Super Oil. The three input variables for Super Oil are the value of last month, last year, and a simple scaled trend variable. The mean error and RMS values of the fitted and forecasted values are calculated as shown below.

The details of ANN are shown in P16-29.WK1 and P16-29A.WK1, following are the weights, RMS in fit and forecast.

FIT   RMS =   .0505   FIT R-SQ.   = .941
FORECAST RMS =   .0666   FORECAST R-SQ. = .673

I1		I0	D6	w04	w05		w14	
0.668	0.732	0.72		0.788	0.0636068	0.2400249		2.034366

w24	w15		w25	I4	O4	I5	O5
-0.24165	1.508543		0.688866	1.227866	0.77344488	1.684775	0.84353576

I3	w36	w46	w56	I6	O6	E6	RMS	D6
1	-7.52978	5.9486	4.77936	1.10275	0.7507	0.0372	0.001386	0.788

MINCASES

The solutions to these Minicases can be found on the Author's Website (http://forecast.umkc.edu) or mailed directly to you. Email can be sent to sad@forecast.umkc.edu or delurgio@cctr.umkc.edu. You must contact the author to get authorization to the private directory on forecast.umkc.edu.

CHAPTER 17

CONTROL, VALIDATION, AND COMBINING METHODS

PROBLEMS

ESTIMATED DIFFICULTY

Elementary		Medium		Hard		Very Hard		Bad	
1 E	2 E	3 E	4 E	5 E	6 E	7 E	8 E	9 M	10 M
11 M	12 M	13 M	14 E	15 E	16 M	17 M	18 E	19 M	20 M
21 M	22 M	23 M	24 M	25 M	26 M	27 H	28 E	29 M	30 E
31 M	32 H	33 H	34 M	35 M					

Minicases are all Very Hard.

17-1. The purpose of tracking signals is to detect when a forecasting system has gone out of control (e.g., series patterns have changed). Either the model is no longer valid because demand has changed or some unusual values have occurred.

17-2 Cumulative summation is the process of summing all errors over time. A disadvantage is that all errors, old and recent are given equal weight; in general, the most recent errors should be given more weight. The TSM_t is $CUSUM_t/MAD_t$. Because it uses $CUSUM_t$, the TSM_t is not more responsive to recent errors.

17-3. Trip points are typically set empirically because of the very real problem of attending to all tripped time series and the inability to predict how many time series will be tripped based on a predetermined trip point. Thus, trip points might vary from period to period.

17-4. If recent errors are low and MAD_t is calculated using equation 17-5, then TSM_t may falsely trip when low forecast errors are encountered and old, higher errors remain in $CUMSUM_t$. This is very undesirable because the TS trips because of low errors, not large errors.

17-5. Because the Autocorrelation tracking signal trips because of positive or negative autocorrelation, it is assumed that it is being used with models that are expected to yield white noise errors. However, white noise errors are not obtained with exponential smoothing models. Thus, exponential smoothing models will trip the control device when used with the autocorrelation tracking signal.

17-6. When a high smoothing constant is used with an simple exponential smoothing model and a relatively random series then

$$F_t = F_{t-1} + \alpha e_{t-1} \qquad e_{t-1} = A_{t-1} - \alpha A_{t-2} + (1-\alpha)F_{t-2}$$

For a random series one-half of the actuals will be above the mean and one-half below and because the series is random without high autocorrelations, typically there will not be long runs above or below the mean. Consequently, as shown above, when an error occurs, that error will likely drive the forecast below the mean using the first equation above. Thus, the forecast will at times "zigzag" about the mean as the actual time series zigzags about the mean. This induces negative correlation in the errors.

17-7. The backward cusum detects out of control situations earlier than other methods.

17-8. A reasonableness test is a simple filter that detects forecasts that are, from a practical and likely a theoretical, standpoint unreasonable. For example, three possible tests might be highlight a forecast if any of the following are true.

Filter 1: If $F_t > 1.50A_{t-1}$, Filter 2: If $F_t < .50A_{t-1}$, Filter 3: If $F_t > 1.20A_{t-s}$ or $F_t < .50A_{t-s}$

17-9. The four methods are simple averages, weighted averages, inversely proportionate weights to the SSE, and regression determined weights. These four methods are described on pages 723 to 728.

17-10. The sum of weights should equal 1.00. However, results with and without regression constants often do not sum to 1.00, thus, this seems to be an inconsistency in the weighting scheme. Also, at times the weight given a model may be negative. In practice, some suggest that the model with a negative weight should be dropped and the constant should be included whether the weights sum to 1.0 or not. However, the research on these problems is still ambiguous. Thus, in a specific application, some experimentation may be advisable.

17-11. The greatest benefits from combining forecasts occurs when the errors of different models have the same RSE and are not correlated. Negative results occur when combining the forecasts of models when different models have greatly different RSEs and errors are highly correlated. In this last situation, it is much better to discard all but the best model.

17-12. The model which is more accurate should be given more weight in the forecasts and the model which is least accurate should be given less weight. Weights inversely proportionate to the Sum of Squared Errors achieves appropriate weights.

17-13. When weighted averages are used, these weights must be estimated some way, either objectively or subjectively. Research has been mixed about how to best weight forecasts, either using regression or inversely proportionate weights. The M1 competition of 1001 series showed that simple averages worked better than inversely proportionate weights for many time series. Clearly, the best weighting scheme of the past may not be the best weighting scheme for the future. Simple averages assume equally likely weights.

17-14. Integrated Aggregate = 567, Vinyl = 317, Leather = 159, Deluxe = 91.

17-15. Integrated Aggregate = 600, Vinyl = 336, Leather = 168, Deluxe = 96.

17-16. The best way to determine a combining method and weights is to determine which works best in fitting in-sample values. In Figure 17-1 and 17-2 equal weight is used to (i.e., a simple average) is taken to calculate the roll-up, aggregate forecast and the group forecasts.

17-17. The number of companies that do not integrate group, item, and combined forecasts is surprising. Most often either political reasons or lack of knowledge explain this omission of an important integration tool.

17-18. The one-number principle states that the expected value used in planning processes throughout the organization should be based on the same forecast. This does not preclude different uses of the forecast, but it does require that there be an agreed upon expected value. By having different departments planning to the same value, the integrity of the planning process is enhanced.

17-19. Thomas Jefferson has noted that "Information is the currency of democracy." Some organizations resemble anything but a democracy. James March has noted that "Information is not innocent " "Information is power," author unknown. Those controlling the information can have greater control of the organization, thus, information and forecasts might wrongly or rightly be withheld. In general, it is the insecure manager who withholds information and is reluctant to participate in integrated processes.

17-20. Missing values can best be estimated by using a forecast. Fit a model to the data before the missing values and then predict the missing value, alternatively, a backcast can be used to predict the missing value. Finally, the mean of a forecast and a backcast can be used to estimate the missing value.

17-21. I have seen several firms with sales in the billions of dollars who do not capture demand nor forecast demand. Several retail and mail order operations seem to excel at capturing actual customer demand. For example, Bass Pro Shops™ of Springfield Missouri has always had an extraordinarily well designed customer order line. Customers commit to an order before the order taker knows if an item is in stock. When the order is ready to "ring-up" for credit card payment, then the demand or stock out is recorded. In contrast, too many other firms do not capture actual demand this way or only measure shipments or processed orders. In general, firms should capture demand and the fulfillment of that demand in order to measure percent fill rates, stock out rates, backorder response times etc. Again, I have been impressed with the systems at Bass Pro Shops in their desire to ship a backorder as soon as possible. I have received items on backorder which were shipped at a cost exceeding the cost of the item. Such displays of commitment to customer service are impressive and not easily forgotten.

17-22. A group forecast error is the error associated with an aggregate forecast such as the Group column of Table 17-8. It is a forecast based on a time series of a single aggregate, group (e.g., product line). In contrast, a cumulative forecast error is one which results from adding up individual errors. When these errors are not highly correlated, then the cumulative error will be less than the individual errors. Errors can be accumulated over time (weeks into months) or space (item 1 to item 4 forecasts). This distinction is so important because these are different concepts and each has advantages in different applications, see also, problem 17-26.

17-23. Table 17-11. Note that there is an error in the heading of Table 17-11. It is corrected below:

ITEM		Actual	Forecast	Error	Percent Error	Cum. Actual	Cum. Error	Cum. %Error
	1	1000	1100	-100	-10	1000	-100	-10
	2	900	1000	-100	-11.1111	1900	-200	-10.5263
	3	900	1000	-100	-11.1111	2800	-300	-10.7143
	4	1200	1000	200	16.66667	4000	-100	-2.5
Total		4000	4100	-100		4000		-2.5

17-24.

ITEM		Actual	Forecast	Error	Percent Error	Cum. Actual	Cum. Error	Cum. %Error
	1	1000	900	100	10	1000	100	10
	2	900	2000	-1100	-122.222	1900	-1000	-52.6316
	3	900	900	0	0	2800	-1000	-35.7143
	4	1200	1000	200	16.66667	4000	-800	-20
Total		4000	4800	-800		4000		-20

17-25.

ITEM		Actual	Forecast	Error	Percent Error	Cum Actual	Cum Error	Cum %Error
	1	1000	900	100	10	1000	100	10
	2	1000	700	300	30	2000	400	20
	3	900	800	100	11.11111	2900	500	17.24138
	4	1200	900	300	25	4100	800	19.5122
Total		4100	3300	800		4100		19.5122

Because all errors are positive, the cumulative percent error is nearly equal to the typical error.

17-26. These principles are so important because they can be used advantageously in different planning processes. In controlling safety stock in a global distribution network, the forecast accuracy is much greater for the aggregate, global demand of the whole distribution network then it is for any single distribution center; this is an application of the group forecasting principle. The cumulative forecasting principle denotes that on average, the errors across the global network will typically cancel out when errors are uncorrelated. The cumulative principle might be used to transship goods from one site to another, while the group error concept might be used to centralize those items with low erratic demands.

17-27. The cumulative percentage errors are dramatically lower than the individual item forecast errors. Because no group forecast was given in the table, there is no way to judge the group forecast error. This omission illustrates the distinction between group and cumulative errors.

Item	1	2	3	4	Group	Cum
Actual	460	676	283	284	1703	1703
Forecast	360	700	300	322		1682
Error	100	-24	-17	-38		21
Percent Error	21.7391	-3.5503	-6.00707	-13.3803		1.23312

17-28. As shown on page 735, equation 17-36, the SBC or BIC of forecasting models are penalized by the number parameters, k, the sum of squared errors, and number of observations. As these increase, the SBC increases. Everything else being equal, that model with the lower SBC is the preferred model.

17-29. The extreme value validation method is a simple procedure to assure that reasonable combinations of extreme values of the independent variables result in reasonable forecasts. We have seen students overfit regression models which were clearly not valid when out-of-sample combinations of independent variables were input to the model even though the individual values of the out-of-sample values were in-sample observations. An important assumption of this method is that reasonable extreme combinations of variables are valid combinations and thus are useful in judging the validity of the estimated relationship. Based on this assumption, if such reasonable combinations yield unreasonable forecasts, then either the model or the "reasonable combination" is invalid.

17-30. Excluding values in the middle of the time series makes time series estimation more difficult and less precise and therefore bootstrapping is more difficult. If the time series is long enough, this problem is eliminated because one-half of the data is still sufficient to fit models.

17-31. a. Split Sample, see page 736,   b. Extreme value, see page 736

   c. Jackknife, see page 737   d. Bootstrap, see page 738

17-32. Answer varies depending on the chosen time series. The minicase examples provide several results which can be used to answer this question.

17-33. Same comment as that for problem 17-32, students who have been filling out the Master Forecasting Summary Table will have several possible examples to use for this question.

17-34. Lowest RSE (SEE) in fitting and forecasting is the univariate ARIMA model while the best combining method in fitting and forecasting is the regression technique. Two combining methods performed worse than the ARIMA univariate model. There were no differences in the relative performance of fit versus forecast, thus, the rankings remained the same.

17-35. The lowest SEE method in fitting was Winter's method while the lowest SEE in forecasting was the univariate ARIMA model, which was significantly better than all other methods including the combining methods. The best combining method in fitting, based on SEE, was the regression method, however, in forecasting, the simple average method was considerably better. The differences in performance may result from large random errors resulting from the small sample size. Such variations in actual applications are common, thus, this example illustrates that what works best in fitting may not be the best in forecasting. Nonetheless, as shown in problem 17-34, it is normally a best procedure to select methods based on in-sample performance or competition.

MINICASES

MINICASE 17-1. Kansas Turnpike, Daily Data. TURNPIKD.DAT

Two models were fitted to this data, one was an ARIMA model, the other a Winter's model exclusive of trend. The details of these models are given in the RATS program M17-2.PRG. Even if you are not familiar with RATS, this program is relatively easy to follow and report to students. The following definitions of terms reported in the table are:

```
WIN  = Results of fitting Winter's model.
BJ   = Results of fitting an ARIMA model.
RES  = Residuals from fitting a model.
AVG  = Results from applying a simple average method.
INV  = Results from applying an inverse combination method.
REG  = Results from applying a regression combination method.
SSE  = Squared errors, either in fit or forecast.
FORE = Forecast result.
FER  = Forecast error.
SFER = Squared forecast error.
```

Series	Obs	Mean	Std Error	Minimum	Maximum
DAY	91	4.00	2.01	1.00	7.00
DATE	91	52967.73	30420.25	6193.00	83093.00
VEH	91	72706.37	6972.60	56242.00	95411.00
SALES	91	72571.68	6468.24	59900.00	91665.00
RESBJ	76	329.80	1873.94	-6788.58	4351.58
RESWIN	76	0.68	1720.99	-5670.91	4900.88
FITBJ	76	73301.08	6140.39	62436.30	88493.28
FITWIN	76	73630.20	6183.61	65036.71	89466.71
RESAVG	76	165.24	1681.77	-6229.75	3909.46
FITINV	76	73482.14	6131.33	64421.55	89028.79
ERRINV	76	148.74	1674.78	-6173.72	4008.86
RESINV	76	148.74	1674.78	-6173.72	4008.86
FITREG	76	73630.88	5949.34	65262.21	88773.11
RES	76	-0.00	1656.98	-6019.10	4038.20
RESREG	76	-0.00	1656.98	-6019.10	4038.20
SSEBJ	76	3574223.66	6275814.73	134.10	46084882.81
SSEWIN	76	2922846.23	4753195.30	0.00	32159180.87
SSEAVG	76	2818444.74	5014309.82	651.01	38809730.69
SSEINV	76	2790114.48	4940757.70	7808.97	38114774.53
SSEREG	76	2709470.43	4764418.98	1663.67	36229609.09
FOREBJ	7	72514.69	5757.49	65879.44	83517.53
FOREWIN	7	69659.03	5717.22	65245.96	81504.49
FERBJ	7	-6765.83	3963.71	-11811.42	-1345.44
FERWIN	7	-3910.17	3133.27	-7596.20	-81.86
FERAVG	7	-5338.00	3506.98	-9399.50	-1147.60
FERINV	7	-5194.85	3465.28	-9157.68	-1127.76
FERREG	7	-5025.23	3295.23	-8730.67	-1272.23
SFERBJ	7	59243026.26	53622045.64	1810198.98	139509758.20
SFERWIN	7	23704293.92	23910572.65	6701.82	57702265.75
SFERAVG	7	39036162.60	37229624.87	1316978.75	88350538.43
SFERINV	7	37279107.84	35759133.92	1271846.15	83863044.21
SFERREG	7	34560294.79	33098217.84	1618572.87	76224660.60

Reported Mean squared errors (Note that these means are Mean Squared Errors).

Fit

Series	Obs	Mean	Std Error	Minimum	Maximum
SSEBJ	76	3574223.66	6275814.73	134.10	46084882.81
SSEWIN	76	2922846.23	4753195.30	0.00	32159180.87
SSEAVG	76	2818444.74	5014309.82	651.01	38809730.69
SSEINV	76	2790114.48	4940757.70	7808.97	38114774.53
SSEREG	76	2709470.43	4764418.98	1663.67	36229609.09

Forecast

Series	Obs	Mean	Std Error	Minimum	Maximum
SFERBJ	7	59243026.26	53622045.64	1810198.98	139509758.20
SFERWIN	7	23704293.92	23910572.65	6701.82	57702265.75
SFERAVG	7	39036162.60	37229624.87	1316978.75	88350538.43
SFERINV	7	37279107.84	35759133.92	1271846.15	83863044.21
SFERREG	7	34560294.79	33098217.84	1618572.87	76224660.60

As shown above, the best individual forecasting method was the Winter's method in fitting and forecasting. In fact, in forecasting, Winter's method was superior to the best combining method which was the regression method.

The correlation between the BJ and Winter's residuals was 0.7504; which apparently, was so high as to have the Winter's model dominate the BJ model. The regression combining method worked quite well here.

```
The estimated weights are:
Simple Average = .5*FITBJ + .5*FITWIN
DISP ((1/3574223.661*76)/(1/3574223.661*76+1/2922846.233*76)) = 0.44987
DISP ((1/2922846.233*76)/(1/3574223.661*76+1/2922846.233*76)) = 0.55013
Inverse Weights = 0.44987*FITBJ + 0.55013*FITWIN
```

The regression weights are shown below:

```
LINREG SALES / RESREG
#CONSTANT FITBJ FITWIN
Dependent Variable SALES - Estimation by Least Squares
7/Year Data From 2:02 To 12:07
Usable Observations      76      Degrees of Freedom      73
Centered R**2      0.928013      R Bar **2    0.926041
Uncentered R**2    0.999504      T x R**2     75.962
Mean of Dependent Variable       73630.875000
Std Error of Dependent Variable  6175.776645
Standard Error of Estimate       1679.529259
Sum of Squared Residuals         205919752.81
Regression F(2,73)                 470.5366
Significance Level of F            0.00000000
Durbin-Watson Statistic            1.902803
Q(19-0)                           22.932563
Significance Level of Q            0.24032517
```

	Variable	Coeff	Std Error	T-Stat	Signif
1.	Constant	2399.2897917	2332.8391302	1.02848	0.30711758
2.	FITBJ	0.3110231	0.1531826	2.03041	0.04595874
3.	FITWIN	0.6577907	0.1521120	4.32439	0.00004770

This experiment is a validation process in that the out-of-sample results confirmed the in-sample fits. We have much greater confidence in Winter's method and the use of the regression combining method.

MINICASE 17-2. Domestic Air Passengers by Quarter. PASSAIR.DAT

Two models were fitted to the logarithms of this time series, one was an ARIMA model, the other a Winter's model with linear trend and additive seasonality. The details of these models are given in the RATS program M17-2.PRG. Even if you are not familiar with RATS, this program is relatively easy to follow and report to students. The following definitions of terms reported in the table are:

```
WIN   = Results of fitting Winter's model.
BJ    = Results of fitting an ARIMA model.
RES   = Residuals from fitting a model.
AVG   = Results from applying a simple average method.
INV   = Results from applying an inverse combination method.
REG   = Results from applying a regression combination method.
SSE   = Squared errors, either in fit or forecast.
FORE  = Forecast result.
FER   = Forecast error.
SFER  = Squared forecast error.
```

The following error statistics are based on the use of the logarithms.

Series	Obs	Mean	Std Error	Minimum	Maximum
DATE	50	880.060000	36.456521	821.000000	942.000000
PASS	50	11916.592375	2921.162808	7025.431137	17164.422700
CARGO	50	1492.875859	501.376036	724.015430	2403.735020
CHART	50	425.526131	229.407712	177.855423	1137.727619
OTHER	50	1212.375795	788.336407	303.208375	2568.013576
TOTAL	50	15047.370161	4210.092217	8339.396250	22147.260790
SALES	50	11916.592375	2921.162808	7025.431137	17164.422700
LPASS	50	9.354418	0.256781	8.857292	9.750594
RESBJ	41	0.005313	0.036279	-0.116895	0.067226
FOREBJ	4	9.702248	0.053186	9.653842	9.755131
RES	41	0.005313	0.036279	-0.116895	0.067226
RESWIN	41	0.004886	0.032391	-0.113118	0.052122
FOREWIN	7	9.711659	0.051434	9.648077	9.793066
FITBJ	41	9.370482	0.223475	8.954614	9.699032
FITWIN	41	9.370910	0.213517	9.003781	9.690788
RESAVG	41	0.005100	0.031901	-0.115006	0.045326
FITINV	41	9.370720	0.217619	8.987255	9.694447
RESINV	41	0.005076	0.031698	-0.114794	0.046089
RESREG	41	0.000000	0.030891	-0.113533	0.038395
FITREG	41	9.375796	0.210609	9.006684	9.689381
SSEBJ	41	0.001312	0.002503	0.000001	0.013664
SSEWIN	41	0.001047	0.002160	0.000000	0.012796
SSEAVG	41	0.001019	0.002247	0.000004	0.013226
SSEINV	41	0.001006	0.002230	0.000001	0.013178
SSEREG	41	0.000931	0.002158	0.000000	0.012890
FERBJ	4	-0.023429	0.016982	-0.038230	-0.004537
FERWIN	4	-0.017878	0.020755	-0.035555	0.006570
FERAVG	4	-0.020653	0.018855	-0.036448	0.001016
FERINV	4	-0.020375	0.019044	-0.036351	0.001573
FERREG	4	-0.015265	0.019644	-0.032528	0.008483
SFERBJ	4	0.000765	0.000768	0.000021	0.001462
SFERWIN	4	0.000643	0.000682	0.000043	0.001264

SFERAVG	4	0.000693	0.000735	0.000001	0.001328
SFERINV	4	0.000687	0.000730	0.000002	0.001321
SFERREG	4	0.000522	0.000538	0.000046	0.001058

The best fitting model was Winter's method and the best forecasting model was also Winter's but not by an extraordinary amount. Based on Minimum Mean Squared Error, the best combining method in fit and forecast was the regression method. This experiment is a validation process in that the out-of-sample results confirmed the in-sample fits. For this data we have much greater confidence in Winter's method and the use of the regression combining method.

The following equations show the calculation of the forecasted errors, squared errors, and the weights used in those calculations.

```
SET FERAVG = LPASS - .5*FOREBJ -.5*FOREWIN
SET FERINV = LPASS - 0.44987*FOREBJ - 0.55013*FOREWIN
SET FERREG = LPASS - 0.2863972175 - 0.3817551720*FOREBJ - 0.5882212751*FOREWIN
SET SFERBJ = (LPASS - FOREBJ)**2
SET SFERWIN = (LPASS - FOREWIN)**2
SET SFERAVG = (LPASS - .5*FOREBJ -.5*FOREWIN)**2
SET SFERINV = (LPASS - 0.44987*FOREBJ - 0.55013*FOREWIN)**2
SET SFERREG = (LPASS - 0.2863972175 - 0.3817551720*FOREBJ -
0.5882212751*FOREWIN)**2
```

MINICASE 17-3. Hospital Census by Month. CENSUSM.DAT

Two models were fitted to this time series, one was an ARIMA model, the other a Winter's model with linear trend and additive seasonality. Before fitting these models all observations were changed into 4-week month equivalents and two outliers were adjusted as below:

ENTRY	ASALES	SALES
1:01	11149.000000000	11149.000000000
1:02	11027.000000000	11027.000000000
1:03	13885.000000000	11108.000000000
1:04	11668.000000000	11668.000000000
1:05	10935.000000000	10935.000000000
1:06	12897.000000000	10317.600000000
1:07	10893.000000000	10893.000000000
1:08	11470.000000000	11470.000000000
1:09	14398.000000000	11518.400000000
1:10	11551.000000000	11551.000000000
1:11	11202.000000000	11202.000000000
1:12	13738.000000000	10990.400000000
2:01	11624.000000000	11624.000000000
2:02	10800.000000000	10800.000000000
2:03	12871.000000000	10296.800000000
2:04	10161.000000000	10161.000000000
2:05	10849.000000000	10849.000000000
2:06	12586.000000000	10068.800000000
2:07	10764.000000000	10764.000000000
2:08	10976.000000000	10976.000000000

ASALES are sales with the repeating 4, 4, and 5 week months, while SALES are sales adjusted so that all months have the equivalent of 4-week months as shown in the above table. Finally, observations in March and April of the second year were found to be outliers, they were equated to the same value last year as shown below.

```
set nsales = sales
set nsales 2:03 2:04 = sales(t-12)
```

The new time series called nsales was subsequently analyzed.

The details of the two forecasting models are given in the RATS program M17-2.PRG. Even if you are not familiar with RATS, this program is relatively easy to follow and report to students. The following definitions of terms reported in the table are:

```
WIN   = Results of fitting Winter's model.
BJ    = Results of fitting an ARIMA model.
RES   = Residuals from fitting a model.
AVG   = Results from applying a simple average method.
INV   = Results from applying an inverse combination method.
REG   = Results from applying a regression combination method.
SSE   = Squared errors, either in fit or forecast.
FORE  = Forecast result.
FER   = Forecast error.
SFER  = Squared forecast error.
```

Series	Obs	Mean	Std Error	Minimum	Maximum
DATE	120	198306.50000	292.27347	197807.00000	198806.00000
ASALES	120	11861.46667	1209.62066	10161.00000	14398.00000
SALES	120	10961.49500	313.71165	10042.40000	11668.00000
NSALES	120	10980.81333	305.47665	10042.40000	11668.00000
RESBJ	96	-11.72832	225.84118	-783.27688	616.80316
PAR	25	0.08081	0.20972	-0.10409	1.00000
FOREBJ	12	11074.18579	276.22092	10317.05053	11359.14938
RESWIN	96	-11.81765	165.72804	-579.51077	388.83886
FOREWIN	12	11113.39934	251.46804	10389.87627	11410.98429
FITBJ	96	10951.54707	291.38586	10068.13574	11687.70987
FITWIN	96	10951.63640	270.34535	10071.82090	11624.00000
RESAVG	96	-11.77298	174.31213	-597.91768	502.82101
FITINV	96	10951.60508	263.00231	10097.59808	11457.48400
RESINV	96	-11.78633	166.30611	-542.51752	468.75402
RESREG	96	-0.00000	161.81349	-505.26874	448.82142
FITREG	96	10939.81875	247.96293	10127.56968	11499.40850
SSEBJ	96	50610.49781	91076.67734	0.01115	613522.67445
SSEWIN	96	27319.33868	52320.51695	0.00000	335832.73611
SSEAVG	96	30206.81546	52662.54305	0.13393	357505.54763
SSEINV	96	27508.53943	48392.84075	0.66155	294325.25602
SSEREG	96	25910.85920	46242.80520	0.00387	255296.49978
FERBJ	12	62.94755	190.84619	-336.14938	376.54947
FERWIN	12	23.73400	136.31697	-155.92850	303.72373
FERAVG	12	43.34077	158.21308	-240.30635	340.13660
FERINV	12	41.37500	155.44098	-230.69713	336.48584
FERREG	12	51.71124	132.47718	-146.71511	289.88744
SFERBJ	12	37349.47428	45537.57538	458.26171	141789.50211
SFERWIN	12	17597.09186	25373.98023	540.56309	92248.10254
SFERAVG	12	24823.85220	32884.27459	81.77499	115692.90519
SFERINV	12	23860.29753	31935.89910	235.54489	113222.72283
SFERREG	12	18761.73800	23653.84006	3.23642	84034.72785

The best fitting model was Winter's method and the best forecasting model was also Winter's by an extraordinary amount. Based on Minimum Mean Squared Error, the best combining method in fit and forecast was the regression method. This experiment is a validation process in that the out-of-sample results confirmed the in-sample fits. We have much greater confidence in Winter's method and the use of the regression combining method.

The following equations show the calculation of the forecasted errors, squared errors, and the weights used in those calculations.

```
SET FERBJ = NSALES - FOREBJ
SET FERWIN = NSALES - FOREWIN
SET FERAVG = NSALES - .5*FOREBJ -.5*FOREWIN
SET FERINV = NSALES - 0.44987*FOREBJ - 0.55013*FOREWIN
SET FERREG = NSALES - 695.40810192 - 0.14603864*FOREBJ - 0.78938538*FOREWIN
SET SFERBJ = (NSALES - FOREBJ)**2
SET SFERWIN = (NSALES - FOREWIN)**2
SET SFERAVG = (NSALES - .5*FOREBJ -.5*FOREWIN)**2
SET SFERINV = (NSALES - 0.44987*FOREBJ - 0.55013*FOREWIN)**2
SET SFERREG = (NSALES - 695.40810192 - 0.14603864*FOREBJ -
0.78938538*FOREWIN)**2
```

We infer that ARIMA was not well suited for this data because of its considerable randomness. Also, we would expect the ARIMA model to perform better in forecasts of greater than 12 months. Alternatively, one might argue that more time should have been spent in ARIMA model building.

MINICASES 17-4 TO 17-10

Because of time and space limitations, the following minicases are not included here. These solutions may be added to the website. However, note that solutions are very much method dependent, thus, it is reasonable to require the student to develop his or her own solution.

MINICASE 17-4. Henry Machler's Hideaway Orchids. MACHLERM.DAT

MINICASE 17-5. Your Forecasting Project.

MINICASE 17-6. Midwestern Building Materials. LUMBER.DAT

MINICASE 17-7. International Airline Passengers. AIRLINE.DAT

MINICASE 17-8. Automobile Sales. AUTO.DAT

MINICASE 17-9. Consumption of Distilled Spirits. SPIRITS.DAT

MINICASE 17-10. Discount Consumer Electronics. ELECT.DAT

PROBLEMS

ESTIMATED DIFFICULTY

Elementary	Medium	Hard	Very Hard	Bad

1 M   2 E   3 M   4 M   5 E   6 E   7 E   8 E   9 E   10 E

11 E   12 M   13 M   14 M   15 E   16 M   17 H

Minicases are all of medium difficulty.

18-1. The most important factors in choosing one method over another are the cost effectiveness or net benefits from the chosen method, and as listed in Table 18-1, availability of data (j), use of external or subjective data (h), horizon length (a), type of application (f), pattern recognition ability (i). While not shown in Table 18-1, the compatibility of the chosen method with the organization can be a very important determinant of a method's effectiveness.

18-2. See the previous question and Table 18-1.

18-3. While very speculative, I believe that the proportion of univariate to multivariate forecasting methodology will likely decrease. In absolute terms, both methods will be used more often. Finally, on a percentage growth basis, multivariate methods will most likely increase the greatest.

18-4. Some very simple random walk models forecast the next period better than more complex ARIMA or causal models. However, these simple random walk models lose their effectiveness very rapidly as the horizon increases. Thus, two models might be used to forecast, a random walk model for one or two period ahead forecasts and a more complex (e.g., seasonal) model for multiperiod forecasts. The practice of using a univariate model for short term forecasting and multivariate or judgmental models for long-term forecasting is common. In general, theoretically, there is nothing wrong with using different models for different horizons, clearly, we desire a single model, however, very often more than one model is better.

18-5. What does "cost" denote? Most often, cost should be discussed in the context of cost effectiveness. Thus, the best forecasting model is the most cost effective, where cost effectiveness is measured by the sum of the cost of forecast errors plus the cost of forecasting. It is this cost which we want to minimize. In a more general, profit or return on investment maximization process, the best forecasting method is one that maximizes either profit or return on investment, the latter being the most important criteria.

18-6. Forecasting ability can be measured directly from error statistics such as RSE, ME, MPE, MAPE in actually forecasting. Explanatory power or ability results from the insights and theory of a model. If a causal model does not forecast as accurately as a univariate model, but nonetheless provides important insights and causal relationships, its explanatory utility is great. In some applications forecasting accuracy is more desirable than explanatory ability, in other applications, the reverse is true.

18-7. The choice of data period should be based on the most logical or effective planning period. On a percentage basis there is much greater variability in smaller time periods than in larger time periods (i.e., forecasts of groups are, in general, more accurate). Also, smaller time periods require projections of more periods, which may or may not be done more accurately.

18-8. 13-month years standardize every month to have exactly four weeks, thus avoiding changes in the number of weeks from month to month and changes in the number of trading days from year to year. Monthly data can be homogenized from year to year by modeling and forecasting the demand after adjusting for trading days as shown on page 754.

18-9. Normally all weeks have 7 days and typically, from year to year have the same calendar effects, such as holidays that occur on Monday etc. There are exceptions such as Christmas, Easter, Passover, Thanksgiving, and the Fourth of July which are celebrated on different days and weeks of the year.

18-10. Typically, forecasts are revised every planning or forecasting period, that is if the period of analysis consists of weeks, then the forecast is regenerated or revised every week unless extraordinary things happens. However, with all rules, there are exceptions.

18-11. Automation potential relates to the ability of current software and software developers to duplicate the abilities of a manager-analyst in identifying, estimating, diagnosing, and forecasting with different methods. Clearly, many univariate methods can be automated, however, sophisticated causal or judgmental methods are difficult to automate. As firms become more knowledgeable of their forecasting needs and become more proficient in the development of Conventional Program Systems (CPS), ES, and ANN the automation potential of different methods increases. Absolute automation potential is relative to the specific organization.

18-12. Univariate and Multivariate ARIMA require the most observations because they are more empirically driven methods. In general, methods that work with fewer observations are not less costly, and in general, when there are fewer observations, the cost to apply a specific forecasting method increases. Judgmental methods require fewer observations but are among the most expensive methods.

18-13. If the methods model and smooth the same relevant patterns, then their accuracy is about the same

18-14. M-competition results related to 1001 time series in which little intelligence was used in the selection of the methods. The conclusions mentioned on page 759 can be generalized when there is no intelligent selection process in choosing the method of forecasting or combining forecasts, however, if expert systems are designed to choose the method of forecasting or combining forecasts, then most of these conclusions are not accurate. For example, when combining forecasts, the level of correlation been fitted errors of different models can be important determinants of whether to combine forecasts and what method should be used in combining those forecasts. Similarly, intelligence can be used to select one method over another method when in-sample forecast error measures are known. Confirming this is the very successful results of the expert system of ForecastPro^{tm} . This product did extremely well in the M3 competition involving 3003 times series.

18-15. Simple combining methods seem to work as well as more complex methods. However, this conclusion only applies if no intelligence is used in selecting one method over the other, that is, the conclusion was based on the choice of using one or the other method on all series, as opposed to selectively using different methods based on in-sample error and correlation measures.

18-16. The conclusions are more often right than wrong. Most students are somewhat surprised when the model that fitted the in-sample time series is not always the best in out-of-sample results. This is particularly insightful when it results from the process of over fitting the in-sample model. The principle of parsimony should be emphasized in this context.

18-17. As mentioned in questions 18-13 and 18-14 the conclusions of the M-competition are most valid under the assumption that no real intelligence is built into the system. An automated forecasting system should have as much intelligence as possible built into it, thus, the selection of the best forecasting method should be based on some simulated out-of-sample forecasting competition as well as user input. The use of in-sample forecasting accuracy should apply to the choice of combining method. When forecasting a single time series where accuracy, not the cost of the forecast is most important, then the results of the M-competition suggest selecting a method based on the characteristics of the time series and other characteristics, much as defined in Table 18-1. We should use as much natural (i.e., human analyst) intelligence as possible in the method selection and model identification, estimation, diagnostics, and forecasting steps. A well designed automated forecasting system will have as much expert system support as is cost effective. Needless to say, this expert system support and development is normally more cost effectively acquired then developed in-house.

MINICASES

Each of the minicases should confirm the results of the M-competition particularly as emphasized in questions 18-13 to 18-17. Relative to the summary in the middle of page 762, students analyzing a minicase using several different methods should be able to confirm these principles. Solution to this question is very much dependent on which chapters and which minicases were assigned.